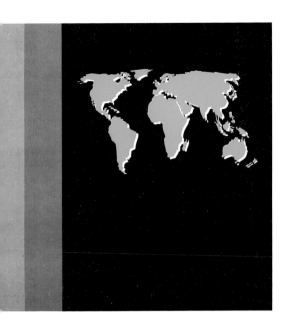

World Development Report 1990

Published for The World Bank
Oxford University Press

Oxford University Press

OXFORD NEW YORK TORONTO DELHI
BOMBAY CALCUTTA MADRAS KARACHI
PETALING JAYA SINGAPORE HONG KONG
TOKYO NAIROBI DAR ES SALAAM
CAPE TOWN MELBOURNE AUCKLAND
and associated companies in
BERLIN IBADAN

ISBN 0-19-520850-1 clothbound
ISBN 0-19-520851-X paperback
ISSN 0163-5085

The Library of Congress has cataloged this serial publication as follows:
World development report. 1978–
[New York] Oxford University Press.
v. 27 cm. annual.
Published for The World Bank.
1. Underdeveloped areas—Periodicals. 2. Economic development—
Periodicals. I. International Bank for Reconstruction and Development.

HC59.7.W659   *330.9′172′4*   *78-67086*

This book is printed on paper that adheres to
the American National Standard for Permanence of Paper
for Printed Library Materials, Z39.48-1984.

World Development Report 1990

POVERTY

Embargo

Not for press publication
or broadcast until

Ne pas publier dans la presse
ni diffuser avant

No deberá publicarse en la
prensa, radio o TV hasta

JULY 16
1990

le 16
JUILLET 1990

el 16 de JULIO
de 1990

WORLD DEVELOPMENT INDICATORS

World Development Report 1990

POVERTY

WORLD DEVELOPMENT INDICATORS

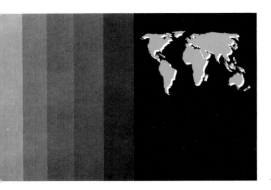

Foreword

This Report is the thirteenth in the annual series addressing major development issues. Like its predecessors, it includes the World Development Indicators, which provide selected social and economic data on more than 120 countries. The Report addresses the most pressing issue now facing the development community: how to reduce poverty. Its main conclusions are summarized below.

The world economy enjoyed moderate growth in the closing years of the decade. But the auspicious picture was not uniform. The industrial countries saw favorable developments in growth, trade, and investment. Real per capita incomes grew (and poverty declined) in South Asia and, even more markedly, in East Asia. But in some countries of Latin America and in most of Sub-Saharan Africa, real per capita incomes, living standards, and investment have slipped. For the poor in these countries, the 1980s was a lost decade.

In 1985 more than one billion people, or almost one-third of the total population of the developing world, were living on less than $370 per capita a year. The percentage of the population living in poverty was especially high in South Asia and Sub-Saharan Africa. Other aspects of the quality of life—already lower, on average, in developing than in developed countries—varied dramatically among regions, with the bleakest figures for regions with the greatest incidence of poverty. For example, in 1985 life expectancy was 76 years for the developed world but only 50 years for Sub-Saharan Africa and 56 years for South Asia. Some regions were close to achieving universal enrollment in primary education, but in Sub-Saharan Africa net primary enrollment was only 56 percent, and in South Asia it was about 75 percent. Women

often constitute a deprived group even among the poor; in most areas literacy rates and wages are much lower for women than for men, and access to social services and employment is more difficult. The plight of poor women is troubling in itself. It is even more troubling because the health and education of mothers greatly influence the well-being and future of their children.

A review of development experience shows that the most effective way of achieving rapid and politically sustainable improvements in the quality of life for the poor has been through a two-part strategy. The first element of the strategy is the pursuit of a pattern of growth that ensures productive use of the poor's most abundant asset—labor. The second element is widespread provision to the poor of basic social services, especially primary education, primary health care, and family planning. The first component provides opportunities; the second increases the capacity of the poor to take advantage of these opportunities. The strategy must be complemented by well-targeted transfers, to help those not able to benefit from these policies, and by safety nets, to protect those who are exposed to shocks.

Although domestic policy is critical to the reduction of poverty, international assistance is needed to support countries' efforts. Simply increasing resources, however, will not solve the problem. Aid is most effective when it complements the recipients' efforts. The allocation of aid should be more closely linked to a country's commitment to pursue development programs geared to the reduction of poverty.

The Report's projections for the 1990s show buoyant growth of about 3 percent a year in the industrial countries and about 5.1 percent in the developing world—compared with the 4.3 percent achieved by developing countries in the 1980s. If this forecast is correct, prospects for improving the quality of life are bright in most regions—except where rapid population growth is expected to offset the beneficial effects of economic growth.

In East Asia and South Asia the number of poor is expected to fall dramatically, and social indicators should continue to improve. The countries of Latin America and the Caribbean, Eastern Europe, and the Middle East and North Africa will see only modest reductions in the number of poor, but improvements in social indicators will continue. In Sub-Saharan Africa the expected growth in gross domestic product of 3.7 percent a year, although significantly higher than in the 1980s, will not be sufficient to offset the effects of rapid population growth, and the number of poor will increase. Even so, adequate provision for the social sectors should allow a rapid reduction in child mortality and a reversal of the decline in primary school enrollment experienced in the 1980s.

The hurdles to be overcome in decreasing poverty throughout the world remain formidable. They are especially daunting in Sub-Saharan Af-rica. Nevertheless, the key measures for combating poverty are known, and the resources to support such an effort are there to be mobilized. Containing the number of poor in Sub-Saharan Africa until population growth can be brought under control and reducing the number elsewhere by 400 million are feasible goals for the century's end. The main obstacle is not the availability of resources but the willingness of governments in both developing and developed countries to commit themselves to these goals.

Like previous World Development Reports, this Report is a study by the staff of the World Bank, and the judgments in it do not necessarily reflect the views of the Board of Directors or the governments they represent.

Barber B. Conable
President
The World Bank

June 1, 1990

This Report has been prepared by a team led by Lyn Squire and comprising Ehtisham Ahmad, Robert L. Ayres, Gary Fields, Helena Ribe, Mark Sundberg, Jacques van der Gaag, Dominique van de Walle, and Michael Walton. The team was assisted by Lara Akinbami, Fernando J. Batista, Robin Burgess, Elaine K. Chan, Pierre Englebert, Carlos Alberto Herran, Kathryn A. Larin, Natasha Mukherjee, and Anna-Birgitta Viggh. The work was carried out under the general direction of Stanley Fischer.

Many others in and outside the Bank provided helpful comments and contributions (see the bibliographical note). The International Economics Department prepared the data and projections presented in Chapter 1 and the statistical appendix. It is also responsible for the World Development Indicators. The production staff of the Report included Les Barker, Kathy Dahl, Connie Eysenck, Kenneth Hale, Jeffrey N. Lecksell, Nancy Levine, Hugh Nees, Joyce C. Petruzzelli, Kathy Rosen, Walt Rosenquist, and Brian J. Svikhart. Library assistance was provided by Iris Anderson. The support staff was headed by Rhoda Blade-Charest and included Laitan Alli, Trinidad S. Angeles, and Maria Guadalupe M. Mattheisen. Clive Crook was the principal editor.

Fondly remembered and acknowledged, too, is Pensri Kimpitak (1945–1990), illustrator and graphics designer for the Report since its inception in 1978, whose final illness prevented her participation in this edition.

Contents

Boxes

Text figures

Text tables

Statistical appendix tables

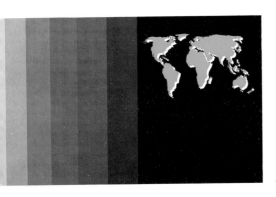

Acronyms and initials

CMEA Council for Mutual Economic Assistance (Bulgaria, Czechoslovakia, German Democratic Republic, Hungary, Poland, Romania, and U.S.S.R.)

DAC Development Assistance Committee of the OECD

DPT Diphtheria, pertussis, and tetanus (vaccine)

EC The European Community (Belgium, Denmark, Federal Republic of Germany, France, Greece, Ireland, Italy, Luxembourg, Netherlands, Portugal, Spain, and United Kingdom)

ECE Economic Commission for Europe

EFTA European Free Trade Association

EGS Employment Guarantee Scheme (Maharashtra State, India)

EPI Expanded Programme on Immunization

EPZ Export processing zone

ESCAP Economic and Social Commission for Asia and the Pacific

Eurostat European Statistical Office

FAO Food and Agriculture Organization

GATT General Agreement on Tariffs and Trade

GDP Gross domestic product

GNP Gross national product

GSP Generalized system of preferences

G-7 Group of Seven (Canada, France, Federal Republic of Germany, Italy, Japan, United Kingdom, and United States)

IBRD International Bank for Reconstruction and Development

ICRISAT International Crops Research Institute for the Semi-Arid Tropics

IDA International Development Association

IFAD International Fund for Agricultural Development

IFC International Finance Corporation

IFPRI International Food Policy Research Institute

IMF International Monetary Fund

LIBOR London interbank offered rate

NATO North Atlantic Treaty Organization

NGO Nongovernmental organization

ODA Official development assistance

OECD Organisation for Economic Co-operation and Development (Australia, Austria, Belgium, Canada, Denmark, Finland, France, Federal Republic of Germany, Greece, Iceland, Ireland, Italy, Japan, Luxembourg, Netherlands, New Zealand, Norway, Portugal, Spain, Sweden, Switzerland, Turkey, United Kingdom, and United States)

OPEC Organization of Petroleum Exporting Countries (Algeria, Ecuador, Gabon, Indonesia, Islamic Republic of Iran, Iraq, Kuwait, Libya, Nigeria, Qatar, Saudi Arabia, United Arab Emirates, and Venezuela)

PPP Purchasing power parity

Unesco United Nations Educational, Scientific, and Cultural Organization

UNDP United Nations Development Programme

UNIDO United Nations Industrial Development Organization

UNICEF United Nations Children's Fund

USAID United States Agency for International Development

WHO World Health Organization

WFP World Food Programme

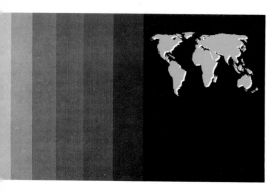

Definitions and data notes

Demographic terms

• *Total fertility rate.* The average number of children that would be born alive to a woman during her lifetime if she were to bear children at each age in accordance with the prevailing age-specific fertility rates.

• *Infant mortality rate.* The probability of dying between birth and age 1, per thousand births.

• *Under 5 mortality rate.* The probability of dying between birth and age 5, per thousand births.

• *Life expectancy at birth.* The number of years a newborn infant would live if prevailing patterns of mortality at the time of its birth were to stay the same throughout its life.

• *Net primary enrollment rate.* The number of children age 6 to 11 enrolled in primary school as a percentage of the population age 6 to 11, adjusted for each country's age structure for primary school.

Country groups

For operational and analytical purposes the World Bank classifies economies according to their gross national product (GNP) per capita. (Other international agencies maintain different classifications of developing countries; a table describing the classifications was included in *World Development Report 1989.*)

Country classifications were revised in the 1989 edition of the *World Development Report* and its statistical annex, the World Development Indicators. The principal changes were: (a) the "developing economies" group was dropped, but references to the specific income groups *low- and middle-income*

economies were retained; (b) all economies with a GNP per capita of $6,000 or more were classified as *high-income economies*, and (c) the subgroups "oil exporters" and "exporters of manufactures" under "developing economies" were dropped. In addition, "high-income oil exporters" is no longer a separate group; "industrial economies" has been renamed *OECD members*, which is a subgroup of the new category *high-income economies;* and a new aggregate, *total reporting economies* and its subcategory *oil exporters* has been added. As in previous editions, this Report uses the latest GNP per capita estimates to classify countries. The country composition of each income group may therefore change from one edition to the next. Once the classification is fixed for any edition, all the historical data presented are based on the same country grouping. The country groups used in this Report are defined as follows.

• *Low-income economies* are those with a GNP per capita of $545 or less in 1988.

• *Middle-income economies* are those with a GNP per capita of more than $545 but less than $6,000 in 1988. A further division, at GNP per capita of $2,200 in 1988, is made between lower-middle-income and upper-middle-income economies.

• *High-income economies* are those with a GNP per capita of $6,000 or more in 1988.

Although the dividing line between low and middle income used in the *World Development Report* has always been a specific level of GNP per capita, editions prior to 1989 were ambiguous about the line between middle income and high income. Industrial market economies and high-income oil exporters were shown separately, but some economies remained in the middle-income group despite having a GNP per capita above that of some countries classified as high-income. The high-income cutoff point of $6,000 removes that anomaly.

Low-income and middle-income economies are sometimes referred to as developing economies. The use of the term is convenient; it is not intended to imply that all economies in the group are experiencing similar development or that other economies have reached a preferred or final stage of development. Classification by income does not necessarily reflect development status. (As in last year's edition of the World Development Indicators, high-income economies classified by the United Nations or otherwise regarded by their authorities as developing are identified by the symbol †.) The use of the term "countries" to refer to economies implies no judgment by the Bank about the legal or other status of a territory.

- *Nonreporting nonmembers* are Albania, Bulgaria, Cuba, Czechoslovakia, German Democratic Republic, Democratic People's Republic of Korea, Mongolia, Namibia, and the Union of Soviet Socialist Republics. In the main tables of the World Development Indicators, only aggregates are shown for this group, but Box A.2 contains key indicators reported for each of these countries.

Analytical groups

For analytical purposes, other overlapping classifications based predominantly on exports or external debt are used in addition to geographic country groups. The lists provided below are of economies in these groups that have populations of more than 1 million. Countries with less than 1 million population, although not shown separately, are included in group aggregates.

- *Oil exporters* are countries for which exports of petroleum and gas, including reexports, account for at least 30 percent of merchandise exports. They are Algeria, Bahrain, Brunei, Cameroon, People's Republic of the Congo, Ecuador, Arab Republic of Egypt, Gabon, Indonesia, Islamic Republic of Iran, Iraq, Kuwait, Libya, Mexico, Nigeria, Norway, Oman, Qatar, Saudi Arabia, Syrian Arab Republic, Trinidad and Tobago, United Arab Emirates, and Venezuela.

- *Severely indebted middle-income countries* (abbreviated to "Severely indebted" in the World Development Indicators) are nineteen countries that are deemed to have encountered severe debt-servicing difficulties. They are Argentina, Bolivia, Brazil, Chile, People's Republic of the Congo, Costa Rica,

Côte d'Ivoire, Ecuador, Honduras, Hungary, Mexico, Morocco, Nicaragua, Peru, Philippines, Poland, Senegal, Uruguay, and Venezuela. The 1989 edition used the category "seventeen highly indebted economies," which did not include the People's Republic of the Congo, Honduras, Hungary, Nicaragua, Poland, and Senegal and did include Colombia, Jamaica, Nigeria, and Yugoslavia.

- *OECD members*, a subgroup of high-income economies, comprises the members of the Organisation for Economic Co-operation and Development except for Greece, Portugal, and Turkey, which are included among the middle-income economies.

Geographic regions (low-income and middle-income economies)

- *Sub-Saharan Africa* comprises all countries south of the Sahara except South Africa.
- *Europe, Middle East, and North Africa* comprises eight European countries—Cyprus, Greece, Hungary, Malta, Poland, Portugal, Romania, and Yugoslavia—all the economies of North Africa and the Middle East, and Afghanistan. For some analyses in the *World Development Report* separate groupings are used for Eastern Europe and for Middle East and North Africa (or Middle East, North Africa, and other Europe, depending on the database used). Eastern Europe comprises the former centrally planned economies in the group (Hungary, Poland, and Romania) and Yugoslavia.
- *East Asia* comprises all the low-income and middle-income economies of East and Southeast Asia and the Pacific, east of and including China and Thailand.
- *South Asia* comprises Bangladesh, Bhutan, India, Myanmar, Nepal, Pakistan, and Sri Lanka.
- *Latin America and the Caribbean* comprises all American and Caribbean countries south of the United States.

Data notes

- *Billion* is 1,000 million.
- *Trillion* is 1,000 billion.
- *Tons* are metric tons. equal to 1,000 kilograms, or 2,204.6 pounds.
- *Dollars* are current U.S. dollars unless otherwise specified.
- *Growth rates* are based on constant price data and, unless otherwise noted, have been computed with the use of the least-squares method. See the technical notes of the World Development Indicators for details of this method.

- *The symbol* .. in tables means not available.
- *The symbol* — in tables means not applicable.
- *The number 0 or 0.0* in tables means zero or a quantity less than half the unit shown and not known more precisely.

All tables and figures are based on World Bank data unless otherwise specified. The cutoff date for all data in the World Development Indicators is April 30, 1990.

Data for secondary sources are not always available after 1987. Historical data in this Report may differ from those in previous editions because of continuous updating as better data become available and because of new group aggregation techniques that use broader country coverage than in previous editions.

Economic and demographic terms are defined in the technical notes to the World Development Indicators.

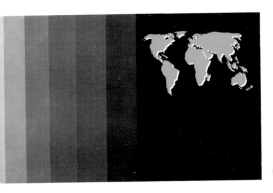

Overview

During the past three decades the developing world has made enormous economic progress. This can be seen most clearly in the rising trend for incomes and consumption: between 1965 and 1985 consumption per capita in the developing world went up by almost 70 percent. Broader measures of well-being confirm this picture—life expectancy, child mortality, and educational attainment have all improved markedly. Viewed from either perspective—income and consumption on the one hand, broad social indicators on the other—the developing countries are advancing much faster than today's developed countries did at a comparable stage.

Against that background of achievement, it is all the more staggering—and all the more shameful—that more than one billion people in the developing world are living in poverty. *World Development Report 1990* estimates that this is the number of people who are struggling to survive on less than $370 a year. Progress in raising average incomes, however welcome, must not distract attention from this massive and continuing burden of poverty.

The same is true of the broader measures of well-being. Life expectancy in Sub-Saharan Africa is just 50 years; in Japan it is almost 80. Mortality among children under 5 in South Asia exceeds 170 deaths per thousand; in Sweden it is fewer than 10. More than 110 million children in the developing world lack access even to primary education; in the industrial countries anything less than universal enrollment would rightly be regarded as unacceptable. The starkness of these contrasts attests to the continuing toll of human deprivation.

This Report is about poverty in the developing world—in other words, it is concerned with the poorest of the world's poor. It seeks first to measure poverty, qualitatively as well as quantitatively. It then tries to draw lessons for policy from the experience of countries that have succeeded in reducing poverty. It ends with a question that is also a challenge: what might be achieved if governments in rich and poor countries alike made it their goal to attack poverty in this closing decade of the twentieth century?

Poverty today

In the countries that have participated in the overall economic progress that has taken place since the 1960s, poverty has declined and the incomes even of those remaining in poverty have increased. In some cases this change has been dramatic. Indonesia, for example, took less than a generation in the 1970s and 1980s to reduce the incidence of poverty from almost 60 percent of the population to less than 20 percent. On a variety of social indicators, some developing countries are now approaching the standards of the developed world. In China, which accounts for a quarter of the developing world's people, life expectancy reached 69 in 1985. But in many countries economic performance was weaker, and the number in poverty fell more slowly. Where rapid population growth was an important additional factor, as in much of Sub-Saharan Africa, consumption per head stagnated and the number in poverty rose.

The 1980s—often called a "lost decade" for the poor—did not, in fact, reverse the overall trend of progress. The incomes of most of the world's poor went on rising, and under 5 mortality, primary school enrollment ratios, and other social indicators also continued to improve. The setbacks of the

1

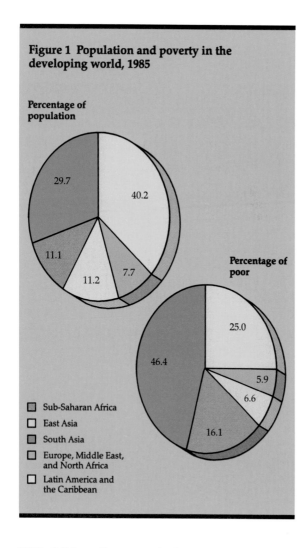

Figure 1 Population and poverty in the developing world, 1985

Percentage of population

29.7
40.2
11.1
11.2
7.7

Percentage of poor

25.0
46.4
5.9
6.6
16.1

☐ Sub-Saharan Africa
☐ East Asia
☐ South Asia
☐ Europe, Middle East, and North Africa
☐ Latin America and the Caribbean

1980s fell heavily on particular regions. For many in Sub-Saharan Africa and Latin America incomes fell during the decade, and the incidence of poverty increased—although the social indicators, at least in Latin America, proved somewhat more resilient.

The burden of poverty is spread unevenly—among the regions of the developing world, among countries within those regions, and among localities within those countries. Nearly half of the world's poor live in South Asia, a region that accounts for roughly 30 percent of the world's population (Figure 1). Sub-Saharan Africa accounts for a smaller, but still highly disproportionate, share of global poverty. Within regions and countries, the poor are often concentrated in certain places: in rural areas with high population densities, such as the Gangetic Plain of India and the island of Java, Indonesia, or in resource-poor areas such as the Andean highlands and the Sahel. Often the problems of poverty, population, and the environment are intertwined: earlier patterns of development

and the pressure of rapidly expanding populations mean that many of the poor live in areas of acute environmental degradation.

The weight of poverty falls most heavily on certain groups. Women in general are disadvantaged. In poor households they often shoulder more of the workload than men, are less educated, and have less access to remunerative activities. Children, too, suffer disproportionately, and the future quality of their lives is compromised by inadequate nutrition, health care, and education. This is especially true for girls: their primary enrollment rates are less than 50 percent in many African countries. The incidence of poverty is often high among ethnic groups and minorities such as the indigenous peoples in Bolivia, Ecuador, Guatemala, Mexico, and Peru and the scheduled castes in India.

In many but not all cases low incomes go hand in hand with other forms of deprivation. In Mexico, for example, life expectancy for the poorest 10 percent of the population is twenty years less than for the richest 10 percent. In Côte d'Ivoire the primary enrollment rate of the poorest fifth is half that of the richest. National and regional averages, often bad enough in themselves, mask appallingly low life expectancy and educational attainment among the poorest members of society.

Policies for attacking poverty

In the 1950s and 1960s many saw growth as the primary means of reducing poverty and improving the quality of life. For example, the Indian Planning Commission viewed rapid growth as the main (although not the only) instrument for achieving this objective. In the 1970s attention shifted to the direct provision of health, nutritional, and educational services. This was seen as a matter for public policy. *World Development Report 1980*, marshaling the evidence available at the time, argued that improvements in the health, education, and nutrition of the poor were important not only in their own right but also to promote growth in incomes, including the incomes of the poor.

The 1980s saw another shift in emphasis. Countries, especially in Latin America and Sub-Saharan Africa, struggled to adjust after the global recession. The constraints on public spending tightened. At the same time, many began to question the effectiveness of public policy, and especially policy toward the poor. Against this background, *World Development Report 1990* reexamines how policy can help to reduce poverty and explores the prospects for the poor during the 1990s.

The evidence in this Report suggests that rapid and politically sustainable progress on poverty has been achieved by pursuing a strategy that has two equally important elements. The first element is to promote the productive use of the poor's most abundant asset—labor. It calls for policies that harness market incentives, social and political institutions, infrastructure, and technology to that end. The second is to provide basic social services to the poor. Primary health care, family planning, nutrition, and primary education are especially important.

The two elements are mutually reinforcing; one without the other is not sufficient. In some countries, such as Brazil and Pakistan, growth has raised the incomes of the poor, but social services have received too little attention. As a result, mortality among children remains unusually high and primary enrollment unusually low, and the poor are not as well equipped as they might be to take advantage of economic opportunities. Some other countries, by contrast, have long stressed the provision of social services, but growth has been too slow. In Sri Lanka, for example, primary enrollment rates and under 5 mortality rates are exceptionally good, but the potential for raising the incomes of the poor has gone to waste for lack of economic opportunity.

Progress has been greatest in the countries that have implemented both parts of the strategy. By promoting the productive use of labor these countries have furnished opportunities for the poor, and by investing in health and education they have enabled the poor to take full advantage of the new possibilities. In Indonesia and Malaysia this approach has brought about a substantial reduction in poverty along with rapid improvements in nutrition, under 5 mortality, and primary enrollment.

Even if this basic two-part strategy is adopted, many of the world's poor—the sick, the old, those who live in resource-poor regions, and others—will continue to experience severe deprivation. Many others will suffer temporary setbacks owing to seasonal variations in income, loss of the family breadwinner, famine, or adverse macroeconomic shocks. A comprehensive approach to poverty reduction, therefore, calls for a program of well-targeted transfers and safety nets as an essential complement to the basic strategy.

During the 1980s many developing countries had to cope with macroeconomic crises. Their experience drew attention to a new concern: the need to frame adjustment policies that give due weight to the needs of the poor. In many developing countries a period of painful macroeconomic adjustment was unavoidable. In the longer term the economic restructuring associated with adjustment is perfectly consistent with the two-part strategy. In the short term, however, many of the poor are at risk. During the transition period the poor can be protected through a judicious mix of macroeconomic policies (for example, pricing policy reforms that benefit poor farmers) and measures to moderate declines in private consumption. Experience also shows that it is possible to shift public spending in favor of the poor, even within an overall framework of fiscal discipline, and to target transfers more accurately. In addition, increased capital inflows can be used to help cushion the impact of adjustment on the poor.

The politics of poverty

The framework of political and economic institutions is important because policies to reduce poverty involve a tradeoff. This tradeoff is not, in the main, between growth and the reduction of poverty. Switching to an efficient, labor-intensive pattern of development and investing more in the human capital of the poor are not only consistent with faster long-term growth; they contribute to it. Since these actions mean that a larger share of income and more public spending will go to the poor, the principal tradeoff, especially in the short run, is between the interests of the poor and those of the nonpoor. The two-part strategy is, therefore, more likely to be adopted in countries where the poor have a say in political and economic decisionmaking.

Although the two-part strategy does involve a politically sensitive tradeoff between the poor and the nonpoor, it is likely to prove more feasible than other strategies. Large-scale redistributions of land have sometimes been successful. In Japan and the Republic of Korea, for example, land redistribution was central to the reduction of rural poverty and laid the basis for the other policies advocated in this Report. Where it can be done, redistribution of land should be strongly supported. But the political obstacles to such reform are great. In most countries the two-part strategy outlined here, which sees investment in education as the best way of augmenting the assets of the poor, is more likely to succeed.

Reaching the poor

Even when macroeconomic adjustment is not a primary issue, the strategy requires an increase in certain categories of public spending that specifically benefit the poor. If these are to be affordable and hence sustainable, they must be cost-effective. Experience since the 1970s shows, however, that reaching the poor with targeted programs can be difficult. Nongovernmental organizations have made important contributions here. Self-selecting programs, which exclude the nonpoor by offering benefits that are of interest only to the poor, are another promising approach. Low-wage public employment programs, for instance, have provided an effective safety net for the poor in certain parts of South Asia and have been especially valuable in preventing famine. Chile's experience suggests that such schemes may also be helpful during recessions.

To be truly cost-effective, interventions must be not merely well targeted but also carefully designed to meet the specific needs of poor people. This means developing technologies suited to the risky environment that confronts small farmers, devising credit schemes to serve small borrowers, combining feeding programs for especially vulnerable groups with education on health and nutrition, and so on. Successful programs have usually involved the poor both at the design stage and during implementation.

Public spending that is well designed and accurately targeted can play an important part in the fight against poverty. But such programs, however cost-effective, are no substitute for efforts to attune the broad stance of economic policy to the needs of the poor. Attacking poverty is not primarily a task for narrowly focused antipoverty projects, vital though these may be. It is a task for economic policy in the large.

Aid

Aid has often been an effective instrument for reducing poverty—but not always. Donors sometimes have other objectives. In 1988 about 41 percent of external assistance was directed to middle- and high-income countries, largely for political reasons. Even when aid has been directed to the poor, the results have sometimes been disappointing—especially in countries in which the overall policy framework has not been conducive to the reduction of poverty.

The world is at a turning point: the geopolitical tensions that have prevailed since World War II are easing rapidly. This offers a unique opportunity to cut military spending and increase international assistance. A cut of just 10 percent in military spending by the countries of the North Atlantic Treaty Organization would pay for a doubling of aid. The resources can be made available—although little will be achieved unless they are used effectively.

The analysis in this Report provides the basis for a better aid strategy. External assistance should be more tightly linked to an assessment of the efforts that would-be recipients are making to reduce poverty. This principle already underlies procedures for allocating the resources of the International Development Association (IDA). Carrying out this principle would mean that countries committed to the two-part strategy would be the main recipients of aid. This reflects the conviction that aid works well only when it complements a sound development strategy.

In countries where policies (on prices and public spending, for instance) are inconsistent with efforts to reduce poverty, external resources would achieve far less. Yet there are many poor people in such countries. Indeed, these are the very countries in which poverty is going to get worse. The judgments that have to be made in such cases will be extremely difficult. Aiming moderate quantities of aid directly at highly vulnerable groups seems the appropriate response. Health clinics that serve the poor, immunization programs for children, and targeted nutrition programs are the sorts of intervention that might be supported by the aid community in such circumstances.

Many countries will fall between these two extremes. In such cases, intermediate amounts of assistance would be appropriate. Careful judgment is needed to determine how this aid can best be used to make policy more responsive to the needs of the poor.

These principles certainly bear on the operations of the World Bank, but they should be regarded as applicable to the aid community as a whole. If the aid strategy outlined here were adopted and followed consistently by bilateral donors, nongovernmental organizations, and multinational agencies, its effectiveness would be greatly increased.

What can be achieved?

The Report projects that if, over the next ten years, the industrial countries grow at about 3 percent a year (the historical trend) and real aid flows increase at a similar rate, per capita incomes in the developing countries will grow by between 5.1 percent a year in East Asia and 0.5 percent a year in Sub-Saharan Africa. With some progress toward adopting the strategy advocated by the Report, the number of poor in the developing world could fall—counting gains and setbacks—by more than 300 million by the end of the century. More determined efforts to reduce poverty could see even greater progress.

This relatively favorable outcome hides marked differences among regions (Figure 2). The number of people in poverty would fall most sharply in East Asia. Progress would be good in South Asia, modest in Latin America and the Caribbean, and negligible in developing Europe, the Middle East, and North Africa. Compared with a reduction of 400 million in poverty elsewhere in the developing world, in Sub-Saharan Africa slow economic growth and rapid population growth would mean an increase of nearly 100 million in the number of poor people. By the end of the century Sub-Saharan Africa will account for more than 30 percent of the developing world's poor, as against 16 percent in 1985.

Progress in other aspects of living standards is expected to continue. By 2000 mortality for children under 5 will range from about 30 deaths per thousand in East Asia to a still-high 135 per thousand in Sub-Saharan Africa. Most regions will be able to achieve universal primary school enrollment with, at most, a modest increase in the share of gross domestic product (GDP) allocated for this purpose. Again, Sub-Saharan Africa is the exception. Universal primary enrollment can be achieved by 2000, but it will cost more than 2.5 percent of GDP, compared with current spending of less than 1.5 percent.

Progress in Asia depends critically on developments in China and India. If economic reform falters in China or if India is unable to maintain its recent momentum, the prospects for reducing poverty will be far less bright. Alternative projections based on slower growth and policies less favorable to the poor show an additional 150 million poor, mainly in India.

The plight of Sub-Saharan Africa is unfortunately all too clear. Even to hold the number of poor at the 1985 level will require a massive effort: GDP growth of 5.5 percent a year, a radical restructuring of industry, improved incentives and technology for agriculture, and increased allocations of resources to primary education, health care, nutrition, and family planning. This cannot be achieved unless governments strengthen their reform efforts and donors increase their assistance.

Slower growth in the industrial countries, higher interest rates, and a smaller-than-expected rise in the terms of trade could combine, as in the 1980s,

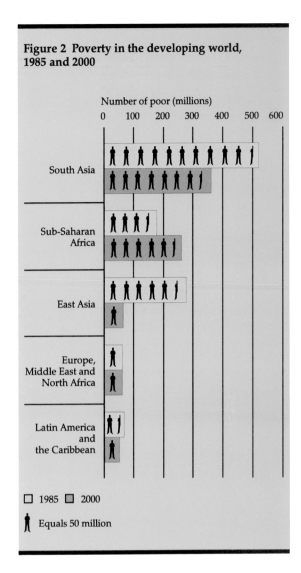

Figure 2 Poverty in the developing world, 1985 and 2000

Number of poor (millions)

1985   2000

Equals 50 million

to pose further obstacles to the reduction of poverty. Trends in regional growth would then diverge more noticeably. Although progress in East and South Asia—the regions with the greatest number of poor—would be relatively unaffected, Latin America would face a serious setback, and an already intolerable situation in Sub-Saharan Africa would deteriorate still further.

The challenge for the 1990s

No task should command a higher priority for the world's policymakers than that of reducing global poverty. In the last decade of the twentieth century it remains a problem of staggering dimensions. Despite the difficulties, which are especially daunting in Sub-Saharan Africa, the means for reducing poverty are at hand. This Report argues that the principal elements of an effective strategy are well understood and that the external resources needed to support it could be made available at little cost to the industrial countries. Where developing countries are committed to reducing poverty, the industrial countries should respond with increased assistance.

Containing the number of poor in Africa and reducing the number elsewhere by almost 400 million (compared with 1985) would be a substantial achievement. It is an ambitious goal—but one that is within reach by the end of the century.

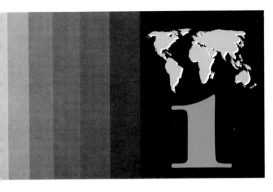

Diverging trends in the world economy

Looking back on the 1980s, much of the world can count itself fortunate. One after another, great dangers appeared, only to recede without serious repercussions. The international debt crisis no longer threatens the integrity of the world's financial system; the recession of the early 1980s, which drove unemployment in Europe to record highs, gave way to one of the longest peacetime expansions of this century; the stock market crash of October 1987 failed to cause a second Great Depression. It was a turbulent period, to be sure. But by the standard of the fears expressed at the time, it was a decade of disasters that never happened. Aptly enough, it closed with momentous changes in several Eastern European countries—changes that mark the beginning of a new and uniquely promising era in the history of the world.

Yet millions of the world's most vulnerable people must take a far gloomier view of the past ten years. Many developing countries have not merely failed to keep pace with the industrial countries; they have seen their incomes fall in absolute terms. The living standards of millions in Latin America are now lower than in the early 1970s. In most of Sub-Saharan Africa living standards have fallen to levels last seen in the 1960s. Such facts, extraordinary as they are, fail to capture the plight of the very poorest, whose lives have remained blighted even as incomes elsewhere in the developing world have risen. For many of the world's poor, the 1980s was a "lost decade"—a disaster indeed.

This Report is about the poor. It is thus about the fundamental issue in economic development: the eradication of poverty from the world. Later chapters will look in greater detail at policies that offer hope for reducing poverty. As in previous Reports,

however, this first chapter begins by examining recent developments in the world economy and the prospects for the 1990s. Just as the external environment of recent years goes some way toward explaining the disappointing performance of many developing countries, so too the economic outlook describes the foundation on which future efforts to attack poverty will have to be built. It will be far easier to reduce poverty if the platform is one of low inflation, lower real interest rates, and open trade than if fluctuating prices, high real interest rates, and restricted trade prevail. As always, progress in the developing countries is closely bound up with the policies of the industrial countries.

Recent developments in the world economy

The 1980s closed happily for the industrial countries—growth was moderate to high, output was at or near potential, unemployment was well down from the levels seen earlier in the decade, inflation was under control, and world trade was expanding strongly. In the principal industrial countries productivity growth accelerated in the late 1980s, and investment grew nearly twice as fast as GDP. Concern over inflation remained, but restrictive monetary policies appeared to be keeping the pressures in check. Commodity prices were fairly stable, although petroleum prices rose by an average of 20 percent over their 1988 level.

Despite a healthy growth of 3.6 percent in the industrial countries, external imbalances were slow to narrow. The United States finished the year with a current account deficit of $106 billion, down by $20 billion from the previous year. The

Table 1.1 Performance indicators in the world economy, 1989

Group and region	Real growth of GDP		Growth of export volume		Gross domestic investment/GDP[a]	
	1980–89	1989	1980–89	1989	1980–89	1989
Industrial countries	3.0	3.6	4.8	7.6	20.9	21.5
Developing countries	4.3	3.3	6.1	8.1	24.3	24.6
Sub-Saharan Africa	1.0	3.5	0.0	10.1	16.1	15.2
East Asia	8.4	5.1	14.7	8.1	30.0	30.7
South Asia	5.5	4.8	6.1	9.6	22.3	21.4
Eastern Europe[b]	1.4	0.0	3.8	2.0	29.4	24.8
Middle East, North Africa, and other Europe	2.9	2.5	6.4[b]	1.4[b]	25.9	24.1
Latin America and the Caribbean	1.6	1.5	4.9	4.4	20.1	20.6

a. Data for 1989 are preliminary.
b. Estimates.

Japanese current account surplus fell by more than 27 percent, to $58 billion, but in the Federal Republic of Germany the surplus rose by more than 14 percent, to $56 billion, and approached that of Japan for the first time in recent history. Although concern over the willingness of capital markets to finance the U.S. current account deficit has eased, saving in the United States and other industrial countries remains low. As a result, these economies continue to absorb a large share of the global supply of capital, and this in turn contributes to high world interest rates.

In 1989 the developing countries saw growth slow to 3.3 percent, as against an average for the decade of 4.3 percent (Table 1.1). Growth was strongest in South Asia and East Asia—the regions with the world's largest concentration of poor people—although it was slower in both cases than the average for recent years. Despite strong export performance, South Asia's growth fell to 4.8 percent from 9 percent in 1988. Incomes in East Asia rose by a healthy 5.1 percent, but that followed a 10 percent rise in 1988. China's growth fell to 3.9 percent, less than half the average for the decade, as the pace of economic reform slowed and the government adopted austerity measures to curb inflation by controlling the expansion of domestic credit.

Elsewhere, growth was less buoyant. Real export growth of 10 percent helped boost growth in Sub-Saharan Africa to 3.5 percent in 1989, one of the decade's strongest years. But because population was growing extraordinarily fast, average per capita income scarcely increased. Some countries, including Burkina Faso, Ghana, Mali, and Mauritius, managed growth of more than 5 percent in 1989, but investment remains severely depressed across the region. In some countries investment

has fallen to less than 10 percent of GDP—a level that is insufficient even to replace worn-out capital.

In 1989 Latin America saw no recovery from the weak growth and falling per capita incomes that had characterized the rest of the decade. Average income growth was 1.5 percent, but differences within the region were great. Brazil achieved 3.5 percent real growth, whereas the rest of Latin America averaged just 0.2 percent. Debt continues to be a major obstacle to growth: net outward transfers of resources to creditors amounted to almost one-fifth of export revenues. A reappraisal of strategies for handling the debt crisis led to several proposals for a new approach in 1989. The Brady initiative, announced in March 1989, calls for case-by-case debt reduction accompanied by official financial support that is conditional on domestic policy reform. Recognition of the need for debt reduction and for full participation both by official agencies and by private creditors marks an important departure from previous debt strategies.

Several agreements providing for commercial debt reduction have already been concluded under the broad guidelines of the Brady initiative. These agreements, which are backed with financial support from the World Bank, the International Monetary Fund (IMF), and the Japanese government, vary in their structure and terms. Mexico's agreement, for example, covers 85 percent of its commercial bank debt. The Philippines bought back a portion of its commercial bank debt at a 50 percent discount and also received some new loans. Costa Rica's existing commercial bank claims were exchanged for new low-interest bonds. The results so far indicate that in addition to reducing the debt burden these agreements will encourage the countries concerned to strengthen their adjustment pol-

Box 1.1 Reform in the Eastern European economies

The countries of Eastern Europe face the task of transforming their command economies into decentralized
and more market-oriented systems. The long-term
gains are likely to be great, but in the short term the
reformers may face steep transitional costs. Different
countries have already adopted their own distinctive
approaches. Poland has decided to ''cross the chasm in
one leap,'' whereas in Hungary reforms have been
more cautious and gradual.

In October 1989 the Polish government announced a
far-reaching plan to first stabilize the economy and
then move quickly to a market-based system. The goals
of stabilization are to reduce inflation—which ran at an
annualized rate of 650 percent during 1989—and to
eliminate the government deficit. Inflation is to be held
down by decreasing real wages, stabilizing food prices,
and increasing interest rates to reduce the demand for
credit. But these measures will not succeed unless the
fiscal deficit is curbed. The plan calls for massive sales
of state enterprises, closure of inefficient plants, cuts in
price subsidies on food and domestic energy, and cutbacks in spending on defense and public administration. It looks toward an ownership system modeled on
that of Western industrial countries. Freedom to establish enterprises is to be codified and restrictions on
housing rentals and sales removed. Some of these
measures will fall heavily on low-income families and
those most dependent on the state.

Hungary's reforms began in 1968, when rigid central

planning was abolished and the state began making
greater use of taxes, subsidies, and price controls to
guide the economy indirectly. During the 1970s and
early 1980s progress was slow. In 1985–86, however,
new impetus for reform came after the stabilization efforts of 1982–84 had failed to address the underlying
structural problems. Wage regulations were made
more flexible, enterprises were given greater autonomy
in setting prices, and foreign trading rights were expanded. The reforms failed, however, mainly because
of lax monetary and fiscal management. Wage increases were allowed to outstrip productivity, and the
state incurred large losses. After 1987 the government
again tried to impose fiscal and monetary discipline
and to stimulate nonruble exports. Although trade performance improved, efforts to curb the fiscal deficit
have been disappointing.

The choice of gradual versus rapid reform is also a
choice between two sets of risks. Rapid reform is likely
to lead to greater dislocation in the short run, whereas
slow reform often creates inconsistencies that thwart
further progress. In Poland a substantial share of the
work force may become unemployed under the
planned restructuring and sale of state enterprises. The
social safety nets being put in place may prove both
costly and inadequate. Hungary took the other path;
the government freed many prices and decentralized
the economy, but large fiscal deficits led in the end to
the failure of the pre-1990 reform efforts.

---

icies. This should help to restore the confidence of
domestic and foreign investors.

The year 1989 was a historic one for Eastern Europe. Many countries in the region saw nothing
less than a political revolution, although a largely
peaceful one, and the pace of change in economic
policy accelerated everywhere (Box 1.1). Suddenly
there has emerged an enormous potential for raising industrial productivity, expanding technological exchange and trade relations, and thereby
boosting incomes in the region.

In the short and medium run, however, adjustment will probably involve significant costs. Average regional incomes failed to grow in 1989, and
Poland's GDP is estimated to have fallen by 1 percent, with a sharper decrease likely in 1990. Ram-
pant open inflation has occurred recently in Poland
and Yugoslavia, but both countries have had early
success after implementing tough anti-inflationary
policies. Elsewhere in the region there are many
signs of repressed inflation.

Expansion of external economic relations may
also pose difficulties. More than half the exports of
the members of the Council for Mutual Economic
Assistance (CMEA)—Bulgaria, Czechoslovakia,
the German Democratic Republic, Hungary, Poland, Romania, and the U.S.S.R.—are within the
region. The adoption of outward-oriented market
reforms will require restructuring of the CMEA
and dismantling of the current accounting practices based on ''transferable rubles.'' Many of
these countries' manufactured exports are unlikely
to be competitive in outside markets.

In other developing Europe, the Middle East,
and North Africa the decade ended with slower
growth. On average, income in the region grew by
2.5 percent in 1989, but this implied no growth in
per capita incomes. Weak export performance
made foreign exchange scarce and curbed investment. Turkey and several countries in North Africa
are finding that debt service is absorbing a large
share of their export earnings.

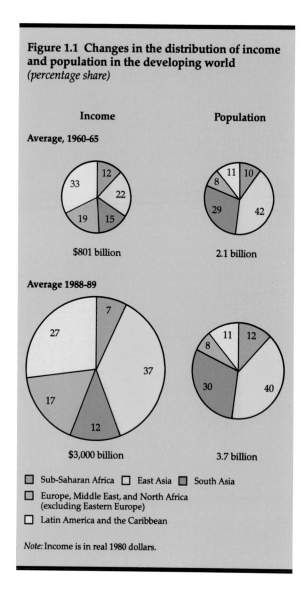

Figure 1.1 Changes in the distribution of income and population in the developing world
(percentage share)

Income   Population

Average, 1960-65

12   33   22   19   15

11   10   8   29   42

$801 billion   2.1 billion

Average 1988-89

7   27   37   17   12

11   12   8   30   40

$3,000 billion   3.7 billion

☐ Sub-Saharan Africa   ☐ East Asia   ☐ South Asia
☐ Europe, Middle East, and North Africa (excluding Eastern Europe)
☐ Latin America and the Caribbean

Note: Income is in real 1980 dollars.

The diverging performance of developing countries in the 1980s

Over the past quarter-century the distribution of income among the developing countries has changed markedly (Figure 1.1). The East Asian countries account for the largest gain; their share of developing country real incomes rose from 22 to 37 percent. All other regions had lower shares by the 1980s, but Latin America and Sub-Saharan Africa slipped furthest, by 6 and 5 percentage points, respectively. Population shares have also changed over this twenty-five-year period, but much more gradually. Population growth has fallen below average in East Asia, leading to a 2 percent drop in that region's share of the developing world's population, whereas fertility rates in Sub-Saharan Africa are well above average, and the population share is rising. In South Asia fertility rates have been successfully reduced since the 1960s, and income growth has been boosted over the past decade. Although South Asia still harbors the largest number of poor, during the past twenty-five years Sub-Saharan Africa's share of the world's poor has grown and incomes in Latin America have gradually deteriorated.

Why have some regions performed so much better than others? In the end, the battle against poverty depends on the answer to this question. Not surprisingly, trends in poverty during the 1980s reflect trends in overall economic performance. Although data are scarce, the evidence shows that where economic performance was good, poverty decreased. Thus, in Asia poverty declined in India, Indonesia, Malaysia, and Pakistan. In many countries of Sub-Saharan Africa, Latin America, and Eastern Europe, however, external and internal shocks caused poverty to increase. In all the countries in these regions for which data are available—Brazil, Colombia, Costa Rica, Côte d'Ivoire, Poland, Venezuela, and Yugoslavia—poverty increased during at least part of the 1980s.

This performance gap should not be regarded as an unchangeable fact of life; per capita incomes did grow almost everywhere during the 1960s. But the regions began to diverge in the 1970s. By the 1980s per capita GDP was growing at 6.7 percent in East Asia and 3.2 percent in South Asia but was falling in both Sub-Saharan Africa and Latin America (Table 1.2). These regional differences found their counterparts in investment. Both Asian regions increased their national saving and investment rates during these periods, in contrast to the declines experienced in Sub-Saharan Africa and Latin America. Domestic policies and external economic factors combined to determine the levels of regional growth and investment.

Domestic factors: the policy environment

The performance of countries in the 1980s varied according to their initial position and their ability to adjust to shocks over the decade. Many East Asian countries had a relatively healthy balance of payments and strong trade performance at the beginning of the 1980s, and their fiscal expenditures were largely under control. When disturbances such as higher world interest rates came along, these countries responded swiftly and succeeded in maintaining stability and restoring growth. In contrast, many countries in Latin America and Sub-Saharan Africa began the decade with greater

Table 1.2 Performance indicators, by developing region, selected periods

Region	Growth of real per capita GDP (percent)			Gross domestic investment/GDP		
	1965–73	1973–80	1980–89	1965–73	1973–80	1980–89 [a]
Sub-Saharan Africa	3.2	0.1	−2.2	16.2	20.8	16.1
East Asia	5.1	4.7	6.7	24.2	29.7	30.0
South Asia	1.2	1.7	3.2	17.1	19.9	22.3
Eastern Europe [b]	4.8	5.3	0.8	28.3	33.8	29.4
Middle East, North Africa and other Europe	5.5	2.1	0.8	23.4	29.2	25.9
Latin America and the Caribbean	3.7	2.6	−0.6	20.7	23.9	20.1

a. Data for 1989 are preliminary.
b. Estimates.

underlying imbalances, often hidden because borrowing had temporarily maintained growth. This group found it much harder to adjust to the shocks of the 1980s.

Successful adjustment requires macroeconomic stability: a low and sustainable rate of inflation, a realistic exchange rate, and a manageable level of fiscal expenditures. It also requires a microeconomic environment that is favorable to new investment. The countries that succeeded in both respects were able to sustain or improve their growth performance during the 1980s.

RESTORING STABILITY. The shocks to interest rates and terms of trade of the 1980s reduced real incomes in most developing countries. Adjustment called for cuts in consumption and in government spending. Countries that were particularly dependent on primary exports or were heavily burdened with debt needed to make even deeper cuts. By and large, the countries that weathered the storm were the ones that acted early. Indonesia, for example, saw its terms of trade decline by 25 percent in 1986; meanwhile, exchange rate movements pushed its ratio of debt to gross national product (GNP) to twice that of Brazil. The government acted promptly by devaluing the rupiah and cutting public spending. The 1986 budget deficit was held to 3.6 percent of GDP despite lost oil revenues; the 1987 deficit fell to just 1 percent of GDP. In both years real GDP growth remained above 3 percent, and it has been even stronger since then.

Government deficits, inflation, and unstable exchange rates are closely related in debtor countries. Large government deficits in the late 1970s and early 1980s were financed mainly by external borrowing. With the halt in foreign loans in the 1980s many governments, particularly in Latin America, increasingly financed their deficits by borrowing at home and by printing money. On

average, inflation in the severely indebted middle-income countries was more than 100 percent between 1980 and 1987, compared with 8 percent in South Asia and 5 percent in East Asia.

The recurrent bouts of high inflation that have plagued Latin America are linked to the tax base, the social structure, and domestic politics (Box 1.2). Severe inflation cripples the economy and deepens economic crises in several ways: it undermines domestic confidence, reduces investment, provokes capital flight, and often leads to a misallocation of scarce foreign exchange. It further encourages dollarization (the use of foreign currency as a medium of exchange), and it shrinks the tax base by driving many economic activities into the informal and illegal sectors. The result is an economy that does not respond to adjustment efforts.

RESTRUCTURING FOR GROWTH. For countries that entered the 1980s with structural problems, raising long-run growth requires adjustment policies aimed at institutional reform and reallocation of resources. Unlike stabilization measures, which often hinge on quick and decisive adjustment, economic restructuring also requires long-term planning. The trade regime, the financial sector, and the domestic regulatory framework are all crucial to this task.

The successful East Asian countries have acted swiftly to stabilize their economies while pursuing gradual reform programs and maintaining a competitive exchange rate. The Republic of Korea, for example, pursued gradual but comprehensive trade reform during the late 1970s and 1980s. Indonesia supported its careful approach toward stable exchange rate management with reforms of the trade regime, the domestic regulatory framework, and the financial system. By contrast, most Latin American and Sub-Saharan African countries entered the decade with overvalued exchange rates

Box 1.2 Politics and economic performance

Several Latin American countries have gone through periods of intense political and economic change driven by a combination of social and redistributive goals, populist politics, and nationalism. Although the policies may come from the left or the right of the political spectrum, they and their consequences share remarkable similarities. Examples include Argentina (1946–49), Brazil (1985–88), Chile (1970–73), and Peru (1985–88). Ironically, the very people these programs set out to help have often been harmed in the process.

In each case the government looked for support to a diversity of groups, especially the urban working class and elements of the rural poor. The leaders promised to accelerate and redistribute growth through state activism. Typically, they came to power after a period of slow growth that was often the outcome of previous austerity programs.

The reformist agenda starts with expansionary macroeconomic policies to promote employment and raise real wages. The results are encouraging. In Chile during the first year of the Allende administration GDP increased by nearly 8 percent and real wages rose by 17 percent. Labor's share of national income grew from 52 to 62 percent in that year. In Peru real wages grew by 27 percent in 1986 under the Garcia administration.

In time the program starts to unravel. Stocks are run down, foreign exchange reserves are depleted, inflation increases dramatically, and devaluations become inevitable. An erosion of external support and of access to foreign borrowing generally accompanies these developments. In Brazil in the second year of the Cruzado Plan (named for the new currency introduced in an effort to stabilize the economy) foreign exchange reserves were exhausted, inflation soared to more than 400 percent, and the exchange rate was sharply devalued. In the final stages the program collapses with a surge of inflation, an outflow of capital, and a sharp drop in real wages. In Chile real wages fell by 10 percent in 1972 and by 32 percent in 1973, to well below their preprogram levels. In Peru real wages fell by 34 percent in 1988, and in Brazil they fell by 29 percent during 1987–88.

The programs have generally reduced investment, promoted capital flight, and left workers worse off. They have also had less visible effects—an erosion of investor confidence and loss of government credibility. Later governments are caught in a double bind. Social pressures to restore growth and stability are intensified, and confidence in government is weakened. Under these circumstances it is difficult to halt inflation through currency reform and a fiscal austerity program without a radical change in the policy environment.

---

that were sustained by high levels of protection and overborrowing. Direct export taxes, nontariff barriers, and quantitative controls on credit and investment were also common. Adjustments were often delayed and hesitant.

Toward the end of the decade many countries in both regions did sharply devalue their currencies and begin substantial reforms of trade and domestic policies. (Some, including Chile, Ghana, and Mexico, were already showing signs of restored growth.) But the response of exports and investment has often been slow. This may be because of continuing uncertainty about the policy regime. Consistent actions are essential to convince the private sector that the policy stance will be maintained. In Sub-Saharan Africa the problems are compounded by the lack of complementary infrastructure, heavy dependence on exports of primary commodities, and weak entrepreneurial and managerial capacity. Adjustment will take longer under these circumstances.

External factors: the global environment

Adverse developments in the world economy also had a part in the falling growth rates of the 1980s.

Weak external demand, declining terms of trade, a diminishing supply of external finance, and a great increase in the volatility of interest rates combined to produce an unusually adverse economic climate.

WORLD DEMAND AND TRADE. Growth in the output and exports of developing countries is closely correlated with demand in the industrial countries (Figure 1.2). During the early 1980s growth in developing countries' exports fell as world growth slowed and industrial countries' imports stagnated. Matters have improved somewhat since 1983; the industrial countries have achieved an average GDP growth of 3.5 percent a year, and the volume of merchandise exports from developing countries has expanded by 6.7 percent a year.

Imported primary commodities from developing countries are used mainly as intermediate inputs; here the link to industrial country production is direct. Demand for developing countries' manufactures is also related to industrial country production and to changes in the pattern of final demand. Between 1965 and 1988 the share of manufactured goods in total developing country

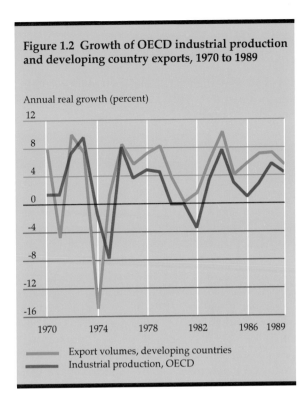

Figure 1.2 Growth of OECD industrial production and developing country exports, 1970 to 1989

Annual real growth (percent)

— Export volumes, developing countries
— Industrial production, OECD

exports increased from 16 to 64 percent. The growing importance of manufactures—notably, electronics, apparel, toys, and other consumer goods—has strengthened the link between industrial countries and East Asian exporters, in particular. The revival in world demand after 1985 had a smaller effect on the exports of other regions. Exports from South Asia have expanded rapidly since 1985 but remain a low share of national output. Latin America's exports have expanded slowly and have only recently regained the level of the early 1970s. Sub-Saharan Africa's exports fell in the early part of the decade and stagnated through 1988 (Figure 1.3).

Many highly indebted developing countries have been running substantial trade surpluses, largely because of their need to service debt. Between 1980 and 1981 the nineteen severely indebted middle-income countries had an average trade deficit of $4 billion; during 1982–89 they achieved an average annual surplus of $26 billion, the equivalent of 3.3 percent of GDP (see Figure 1.4). This improvement has come largely through a reduction in imports. It bears witness to the squeeze on investment and consumption caused by the austerity programs undertaken in many of these countries. Unfortunately, however, the decline in imported intermediate and investment goods has had adverse long-term effects.

EXTERNAL TERMS OF TRADE. For many of the poorest developing countries the purchasing power of exports depends on the prices of a few primary commodities—cocoa beans in Ghana, copper and coffee in Papua New Guinea, and so on—in relation to the prices of imports, which are mainly manufactured goods. Prices for primary commodities, especially tropical products and food crops, fluctuate sharply with global supply and demand. During the 1980s prices for many primary commodities fell to their lowest levels since World War II. Nonoil commodity prices declined for most of the decade, although they recovered a little in 1988. By 1989 average commodity prices were still 33 percent lower than in 1980. Oil prices also fell steadily between 1980 and 1985, but most developing countries import oil, and so they benefited.

The decline in the terms of trade during the 1980s has been most pronounced in Sub-Saharan Africa and Latin America, although by the standards of the 1970s both regions started the decade in a favorable position (Figure 1.5). The fall in prices during the 1980s cost Latin America and Sub-Saharan Africa 13 and 15 percent, respectively, of their exports' real import purchasing power relative to the 1970s. In both regions

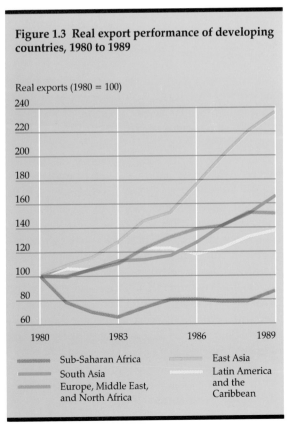

Figure 1.3 Real export performance of developing countries, 1980 to 1989

Real exports (1980 = 100)

— Sub-Saharan Africa
— South Asia
— Europe, Middle East, and North Africa
— East Asia
— Latin America and the Caribbean

13

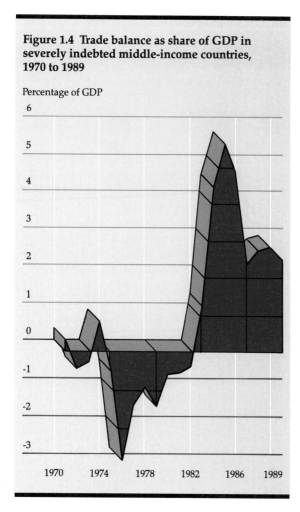

Figure 1.4 Trade balance as share of GDP in severely indebted middle-income countries, 1970 to 1989

Percentage of GDP

ments. After 1984 this changed dramatically. Between 1984 and 1989 total net transfers were −$153 billion, bringing the average annual flow to −$25 billion, or about 15 percent of the region's exports. The halt in commercial lending coincided with, and was partly provoked by, falling terms of trade and rising real interest rates—both of which pushed up the need for financing. Official lending was also scaled back, compounding the difficulties. Some countries in East Asia also found themselves deep in debt in the early 1980s, but they have coped more easily with the problem. Strong current account surpluses have reduced the region's borrowing needs, and the corresponding capital outflow has in some cases taken the form of accelerated amortization payments.

In Sub-Saharan Africa the story is very different. Commercial borrowing has been a significant source of funds only for a handful of middle-income or resource-rich countries. Between 1984 and 1989 only 6 percent of net flows came from private sources. As a result, more than 65 percent of the stock of foreign debt in the region is official,

roughly two-fifths of this loss was attributable to the effect of lower petroleum prices on oil exporters. Losses elsewhere were much less pronounced.

EXTERNAL FINANCE. Debt can safely be used to finance investment only if the investment generates the revenues that will be needed to repay the loan. The debt accumulated by many developing countries in the 1970s and early 1980s failed this test—although this was partly because of unforeseeable circumstances. The international financial markets responded by halting most voluntary lending to the principal debtors after 1983. The threat of default kept banks from withholding finance altogether, but most of the loans went toward rolling over the debt and capitalizing interest payments in arrears.

Until 1983 Latin America regularly experienced a positive net transfer of long-term debt (excluding IMF credit): borrowing outpaced total debt repay-

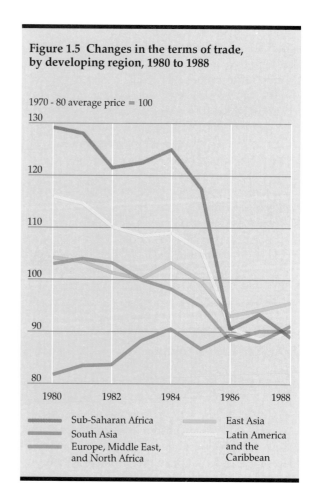

Figure 1.5 Changes in the terms of trade, by developing region, 1980 to 1988

1970 - 80 average price = 100

Sub-Saharan Africa	East Asia
South Asia	Latin America and the Caribbean
Europe, Middle East, and North Africa	

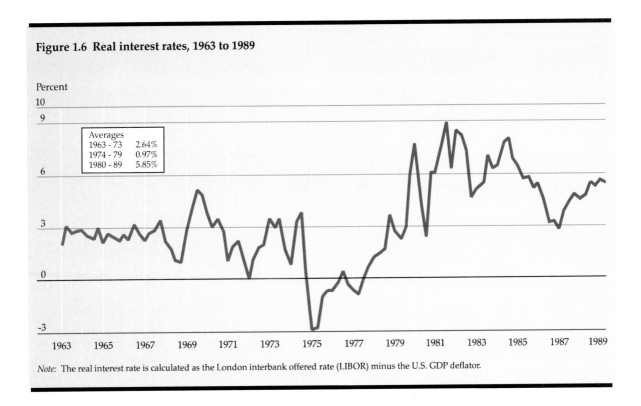

Figure 1.6 Real interest rates, 1963 to 1989

Percent

Averages	
1963 - 73	2.64%
1974 - 79	0.97%
1980 - 89	5.85%

Note: The real interest rate is calculated as the London interbank offered rate (LIBOR) minus the U.S. GDP deflator.

and in 1988 more than half of this was concessional. Although debt remains a serious obstacle to growth, the region has continued to receive large amounts of aid, and net transfers remained positive through the 1980s. The structure of South Asian debt resembles that of Sub-Saharan Africa, but the region's high ratios of debt service to exports have been manageable thanks to relatively strong growth and prudent borrowing.

INTEREST RATE VARIABILITY. Floating rate debt became commonplace during the high-inflation years of the mid-1970s. As long as real interest rates remain constant, floating rate debt should impose no additional burden on debtors. It was the combination of world recession, worsening terms of trade, and a rise in real interest rates that brought on the debt crisis.

Real interest rates were exceptionally high during the 1980s. On average, they were more than twice as high as in the 1960s and nearly six times higher than in 1974–79, when the developing countries took on a large share of their debt (Figure 1.6). High rates were caused by a decline in industrial country savings, by lack of progress in dealing with global current account imbalances, and by large swings in the major currencies, perhaps accompanied by greater uncertainty regarding future exchange rate movements.

The additional burden of high real interest rates, in relation to their 1963–80 average, was roughly $8 billion a year for Latin America during the 1980s, or close to 1 percent of the region's GDP. Much of the cost was concentrated between 1982 and 1985, after the debt crisis first erupted. In 1984 alone this interest rate shock is estimated to have cost 1.8 percent of Latin America's GDP. The cumulative shock to Sub-Saharan Africa and South Asia was milder—less than one-third of that experienced in Latin America.

Prospects for the 1990s

The interaction of unfavorable external events and inappropriate domestic policies has placed some countries on a persistent downward path. Several of the severely indebted countries have become progressively further removed from normal financial relations. The prospects for these countries depend on credible changes in domestic policy and on a response by the international community that will provide a breathing space for the adjustment process.

If the patterns of regional income growth seen in the 1980s were to be repeated in the 1990s, the results would be disastrous for most of Sub-Saharan Africa as well as for parts of Latin America and South Asia. Sub-Saharan Africa, which today

Table 1.3 Prospects for the 1990s

	Real GDP growth rates			Real GDP per capita growth rates		
Group and region	Trend, 1965–80	Recent experience, 1980–89	Forecast, 1989–2000	Trend, 1965–80	Recent experience, 1980–89	Forecast, 1989–2000
Industrial countries	3.7	3.0	3.0	2.8	2.5	2.6
Developing countries	5.9	4.3	5.1	3.4	2.3	3.2
Sub-Saharan Africa	5.2	1.0	3.7	2.0	−2.2	0.5
East Asia	7.3	8.4	6.6	4.8	6.7	5.1
China	6.4	10.1	6.8	4.1	8.7	5.4
Other	8.1	6.4	6.3	5.5	4.2	4.6
South Asia	3.6	5.5	5.1	1.2	3.2	3.2
India	3.6	5.6	5.2	1.2	3.5	3.4
Other	3.9	5.0	4.8	1.2	2.2	2.4
Eastern Europe	5.3[a]	1.4[a]	1.9	4.5[a]	0.8[a]	1.5
Middle East, North Africa, and other Europe	6.3	2.9	4.3	3.9	0.8	2.1
Latin America and the Caribbean	6.0	1.6	4.2	3.4	−0.6	2.3

a. Estimates.

has a population of about 450 million, would have an additional 165 million people, and per capita incomes would be 20 percent lower than today's near-subsistence levels. The countries of Latin America would have an additional 85 million people and average incomes 6 percent lower than today's.

The outlook, however, is for stronger performance during the 1990s (Table 1.3). The developing countries should grow, on average, by 5.1 percent a year, compared with 4.3 percent in the 1980s. This judgment reflects confidence that a combination of improvements in domestic policy and greater external assistance will gradually bring growth to closer to its long-run potential by the end of the decade. The disturbances of the 1980s are assumed not to recur, although the process of recovery will be gradual. Real commodity prices are expected to dip in the short run but then rise gradually and grow at an average 0.2 percent over the decade. Real interest rates should ease to between 3 and 4 percent over the decade, as against an average of nearly 5.5 percent in the 1980s.

The industrial countries should grow at roughly 3 percent a year—close to their long-run potential. This outlook takes into account the high rates of investment achieved since the mid-1980s and the productivity growth evident in several countries. In the short run, growth in the United States is projected to slow to between 2.0 and 2.5 percent owing to a decrease in private and government aggregate demand. The U.S. current account deficit will remain below 2 percent of GDP in the early 1990s, but smooth financing of the deficit should

prevent any disruption of global financial markets. Over the course of the decade lower U.S. government spending (especially on defense), a gradual depreciation of the dollar, and buoyant growth in the other industrial countries should help to correct the U.S. fiscal and current account deficits.

International political developments should make deficit correction in the United States easier and help to spur more vigorous growth in Europe. The strategic arms negotiations between the Warsaw Pact countries and the members of the North Atlantic Treaty Organization, as well as unilateral decisions by the U.S.S.R. and the United States to pare defense expenditures, will release resources for other uses (Box 1.3). (The members of the Warsaw Pact are Bulgaria, Czechoslovakia, the German Democratic Republic, Hungary, Poland, Romania, and the U.S.S.R.)

Despite this generally favorable outlook, the legacy of the 1980s remains evident. Although all regions are expected to have positive per capita income growth, Latin America and Sub-Saharan Africa are unlikely to achieve their long-run potential. With the reduction of debt under the Brady initiative, per capita income growth in Latin America might rise to 2.3 percent, as against an average of 3.4 percent a year between 1965 and 1980. If this projection is correct, the number of poor people in Latin America is unlikely to decrease during the decade. In Sub-Saharan Africa per capita incomes are not likely to rise in the first half of the decade, although growth of about 1 percent a year is forecast for 1995–2000. The combination of low income growth and high fertility rates implies that the

Box 1.3 World military expenditures in the 1990s

In the 1980s world military expenditures grew to unprecedented peacetime levels; at an estimated $1 trillion (Box figure 1.3), they accounted for roughly 5 percent of total world income. (Owing to data imperfections and methodological differences, estimates vary from source to source. The numbers shown here are given only as an example of the potential benefits from reductions in military spending.) But the decade that began with accelerated spending has ended with the promise of a sharp decrease. In 1989 defense expenditures in the U.S.S.R. fell by an estimated $20 billion, or 6 percent of the defense budget. The United States is also scaling back defense spending, perhaps by as much as 10 percent over the next four years. Much deeper cuts may be feasible.

Success hinges on the Strategic Arms Reduction Talks and the Negotiations on Conventional Armed Forces in Europe. These talks seek to establish an acceptable parity in strategic and conventional forces between the Warsaw Pact countries and the countries of the North Atlantic Treaty Organization. Some analysts

estimate that by the end of the decade defense outlays could be brought to half their current levels without jeopardizing the military balance between the superpowers.

The net impact of reduced defense costs on industrial and developing countries will depend on how the "peace dividend" is used. In the United States a conservative estimate puts annual savings over the next four years at about $45 billion, roughly three times the total spent each year on foreign assistance. These resources could be used to cut the fiscal deficit, boost spending on domestic programs, assist industries affected by the cutbacks, or expand the U.S. commitment to development assistance abroad.

Reining in defense spending in developing countries should also be a priority over the coming decade. On average, defense accounts for one-fifth of government spending. Moreover, the high import content of defense expenditures exacerbates the balance of payments difficulties and foreign exchange constraints faced by many developing countries.

Box figure 1.3 Defense expenditures, 1987

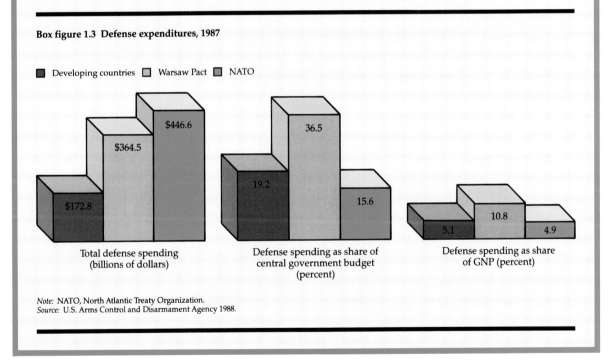

Note: NATO, North Atlantic Treaty Organization.
Source: U.S. Arms Control and Disarmament Agency 1988.

---

number of poor in the region is likely to swell rapidly.

Even this grim prospect assumes that Sub-Saharan Africa perseveres with adjustment and continues to receive debt relief and financial aid. As discussed in detail in a recent World Bank report (*Sub-Saharan Africa: From Crisis to Sustainable*

Growth), the region will need to sustain and deepen reforms to rationalize the incentive system, develop domestic infrastructure, diversify the productive base, and improve the efficiency of investment. If this can be done, export volume could grow at about 3 percent a year over the decade, allowing the region to increase imports commensurately while raising the share of investment in national expenditure. The projection also assumes the reduction or rescheduling of all official bilateral debt falling due over the decade, in accordance with the terms adopted by the Group of Seven (G-7) countries in 1988. (The Toronto summit laid out terms for rescheduling concessional bilateral claims and partially reducing nonconcessional bilateral claims on low-income African countries that are following adjustment policies supported by the World Bank or the IMF.) The gains from this assistance are projected to amount to only 10 percent of the countries' current long-term nonconcessional debt by the end of the decade. Clearly, the plan will not relieve the region of its debt burden, but it will ease the financial strain of debt service.

The projected per capita growth of 2.3 percent a year in Latin America will also depend on further policy reform and a significantly lighter debt service burden. The projections assume lower interest rates and buoyant exports (growth in volume of 4.9 percent a year). They also assume a restoration of creditworthiness and a return to precrisis investment levels by the middle of the decade. The current debt reduction strategies will need to be strengthened to ensure sufficient financing for new investment.

For other developing regions the outlook is more favorable. Per capita incomes in South Asia appear set to continue growing at 3.2 percent a year—nearly three times as fast as between 1965 and 1980. India, in particular, is forecast to lead the region with a 3.4 percent growth in per capita GDP—enough to allow substantial progress in reducing poverty. A critical assumption in the projection for India, however, is that the policies that allowed investment, productivity, and exports to expand rapidly in the 1980s will be maintained. With careful management of the real exchange rate, export volume could grow at a robust 8 percent a year. If measures are taken to restrain the fiscal deficit, this rise should prevent debt service costs from undermining growth.

The countries of East Asia are expected to continue the prudent and flexible macroeconomic policies that have worked so well in the past. The region's real per capita income is projected to grow at 5.1 percent a year. This would mean that average incomes would rise by a further 65 percent by 2000 and that poverty would be nearly eliminated. Strong global demand for the region's exports, particularly in Japan, will help to offset the effects of a slackening U.S. domestic market. Manufactured exports from China and Indonesia are ex-

pected to expand by more than 9 percent in real terms during the decade. In the high- and middle-income countries of the region exports will matter less for growth as rising domestic demand assumes greater importance.

China's economy is projected to perform well, although growth of per capita income is expected to fall from the 8.7 percent a year achieved in the 1980s to about 5.4 percent. Austerity measures designed to restrain domestic inflation and rein in foreign and domestic borrowing will put a brake on growth early in the decade. Continuing reforms in pricing and labor markets and further decentralization of investment and management should help to bring about sustained advances in productivity.

Considerable uncertainty surrounds the outlook for Eastern Europe. Needed economic reforms, combined with strong anti-inflationary measures, will depress growth for a time despite generous external assistance. Dismantling worker-managed firms and privatizing state enterprises will create open unemployment on a large scale. In the medium run, however, the prospects for boosting productivity and attracting new investment from Western Europe are good. By the end of the decade growth should be robust, and over the decade as a whole per capita income is expected to grow by 1.5 percent a year.

Per capita GDP in other developing Europe, the Middle East, and North Africa is expected to increase at 2.1 percent a year. Thanks to steady growth in world demand for oil and to an expected decline in the share of output from countries that are not members of the Organization of Petroleum Exporting Countries (OPEC), oil prices are forecast to rise 3 percent a year in real terms. This will strengthen the region's terms of trade. Debt service, however, will continue to be a drain. Morocco is the only North African country with commercial debt big enough to merit consideration for relief under the Brady initiative, but several other countries have debt-to-exports ratios that put them nearly on a par with many of the severely indebted countries.

Risks in the outlook

These forecasts inevitably rest on assumptions that may turn out to be wrong. By modifying some of the assumptions, it is possible to estimate ranges for the forecasts. This exercise also confirms the important influence that fiscal and monetary policies in the industrial countries have on developing countries. The fiscal policies of the United States have particularly large international repercussions because of the country's size and the pivotal role of the dollar in global financial markets. The persistence of current account imbalances among the United States, Japan, and Europe is largely the result of the drop in saving in the United States—a decline for which both the government and households are responsible. Overall savings in the United States have fallen by about 3 percent of GNP since the early 1980s. If savings in the United States and other industrial countries fail to rise as projected—perhaps because the United States fails to cut its federal deficit—then real interest rates will remain high in the 1990s. Under this scenario, and assuming that the industrial countries continue to tighten their monetary policies, industrial country growth rates are likely to be about 0.5 percent lower over the decade, and real interest rates will probably hold steady at about the 1980s average of 5.5 percent.

This situation would damage the growth prospects for developing countries through four main channels. First, slower industrial country growth would dampen import demand for developing country exports. Second, higher real interest rates would increase the debt service burden on countries with floating rate debt and those undertaking new borrowing. Third, commodity prices would be likely to weaken, worsening the terms of trade for exporters of primary commodities. Finally, the slower-growing industrial countries would probably be less generous in their assistance to developing countries.

Developing countries that have heavy commercial debts and depend on exports of primary commodities would be the most vulnerable to this turn of events. Over the decade real income growth in the developing countries as a group would be about 0.7 percent lower than the forecasts presented in Table 1.3. Asia would be least affected since, compared with the group as a whole, the region holds less commercial debt, has a greater share of manufactures in exports, and (except for the export-led countries) is less dependent on trade. Real income growth in South and East Asia would be lower by about 0.6 percent. Latin America would be worst affected; its average real growth would be reduced by about 1.0 percent over the 1990s. In Sub-Saharan Africa a low share of floating rate debt offsets the region's high dependence on commodity exports. As in Asia, income growth would decline by 0.6 percent, but because of the region's growing population, a slowdown there would mean that per capita incomes would fall over the decade. The outlook for the incidence of poverty in Sub-Saharan Africa would worsen accordingly.

Coordination of policies among the principal industrial nations (notably, to stabilize exchange rates) became an important factor in international economic relations during the 1980s. At their annual summits, however, the G-7 countries have as yet failed to give due consideration to the effects of their policies on the developing world. Finding solutions to the problems faced by developing countries, especially those that did not share in growth during the 1980s, will increasingly rest on coordinated efforts that recognize these linkages. There are two tasks of immediate importance: to ease the debt burden on developing countries and to lower barriers to world trade.

Dealing with debt in the 1990s

The goal of the highly indebted countries has not changed: as in the 1980s it is to return to sustained growth and external creditworthiness. That these countries have failed to restore growth and are now more deeply indebted than at the outset is testimony to the difficulty of their task. Since the debt crisis began, many severely indebted countries have restrained imports, raised exports, and thereby generated trade surpluses. These adjustments, however, have been made at the cost of compressed consumption and wages, lower investment and output, and frequent recourse to inflationary financing of government deficits. A strategy is needed to break this pattern in the 1990s.

Among the severely indebted countries a distinction must be made between low- and middle-income countries because of their significant structural differences (Table 1.4). The severely indebted low-income countries—twenty-six in all, most of them in Sub-Saharan Africa—suffer from deeply rooted structural weaknesses. Most have weak financial and infrastructural bases, depend on a narrow range of primary commodities for exports, and are crippled by low nutritional and educational standards. Rapid population growth exacerbates their difficulties. In contrast, the middle-income debtors are well endowed with natural resources and skilled labor and have well-developed industrial bases.

For all the severely indebted countries the main challenge is to design and implement credible policy reforms to foster growth. The direct benefits

Table 1.4 Comparative indicators for severely indebted low- and middle-income countries
(percent, unless otherwise specified)

Indicator	Low income	Middle income
Average population growth (1988)	3.1	2.0
GNP per capita (1988 dollars)	274.0	1,782.0
Gross domestic investment as a share of GDP (current prices, 1987–88)	14.4	22.4
Exports as a share of GDP (1987–88)	19.4	16.3
Imports as a share of GDP (1987–88)	23.3	13.7
Share of manufacturing in exports (1987–88)	6.2	45.0
Share of nonfuel commodities in exports (1987–88)	52.5	39.3
Official development assistance as a share of GDP (1987)	8.2	0.5
Under 5 mortality rate (per thousand, 1985)	191	84
Primary net enrollment rate (1985)	50	89

Source: World Bank 1989f and World Bank data.

that can be won through negotiations cannot by themselves lift the constraints imposed by chronic indebtedness; they must go hand in hand with the indirect benefits of restored credibility, higher private investment, and the repatriation of flight capital. New measures are needed to encourage investment, improve the allocation of resources, and raise, in a less distortionary way, domestic revenues for financing government. The outlook for growth and renewed creditworthiness would then be bright.

In most cases official creditors account for more than four-fifths of the total debt of the severely indebted low-income countries. The principal creditor governments are trying to reduce the debt burden of this group through the mechanisms agreed to at the 1988 Toronto summit. Sixteen Sub-Saharan African countries have rescheduled under the new protocol. The Special Program for Africa, which provides concessional balance of payments assistance to low-income countries that are undertaking significant reforms, is expected to be extended beyond 1990, when the current program ends. These, together with the IMF's Enhanced Structural Adjustment Facility, are the main sources of multilateral concessional assistance.

Even with favorable commodity prices and export growth over the next decade, the severely indebted low-income countries will need further assistance, including debt reduction, if they are to maintain per capita consumption and increase investment at the same time. They face structural impediments to growth that will take several years to overcome. In the meantime, debt service, even after the Toronto reschedulings, will continue to cost an average of 5 percent of GDP during the 1990s.

The Brady initiative is directed at the nineteen middle-income countries with predominantly commercial debt. In this group the potential for restoring growth is greater. Experience with the Brady initiative so far suggests that it is possible to strengthen adjustment programs and mobilize private investment through partial debt reduction (see Box 1.4). But there is room for improvement. For a variety of reasons, foreign commercial creditors remain reluctant to provide much new lending. Alternative profit opportunities and doubts about the prospects for debt-distressed countries, even with Brady programs in place, have accelerated the exit of commercial banks. Changes in banking regulations in creditor countries could encourage banks to take part in debt reduction programs and grant new loans. The official financial resources available under the Brady initiative amount to $30 billion to $35 billion. This is a significant amount of assistance—enough to reduce the annual debt service of the severely indebted middle-income countries by an estimated $6 billion a year between 1990 and 1993. But it is not enough to support programs for all nineteen Brady countries. Additional financing from bilateral official sources may become necessary.

Insurance against shocks is also likely to be part of any successful strategy. A 10 percent deterioration in the terms of trade, or a 2 percent rise in world interest rates, could erase the gains from debt reduction under the new approach. Protection against such contingencies is needed. One possibility is commodity-linked bonds, which spread the risk between creditors and debtors in the event of a severe drop in commodity prices. Another is to include provisions for severe output price shocks. These provisions might mirror the upside recapture clauses in the recent Mexican agreement and link lower export prices to lower debt repayment.

Policy reform to encourage investment and growth in export industries is an explicit part of the new strategy. Stronger exports would make it easier to finance imports and service debt and would thereby help to restore creditworthiness. Clearly, however, such export-based growth would be hindered by greater protectionism in the industrial countries. Efforts to improve global trade relations should be seen as an important part of the broader strategy for reducing debt and restoring growth in the middle-income debtor countries.

Changes in the world trade system

During the 1990s developing countries' export volumes are expected to grow at 6 percent a year—the same as during the 1980s. Domestic policy is critical for such growth, but just as essential will be the strengthening of the General Agreement on Tariffs and Trade (GATT) through the Uruguay Round, which is scheduled for completion by the end of 1990.

Although successive GATT rounds have cut industrial country tariffs significantly, the use of nontariff barriers has been on the rise lately. In the United States nontariff barriers on steel, automobiles, and textiles are estimated to be equivalent to an additional tariff of about 25 percent, raising protection to the level of the early postwar years. In 1989 the United States warned Brazil, India, and Japan that it might take unilateral steps to protect trade by using its "Super 301" legislation. Trade frictions with the United States have been reduced through bilateral discussions, but the threat of unilateral action remains. Voluntary export restraints,

especially on more sophisticated manufactured goods, have proliferated. More than 120 such restraints affected the exports of developing countries in 1988.

The Uruguay Round offers a chance to create a truly global trade regime under the GATT. The expansion of country and product coverage suggests that new ground may be broken. More countries than ever before are active members of the GATT, and several developing countries that had been nominal signatories are now full partners in the negotiations. The talks are covering virtually every kind of trade—not just conventional merchandise but also agriculture, services, investment measures affecting trade, and intellectual property rights.

Open trade relations are ultimately in everybody's interest. Protection in the industrial countries preserves only a small number of jobs, and at great cost to consumers. In the United States, for example, the cost of protecting each job in the textile industry is roughly four times the annual wage of the average textile employee. Protection in developing countries burdens consumers and industries that need imported inputs, and it creates an environment that rewards inefficiency. Competitive industries—the automobile industry in Korea, for instance, and the production of commuter airplanes in Brazil—have sometimes been built behind protectionist walls, but such success is rare, and failure is all too common.

Box 1.5 Going bananas in the European Community, 1992

World trade in bananas totals about $2 billion a year, and 30 percent of this is sold in the European Community. Although these imports are regulated by the EC, exceptions to existing rules protect the rights of some countries to grant preferential arrangements to traditional suppliers. For example, Italy imports bananas from Somalia and Britain from Jamaica and the Windward Islands. Belgium, Denmark, and Luxembourg have set a flat 20 percent tariff on bananas from other than African and Caribbean countries. Germany, the only country with essentially unrestricted trade, imports mainly from the efficient "dollar banana" countries in Central and South America.

After 1992 a common agreement on banana imports will be in place. It is still unclear what form this agree-ment will take, but it will have important effects on the division of export earnings among banana producers. Box table 1.5 reports the simulated effects on the banana market of a move to free trade.

Moving to free trade would lower the price that protected exporters receive by 49 percent, and they would suffer a loss of $209 million. Developing country exporters in the dollar banana countries would gain an estimated $61 million from the move to free trade. The largest net gains ($386 million) would go to the Europeans themselves, mainly as a result of the 24 percent drop in import prices. Non-European importers (principally the United States) would lose an estimated $46 million owing to the rise in world prices.

Box table 1.5 The impact on the banana market of moving to free trade in the European Community

Group	Price effects (percent change) [a]	Volume effects (percent change)	Revenue effects (millions of dollars)
Exporters			
Protected [b]	−49	−46	−209
Other suppliers	4	12	61
Importers			
European protected markets [c]	−24	15	394
European unprotected markets [d]	1	1	−8
Rest of world	2	−1	−46

Note: Prices are based on 1987 data.
a. Average retail prices are used for importers and f.o.b. export prices for exporters.
b. Canary Islands, Guadaloupe, Jamaica, Madeira, Martinique, Somalia, the Windward Islands, and other African, Caribbean, and Pacific (ACP) countries. (European imports of bananas from the Pacific states are, however, negligible.)
c. France, Greece, Italy, Portugal, Spain, and the United Kingdom. French prices are used to represent the market.
d. German prices represent the market.
Source: Borrell and Yang 1990.

"Project 1992," the effort to create a single European market, is likely to have a great effect on world trade. The European Community (EC) will become the largest market in the world, with a population of 320 million and a GDP of about $6 trillion. It will account for about 30 percent of developing country exports. And this huge market may well expand during the next decade to include several members of the European Free Trade Association (EFTA) and some Eastern European countries. (Indeed, the German Democratic Republic is already likely to be included.)

The effect on the developing countries will depend on whether the trade-creating effects of greater efficiency and growth outweigh the trade-diverting effects of external barriers to entry. It has been estimated that the 1992 program could boost European GDP by as much as 5 percent in five to ten years, leading to an increase of about $4 billion in imports of primary commodities from developing countries. The EC Commission, however, has estimated that the removal of internal barriers may reduce Europe's manufactured imports by 10 percent, and the developing countries would bear part of that loss of trade. The possibility that trade diversion could outweigh trade creation is greater for manufactures, especially if the gains in EC output come about through trade diversion rather than as a result of higher productivity. The net impact on the main developing country exporters to Europe might then be severe. This risk would increase still further if the EC adopted special trade arrangements with Eastern Europe; other developing countries compete with Eastern Europe in supplying manufactured goods to European markets.

Much depends on what form Europe's common

external trade barriers take. Will Europe remove its trade restrictions and reduce tariffs—perhaps as part of the Uruguay Round (Box 1.5)? Or will it replace trade restrictions with tariffs or adopt other nontariff barriers, such as uniform quality standards and content requirements? All developing country exports—tropical and temperate agricultural goods, manufactures, and services—will be affected directly and indirectly by these decisions. The greatest threat is that new trade barriers will proliferate, encouraging retaliation elsewhere.

What does this mean for the poor?

The aggregate statistics examined in this chapter are important for understanding events in the world economy, but they do not show what is happening to people, especially the poor. The rest of the Report addresses this question directly. How the poor earn their living, the adequacy of their health care, and their access to education and other public services will be examined in detail. But this chapter's findings concerning the differences in regional economic performance are immediately relevant. Although growth in average per capita incomes does not automatically improve the well-being of the poor, it is a crucial factor. Figure 1.7 shows sharp regional differences in recent and forecast income growth. What do these differences mean for the poor?

The next two chapters examine the current extent of poverty and the consequences for the poor of recent economic performance. Has rapid per capita growth in East and South Asia really reached the poor? Who suffers most from falling incomes in Sub-Saharan Africa? Chapters 2 and 3 lay the foundation for the discussion of public policies in Chapters 4 through 8. The final chapter reexamines the implications of the divergent re-

gional performances projected for the 1990s and asks how they will affect the outlook for reducing global poverty at the start of the next century.

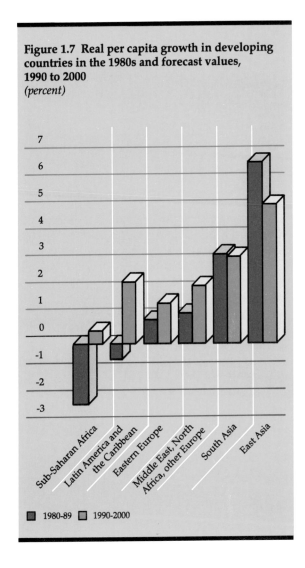

Figure 1.7 Real per capita growth in developing countries in the 1980s and forecast values, 1990 to 2000

(percent)

Legend: ■ 1980-89 □ 1990-2000

What do we know about the poor?

Reducing poverty is the fundamental objective of economic development. It is estimated that in 1985 more than one billion people in the developing world lived in absolute poverty. Clearly, economic development has a long way to go. Knowledge about the poor is essential if governments are to adopt sound development strategies and more effective policies for attacking poverty. How many poor are there? Where do they live? What are their precise economic circumstances? Answering these questions is the first step toward understanding the impact of economic policies on the poor. This chapter draws on a number of detailed household surveys done over the past ten years or so, including some conducted by the World Bank, to estimate the number of poor people and to establish what is known about them.

Three poor families

We begin by focusing on the people this Report is intended to help—by telling the stories of three poor families living in three different countries. These families have much in common. For them, the difference between a tolerable quality of life and mere survival depends on their capacity to work and on their opportunities to work. Lack of education, landlessness, and acute vulnerability to illness and seasonal hard times affect all of them to varying degrees. Problems such as these are at the core of poverty.

A poor subsistence farmer's household in Ghana

In Ghana's Savannah region a typical family of seven lives in three one-room huts made from mud bricks, with earthen floors. They have little furniture and no toilet, electricity, or running water. Water is obtained from a stream a fifteen-minute walk away. The family has few possessions, apart from three acres of unirrigated land and one cow, and virtually no savings.

The family raises sorghum, vegetables, and groundnuts on its land. The work is seasonal and physically demanding. At peak periods of tilling, sowing, and harvesting, all family members are involved, including the husband's parents, who are sixty and seventy years old. The soil is very low in quality, but the family lacks access to fertilizer and other modern inputs. Moreover, the region is susceptible to drought; the rains fail two years out of every five. In addition to her farm work, the wife has to fetch water, collect firewood, and feed the family. The market town where the husband sells their meager cash crops and buys essentials is five miles away and is reached by dirt tracks and an unsealed road that is washed away every time the rains come.

None of the older family members ever attended school, but the eight-year-old son is now in the first grade. The family hopes that he will be able to stay in school, although there is pressure to keep him at home to help with the farm in the busy periods. He and his two younger sisters have never had any vaccinations and have never seen a doctor.

A poor urban household in Peru

In a shantytown on the outskirts of Lima a shack made of scraps of wood, iron, and cardboard houses a family of six. Inside there is a bed, a table, a radio, and two benches. The kitchen consists of a small kerosene stove and some tins in one corner. There is no toilet or electricity. The shantytown is provided with some public services, but these tend to be intermittent. Garbage is collected twice a week. Water is delivered to those who have a cement tank, but this family has been unable to save enough for the cement. In the meantime, the mother and eldest daughter fill buckets at the public standpipe 500 yards away.

Husband and wife are Indians from the same mountain village in the Sierra. Neither completed primary school. They came to Lima with two children almost four years ago, hoping to find work and schools. Although they have jobs, the economic recession of the past few years has hit them hard. Better-off neighbors who arrived in Lima three to six years before they did say that it was easier to get ahead then. Still, husband and wife are hopeful that they will soon be able to rebuild their house with bricks and cement and, in time, install electricity, running water, and a toilet like their neighbors. They now have four children, after losing one infant, and the two oldest attend the local community school, recently built with funds and assistance from a nongovernmental organization (NGO). All the children were given polio and diphtheria-pertussis-tetanus (DPT) inoculations when a mobile clinic came to the shantytown. Community solidarity is strong, and a community center is active in the shantytown.

The father works in construction as a casual laborer. The work is uncertain, and there are periods when he must take any odd job he can find. When he is hired on a construction site, however, it is frequently for a month or so. His wife worries that he will be injured on the job like some of his fellow workers, who can no longer work and yet receive no compensation. She earns some income doing laundry at a wealthy person's house twice a week. To get there she must take a long bus ride, but the job does enable her to look after her one- and three-year-old children. She is also in charge of all domestic chores at home. When she is away from the house for long periods, the two oldest children take morning and afternoon turns at school so as not to leave the house unattended. There have been many burglaries in the neighborhood recently, and although the family has few possessions, radios and kerosene stoves are much in demand. The family lives on rice, bread, and vegetable oil (all subsidized by the government), supplemented with vegetables and, occasionally, some fish.

A poor landless laborer's household in Bangladesh

In a rural community in a drought-prone region of Bangladesh a landless laborer and his family attempt to get through another lean season.

Their house consists of a packed mud floor and a straw roof held up by bamboo poles from which dry palm leaves are tied to serve as walls. Inside there is straw to sleep on and burlap bags for warmth. The laborer and his wife, three children, and niece do not own the land on which the shack is built. They are lucky, however, to have a kindly neighbor who has indefinitely lent them the plot and a little extra on which they are able to grow turmeric and ginger and have planted a jackfruit tree.

The father is an agricultural day laborer and tends to be underemployed most of the year. During slow agricultural periods in the past he could sometimes find nonagricultural wage labor—for example, in construction in a nearby town—but he lost the strength to do much strenuous work after a bout of paratyphoid. He therefore engages in petty services around the village for very low pay.

The wife typically spends her day cooking, caring for the children, husking rice, and fetching water from the well. She is helped in these tasks by her thirteen-year-old niece, whose parents died in a cholera epidemic some years ago. The woman and her niece are always on the lookout for ways to earn a little extra. Such work as husking rice, weeding fields, and chopping wood is sometimes available from better-off neighbors. The nine-year-old son attends school a few mornings a week in a town an hour's walk away. The rest of the day he and his seven-year-old sister gather fuel and edible roots and weeds. The sister also looks after the baby when her mother or cousin cannot.

The household spends about 85 percent of its meager income on food—predominantly rice. Family members are used to having only two meals a day. They hope to struggle through to the rice harvest without having to cut down and sell their jackfruit tree or the bamboo poles supporting their roof.

Measuring poverty

These are the people behind the statistics. Lifting them out of poverty will depend to a large extent on a better understanding of how many poor there are, where they live, and, above all, why they are poor. None of these questions turns out to be straightforward. To begin with, it is necessary to be more precise about what "poverty" really means.

Poverty is not the same as inequality. The distinction needs to be stressed. Whereas poverty is concerned with the absolute standard of living of a part of society—the poor—inequality refers to relative living standards across the whole society. At maximum inequality one person has everything and, clearly, poverty is high. But minimum inequality (where all are equal) is possible with zero poverty (where no one is poor) as well as with maximum poverty (where all are poor).

This Report defines poverty as the inability to attain a minimal standard of living. To make this definition useful, three questions must be answered. How do we measure the standard of living? What do we mean by a minimal standard of living? And, having thus identified the poor, how do we express the overall severity of poverty in a single measure or index?

Measuring the standard of living

Household incomes and expenditures per capita are adequate yardsticks for the standard of living as long as they include own production, which is very important for most of the world's poor (Box 2.1). Neither measure, however, captures such dimensions of welfare as health, life expectancy, literacy, and access to public goods or common-property resources. Being able to get clean drinking water, for example, matters to one's standard of living, but it is not reflected in consumption or income as usually measured. Households with access to free public services are better off than those without, even though their incomes and expenditures may be the same. Because of these drawbacks, this Report supplements a consumption-based poverty measure with others, such as nutrition, life expectancy, under 5 mortality, and school enrollment rates.

The poverty line

All the measures described above are judged in relation to some norm. For example, we deem life expectancies in some countries to be low in relation to those attained by other countries at a given date. The choice of the norm is particularly important in the case of the consumption-based measures of poverty.

A consumption-based poverty line can be thought of as comprising two elements: the expenditure necessary to buy a minimum standard of nutrition and other basic necessities and a further amount that varies from country to country, reflecting the cost of participating in the everyday life of society. The first part is relatively straightfor-

Box 2.1 How should we measure living standards?

Current consumption (including consumption from own production) reflects households' ability to buffer their standard of living through saving and borrowing, despite income fluctuations. To that extent, consumption is a better measure of well-being than income. A study of Sri Lanka, however, found that both consumption and income indicators identified the same people, by and large, as poor. Furthermore, current consumption may not be a good measure of a household's typical standard of living (although it is probably better than current income). In another study, which looked at a set of Indian households over nine years, 54 percent of households, on average, were deemed poor on the basis of current-year consumption. Slightly fewer, 50 percent, were deemed poor on the basis of their nine-year mean consumption.

Another problem is that different households may face different prices. In developing countries prices often vary between urban and rural areas. A study of Sri Lanka that allowed for this difference found that price

variability made little difference to estimates of poverty. In bigger countries, however, rural-urban differences are a more significant problem. In Indonesia, for example, regional price differentials are large and affect regional comparisons of poverty.

Household size and composition are also relevant. Researchers estimate "equivalent adult scales" based on the consumption needs of individuals according to age, sex, and activity. Allowing for household composition in the Sri Lanka estimates, however, yielded a poverty estimate similar to that based on the per capita measures; the overlap in classifying people as poor was 90 percent.

Such corrections typically assume that the distribution of consumption within the household is equal. What if this is not the case? A recent study of data for the Philippines concluded that allowing for inequality in distribution might change the figures for the overall incidence of poverty but not the pattern across socio-economic groups.

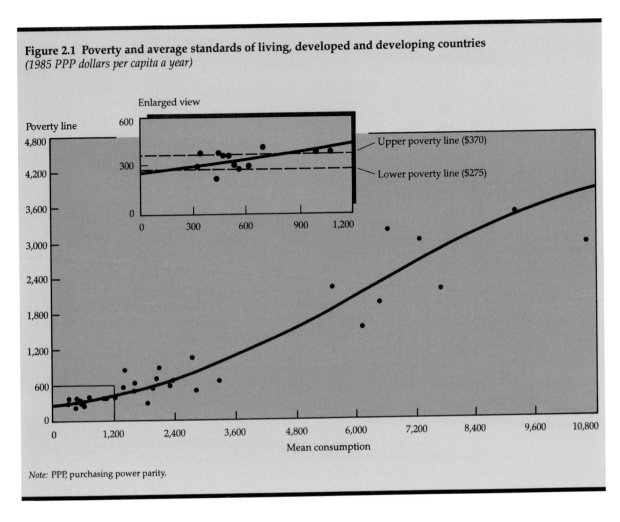

Figure 2.1 Poverty and average standards of living, developed and developing countries
(1985 PPP dollars per capita a year)

Enlarged view

Poverty line

Upper poverty line ($370)

Lower poverty line ($275)

Mean consumption

Note: PPP, purchasing power parity.

ward. The cost of minimum adequate caloric intakes and other necessities can be calculated by looking at the prices of the foods that make up the diets of the poor. The second part is far more subjective; in some countries indoor plumbing is a luxury, but in others it is a "necessity."

The perception of poverty has evolved historically and varies tremendously from culture to culture. Criteria for distinguishing poor from nonpoor tend to reflect specific national priorities and normative concepts of welfare and rights. In general, as countries become wealthier, their perception of the acceptable minimum level of consumption—the poverty line—changes. Figure 2.1 plots country-specific poverty lines against per capita consumption (both in 1985 purchasing power parity—PPP—dollars) for thirty-four developing and industrial countries. The poverty threshold rises slowly at low levels of average consumption but more sharply at higher levels.

When discussing poverty within countries, this Report uses country-specific poverty lines. In this chapter and in Chapter 9, however, a universal poverty line is needed to permit cross-country comparison and aggregation. This global poverty line is inevitably somewhat arbitrary. Rather than settle for a single number, this chapter employs two: $275 and $370 per person a year. (The amounts are in constant 1985 PPP prices.) This range was chosen to span the poverty lines estimated in recent studies for a number of countries with low average incomes—Bangladesh, the Arab Republic of Egypt, India, Indonesia, Kenya, Morocco, and Tanzania (see the inset in Figure 2.1). The lower limit of the range coincides with a poverty line commonly used for India.

How much poverty is there?

Once the poor have been distinguished from the nonpoor, the simplest way to measure poverty is to express the number of poor as a proportion of the population. This *headcount index* is a useful measure, although it is often criticized because it ignores the extent to which the poor fall below the poverty line. The income shortfall, or *poverty gap*, avoids this drawback. It measures the transfer that would bring the income of every poor person exactly up to the poverty line, thereby eliminating poverty. This Report relies on both the headcount index and the poverty gap. Box 2.2 discusses some other measures.

The use of the upper poverty line—$370—gives an estimate of 1,115 million people in the developing countries in poverty in 1985. That is roughly one-third of the total population of the developing world. Of these, 630 million—18 percent of the total population of the developing world—were extremely poor: their annual consumption was less than $275, the lower poverty line. Despite these massive numbers, the aggregate poverty gap—the transfer needed to lift everybody above the poverty line—was only 3 percent of developing countries' total consumption. The transfer needed to lift everybody out of extreme poverty was, of course, even smaller—just 1 percent of developing countries' consumption. Mortality for children under 5 averaged 121 per thousand for all developing countries, aggregate life expectancy was 62 years, and the overall net primary school enrollment rate was 83 percent. These figures hide considerable variation within and among countries. Table 2.1 sets out a detailed regional breakdown of these estimates.

Although care has been taken to make the table as precise as possible, the margins of error are inevitably wide, and the figures, it must be stressed, are only estimates. The quality of the underlying data varies. Reputable household income and expenditure surveys have been used where available. These surveys encompass 2.5 billion people, or almost 75 percent of the total. For other countries, including most of Sub-Saharan Africa, extrapolations have been made on the basis of indicators that are strongly correlated with the measures of poverty derived from the household surveys. The notes to Table 2.1 give calculations of the potential imprecision of the estimates as a result of inadequacies in the data.

Nearly half of the developing world's poor, and nearly half of those in extreme poverty, live in South Asia. Sub-Saharan Africa has about one-third as many poor, although in relation to the region's overall population, its poverty is roughly as high. Table 2.1 also shows that both South Asia and Sub-Saharan Africa have low scores on several other social indicators; in Sub-Saharan Africa, in particular, life expectancy and primary school enrollment rates are alarmingly low, and under 5 mortality rates are alarmingly high. The Middle Eastern and North African countries have the next highest poverty, according to all the indicators. They are followed by Latin America and the Caribbean and by East Asia. China's overall performance is impressive, although the size of its population means that a relatively low headcount index still translates into large numbers of poor.

The characteristics of the poor

If governments are to reduce poverty or to judge how their economic policies affect poverty, they need to know a lot about the poor. For example, information on how the poor derive and spend their incomes can help policymakers assess how changes in relative prices will affect real income. Policies targeted directly to the poor can hardly succeed unless governments know who the poor are and how they respond to policies and to their environment. Unfortunately, gathering this sort of information is not always easy. The poor are heterogeneous, and data about their characteristics are patchy. The following discussion looks at where the poor live, the size and composition of their households, what they do for a living, what they own and purchase, what risks they face, and how they fit into the society around them.

Rural and urban poverty

In many countries poverty has a significant regional dimension. In general, it is more common in areas with low average incomes, but the link is sometimes surprisingly weak. Figure 2.2 plots the headcount index of poverty (in the upper panel)

and the infant mortality rate (in the lower panel) against average monthly consumption per capita for urban and rural areas in India. At any given level of consumption, the headcount index and (especially) the infant mortality rate can vary widely. This underlines the need to look beyond average incomes to the distribution of income and the provision of social services.

Poverty as measured by low income tends to be at its worst in rural areas, even allowing for the often substantial differences in cost of living between town and countryside. The problems of malnutrition, lack of education, low life expectancy, and substandard housing are also, as a rule, more severe in rural areas. This is still true in Latin America, despite high urbanization rates. The importance of rural poverty is not always understood, partly because the urban poor are more visible and more vocal than their rural counterparts. In 1980 El Salvador's infant mortality rate was 81 per thousand live births in rural areas and 48 in the towns; the incidence of malnutrition was five times higher in Peru's Sierra than in Lima. Table 2.2 confirms that in many countries rural poverty is a critical factor in the overall incidence and depth of poverty.

The extent of poverty can vary greatly among rural areas within the same country. The acute deprivation in Brazil's Northeast Region, which has more than 50 percent of the country's poor but only 27 percent of its total population, is well

Table 2.1 How much poverty is there in the developing countries? The situation in 1985

	Extremely poor			Poor (including extremely poor)			Social indicators		
Region	Number (millions)	Headcount index (percent)	Poverty gap	Number (millions)	Headcount index (percent)	Poverty gap	Under 5 mortality (per thousand)	Life expectancy (years)	Net primary enrollment rate (percent)
Sub-Saharan Africa	120	30	4	180	47	11	196	50	56
East Asia	120	9	0.4	280	20	1	96	67	96
China	80	8	1	210	20	3	58	69	93
South Asia	300	29	3	520	51	10	172	56	74
India	250	33	4	420	55	12	199	57	81
Eastern Europe	3	4	0.2	6	8	0.5	23	71	90
Middle East and North Africa	40	21	1	60	31	2	148	61	75
Latin America and the Caribbean	50	12	1	70	19	1	75	66	92
All developing countries	633	18	1	1,116	33	3	121	62	83

Note: The poverty line in 1985 PPP dollars is $275 per capita a year for the extremely poor and $370 per capita a year for the poor.

The headcount index is defined as the percentage of the population below the poverty line. The 95 percent confidence intervals around the point estimates for the headcount indices are Sub-Saharan Africa, 19, 76; East Asia, 21, 22; South Asia, 50, 53; Eastern Europe, 7, 10; Middle East and North Africa, 13, 51; Latin America and the Caribbean, 14, 30; and all developing countries, 28, 39.

The poverty gap is defined as the aggregate income shortfall of the poor as a percentage of aggregate consumption. Under 5 mortality rates are for 1980–85, except for China and South Asia, where the period is 1975–80.

Source: Hill and Pebley 1988, Ravallion and others (background paper), and United Nations and World Bank data 1989.

known. Regional disparities are equally stark in many other countries. Thailand's Northeast Region, Côte d'Ivoire's Savannah, Indonesia's Nusa Tenggara, the Andean highlands of Bolivia, Ecuador, Guatemala, and Peru, rural Gansu Province in China, parts of the central Asian region of the U.S.S.R., and Appalachia in the United States are all areas of concentrated poverty.

Many of the poor are located in regions where arable land is scarce, agricultural productivity is low, and drought, floods, and environmental degradation are common. In Latin America, for example, the worst poverty occurs predominantly in arid zones or in steep hill-slope areas that are ecologically vulnerable. Such areas are often isolated in every sense. Opportunities for nonfarm employment are few, and the demand for labor tends to be highly seasonal. Others among the poor live in regions that have a more promising endowment of natural resources but lack access to social services (education and health) and infrastructure (irrigation, information and technical assistance, transport, and market centers).

Although urban incomes are generally higher and urban services and facilities more accessible, poor town-dwellers may suffer more than rural households from certain aspects of poverty. The urban poor, typically housed in slums or squatter settlements, often have to contend with appalling overcrowding, bad sanitation, and contaminated water. The sites are often illegal and dangerous. Forcible eviction, floods and landslides, and chemical pollution are constant threats. Some of these people are migrants from the countryside who are seeking better-paid work. For many, particularly in Latin America, migration is permanent. For others, as in East Africa and parts of Southeast Asia, it may be temporary, reflecting (for example) seasonality in agriculture. The effect that migration to the towns has on poverty depends crucially on whether urban employment opportunities are better or worse than in rural areas. The evidence suggests that urban areas do offer more opportunities for higher-paid work, and this implies that, on balance, urbanization helps to reduce poverty.

What are the demographic characteristics of the poor?

Households with the lowest income per person tend to be large, with many children or other economically dependent members. In Pakistan in 1984 the poorest 10 percent of households had an average of 7.7 members, of whom 3.3 were children under age 9. The corresponding national averages were 6.1 and 2.0. Lack of a fit male adult can be crucial, especially if women have small children to care for or are culturally discouraged from taking paid employment.

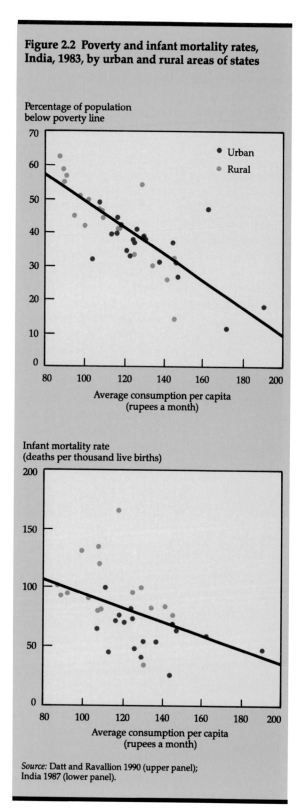

Figure 2.2 Poverty and infant mortality rates, India, 1983, by urban and rural areas of states

Percentage of population below poverty line

• Urban
• Rural

Average consumption per capita (rupees a month)

Infant mortality rate (deaths per thousand live births)

Average consumption per capita (rupees a month)

Source: Datt and Ravallion 1990 (upper panel); India 1987 (lower panel).

Table 2.2 Rural and urban poverty in the 1980s

Region and country	Rural population as percentage of total	Rural poor as percentage of total	Infant mortality (per thousand live births)		Access to safe water (percentage of population)	
			Rural	Urban	Rural	Urban
Sub-Saharan Africa						
Côte d'Ivoire	57	86	121	70	10	30
Ghana	65	80	87	67	39	93
Kenya	80	96	59	57	21	61
Asia						
India	77	79	105	57	50	76
Indonesia	73	91	74	57	36	43
Malaysia	62	80	. .	. .	76	96
Philippines	60	67	55	42	54	49
Thailand	70	80	43	28	66	56
Latin America						
Guatemala	59	66	85	65	26	89
Mexico	31	37	79	29	51	79
Panama	50	59	28	22	63	100
Peru	44	52	101	54	17	73
Venezuela	15	20	. .	. .	80	80

Does family size determine living standards, or is it the other way around? The decision to have many children can be a sensible response to poverty. Mortality is high for children in destitute families, but it is essential to ensure that some children survive to support the household in the parents' old age, if not sooner. Even before they can earn income, children can free adults from various domestic tasks. Still, many poor parents report that they want no more children and that their last-born child had been unwanted. These couples often lack access to modern family planning services.

In the rural areas of many developing countries the aged often rely on the extended family—a structure that tends to be stable over time. In urban areas multigenerational households are more likely to break up, and the elderly are becoming more vulnerable. Moreover, traditions such as kinship in Africa and the duty of sons in India and Bangladesh to care for widowed mothers may be in decline. In India widows without an adult son are already a particularly underprivileged group.

Poverty and hunger among children is of particular concern. The very young are highly susceptible to disease, and malnutrition and poverty-related illnesses can cause permanent harm. Child poverty is strongly self-perpetuating. Child labor is common; many households depend on it, and much of the work has the social purpose of engaging the child in family activities. But work is often at the expense of schooling. For many poor people the opportunity costs of sending children to school outweigh the future benefits—especially for girls, whose economic value is often reckoned to be lower in various parts of the world. Some of the work that children do is highly exploitative; cases of debt bondage and of long hours worked in unhealthy conditions for low wages are widely documented.

Are women poorer than men? The data on incomes are too weak to give a clear answer. But the available figures on health, nutrition, education, and labor force participation show that women are often severely disadvantaged. For example, data for 1980 indicate that the literacy rate for women was only 61 percent of that for men in Africa; the figures were 52 percent in South Asia, 57 percent in the Middle East, 82 percent in Southeast Asia, and 94 percent in Latin America. Women face all manner of cultural, social, legal, and economic obstacles that men—even poor men—do not. They typically work longer hours and, when they are paid at all, for lower wages. A study in Nepal found that, on average, poor women worked eleven hours a day, men seven-and-a-half. In many developed countries the poorest include large numbers of single-mother households. Poor female-headed households are also increasingly common in southern Africa and Latin America. In Brazil female-headed households account for 10 percent of all households but for 15 percent of the poor.

Assets

The poor usually lack assets as well as income. In local economies in which wealth and status come from the land, disadvantaged households are typi-

cally land poor or landless. Poverty is highly correlated with landlessness in South Asia, southern
Africa, and much of Latin America. (See the data
in Table 2.3 for Bangladesh.) When the poor do
own land, it is often unproductive and frequently
lies outside irrigated areas. The poor are usually
unable to improve such plots, since they lack income and access to credit.

Many of the poor have access to land without
having ownership rights. Tenancy is common—
although the poorest are often locked out of these
arrangements because they lack the other resources needed for farming. Tenancy does not provide collateral or a secure hedge against risk, and
access to the land from one year to the next is often
uncertain.

In other cases the poor have access to land that is
owned by the community or is common property.
Such arrangements are increasingly jeopardized
by population pressure, privatization, overex-
ploitation of resources, and deterioration of the environment. Studies of Rajasthani villages in India
over twenty years found that the income earned
from common-property resources has declined for
all these reasons. In the Sahel region of Africa
common ownership of the (generally unproductive) land is considered a principal cause of overgrazing and deforestation. Environmental degradation of common-property resources can badly
hurt the assetless poor. Improving their access to
income-earning opportunities while protecting the
environment is an important policy issue.

The poor are also lacking in human capital.
Everywhere, they have a lower level of educational
achievement than the population at large. (Figure
2.3 illustrates this with data from India.) Poor
women often have too many children, spaced too

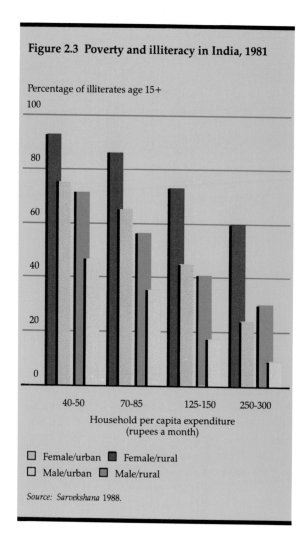

Figure 2.3 Poverty and illiteracy in India, 1981

Percentage of illiterates age 15+

Household per capita expenditure
(rupees a month)

☐ Female/urban   ■ Female/rural
☐ Male/urban   ◼ Male/rural

Source: Sarvekshana 1988.

close together, to the detriment of their health. The
poor frequently suffer from hunger and malnutrition and from related illnesses. This undermines
their capacity for labor—often their main or only
asset.

The ownership of assets directly affects income
opportunities (Box 2.3). Without assets such as
land, the poor must hire out their labor. Without
adequate human capital, they are limited to unskilled work. The elderly and the incapacitated
may not even be able to offer their labor and may
be forced to rely on charity. The importance of assets, broadly defined, suggests that policies should
seek to increase the assets owned by the poor—
especially skills, health, and other aspects of human capital and, in agricultural economies, land.

Sources of income

Besides having lower incomes and fewer assets
than the nonpoor, the poor often have distinctive
sources of livelihood. Most of the destitute mix

**Table 2.3 Poverty and landholding
in Bangladesh, 1978–79**

Landholding class (acres of land owned)	Percentage of total households in class	Mean income (taka a month)	Mean land-holdings (acres)	Headcount index (percentage of population)
Landless	7.1	508	0	93
0–0.5	36.1	560	0.1	93
0.5–1.0	10.5	711	0.7	84
1.0–1.5	8.9	783	1.2	78
1.5–2.5	12.1	912	2.0	68
2.5–5.0	13.8	1,163	3.5	45
5.0–7.5	5.7	1,516	6.0	23
7.5+	5.8	2,155	14.0	10
Total	100.0	865	2.1	70

Source: Ravallion 1989b.

Box 2.3 Village-level perspectives on asset poverty

Much has been learned about asset poverty from village studies. In Palanpur, a well-studied village in India's Uttar Pradesh State, the most disadvantaged groups were invariably landless casual laborers for whom work was not available on a regular basis and households without an able-bodied male. In 1983–84 all households with both these characteristics were found to be poor. They had very few opportunities for raising their incomes. Self-employment was either restricted to certain castes or required skills and physical capital that poor households lacked. As entry to regular wage employment was also limited, poor men had no choice but to take occasional agricultural work. Local tradition denied even this option to most women.

In Kenya, where population pressure on the land has been rising, landholding was found to be an important determinant of welfare. Another study, however, suggests that among smallholders education is more important; it enables family members to bring in urban wages that can then be invested in farm innovation and higher productivity.

A study of rural Tanzanian households in 1980 found that the poorest in the twenty sampled villages did not possess significantly less land or labor resources than others. Differences in living standards were largely attributable to differences in human capital and in ownership of nonlabor resources such as livestock. The poorer households were less likely to participate in market transactions than the nonpoor, since they lacked the resources to grow cash crops and could not take the chance of a bad harvest that would leave them dependent on the market for their food needs. The poor also had much lower rates of return on work away from the family farm. Weak skills restricted them to marginal pursuits such as handicrafts, while the better-off captured more lucrative wage employment.

---

many different earning activities. It is common for the poor to work as cultivators, hunters and gatherers, small artisans, petty traders, and wage laborers at various times of the year. The poor are rarely self-sufficient. They need cash to buy small household items such as soap, clothes, salt, and cooking oil, and they have to pay taxes and medical and school costs. So they need to sell at least some of their produce or obtain some paid work.

Agriculture is still the main source of income for the world's poor. We have seen that the greatest numbers of the poor, including the very poorest, are found overwhelmingly in rural areas. Their livelihoods are linked to farming, whether or not they earn their incomes directly from it. The demand for nonfarm goods and services often depends on the health of the farm economy. To help the rural poor, policies should strive to raise agricultural productivity—through investment in infrastructure and through appropriate pricing, for example.

Within agriculture, there are two groups of poor: the self-employed and wage laborers. The distinction is often imprecise. Many casual farm laborers also own tiny plots of land. These plots are not sufficient to ensure family survival, but if they are productive, they can provide extra income and some collateral against risk. Most of the poor in Botswana, Côte d'Ivoire, Ghana, Kenya, Nigeria, and Tanzania are small-scale agriculturalists or pastoralists. In 1981–82 the poorest tenth of Kenya's population earned two-thirds of its income from farming. In Côte d'Ivoire in 1985 most poor households were headed by self-employed cultivators. (This group also had the lowest literacy rate and the largest poverty gap.) In these African countries agricultural wage earners are still relatively unimportant among the poor. The situation is somewhat different in southern Africa; there many households hire out their labor, although not necessarily in farming.

Agricultural self-employment is also important in Southeast Asia. In Thailand a study of 1981 data found that 75 percent of poor rural households were self-employed in agriculture; for nonpoor rural households the figure was 64 percent. Seventeen percent of all households, poor and nonpoor, depended primarily on agricultural wage labor. Recent data for Indonesia indicate that in 1987 households that were self-employed in farming (as tabulated by the principal activity of the head of household) accounted for 58 percent of the poor and 41 percent of the total population. Farm wage laborers, in contrast, accounted for only 14 percent of the poor and 9 percent of the population.

The picture is more varied in South Asia. In India households self-employed in agriculture accounted for 35 percent of poor rural households in 1977–78 and for 46 percent of all rural households. Households engaged in agricultural labor accounted for a further 44 percent of poor rural households but for only 30 percent of all rural households. Figures for Pakistan suggest that among the poor there are fewer farm laborers than own-account cultivators; the opposite is true for Bangladesh.

In Latin America most of the poor are small-scale farmers, but few derive adequate subsistence from their plots. In the plantation economies of Central America, especially in Costa Rica, wage labor in agriculture is important. Peru's poor are mainly small farmers and herders. In a survey conducted in 1985–86, 78 percent of the heads of poor households said they were self-employed and 71 percent said they worked in farming; the corresponding figures for all Peruvians were 60 and 40 percent. In the Sierra, Peru's poorest region, the numbers are even higher. In Mexico, too, poverty is concentrated among cultivator families.

Rural nonfarm employment mainly consists of cottage industries, services, and commerce. In Asia, Sub-Saharan Africa, and Latin America rural nonfarm work tends to be highly seasonal or part-time. In Asia wages in these jobs are generally lower than wages in agriculture. The poor are concentrated in traditional industries with low skill and capital requirements and very low labor productivity. Their products are normally intended for home consumption or for the local market. Demand is an important constraint on nonfarm economic activities, which depend heavily on the primary farm sector. In areas in which agricultural incomes have grown, nonfarm employment has flourished and wages have risen. Nonfarm employment is particularly important in providing work in slack seasons for landless laborers and women from poor households.

In some of the poorest villages in Thailand, for example, woven bamboo baskets and other forest by-products provide extra income for rice farmers. Forest protection laws make this a risky and unprofitable business—another illustration of how the loss of common-property resources harms the poor in the short term. Studies have found that virtually all poor farmers in western Guatemala and the northernmost region of the Peruvian Sierra supplement their farming income with artisanal production and petty trade. In the poorest households much of this additional work is done by women.

Informal sector jobs of one sort or another—generally the jobs that pay least—are the main source of livelihood for the urban poor. In Brazil in 1985 an estimated 75 percent of heads of poor families worked in the informal sector, compared with 35 percent of the population as a whole. Disadvantaged urban groups are largely self-employed. They sell services and engage in trade or work on a casual basis in construction, manufacturing, and transport. Some are full-time beggars, garbage sift-

ers, prostitutes, or pickpockets. Incomes are low and insecure. In Bombay poverty was found to be more common among casual workers than among regular employees, and there was little mobility between the two forms of employment. About half the urban poor in Pakistan are self-employed, mostly in trade and manufacturing. They are generally less skilled than people who work for wages.

Transfers can be an important source of income for some of the poor. In most developing countries transfers are made by relatives and friends or through village support systems rather than by the government. Transfers accounted for 9 percent of the incomes of poor Kenyan smallholders in 1974–75. In rural Java transfers are targeted toward the sick and elderly; in urban areas the unemployed receive assistance. For the most disadvantaged households, transfers can be crucial.

How does income variability affect the poor?

Because incomes fluctuate, a static picture of poverty can be deceptive. Evidence indicates that some people move in and out of poverty, whereas others never cross the poverty threshold (Box 2.4).

Households deliberately diversify their sources of income to reduce the risk that adverse circumstances will cause a sharp drop in income. But living standards still fluctuate considerably—with the weather, with the time of year, because of the death of the family breadwinner, and so on. If households are unable to cushion a fall (through, for example, borrowing or insurance), an unfavorable turn of events, especially an unexpected one, can be catastrophic. The poorest households are the most vulnerable and the least able to protect themselves from contingencies. One study tells how a young household in Guinea fell into destitution and eventually disintegrated after the father contracted river blindness. As he became progressively incapacitated, the mother's work load multiplied and her health deteriorated, along with the children's. Soon the family was unable to feed itself. In time, various members of the household succumbed to illness or left the village. After fifteen years what remained of the household was entirely dependent on village charity.

Often, unanticipated events affect the poor not merely in certain localities but nationwide. For instance, a sudden decline in the terms of trade, followed perhaps by policy changes intended to cope with that decline, may change relative prices in ways that hurt the poor. Others may gain from the same events. Real currency devaluations, for ex-

Box 2.4   Moving in and out of poverty in rural India

How much of the poverty that we observe at any one date is persistent and how much is transient, reflecting variability in individual incomes over time? Data collected by the International Crops Research Institute for the Semi-Arid Tropics (ICRISAT), based in Hyderabad, India, track the incomes and consumption of 211 agricultural households in central India between 1975 and 1983. Drought conditions are common in this region.

In Box figure 2.4a the percentage of households deemed to be poor fluctuates over time around a generally downward trend, from 64 percent at the beginning of the period to a low of 41 percent in 1982; the average proportion of poor was 50 percent. For each year the poor are divided into those who were poor in the previous period and those who were not, and the same is done for the nonpoor. On average, 84 percent of the poor at each date had been poor in the previous period, and 16 percent were newcomers to poverty. Of the

Box figure 2.4b Number of years in poverty, sample villages, India

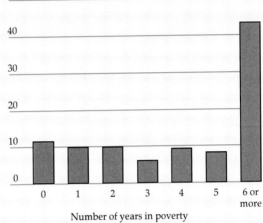

Percentage of households

nonpoor, 75 percent had been nonpoor in the previous period, and 25 percent had moved out of poverty. The income fluctuations are large: more than half the households that moved into poverty did so with incomes of less than 80 percent of the poverty line, and more than half of those who moved above the poverty line moved at least 20 percent above it.

Box figure 2.4b shows the number of years (not necessarily consecutive) that were spent in poverty. Only about 12 percent of households were never poor during the nine years. At the other extreme, 44 percent were poor for six or more years, and 19 percent were poor in every year. Thus, most households in these villages do experience poverty at one time or another. Whereas 50 percent are poor in a typical year, nearly 90 percent of the households are poor for at least one of the nine years. The transient component is large. Yet it is also clear that there is a substantial core of persistent, chronic poverty in these villages—poverty experienced by the same households year after year.

Box figure 2.4a Dynamics of rural poverty, sample villages, India

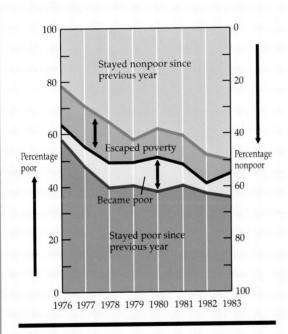

ample, usually benefit farmers who are net suppliers of internationally traded produce while hurting the urban poor, who are typically net consumers of tradable goods. In some parts of the world—such as Afghanistan, Central America, Indochina, Iran,

Iraq, Lebanon, southern Africa, and Sri Lanka—many of the poor are uprooted people fleeing from wars, persecution, famine, and natural disasters. Previously, they may not have been poor. In Angola and Mozambique about 8.5 million people

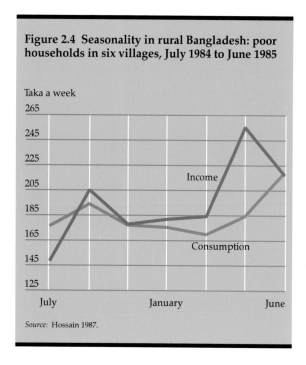

Figure 2.4 Seasonality in rural Bangladesh: poor households in six villages, July 1984 to June 1985

Taka a week

Income

Consumption

July   January   June

Source: Hossain 1987.

have become war refugees. Poverty in these countries reflects a massive destruction of rural infrastructure and productive assets.

Incomes in rural households vary substantially according to the season. For example, wage work is readily available only at certain times of the crop year, and it often depends on the weather. In many African countries the dry season puts an extra burden on women, who may have to walk miles to find water. In some busy seasons heavy agricultural work coincides with depleted food stocks and higher prices. Undernutrition and illnesses are more common at certain times of the year. The rains typically increase water contamination and the incidence of waterborne diseases. Acute weight loss during the "hungry season" has been documented among farmers in The Gambia; adult weight fluctuated as much as 4.5 kilograms within one year. In northeast Ghana losses of 6 percent of body weight were recorded. Among women farmers in Lesotho the figure was 7 percent, and for pastoralists in Niger it was 5 percent. For vulnerable groups such as children, the aged, and others whose biological defenses are already weakened, seasonal weight change can be extremely damaging.

Most of the rural poor, however, can cope reasonably well with normal seasonality. Saving and dissaving help to smooth consumption over the

ups and downs. Figure 2.4 shows consumption and income over the course of a year for 178 poor households in Bangladesh. Consumption is clearly smoother than income, which varies markedly with the crop cycle. For these households, earnings from labor are less than consumption in most periods, and the remaining sources of income—transfers, asset sales, and borrowing—small as they are, can be crucial to survival. Widespread indebtedness to local moneylenders and shopkeepers has been reported for various countries. Friends and family are often a preferable source of small amounts of credit, but they are likely to have little to spare. (One study of the Philippines described extensive short-term borrowing and lending among poor families as a form of shared poverty.) Borrowing may often be the only way to maintain a minimum level of consumption.

Credit is rarely available for accumulating productive assets. Savings and borrowings often have to be held in unproductive forms such as cash or grain to hedge against future calamities. The poor have few opportunities to obtain insurance, and they are not able to use credit and savings to bolster their capacity for bearing risk or to become entrepreneurs. Those on the edge of survival can not afford to gamble.

Another way of coping with risk is to diversify income sources. A study of rural Java found that the poorest landless households coordinate their members' activities much more carefully than do asset-owning households. The main purpose of this coordination is to establish a steady stream of income. The household may adjust its overall supply of labor, either through hours worked or through changes in labor force participation. Members of the household may migrate in search of work. Farmers are known to intercrop and to choose crops that are quick to mature or are more resilient, even though they may have lower yields and be less valuable.

How do the poor spend their incomes?

Over a typical year the poor spend nearly all their incomes on consumption of one sort or another, and at least half of this consumption is likely to be in the form of food. Data for both Côte d'Ivoire and Peru in 1985 indicate that about 70 percent of the expenditure of poor households goes for food; the corresponding figure for all households is about 50 percent. A high proportion of the food budget—60 percent in the case of the Indonesian poor, for instance—is devoted to the local food staple.

The relative prices of food staples can be crucial to the welfare of the poor. The number of rural poor who rely on the market for their consumption depends on the distribution of access to productive land. It is typically the "not so poor" who are net suppliers of farm produce and so benefit from higher prices. The poorest of the poor consume more of the food staple than they produce, and they rely on agricultural wages, which may be slow to respond to changing prices.

Poverty is often the fundamental cause of malnutrition. Yet nutrition need not be very responsive to changes in income. The poor may spend a rise in income on "better" food (rather than on more nutritious food) or on other things altogether. In Indonesia one study found that when income rose by 10 percent, calorie intake for the average household increased only 1.5 percent. For the poorest tenth of households the increase was 4 percent.

Within the household the distribution of consumption often favors males and income-earning adults. This finding has been documented in various countries, including Bangladesh, Ghana, Guatemala, India, and Papua New Guinea. Poor households are more likely to invest in education for boys than for girls. A series of studies in Brazil, India, Kenya, Malawi, and other countries indicates that a larger proportion of women's than of men's income tends to be spent on household nutrition and basic welfare. Of the studies conducted in India, one covering twenty villages in the south found that 80 to 100 percent of women's wage income was devoted to family maintenance, whereas men committed between 40 and 90 percent of their earnings. This suggests that raising women's incomes directly is a good way to reach children as well as to strengthen women's status and bargaining power within the household.

What is the position of the poor in the society around them?

In general, the poor have less access to publicly provided goods and infrastructure than do other groups. On the whole, governments fail to reach the rural poor. Even in urban areas poor neighborhoods are less well supplied with services than well-to-do ones. Data for Latin America show that the pattern of social expenditures is regressive in most countries. In Brazil, according to some esti-

mates, it is only slightly more equal than the distribution of income, which is known to be among the most unequal in the world. The primary school enrollment rate for the wealthiest 20 percent in Côte d'Ivoire is twice that of the poorest 20 percent. In both India and Nepal enrollment rates for the top 10 percent of families are 50 to 100 percent higher than for the poor. Morbidity and mortality figures tell a similar story. Access is not the only issue; use of services by the poor can also be low. But the fact remains that fewer social services are available to the poor.

There are exceptions. In Eastern Europe and in a few low-income and lower-middle-income countries—including Chile, China, Costa Rica, Cuba, Mauritius, and Sri Lanka as well as India's Kerala State—governments have tried hard to provide basic services widely and have largely succeeded. For example, in Sri Lanka 93 percent of the population has access to health services. Chile's social services are carefully targeted toward the neediest. Through its commune organization China was able to meet certain basic needs such as health care, education, and family planning services for most of its people.

The poor are often set apart by cultural and educational barriers. Illiterate people may be intimidated by officials or may simply lack information about programs. Sometimes the design of the services unintentionally adds to the problem. Agricultural extension programs, for example, are usually geared toward men even where—as is often the case—many, if not most, cultivators are women. The requirement that birth certificates be produced for admission to school in urban areas of India prevents poor migrant women from enrolling children and taking needed work. The poor play little part in politics and are often, in effect, disenfranchised.

In many countries poverty is correlated with race and ethnic background. Indigenous peoples in Bolivia, Ecuador, Guatemala, Mexico, and Peru are disproportionately represented among the poor. Scheduled castes and tribal peoples are among those most at risk of poverty in India and Bangladesh. In Australia the aborigines are prominent among the poor. In the United States 45 percent of all black children were poor in 1984, compared with 17 percent of white children. In South Africa the mortality rate for white infants averaged 12 per thousand live births between 1981 and 1985; for black Africans it was estimated to fall between 94 and 124. The risk of contracting tuberculosis—a disease closely associated with poverty—was twenty-two times greater for blacks than for whites in South Africa, excluding the homelands, and fifty-five times greater in Transkei.

From diagnosis to treatment

This chapter's survey of what we know about the poor points to two overwhelmingly important determinants of poverty: access to income-earning opportunities and the capacity to respond. When households have secure opportunities to use their labor to good purpose and household members are skilled, educated, and healthy, minimal standards of living are ensured and poverty is eliminated. When such opportunities are lacking and access to social services is limited, living standards are unacceptably low. The living standards of many in the developing world are also highly vulnerable to a variety of misfortunes, ranging from illness to drought. Inability to cope with shocks can render relatively well-off households poor and lead to starvation and death for those already impoverished. These facts set the agenda for the rest of this Report.

3

Progress on poverty: lessons for the future

Over the past twenty-five years the developing countries have made tremendous progress. Consumption per capita has increased by nearly 70 percent in real terms, average life expectancy has risen from 51 to 62 years, and primary enrollment rates have reached 84 percent (Table 3.1). These remarkable gains, if evenly spread, would have gone a long way toward eliminating poverty—but, of course, they have not been evenly spread. Some countries have done much better than others. An examination of why this is so—of the reasons for successes and failures—can suggest practical solutions to the problem of poverty.

This chapter draws on past trends to identify the key factors behind rapid and sustained improvement in the living standards of the poor. The elements of the broad strategy that emerge from this analysis are then discussed in more detail in Chapters 4 through 7.

Changes in poverty

If history is to guide future policy toward poverty, it is important to be as accurate as possible about what has actually happened. Unfortunately, weak-

nesses in the data make it impossible to be precise. The evidence points to considerable progress in reducing poverty, especially in the 1960s and 1970s; the picture for the 1980s is mixed. In some regions the poor have suffered serious setbacks, whereas in others the progress of previous decades has continued and has even accelerated.

General indicators

Since there is no universally accepted indicator of welfare, it is necessary to look at several different measures. We begin with a review of changes in consumption per capita, life expectancy, and educational attainment. Figure 3.1 reveals that although all regions have made good progress in life expectancy and primary enrollment, the gains in consumption per capita have differed considerably. South Asia, for example, recorded an improvement of only 30 percent from a very low base, and consumption per capita in Sub-Saharan Africa stagnated. There are two implications. First, improvements in social indicators such as life expectancy and primary enrollment can occur independent of increases in consumption. And second, since many of the world's poor live in South Asia and Sub-Saharan Africa, the substantial increase in consumption per capita in the developing world as a whole has not led to an equally impressive reduction in poverty.

Focusing on regional averages, however, provides only indirect evidence about the poor. How much, if at all, have the poor participated in the general improvement shown in Figure 3.1? To answer this question it is necessary to move from aggregate data to survey results.

Table 3.1 Twenty years of progress in developing countries

Indicator	1965	1975	1985
Consumption per capita (1985 PPP dollars)	590	780	985
Life expectancy (years)	51	57	62
Primary net enrollment rate (percent)	73	74	84

39

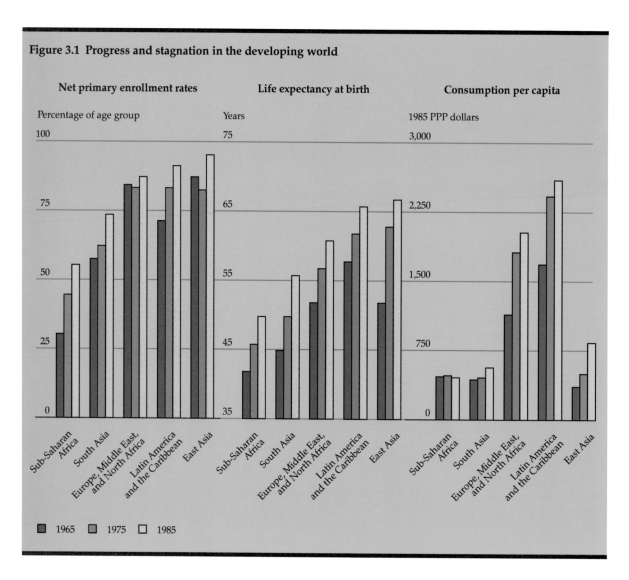

Figure 3.1 Progress and stagnation in the developing world

Net primary enrollment rates
Percentage of age group

Life expectancy at birth
Years

Consumption per capita
1985 PPP dollars

■ 1965   ■ 1975   □ 1985

What has happened to the incomes of the poor?

Surveys that cover periods of at least ten years are available for eleven countries, which together account for 40 percent of the total population of the developing world and for 50 percent of the poor (Table 3.2). The surveys for earlier years are generally less reliable than more recent ones, and the results should therefore be interpreted as indicating trends rather than precise magnitudes. Note also that, in contrast to the exercise in Chapter 2, this chapter uses country-specific poverty lines. Comparisons between countries should be made with this difference in mind.

Table 3.2 reveals considerable progress in reducing the incidence of poverty. Indonesia, for example, cut its headcount index by 41 percentage points in just seventeen years. (Box 3.1 describes this change from the perspective of one village.) Even countries that are often thought to have fol-

lowed inegalitarian paths of development, such as Brazil and Pakistan, have succeeded in reducing the headcount index. More important, India, the country with the world's greatest concentration of poor, cut the incidence of poverty by 11 percentage points in just eleven years.

In some countries rapid population growth has increased the absolute number of poor. Nevertheless, as the changes in the average income shortfall show, the poor are better off even though they may have remained poor. In Morocco, for example, the number of people below the poverty line increased by almost a million, but their average expenditure rose from 54 percent of the poverty line to 64 percent. In sum, therefore, the evidence suggests that there has been considerable progress in reducing the incidence of poverty, a more modest reduction in the number of poor, and achievement of somewhat better living standards for those who have remained in poverty.

A weakness in this assessment is the lack of reliable data for Sub-Saharan Africa. The discussion of diverging trends in Chapter 1 and the evidence of stagnant consumption per capita in Figure 3.1 suggest that progress in reducing poverty has probably been slowest in that region. Even assuming that the distribution of income did not worsen between 1965 and 1985, the number of Africans in

Table 3.2 Changes in selected indicators of poverty

Country and period	Length of period (years)	Headcount index		Number of poor (millions)		Average income shortfall (percent)	
		First year	Last year	First year	Last year	First year	Last year
Brazil (1960–80)[a,b]	20	50	21	36.1	25.4	46	41
Colombia (1971–88)[a]	17	41	25	8.9	7.5	41	38
Costa Rica (1971–86)[a]	15	45	24	0.8	0.6	40	44
India (1972–83)	11	54	43	311.4	315.0	31	28
Indonesia (1970–87)	17	58	17	67.9	30.0	37	17
Malaysia (1973–87)[a]	14	37	15	4.1	2.2	40	24
Morocco (1970–84)	14	43	34	6.6	7.4	46	36
Pakistan (1962–84)[a,b]	22	54	23	26.5	21.3	39	26
Singapore (1972–82)	10	31	10	0.7	0.2	37	33
Sri Lanka (1963–82)[a]	19	37	27	3.9	4.1	35	29
Thailand (1962–86)[a,b]	24	59	26	16.7	13.6	..	35

Note: This table uses country-specific poverty lines. Official or commonly used poverty lines have been used when available. In other cases the poverty line has been set at 30 percent of mean income or expenditure. The range of poverty lines, expressed in terms of expenditure per household member and in PPP dollars, is approximately $300–$700 a year in 1985 except for Costa Rica ($960), Malaysia ($1,420), and Singapore ($860). Unless otherwise indicated, the table is based on expenditure per household member. The headcount index is the percentage of the population below the poverty line. The average income shortfall is the mean distance of consumption or income of the poor below the poverty line, as a proportion of the poverty line.
a. Measures for this entry use income rather than expenditure.
b. Measures for this entry are by household rather than by household member.

Box 3.1 Development in a Javanese village

The story of Balearjo, an East Javanese village of almost 4,000 people, shows what declining poverty means for individuals. The village is about eight kilometers from the town of Gondanglegi and is connected to the outside world by bumpy but passable dirt roads. Although Balearjo is still somewhat poorer than its neighbors, research conducted in 1953 and 1985 shows that the lives of its inhabitants improved greatly in the intervening years. Rice yields increased dramatically, from 2 tons to 6 tons of paddy per hectare for the wet season crop, and the wage for a day's work increased from 2 kilograms of rice in 1953 to nearly 4 kilograms in 1985.

In 1953 the village would have been considered poor by most definitions. Rice was available for only four months; the diet for the rest of the year consisted of corn and, when that ran out, cassava. Clothes were worn until they were in tatters, and few people had shoes. A typical house was made of thatch and bamboo, with an earthen floor. Furnishings were sparse and uncomfortable. Few villagers could read, and few had traveled any distance from the village. A daily paper brought from a nearby town supplied the only outside news.

By 1985 things had changed. Rice was available throughout the year. Clothing was much better, and shoes were commonplace. Most villagers had radios, and some even had television sets. More than 90 percent of the houses were made of colorfully painted brick and stucco, with partial cement floors. Furnishings were more extensive and included chairs and tables bought from stores. Literacy had improved dramatically thanks to two primary schools, one financed by the village and the other by the central government. Travel outside the village was common, and knowledge of national events, provided through hourly radio broadcasts, was widespread. In 1953 villagers relied on homemade kerosene lamps that provided little illumination, but by 1982 electric power lines had reached Balearjo, and by 1985 many households had electric light.

Such burdensome activities as rice pounding and shoulder transport had disappeared, relieving women of some of their most exhausting tasks. Higher incomes had led to demands for new products and services and hence to more productive work, such as construction, trade, and small manufacturing. Growing specialization was also evident: houses in 1953 were constructed by the owners with the help of neighbors, but by 1985 most of the work was done (and done better) by full-time carpenters.

The absence of reliable intertemporal statistics on income distribution in most Sub-Saharan African countries makes any comprehensive account of trends in poverty there impossible. The Social Dimensions of Adjustment project is beginning to address this problem, and surveys have been conducted in three countries. For now, however, an assessment of past trends in poverty has to rely on a few household surveys, supplemented by village studies, and on aggregate statistics for income, consumption, and population.

Tanzania is one of the few Sub-Saharan African countries for which large-scale urban and rural household surveys have been conducted over a period of several years. The surveys show that real rural living standards declined at an average annual rate of 2.5 percent between 1969 and 1983. The decline in urban areas was even more dramatic; real wages fell by 65 percent over the period. Real private consumption per capita has fallen by 43 percent since 1973, and food purchases have moved away from meat, dairy products, and vegetables toward cheap starches and beans. Small-scale village surveys have revealed worsening social indicators despite government efforts to provide services.

In Nigeria trends in poverty have followed a somewhat different pattern. The rise in world oil prices and in Nigerian oil production increased per capita consumption and income throughout most of the 1970s, but the economic reversal of the early 1980s has had a severe effect on the country's poor. Consumption has plummeted by 7 percent a year, and standards of living were lower in the mid-1980s than in the 1950s. Analyses of caloric intake show no improvement between 1952 and 1985. The economic crisis of the 1980s was so severe that it more than canceled out the progress of the previous twenty years.

Ghana has only recently begun to see rising living standards after two decades of negative growth. In 1985 nearly 60 percent of the population lived on less than $370 a year. Botswana has been one of the few African countries to achieve rapid growth (nearly 9 percent a year since 1965), but even there almost 50 percent of the population had incomes of less than $370 a year in 1985–86. With few exceptions, the evidence supports the conclusion that poverty in Sub-Saharan Africa is severe and has been getting worse.

poverty would have increased by 55 million. Data from small local surveys and other evidence support this general conclusion (Box 3.2).

Table 3.2 deals with periods of at least ten years and may therefore mask the effect of short-run recessions. Many observers have argued that the recession and adjustment of the 1980s were particularly harmful to the poor. Table 3.3 presents evidence on changes in poverty in the 1980s. The data reveal continued progress in several East Asian and South Asian countries. India, Indonesia, Malaysia, and Pakistan—which accounted for more than 40 percent of the world's poor in 1985—managed to reduce the incidence of poverty in the 1980s. China, although it suffered a reversal after 1985, also saw a decline in poverty during the early 1980s. In the regions most severely affected by the recession, however, poverty has increased. In all the Latin American countries in the table, including Brazil, the incidence of poverty increased for at least some part of the 1980s. In Sub-Saharan Africa the only data available, those for Côte d'Ivoire, display a slight increase in the mid-1980s. Finally, the problems of Eastern Europe are clear: Poland and Yugoslavia experienced a sharp rise in poverty.

Social progress and the poor

In principle, a similar analysis for the social indicators shown in Figure 3.1 would be desirable, but distributions of social indicators are not usually available. We do know, however, that the nonpoor usually have access to social services before the poor do. Thus, only if the percentage of the population with access to social services exceeds the percentage of nonpoor can we conclude that some of the poor are being reached.

Table 3.4 compares the percentage of nonpoor in the population with primary enrollment rates and the percentage of children immunized. In East Asia universal primary enrollment had almost been reached by 1985, implying that most of the poor had access to primary education. In Sub-Saharan Africa the enrollment rate is only slightly higher than the percentage of nonpoor, and it is therefore probable that few of the poor are being reached. The other regions occupy an intermediate position. Health coverage, as measured by the percentage of children immunized, follows a similar regional pattern, but at lower levels. The evidence suggests that many poor people have benefited from the expansion in education (except in Sub-

Saharan Africa) but that less progress had been made up to 1985 in extending health care to the poor. Further expansion in coverage will mainly benefit the poor.

Regional averages mask the tremendous achievements that some countries have made in providing social services to their populations. Colombia, where mortality for children under 5 fell from 135 per thousand in 1965 to 42 per thousand by 1985, and Costa Rica, where 95 percent of the population has access to primary health care, show what can be done. Even in regions with poor overall performance, some countries have managed to make great strides. Botswana, for example, has achieved universal primary enrollment, and its under 5 mortality rate fell from 165 to 70 per thousand during the past two decades. The sheer scale of the improvements in these countries suggests that the poor must have participated in the overall progress. At the other end of the spectrum are countries that have done much worse than regional averages indicate. In Pakistan the net enrollment ratio has hardly improved in the past twenty years—it was only 43 percent in 1985—and an estimated 36 percent of the population lacks access to health care.

Recently, concern has centered on the effect of the recession of the early 1980s on the provision of social services to the poor. In Sub-Saharan Africa and Latin America, the two regions worst affected by recession, roughly half the countries for which information is available experienced substantial declines in real per capita spending on education and health. The social indicators for the early 1980s, however, tell a somewhat less gloomy story, at least in Latin America.

Figure 3.2 shows that progress in under 5 mortality and primary school enrollment rates continued into the 1980s in most of the developing world. Progress was least in the region with the

Table 3.3 Changes in poverty in the 1980s

Country and period	Length of period (years)	Headcount index First year	Headcount index Last year	Number of poor (millions) First year	Number of poor (millions) Last year	Average income shortfall (percent) First year	Average income shortfall (percent) Last year
Brazil (1981–87)[a]	6	19	24	23.1	33.2	..	..
China (1985–88)[a,b]	3	10	14	79.2	101.3	25	24
Colombia (1978–88)[a]	10	24	25	6.0	7.5	36	38
Costa Rica (1977–83)[a]	6	29	36	0.6	0.9	44	39
Costa Rica (1983–86)[a]	3	36	24	0.9	0.6	39	44
Côte d'Ivoire (1985–86)	1	30	31	3.1	3.3	33	26
India (1977–83)	6	50	43	324.9	315.0	29	28
Indonesia (1984–87)	3	28	17	45.4	30.0	24	17
Malaysia (1984–87)[a]	3	15	14	2.3	2.2	26	24
Pakistan (1979–84)	5	21	20	17.1	18.7	19	19
Poland (1978–87)[a]	9	9	23	3.3	8.6	..	..
Thailand (1981–86)[a,c]	5	20	26	9.5	13.6	27	35
Venezuela (1982–87)[a]	5	12	16	1.9	3.0	26	31
Yugoslavia (1978–87)[a]	9	17	25	3.8	5.7	..	..

Note: See note to Table 3.2 for definitions. The range of poverty lines, expressed in terms of expenditure per household member and in PPP dollars, is approximately $300–$700 a year in 1985 except for Costa Rica ($960) and Malaysia ($1,420).
a. Measures for this entry use income rather than expenditure.
b. Rural only.
c. Measures for this entry are by household rather than by household member.

Table 3.4 Have social services reached the poor in developing countries?

Indicator (1985)	Sub-Saharan Africa	East Asia	South Asia	Europe, Middle East, and North Africa	Latin America and the Caribbean	All developing countries
Percentage of nonpoor in population	53	79	49	75	81	67
Primary net enrollment rate (percent)	56	96	74	88	92	84
Percentage of children immunized	47	73	43	63	65	58

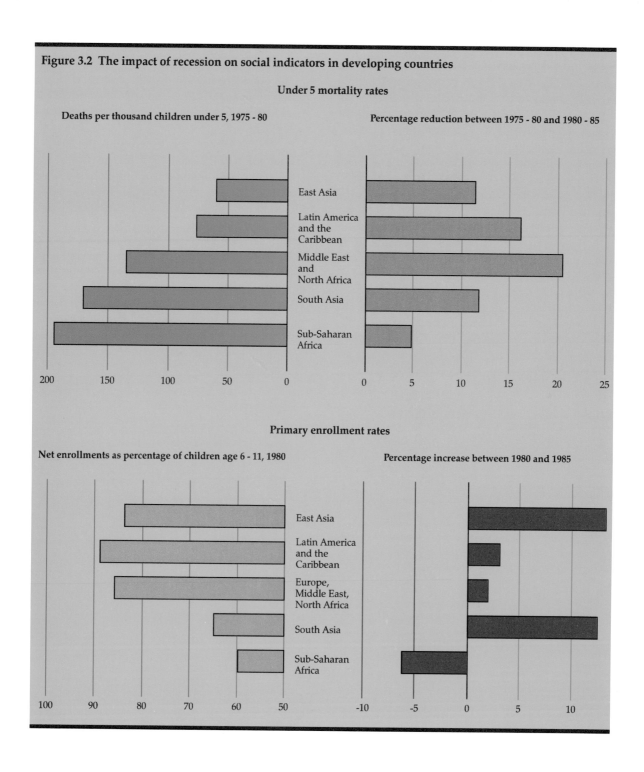

Figure 3.2 The impact of recession on social indicators in developing countries

Under 5 mortality rates

Deaths per thousand children under 5, 1975 - 80

Percentage reduction between 1975 - 80 and 1980 - 85

East Asia

Latin America and the Caribbean

Middle East and North Africa

South Asia

Sub-Saharan Africa

Primary enrollment rates

Net enrollments as percentage of children age 6 - 11, 1980

Percentage increase between 1980 and 1985

East Asia

Latin America and the Caribbean

Europe, Middle East, North Africa

South Asia

Sub-Saharan Africa

greatest needs, Sub-Saharan Africa. That region had the highest mortality for children under 5 and the lowest enrollment rate at the start of the period; it saw the smallest improvement in under 5 mortality of all the regions, and its enrollment rate actually declined. By contrast, in several Latin American countries under 5 mortality declined at an increasing rate. Brazil, Chile, and Colombia, for

example, recorded higher rates of decline in the late 1970s and early 1980s than in the 1960s and 1970s.

Changes in nutritional status are another measure of the impact of recession. Data on nutrition are not always national in coverage, but they are nonetheless of special interest because they are often drawn from areas in difficulty. Evidence from the regions most affected by recession echoes the patterns already noted. In Latin America malnutrition has continued to decline steadily in Chile, Colombia, and Costa Rica, but progress has halted in Uruguay and Venezuela, and there are signs of worsening in Guatemala and Peru. In Sub-Saharan Africa malnutrition is on the rise, and the number of underweight children has grown substantially. Two broad patterns can be discerned. In Benin, Burkina Faso, Ghana, and Togo malnutrition rose sharply in the mid-1980s, then declined until 1986, and is now rising again. Ethiopia, Lesotho, Madagascar, Niger, and Rwanda have seen a more persistent trend of rising malnutrition around marked seasonal fluctuations. (The patterns for Ghana and Lesotho are shown in Figure 3.3.)

An overall assessment

Although circumstances vary enormously from country to country, this review shows that there has been a significant long-run improvement in under 5 mortality, life expectancy, and primary enrollment. In these respects the situation in the early to mid-1980s was substantially better in every region than in the 1960s and 1970s. Except in Sub-Saharan Africa, the incomes of the poor have also risen, in some cases substantially.

In recent years, however, much depended on where the poor lived. Most of the poor became better off on every measure, but that is because most of them live in South Asia and East Asia. In many countries of Latin America and Eastern Europe the incomes of the poor have declined—although social indicators have proved more resilient and in some countries have improved faster than before the recession of the 1980s. Sub-Saharan Africa's poor fell further behind in the 1980s; the decline that started in the 1970s has continued and in some cases has accelerated.

Regional differences aside, the review also showed that some countries have been much more successful than others in reducing poverty. Table 3.5 shows this for two key indicators—the headcount index and the under 5 mortality rate—for ten countries. The next part of this chapter draws on country experience to identify the factors underlying these differences.

Factors influencing country performance

Public policy is critical both in reducing poverty, as measured by income, and in improving social indicators. Policy affects incomes indirectly, through

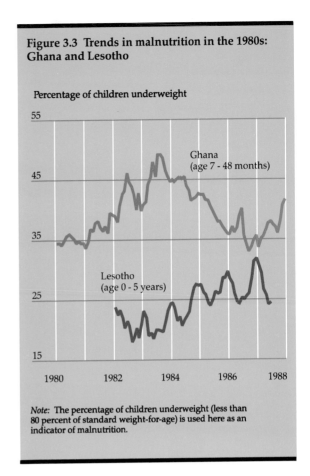

Figure 3.3 Trends in malnutrition in the 1980s: Ghana and Lesotho

Percentage of children underweight

Ghana (age 7 - 48 months)

Lesotho (age 0 - 5 years)

Note: The percentage of children underweight (less than 80 percent of standard weight-for-age) is used here as an indicator of malnutrition.

Table 3.5 Variation in country experience

Country and period	Average annual reduction		
	Headcount index (percentage points)[a]		Under 5 mortality (percent)[b]
Indonesia (1970–87)	2.34	(58)	3.3 (146)
Malaysia (1973–87)	1.66	(37)	3.7 (46)
Brazil (1960–80)	1.45	(50)	2.8 (107)
Pakistan (1962–84)	1.43	(54)	1.8 (200)
Costa Rica (1971–86)	1.41	(45)	9.3 (35)
Thailand (1962–86)	1.40	(59)	4.4 (70)
India (1972–83)	1.04	(54)	1.8 (199)
Colombia (1971–88)	0.91	(41)	7.2 (64)
Morocco (1970–84)	0.64	(43)	5.6[c] (136)
Sri Lanka (1963–82)	0.51	(37)	2.8 (66)

Note: Use of the income shortfall rather than the headcount index yields essentially the same ranking.
a. Initial level in parentheses.
b. 1975–80 rate in parentheses.
c. 1977–81.

the rate and pattern of economic growth. It has a more direct effect on social indicators, mainly through the government's expenditure program. The two issues—higher incomes and improved social indicators—are clearly linked. Each supports the other in a variety of ways. But since the direct

Table 3.6 Social sector spending as a percentage of GNP

Sector and country	1975	1985
Primary education		
High enrollment rate		
Botswana	2.1	2.8
Tunisia	1.9	2.3
Chile	1.4	2.2
Thailand	1.6	2.0
Low enrollment rate		
Nepal	0.7	1.0
Ghana	1.1	0.7
Pakistan	0.6	0.7
Haiti	0.6	0.6
Health		
Low under 5 mortality		
Chile	2.5	2.1
Mauritius	2.0	2.0
Malaysia	1.9	1.8
Sri Lanka	1.7	1.3
High under 5 mortality		
Ethiopia	0.8	1.2
Burkina Faso	0.8	0.9
India	0.3	0.3
Pakistan	0.3	0.2

effect of policy on social indicators is easier to measure, that is a good place to start.

Improving social indicators

The countries that have succeeded in providing primary education and health care to the poor are those that have made adequate provision for the purpose in their budgets (Table 3.6). In 1985 spending on primary education as a percentage of GNP was more than four times higher in Botswana, where the enrollment rate was 99 percent, than in Haiti, where it was only 55 percent. Similarly, in countries that have achieved broad provision of health care, such as Chile and Mauritius, spending as a percentage of GNP is several times greater than in countries such as India and Pakistan, where under 5 mortality remains exceptionally high and the percentage of children immunized is low.

But increased government spending is not always the answer to improving the well-being of poor people. Better allocation of expenditures within the sector and more efficient use of funds are often more important. It is clear, however, that through well-directed public expenditures even low-income countries can dramatically improve so-cial services. Within the sample of ten countries identified in Table 3.5, public spending is an important part of the explanation for variations in mortality of children under 5. The best performers are Sri Lanka among low-income countries and Costa Rica in the middle-income group. Both countries have had a long-standing commitment, dating to the first half of the century, to providing social services.

Raising incomes

Isolating the factors that influence the incomes of the poor is more complex than is the case with social indicators. As a preliminary step, changes in the incomes of the poor can be "explained" by decomposing them into the part attributable to overall economic growth and the part attributable to changes in the inequality of income (Box 3.3). It has been argued that inequality worsens at first with development and improves only later. This idea was encapsulated in the "Kuznets curve," which posits an inverted-U relationship between inequality and average income. The curve implies the possibility of a conflict between growth and poverty. In the extreme, the inequality of income may worsen fast enough at the outset of economic growth for poverty to increase; growth would be "immiserizing."

Table 3.7 presents a simple test of this view. It shows the change in poverty, as measured by the headcount index of Tables 3.2 and 3.3, and compares it with a simulated change in poverty. This is the change that would have occurred if inequality had remained constant—that is, if everyone had received the same percentage increase in income. If the actual decrease in poverty is less than the simulated decrease, growth has increased inequality, and the poor have gained less than the nonpoor. If the actual decrease is bigger than the simulated decrease, the opposite is true.

Table 3.7 looks both at periods of long-term growth and at short-term recessions. In general, long-term growth has had only a limited effect on inequality, but it has tended to reduce it. In India, for example, the actual and simulated changes in poverty are almost exactly the same. This implies that the poor enjoyed approximately the same percentage increase as everyone else and that the income attributable to growth was distributed in the same way as the initial income.

In some countries—Colombia, for example—long-term changes in inequality have been more important. But these and other cases lend no sup-

Box 3.3 The mechanics of changes in poverty

For any given increase in the incomes of the poor, the reduction in poverty depends on where the poor are in relation to the poverty line. If they are concentrated just below the line, the increase in their incomes will have a bigger effect on poverty than if they are spread more evenly.

Box figure 3.3 shows the cumulative distribution function—that is, the percentage of persons who receive no more than a particular income, expressed as a function of that income. For example, with the poverty line set at 30, the curve on the left in each figure shows that 50 percent of the population is poor. A 50 percent increase in income will shift the distribution function to the right. The reduction in the incidence of poverty is 37 percentage points in the upper panel of the figure but only 27 percentage points in the lower panel.

The difference in outcome arises from differences in the slope of the distribution function at the poverty line. If the slope is very steep (implying less inequality in the region of the poverty line), as in the upper panel, a large number of people is concentrated just below the line. An increase in income moves many people above the line, and the incidence of poverty falls substantially. If the slope is less steep (implying greater inequality around the poverty line), as in the lower panel, few people are located immediately below the poverty line. In this case the same increase in income moves only a few of the poor above the line, and the reduction in the incidence of poverty will be much smaller.

For example, starting from the latest available distributions, a 10 percent increase in the incomes of the poor in Bangladesh and India would reduce the incidence of poverty by about 7 percentage points. Where the distribution of income is more unequal, as in Venezuela and Brazil, the corresponding figure would be only 3 percentage points.

Box figure 3.3 Different initial conditions: the impact on poverty reduction

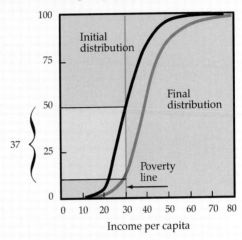

Heavy concentration of poor just below poverty line

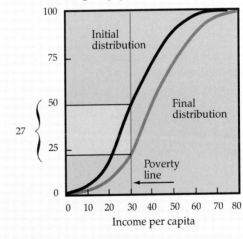

Lower concentration of poor just below poverty line

port to either the Kuznets or the immiserizing-growth hypothesis. In the low-income countries inequality consistently improves (contrary to the Kuznets hypothesis), and there is no case in which the effect of growth is offset by changes in inequality (contrary to the immiserizing-growth hypothe-sis). In short, growth reduces poverty. Even so, where inequality has worsened, as in Brazil, the implications for poverty are significant. If inequality had declined as in Malaysia, Brazilian poverty would have fallen by 43 percentage points between 1960 and 1980 rather than by 29. The pattern

Table 3.7 Poverty, economic growth, and recession

Country and period	Length of period (years)	Observed reduction in poverty (percentage points)[a]	Simulated reduction in poverty (percentage points)[b]	Annual growth of mean income or expenditure (percent)
Long-run growth				
Indonesia (1970–87)	17	41	35	3.4
Thailand (1962–86)	24	33	30	2.7
Pakistan (1962–84)	22	31	26	2.2
Brazil (1960–80)	20	29	34	5.1
Malaysia (1973–87)	14	23	19	4.0
Singapore (1972–82)	10	21	19	6.4
Costa Rica (1971–86)	15	21	22	3.5
Colombia (1971–88)	17	16	8	1.1
India (1972–83)	11	11	10	1.0
Sri Lanka (1963–82)	19	10	8	0.9
Morocco (1970–84)	14	9	1	0.2
Short-run recession				
Costa Rica (1983–86)	3	12	13	10.9
Indonesia (1984–87)	3	11	9	5.0
India (1977–83)	6	7	2	0.8
Malaysia (1984–87)	3	1	−1	−0.7
Pakistan (1979–84)	5	1	4	1.2
Colombia (1978–88)	10	−1	−1	−1.2
Côte d'Ivoire (1985–86)	1	−1	−5	−5.4
China (1985–88)[c]	3	−4	5	6.7
Brazil (1981–87)	6	−5	1	0.9
Venezuela (1982–87)	5	−5	−6	−4.5
Thailand (1981–86)	5	−6	0	0.0
Costa Rica (1977–83)	6	−7	−8	−3.4
Yugoslavia (1978–87)	9	−7	−12	−2.9
Poland (1978–87)	9	−14	−17	−1.2

a. Absolute change in the headcount index on the basis of the definition of absolute poverty in the specific country.
b. The simulation assumes that the inequality of income remains unchanged.
c. Rural only.

of growth as well as its rate is thus an important determinant of changes in poverty.

As the lower part of Table 3.7 shows, in the 1980s the link between growth and poverty reduction is still there, but it is weaker than before. By and large, economic growth reduces poverty and economic decline increases it. Fluctuations in inequality, however, were larger in the 1980s. In Malaysia, for example, poverty decreased even though mean income also declined. This suggests that external shocks or important policy changes can alter the incidence of poverty by way of changes in the inequality of income, whereas in more stable periods economic growth is the dominant influence on poverty.

Would the conclusion that growth reduces poverty change if attention were shifted from the poor to the very poor? The country-specific poverty lines used in this analysis define 20 to 50 percent of the population as poor. If we turn to the poorest tenth of the population, we find that in periods of stable growth this group enjoyed a larger-than-

average percentage increase in income in all countries except Brazil and Costa Rica, where inequality worsened. In Brazil the poor nevertheless enjoyed a substantial increase in income; in Costa Rica they suffered a loss. In general, therefore, the poorest of the poor participated fully in economic growth.

No simple pattern emerged during the 1980s. In about half the countries the very poor suffered more, or advanced less, than the average citizen. In Colombia, for example, mean income for the entire population fell by 11 percent between 1978 and 1988, whereas for the poorest tenth it fell by more than 20 percent. In contrast, the poorest households in other countries did much better than the rest of the population. In Malaysia average incomes fell by 2 percent between 1984 and 1987, but the mean incomes of the poorest actually increased by 9 percent.

These conclusions shed some light on the differing experience of the countries identified in Table 3.5. Economic growth was clearly important—in the two countries that experienced the fastest reduction in poverty, per capita income grew by more than 3 percent a year, whereas the two countries that reduced poverty least had growth rates of less than 1 percent. In egalitarian economies (Indonesia, for example) economic growth that preserved the existing degree of inequality was sufficient to reduce poverty quickly. Where the initial distribution of income was less equal, as in Colombia, changes in inequality were an important complement to overall growth.

Economic growth and changes in inequality, however, are not instruments of policy; they are consequences. What were the policies that, in egalitarian economies such as Indonesia, spurred growth and even slightly reduced the initial degree of inequality? And what were the policies that, in inegalitarian economies such as Colombia, enabled the poor to benefit more than proportionately from growth? The answer lies in the factors that determine the incomes of the poor.

OWNERSHIP OF ASSETS. Redistributing the existing stock of assets to the poor has sometimes proved successful, but this is the exception rather than the rule. Large redistributions of land have been associated with rapid reductions in poverty, but they have occurred only in times of great political upheaval. Distribution of new capital (that is, investment) in favor of the poor has been more common. In particular, investment in human capital through primary health care and education has been an important part of the approach adopted by several countries. Whether this raises incomes, however, depends on the opportunities that are available for using the new skills.

RETURNS TO ASSETS. Since poverty is largely a rural phenomenon and since many of the poor depend, directly or indirectly, on the farm sector for their incomes, growth that raises agricultural productivity and the return to farm labor ought to be particularly effective in reducing poverty. The contrast between Indonesia and India illustrates this point. Between 1970 and 1987 poverty in Indonesia declined by 41 percentage points; over the same period the purchasing power of agricultural value added rose by 2.6 percent a year per rural dweller. Between 1984 and 1987, a period of especially rapid decline in poverty, purchasing power grew by 5.0 percent a year. In contrast, in India poverty decreased by 11 percentage points, and agricultural purchasing power grew by less than 0.4 percent a year. Most of the decline in poverty in India—7 percentage points between 1977 and 1983—took

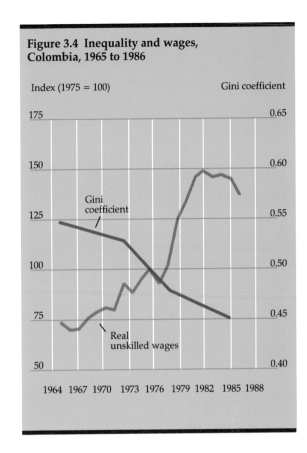

Figure 3.4 Inequality and wages, Colombia, 1965 to 1986

place at a time when agricultural purchasing power was growing at 1.5 percent a year. Econometric analysis confirms that rural poverty in India has a strong negative link to farm incomes.

In India and Indonesia the initial distribution of income was fairly equal, and growth was able to reduce poverty even though the degree of inequality remained the same. Where the initial distribution is less equal, growth must shift the pattern of returns in favor of the poor if it is to have much effect. Colombia is one of the few Latin American countries that has managed to improve an initially very unequal distribution of income. Its Gini coefficient (a measure of inequality in which 1 represents complete inequality and 0 perfect equality) fell from 0.54 to 0.48 between 1971 and 1978, and its incidence of poverty fell by 2.9 percentage points a year. As Figure 3.4 shows, the return to poor people's most important asset—unskilled labor—had to rise sharply for this to come about. Between 1971 and 1978 real unskilled wages increased at 6.6 percent a year, as against 3.9 percent for GNP per capita. This shifted the distribution of income in favor of the poor. Box 3.4 illustrates what happened to wages and poverty in a period

49

of economic growth—the industrial revolutions in the United Kingdom and the United States.

Returns to the assets of the poor can also be increased through higher productivity. In Malaysia investing in the poor contributed to rapid growth, with some improvement in a fairly unequal distribution of income and a decrease in poverty of 23 percentage points between 1973 and 1987. During this period average labor earnings for rural workers rose by almost 75 percent. Studies suggest that better education accounted for roughly one-quarter of the rise in farm earnings and about three-quarters of the rise in nonfarm earnings. By investing in the human capital of the poor and providing an environment in which new skills could be productively used, Malaysia improved both the short-run welfare of the poor and the prospects for raising incomes in the medium term.

Sri Lanka has been less successful in realizing the potential increase in productivity made possible by social spending. Between 1970 and 1985 it allocated about 10 percent of GDP to social expenditures, and coverage was widespread. Although social indicators improved, the incomes of the poor did not rise significantly. Poverty declined by only 0.5 percentage points a year during the 1960s and 1970s.

Another way of increasing the productivity of the assets of the poor is to provide better physical infrastructure. For example, Indonesia used its oil receipts to improve and extend infrastructure throughout rural Java and thus provide access to markets for most of the country's poor. In contrast, the inadequate infrastructure in much of Sub-Saharan Africa continues to deteriorate.

TRANSFERS. All the countries listed in Table 3.5 have used transfers, usually in the form of food subsidies. In countries such as Indonesia and Thailand moderate transfers—about 0.2 percent of GDP—have proved to be consistent with rapid growth. Other countries have gone much further. In the late 1970s Egypt's transfers (which, although they reached the poor, went mainly to the nonpoor) amounted to 7 percent of GDP. Such heavy use of transfers can cause severe macroeconomic difficulties, and by reducing growth, it condemns future generations to poverty.

Transfers are unlikely to be the answer to poverty—certainly not in low-income countries with large numbers of poor. One reason is the sheer size of the problem. Transfers of at least 15 percent of current GDP would be needed to eliminate poverty in Bangladesh—and this assumes that the transfers would not "leak" (as they usually do) to the urban middle class. In some middle-income countries the situation is different; transfers amounting to only 1.1 percent of current GDP could eliminate poverty in Brazil. Because of leakage and administrative costs, however, much more than this would be required in practice.

Explaining successful performance

Armed with this account of the factors that have influenced poverty, we can review the performance of the countries listed in Table 3.5. The three East Asian countries—Indonesia, Malaysia, and Thailand—demonstrate the benefits of an appropriate balance between policies that spur growth and policies that enable the poor to participate in growth. All three achieved and sustained annual GDP growth rates of more than 6 percent. This growth—relatively labor-intensive, with agriculture to the fore—generated demand for the factors of production owned by the poor. These countries also provided for adequate social spending. As a result, they have achieved universal primary education, and their infant mortality rates are lower than those of many countries with similar incomes. The improvement in the skills and quality of the labor force enabled the poor to seize the opportunities provided by economic growth.

In other countries the creation of opportunities for the poor and the development of their capacity to respond have not always been as well balanced. Brazil's GDP growth exceeded that of every other country in the sample, and Pakistan equaled the 6 percent annual growth achieved by the East Asian countries. Yet in neither country did social indicators improve rapidly. Brazil has one of the highest mortality rates for children under 5 among the middle-income countries, and Pakistan has one of the lowest rates of primary school enrollment in the world. The failure to improve the skills of the labor force has limited poor people's ability to benefit from growth. In each case the headcount index fell, but less quickly than in Indonesia or Malaysia.

So, it is possible to have economic growth without much social progress. The converse is also true: social indicators can be improved even in the absence of rapid economic growth. Between 1971 and 1978 in Colombia and between 1971 and 1977 in Costa Rica poverty declined rapidly, under 5 mortality fell at an extraordinary rate, and GDP grew at 5 to 6 percent a year. The recession of the early 1980s brought stagnant or declining GDP per capita and put an abrupt halt to the improvement

in poverty—the headcount index remained roughly constant in Colombia and increased in Costa Rica. Still, under 5 mortality continued to fall, demonstrating that efforts to improve social indicators can yield results even during a recession. Similarly, the experience of Sri Lanka shows that remarkable social progress can be achieved even at low levels of income. The benefits of Sri Lanka's long-standing support for the social services can be seen in its under 5 mortality rate, which was 66 per thousand in 1980—an impressive achievement for a low-income country.

Yet, as the experiences of India, Morocco, and Sri Lanka show, low GDP growth makes it difficult to reduce poverty. This suggests an important distinction: raising the incomes of the poor (and thus lifting people above the poverty line) requires broadly based economic growth, but making the poor better off in other respects—by reducing child mortality, for instance—can be brought about through specific public actions.

A key conclusion emerges from all this: the countries that have been most successful in attacking poverty have encouraged a pattern of growth that makes efficient use of labor and have invested in the human capital of the poor. This two-part approach is the basic strategy for the reduction of poverty proposed in this Report. Both elements are essential. The first provides the poor with opportunities to use their most abundant asset—labor. The second improves their immediate well-being and increases their capacity to take advantage of the newly created possibilities. Together, they can improve the lives of most of the world's poor.

Some among the poor—for example, the infirm, the aged, and those in resource-poor areas—may not benefit even from successful implementation of the two-part approach. Others, although benefiting, will remain highly vulnerable to personal disasters such as death of the family breadwinner and to national calamities such as drought or economic recession. A comprehensive approach to poverty, therefore, requires that the basic strategy be supplemented by a system of well-targeted transfers and safety nets.

What is the critical tradeoff?

Discussions of policy toward the poor usually focus on the tradeoff between growth and poverty. But the review of country experience suggests that this is not the critical tradeoff. With appropriate policies, the poor can participate in growth and

Box 3.5 Political coalitions and the poor

Bringing about reforms that are intended to reduce poverty is not necessarily a matter of simply pitting the poor against the nonpoor. Although many economic policies benefit the rich at the expense of the poor, others link the fortunes of both groups and can draw support from coalitions that cut across the poor-nonpoor divide.

Policy coalitions often form across the income spectrum when sectoral interests are at issue. Tariff, exchange rate, and food pricing policies often have effects that differentiate more between the agricultural and industrial sectors than across income levels. In many African and Latin American countries the agricultural sector has long suffered from policies that favor industry and cities. For example, food prices are frequently kept low, which benefits the urban poor, industrial workers, and enterprise owners at the expense of the entire rural sector, including the rural poor.

Coalitions of the poor and nonpoor also form along geographic lines—to promote the flow of resources to an entire region, such as Brazil's Northeast, or to push for interventions such as an irrigation project that will help a specific locale. Entire districts in India have pressed to be included within irrigation command areas in the expectation of increased productivity for both large and small farmers.

Service providers and recipients may also form coalitions. Pressures on governments to finance social services often come as much from the middle-income providers of services as from the beneficiaries. Teachers, medical personnel, social workers, and other middle- and upper-income service providers themselves benefit when the government devotes more resources to social services, and they often have the voting power

and organizational capacity to lobby successfully for greater investments in the development of human resources. Kenya and Sri Lanka, which spend relatively high amounts on primary education, not surprisingly have powerful teachers' unions. The expansion of primary education in Peru was largely attributable to the efforts of political parties to win teachers' votes.

In Argentina, Chile, and Peru the success of tax and other policy reforms to benefit the poor has generally turned on the stance of white-collar workers, professionals, bureaucrats, and small- and medium-size business interests. Redistributive policies were more likely to succeed when these sectors shared in transfers directed primarily to the poor. The same is no doubt true in many other countries. The Maharashtra Employment Guarantee Scheme in India transfers income from the urban nonpoor to the rural poor, but it nevertheless enjoys wide political support. The urban nonpoor see the reduction of migration to Bombay as a benefit, and landowners may look favorably on the scheme because it helps to stabilize the rural labor force and because it creates infrastructure in the countryside. By contrast, when Sri Lanka switched from a general food subsidy and ration scheme to a food stamp program during 1979–80, the fall in implicit transfers to the nonpoor undermined support for the scheme.

In sum, the political economy of poverty reduction is complex and varies greatly according to country and historical circumstances. As this brief review illustrates, policies to benefit the poor have been proposed and successfully implemented under a diversity of conditions. But experience shows that success is often built on objectives and strategies that are shared to some degree by the poor and at least some groups among the nonpoor.

contribute to it, and when they do, rapid declines in poverty are consistent with sustained growth.

If policies can be identified that both reduce poverty and contribute to growth, why have more countries not adopted them? The answer lies in political feasibility. The strategic choices that governments make reflect both economic and political factors. Countries differ enormously in their political culture, in the nature of their political organizations, in their leadership, in their bureaucratic processes, and so forth. This section investigates one aspect of the complex interaction between political and economic factors.

Policies that help the poor but impose costs on the nonpoor will encounter resistance whether or not they increase national income. The nonpoor are usually politically powerful, and they exert a

strong influence on policy. Giving the poor a greater say in local and national decisionmaking would help to restore the balance. But since political power tends to reflect economic power, it is important to design poverty-reducing policies that will be supported, or at least not actively resisted, by the nonpoor. Sometimes it is possible to build coalitions that bring together the poor and certain nonpoor groups that have an interest in reform (Box 3.5). As a rule, however, avoiding resistance by the nonpoor will call for policies that put the least burden on the majority.

Increasing assets

Governments that seek to increase the assets of the poor have pursued two approaches—redistribution of existing assets (such as land) and increased public investment in the human capital of the poor. Both policies are beneficial to the poor. The experience of Japan and Korea provides an example of significant land redistributions that led to a marked and sustained decline in poverty. Colombia and Malaysia illustrate the benefits of increasing human capital.

The lower panel of Figure 3.5 uses the framework described in Box 3.6 to illustrate the benefits to the poor under each approach. Land redistribution brings an immediate and lasting gain; higher spending on education brings no improvement in the short run but a rapid increase later. (The policies were calibrated to ensure the same increase in the incomes of the poor by the tenth year.)

Do the two policies' effects on long-term growth make one preferable to the other? In principle, both policies have growth-increasing and growth-reducing effects. The land reform, for instance, might reduce saving (since the poor tend to save a smaller proportion of their income than the rich), and that would be bad for growth. But it might also encourage the more efficient use of land, which would be good for growth. Investment in education improves the quality of the work force (good for growth) but requires, at least in the short term, higher taxes to finance the increase in public spending (bad for growth). On balance, there may be little to choose between the two approaches.

The policies, however, differ strikingly in their effects on the distribution of income and thus in their political feasibility (see the upper panel of Figure 3.5). Land redistribution causes an immediate and permanent loss of consumption for the nonpoor—which is why it is resisted so strongly. Extra spending on education can be built up more gradually so that the increased burden of taxation on the nonpoor is paid entirely out of increments to income. The second approach, therefore, is likely to be more feasible. Moreover, some nonpoor groups—for example, industrialists who need a skilled labor force—stand to gain from the human capital policy and would be likely to support it.

This does not imply that governments should reject asset redistribution or that asset redistribution and investment in the poor are mutually exclusive. Indeed, a relatively egalitarian distribution of land increases the effectiveness of other policies aimed at reducing poverty. It does suggest, however, that tilting the distribution of new investment in favor of the poor (as advocated in *Redistribution with Growth*, by Chenery and others) is likely to be more popular than reshuffling the stock of existing assets. If redistribution is impossible, the case for spending more on education and other forms of investment in human capital is all the stronger.

Increasing income

A similar comparison can be made between a current transfer of income and growth that raises the

---

Box 3.6 Tradeoffs and poverty: a simple simulation model

The simulation model underlying the results of this section captures two tradeoffs—that between poverty and growth and that between the poor and the nonpoor. The severity of the tradeoffs depends on two factors.

The first is the immediate economic cost of raising the revenues necessary to finance transfers and social programs. Higher taxes are likely to reduce economic efficiency (and hence GNP), at least to some extent. Moreover, not all of the increased public spending will find its way to the intended beneficiaries. Similarly, some of the rise in taxes will fall on the poor. So, to deliver a net benefit of $1 to the poor, more than $1 will have to be raised in taxes. In the model, a net transfer of 0.5 percent of GNP to the poor reduces GNP by 0.4 percent and the consumption of the nonpoor by 1.0 percent. Policies that allow a reduction in taxation, such as the elimination of subsidies to capital, have the reverse effect.

Second, if the nonpoor save more than the poor, transferring income from the nonpoor to the poor will reduce national saving. This in turn will mean slower economic growth. A net transfer of 0.5 percent of GNP reduces the growth rate of GNP by 0.1 percentage points and that of the consumption of the nonpoor by 0.12 percentage points. The productivity of capital, however, is assumed to be independent of ownership. Thus, increased investment in the human capital of the poor, for example, will increase growth to the same extent as investment elsewhere in the economy.

The model depicts growth in a one-sector economy. It consists of a single production function that combines factors of production and yields national income; a submodel that distributes national income to the poor and the nonpoor according to their ownership of factors of production; a set of taxes and transfers that determines disposable income by income class; saving rates by income class; and a "cost" function that measures the loss of GNP arising from taxation.

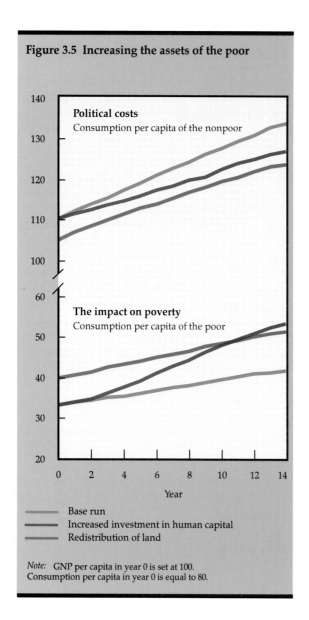

Figure 3.5 Increasing the assets of the poor

Political costs
Consumption per capita of the nonpoor

The impact on poverty
Consumption per capita of the poor

Year

Base run
Increased investment in human capital
Redistribution of land

Note: GNP per capita in year 0 is set at 100.
Consumption per capita in year 0 is equal to 80.

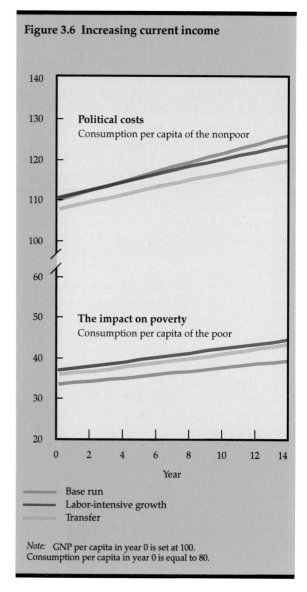

Figure 3.6 Increasing current income

Political costs
Consumption per capita of the nonpoor

The impact on poverty
Consumption per capita of the poor

Year

Base run
Labor-intensive growth
Transfer

Note: GNP per capita in year 0 is set at 100.
Consumption per capita in year 0 is equal to 80.

returns to assets owned by the poor. Some countries, such as Sri Lanka, have relied heavily on subsidies; others, such as Colombia, have increased the return to labor through policies that promote its more efficient use. Both approaches can benefit the poor. In the lower panel of Figure 3.6 the transfer has been chosen to ensure the same increase in income over the simulation period as with policies that remove biases against the use of labor.

As before, both policies affect growth. But in this case there is a stronger presumption—confirmed by the model—in favor of removing the biases against the use of labor. This policy produces an immediate gain in efficiency, and the level of GNP rises. Thereafter, the effect of the policy on growth

will depend on the interaction of many different factors. By contrast, an increase in the transfer is likely to reduce both the level and the future growth of income. Higher taxes will be needed to finance the increase, and long-term saving will be lower; both are bad for growth.

This initial preference for the labor-promoting approach is greatly strengthened by considerations of political feasibility. Here, as before, the difference between the two policies is striking (see the upper panel of Figure 3.6). Whereas transfers reduce the present consumption of the nonpoor, switching to a more efficient use of labor increases their consumption initially and leads to only somewhat slower rises in the future. Transfers are therefore far more likely to encounter political resistance. Moreover, some among the nonpoor, such as investors in labor-intensive industry, stand to gain from the removal of biases against the use of labor and may therefore support such reforms. Again, however, the two approaches are not mutually exclusive. Indeed, some transfers will clearly be necessary for those who cannot participate in growth.

As with the review of country experience, this analysis suggests that a more efficient use of labor, coupled with increased investment in the human capital of the poor, reduces poverty and increases national income. The two-part strategy proposed in this Report thus entails no tradeoff between income and growth on the one hand and poverty on the other. The tradeoff between the poor and the nonpoor remains—but the strategy achieves a substantial reduction in poverty with a smaller cost to the nonpoor than under other approaches. It may therefore be politically more acceptable.

A tradeoff between growth and poverty does emerge during the economic restructuring that follows, for instance, a permanent fall in the terms of trade. The need to change the pattern of production makes investment even more important than usual, and as a result, policies that reduce investment become more "expensive" in terms of future growth. Yet the poor are especially vulnerable during adjustment. Protecting them at such times becomes both more urgent and more difficult. Transfers must be targeted with special care if the poor are to be protected at reasonable cost. The case for transfers in the event of a temporary shock is much more clear-cut. The value of investment is not affected by a drought, for example—but the value of a transfer to prevent death from famine is certainly increased.

The next four chapters turn from a broad view of approaches to development to a more detailed discussion of specific policies. How are governments to promote efficient, labor-intensive growth together with investment in human capital? Chapter 4 concentrates on the first element of the strategy by identifying the policies that have encouraged a pattern of growth that uses labor more efficiently. Chapter 5 turns to the second component and examines the delivery of social services to the poor. Chapter 6 discusses the role of transfers and safety nets in helping those who may not benefit from the policies recommended in Chapters 4 and 5 as well as those who may suffer income-reducing shocks. And Chapter 7 asks how all these policies need to be modified to cope with recession and restructuring.

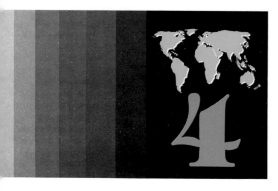

Promoting economic
opportunities for the poor

Ensuring that the poor participate in and contribute to growth requires the adoption of appropriate economywide and sectoral policies and of measures to help the poor grasp new income-earning opportunities. This chapter examines policies that will:

• Encourage a pattern of growth that increases the efficient use of the assets owned by the poor
• Expand the access of the poor to land, credit, infrastructure, and productive inputs.

As noted in Chapter 3, there are strong complementarities among growth, poverty reduction, and human capital. Investment in human capital, which is critical for enabling the poor to seize expanded opportunities, is discussed in Chapter 5.

The pattern of growth and the incomes of the poor

Most of the poor in developing countries depend on income from labor—from work on their own land, from wages, or from other self-employment. The countries that have succeeded in reducing poverty over the long term have encouraged broadly based rural development and urban employment, thereby increasing the returns to small-farm production and wage labor. Successful approaches to development, however, have varied according to the initial economic conditions. In Thailand in the 1960s and Kenya in the 1970s the rising productivity of small farms spurred growth in nonfarm incomes. In Malaysia in the 1970s expansion of urban employment played an equally important role.

Since labor is an abundant resource, encouraging its use is generally consistent with rapid and efficient growth. Yet most countries have adopted policies that are implicitly biased against labor. In particular, although agriculture is the principal labor-intensive sector, almost all developing countries have taxed agricultural output. Governments have done this for two reasons: to finance public spending (it is administratively easy to tax agricultural output) and to protect manufacturing, especially in the early phases of industrialization. Country experiences suggest two conclusions.

• Successful rural development entails avoiding excessive taxation of agriculture, providing strong support for rural infrastructure, and making technical innovations accessible to small farmers.
• A rising urban demand for labor (in industry and services) plays an increasing role as incomes rise. Governments can foster urban job creation by avoiding severe distortions in product and factor markets and by providing suitable urban infrastructure.

Government policy and rural development

The expansion of agriculture is the driving force behind effective rural development, which in turn lays the foundation for broadly based, poverty-reducing growth. The poor benefit directly if they are farmers, and they benefit indirectly from growth in demand for farm labor and for the products of the rural nonfarm sector. Especially in low-income countries, there is a strong association between growth in agricultural purchasing power and rural wages—a key welfare indicator for the

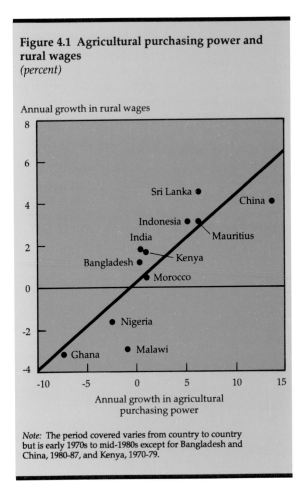

Figure 4.1 Agricultural purchasing power and rural wages
(percent)

Annual growth in rural wages

Note: The period covered varies from country to country but is early 1970s to mid-1980s except for Bangladesh and China, 1980-87, and Kenya, 1970-79.

sia enjoyed an agricultural growth rate of 5 percent a year over that decade. Ghana, in contrast, taxed agricultural commodities to the tune of 63 percent and spent only 3 percent of value added on support. Its farm output fell by more than 1 percent a year.

In some cases taxes can be offset by effective public support. Thailand's total taxation on agricultural commodities amounted to 43 percent of output value, with the burden falling mainly on rice and rubber. But substantial public support for infrastructure and services made up for these outflows. Figure 4.3 shows the pattern of gross and net flows to the sector. It excludes spending on

rural poor (see Figure 4.1). Moreover, agricultural growth helps the rest of the economy. Typically (as noted in *World Development Report 1986*) countries with rapid agricultural growth have also had rapid industrial growth.

The main policies that affect agricultural performance are taxation and public support for agricultural development. In quantifying taxation it is important to take account of both direct taxes on agricultural products and the indirect taxes that are implicit in industrial protection and overvaluation of the exchange rate. As Figure 4.2 shows, these indirect taxes can add substantially to the overall tax burden.

The range of experience is wide, but countries that have performed well have usually taxed moderately and provided strong support. For example, in the 1970s total taxation of agricultural commodities in Malaysia was a relatively low 19 percent of the value of output (at international prices); government spending for direct support of agriculture was 10 percent of the sector's value added. Malay-

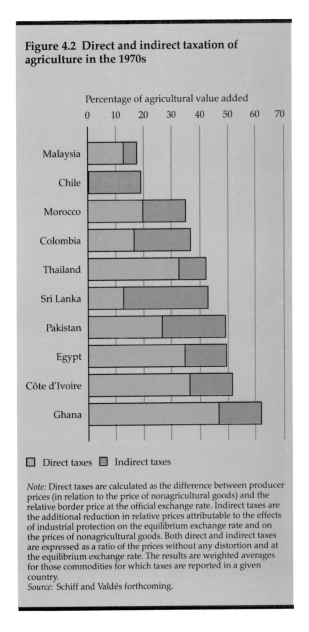

Figure 4.2 Direct and indirect taxation of agriculture in the 1970s

Percentage of agricultural value added

☐ Direct taxes ☐ Indirect taxes

Note: Direct taxes are calculated as the difference between producer prices (in relation to the price of nonagricultural goods) and the relative border price at the official exchange rate. Indirect taxes are the additional reduction in relative prices attributable to the effects of industrial protection on the equilibrium exchange rate and on the prices of nonagricultural goods. Both direct and indirect taxes are expressed as a ratio of the prices without any distortion and at the equilibrium exchange rate. The results are weighted averages for those commodities for which taxes are reported in a given country.
Source: Schiff and Valdés forthcoming.

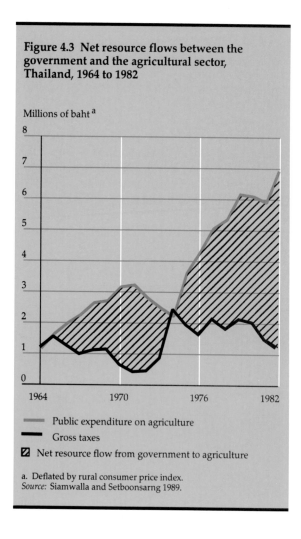

Figure 4.3 Net resource flows between the government and the agricultural sector, Thailand, 1964 to 1982

Millions of baht [a]

(chart showing years 1964, 1970, 1976, 1982 on horizontal axis; 0 to 8 on vertical axis)

— Public expenditure on agriculture

▬ Gross taxes

▨ Net resource flow from government to agriculture

a. Deflated by rural consumer price index.
Source: Siamwalla and Setboonsarng 1989.

rural roads and the effects of the country's indirect taxation (which is about 15 percent of value added), but the overall pattern is clear; substantial public spending led to net flows into the sector after the early 1960s. This spending supported expansion of the land frontier and crop diversification—generally toward less heavily taxed commodities such as cassava. Like Malaysia, Thailand was strikingly successful in reducing poverty.

A World Bank study of six African countries, "Managing Agricultural Development in Africa," offers further contrasts between good and bad performers. The countries with the most successful agricultural sectors (especially Cameroon and Kenya) were also the best performers in GDP per capita and manufacturing output. These countries taxed farming less severely than the others, partly by avoiding acutely overvalued exchange rates. They also invested in an institutional and infrastructural environment that supported diversified agricultural growth, much of it in the small-farm

sector. By contrast, Nigeria, Senegal, and Tanzania sought capital-intensive industrialization. They imposed heavy direct and indirect taxes on farming and provided only weak public support for infrastructure and institutions. Like Ghana in the 1970s, they failed dismally to spur growth in agricultural output and in nonfarm output and total labor demand.

Policy within the agricultural sector influences not just the growth of the sector but also the extent to which this growth reduces poverty. When product pricing and support are biased in favor of large farmers, the poor benefit less. For example, policy in Malawi contains biases in the form of pricing that discriminates in favor of large estates and against small farmers in the tobacco sector. Small-farm tobacco production has grown only slowly. In Zimbabwe before independence the entire system of infrastructure and services was intended to help large farmers. When this bias was partially redressed in the 1980s, smallholder maize and cotton production grew rapidly. In many Latin American countries, too, support services are designed mainly in the interests of large farmers.

Other aspects of policy may add to the bias against labor. Credit subsidies, for instance, foster excessive mechanization, and research suggests that they have reduced the demand for farm labor in India. A highly unequal land distribution also limits the extent to which the poor gain from agricultural growth. Brazil shows that transfers of resources to the sector can fail to have much effect on poverty if policy within the sector is biased against the poor and if the poor have little access to land (Box 4.1).

INFRASTRUCTURE AND TECHNOLOGY. Public programs to provide services, infrastructure, research, and technology for agriculture have a decisive influence on the level and pattern of agricultural growth and on private investment in the sector. A study of fifty-eight countries during 1969–78 found that a 1 percent increase in irrigation coverage was associated with a rise in aggregate crop output of 1.6 percent and that a 1 percent increase in paved roads was associated with a rise in output of 0.3 percent. Investments in infrastructure also help to improve and maintain natural resources. Cost-effectiveness, however, is important. An analysis of completed Bank-supported projects to create infrastructure in agriculture found that economic rates of return averaged 17 percent—well above the 10 percent used to qualify a project as successful. (In Africa, however, performance is much

Box 4.1 Agricultural policies in Brazil favor large farmers

Brazil has promoted agriculture and has achieved rapid growth in the sector. But its record on poverty is disappointing. One reason is that biases within the agricultural sector, notably in taxation and subsidized credit, favor large farmers and work to the disadvantage of labor. These biases interact with the highly inequitable initial land distribution to reduce the gains to the poor from growth. Brazil vividly demonstrates that promoting agriculture is not enough. Policies within the sector also matter.

Land and agricultural taxation

Brazil's income tax greatly favors agriculture in relation to other sectors, but only the rich can reap the benefits. Through special provisions in the income tax code, corporations can exclude up to 80 percent of agricultural profits from their taxable income, and individuals can exclude 90 percent. Fixed investments can be fully depreciated in the first year and can even be depreciated two to six times over. This, together with high inflation, encourages corporations and the rich to overinvest in land. The result has been the accumulation of large landholdings and increases in land prices that exceed growth in land productivity. The poor do not benefit from the tax breaks (they pay no income tax), and they cannot afford to buy land. Many move to frontier areas in search of unclaimed land.

A progressive land tax could offset the bias in the income tax. Brazil tried this but failed because of widespread evasion and many exceptions. One such exception, intended to encourage land use, reduces the tax by up to 90 percent if owners use the land to graze cattle. This promotes the conversion of forestland to uneconomic livestock ranching, reduces the demand for labor, and has harmful environmental consequences.

Subsidized credit

Agricultural credit has been exceptionally distorted in Brazil. Until recently, real interest rates on official credit were negative, and real interest rates on loans for agriculture were lower than in the nonagricultural sector. The difference in credit terms between sectors has been capitalized in the price of land. Although subsidies raise profits in agriculture, they have mainly benefited large farmers and have encouraged excessive mechanization, again reducing the demand for unskilled labor. Poor people who lack land titles have not benefited from credit subsidies.

Agricultural policies in Brazil have reduced labor demand and have made it almost impossible for a poor person to buy land and become a farmer. Opportunities for unskilled workers to acquire skills by becoming long-term workers have been substantially reduced by subsidized mechanization.

lower because of weak institutions and poor project implementation.)

Better infrastructure can lead to increased productivity, technical change, and strengthened market linkages. Irrigation and water control have been crucial for higher yields (through the adoption of modern varieties and multiple cropping) and reduced variability of output in the past twenty years in South and East Asia. And although landowners are likely to enjoy the biggest absolute gains, the income gains from infrastructure can be widely dispersed. In Andhra Pradesh, India, for example, the monthly per capita expenditure for small farm units and wage-earning households in 1983 was 35 percent higher in irrigated than in nonirrigated districts. A study of Bangladeshi villages found that infrastructural development is associated with a rise in the incomes of all households, including the poor and landless (Box 4.2). Much of the increase was a result of changes in the way labor is used.

Infrastructure projects benefit many, but they can sometimes affect certain subgroups adversely unless planners anticipate and prevent such potential effects. For instance, thirty-nine dam projects approved for financing by the World Bank in twenty-seven countries during 1979–85 brought considerable benefits to people in the command areas but also entailed relocation of about 750,000 inhabitants of reservoir areas. Such displacement can cause profound distress, disruption of social and productive structures, increased poverty, and environmental damage. The issue has not always been adequately addressed by governments and aid agencies. During the 1980s, however, the treatment of populations displaced by infrastructure projects improved considerably. Resettlement plans are becoming integral components of the projects, which also include funds for acquiring land and providing infrastructure and services for the resettled areas.

Technological change is vital for agricultural growth. The record of the past thirty years clearly supports the argument for public funding for agri-

Box 4.2 Infrastructural development and rural incomes in Bangladesh

A study of sixteen villages in Bangladesh shows how the development of infrastructure—roads, electric power, banks, markets, schools, and health centers—affects the incomes of rural households. The study divided the villages into those that had and had not benefited from the provision of public infrastructure. With other factors controlled, the study found that greater infrastructural development was associated with a one-third increase in average household incomes. Crop income increased by 24 percent, wage income by 92 percent, and income from livestock and fisheries by 78 percent. These three changes largely benefited the poor. Income from nonfarm businesses increased by 17 percent; this largely benefited the nonpoor.

Roads, electricity, and other economic services encouraged the production of new farm products (including perishable commodities) and higher output in transport, construction, services, and small-scale industries. All this had a substantial effect on the pattern of labor demand. Although households worked roughly as many days a year in developed as in undeveloped villages, in the developed ones they spent less time on family labor, which had low implicit returns, and much more on wage labor, especially in the relatively high-paying nonfarm sector. Poor households with few physical assets, including landless households, gained substantially.

cultural research and for dissemination of new technologies in small-scale production. Many in the 1970s thought that the Green Revolution would do little or nothing to help the poor, but recent appraisals suggest that most of these fears were unfounded. In Asia and Latin America (the main areas in which the new varieties were adopted) small farmers and laborers alike have benefited—although most studies have found that small farmers adopt new varieties with a lag of three years or so because they are less willing or able to take risks. Better access to new varieties as well as to water, chemical inputs, and credit has encouraged small farmers to switch more quickly. Extension services designed for small farmers have also helped. Where policies and support were inadequate, as in much of Sub-Saharan Africa, few small farmers have adopted the improved technologies, and both overall growth and the incomes of the poor have suffered.

There is also evidence of a link between technology and wages. Detailed country studies often find that new technologies give an initial boost to the demand for agricultural labor because total labor use is greater over the course of the year. Rural wages increased in many states in India and Pakistan between the mid-1960s and the mid-1970s and in Java, Indonesia, between the mid-1970s and the early 1980s. The demand for farm labor may have slowed in India from the late 1970s owing to labor-saving innovations, sometimes encouraged by subsidies to mechanization. But slow growth in farm employment has been offset by the buoyancy of the nonfarm sector. There has been some concern that modern technologies and mechanization may have reduced employment opportunities and incomes for women, but the evidence does not, in general, support this view (Box 4.3).

FARM-NONFARM LINKAGES. Growth in the rural nonfarm economy is important in creating rural employment and in raising labor incomes. Small, labor-intensive enterprises are the most common. Nonfarm activities typically account for 20 to 30 percent of rural employment in Asia and Latin America and for 10 to 20 percent in Africa. If rural towns are included, the proportions rise substantially. A study in India found that employment in the nonfarm sector grew 35 percent in the 1970s, compared with 14 percent for employment in agriculture; without that growth, rural wages would have risen much more slowly. In Kenya among smallholder families per capita income from nonfarm sources climbed 14 percent a year between 1974–75 and 1981–82; incomes from farm employment rose only 3 percent a year.

Although the nonfarm sector has often expanded faster than the farm sector, agriculture is usually the key to the growth of nonfarm activities. An expanding farm economy demands inputs from and supplies raw materials to transport, processing, and marketing firms. Rising farm incomes lead to greater demand for consumer goods and services. A study found that spending on locally produced nonfoods accounted for 33 percent of the increase in household expenditures in rural areas of Malaysia and India and for 15 percent of increased spending in Sierra Leone and Nigeria. More generally, the study found that every dollar increase in agricultural income led to an income increase of about eighty cents elsewhere in the economy in the Asian cases and fifty cents in the African cases. This difference reflects the lower population densities and poorly integrated mar-

Box 4.3 The impact of technological change on women

Modern seed varieties, irrigation, and the increased commercialization of crops have commonly been accompanied by the greater use of hired labor, mostly from landless households. The new technologies have also had important implications for the division of household labor. Wage labor has replaced unpaid labor, and in some cases male labor has replaced female labor. This has raised concerns that technological change has harmed women.

The substitution of hired labor for family labor usually improves the household's standard of living. In the Philippines, for example, the new technologies raised farming incomes, allowing households to hire labor and purchase labor-saving farm implements. This reduced the number of hours worked by family members in low-productivity jobs on the farm and allowed them to engage in other, more productive, activities such as trade or raising livestock. In addition, greater demand for hired labor provided jobs to landless workers.

Modern varieties have, in general, raised the demand for hired female labor. They usually require more labor per acre—particularly in tasks typically done by women, such as weeding, harvesting, and postharvest work. A study of three Indian states concluded that the use of hired female labor was greater on farms that had adopted modern varieties than on those that had not.

Other studies for India and Nepal have found that the overall use of hired female labor rose substantially with the introduction of modern varieties.

In some cases, however, mechanization has led to lower female employment. The outcome has often depended on the tasks mechanized. When predominantly female tasks were given over to machinery, women were displaced. This happened in Bangladesh, Indonesia, and the Philippines with the replacement of the finger knife as a harvesting tool and the introduction of direct seeding and portable mechanical threshers. In Bangladesh most of the postharvest work had been done by women using the *dheki* (a foot-operated mortar and pestle). When the dehusking and polishing of grain were mechanized, these operations were turned over to men, who now operate the modern mills. A study in the Indian states of Kerala, Tamil Nadu, and West Bengal found that where chemical fertilizers have replaced cow dung, men rather than women now apply the fertilizer because women lack access to the information provided by extension services.

When women were displaced, the effect on their incomes and on household welfare depended on whether they found more productive jobs elsewhere. Overall nonfarm employment did increase, but data classified by gender are scanty.

---

kets in Africa. Public investments in rural infrastructure (in electricity, transport, water, banks, telephones, schools, and so on) can greatly strengthen these linkages.

The pattern of urban and industrial growth

Growth in urban employment and wages is the second broad determinant of the pace of poverty reduction—through its direct influence on the existing urban poor and through the opportunities it creates for migration from rural areas (Box 4.4). Growth of urban employment is especially important in middle-income developing countries, but it matters increasingly everywhere. Governments can affect the urban demand for labor by altering the incentives and regulations that face workers and their employers and by providing, or failing to provide, adequate urban infrastructure.

INCENTIVES AND REGULATION. The demand for urban labor depends partly on government policy toward the markets for goods and capital as well as

on policy toward the labor market itself. Often, industrial protection reduces both the level and growth of labor use in the formal sector. As a rule, the greater the degree of protection, the greater the capital intensity of production; this is illustrated with data for India in Table 4.1. A more neutral trade regime would therefore increase the demand for labor. Some of this expansion in demand would probably come from increased exports, but the main reason for reducing protection is to use resources—including labor—more efficiently. Greater neutrality in the trade regime can support a more labor-intensive pattern of industrial expansion in import-competing as well as exporting sectors. A study of ten countries in the 1970s confirms this view. In addition, it found that in Indonesia, Pakistan, and Tunisia labor demand would have increased more from better use of resources within the import-competing sector than from a shift between the two sectors.

The contribution of manufacturing to employment over time differs greatly from country to country (Table 4.2). The growth of manufacturing

Box 4.4 Does rural-to-urban migration help or hurt the poor?

Most studies have found that people migrate mainly for economic reasons. Poverty, both absolute and relative, and income variability, which leads to greater vulnerability, cause people to move. In Botswana households "place" different members of the household in different labor markets so that, for example, the effects of a drought on rural incomes will be offset by remittances from members working in urban areas. In rural India households often marry their daughters into distant and dispersed (although still kinship-related) households. In almost all cases rural-urban migrants increase their incomes. Most migrants have jobs waiting for them or find one within a month or two. In the Ludhiana District of Punjab, India, 78 percent of migrants had a job after one month and 94 percent after two months. A study of the poorest of the urban poor, the Calcutta pavement dwellers, found that migrants were better off after moving. In Colombia rural-urban migrants had higher incomes than comparable people in their rural places of origin; the gains were even higher for the better educated.

The poorest are likely to be underrepresented in rural-urban migration. The study of Punjab's Ludhiana District showed that only 15 percent of rural outmigrants belonged to the lower classes, although they accounted for more than 24 percent of the sample. In a study of forty North Indian villages, only 5 percent of the working migrants came from farm-labor households, although such households made up 19 percent of the villages' population. The poorest may stay at home because they are less educated. In Kenya the probability that an educated person will leave the village is five times greater than for an uneducated person; in Tanzania 90 percent of the men who left their villages had some schooling.

The poor who do not migrate may still benefit indirectly. Rural-urban migration has tightened the rural labor market in many countries. In addition, remittances help those who stay behind. In Kenya remittances helped to lift some of the poorest households out of the lowest income class and contributed to agricultural innovation, partly by reducing income variability. There is little evidence to suggest that migration worsens poverty in the sending areas.

The impact of migration on the urban poor is also of interest, but information is sparse. Migration, it might seem, will hold down urban wage rates for unskilled work in the informal sector. Evidence from Colombia showed that migrants had higher incomes than urban natives of similar education. But there is no evidence that migration causes the incomes of natives to fall.

Some countries have tried to reduce migration on the grounds that it leads to excessive and costly urbanization. With few exceptions, these efforts have failed to stem rural-urban migration significantly or to redirect migrants to secondary towns. An urban bias in policy could lead to more migration than is socially desirable. The appropriate policy is to focus on direct remedies—such as reducing the biases against agriculture in pricing and improving the social and economic infrastructure of rural areas.

Table 4.1 Effective protection and labor intensity of manufacturing, India, 1986

Degree of effective protection of industry	Share of fixed capital (percent)	Share of employment (percent)	Fixed capital per worker (thousands of rupees)
High	53	19	93
Medium	4	3	32
Low	43	78	18
All industries	100	100	32

Source: World Bank 1989b.

employment depends on both the growth and the labor intensity of the sector. The middle- and low-income countries of East Asia again stand out. Many of the countries that saw manufacturing employment rise quickly also had thriving farm sectors. Policies that avoid discriminating against agriculture go hand in hand with a more broadly labor-intensive pattern of development. No coun-try opted for an entirely neutral trade regime, but incentives were far less distorted in Korea, Malaysia, and (after the mid-1970s) Thailand than in Argentina, Pakistan, or Tanzania.

FACTOR MARKET INTERVENTIONS. When governments intervene in the markets for capital and labor, they often exacerbate the antilabor bias of protection. Many countries make imports of capital goods cheap (through low tariffs and overvalued exchange rates), offer tax breaks for investment in capital equipment, and subsidize credit—all of which tend to reduce the price of capital. Subsidized energy prices often exacerbate this bias and, furthermore, have adverse environmental consequences. In contrast, social security taxes, labor regulations, and high wages (especially in industries in which competition among producers is weak) all tend to raise the cost of labor in the formal sector. A study of incentive structures in ten

Table 4.2 The contribution of manufacturing to employment, selected countries, 1970 to 1980
(percent)

Country	Manufacturing employment as share of total labor force		Increment, 1970–80[a]
	1970	1980	
Korea, Rep. of	7	14	36
Malaysia	9	16	33
Indonesia	6	9	23
Brazil	7	10	19
Thailand	5	7	13
Colombia	5	6	10
India	2	3	5
Zambia	3	3	4
Kenya	2	2	4
Tanzania	1	1	2
Pakistan	2	2	1
Argentina	17	13	−21

Note: The figures are based on registered employment in manufacturing.
a. The ratio of the increase in manufacturing employment to the increase in the labor force.
Source: United Nations Industrial Development Organization and World Bank data.

countries found that government intervention raised the relative price of labor in all cases in the early 1970s. The increase was 11 percent in Korea, between 30 and 50 percent in Argentina, Brazil, and Côte d'Ivoire, almost 90 percent in Tunisia, and more than 300 percent in Pakistan.

Labor-market policies—minimum wages, job security regulations, and social security—are usually intended to raise welfare or reduce exploitation. But they actually work to raise the cost of labor in the formal sector and reduce labor demand. Studies from the 1970s and 1980s found that job security regulations reduced the long-term demand for labor by an estimated 18 percent in India and 25 percent in Zimbabwe. There is little poverty, in any case, in the formal sector. Yet by trying to improve the welfare of workers there, governments reduced formal sector employment, increased the supply of labor to the rural and urban informal sectors, and thus depressed labor incomes where most of the poor are found.

THE ROLE OF THE INFORMAL SECTOR. In most developing countries the informal sector plays a prominent role in providing employment and incomes. It has been estimated to account for 75 percent of urban employment in many countries in Sub-Saharan Africa and for 85 percent in Pakistan. It also accounts for most of the poverty in urban areas. In Côte d'Ivoire, for example, the incidence of urban poverty in the informal sector is more than three times that in the formal sector.

The informal sector is very diverse in its income structure and activities. It is dominated by one-person firms and small-scale entrepreneurs that employ a few apprentices (often relatives) and hired laborers. Firms are not covered by government labor regulations, and there are no restrictions on entry. But many in the informal sector pay indirect taxes and fees—license fees for small repair shops and street vendors, for example. Wages are generally lower than in the formal sector, especially for apprentices. But there is also a high degree of inequality, and many entrepreneurs do much better than workers in the formal sector. Activities range from efficient manufacturing, transport, and trading enterprises to marginal work such as collecting and recycling trash. Most of the sector's production is for consumption—especially by low-income households—and little is exported.

As in the rural nonfarm sector, growth in the urban informal sector depends on the rest of the economy and, in particular, on the demand for nontraded goods and services. But preferential treatment for large firms has undermined the informal sector. Subsidized capital for one part of the economy implies fewer resources for the rest.

Some countries have tried to offset these biases. India, for example, has provided cheap credit for small enterprises and has restricted competition from larger firms. This kind of approach rarely works. Protection and constraints on the entry of large firms into labor-intensive activities have tended to reduce any gains in employment, especially since credit subsidies have led many small firms to adopt relatively capital-intensive techniques. Distortions in product markets, particularly biases in the structure of protection among industries, have probably been a more important influence on the demand for labor. Indeed, evidence suggests that small firms in the manufacturing sector are not necessarily more labor-intensive than large firms in the same line of business. In Korea labor intensity within industries seldom varies by a factor of more than three, whereas across industries it varies by a factor of more than a hundred.

Most countries have further undermined informal employment through heavy regulation. In Indonesia, where most of the informal sector is thriving, restrictions on pedicabs have steadily increased, and pedicabs are now completely banned from Jakarta. In Zimbabwe street vendors and small-scale enterprises are excluded from many parts of the towns, and small businesses have to struggle to acquire land titles. A study of

Peru found that a prospective entrepreneur who wanted to set up a small garment factory had to spend 289 working days dealing with regulations; in Lima it took more than two years to register a minibus route. In addition to removing biases that favor larger firms, light regulation together with the provision of appropriate urban infrastructure is the best way to facilitate growth in the informal sector.

URBAN INFRASTRUCTURE AND POVERTY. Urbanization will make increasing demands on infrastructure. Investments in infrastructure can make inroads on poverty both by improving living conditions and by promoting employment. Indeed the two go together. In many cases roads, water, sanitation, electric power, and other services for low-income areas help small businesses as well as households because many informal businesses are based in the home. Studies on Colombia and Korea show that access to public utilities is essential for small new firms. In Nigeria, as in many other African countries, weak urban infrastructure inhibits the growth of small firms that cannot afford, for example, their own power generators or water facilities.

Increasing the participation of the poor in growth

Growth that creates opportunities for the poor will have a greater impact on the poor if they have access to land, credit, and public infrastructure and services. Many countries have adopted programs to this end.

Increasing access to land

Policies to redistribute land have deservedly received much attention. In addition, policies that expand tenancy, provide clear land rights where traditional systems fail, and improve the management of common-property resources can create opportunities for many of the rural poor. Such policies should help reduce poverty and make the land more productive at the same time.

REFORMING PROPERTY RIGHTS. In the twentieth century virtually all the major redistributions of property rights in land were precipitated by social revolution, defeat in war, or national liberation from colonial rule. Many of these upheavals led to large-scale collective forms of organization, as was the case in China, Cuba, Ethiopia, the Democratic People's Republic of Korea, the U.S.S.R., and

Vietnam. The old agrarian order was swept away entirely and no compensation was paid. Elsewhere, reform helped existing tenants, smallholders, or new settlers by transferring individual rights; Egypt, India, Iran, Japan, Kenya, and the Republic of Korea are examples. In some cases compensation was paid, but it was usually based on depressed land prices.

In China, Japan, and the Republic of Korea, land reforms were extensive. They affected the poor in two ways. First, rural households benefited from the reallocation of rents and from new opportunities to use the family's resources. Second, together with favorable incentives for agriculture and strong local institutions, they provided the basis for broadly based poverty-reducing growth.

In the absence of a major upheaval, land reforms have rarely gone so far, and as a result their impact on the poor has been modest. In Egypt, India, and Iran the reforms made owners out of former tenants but favored the better-off farmers. Redistributions in Bolivia and Mexico attacked the inefficiency and inequity of the "hacienda" system, but since subsequent policies failed to sustain growth of productivity in smallholder agriculture, the effect on the poor was muted. In Bolivia, moreover, most of the land was given to large agricultural companies for livestock raising and forestry. And although more than half a million rural people gained access to four million hectares of land, many still lack land titles. This makes transactions difficult and limits the use of land as collateral.

In most circumstances, political realities forbid reform to stray far from the status quo. Where expropriation is not possible, the cost of compensating the former owners becomes a major difficulty, especially when policy distortions have driven up the price of land. Land reform can be expensive in other ways, too: there is the cost of mapping and registering the new owners' holdings and of providing infrastructure and services to raise productivity on the new farms.

The chances of successful land reform are greater if aid is available, as in the case of Kenya. A project in northeast Brazil also suggests that more modest land transfers to small farmers are feasible despite all the difficulties and that, when supported with adequate investment, they help to raise farm incomes (Box 4.5).

IMPROVING TENANCY. Many governments have tried to make tenancy more secure and thus, in effect, to transfer ownership rights. Some of these reforms have been successful—in the Philippines,

BALANCING INDIVIDUAL AND COMMON PROPERTY. Africa's traditional forms of land ownership seem to be evolving toward individual property rights. This is mainly because of population growth and the increasing commercialization of agriculture. But this shift toward individual land rights tends to undermine the ability of traditional systems to ensure that all members of the extended family have access to land. This feature of their land systems has helped some countries in Africa to avoid the extremes of poverty and landlessness that are common in much of Asia and Latin America: traditional systems have provided secure land tenure and encouraged farmers to invest in their land (Box 4.6). In such cases, encouraging individual land registration and titling may be undesirable. Where traditional systems have failed to provide clear land rights, land titles and registration are useful.

Common pasture and forest resources are important for poor rural households. They provide fuelwood, fodder, and employment to those who otherwise have few land rights. When the population is growing rapidly, or when there is open access to these land resources and traditional community management has broken down, the commons are often overused and degraded. This hurts those who depend most on the common resources as a safety net. Policies to privatize these resources have often failed to protect the interests of those with existing rights to the land or to create the basis for a viable and equitable system. Small farmers have sometimes been forced, as a result, to sell their individual holdings. Common-property resources should receive greater attention. They need to be better protected and better managed. Investment in research on how to use these fragile resources would be money well spent.

Increasing access to credit

Credit can help the poor to accumulate assets and to cushion their consumption in hard times. But extending credit to the poor is costly to the lender. Transaction costs are high, and the risk may be great owing to lack of collateral. Moreover, other borrowers, such as large-scale farmers, may have preferential access for cultural or ethnic reasons. Many governments have therefore tried to expand credit for the poor through large-scale subsidized credit programs and other measures. Several rationales have been given for these policies: the poor cannot afford market interest rates; formal lenders are too cautious; informal lenders are too

for example, and in West Bengal and Kerala, India, where tenants' rights became inheritable. But tenancy reform has usually failed. Landlords have thwarted the new legislation by evicting tenants or concealing tenancy as wage labor. In Brazil, where tenancy laws limit owners' share of output and make it hard to evict tenants and sharecroppers, semiskilled workers have difficulty in gaining access to land. Landowners prefer informal and very short-term tenancy agreements. Or they may evict the tenants and use the land for forestry, livestock, or mechanized production or even leave it idle. In India and Pakistan the area cultivated by pure tenants has shrunk dramatically over the past thirty years.

Tenancy law is evidently not the best way to expand tenancy or to protect tenants' rights and incomes. Tenants' bargaining power can probably be strengthened most effectively through policies that raise the demand for labor and thus boost unskilled wages—the return to the best alternative for the potential tenant. Such policies are better suited for improving the chances for the landless to become tenants and enabling their households to increase the returns to their farming skills.

Box 4.6   Land tenure systems in Sub-Saharan Africa: the case of Rwanda

Some African land tenure systems retain from earlier forms of communal ownership features that give the poor guaranteed access to at least a small piece of land and at the same time motivate farmers to conserve the long-term productivity of their holdings. Rwanda offers a good example. It has one of the highest population densities in Africa (445 inhabitants per square kilometer of arable land in 1986), and employment opportunities outside farming are few (90 percent of the work force is in agriculture). Yet landlessness is almost nonexistent. For example, in Ruhengeri Prefecture, a densely farmed area, about 98 percent of rural households cultivate at least 0.1 hectares, and 75 percent work at least 0.3 hectares. The distribution of land is also relatively equitable. This contrasts sharply with similarly populated areas in Asia, where 30 percent or more of the rural households may be landless.

Survey data from a World Bank research study in three prefectures (Butare, Gitarama, and Ruhengeri) show that 22 percent of rural households did not inherit any land. About half the households in this group obtained some land from state allocations at or shortly

after independence. The rest obtained most of their land in the form of transfers (gifts and loans) from within their extended families. These transfers typically provide secure rights to the land and hence give farmers the incentive to use it efficiently and conserve its productivity. This is essential, given Rwanda's mountainous terrain and the potential for erosion.

The ability of the extended family to exercise some control over land transfers is a key feature of the Rwandan land tenure system. Households that borrow land rarely claim any permanent transfer rights over it, even though they may have the right to farm it on a long-term basis. Even land that is inherited or received as a permanent gift cannot always be freely transferred to others by the recipient. But the lack of full land transfer rights in this case does not appear to have affected farmers' investment behavior in improving and conserving land or the level of productivity that is achieved. What is crucial seems to be the right to bequeath land to family members. Without this right, levels of investment and use of modern inputs are significantly lower.

---

exploitative. But this approach turned out to be misguided.

SUBSIDIZING CREDIT FOR THE POOR. Despite, or because of, many years of trying to channel greater amounts of formal credit to the poor, only 5 percent of farms in Africa and 15 percent in Asia and Latin America have had access to it. In Bangladesh, after more than a decade of subsidies, only 15 percent of smallholders and 7 percent of the landless households had received institutional credit. Cheap credit has become a transfer program for the nonpoor. In Brazil these implicit transfers, at their peak in the early 1980s, were estimated to be as high as $3 billion to $4 billion a year (between 1.2 and 1.6 percent of GDP). In addition, artificially low interest rates and credit regulations distort the allocation of resources and lend themselves to patronage and corruption. They have damaged the financial sector and have failed to expand credit to the poor.

Studies of formal subsidized credit programs in Sub-Saharan Africa, the Middle East, and Latin America have found that loans in arrears range from 30 to 95 percent. Subsidized borrowers are less reliable than unsubsidized ones. A detailed study of three Indian villages found that about 60 percent of borrowers were in arrears in the two villages in which institutional credit accounted for

two-thirds of total credit; in the other village institutional credit was a smaller part of the total, and only 17 percent of borrowers were in arrears. And repayment rates were generally lower for large farmers than for small ones. So it is not poverty, as such, that makes borrowers unreliable.

Moreover, experience shows that the poor are willing to pay market interest rates. Bangladesh found that small farmers continued to demand loans even when the interest rate was about 30 percent a year. The poor, in any case, borrow routinely on the informal market, where rates are frequently very high. Moneylenders in rural Sri Lanka commonly charge rates of 25 to 50 percent for a growing season.

Where subsidized credit has reached the poor, other questions arise. By 1988, India's Integrated Rural Development Program (IRDP) covered 27 million rural families. A sample study in Uttar Pradesh found that almost 60 percent of investments had been retained for four to five years. But in 1986, 59 percent of IRDP loans were in arrears. The study in Uttar Pradesh showed, moreover, that only 7 percent of households that had repaid their loans were receiving additional credit. Thus, although the IRDP has succeeded in increasing the asset holdings of large numbers of disadvantaged households, it has not established sustainable financial services for the poor.

Box 4.7 Learning from informal finance in Sub-Saharan Africa

Informal finance takes many different forms: saving and loan associations, rotating funds, mobile bankers and moneylenders, financial dealings among family and friends, and so on. Despite their flexibility, these arrangements are usually strict and well run.

Rotating associations, known in some African countries as *susus* or *tontines*, are flexible and creative. People pay an agreed sum into a fund, out of which loans are then made to members on a rotating basis. In Ghana susus have evolved into growing credit and saving facilities. Daily contributions range between 10 and 500 cedis ($0.04—$2.00). Collectors visit markets daily to accept deposits, no matter how small, mainly from market women. In rural areas collectors make their rounds early in the morning before farmers go to the field and again in the evening after they come back. Monthly deposits reach millions of cedis. A study in Tamale, in Ghana's Northern Region, found that monthly deposits by an average collector range from approximately 1.5 million cedis to 2.0 million cedis. A typical Northern rural bank might hold savings of 10 million cedis. The informal system evidently mobilizes a significant volume of savings.

Seeing the advantages of this approach, Ghana's State Insurance Corporation began a susu-like program in February 1987. Money Back, as it is called, provides life insurance and investment services primarily to small- and medium-scale businesses. As with the susu, clients deposit an agreed contribution, and staff members visit markets daily to collect. Money Back works in a way that people find familiar, it provides clients with security for their savings, and it attracts funds that the formal banking system, on the whole, would not. The Money Back program is still in its early stages, but it is increasingly popular. It may grow into a regionwide or nationwide program.

In other African countries informal arrangements have grown into relatively large financial organizations. In Cameroon, Côte d'Ivoire, Guinea, Mali, and Senegal savings "clubs"—which include, for example, rotating funds and credit unions—have been established. These arrangements are based on personal loyalties, but they also function effectively as financial intermediaries that give mutual loan guarantees. The Cameroon Cooperative Credit Union League provides services to 231 credit unions with about 62,000 members and savings of about $33 million.

Thus, cheap credit programs have not helped the poor. Public funds are better spent on infrastructure and services, such as agricultural extension and market information. A viable, undistorted financial sector will help to make the best use of this investment.

DEVELOPING FINANCIAL INSTITUTIONS FOR THE POOR. Subsidized formal finance has failed. But is there scope for expanding informal finance, the most common source of credit for the poor? Informal lenders, operating on low fixed costs, offer low-income clients small loans on the basis of personal or business acquaintance. Because informal lenders know a lot about their clients, they can be flexible about collateral and repayment schedules. There are lessons here for formal lenders (Box 4.7).

Despite its popularity and potential, informal finance has drawbacks. Its separation from larger financial markets limits the lenders' access to funds and reduces competition, and it rarely provides term finance or large loans. Some of these difficulties may be overcome through links between informal and formal finance, but much remains to be learned about these linkages.

The limitations of both formal and informal finance have led governments, donors, and NGOs to adopt a variety of innovative credit programs targeted to the poor. These vary enormously in coverage (Table 4.3), but successful programs have certain features in common. Most have chosen not

Table 4.3 Diversity in the coverage of credit programs

Program	Year	Coverage[a]
MicroFund (Philippines)	1989	730
Production Credit for Rural Women (Nepal)	1989	6,640
Association for Development of Microenterprise (ADEMI) (Dominican Rep.)	1988	19,430
Small-scale Enterprise Program (Calcutta)	1988	36,000
Working Women's Forum (Madras)	1988	50,000[b]
Small Farmer Development Program (Nepal)	1989	78,520
Saving Development Foundation (Zimbabwe)	1985	250,000[b]
Grameen Bank (Bangladesh)	1988	413,000
Kupedes (Indonesia)	1988	1,300,000[c]
Badan Kredit Kecamatan (BKK) (Indonesia)	1982	2,700,000

a. Cumulative membership.
b. Approximate figure.
c. Number of beneficiaries in 1988.

Table 4.4 Grameen Bank loans, by purpose of loan and sex of borrower, 1985
(percentage of current loan amount)

Purpose of loan	Male borrowers	Female borrowers	All borrowers
Crop cultivation	4.0	4.6	4.3
Livestock, poultry raising, and fisheries	18.5	44.6	31.9
Processing and manufacturing	18.6	29.9	24.4
Trading and shopkeeping	49.7	18.7	33.8
Transport and other services	9.2	2.2	5.6

Source: Hossain 1988.

to subsidize interest rates. Instead, they have tried to adapt themselves to the needs of the poor by reducing transaction costs to both lender and borrower. Programs with high borrowing rates and strict terms, especially those that link repayment to future lending, stand a better chance of reaching the poor.

Group lending is one approach for reaching poor people. Typically, under such schemes one member's failure to repay jeopardizes the group's access to future credit. Joint liability among a group of borrowers reduces the risk of default and makes it cheaper to reach dispersed clients. The best-known example of this approach is the Grameen Bank in Bangladesh. It has successfully served extremely poor people—83 percent of them women—and its loan recovery rates exceed 95 percent. Table 4.4 shows how the poor use Grameen Bank credit. The Working Women's Forum in Madras, India, has also achieved recovery rates of between 90 and 95 percent. In both cases loan recovery far exceeds the national averages for commercial banks. Small, self-selected groups—such as those in the Grameen Bank or in Nepal's Small Farmer Development Program and Production Credit for Rural Women Program—usually offer the best base for such schemes.

The Zimbabwe Agricultural Finance Corporation demonstrates that group lending can decrease administrative costs. Because it lends only to established groups, its costs are a minuscule 1 percent of loan capital. If lenders must incur the costs of setting up the groups, however, the overall costs of group lending can exceed the costs of lending to individuals. At the Grameen Bank expenses as a share of outstanding loans are 16 to 25 percent for new branches, dropping to 6 percent after three years.

Group lending may not always be appropriate or necessary. Badan Kredit Kecamatan (BKK), an Indonesian public program, provides individual loans without collateral primarily to low-income women, without relying on groups. It contains its processing costs by making tiny initial loans ($5 is the limit) on the basis of character references from local officials and by using one-page loan applications that are processed in less than a week. The program's local units are autonomous. To reach the poor, they disburse their loans quickly from accessible village outposts. Since the program's loans are small and loan terms have been strict, the nonpoor tend to look elsewhere for credit. Finally, the program encourages borrowers to repay by making repayment a condition for approving new loans, and it has strong incentives for loan officers to expand the client base and maintain high collection rates. The BKK has managed both to reach the poor and to remain financially viable. It serves more than 35 percent of Java's 8,500 villages, and in 1987 it earned profits of $1.4 million—a 14 percent return on the loan portfolio.

Some credit programs have targeted microenterprises, often in urban areas, with packages of credit, training, and technical assistance. The programs that have emphasized credit have been the most successful. Schemes such as MicroFund in Manila, Philippines, and ADEMI in Santo Domingo, Dominican Republic, have targeted the poor—especially poor women, many of whom work in very small enterprises. Microenterprise lending can have a considerable impact on incomes. The average income of new borrowers from the Small-Scale Enterprise Credit Program in Calcutta rose by 82 percent, and that of borrowers from the Kupedes program in Indonesia increased from $74 to $183 after an average of three years. Most microenterprise credit programs receive subsidies to help cover their initial costs. Experience has shown that the more successful programs, such as Kupedes, can become financially viable if they charge market-based interest rates and keep operating costs low.

Experience also highlights the importance of savings. The Savings Development Foundation in Zimbabwe generated considerable savings by organizing households into neighborhood groups and devising a simple system of financial record-keeping that illiterate people could understand. By 1985, 250,000 members had saved enough to place bulk orders for fertilizer and seeds, improve their housing, and meet other basic needs. Rural women, who account for 97 percent of the program's participants, acquired new skills while becoming financially more independent.

Although successes are none too common, they suggest that well-designed programs can give disadvantaged groups access to credit and still remain financially viable. Institutions of this kind should be supported with limited subsidies to help cover their initial administrative costs (but not interest rates) and to encourage innovation; with time, as costs decline, the subsidies should be withdrawn. Programs such as BKK, Kupedes, the Grameen Bank, and ADEMI have demonstrated the potential for raising the productivity and incomes of the poor. Because of their example, the number of similar schemes, although still small, has grown rapidly in recent years.

Improving access to infrastructure and technology

Public investment in technology and infrastructure is critical in raising incomes and reducing poverty. The extent to which the poor benefit, however, depends on the design and effective implementation of the programs.

ADAPTING TECHNOLOGIES FOR SMALL FARMERS. Technological improvements in agriculture have helped small farmers in some regions more than in others. The Green Revolution benefited many smallholders in Latin America and Asia, but in Sub-Saharan Africa relatively few small farmers use improved high-yielding varieties. In Malawi, after twenty years of agricultural research and extension, only 5 percent of farmers have adopted hybrid maize. This slow acceptance reflects severe biases against peasant agriculture. Many countries have encouraged and subsidized large-scale mechanized commercial farming, which is beyond the reach of most smallholders. In addition, supplies of inputs are unreliable, and storage facilities are lacking. More important, indigenous farm-research institutions are weak. As a result, there has been too little emphasis on developing and disseminating varieties and techniques that are appropriate for small-scale rainfed farms.

In addition to removing biases against small farmers, countries need an indigenous capacity to do adaptive agricultural research. International research centers initiate much of the scientific work necessary for technological change, but countries need to be able to identify relevant technologies and adapt them to the specific requirements of different farm locations. In Cameroon, for example, a public sector agency, the Société de Développe-

ment du Coton du Cameroon, adapted the existing research on cotton to the local environment and substantially improved the productivity of smallholders. Farmers should be more directly involved in the selection of research topics. Adaptive research needs to be broadened to include, for example, soil and livestock management techniques in addition to the traditional stress on crop husbandry. To make all this feasible, countries will also need well-trained extension workers to act as a bridge between small farmers and researchers.

PRODERO in Honduras has improved the productivity of small farmers by involving them in planning and testing new agricultural technologies. The project targeted farmers who owned less than five hectares in the isolated western states of Copan, Lempira, and Ocotepeque. To combat soil erosion, it developed low-cost methods of conservation and fertilization. Average maize yields increased by more than 300 percent.

Farming systems research is an approach that listens to farmers and pursues a broad research agenda. It looks at the entire farming system—cropping patterns, livestock and irrigation management, the division of labor among household members, and so on. The results in Zambia, Zimbabwe, and the Indian state of Bihar (Box 4.8) have been encouraging.

PROVIDING RURAL INFRASTRUCTURE. Poor farmers typically have less access to public infrastructure than more prosperous farmers. Rural roads and electricity, for example, are first extended to the relatively well-off. The supply of water to marginal farmers is especially erratic and inadequate. In India the low quality of canal construction and maintenance means that surface irrigation reaches only part of the intended area. Small farmers cannot afford deepwells, tubewells, or pumpsets.

Successful infrastructure projects have usually delegated to the local level as much responsibility for administration and maintenance as possible. This has required some effort in building local institutions, involving local people, and designing infrastructure with these needs in mind. *World Development Report 1988* showed that delegating public responsibility to local organizations can make infrastructure projects more effective and benefit the poor.

The National Irrigation Administration (NIA) in the Philippines has worked with user groups to improve maintenance and distribution. It employs community organizers to help form groups of water users and then negotiates with each group over

Box 4.8 Developing appropriate technologies for subsistence farmers in Bihar

The Rural Women's Agricultural Development Project, which is sponsored by the Birsa Agricultural University in Bihar, demonstrates how farming systems research can help to improve the incomes of the poor. The project targets poor tribal farmers in the drought-prone Chota Nagpur Plateau, where illiteracy rates reach 90 percent and 85 percent of the farmers possess less than five acres of land. Women perform at least half of the preharvest and four-fifths of the postharvest work. They depend mainly on rice-based rainfed farming for their livelihood. Inappropriate farming practices and insufficient use of inputs contribute to low productivity.

The local culture makes it difficult for male extension workers to advise female farmers or to be advised by them. Women with tribal backgrounds have therefore been hired as extension workers. They work through *mahila mandals* (women's groups).

Since farmers refused to adopt costly new technologies, researchers worked with them to develop a simple dugwell system that allows vegetables to be grown during the dry season, when land had previously been left fallow. Farmers have also been taught to diversify to higher-value crops. Farmers, extension workers, and researchers analyzed the problems together. They then developed a package that combined new and indigenous technologies, tested the technologies both on-station and on-farm to adapt them to varying local conditions, and disseminated the package to participating villages.

The gains are illustrated by the experience of one farmer. In 1982 she had planted 2.5 acres of rice and millet in the rainy season, 0.5 acres of cauliflower in the winter, and no crops in the summer. In 1987 she planted her 2.5 acres with rice and potatoes during the rainy season and with wheat, cauliflower, peas, and carrots in winter. In the summer she planted 1.25 acres of cabbage and okra.

Diversification and irrigation raised cropping intensities and incomes. Cropping intensity rose, on average, from 95 percent in 1981–82 to 145 percent in 1986–87. Gross income per household increased more than four times in real terms.

---

the quantity of water delivered. User groups allocate water and costs among themselves and share construction and maintenance responsibilities. Between 1981 and 1984 this allowed a 38 percent drop in the NIA's per hectare spending on operation and maintenance. The efficiency of water use and distribution improved, and the access of small farmers to irrigation increased. The NIA, which had started as a pilot project in 1976, covered more than 35,000 hectares by 1986. The Gal Oya irrigation project in Sri Lanka was modeled on the Philippine program. There too the introduction of user groups almost doubled the efficiency of water use, and the improved irrigation system now reaches the poorer farmers downstream.

Both schemes were based on pilot projects, and both embody a flexible design. The designers experimented extensively with the composition and responsibilities of user groups and with ways to integrate these groups with the national administration. Their success has led such countries as Malaysia and Thailand to introduce similar systems.

Local organizations are more likely to succeed if they are legally recognized by the central government and if the government provides support in the form of guidelines, training, and information systems. It is also crucial to establish management systems that define clear lines of responsibility for agency managers and performance criteria that are linked to budget allocations and create incentives for greater local responsibility. In the case of the NIA, farmer groups were required to repay construction costs, which increased their ownership of the program and the accountability of managers. In turn, each regional office was expected to achieve financial viability, and managers' performance was evaluated by their actual recovery of costs from farmers.

Another illustration of the importance of local institutions is the Aga Khan Rural Support Program in northern Pakistan. This NGO-managed project supports commercialization in subsistence villages. It has created village organizations, built productive physical infrastructure, developed financial services, and provided support systems and training for production and marketing. The local organizations carry out many tasks and have avoided the need for coordination with ministries. The program has recorded household participation rates of up to 97 percent in Gilgit District and has achieved average rates of return of 33 percent for irrigation schemes and other projects.

More targeted approaches are especially important in remote regions where poor people are isolated from markets and services. In order to reach the most disadvantaged—tribal groups, the landless or near landless, and, in some societies, women—it is essential to work with organizations such as local groups, NGOs, and private operators, that know their needs. The International Fund for Agricultural Development (IFAD) has carried out many projects that target the poorest. IFAD uses pilot programs and flexible designs and usually relies on forming groups to reach the target population. A rural development project in Cameroon, designed to improve coffee production by farmers who own less than two hectares, is one example. A similar approach has been used by NGOs in Bangladesh, where landless groups operate irrigation equipment and sell water to farmers (Box 4.9).

The lessons of recent experience in rural infrastructure and technology programs are broadly as follows. Local institutions can mobilize resources such as savings and labor. They can help to ensure that project benefits reach the poor, that specific local needs are met, and that the projects remain financially viable. Successful programs have not relied exclusively on government agencies, which can provide effective central support but often lack both the field staff and the flexibility to work at the local level. Instead, they have employed a mixture of institutions—NGOs, private operators, and lo-cal groups. Large programs that start as pilot projects seem to have a better chance of success. A pilot project may slow the scheme down and use up valuable management time, but the benefits usually outweigh these costs.

Reaching resource-poor areas

Increasing numbers of poor people live in areas that have little agroclimatic potential and are environmentally fragile. Examples include the Loess Plateau in China, the highlands of Bolivia and Nepal, the desertic African Sahel, and much of the humid tropics. Population pressure in these areas has decreased the productivity of the land and increased its vulnerability to flooding and soil erosion. This raises the question of the links between poverty and environmental degradation.

These regions need a special development strategy, for three reasons. First, their potential for growth is limited. Second, they are increasingly occupied by poor people with the fewest skills and the least access to infrastructure and supplies. Third, environmental degradation in these regions adversely affects both the immediate area and regions downstream or downhill.

The causes of these growing pressures on natural resources are complex and interconnected. In many countries poor farmers are being margina-

---

Box 4.9 Groundwater irrigation in South Asia: reaching the landless

In the Gangetic Plain groundwater is one of the few remaining natural resources that can be exploited to reduce rural poverty. Recent efforts to help the landless poor benefit directly from groundwater irrigation have been based on groups. Proshika and the Grameen Bank have organized new groups and have called on existing ones to buy and operate irrigation equipment and sell water to farmers.

Five points stand out in the groups' performance to date. (1) In certain technical respects (for example, the area irrigated with equipment of a given capacity), the groups are at least as effective as private management. (2) Some groups have successfully promoted the use of high-yielding varieties by their customers. (3) The groups invest some of their higher incomes in other activities, such as fisheries, poultry raising, or cottage industries. (4) They help farmers to spread the risks associated with irrigation and to reduce the costs of organizing farmer cooperatives, settling conflicts, and so on, which can be high for minor irrigation. (5) The repayment rates achieved by Proshika (75 percent) and the Grameen Bank (more than 75 percent) are much higher than is usual for agricultural loans.

The biggest drawback is the demands this approach makes on management. Most groups require costly managerial and technical assistance, and they often need help in mediation with water users. Problems such as technical deficiencies in pump operation and maintenance, difficulties in obtaining satisfactory pump locations, and struggles over contracts with water users have led the Grameen Bank to assume direct management of some groups.

After more than a decade Proshika has reached only about 300 groups covering 6,000 irrigated acres. It is unlikely that such groups can become a significant force in groundwater management. But the groups have managed to reach the poorest of the poor, who are usually excluded from rural development initiatives. The reasons for their success are just beginning to be understood and merit further study.

Box 4.10   Protecting the environment and reducing poverty: China's experience in the Loess Plateau

In China's Loess Plateau, programs combining erosion control with improved crop- and animal-raising practices have reduced chronic soil erosion and increased rural incomes. This success follows several earlier failures. It suggests that economic and sustainable agriculture in such areas requires a mixture of technical, social, and policy actions. It also confirms the importance of research in pilot stations prior to broad implementation.

The Loess Plateau extends over about 630,000 square kilometers of northwestern China. Rainfall is barely sufficient for agriculture and is often concentrated in sporadic, heavy falls in the summer. Agricultural expansion and exploitation have progressively removed the plateau's vegetative cover, contributing to erosion and degradation of the soil on most of the plateau. Streams carry silt to the Yellow River, creating problems for downstream irrigation works and causing dangerous increases in the height of the riverbed.

The situation worsened during the 1960s and 1970s. As part of the national policy of self-sufficiency in grain, farmers on the plateau were encouraged to switch from pasture-based livestock and limited grain production to extensive grain cultivation. This exacerbated land degradation and led to declines in agricultural productivity and income. By the mid-1980s more than five million people on the plateau's rainfed uplands were surviving on incomes of less than $50 a year.

In the late 1970s the government initiated research and development to improve erosion control and agricultural production in the area. Erosion control experiment stations were established in Mizhi County (Shaanxi Province) and Dingxi Prefecture (Gansu Province). The strategy is designed to reverse environmental degradation by replacing the existing extensive cropping system with intensive cropping on terraces and reclaimed flatland and by converting unterraced hills to fodder and tree-crop production. Specific measures include constructing new terraces to reduce erosion and increase crop yields, introducing improved pasture species, eliminating uncontrolled grazing on unterraced hillsides, planting trees and shrubs on the steepest hillsides, and constructing soil dams to create cultivable flatlands by impounding loess sediment. These measures require that much of the steeply sloped land that is now being cultivated be taken out of crop production. Higher yields on existing and newly created flatland and terraces are therefore essential for raising production and farm incomes.

The initial results have been favorable. The per capita gross value of output has doubled, output has been diversified, and soil erosion has been reduced. Despite a decrease in the area sown to grain, greater yields on improved terraces and intensively cultivated flatland have helped to increase total per capita grain production by more than 30 percent. Expanded pastureland supports more sheep, and the volume of animal products has increased. Cost-benefit analysis indicates that the financial and economic rates of return range from 13 percent for construction of soil dams to 25 percent for the terracing of gently sloped land for crop production.

The government is now encouraging adoption of the erosion control program throughout the Loess Plateau by limiting cultivation on steep, unterraced land and by providing credits for constructing terraces and planting pasture species. Participating households receive full rights to land use and rights to the output of trees and fodder from hillsides they have converted. The agricultural development component of the Gansu project, which is assisted by the World Bank, is supporting implementation of the strategy over about 200,000 hectares in the Guanchuan Basin in Dingxi.

---

lized and pushed to frontier areas. In addition, population growth and the commercialization of agriculture have forced farmers who once relied on environmentally sustainable forms of cultivation to use their land more intensively. That might be desirable under certain systems of land and livestock management, but the intensification of traditional farming methods, such as slash-and-burn agriculture, has damaged the productivity of these marginal areas. Overgrazing, unmanaged irrigation, and an ever widening search for fuelwood all accelerate the decline.

Policies that discriminate against smallholders in granting access to land and forests make matters still worse. For example, land policies have directed population movement away from the most productive land by giving a few large estates preferential access (as in Malawi) or by limiting migration (as in Tanzania). Insecure land tenure and encroachment on common and state lands encourage soil-mining practices that diminish the longer-term productivity of the land. Policies that promote industrial extraction from these areas (such as pulp subsidies to Indian rayon mills) can add to the pressures on the resource base.

Providing infrastructure to develop these resource-poor regions may be neither cost-effective nor viable. A better strategy would start with investment in education and training to spur outmigration to areas of better potential. Spending to meet basic needs such as health care and drinking water will also be required. Outmigration would be most effective in countries where labor demand is growing strongly in other regions.

Experience, however, shows that migration is only a partial solution. Growth in the areas of greater potential is usually not high enough; many resource-poor regions have rising populations despite outmigration. Therefore, additional investments will be necessary. These will involve training poor farmers in better techniques for farming, animal husbandry, and soil and moisture conservation, increasing the opportunities for diversification and off-farm employment, and providing local user groups (such as the village forestry associations in Korea and the rangeland management associations in Botswana) with rights to manage degraded communal lands. In addition, policies to make land tenure more secure in areas in which traditional tenure systems have broken down will discourage farmers from mining the soil for short-term gains.

In many of these areas farmers can adopt low-cost, low-input technologies that would increase and stabilize yields, diversify production, and maintain the resource base. One such technology, contour cultivation, has raised yields substantially—by between 6 and 66 percent on slopes of up to 32 percent. When contour cultivation is supported by a vegetative barrier—vetiver grass, for example—the benefits are even greater. Vetiver grass has been used for many years in the Caribbean, Kenya, and South Asia. It holds soil while allowing for water filtration, and it is cheap to establish, manage, and maintain. But it is not appropriate everywhere; it is ineffective in parts of the Sahel where soil and moisture are insufficient.

In some regions more substantial interventions will be required. Programs that target only a few households or villages cannot prevent soil erosion or protect watersheds. Box 4.10 describes how improved technology for terraced lands and more appropriate land tenure policies have decreased land degradation and poverty in China's Loess Plateau.

Reaching the poor in these regions will be difficult. Without effective measures, the situation is likely to grow worse for the foreseeable future. International research institutes have recognized the urgency of the problem and have increased their funding for research in marginal areas. The International Rice Research Institute in the Philippines, for example, now devotes 12 percent of its budget to upland rice cultivation alone. In many countries government subsidies to develop and improve low-return farming activities may be the only way to reduce poverty in these regions.

Policies for poverty-reducing growth

Achieving a pattern of development that successfully reduces poverty requires policies that provide opportunities to the poor and enable them to participate in growth. To accomplish this, policies must be attuned to three broad tasks.

First and foremost, economywide and sectoral policies must encourage rural development and urban employment. Experience indicates that this requires moderate taxation of agriculture and relatively undistorted product and factor markets. It also requires public provision of infrastructure and an environment that makes technical change accessible to small farmers and the urban poor.

Second, specific policies are needed to improve the participation of the poor in growth by increasing their access to land, credit, and public infrastructure and services. Land transfers can reduce poverty, but they succeed only in special circumstances. Other policies to increase and secure access to land can also reduce poverty. Subsidized credit programs have failed to reach the poor, but approaches such as group lending offer a promising alternative. Flexible programs that involve the intended beneficiaries, build institutions, employ NGOs and local groups, and respond to local needs are the best way of molding infrastructure, services, and technology to the needs of the poor.

Third, resource-poor regions, where poverty and environmental degradation are interrelated, require a different approach. Since the potential for growth in these regions is limited and the population is increasing, policies that facilitate outmigration are essential. But in many of these regions additional investments, which are likely to require government subsidies, will still be necessary to meet basic needs, maintain or increase yields, and preserve natural resources.

Delivering social services to the poor

Efforts to reduce poverty are unlikely to succeed in the long run unless there is greater investment in the human capital of the poor. Improvements in education, health, and nutrition directly address the worst consequences of being poor. But there is ample evidence that investing in human capital, especially in education, also attacks some of the most important causes of poverty. Social services are therefore an essential part of any long-term strategy for reducing poverty.

Social sector policies

In the developing world as a whole, the past three decades have seen tremendous progress in social indicators. But the advances have been uneven among regions and among socioeconomic groups within countries. Progress in the social sectors requires a long-term commitment to making education, health care, and other social services accessible to all levels of society. Where that commitment is lacking and where government policies have failed to reach the poor, social needs remain staggeringly high.

Progress in health

In the past few decades the developing countries have made great strides in health. In China over the past twenty-five to thirty years, for instance, the total fertility rate fell from 6.4 to 2.4 children per woman, and the infant mortality rate dropped from 90 to 32 per thousand live births; life expectancy increased from 52.7 to 69.5 years. Here, as in other countries, no single factor accounts for the improvement. China's remarkable performance

owes as much to safe drinking water, improved sewage disposal, and other sanitation measures as to broad immunization coverage and mass campaigns against parasitic diseases. It has much to do with the provision of basic health care and affordable drugs to even the most remote parts of the country. It reflects the successful drive to reduce fertility and to increase, through legislation, the age of first delivery, as well as great efforts to provide education on health and nutrition. And it would probably have been impossible without a safety net that, among other things, guaranteed minimum food rations to even the poorest rural people.

China's performance is exceptional. But it teaches an important general lesson: large improvements in the health of the population can be achieved if there is a broad and lasting political commitment, with a consistent emphasis on preventive measures and basic curative care. In other words, social progress is not merely a by-product of economic development. Policies matter. Where progress has been better than average, strong interventions based on a long-term commitment to social progress lay behind it.

Costa Rica provides another example. Its mortality rate for children under 5 fell from 112 per thousand in 1960–65 to 24 in 1980–85. Since the 1960s the proportion of underweight children under 6 has dropped from 14 to 2 percent. Life expectancy is comparable to that in the industrial world. In the 1970s the country embarked on several far-reaching health and nutrition initiatives, including the first National Health Plan (1971), the Universal Social Security Law (1971), and rural and community health programs (1973 and 1976). A family planning program was introduced in 1968; by using the available rural health infrastructure, it has succeeded in reaching people in the countryside as well as the urban poor. The total marital fertility rate declined from 7.6 in 1960 to 3.4 in 1980. These achievements did not come cheaply; by 1985 Costa Rica was spending 23 percent of its government budget on health. Such high spending was sustainable only because the country devoted just 3.2 percent of its budget to military outlays between 1975 and 1985.

Other countries, too, have been able to raise health standards to well above the level that might be expected on the basis of their per capita GNP. In Cuba, for instance, life expectancy is high, and Sri Lanka reduced its under 5 mortality rate from 101 per thousand in 1960 to 35 in 1985. In all these cases the government has taken the leading role.

Government spending on health usually rises with economic development. Through training medical personnel, investing in clinics and hospitals, licensing practitioners, testing drugs, and running subsidy and insurance schemes, in addition to directly providing medical care, the public sector is the dominant player in health. Government efforts have helped bring about an increase in the number of doctors, nurses, and hospital beds per thousand population throughout the developing world. Such summary health measures as life expectancy and under 5 mortality have improved dramatically (Figure 5.1). It is widely believed that many of the economic problems in the developing world (as well as in the industrial world) can be attributed to excessive or inappropriate government intervention. Yet much of the social progress observed during the past two decades is clearly a direct result of government action.

Another factor behind the improvement in world health has been the effort of the international health community to focus on affordable, low-technology child survival techniques such as immunization and the use of oral rehydration therapy (ORT) for diarrheal dehydration. In this field it is no exaggeration to talk of a public health revolution. This progress has been possible because of a unique coalition of bilateral development agencies and United Nations agencies, notably the World Health Organization (WHO) and the United Nations Children's Fund (UNICEF). When in 1974 the World Health Assembly announced a new immunization drive, immunization services were reaching less than 5 percent of the children in the developing world. Just fifteen years later, the Expanded Programme on Immunization (EPI) had extended its polio and DPT coverage to about 60 percent (as measured by the number of children receiving a third dose of vaccine before age 1). Many countries—for example, Egypt, Mexico, Peru, Thailand, and Zaire—have made good progress in training workers to use ORT. Much remains to be done, but after less than a decade one-third of all families in the developing world now have access to this treatment.

Progress in education

As in health, the developing countries have made great advances in education over the past two decades. Between 1965 and 1985 the number of primary schools in low-income countries (excluding China) increased by almost 60 percent, to more than 775,000. In middle-income countries the number more than quadrupled, to nearly 950,000. (During the same period the number of school-age children grew 69 percent in low-income countries and 48 percent in middle-income countries.) Between 1965 and 1985 the number of teachers went up 55 percent in low-income countries, 175 percent in lower-middle-income countries, and 120 percent in upper-middle-income countries.

Most of the schools in developing countries are public schools that are built, financed, and staffed by the government. The share of education spending allocated to capital expenditures—essentially, school construction—reflects the big push of the 1960s to improve access to schooling. In 1965 low- and middle-income countries spent 21 and 14 percent, respectively, of their total education budgets on building schools; twenty years later the share had fallen to 12 percent in both cases. Most teacher training programs, both for primary and for secondary school teachers, are run by governments. As in health care, spending on education rises with the level of development, and so do standards of attainment (Figure 5.2).

As a result of this commitment to education, and especially primary education, net enrollment rates grew, on average, 5.7 percent a year between 1965 and 1975 in low-income countries, 5 percent in lower-middle-income countries, and 2.3 percent in upper-middle-income countries. During the late 1970s enrollment continued to grow faster than population. By 1985 there was enough primary school capacity in most middle-income countries to enroll virtually all children; in the low-income countries capacity still fell short of that goal.

Figure 5.1 Trends in health expenditure, number of physicians, and health outcome

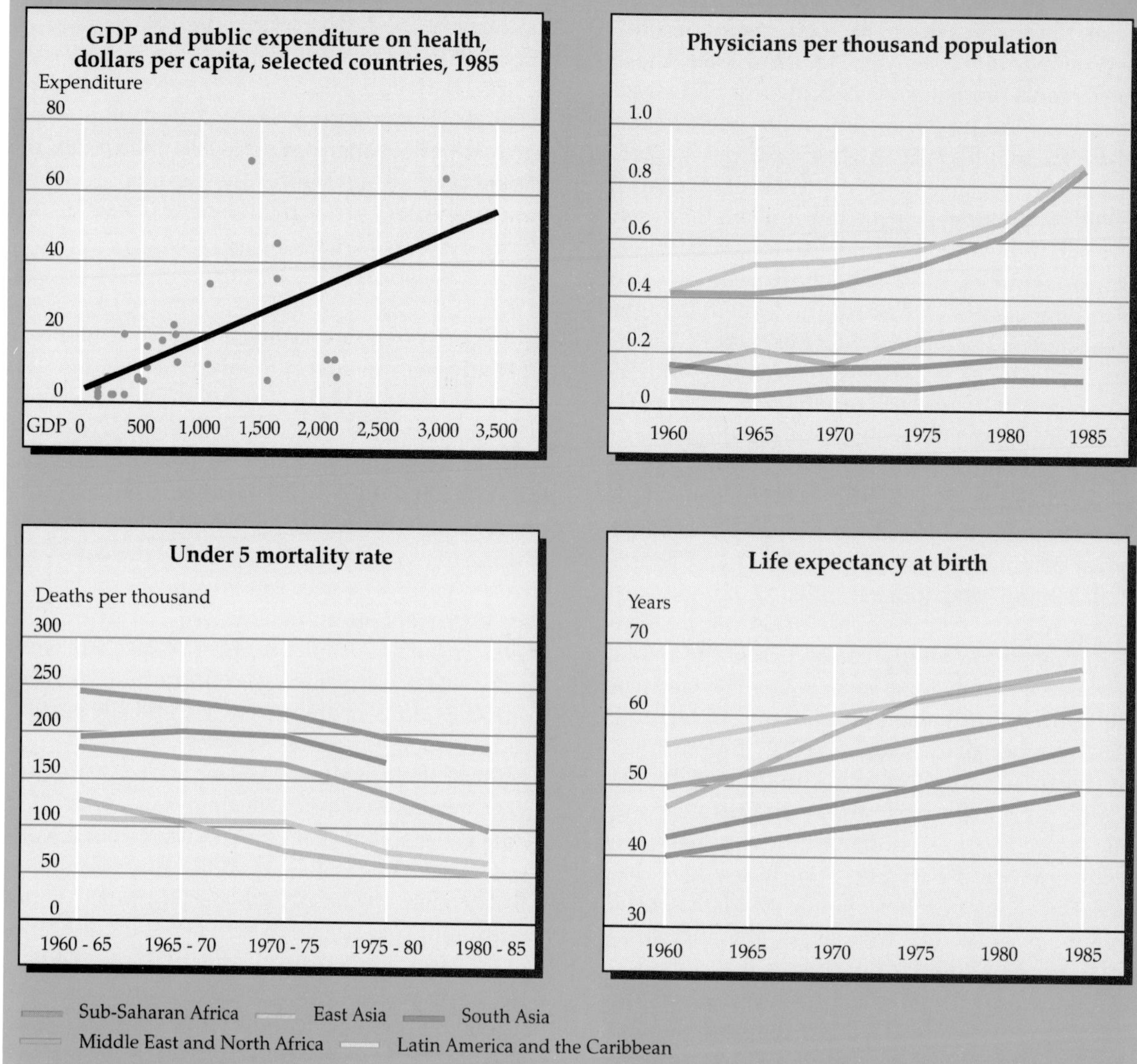

GDP and public expenditure on health, dollars per capita, selected countries, 1985

Physicians per thousand population

Under 5 mortality rate

Life expectancy at birth

Sub-Saharan Africa — East Asia — South Asia
Middle East and North Africa — Latin America and the Caribbean

Note: For life expectancy, data for East Asia 1960 include the average life expectancy for China for 1963 - 67 .

Sources: Hill and Pebley 1988 and World Bank data.

Continuing needs

Despite great progress in both health and education, an immense task remains. About 30 million children under 5 die every year from causes that would not usually be fatal in developed countries. About 110 million children worldwide (almost 20 percent of the relevant age group) receive no primary education. More than 90 percent of them live in low- and lower-middle-income countries.

Governments deserve credit for the achievements to date. But their justifiably heavy outlays on health and education would do more good—and would go a long way toward meeting the problems that remain—if they were better spent. Government spending on social services is inefficient in many ways. Above all, it tends to be skewed away from the people who need it most—the poor.

On average, an estimated 70 to 85 percent of the

developing world's total health spending, both public and private, goes for curative care. Between 10 and 20 percent is spent on preventive care and the remaining 5 to 10 percent on community services such as mosquito control and health education. Within the curative sector, hospitals often account for more than 80 percent of the cost. Yet it is well known that preventive and community services are far more effective in reducing morbidity and mortality. If public resources tied up in hospitals were redirected to the lower levels of the health care system, many diseases could be pre-vented altogether or treated earlier at less cost. The heavy financial demands of the curative sector also lead to internal inefficiencies—hospitals without equipment and clinics without drugs—because salaries crowd out other spending.

The result is that the poor often lack access to even the most basic services. The proclaimed goal of free health care for all often means low-quality care in the cities and none at all for the rural poor. Even in China in 1981 government spending per capita on health care was more than three times higher for urban dwellers than for rural people.

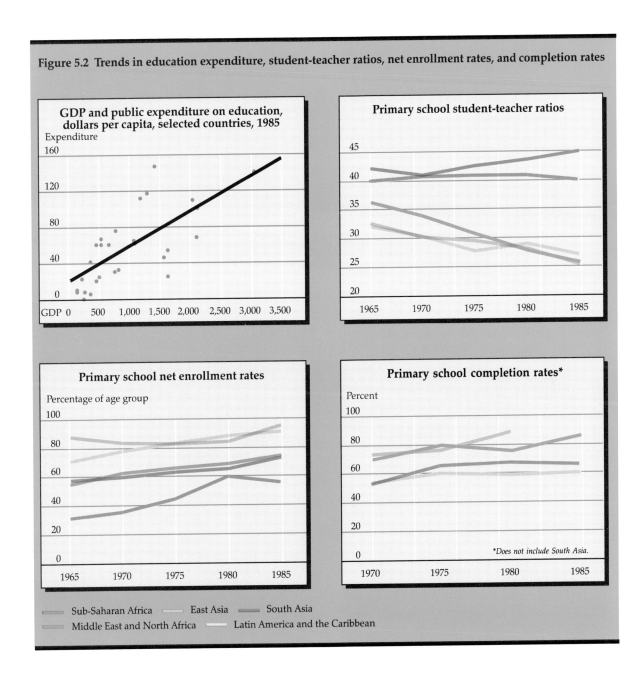

Figure 5.2 Trends in education expenditure, student-teacher ratios, net enrollment rates, and completion rates

Seventy percent of Senegal's physicians and pharmacists, 60 percent of its midwives, and 40 percent of its nurses are concentrated in the Dakar–Cap Vert region, where less than 30 percent of the population lives. In Peru two-thirds of all doctors live in the capital, serving just 27 percent of the population; in most rural areas, where the majority of the poor live, there is only one doctor for every 10,000 or more inhabitants.

In short, the overall expansion of the health care system has shortchanged the most important services: preventive care and basic curative care. The poor have not benefited proportionally from the larger numbers of doctors, nurses, and health care facilities, from the increased availability of affordable drugs, or from public health services such as water and sanitation. As a result, the link between poverty and illness remains strong both for chil-

---

Box 5.1 Adult health: a neglected issue of growing importance

Adult health is a relatively new issue in public health policy in developing countries. Most public health efforts in developing countries have emphasized child and infant health. Yet half the population in the developing world is between ages 15 and 60. Children depend on these adults, and so does the economy. More than anybody else, the poor depend on good health to maintain the productivity of their only asset—labor. The loss of the family breadwinner to death or debilitating disease may force a whole household into poverty.

Each year in developing countries ten million young adults die. Respiratory diseases, malaria, diarrhea, cardiovascular diseases, cancers, chronic obstructive lung diseases, sexually transmitted diseases (including acquired immune deficiency syndrome—AIDS), diabetes, tuberculosis, and injuries are widespread. In Guinea-Bissau and Sierra Leone, for example, the chance at age 15 of surviving to 60 is less than 50 percent; in most developing countries it is between 50 and 75 percent (as against 85 percent in developed countries). Diseases such as onchocerciasis, epilepsy, and leprosy—which raise morbidity rather than mortality—are not captured in those figures.

As Box figure 5.1 indicates, adult mortality is highest in low-income countries. Life expectancy at 15 in the developing world is seven years less than in industrial countries. Fertility and mortality rates are falling in most developing countries, but the adult population is still growing. This demographic transition is happening alongside a health transition: chronic diseases are becoming more important.

In Colombia high rates of parasitic infections in adults are associated with less education and lower income. In Peru and Côte d'Ivoire poor rural households lose half as many more working days because of illness as households in poor urban areas. In Bahrain disability and low economic status go together; according to a 1981 census people with disabilities were three-and-a-half times more likely to be illiterate, twelve times less likely to have a college degree, and three-and-a-half times less likely to be employed. In Kenya bad health among adults is strongly linked to low economic status, poor household sanitation, and inadequate nutrition.

Policies that succeed in reducing poverty in developing countries will usually improve adult health too. Improvements in drinking water, sanitation, housing, and nutrition check the spread of tropical diseases. Less crowding and better housing prevent the transmission of tuberculosis and other viral respiratory diseases. Specific preventive measures are needed for a range of other illnesses: vaccination for tetanus, education and taxation for diseases linked to alcohol and cigarettes, and, especially in Africa, sex information campaigns for AIDS.

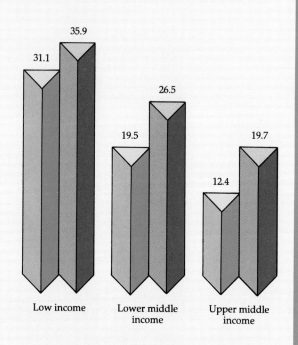

Box figure 5.1 Adult mortality in the developing world

Note: Adult mortality is the probability at age 15 of dying before age 60, expressed as a percentage.

dren (as stressed in Chapter 2) and for adults (Box 5.1).

In education, too, government policy has favored higher-level training over services that would benefit the poor. It is well known that tertiary education yields the lowest social rate of return, but many countries nonetheless spend a disproportionate share of their education budgets on that level.

In West Africa, in addition to free tuition and regular government subsidies to the colleges, students in higher education often receive living allowances. It is estimated that these living allowances account for nearly half of the total spent on higher education. Only 2 percent of the relevant age group in Sub-Saharan Africa goes on to higher education, but that level accounts for 22 percent of the region's public education budget. Brazil spends 9 percent of its public education budget on secondary education and 23 percent on higher education. In Chile, Costa Rica, the Dominican Republic, and Uruguay people in the top one-fifth of the income distribution receive more than 50 percent of the subsidies for higher education; the poorest one-fifth receives less than 10 percent.

In India education is heavily biased in favor of urban dwellers and males. Urban literacy rates are twice as high as rural rates, and females in both rural and urban India have lower literacy rates than males. In Pakistan 63 percent of the boys in the relevant age group are enrolled in elementary school, but only 32 percent of the girls are. In rural areas enrollment rates for girls are as low as 20 percent.

But the problems in education go well beyond enrollment rates. Low enrollment figures are often accompanied by high dropout rates. In low-income countries more than 40 percent of those who enter primary school fail to finish, and even in upper-middle-income countries completion rates are only 85 percent. As a result, illiteracy remains widespread in the developing world.

The low quality of education goes a long way toward explaining the weak performance of children in developing countries. Governments have stressed quantity over quality. Many countries spend less each year on textbooks and other materials; in low-income countries teaching materials account for less than 3 percent of recurrent expenditures.

Until the 1980s textbooks were often not provided to students at all. In the Central African Republic the national student-to-textbook ratio was between ten and twenty to one. In Brazil only 23 percent of all schools had received first-grade textbooks by the early 1980s, in the Dominican Republic fewer than 20 percent of eighth-grade students in public schools had mathematics textbooks, and in Botswana fewer than 20 percent of primary school students had access to science or social studies textbooks. A 1983 study in the Philippines reported that only 32 percent of fifth-grade science teachers used textbooks frequently; another in Botswana showed that teachers used textbooks only 12 percent of the time. Teachers' guides are seldom available.

So it is hardly surprising that repetition rates are high and that many of those who complete primary school have learned very little. In various tests conducted in about forty countries students in low- and lower-middle-income countries answered only 40 percent of the questions correctly. In particular, reading comprehension appeared to be weak.

To make matters worse, there is a recent trend, mainly in low-income countries, toward lower primary enrollment rates. In the face of tight budgetary constraints, many African countries are failing to expand their education systems to keep up with population growth. (Ghana, Liberia, Mali, and Tanzania are but a few examples.) The sharpest declines in enrollment are observed in low-income countries that have suffered from war or internal strife. Afghanistan's enrollment rate fell 40 percent between 1980 and 1985; during the same period Somalia's also fell 40 percent. In Ethiopia and Mozambique, after considerable progress in earlier years, growth in enrollment has ceased.

Extra spending on social services in general will not automatically help the poor. The existing pattern of provision needs to be tilted in their favor in terms of both the quantity and the quality of services. The most important measures in the social sectors for improving the living conditions of the poor are also the most basic: expand and improve primary education and primary health care.

Investing in people

There is overwhelming evidence that human capital is one of the keys to reducing poverty. Moreover, improvements in health, education, and nutrition reinforce each other. But the poor generally lack access to basic social services. There is too little investment in their human capital, and this increases the probability that they and their children will remain poor. To break this vicious circle, governments must make reaching the poor a priority in its own right.

Box 5.2 Education and economic growth

Many studies of farm productivity, family enterprises, and wage earners have demonstrated the effects of education on output and productivity. As Box table 5.2 shows, the returns to education are substantial. Although the impact of education on aggregate real output has been less well documented, a recent study of the determinants of real GDP covering fifty-eight coun-

benefiting fully from their greater skills. The results suggest that there may be thresholds in the returns to education. For example, about four years of education seem to be needed to attain functional literacy. Investments may yield substantial returns only when they are big enough to push the economy over such a threshold.

Box table 5.2 Average social returns to education
(percent)

Region	Primary education	Secondary education	Higher education
Sub-Saharan Africa	26	17	13
Asia	27	15	13
Latin America and the Caribbean	26	18	16

Source: Psacharopoulos 1985.

tries during 1960–85 strongly suggests that education can contribute significantly to aggregate output. An increase of one year in average years of education may lead to a 3 percent rise in GDP.

The results of this research differ from region to region (Box figure 5.2). For most groups of developing countries the effect of education on GDP is clearly positive, and (within the range examined) the higher the initial level of education, the greater the benefits from increasing it. This underscores the importance of investing in education. Sub-Saharan Africa is an exception; there, increasing average years of education by one year, from 3.25 (in 1985) to 4.25, is expected to have a negligible effect on output. This reflects many factors: unfavorable local conditions, the lack of complementary inputs, inadequate institutional capability, and other economic obstacles that prevent people from

Box figure 5.2 The effect on real GDP of one additional year of education per person

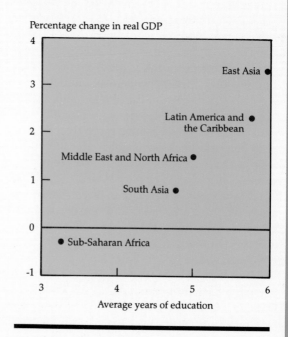

Education and productivity

The principal asset of the poor is labor time. Education increases the productivity of this asset. The result at the individual level, as many studies show, is higher income. More recent research also points to a strong link between education and economic growth (Box 5.2).

In the wage sector the individual returns to education are consistently above returns to conventional investments. It is true that most people in the developing world do not work for wages and that many of the poor are self-employed in agriculture or in small family enterprises. But this does not weaken the case for investing in education. Educated farmers are more likely to adopt new

technologies, and virtually all studies on agricultural productivity show that better-educated farmers get a higher return on their land. One study on Africa found that farmers who have completed four years of education—the minimum for achieving literacy—produce, on average, about 8 percent more than farmers who have not gone to school. Numeracy and literacy were identified as the essential skills. Studies in Korea, Malaysia, and Thailand confirm that schooling substantially raises farm productivity.

A growing number of the poor in the developing world find employment in the nonagricultural nonwage sector—mostly in the informal economy. Not all these workers are poor, but many of the self-employed do belong to the poorest segments of society, and employment in the informal sector makes up the main part of their family income.

Studies on how education influences informal sector productivity are scarce, but the few that do exist point to benefits. More education gives the worker a wider range of self-employment options and allows him or her to choose more profitable alternatives (for example, modern trade rather than traditional handicrafts). Within most subsectors earnings per hour rise with years of education, just as in the wage sector. The precise effects vary by type of activity and sometimes differ between men and women. In Peru returns to an extra year of primary education are estimated to be as high as 33 percent for women self-employed in the retail textile sector. Postprimary education appears to have a relatively high payoff—14 percent—for men in the service sector. A study of small and medium-size enterprises in Colombia showed that the entrepreneur's background—skills, education, and experience in previous jobs—strongly influences both the technical efficiency and the profitability of the enterprise.

There can be little doubt that educating the children of the poor greatly improves their chances of escaping poverty. Since labor is the one scarce resource on which all able-bodied poor can rely, increasing the productivity of this labor is clearly the most effective way to combat poverty.

Other benefits of education

The effectiveness of education as a weapon in the fight against poverty goes well beyond productivity in the labor market. One year of mother's education has been associated with a 9 percent decrease in under 5 mortality. The children of better-educated mothers, other things being equal, tend to be healthier. The effects of education on fertility appear to be more complicated. At low levels of education a few extra years of schooling may actually lead to increased fertility, but after that there is a strong negative effect. In what *World Development Report 1980* called the "seamless web of interrelations" among social services, education plays the central role.

Health, nutrition, and productivity

The effect of better health and nutrition on productivity is less well documented than the effect of education. An increasing number of studies, however, show a positive effect on agricultural productivity, especially for the activities in which most of the poor are engaged. Among sugarcane workers in Guatemala productivity increased with better nutrition. The productivity of workers in Indonesia who received iron supplements for two months rose by between 15 and 25 percent. Increased calorie intake in Sierra Leone substantially raised farmers' productivity. A study for India shows a significant link between wages and weight-for-height (a measure of short-term nutritional status) among casual agricultural laborers. Another study found that the effect was especially marked in the peak agricultural season, when more energy is required for harvesting. Estimates for Sri Lanka show a significant positive effect of energy intake on real wages.

Nutrition and learning

Just as the education of parents has a positive effect on child nutrition, better nutrition improves the child's capacity to learn. Studies in many developing countries (China, India, and Kenya, among others) consistently show that protein-energy malnutrition is related to lower cognitive test scores and worse school performance. Micronutrient deficiencies are also linked to school performance. A study of Indonesia found that iodine deficiency reduced cognitive performance among nine-to-twelve-year-old children. Iron deficiency decreases the child's alertness, which in turn affects learning. In Thailand providing iron supplements to schoolchildren has improved test scores. Vitamin A deficiency has long been associated with blindness and the severity of measles; a milder deficiency affects growth, including brain development.

The health benefits of adequate energy, protein, and micronutrients are important by themselves. Because of the positive effect of better health and nutrition on productivity, investment in these areas also contributes to reducing poverty. And if the full benefits of education are to be realized, pupils must be adequately nourished. There are many inexpensive things that governments can do. Providing vitamin A capsules twice a year and giving doses of iodine once every three years would go a long way toward eliminating nutritional disorders among school-age children.

Poverty and population growth

Poverty and rapid population growth reinforce each other in a number of ways. Low wages (especially for women), inadequate education, and high infant mortality—all linked to poverty—contribute to high fertility rates and thus to rapid population growth. Increased education for girls and women is one of the most powerful ways of reducing fertility. Greater opportunities for women in the wage sector have an independent negative effect on fertility and offer other benefits as well. When women work, parents may decide they need fewer boys to support them in old age, and if mothers work for reasonable wages, the opportunity cost of bearing an additional child is relatively high.

High infant mortality is consistently associated with high fertility. Studies from places as diverse as Colombia, Egypt, and India show that parents who have lost a child expect to have more children than do similar parents who have not. Reducing mortality among children is a necessary step toward reducing fertility.

Thus, the link leading from poverty (low wages, low income, and high mortality) to high fertility is well established. How does high fertility or, more generally, rapid population growth affect poverty? At the national level, the relationship is not simple. In the short run an increase in population will result, almost by definition, in lower per capita income growth, but in the longer run the larger number of productive workers may accelerate growth. It can even be argued that some countries —particularly in the West—need faster population growth even to sustain their current economic performance.

On the negative side, in many high-fertility countries about 45 percent of the population is under 15. This puts enormous pressure on the schools. Spending on education in the developing world is much lower than in the industrial countries to begin with, and the scarce resources have to be spread over a much larger proportion of the population. As a rule, the poor are last in line. The same holds for other sectors, such as health care and water supply. So, if investing in human capital is necessary for reducing poverty, rapid population growth will make the task much more difficult in many poor countries.

Population growth also affects the labor market. Rapid growth of the labor force does not necessarily lead to unemployment and poverty: if investment in capital is adequate, an expanding economy could absorb the additional labor and may indeed depend on it. But most countries invest too little to absorb a population that is growing at 3 to 4 percent a year. Low wages and growing poverty are the likely results.

At the household level, high fertility can damage the health of both mother and child. The mother's health suffers from closely spaced pregnancies, and her health in turn affects the child's health at birth and in the critical early years. Providing family planning services is one of the most effective policies for better health.

Family planning

Having too many children puts mothers at risk and compounds the problems of poverty (Box 5.3). Most developing countries recognize the importance of reducing population growth. Lower fertility is not an end in itself, but it makes other interventions more effective in improving overall welfare. Providing family planning services is the most direct way to reduce fertility, although lowering infant and child mortality and creating better education and work opportunities for women also help. Again, appropriate policies reinforce each other: better-educated women make more use of modern contraceptives (when they are available) than do the uneducated.

In many countries family planning services are virtually nonexistent, despite the apparent demand. In Ghana, for example, 20 percent of women in rural areas and 28 percent in the cities say they want no more children, yet modern family planning services reach less than 7 percent of the women. Ghana's fertility rate is 6.4. In Indonesia, where about half of the women want no more children, family planning services reach 44 percent of all women. Indonesia's fertility rate is 3.3.

Family planning programs, where they have been implemented, have brought birthrates down. In Costa Rica, Korea, and Singapore, for instance, birthrates fell by 35 to 48 percent between 1965 and 1985. Other factors in reducing birthrates, however, should not be overlooked. Rapidly developing economies can bring about some modest declines, even with weak family planning programs. But in the poorest countries (such as India and Indonesia) strong family planning programs are necessary to slow population growth.

Providing access for the poor

Providing the poor with access to social services requires a clear commitment. This must be reflected in the infrastructure and organization of the social sectors and in the way they are financed. Much can be learned from decades of experience in countries at different levels of development and with varying needs.

Infrastructure and organization

The biggest obstacle for the poor in gaining access to health and education services is the lack of

Box 5.3 Safe motherhood

In many developing countries pregnancy and child-birth account for more than a quarter of all deaths of women of childbearing age. About half a million women, 99 percent of them in the developing world, die in childbirth each year (see Box figure 5.3). Of every 100,000 women who give birth in Africa, from 200 to 1,500 may die, compared with fewer than 10 in most developed countries. By contrast, of every 100,000 African women who take the contraceptive pill for a year, perhaps one will die. About three-quarters of maternal deaths are from one of five causes: hemorrhage, infection, toxemia, obstructed labor, and abortion (particularly unsafe abortions, performed by untrained personnel in unhygienic conditions). Because women in many developing countries, and especially in the poorer areas, tend to have many pregnancies, the cumulative lifetime risk of dying in pregnancy may reach one in twenty. Most of these maternal deaths could be prevented by relatively cheap and simple measures.

A woman's health and nutritional status substantially affect her capacity to withstand difficulties during pregnancy, childbirth, and the postpartum period, to produce a strong, healthy baby, and to nurse and care for her baby. Most pregnant women in developing countries are anemic, and many teenage mothers are not yet fully grown. Women could help themselves if they had basic information about nutrition and health. Improving women's income, education, health, and nutrition could greatly reduce maternal mortality and morbidity.

Family planning information and services can also improve maternal health by enabling women to time and space pregnancies. In many countries 25 to 40 percent of maternal deaths could be averted by avoiding unwanted pregnancies. The three essential elements are prevention of complications, routine care, and backup for high-risk emergency cases. Existing programs could be modified to stress:

- *Stronger community-based health care*, relying on nonphysician health workers, to screen pregnant women, identify those at high risk, and refer them for help; to provide good prenatal care and ensure safe delivery for women at less risk; to provide family life education and family planning services; and, in general, to promote better family health and nutrition
- *Stronger referral facilities*—hospitals and health centers with beds—to act as a backup network, to take care of complicated deliveries and obstetrical emergencies, and to provide clinical and surgical methods of family planning
- *An "alarm" and transport system* to transfer women with high-risk pregnancies and emergencies from the community to the referral facilities.

Box figure 5.3 Estimated number of annual maternal deaths, by region

Every year half a million women die in childbirth.

Maternal deaths per 100,000 live births

140,000

308,000

34,000

6,000

■ Sub-Saharan Africa ■ Asia ■ Latin America and the Caribbean □ Developed countries

Equals 30,000 deaths

physical infrastructure, especially in rural areas. The urban bias in the provision of services affects both quantity and quality. The sheer lack of facilities makes necessary a continued expansion of appropriate services, especially rural health clinics and primary schools. This will almost certainly benefit the poor. Improving quality will require more funds, better use of the available resources, and greater accountability in administration.

EDUCATION. Governments in middle-income countries have by and large been able to build enough schools and train enough teachers to make universal primary education possible. Low-income countries, however, still have a long way to go. For example, in Bhutan and Mali net primary school capacity is only about 20 percent, approximately the same as net enrollment rates. Since these countries are faced with the prospect of sluggish economic growth and rapid population growth, it will take an extraordinary effort to provide the necessary infrastructure for achieving universal primary education in the foreseeable future. Given the extremely low incomes of most households in these countries, public provision of education will be needed.

In some countries the private sector can help to make schooling more widely available. Pakistan in 1979 reversed its nationalization decision of 1970 and again allowed private schools to provide education. The education system has expanded quickly, especially at the lower levels. In the Karachi region, for instance, private institutions in 1985 accounted for 25 percent of primary enrollment. Because of the relatively large fees charged, these private institutions are unlikely to serve the poor. But where demand exceeds supply and budget constraints are tight, greater reliance on the private sector will allow the government to direct more of its scarce resources toward education for the poor.

In general, the public sector will remain the dominant supplier of primary education in middle-income countries as well, although here there is more scope for private provision. In 1980–81 Chile reformed its education system and embarked on a policy of developing private education, partly supported by public finance, with the aim of improving quality and increasing enrollment. The government encouraged the private sector to provide education through a per student payment system that forced the public schools to compete for students. It transferred responsibility for primary and secondary public schools to the municipalities and placed vocational schools under nonprofit private

sector organizations in the hope of making the schools more responsive to labor market demands. The Ministry of Education allocates resources to the public schools on the basis of enrollment and dropout rates. Private schools that provide tuition-free education receive the same subsidies. Implementing the reforms was difficult—the monetary transfers had to be suspended during the economic crisis of 1982–83—but enrollment in subsidized private elementary schools doubled between 1980 and 1987, and the proportion of all education subsidies received by the poorest 30 percent of students rose from 29 percent in 1974 to 38 percent in 1986.

Simply expanding the education system is not enough. In many countries the curriculum needs to be improved, the schools need more textbooks, and the teachers need better training, more time for teaching basic skills, and better pay and working conditions. School managers need more authority to control resources, and they must be made more accountable to the local community.

Narrower interventions can sometimes be successful in reaching disadvantaged groups. In Bangladesh, for instance, a scholarship project for secondary school girls in the Sharasti Upazila region, funded by the U.S. Agency for International Development (USAID), has been in place since 1982. Before the project started, 27 percent of the secondary school students in the area were girls. By 1987 the percentage had risen to 44 percent. The project has also greatly reduced the dropout level for female students, from 15 percent before the program started to 4 percent in 1987. In Nepal in the 1970s the United Nations Educational, Scientific, and Cultural Organization (Unesco) sponsored a project that included a teacher training component designed to increase the number of women teachers. During the project period the number of girls enrolled in school rose from 13 to 29 percent of the age group.

HEALTH. Although the government is usually the dominant provider of health care, in many countries the private sector also provides some (mostly curative) services. The case for the state's being sole provider of curative care is weak. There is undoubtedly a need for heavy intervention, but this need not mean putting every doctor and nurse on the government payroll. Although different countries have different needs, several broad principles hold. First, the state should take responsibility for health interventions that have a public-good character (for example, clean air and traffic safety) or that generate benefits to the community in addition to private benefits (for example, immunization against communicable diseases). Second, in curative care the main role of the state as a provider of services should be to supply basic services in those regions that the private sector is unlikely to serve. Third, if a private delivery system is in place, the state should make sure that the poor have access to basic care. In many countries, in other words, the government should continue to expand basic services but with a greater emphasis on access for the poor.

Chile again offers an example. Expansion of primary health care services, with an emphasis on vulnerable groups such as mothers and young children, was part of the reforms implemented after 1974–75. New financing mechanisms were used to promote increased coverage. The government encouraged the private sector to offer prepaid health insurance plans that were to be financed through payroll deductions. User fees were introduced on the basis of ability to pay.

Perhaps the most important aspect of the reforms was the decision to decentralize responsibility for delivering primary health care and public health care services. In many countries primary health care programs are designed and implemented by highly centralized administrations. Building health centers and training health workers can be managed from the center, but supplying services calls for decentralized management. In

1980 a USAID project in Nicaragua used surveys to establish local needs and involved village health committees in building wells, latrines, and health posts. A preschool child care program in Colombia is managed by parents' associations (Box 5.4). In Thailand villagers have helped to build wells and health and nutrition centers. Women in a Bangladesh village maintain new latrines and sewage systems (Box 5.5). With UNICEF's assistance, women's NGOs in Indonesia have produced training booklets about child survival for twelve different religious groups. By January 1988 these booklets had reached about 7 million women at a cost of 10 cents a woman.

Chile has transferred responsibility for many public health services from the central government to municipalities. The reforms are incomplete, but coverage has already been broadened substantially. The capacity of municipal health posts, for instance, has gone up 45 percent since the reforms, and the number of service hours offered has increased by more than 80 percent in rural areas. Chile's long-term commitment to improving its basic health services is having results. Infant mortality declined from 103 per thousand in 1965 to 21 per thousand in 1985, and maternal mortality was reduced from 131 to 47 maternal deaths per 100,000 live births during the same period.

China also illustrates the importance of local involvement in the provision of basic health care. After the introduction of the economic responsibil-

---

Box 5.4 A community child care and nutrition program in Colombia

An estimated 25 percent of Colombia's population lives below the poverty line. In the towns the worst poverty is borne disproportionately by children, who are at risk from malnutrition, illness, neglect, isolation, and violence. To address these problems, the Colombian government and local NGOs developed a system of preschool child care that includes a feeding program and health monitoring.

The target group—children age 2 to 6 and their parents—is drawn mainly from the poorest 20 percent of the population. A group of parents selects a "community mother" to provide day care and other services for fifteen children in her home. With help from the National Family Welfare Institute, the community mother receives training, a small monthly stipend, and a credit to upgrade the home to minimum standards of hygiene and safety. The institute also provides food, including a domestically produced nutritional supple-

ment, to meet 80 percent of the daily requirements of each child. The service is much in demand. It started on a broad scale in 1987 and by late 1989 had served half a million children. Its goal is to reach all children at risk—more than a million of them—by 1994.

Participating children receive improved nutrition and care as well as exposure to preschool learning activities. Community mothers are benefiting from additional income, and parents—often single female heads of household—gain an opportunity to seek remunerative employment outside the home. The cost of the program, at about $11 a month per child, compares well with $33 a month for day care provided through the institute's centers. In addition, the program's subsidies are better targeted to the poor; day care centers largely serve a middle- and lower-middle-income clientele.

Box 5.5   Mirzapur, Bangladesh: water supply, sanitation, and hygiene education

Bangladesh, heavily populated and one of the poorest countries in the world, suffers from endemic health problems. The mortality rate for children under 5 was 204 per thousand in 1980–85—the highest in Asia and one of the highest in the world. Diarrheal diseases account for 29 percent of all deaths of children under age 5 and for roughly one in five deaths in all older age groups. Sixty percent of children under 5 experience moderate to severe malnutrition. These problems stem, at least in part, from the poor quality and management of Bangladesh's water, which in turn are linked to frequent floods.

More than 82 percent of rural villagers say they use tubewell water for drinking, but only 12 percent use it for all their domestic needs. This means that the vast majority still uses fecally contaminated surface water for other purposes, such as bathing and washing utensils and clothes.

In 1984 the Interregional Handpump Project, sponsored by the United Nations Development Programme and the World Bank, initiated a study on the health impact of handpump water supplies, pit latrines, and hygiene education in the Mirzapur region of Bangladesh. The project sought to encourage people to use well water instead of surface water for domestic purposes by supplying new and more efficient Tara handpumps. It also introduced hygienic water-sealed la-

trines. An important element of the project was an education program designed to persuade villages to use handpumps for all domestic purposes, to consume more water, to store it hygienically, and to use and maintain the water-sealed latrines.

One hundred and forty-eight Tara handpumps and 754 latrines—one for every household—were provided. Villages made a financial contribution for the equipment. Classes in hygiene were complemented by further training and household visits over several months. Twelve local women were trained to empty the latrine pits. They were paid about $1.30 each per pit—much less than the price quoted by professional sweepers.

The project achieved high rates of handpump water consumption. The villagers used and stored water more hygienically than before, and 90 percent of the latrines were in regular use.

The effect of the project on health was evaluated through a series of surveys. In the baseline year the incidence of diarrheal diseases in the project area was similar to that in a control area. After the intervention the incidence of persistent diarrhea was 40 percent lower in the project villages than in the control area, and child dysentery was 30 percent lower. In the last two years of the project, children in the project area suffered from diarrhea for, on average, thirty-five days, compared with sixty-three days in the control area.

---

ity system, village-based rural health insurance programs collapsed. Local communities responded with a variety of schemes to secure adequate financing for basic care—from health maintenance organizations with prepaid insurance in some of the larger cities to arrangements that finance village health posts out of charges for sales of medicine and for curative treatment.

Financing health and education

Public funds provide most of the resources for the social sectors. The demand is increasing: basic services need to be expanded so as to reach the poor, and rapid population growth in some regions and aging populations in others add to the burden on all the social services. But the supply of funds is being squeezed. Slow economic growth, tight budget constraints, and competing calls on the government purse from outside the social sectors mean that priorities must be examined carefully.

A shift in the allocation of funds from higher-level services to basic health and primary educa-

tion will serve both efficiency and equity objectives. Recommending such a shift does not mean denying the importance of higher-level services. Any country that wants to compete in the world economy needs a comprehensive education policy that includes spending on higher education, science and technology, and professional training. Hospitals are an essential part of a balanced health care system, and they are the educational and research institutions that train new staff and generate new knowledge. These considerations, however, do not justify using higher-level services as a means of transferring government money to privileged students and urban patients from middle- and upper-class backgrounds. Financial reform, including greater reliance on alternative financing mechanisms such as student loans and health insurance plans, can free up resources that can be used to expand and improve basic services and provide better access to the poor.

In many cases more government spending on the social services (especially at the cost of military expenditures) would be fully justified. In some

Table 5.1 Expenditures on primary education as a percentage of GDP, 1985 and 2000

Region	1985	2000 (at current enrollment rates)	2000 (universal enrollment)
Sub-Saharan Africa	1.41	1.35	2.53
East Asia	1.42	0.60	0.60
South Asia	0.95	0.63	1.08
Eastern Europe	1.17	0.71	0.71
Middle East and North Africa	2.05	1.47	1.76
Latin America and the Caribbean	1.06	0.83	0.92

cases it is likely to be necessary. This is illustrated by Table 5.1, which shows the estimated cost of achieving universal primary education by 2000. Projections for population and economic growth suggest that many regions will be able to achieve that goal by allocating to primary schooling a similar percentage of GDP as in 1985, or even a smaller share. In Sub-Saharan Africa, however, although enrollment levels can be raised significantly, reaching universal primary enrollment will take an extraordinary effort, including a generous increase in foreign aid. Growth in GDP of 3.7 percent a year, combined with an expected increase of 3.4 percent a year in the population age 6 to 11, will require an 85 percent increase in the share of GDP allocated to primary schooling, from 1.4 to 2.5 percent. In some countries outside Africa, too, more spending on education and other social services will be necessary.

But much can also be gained in two other ways: (1) by shifting current outlays to more efficient uses (for example, by emphasizing primary education over higher education and village health posts over city hospitals) and (2) by trying harder to recover the costs of certain services.

How much scope is there for charging for services? Recent evidence shows that the demand for medical care is sensitive to its price—more so for the poor than for the rich. This implies that if fees are collected (or increased), the poor will be the first to drop out and that health services for poor areas will have to be heavily subsidized. This need not mean that service is entirely free; nominal fees could be charged in poor areas. Charging higher fees in better-off regions or in the richer parts of cities makes good sense and can generate substantial revenues. In addition, fees should be considered for those types of care (especially hospital care) that yield mostly private benefits; this would allow more resources to be devoted to public health measures and preventive care.

There is also ample evidence that people are willing to pay for higher education. Higher fees for secondary and higher education would garner resources for improving the quality of education in general and, where necessary, for expanding primary education. The effect of fees on the demand for primary education is less clear. If there are few public schools, private schools can charge substantial fees by catering to the rich. But if the aim is to increase the enrollment rates of the poor, fees are counterproductive.

Both approaches—shifting resources from higher levels of care to basic services and introducing fees for those who can afford them—transfer resources from the rich to the poor. If reducing poverty is a primary objective, this policy is fully justified.

Creating demand

Even when cheap or free social services are available, the poor may not take advantage of them. There are two reasons: they may not understand the benefits being offered, or they may be deterred by the private costs—such as working time forgone in visiting a health center or loss of household income when a child goes to school.

Family planning is a good example of why poor people may not use social services. Health education campaigns are needed to explain the benefits of lower fertility and to describe the various birth control techniques. But even when family planning services are available and understood, it may not be in the household's private interest to have fewer children. For instance, having fewer children may make it possible to give each child a better education, but the benefits may not be felt for years. Where national policies have produced a population growth rate that is faster than socially desirable, governments need to encourage family planning by strengthening the private incentives. Singapore, for instance, uses tax incentives and housing policies to make having smaller families more attractive. China has used bonuses, access to education, and housing privileges in the same way. Thailand combines community involvement, extensive public education, mass sterilization campaigns, rural development programs, and direct benefits for households with fewer children (Box 5.6).

Girls' education is another case in point. The private and social returns to women's education at the primary and secondary levels are at least equal to the returns to education for men. Still, parents often prefer to invest only in their sons' education.

Box 5.6 Family planning buffaloes and vasectomy festivals in Thailand

Thailand is the home of one of the most successful and effective family planning programs in the world. The program relies on the use of media, economic incentives, and community involvement to increase the use of contraception.

Thailand's striking approach stresses the immediate practical benefits from lowered fertility and uses methods that mix humor and audacity. The program is run by an NGO, the Population and Community Development Association (PDA), with the support of the Ministry of Public Health.

The Community Based Family Planning Services (CBFPS), a PDA program, was initiated in 1974 and now reaches more than 16,000 villages and 17 million people—one-third of the nation's population. The key message links population growth to low standards of living and family planning to economic gains. To convey this message, taboos surrounding birth control had to be broken down. Birth control carnivals, games, condom-blowing balloon contests, raffles, village fairs, and weddings have served as occasions for promoting family planning joyfully.

Vasectomy marathons are held on Labor Day and on the king's birthday. In 1983 a team of forty doctors and eighty nurses performed a record-breaking 1,190 vasectomies during the one-day festival. The PDA also delivers free, convenient, and efficient vasectomy services in clinics and mobile units. Between July 1980 and June 1984 it performed 25,412 vasectomies.

Registered family planners may also rent cattle for plowing their fields—family planning buffaloes—at half the regular price. They are encouraged to market some of their products through the CBFPS at prices about 30 percent higher than regular middlemen offer and to buy fertilizer and seeds at 30 percent below local market prices. Under a similar program villagers who practice contraception may have their goods transported to the marketplace at a discount or may receive free piglets.

In 1985 about 60 percent of all Thai couples practiced some form of birth control. The total fertility rate fell from 6.1 in 1965–70 to 2.8 in 1985, as against an average 4.1 for lower-middle-income countries.

Measures such as increasing the number of female teachers or paying parents to send their girls to school (as in Bangladesh) may help to reduce the present inequalities. But longer-term policies to increase women's participation in the labor market will be needed if the bias against girls' education in some parts of the world is to be eliminated.

Lessons for the next decade

The past three decades have seen tremendous progress in improving health, nutrition, and education in the developing world. In many cases progress has been considerably faster than that of the industrial world when it was at a comparable stage of development. But it has been uneven. The poor of the developing countries continue to suffer from illiteracy, sickness, malnutrition, and early death.

If the trends prevailing since the 1960s were to continue, universal primary enrollment would be a fact by the end of the century in East Asia and Latin America. The countries of the Middle East and North Africa would approach that goal, and in South Asia and Sub-Saharan Africa enrollment rates would rise from the current 74 and 56 percent to 88 and 86 percent, respectively. Unfortunately, in Sub-Saharan Africa this long-term trend stalled,

and indeed went into reverse, in the 1980s. If recent trends prevailed, Sub-Saharan Africa's enrollment rate would be a paltry 46 percent in 2000. The pace of progress has increased recently in South Asia, and universal enrollment might be reached there by 2000 (Table 5.2).

A similar picture emerges for mortality among children. If long-term trends continued, all regions would make progress, but under 5 mortality in Sub-Saharan Africa will remain high if the slowdown in the 1980s is not reversed. The experience of the 1980s indicates that accelerated progress can be expected in South Asia, the Middle East and North Africa, and Latin America. The total fertility rate is likely to come down in every region but will still be a high 5.4 in Sub-Saharan Africa by 2000.

Thus, the picture is mixed. Although the outlook is for steady progress in the long run, more recent experience shows that in some cases progress has accelerated and in others has slowed or reversed. Even if the long-term trends prevail, in thirty-six countries of Sub-Saharan Africa, South Asia, and Latin America, under 5 mortality rates will still be at least ten times higher than in the industrial world. That is, in 2000 almost ten million children under 5 will die in the developing world, for broadly the same reasons that children were dying there in 1900.

Table 5.2 Projections of social indicators to 2000

| Region | Net enrollment rates (percent) | | | Under 5 mortality (per thousand) | | | Total fertility rate[e] | |
	1985	Long-term trend[a]	Short-term trend[b]	1985	Long-term trend[c]	Short-term trend[d]	1985	2000
Sub-Saharan Africa	56	86	46	185	136	153	6.1	5.4
East Asia	96	100	100	54	31	33	2.7	2.2
South Asia	74	88	100	150	98	83	4.7	3.4
Middle East and North Africa	75	94	95	119	71	65	5.1	3.9
Latin America and the Caribbean	92	100	100	75	55	32	3.6	2.5

Note: All data are weighted except that for under 5 mortality, short-term trend. All mortality data are projected to 2000–05.
a. Based on the 1965–85 trend.
b. Based on the 1980–85 trend.
c. Based on the trend used by the United Nations.
d. Based on 1975–80 to 1980–85 except for South Asia, 1970–75 to 1975–80.
e. The total fertility rate is the average number of children that would be born alive to a woman during her lifetime if she were to bear children in accordance with the prevailing age-specific fertility rates. It is based on 1985–90 and 2000–05.
Source: United Nations and World Bank data, except for under 5 mortality, short-term trend, from Hill and Pebley 1988, and fertility, from Bulatao 1989.

To avert that shameful prospect, governments, in cooperation with the international community, must make a long-term commitment to improving the social infrastructure that serves the poor. The key elements of such a commitment are clear. First, provide the basic services that the poor need most.

Second, make the existing services more effective. With these principles as the guide, equity and efficiency can go hand in hand. Improving the quality of life of the poor will then become an achievable goal—and the progress made in the past will stand as a sign of what can be done in the future.

Transfers and safety nets

Not all the poor will benefit from the policies discussed in Chapters 4 and 5. In the first place, it may take a long time for some of the poor—including the working poor and those in remote regions—to fully participate, and the old or disabled may never be able to do so. Second, even among those who do benefit from the policies, there will be some who remain acutely vulnerable to adverse events. The first group can best be helped through a system of income transfers. The second group requires a safety net—some form of income insurance to help people through short-term stress and calamities. This is particularly important when food security, and hence survival, is threatened.

As a rule, government interventions will blend elements of both redistribution and insurance. This chapter examines a range of policies under the following headings:

- Food pricing and distribution
- Public employment schemes
- Social security

These complement the policies described in previous chapters and form a crucial ingredient in the overall strategy. Some of them have a surprisingly long history (Box 6.1).

Individuals, families, and communities have ways of coping with poverty. Individuals and families redistribute and stabilize consumption, diversify income sources, migrate, and give and receive transfers. In many parts of Sub-Saharan Africa the term for being poor is synonymous with lacking kin or friends. At the community level these "social security" arrangements are sometimes quite sophisticated. For example, fishing villages in South Asia, Sub-Saharan Africa, and Latin America often provide for the subsistence needs of old fishermen or of poor fishing families whose male income earners have died. Old fishermen are commonly assigned comparatively easy tasks on shore, and children from needy families are allowed to take some fish from each boat. In some Senegalese villages retired fishermen are granted a fixed share of the catch. This "tax" is paid not only by local fishermen but also by fishermen from other areas. Fishing communities are often well suited to such arrangements because they have a high degree of social homogeneity.

But many of the poor, particularly those of concern in this chapter, are inadequately protected by these strategies. There are limits to what those unable to work can do to protect themselves, and limits to what the households looking after them can do to raise household income to tolerable levels. Growing evidence points to the dissolution of family and ethnic ties and the weakening of community support systems in many developing countries. In addition, coping arrangements that work well in normal times may fail when they are needed most. Poor, vulnerable households, on the margin of subsistence at the best of times, will be hard pressed to protect themselves in the face of a series of shocks. And the effectiveness of community insurance depends crucially on the extent to which local incomes are affected simultaneously. Unanticipated shocks such as severe agricultural fluctuations, deterioration in the terms of trade, and famines can create hardship for entire communities.

The state therefore has a role in aiding households or communities in times of insecurity and in

Box 6.1 The historical antecedents of public action

Public food distribution has a history of several thousand years. In Egypt storage of food by the state, accompanied by subsidized sales and public distribution to the needy, has existed since the time of the pharaohs. It was considered to be the moral responsibility of rulers and was an important element in maintaining social stability when crises arose because of shortfalls in domestic production, military demands, and disruptions of trade. The distribution of a grain or bread ration in ancient Rome and Greece was limited to crisis periods precipitated by war or climatic instability. As rural transport and irrigation systems have been developed and private and public food distribution systems have improved, the ability of governments to avert famine has gradually increased.

Public provision of employment also has a long history as a means of reducing poverty. As early as the fourth century B.C. Indian rulers were advised that when natural calamities struck, subjects should be employed in building forts or waterworks in return for food. Employment on public works later became the main element of strategies for famine prevention in India, and it has proved effective. In eighteenth- and nineteenth-century Europe the poor qualified for relief if they agreed to provide labor or to live in squalid poorhouses. Victorians considered this approach preferable to charitable transfers, which they thought induced laziness. Perhaps the most significant use of public works as relief was the Works Progress Administration, which provided employment for one-fifth of all U.S. workers during the Great Depression of the 1930s.

At the turn of the century assistance to the poor consisted mainly of charitable transfers and poor relief based on stringent needs testing that stigmatized the recipients. These forms of assistance were increasingly challenged on moral grounds as demeaning to the recipients, and the world wars and the Depression created demand that they could not meet. The rise of the modern industrial state allowed the development of formal social security systems based on contributions from workers and employers and on wide coverage. Publicly provided pensions for the aged were an important feature of the new systems. Unemployment provisions were instituted after the Depression. Following World War II coverage became universal, with family allowances and a minimum level of benefits for the sick, unemployed, and aged. The existence of guaranteed public health, income support, and insurance systems has provided to the poor in most developed countries a degree of security that developing countries still lack.

---

ensuring minimum levels of provision to those unable to gain from the growth process. Effective policies will take into account what individuals and households can do to protect themselves and what their limitations are. Government interventions should also try to involve people in the solutions rather than treat them as passive recipients of relief.

Public provision of transfers and safety nets

In assessing policy alternatives, the tests are effectiveness in reaching the poor and the extent to which the policies compromise other objectives. For many practical purposes, these can be measured by considering cost-effectiveness—the budgetary cost of delivering a given amount of benefit.

Benefits usually change the way the poor and others behave, and this affects cost-effectiveness. For instance, a public employment program targeted at landless laborers may have important second-round effects on local agricultural wages; the program's overall effect on the incomes of the poor may be greater than the wages participants earn in public employment. This has been observed in various public employment schemes in South Asia. By contrast, child feeding programs may have less than their expected impact if the allocation of food within the household shifts toward other family members.

In measuring the benefits to the poor, governments must also take account of the method of financing. If transfers are financed by printing money, the loss to the poor from the ensuing inflation may well exceed the nominal income transfer. But if progressive taxation is used to finance a policy, the system may be highly redistributive even if the benefits go to the rich as well as to the poor. Often, schemes are financed by cutting spending on other social programs. The net effect on the poor will then depend on the balance between the benefits lost and gained.

Targeting benefits to the poor can be an important way of increasing cost-effectiveness. There are exceptions, but for a given budgetary outlay, schemes that target benefits to the poor are likely to have a greater impact on poverty than universal schemes. The exceptions arise when targeting is

Box 6.2 Reaching the poor through public action

Ideally, government policy would identify the poor without cost and would channel benefits exclusively to them. In practice, policymakers lack information on individual living standards, and the costs of obtaining this information can be high. *Means testing* and other forms of targeting have social costs or cause distortions because they lead to changes in behavior. In the United Kingdom means testing for supplementary benefits requires an elaborate administrative machinery for verification and recordkeeping. In developing countries the identification of income and assets is even more difficult, especially in rural areas, and the administrative problems are likely to be daunting. As a rule, means testing is simply not feasible in these countries.

An alternative is *indicator targeting*. The basic idea is simple. Correlates of poverty are identified from sample surveys or other information, and direct benefits are allocated accordingly. In general, it is less costly to identify the correlates, which may include region of residence, landholding, nutritional status, sex, age, and race, than to measure incomes. Food subsidy schemes in Colombia have successfully combined geographic targeting with further targeting based on household-specific characteristics. The trouble is that the easily monitored correlates of poverty are often imperfect: some poor people will be missed, and some of the nonpoor will receive benefits. Indicator targeting can also lead to incentive effects—for instance, nonpoor people might migrate to target areas. The challenge is to find good indicators of poverty that can be monitored easily by administrators but cannot be altered easily by the nonpoor. Caste status (in India), widowhood, and old age may be good examples.

A good way to design targeted programs is to make benefits contingent on work, as in rural public employment schemes. Another is to subsidize goods that are mainly consumed by the poor. Such policies are called *self-targeting* because the "cost" they impose will (ideally) make participation desirable only for the truly poor. For example, work in return for wages that are generally lower than other unskilled wages will dissuade those with better jobs or other means of livelihood. This screening method is a key component of employment schemes in both Bangladesh and India. Often, self-targeting is more cost-effective than uniform provision.

---

administratively costly or imposes substantial losses on the poor (such as income forgone in queuing for food rations). One promising avenue is to use incentives as a screening device so that the poor are encouraged to participate and the nonpoor are discouraged (Box 6.2).

In practice, the success of public intervention involves more than cost-effectiveness. The demands made by different sections of the population, and their ability to exert pressure on the authorities, are often more influential than the government's economic calculations. Fine targeting based on a single-minded concern for cost-effectiveness can reduce public interest in the vigorous implementation of government programs to help the poor. For example, in the late 1970s Sri Lanka replaced a universal food subsidy with a less costly targeted food stamp program. In time, the benefits delivered by the new program declined. The middle classes no longer gained from the scheme, and although the new program was more cost-effective, it lost crucial political support. Similarly, a food subsidy directed to poor consumers in Colombia was so tightly targeted that it lacked an effective political constituency, and it was dropped at a change of administration. The analysis of public policy has to be alive to these considerations of political economy.

Food pricing and distribution policies

The poor spend a large part of their incomes on food and can be highly vulnerable to any setback in their ability to obtain it. An important way to protect the living standards of the poor is by guaranteeing their food security—that is, by making sure that they can acquire adequate food at all times. The developing countries have adopted various forms of food subsidy: general food price subsidies, food rations, food stamps, food distribution policies, and food supplementation schemes. These policies can be used to raise the real incomes of the direct beneficiaries, and they can provide a safety net to protect a wider group of the poor against collapses in their real incomes.

General food price subsidies

General food price subsidy schemes supply unlimited amounts of subsidized food to anyone who wishes to buy it. Brazil, China, Colombia, Egypt, Mexico, Morocco, Pakistan, Sudan, Thailand, Tu-

Table 6.1 Distribution of the annual income transfer from the general food subsidy, Egypt, 1981–82

Type of household and income level	Amount of transfer (Egyptian pounds)	Transfer as percentage of household expenditure
Urban		
Poorest quartile	15.4	8.7
Richest quartile	18.1	3.4
Rural		
Poorest quartile	11.9	10.8
Richest quartile	15.2	2.7

Source: Alderman and von Braun 1984 and Alderman 1989.

nisia, and, before 1979, Sri Lanka have all operated schemes of this kind, some national and some regional. Costs ranged from less than 1 percent of total public expenditures in Colombia in 1978–80 to 10–17 percent in Egypt between the mid-1970s and 1984. The experience of Egypt well illustrates some of the advantages and drawbacks of these schemes.

Egypt's marketwide food subsidy program has been costly, but it has succeeded in reaching the poor. In 1981–82 the transfer value represented a sizable portion of the total expenditure of the poorest urban and rural groups—8.7 and 10.8 percent, respectively (Table 6.1).

A common feature of these schemes is that the rich receive a greater allocation per capita than the poor, although this amount often accounts for a smaller share of income. In Egypt urban households in the top quartile received 18.1 Egyptian pounds (equivalent to 3.4 percent of household expenditures), compared with 15.4 Egyptian pounds and 8.7 percent of household expenditures for urban households in the lowest quartile. All benefits going to the nonpoor add to the budgetary cost of reducing poverty. Indeed, if general subsidies are to provide reasonable transfers to the poor, they become very expensive. In Egypt only about twenty cents of each dollar spent reached those in the lowest quartile.

The bulk of Egypt's price subsidy transfer is made by subsidizing bread and wheat flour sold at bakeries and flour shops. Administrative ease is one advantage of general food subsidies. Since most subsidized commodities can be sold through private outlets, public involvement in distribution is not necessary. Central administration of the price mechanism and low investments in infrastructure help to contain transfer costs. In many countries, however, general price subsidies fail to reach many of the poor. Outlets for sale of subsidized goods are often concentrated in urban areas, either by design or because market channels bypass rural consumers. Rural consumers must have access to markets if price subsidies are to help to reduce rural poverty.

A better way to reach the poor is to limit subsidies to commodities that are consumed mainly by the poor and that form a significant part of their food expenditures. Such goods are not always available and are not always easy to subsidize. But there are examples. In Egypt benefits from subsidies on coarse flour accrue mainly to low-income groups. Shifting Brazil's general subsidy to cassava and away from wheat, milk, beef, and vegetable oils, which are heavily consumed by the higher-income sections of the population, would improve targeting to the poor. The choice of commodity may also influence distribution between sectors. For example, Mexico has a consumer subsidy on maize tortillas. Since outlets are concentrated in urban areas and urban consumers buy tortillas whereas rural consumers make them at home, the subsidy has an urban bias. In Egypt the urban poor gain more from the bread subsidy than do the rural poor, but the reverse is true for the wheat subsidy.

Better targeting of price subsidies to the poor is possible when the government knows where the poor live. The Pilot Food Price Subsidy Scheme in the Philippines is an example of how to improve cost-effectiveness by combining geographic targeting and consumer price subsidies. The National Nutrition Council's anthropometric reports helped to identify poor villages with high rates of child malnutrition. Seven villages were selected to receive price discounts on rice and cooking oil—goods that account for a large part of food expenditures. These were sold through local retailers and were available to all villagers. The scheme improved the nutritional status of both preschoolers and adults. It was highly cost-effective; eighty-four cents out of each dollar spent were transferred. This, however, did not include setup costs for extensive growth monitoring, which have to be taken into account in determining overall cost-effectiveness. Few countries have in place the national nutrition surveillance systems needed to run such schemes.

Rationed food subsidies

An alternative to a general subsidy is to provide a quota, or ''ration,'' of subsidized food to households while permitting unlimited sales on the open

93

Table 6.2 Distribution of the monthly transfer from food subsidies, Sri Lanka, 1978–79

Subsidy and household income level	Amount of transfer (rupees)	Transfer as percentage of per capita expenditure
General wheat and bread subsidy		
Poorest quintile	4.3	7.6
Richest quintile	7.8	3.8
Targeted rice ration		
Poorest quintile	11.1	19.6
Richest quintile	3.3	1.6

Source: Edirisinghe 1987 and Alderman 1989.

market. Schemes of this type operate or have operated in Egypt and in South Asia (Bangladesh, India, Pakistan, and Sri Lanka). In addition to transferring income, ration schemes ensure access to a regular supply of basic staples at reasonable prices. The absolute transfer under a general ration is similar for all income groups. Thus, rations tend to be more progressive than general food subsidies. For example, the absolute transfer to the richest quartile in urban areas under Egypt's general food subsidy was 20 percent greater than that received by the poorest quartile, whereas with the general ration the rich received 5 percent less than the poor.

The Sri Lankan general rice ration scheme, which operated between 1942 and 1978, had a large impact on poverty both because the benefits that reached the poor were high and because there was extensive coverage of different types of poor people. To reduce costs, the government in 1978 restricted distribution to the poorest half of the population. The targeted scheme can be compared with the general subsidy on wheat and bread of the same period. As Table 6.2 shows, benefits to the poor from the curtailed rice ration are greater both in absolute terms and in relation to income. Given adequate coverage of the poor, targeted rations thus represent an improvement over both general subsidies and unrestricted rations.

A similar pattern of transfers is seen in the distribution of foodgrains through fair-price shops in certain states of India. In Kerala in 1977 the poorest 60 percent of the population received 87 percent of the foodgrains distributed. Kerala is unique in that rations are spread fairly evenly between the rural and urban populations. In other parts of India as well as in other countries, including Bangladesh and Pakistan, the benefits of ration systems have gone disproportionately to urban consumers— although poverty is mainly a rural phenomenon in South Asia.

As is true of general subsidies, ration schemes are often limited in coverage because the infrastructure and retail networks needed to implement the systems in rural regions are lacking and because of a desire not to upset production incentives. These are often compounded by a lack of political will to assist the rural poor. Guaranteeing large sections of the population a basic ration on a long-term basis may place a great burden on the government in terms of both administrative capability and cost.

In the past ration programs have often been set up for political purposes and have rarely been targeted to the neediest. But it is possible to introduce a degree of self-selection and better targeting into rationing schemes without costly means testing. Ration outlets can be strategically located in poor neighborhoods. The quantities distributed should be small enough to allow poor households without much cash to participate. The opportunity cost of buying a restricted quantity at a ration shop located in a slum is greater for the rich than for the poor. In Northeast Brazil small amounts of subsidized basic foods were sold through shops in poor neighborhoods that the well-to-do regarded as unsafe; the inconvenience of the locations and the limit on the size of purchase further discouraged affluent nonresidents from participating. The quality of the subsidized commodity can also be lower than that available on the open market. This method was used to skew the benefits of Pakistan's pre-1987 ration system toward lower-income groups. In Bangladesh better targeting has been achieved by offering a choice of wheat or a larger quantity of sorghum. Poorer households tend to opt for the latter, thus improving the nutritional impact of the program.

Food stamps

Food stamps are similar to ration schemes except that the quota is measured in terms of nominal currency units rather than in commodity weights or volumes. In practice, this means that the value of the food stamps is often eroded by price inflation. Food stamps are usually more finely targeted to needy groups than are rations.

In the face of fiscal crisis, Sri Lanka in 1979–80 replaced its four-decade-old general food subsidy and ration schemes with a food stamp program. The total transfer was lower, and the reduction in administrative machinery led to substantial savings. Stamps for food and kerosene were targeted to families with self-reported incomes of less than

300 rupees a month—roughly 50 percent of the population. The government had removed all other subsidies on food by 1980. The share of food subsidies in GNP dropped from 5.0 to 1.3 percent between the mid-1970s and 1984, and their share in total government expenditure fell from 15 to 3 percent during the same period. But the value of food stamps, which was fixed in nominal terms, quickly eroded in the 1980s, falling from 83 percent of the benefits of the general subsidy at the time of introduction to 43 percent in 1981–82.

Targeted food stamps yield a more progressive pattern of transfers than general food subsidies. Jamaica's food stamp scheme was introduced in 1984 to protect vulnerable groups from the full impact of exchange rate movements and reduced public spending. Stamps are targeted to pregnant and lactating women and to children under 5 through registration at primary health care clinics. This system encourages preventive health care and successfully screens out wealthier households, which tend to use private facilities. Coverage is high among the intended beneficiaries, and this part of the program is markedly progressive. Poor, aged, and handicapped people who are already on welfare programs, as well as households that report total income of less than 2,600 Jamaican dollars a year, are also eligible for food stamps. This component is less well targeted; there is both incomplete coverage of eligible households and leakage to nontarget ones.

Jamaica reinstated a general food subsidy in 1986. Table 6.3 shows that although coverage is wider under the general subsidy scheme, targeting through food stamps has a larger impact on the incomes of the poor, and at about half the cost. Administrative costs (which are not reflected in the table) are kept low by relying on existing government networks. The value of the stamps has eroded over time, although adjustments were made in 1988 and 1989 and more are expected in 1990. The Jamaican food stamp program is cost-effective and, with some modifications, can be further improved. Its success, however, owes much to the availability of a highly developed health and administrative apparatus and the presence of political will. Both are lacking in many countries.

Supplementary feeding programs

Supplementary feeding programs are a form of highly targeted ration or in-kind transfer scheme. Their main objective is to reduce undernutrition. Government and nongovernmental agencies dis-

Table 6.3   General and targeted subsidies, Jamaica, 1988
(percent)

Item	General subsidy	Targeted subsidy (food stamps)
Cost as share of government expenditure[a]	3.0	1.6
Proportion of transfer going to		
Poorest quintile	14.0	31.0
Richest quintile	26.0	8.0
Transfer as share of expenditure per recipient		
Poorest quintile	2.3	9.5
Richest quintile	0.1	1.0
Proportion of households covered		
Poorest quintile	100.0	51.0
Richest quintile	100.0	6.0

a. Does not include administrative costs.
Source: Jamaica Statistical Institute and World Bank 1988 and 1989.

tribute subsidized or free food through noncommercial channels such as nutrition and health centers for direct or home consumption or through schools to those deemed specifically vulnerable to nutritional and health risks. Children under 5, schoolchildren, mothers, and mothers-to-be are the main beneficiaries. Additional targeting on the basis of growth monitoring, health status, location, or income can be used to identify the neediest members within these groups. The scope of these operations can be expanded to cover wider sections of the population in time of crisis.

The case for food supplementation as an immediate response to severe malnutrition is undeniable. Measuring the benefits of these schemes, however, is far from easy. Anthropometric criteria are often used, but they require careful measurement and may not capture other important benefits (such as increased activity levels) realized by people who are not severely malnourished. Evaluations on this basis have tended to show that the nutritional impact on target groups is limited and is achieved at high cost. Distribution is often indiscriminate, and leakage through food sharing or substitution of home consumption has been estimated to be as high as 30 to 80 percent. Studies of large-scale untargeted school feeding programs show little evidence of significant nutritional improvement—although the effects on enrollment, attentiveness, and school performance may be significant and important in their own right.

Feeding programs are sometimes ineffective because they fail to recognize that malnutrition is not always the result of lack of food. Parasitic diseases and other health problems are often to blame. Undernourished people with acute diarrhea, for example, are able to absorb far fewer nutrients. To be effective, therefore, nutrition programs will frequently need to be combined with health programs—including maternal care, immunization, sanitation, deworming, oral rehydration therapy, and micronutrient supplementation. Education in primary health and nutrition is also crucial where local practices are inappropriate. Education programs in Indonesia and the Dominican Republic have significantly improved nutrition at low cost and without any food transfers. Households may be unable to respond owing to lack of resources. In this case it is appropriate to combine nutrition education with cash or food transfers.

It is often cost-effective to deliver nutrition services through the health care system—provided, of course, that an extensive health system is already in place. In much of Sub-Saharan Africa and South Asia this is not the case, and alternative delivery mechanisms must be sought in the short term. But in Latin America and much of East Asia, provision through the existing social infrastructure can be achieved at relatively low cost. International NGOs such as Freedom from Hunger, OXFAM, and Save the Children (as well as a host of local NGOs) have promoted health and nutrition alongside community development.

Tight budgets and the proven ineffectiveness of indiscriminate provision make it essential to identify those in need. In schemes in Brazil and Bangladesh targeting both by geography and by self-reported income supplements the criterion of a household's containing a "vulnerable" member. Self-selection can be introduced through the choice of food available or through a requirement to attend public clinics that only provide basic services. In Chile changing milk distribution from the workplace to public clinics greatly improved the effectiveness of the program. Individual nutritional monitoring also has a role. In several programs, including the World Bank–assisted Tamil Nadu Integrated Nutrition Program in India and the Iringa Nutrition Program in Tanzania, extensive monitoring of children, carried out within the community, identified the needy and led to heightened awareness of nutritional problems.

In Tamil Nadu targeted food supplements are combined with a range of nutrition and health measures. A 53 percent reduction in severe malnutrition was achieved within the first two years. The program in Tanzania's Iringa Province emphasizes maternal and child health, water and sanitation, household food security, child care, and nutrition education. By providing child care the scheme encouraged the participation of very poor women with heavy demands on their time. Between 1984 and 1988 it reduced severe malnutrition by 72 percent and moderate malnutrition by 32 percent. The program had fairly low costs and benefited from the existence of village organizational structures and Tanzania's well-developed rural health care infrastructure. Bangladesh's Vulnerable Group Development Program broadened its emphasis on food supplementation for poor, nutritionally vulnerable women and children to include women's training centers and shelters. It is currently exploring savings and credit schemes.

Thus, delivering basic services through existing health care systems can be highly cost-effective. This approach has been successful in removing basic deprivations in countries as diverse as Chile, China, Costa Rica, Cuba, Jamaica, Korea, and Sri Lanka.

Food policies in famines

Public policies in food trade and distribution can play an important role in a system of famine prevention. Areas facing a bad harvest often see food prices spiral as traders anticipate scarcity. Food-grain markets have often overreacted to impending shortages. For example, in the 1974 famine in Bangladesh, rice prices increased sharply even before floods caused supplies to decline. Public distribution from stocks or imports can stabilize prices and avert potentially disastrous drops in the purchasing power of the poor. In 1984 the Kenyan government responded swiftly to early signs of a shortfall by organizing commercial food imports. These arrived three months before food aid did, just as domestic stocks of maize were exhausted. Zimbabwe relied heavily on its own stocks. Botswana and Cape Verde made use of food aid; Cape Verde sold the food on the open market to finance public employment programs.

Food security need not imply distribution of food through public channels. Private trade can often help in stabilizing prices and distributing supplies. Holding large food stocks can be more costly than relying on external trade—although this depends on a country's foreign exchange position and on how quickly trade can respond in an emergency. Buffer stocks in key locations to bridge the gap before imports arrive may be the best option. In the longer term better internal food mar-

Box 6.3 Drought relief in Africa: food interventions in Botswana

Like many other African countries, Botswana had to cope with episodes of severe drought in the 1980s. Unlike some other countries (for example, Ethiopia, Mozambique, and Sudan), it has succeeded, through appropriate policies, in avoiding the worst effects of famine.

During the 1979–80 drought, relief in Botswana relied almost entirely on transporting food aid into famine-affected areas and distributing it to the destitute. Because of logistic difficulties, this approach was unsuccessful. Beginning in 1980 Botswana implemented a broad, integrated program for drought relief and recovery that combines food supply management, employment generation, and agricultural assistance.

Effective food supply management lies at the core of the program. Botswana received large amounts of food aid in 1982–87, but its relief efforts did not depend on the timely arrival of these supplies. Large-scale imports of food from South Africa were combined with support for rural incomes through public works and grants. Private traders and retailers were used to distribute food. Food prices remained broadly uniform across the country during the drought period.

''Take-home'' rations were distributed to all households that contained children under 10, pregnant and lactating women, and destitutes. The government set up a special trucking operation to supply maize to remote areas. Between one-third and two-thirds of the population received free rations during the drought. Intensive feeding was provided for malnourished children at health facilities, and a feeding program for primary school children was maintained throughout. Health measures, including efforts to provide a clean and dependable supply of water, were also important.

Despite large decreases in domestic food production, the program was effective: the percentage of children who were undernourished had fallen by 1986 to less than predrought levels (see Box figure 6.3). There were no deaths from starvation.

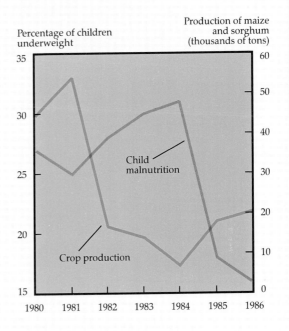

Box figure 6.3 Child malnutrition and crop production in Botswana, 1980 to 1986

Note: The percentage of children underweight, defined here as the percentage of children age 0 - 59 months below 80 percent of expected weight-for-age, is used as an indicator of malnutrition.

The reporting system for underweight children changed at the end of 1984. As a result, the subsequent drop in malnutrition may be slightly overaccentuated.

Source: Morgan forthcoming.

kets and complementary rural infrastructure should reduce the need for government intervention.

Direct feeding and food transfer programs are necessary during crises. Research in Africa and India shows that such measures are especially effective when used in conjunction with efforts to restore the purchasing power of the poor. Cash transfers are often more effective than food rations: cash is faster to move and easier to administer, and it does little or no harm to producers and hence to future food security. But for this approach to work food must be available elsewhere in the affected country, and trade and markets have to work reasonably well (Box 6.3).

Public employment schemes

Rural public employment schemes have two functions. The first is to maintain and create rural infrastructure—examples are road-building, irrigation, soil conservation, and afforestation programs. The second, and the more important in this context, is to reduce poverty by providing employment to those in need. In this vital task, public employment schemes are often cost-effective. Since poor people are willing to work for low wages, public employment programs can offer wages that screen out the nonpoor so that resources can be used more effectively. In two large rural schemes in South Asia—the Maharashtra

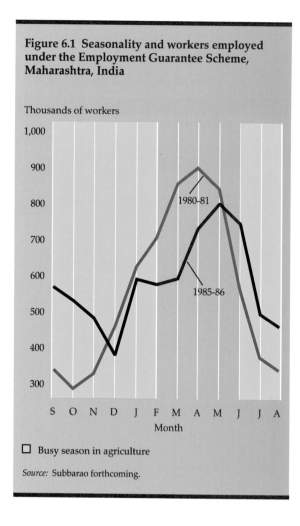

Figure 6.1 Seasonality and workers employed under the Employment Guarantee Scheme, Maharashtra, India

Thousands of workers

1980-81

1985-86

S O N D J F M A M J J A

Month

□ Busy season in agriculture

Source: Subbarao forthcoming.

Employment Guarantee Scheme (EGS) in India and the Food for Work Programme in Bangladesh—the proportion of participants with incomes below the poverty line was at least 90 percent in the early 1980s. The schemes have attracted people who are often excluded from other programs—for example, women and members of scheduled castes in the case of the Maharashtra scheme. Many countries in Latin America and Sub-Saharan Africa run similar programs.

The EGS began in the early 1970s. Its objective is to provide on request employment at a stipulated wage, within fifteen days, and no more than five kilometers away from the participants' home villages. An unemployment allowance is paid when this is not possible. About three-quarters of the EGS budget is spent on wages. The current scheme provides guaranteed employment year-round. Political commitment to the program is firm, and the effect on employment appears to be significant. In 1984–85, 180 million person-days of

employment were provided, representing 3 percent of total rural employment. This has undoubtedly displaced some alternative employment, but the rural unemployment rate in Maharashtra has declined markedly in relation to that of other states. There is evidence that the proportion of poor has also declined faster than would have been expected on the basis of initial conditions and the growth of output.

Are these schemes more cost-effective than food-pricing and food-distribution policies? They appear to target the poor well, but it is important to examine the costs incurred by those who participate. If the participants join a public employment scheme, they are likely to lose some of their previous income. Although such losses are difficult to measure, a study for Bangladesh concluded that the forgone earnings of participants in the Food for Work Programme were equivalent to about one-third of their gross earnings from the program. Net income gains to the poor—and especially the poorest—appear to be a sizable proportion of the governments' wage disbursements.

Since these schemes usually produce economic assets such as roads, they may have second-round effects on the incomes of both the poor and the nonpoor. It is claimed that in Maharashtra a disproportionate share of these extra benefits has gone to the rural rich and that this has been an important factor in achieving political support for the EGS. Other second-round effects are possible. The EGS may bid up wages in general (although it has tried to avoid recruiting during peak periods of agricultural demand). Rural public employment schemes may help labor markets to work better by reducing wage differentials between the sexes and among ethnic groups.

Since the EGS is partly intended to absorb economic shocks, its employment has been highly seasonal and has varied from one year to the next—although this variability has declined as the scheme has grown and the wage rate has risen (Figure 6.1). By providing work, and hence purchasing power, when it is most needed, the EGS has not merely raised average earnings over the course of the year but has also reduced fluctuations from week to week and month to month (Box 6.4). A study of landless households in a drought-prone region showed that families in villages with access to the EGS had incomes that were much less variable than in other villages. The same study examined other income-stabilization policies such as crop insurance and found them less effective. Reducing fluctuations in income can matter as

Box 6.4   At a rural public employment site in India . . .

It is May 1986 in a rural area of Maharashtra State. Lata is one of a group of fifteen women working on a soil conservation project organized by local officials under the state government's Employment Guarantee Scheme. On this project she is shifting soil and doing light digging. Lata is in her mid-twenties, married, with two children, three and seven years old. The youngest child is nearby, playing with other children at the crèche that has been set up at the project site. This allows the eldest child to stay at the school in their village rather than look after her younger brother, as she often does when both parents are working. Lata's husband is doing agricultural work on a nearby farm. Their village is about three miles away. The family is landless, and Lata and her husband earn about 80 percent of their income from casual agricultural labor. Their total income over the past year was about 3,000 rupees, which, for a family of four, is below the rural poverty line in Maharashtra.

The region lacks irrigation, and the land is not very productive. As a result, there is little multiple cropping and the family's work is highly seasonal. Employment is particularly scarce at this time of the year. The family cannot afford to save much and would have a hard time getting by without the EGS. Things will improve in a month or so, when the monsoon crop is cultivated.

Lata seeks EGS work at this time in most years. Her husband does so less often, as he can usually find some work at a better wage rate. For Lata the EGS wage on a typical day is better than she could hope to get in the village now, even if she could find the work. On this job she has been averaging about 6 rupees a day. Lata likes having the wage paid partly in the form of food, since her husband has more say over how cash is spent. She is also pleased that EGS piece rates are the same for men and women; the men in her village usually get more for the same agricultural work.

Like all women on EGS projects, Lata is rarely allowed to do the more strenuous and better-paid jobs, such as breaking rocks for digging irrigation tanks—although she knows she can do much of that kind of work. Because of the complex EGS wage rate schedule, Lata's wages vary from day to day and site to site, even though she is working just as hard. Sometimes there are long delays before projects start and breaks of many days between projects. In the past year an illness kept her out of work for ten days. If she can stay fit, by next month she will have worked about sixty days on EGS projects over the course of the year. That accounts for about a quarter of the paid work she does. With her EGS wages the family buys shoes, clothing, and fuel as well as extra food.

---

much to the poor as raising average incomes. It can prevent acute distress and avoid the need for costly forms of adjustment such as selling productive assets.

Public employment schemes can have a vital role to play in preventing famine. This has long been so in India, and such programs were used extensively in Sub-Saharan Africa in the 1980s. In Botswana (Box 6.5), Cape Verde, and Kenya, strategies based in part on provision of employment have saved many thousands of lives over the past decade. Public employment projects can also soften the impact of recession, as in Latin America during the 1980s. Chapter 7 looks in more detail at how Bolivia, Chile, and Peru implemented their programs.

Perhaps the most important question in designing public employment programs is whether to provide an employment guarantee. A guarantee improves the schemes' effectiveness as a safety net (and may therefore attract more political support from groups that do not currently gain from the program). With a guarantee in place, the number of participants in the program will increase or de-

crease in response to changes in incomes from other sources; this can serve as an early warning of impending crises, such as famine. Some say that the EGS (which offers a guarantee) has helped to mobilize the rural poor as a political force. In Maharashtra the guarantee has helped to develop backward and resource-poor areas, where the demand for jobs is often highest. And it has also acted as a check on the power of local officials, who might otherwise extract side payments from workers.

The main drawback of a guarantee is its implications for the budget. The government can still keep its long-term financial commitment to the program within limits, provided that it can set the wage rate at an appropriate level. But this is not always possible. The Maharashtra scheme is now required to pay wages at the statutory minimum rates, which are higher than market rates. This requirement implies substantial budgetary outlays and potentially high social costs in lost output from alternative employment.

In Maharashtra the EGS is largely financed by taxes on the more prosperous groups in the urban

Box 6.5 Drought relief in Africa: public employment in Botswana

The food interventions under the Drought Relief Programme in Botswana that were discussed in Box 6.3 were complemented by the Labor-Based Relief Programme (LBRP), which provided the rural poor in drought-stricken areas with opportunities for earning cash income on village-improvement projects. Although the program fell short of offering guaranteed employment, it did provide employment for between 60,000 and 90,000 persons each year during the drought period. Wages were set high enough to provide a meaningful return yet low enough so as not to attract the relatively well-off. Village committees identified projects and selected participants, more than 80 percent of whom were women. It has been estimated that LBRP projects replaced almost one-third of the losses in rural incomes caused by crop failures between 1983 and 1985.

In addition to stabilizing incomes and generating purchasing power, the program protected rural assets: the poor did not have to sell cattle or other assets to survive. Furthermore, people who might have been forced to migrate were able to stay. The percentage of traditional household farms with arable land fell by less than 17 percent, and the total number of households engaged in farming declined by less than 5 percent. The productive value of the works created was considerable. Other measures, including distribution of free seed and grants for destumping, clearing, and plowing arable land, facilitated the transition from relief to recovery.

Taken as a whole, the Drought Relief Programme has been successful in preventing human suffering and preserving the productive potential of the rural economy in the midst of a severe and protracted crisis. Although Botswana is rich in comparison with other Sub-Saharan African countries, the critical element in the program's success was the government's commitment to protecting the poor. The Drought Relief Programme has become part of the election platform for the ruling party, whose constituency is found mainly in rural areas. Components of the drought program—food distribution, for instance—have become permanent features of the benefits entitlement system. This means that the institutions and infrastructure will already be in place when drought threatens again.

---

sector. Because the EGS is seen as one way of reducing the migration of rural laborers to Bombay, urban groups have not opposed this method of raising funds. Other schemes, as in Bangladesh, have used foreign food aid and have paid wages in kind. In Cape Verde, as already noted, proceeds from food aid sold on the open market have been used to run the programs. Donor restrictions on the monetization of food aid may prevent governments from taking this route and may reduce cost-effectiveness. For example, rural public employment schemes financed with food aid may not have access to other funds for necessary nonlabor inputs and materials. (This was an issue in Bangladesh in the 1980s.) Still, the role of foreign aid in financing these programs, particularly in periods of stress, should be developed.

If public employment programs are to act as a form of insurance, the government—like any insurer—must be willing to pay up when things go wrong. Governments are in a better position to cover this risk than are poor households. Any scheme, however, should clearly be consistent with long-term budgetary requirements.

A further policy issue in the design of the schemes is their use of nonlabor inputs. The rule followed by the EGS, for example, is that wages must account for at least 60 percent of variable costs. This has sometimes made it difficult to find suitable projects. For example, the materials for a sealed road will cost more than the rule allows, yet unsealed roads are soon washed away. If longer-lasting assets—many of which would help the poor—are to be created under the programs, such restrictions may have to be relaxed. It must be kept in mind, however, that creating the asset is not the main objective: public employment schemes that seek to reduce poverty directly need to be more labor-intensive than a conventional calculation of economic benefits would dictate.

Projects will be all the more successful if they create or maintain assets that are especially beneficial to the poor. Rehabilitation of agricultural land, reforestation, and erosion control all benefit the poor in environmentally degraded regions, both in the short and in the long term. Public employment schemes are commonly used in various African countries—including Ghana, Kenya, Lesotho, Malawi, Mozambique, Tanzania, and Zimbabwe—to build and maintain infrastructure that will improve the quality of life of the poor.

Caring for those left out

Some of the poor will not be adequately reached by the policies discussed so far. For example, concern for the aged and infirm in developing countries is increasing. This is partly because of a shift in demographic profiles—the population is aging in large parts of the world, including Latin America, China, and South Asia—and partly because of a weakening of traditional family- and community-based social security arrangements. The aging of the population in many developing countries will continue. Not all old people are poor, but provision for the elderly poor is an increasingly important issue.

Beginning around the turn of the century, the rise of a large industrial labor force led to the evolution of social security systems in developed countries. Benefits are provided to the elderly, the disabled, surviving spouses, and children through a combination of social insurance (such as pensions) and social assistance (for example, health services). The revenue base is wide, with contributions from workers and employers; coverage is almost universal; and the scale of benefits has been significant, accounting for 15 to 25 percent of GDP in most OECD countries in the late 1970s. Reductions in the incidence of poverty in developed countries, particularly among the elderly, have been strongly linked to the growth of these systems.

Attempts to transplant such systems to developing countries have, however, met with little success. Latin American countries have had the longest experience with formal social security, and even there the programs have failed to reach many needy elderly people and other poor individuals. By and large, coverage has been limited to people employed in the formal sector in urban areas. Chile and Costa Rica are exceptions: both have well-organized urban and rural labor markets and a strong political and social commitment to social welfare systems.

The best policies for protecting the elderly poor and others who are left out will vary from country to country. In Chile and Costa Rica universal coverage is feasible, and other countries with similar characteristics would be well advised to adopt such programs. In Eastern Europe the large size of the wage employment sector suggests that formal social security will have a big role in reducing poverty among the aged and those unable to work. But these cases are not typical of the developing world. In most poor countries formal social security would fail to reduce the worst poverty, since many among the very young and aged poor, the sick, and the disabled would not qualify for benefits. Where formal schemes are already in place or are being introduced, it is important to ensure that

their financing does not become a burden on the truly poor.

A more promising approach for some countries involves transfers based on indicators of need that can be monitored through local health care and community-based systems. Preventive and basic health care could be provided to the elderly and infirm poor and could be supplemented by cash or in-kind transfers when necessary. Self-selection in attending local clinics will achieve a degree of targeting. On the whole, such arrangements are rare, but there are some examples. In rural China, for instance, the community has a moral responsibility for providing basic necessities to elderly people without relatives and to widows and orphans, and the central government helps poorer areas carry out this duty. China also has "houses of respect" for those without relatives who are not capable of living alone. And in some Islamic countries religious land and wealth taxes have been used to finance assistance to those identified as needy at the local level. In India some states administer pension schemes for the elderly and for destitute widows. In Kerala State agricultural workers over 60 with incomes below a specified level receive pensions. Verification is done by local community committees that include representatives of minority groups. In countries in which the aged and disabled poor are concentrated in the agricultural and informal sectors, a well-developed public health care system, coupled with state support for developing and fostering local and community provision, may be the best answer.

The role of transfers and safety nets

This chapter began by identifying two broad groups in need of special attention: those unable to participate in the growth process and those who may be temporarily in danger when events take an unfavorable turn. The first group needs a system of transfers that will ensure them an adequate standard of living. The second group is best served by a variety of safety nets.

The appropriate mix of policies will vary enormously from country to country. It will depend on a host of factors—economic, political, social, and cultural. There are, however, some broad guidelines.

Most food-based policies, including general subsidies, ration schemes, and food stamp schemes, make severe administrative demands on the government. Their potential is greatest in urban areas or in more developed areas that have adequate infrastructure. In all cases, targeting is essential for cost-effectiveness. Targeting can be achieved through the choice of commodity to be subsidized, by locating distribution outlets in poor neighborhoods, or by means of indicators. In South Asia it may be best to reform the present ration systems, building on experience and practical knowledge, rather than to try an entirely new approach.

If the proportion of wage and salary earners is high and acute poverty is usually related to old age, disability, and unemployment, formal social security systems should be developed or their coverage widened. Such systems, which provide old age pensions and unemployment, disability, health, and surviving-spouse benefits, are feasible in many urban areas.

But most of the poor in the developing world live in rural areas, and it is there that the need for effective transfers and safety nets is greatest. For those who are able to work or who have family members who can work, well-designed rural public employment schemes can provide insurance against a risky agricultural environment. The key to such schemes' success in reaching the poor is that they offer unskilled work to anyone who wants it at a wage rate that only the poor find attractive. Thus, targeting is achieved through self-selection by the poor. The infrastructure built and maintained under these programs can yield high economic returns. Links to remote regions and the rehabilita-

tion of environmentally degraded lands are crucial to the reduction of poverty in Sub-Saharan Africa and in the poor rural areas of most other regions. Public employment schemes, appropriately tailored to local conditions, are a promising way to achieve these goals while providing employment opportunities and stabilizing the incomes of groups at risk.

Complementary food-based interventions will be needed for those who are unable to work. Direct food distribution and feeding programs face logistic difficulties but are often the best way to attack severe malnutrition. Special operations to supply staples to the poor in remote areas and other high-risk regions in times of insecurity will continue to be essential in many countries of Sub-Saharan Africa, Latin America, East Asia, and South Asia in the near future. Feeding programs and transfer schemes administered through existing public health systems are also the best way of helping the elderly poor, pregnant women, and children in rural areas. These programs should be integrated with other measures, including improvements in health, sanitation, and education. The development of infrastructure to provide widespread access to basic nutrition, health, and sanitation services should be a top priority for any country.

The 1980s: shocks, responses, and the poor

Many countries experienced macroeconomic difficulties in the 1980s as the debt crisis and international recession brought structural weaknesses into the open. But when structural adjustment issues came to the fore, little attention was paid to the effects on the poor. Macroeconomic issues seemed more pressing, and many expected that there would be a rapid transition to new growth paths. As the decade continued, it became clear that macroeconomic recovery and structural change were slow in coming. Evidence of declines in incomes and cutbacks in social services began to mount. Many observers called attention to the situation, but it was UNICEF that first brought the issue into the center of the debate on the design and effects of adjustment. By the end of the decade the issue had become important for all agencies, and it is now reviewed in all adjustment programs financed by the World Bank. As UNICEF advocated, attention is focused both on how adjustment policies affect the poor and on the specific measures that can be taken to cushion the short-term costs.

Short-run policy and household welfare

The starting point for adjustment is macroeconomic disequilibrium. Whether the causes are external or internal, the usual symptoms are an unsustainable current account deficit, internal financial problems—often linked to high inflation—and slow growth. Adjustment has two objectives: reducing the demand for imports and domestic goods to stabilize economic conditions and restructuring the economy to reach a higher growth path. Many policies, notably exchange rate and fiscal

measures, can have both demand-reducing and restructuring effects. For example, changes in public spending can involve both generalized cuts and deliberate shifts in composition, either to squeeze demand in a particular way or to support economic restructuring.

This chapter is concerned with the effects on the poor of demand-reducing and restructuring policies. Since restructuring calls for a more efficient use of labor, it is fully consistent with the policies advocated in this Report for the long-run reduction of poverty. In Indonesia restructuring policies mainly focused on the industrial sector, whereas in Tanzania the emphasis was on agriculture. But in both cases the changes will help the poor over the medium to long term by promoting the demand for labor.

The short-run effects of adjustment, however, can create difficulties, for two reasons. First, the process of economic restructuring is often sluggish and uneven. Firms and labor markets take time to adjust, and in the meantime economies can suffer higher unemployment or underemployment and labor incomes may decline. Second, demand-reducing measures may be unavoidable, and these are likely to hurt the consumption of the poor and the nonpoor alike. The need for cuts in public spending can lead to a particularly sharp short-run conflict with two essential parts of the strategy advocated in this Report—delivering social services and providing transfers and safety nets.

Changes in the economy affect poor households through two main channels: markets, which determine private incomes and the cost of consumption, and public services. Developments in agricultural and labor markets are the main determinants

Box 7.1 Macroeconomic adjustment, household responses, and the role of women: the experience of an urban community in Ecuador

Studies of the impact of economywide events on households are surprisingly rare. One such study was based on fieldwork in a low-income section of Guayaquil, Ecuador's largest city, between 1978 and 1988. That was a period of boom and bust in the economy, driven partly by changes in the international oil market.

In 1978 the prospects for Indio Guayas, a rapidly expanding community largely made up of households in low-wage employment, looked good. A decade later real wages had fallen by up to one-half, the prices of some foods had soared, and local public health and education services, which had expanded rapidly in the boom of 1978–82, had been cut.

Recession and adjustment had widespread effects. Most men were still working full-time, but at lower wages. In response to falling incomes, the proportion of women working rose from 40 to 52 percent between 1978 and 1988. Many women had reentered the labor force despite having young children at home, and others devoted more hours each day to paid work. Household composition was changing, with married sons or daughters staying in the homes of their parents. Eating habits changed: households consumed much less milk, fish, eggs, and fresh fruit, shifted from potatoes to plátanos, and in some cases cut out meals—first supper, then breakfast. A survey of children at a local health

center in 1988 found that 80 percent were suffering from malnutrition.

In this community, as in many others, women have to balance several roles. In addition to earning income, many women spent more time on community activities, notably to arrange NGO services to replace declining public services. This put greater pressure on their role in the family—only rarely have men taken on more household tasks. For women with young children, going out to work created even more difficulties. There is evidence that more women are taking control of their fertility; in 1988 more than 40 percent had undergone surgical sterilization. Teenage daughters were often a help to mothers, but at the cost of schooling and adequate parental attention. There was concern in the community about teenage boys who were roaming the streets or using drugs. Increased domestic violence, often stemming from disputes over the allocation of men's wages to household needs, was also reported.

Many in this community are worse off than before. Most men earn less in real terms, and many have resorted to temporary migration. Women have been forced to supplement household incomes, adding to the pressures they already faced. Children have often paid the price in poorer nutrition, impaired education, and loss of parental care.

---

of incomes; pricing and subsidy policies influence the prices that households face. Public spending on services, especially in the social sectors, can affect both the current welfare and the human capital of the poor.

The poor are not passive in the face of these developments: they adapt. Households draw down their savings and alter their expenditures—notably, in the direction of cheaper sources of calories. Laid-off workers move into the urban informal sector or return to rural areas. Secondary workers (often women) enter the labor force, usually in relatively low-return activities. And households adjust their relationships with each other. For example, the level of gifts or remittances may change, and families may regroup. Box 7.1 looks at the consequences of recession and adjustment for a low-income urban community in Guayaquil, Ecuador.

Macroeconomic policy and the poor

The evidence on poverty in the 1980s outlined in Chapter 3 suggests that developing countries can

be placed in one of three broad groups. First are the countries that have made progress thanks to steady growth (as in China and India) or to the effective handling of macroeconomic disturbances (as in Indonesia and Malaysia). Second are those in which poverty has worsened because of recession; this group includes most of the severely indebted middle-income countries and Eastern Europe. And third are the low-income countries (most of Sub-Saharan Africa as well as such countries as Bolivia) in which slow long-term growth and macroeconomic crises have led already acute poverty to become worse.

A review of these three groups suggests that the mix and timing of adjustment measures are crucial. The best approach seems to combine two elements: (1) swift action on certain fundamental policies that are designed to provide the context for future growth and (2) macroeconomic policies that can moderate reductions in private consumption in the transition period. Such a mix can support effective adjustment and a relatively favorable outcome for the poor.

Swift action is essential on policies that have to

Box 7.2 Macroeconomic policies and the poor in Ecuador: results from a modeling analysis

Box 7.1 described the fortunes of a poor urban community in Ecuador during the 1980s. That account, however, sheds little light on macroeconomic causes of welfare changes. A model is helpful for understanding these causes. The model used here is designed to take account of both short-run macroeconomic developments and sectoral developments. It is based on a description of Ecuador's socioeconomic characteristics and contains three urban and four rural social groups. Box figure 7.2 shows alternative paths for Ecuador's GDP, private investment, and rural and urban poverty. It compares a "no-shock" case with two different policy responses to an adverse external shock. The shock is similar to the one that Ecuador actually experienced: a combination of a fall in the terms of trade (owing to a decline in the price of oil) and reduced access to foreign financing.

With no external shock, there is steady progress in reducing poverty. Most of this decline occurs in the rural sector, especially through rural-urban migration;

Box figure 7.2 Results of three scenarios for GDP, investment, and rural and urban poverty, Ecuador

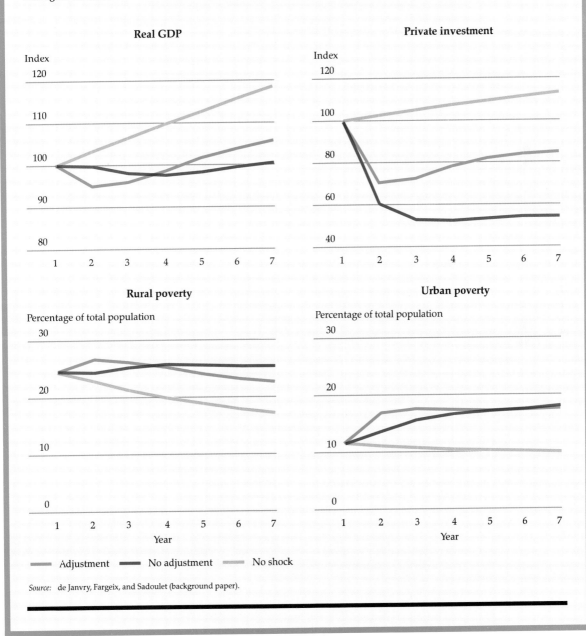

Source: de Janvry, Fargeix, and Sadoulet (background paper).

105

Box 7.2   *(continued)*

urban poverty improves much more slowly.

The "no adjustment" case assumes an essentially passive stance in fiscal and monetary policy but a flexible exchange rate policy. Maintaining public spending moderates the fall in national income in the short run but leads to a real exchange rate depreciation of almost 20 percent, higher inflation, higher real interest rates (because of increased domestic financing of the fiscal deficit), and a 40 percent decline in private investment. This is a pattern seen in many Latin American countries. Welfare losses are moderate in the short run, for both the urban poor (maintaining spending leads to only small declines in labor demand and public services) and the rural poor, who benefit from higher agricultural prices thanks to the depreciation. But the gains are short-lived. The shock reduces GDP in the second and third years, and low investment delays the transition to the new growth path. Poverty worsens steadily.

The "adjustment" case involves fiscal and monetary contraction and substantial depreciation of the real exchange rate, leading to a larger short-run reduction in GDP than in the "no adjustment" case. A decline in investment—private investment falls by 30 percent in the first year—again moderates short-run consumption losses. But the domestic fiscal and monetary situation is more favorable than in the "no adjustment" case,

and inflation is lower. These conditions support a rapid recovery after the third year as the economy shifts onto a new growth path with a stronger orientation toward tradable activities, notably in the agricultural sector. In the short run GDP is lower than in the "no adjustment" case, largely because of reduced demand. But GDP is higher and grows more rapidly in the medium term.

The clear beneficiaries are the rural poor. They are protected in the short run, in relation to their urban counterparts, by the depreciation of the real exchange rate (increased farm incomes partially offset the effects of declining wages), and they benefit in the long run from a growth strategy with a stronger agricultural orientation. After seven years rural poverty is down to its initial level and is falling steadily. Urban poverty rises because of the initial contraction of demand and the associated fall in real wages. Recovery along the new growth path is only a minor moderating force by the end of the period; in Ecuador's case this reflects the high initial proportion of the urban labor force in services and other nontradables—sectors that grow relatively slowly. In the longer term the outcome for the urban poor would be more favorable because of urban-rural migration and the expansion of urban production of tradable goods.

---

do with economic restructuring. Especially important are policies that concern relative prices and the management of public sector resources, including the budget and public enterprises. Poverty cannot be reduced in the long term without broadly based growth. But some policy changes can also help the poor in the shorter term. Exchange rate depreciation and other measures designed to raise agricultural prices will increase the incomes of some of the rural poor, especially small farmers.

Macroeconomic management can soften the impact of adjustment on consumption in several ways. The government might plan for a temporary "pause" in investment, for increased foreign capital flows, and for temporary increases in transfers from the budget. Some of these measures—public spending on investment, for instance—are directly subject to government control. Others, notably private investment, will respond to other aspects of the economic environment. When transfers are used, the budget deficit will be higher than otherwise; this will be justified only if effective action is taken on other aspects of public finance to ensure

that the deficit is consistent with both short- and long-run objectives for inflation, investment, and savings.

Analyzing alternative packages is difficult. One approach is to use a model that consistently incorporates macroeconomic factors, markets, and the determinants of household welfare (Box 7.2). A modeling approach helps to clarify issues but cannot do full justice to the complexities of the real world. In this review we therefore rely more on the differing experiences of the countries in the three groups outlined above.

Adjustment is conditioned by initial macroeconomic imbalances, the depth of structural problems, and the severity of external shocks. The first group of countries, typified by many in East Asia, entered the decade with relatively stable macroeconomies, flexible production and trade structures, and a history of investment in human capital. These countries suffered relatively mild shocks, taking the decade as a whole (Table 7.1). As a result, adjustment there did not require a sustained reduction in demand. Countries in the second group, including many in Latin America, were living beyond their means at the beginning of the decade, and they suffered larger shocks. Their adjustment was inextricably tied up with the reduction of demand. These countries also had a greater need for economic restructuring than the first group. The third group, dominated by Sub-Saharan Africa, started the 1980s with substantial macroeconomic imbalances and severe structural weaknesses, and it experienced the worst shocks. In discussing each of the groups in more detail, it is helpful to focus on one or two representative countries.

The benefits to the poor of effective action

Indonesia and Malaysia represent the first group. In Indonesia progress in reducing poverty was the result of gains across the board; in Malaysia reductions in rural poverty outweighed a small rise in urban poverty (Figure 7.1). These successes are the result of effective adjustment. Both countries acted swiftly on policy fundamentals while relying on changes in investment, debt, and public spending to prevent or moderate declines in consumption.

These countries needed to adjust because of the fall in the prices of oil and other commodities. Once it became clear that the shocks were not temporary, both countries acted decisively to stabilize their economies and establish a framework for economic restructuring. They adjusted their fiscal policies, depreciated their currencies, liberalized their

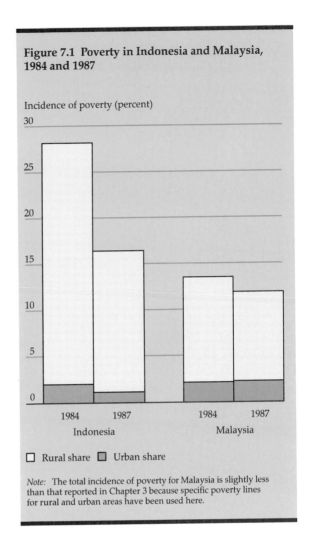

Figure 7.1 Poverty in Indonesia and Malaysia, 1984 and 1987

Incidence of poverty (percent)

Indonesia: 1984, 1987   Malaysia: 1984, 1987

☐ Rural share ☐ Urban share

Note: The total incidence of poverty for Malaysia is slightly less than that reported in Chapter 3 because specific poverty lines for rural and urban areas have been used here.

Table 7.1 External shocks in the 1980s, by region
(percentage of GDP)

Region and country	Terms of trade shock[a]	Interest rate shock[b]	Total
Sub-Saharan Africa	−10.1	−4.4	−14.4
East Asia (excluding China)	−3.9	−4.3	−8.1
China	−0.6	−0.6	−1.2
South Asia (excluding India)	−7.9	−2.3	−10.2
India	−4.6	−1.0	−5.6
Latin America and the Caribbean	−6.3	−4.0	−10.3

Note: Numbers may not sum to totals because of rounding. The table shows changes in external conditions for 1985–88 compared with the average for 1970–80; it thus gives a measure of those shocks that persisted into the second half of the decade. Aggregations by region are not weighted.
a. The difference between changes in export prices and changes in import prices between the two periods. Prices are in dollars and are weighted by the share of exports or imports in GDP.
b. Calculated from changes in the real interest rate weighted by the debt-to-GDP ratio. The real interest rate is derived from the implicit nominal interest rate (the sum of public and private interest payments less interest receipts on reserves divided by total debt) and from U.S. inflation.

trade regimes where necessary, and deregulated their industries. These policies raised the relative price of agricultural goods (Table 7.2), which protected the incomes of farmers in the short run and encouraged continued growth in farm output. The gains were fully passed through in the case of export crop farmers, who are a significant part of the farming population in both countries. Rice farmers in Indonesia also enjoyed significant gains. Well-developed rural infrastructure and markets—the fruits of the policies and investments of previous decades—greatly reinforced the benefits to farmers. The governments gave a high priority to maintaining public infrastructure, despite the need for fiscal stringency.

Although restructuring was effective, demand-reducing policies were also necessary. But these policies had only a moderate impact on private consumption. Investment was high at the beginning of the adjustment, following the increase in revenues from oil exports in the early 1980s, and

Table 7.2 Changes in key variables, Indonesia and Malaysia, 1984 and 1987
(1984 = 100, unless otherwise indicated)

Indicator	Indonesia 1984	Indonesia 1987	Malaysia 1984	Malaysia 1987
GDP per capita	100	107	100	98
Private consumption per capita	100	107	100	85
Fixed investment as a percentage of GDP	22	19	32	23
Real effective exchange rate[a]	100	55	100	76
Agricultural terms of trade	100	116	100	129
Urban wage	100	115	100	97
Rural wage	100	115	100	99

a. In terms of foreign currency per unit of domestic currency.

there was room for a "pause" in investment without a decline to unusually low levels (Figure 7.2). Both countries cut public investment substantially, especially in capital- and import-intensive activities. Private investment declined in response to the contraction in economic activity, tighter monetary conditions, and greater uncertainty. The convincing character of the adjustment policies provided the basis for a recovery in private investment,

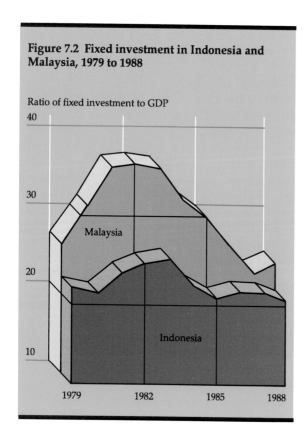

Figure 7.2 Fixed investment in Indonesia and Malaysia, 1979 to 1988

Ratio of fixed investment to GDP

Box 7.3 The poor in Eastern Europe in the years of crisis

The evolution of poverty in Eastern Europe in the 1980s was dominated by macroeconomic developments. As in many highly indebted countries, structural defects were masked by overborrowing in the 1970s. Box figure 7.3 shows the pattern of changes in poverty in Poland and Yugoslavia. Whereas Poland was, until recently, a centrally planned economy, Yugoslavia has followed decentralized socialist policies since the 1950s.

Demand-reducing measures, coupled with halting attempts to reduce subsidies, led to declines in real urban wages in both countries and to increased unemployment in Yugoslavia. This was in spite of substantial declines in investment, which in turn helped protect overall private consumption. Farm incomes fell less sharply because of exchange rate changes (notably in Yugoslavia) and because farm households have greater access to the "second" economy that operates outside official markets. Urban poverty increased substantially.

Although reform was already under way in some Eastern European countries in the 1980s, much more radical measures are being implemented or are under consideration in the 1990s. These steps are likely to put added pressure on urban labor. A substantial shakeout of employment from the state sector will be necessary; the private sectors of these economies, although growing fast, are still very small. Subsidies are a major problem; in 1988 they were 14 percent of GDP in Poland, 12 percent in Hungary, and 9 percent in Yugoslavia. The task is clearly immense. Even so, the principle of effective and early action on policy fundamentals, together with measures to smooth consumption, applies here too.

which was already beginning in 1988. Despite lower receipts from the oil sector, the governments were able to contain the budget deficits through reduced public investment, greater stringency in current spending, and increased revenues (notably, in Indonesia, from higher domestic fuel prices). In Malaysia overall fiscal control proved consistent with holding the consumer price of rice steady in nominal terms, thus increasing the fiscal transfers to rice consumers. Indonesia was able to combine adjustment and an increase in foreign borrowing without losing its creditworthiness. Concessional assistance also made a valuable contribution.

Box figure 7.3 Poverty and wages in Poland and Yugoslavia

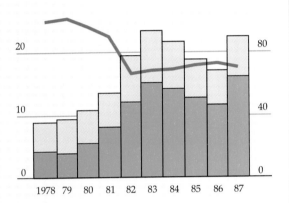

Poland

Incidence of poverty
(percent)

Real wages (1978 = 100)

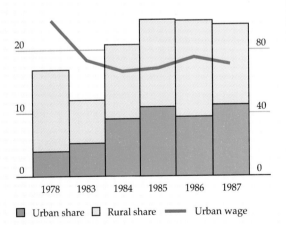

Yugoslavia

Incidence of poverty
(percent)

Real wages (1978 = 100)

■ Urban share   □ Rural share   ▬ Urban wage

Note: For Poland wages are adjusted for shortages of consumer goods in 1980 and 1981.
Source: Milanovic (background paper) and Posarac (background paper).

This mix of measures achieved macroeconomic stability with only moderate losses in welfare and (especially in Indonesia) fostered a political environment that supported strong adjustment. Initially favorable structural conditions helped short-run macroeconomic management as well as restructuring. The three most important factors at the beginning of the decade were a well-managed fiscal policy, high investment, and a relatively low debt burden.

The outcome for the poor was favorable. In both countries most of the poor are farmers, and land distribution was relatively even. Smallholders were able to benefit from higher farm incomes. Urban and rural households that depended on wages were potentially more vulnerable to the price increases associated with devaluation in both countries and with the declines in national labor demand as a result of recession in Malaysia. Wages did fall in Malaysia, causing the small rise in urban poverty seen in Figure 7.1, but in rural areas higher incomes for farm and nonfarm enterprises offset that effect. The decline in real wages was also moderated by a fall in the share of profits, especially in nontradables, and by the policy of stabilizing rice prices. Although public wages declined in Indonesia, the overall buoyancy of the labor market (thanks to deregulation and the rapid growth of nontraditional exports) appears to have raised real wages in the private sector. Survey evidence for Indonesia indicates that the incomes of poor households went up for all sectors and occupations.

The problem of sharply reduced demand

The second group consists of middle-income countries that were living beyond their means at the beginning of the decade as a result of easy borrowing in the past. There, reductions in demand were unavoidable, and there was little scope for using debt to smooth consumption. Because of these unfavorable initial conditions, it was hard to avoid a squeeze on the incomes of the poor in the wake of the debt crisis. In many of these countries the poor depend heavily on the labor market and are therefore vulnerable to a widespread drop in the demand for labor. The group includes much of Latin America and parts of Eastern Europe (Box 7.3). Many are severely indebted. Brazil and Costa Rica can serve as examples. Both experienced a sharp increase in poverty when wages fell in 1983 (Figure 7.3). Costa Rica was able to reverse this trend—by 1986 poverty was below the level of the late

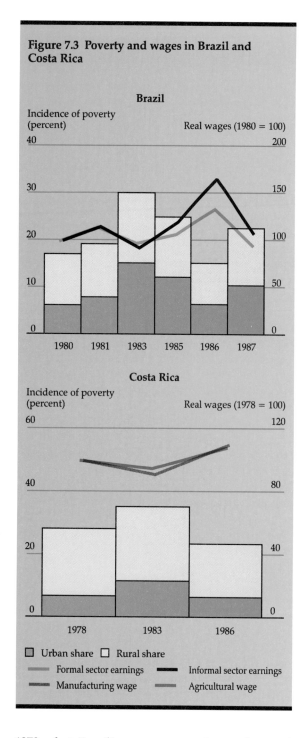

Figure 7.3 Poverty and wages in Brazil and Costa Rica

Brazil

Incidence of poverty (percent)

Real wages (1980 = 100)

Costa Rica

Incidence of poverty (percent)

Real wages (1978 = 100)

☐ Urban share ☐ Rural share

— Formal sector earnings ▬ Informal sector earnings
▬ Manufacturing wage — Agricultural wage

employment stagnated. Policy had much to do with the subsequent outcome. Failure to reduce the deficit undermined the effort to tackle inflation. High domestic borrowing by the public sector raised real interest rates and expanded the share of financial profits in the economy (at the cost of the shares of labor and of nonfinancial profits). In 1986 the Cruzado Plan sparked an economic boom that reduced poverty substantially. But the rise in consumption and wages was not sustainable, owing to rising imports and resurging inflationary pressures. When the inevitable contraction came, poverty rose again. In 1987 the incidence of poverty was higher than at the beginning of the decade. The country faced continuing fiscal difficulties and a larger debt burden. Brazil had undergone the recession of 1983 for nothing.

Brazil's policies led to high inflation and (through widespread import controls) an appreciated real exchange rate, in relation to what it would otherwise have been. Each of these effects had complex implications for poverty. In general, however, they made the poor worse off. The "inflation tax" is probably much more regressive than traditional tax instruments. And greater depreciation would have helped the rural poor—although to a smaller extent than in Malaysia, because more of Brazil's rural workers depend on wages. Evidence from the Philippines, another middle-income country that failed to adjust adequately in

1970s—but Brazil's recovery was incomplete and faltering. The difference can be linked to action on policy fundamentals.

Brazil failed to act decisively on the fundamentals: its public sector deficit (adjusted for inflation) remained high, and its real exchange rate did not change significantly (Table 7.3). The recession of 1983 was probably unavoidable. Poverty increased because of falling wages and incomes in urban and rural areas; informal employment grew as formal

Table 7.3 Changes in key variables, Brazil, 1980 to 1987

(1980 = 100, unless otherwise indicated)

Indicator	1980	1981	1983	1986	1987
GDP per capita	100	92	87	99	100
Private consumption per capita[a]	100	92	89	99	96
Fixed investment as a percentage of GDP	23	23	18	19	22
Public sector deficit as a percentage of GDP[b]	3.6	6.2	4.2	3.6	5.5
Annual inflation (percent)	90	108	141	144	209
Real effective exchange rate[c]	100	92	118	108	100
Formal sector earnings	100	115	98	135	95
Informal sector earnings[d]	32	37	30	53	35

a. Adjusted with the use of the GDP deflator.
b. The public sector deficit is the operational deficit after deducting the component of nominal interest payments that can be attributed to inflation.
c. In terms of foreign currency per unit of domestic currency.
d. The index of informal sector earnings is in relation to the 1980 formal sector wage.

The recession of 1983–85 in the Philippines illustrates the costs to the poor of declining labor demand, lack of real exchange rate movement, and inflation. As in many highly indebted countries, the crisis had its roots in past overborrowing and structural defects. Stabilization began with a nominal devaluation and strict import controls, followed by drastic cuts in public spending and a tight monetary policy. The effects were initially stagflationary: a sharp decline in output, faster inflation, and an appreciating real exchange rate. The currency did not depreciate in real terms until 1986.

How did all this affect the poor? An econometric study that used quarterly data for 1980–86 found that contraction in the labor market and increases in inflation reduce still further the share of the poor in national income; depreciation of the real exchange rate works in the opposite direction. The results indicate that when the inflation rate increases by 10 percent, the share of the poorest fifth of the population falls by 10 percent (other things being equal). By contrast, when the real exchange rate depreciates by 10 percent, the share of the poorest fifth rises by 20 percent. The study also found that lower public spending and higher real interest rates lead to smaller decreases in the incomes of the poor than of the rich.

Why is this? Recession and contraction in the labor market cause declining labor productivity and rising underemployment, which hit the poor hard. Accelerating inflation also hurts the poor because nominal wages fail to keep pace and because the poor lack access to assets that are protected from inflation. The poor gain from real exchange rate depreciation because exports are intensive in unskilled labor (and are often produced by peasants) and because tradables account for only a small part of the consumption basket of most poor people in the Philippines. Government spending mainly benefits the middle classes, and cuts here hurt the poor less.

The country's approach to stabilization was unfavorable to the poor in this period. If the government had chosen not to ration imports, relative prices would have changed more sharply and without such a large rise in inflation. Demand reduction through changes in fiscal and monetary policy was necessary, but greater reliance on changes in relative prices would have moderated the recession and protected the poor. Changes in the composition of public expenditures, although politically difficult, could also have made adjustment less painful for the most vulnerable.

the early 1980s, supports the view that real depreciation and lower inflation help the poor (Box 7.4). In Brazil and the Philippines alike, high inflation and overvalued exchange rates, combined with general uncertainty, also encouraged capital flight, which benefited the rich and hurt the poor.

Costa Rica stands in sharp contrast to Brazil. It suffered a deeper recession at the beginning of the period but undertook a substantial macroeconomic adjustment. Between 1980 and 1986–87 the government cut its budget deficit from 8 percent of GDP to 2–3 percent, and the real effective exchange rate depreciated by 30 percent. By 1986 output and wages had recovered and inflation had declined. These changes account for the significant improvement in poverty seen in Figure 7.3.

The success or failure of efforts to protect the poor does not depend on whether the government attempts to cushion the decline in consumption during adjustment. The successful and the unsuccessful alike have taken this route. Indeed, in both Latin America and East Asia the counterpart of a cushioned fall in consumption was lower investment (Figure 7.4). But Latin America's investment rate is now 27 percent lower than in the early 1980s—and far below East Asia's. This illustrates

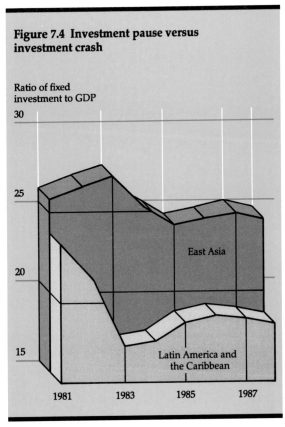

Figure 7.4 Investment pause versus investment crash

Ratio of fixed investment to GDP

East Asia

Latin America and the Caribbean

1981   1983   1985   1987

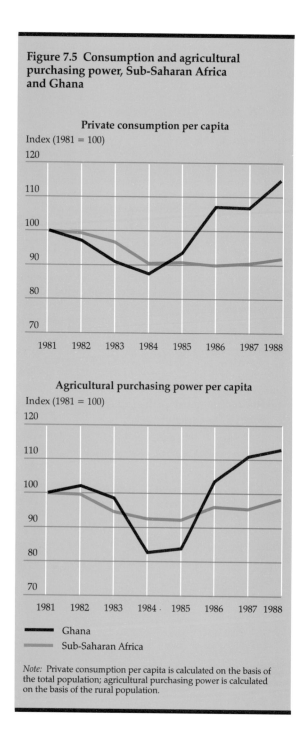

Figure 7.5 Consumption and agricultural purchasing power, Sub-Saharan Africa and Ghana

Private consumption per capita

Index (1981 = 100)

Agricultural purchasing power per capita

Index (1981 = 100)

━━━ Ghana

━━━ Sub-Saharan Africa

Note: Private consumption per capita is calculated on the basis of the total population; agricultural purchasing power is calculated on the basis of the rural population.

the limits of a pause in investment as a way of cushioning consumption: a pause makes sense only if it is followed by an investment recovery that prepares the way for future growth in output—as in Costa Rica and Malaysia. Otherwise a country may start with a smaller reduction in consumption but end with a permanently lower level.

A substantial reduction in demand was unavoidable in Brazil and Costa Rica. As a result, some

decrease in the incomes of the poor was probably inevitable, even with significant declines in investment. As the model described in Box 7.2 illustrated, governments can maintain spending above sustainable levels only temporarily and at great cost. But with appropriate policies, governments can minimize the decline. Demand-reducing measures that moderate inflation and lead to a more competitive real exchange rate hurt the poor less than the alternatives. This is even more the case if the measures are resolute enough to maintain domestic economic stability and thus prevent capital flight. In the 1990s avoiding a further squeeze on living standards will require an increased inflow of capital; where policy reform is on course, this will be warranted. Beyond the short term, however, the only way to help the poor is to bring about sustainable recovery based on a growth path that involves efficient use of labor and widespread investment in human capital.

The problem of severe distortions

Sub-Saharan Africa dominates the group of low-income countries with severe distortions. These distortions were exacerbated by the macroeconomic shocks of the 1980s, and the region suffered badly. By the end of the decade many countries had initiated significant reform programs. As in the other groups, balancing the need to adjust with the need to protect the poor called for a mixture of (in some cases radical) changes in fundamental policy and measures to cushion consumption. Ghana provides an illustration. Like many

Table 7.4 Changes in key variables, Ghana, 1980 to 1988

(percent, unless otherwise indicated)

Indicator	1980–84	1985–88
Average growth rate		
GDP per capita	−4.1	1.7
Private consumption per capita	−3.4	1.6
Agricultural purchasing power per capita[a]	−10.3	10.6[b]
Share of GDP		
Fixed investment	5.0	9.9[b]
Fiscal deficit	4.2	0.5
Foreign aid receipts	0.8	3.8
Average value		
Real effective exchange rate[c]	172	32
Black market premium (percent)[d]	597	62

a. This is the growth in nominal value added in agriculture per capita rural population, deflated by the consumer price index as a rough measure of terms of trade gains for farmers.
b. 1985–87.
c. Based on the official exchange with 1980 = 100 and expressed in terms of foreign currency per unit of domestic currency.
d. The percentage of the black market exchange rate above the official rate—this had declined to 4 percent by 1988.

countries in this group, its economy has suffered from serious distortions, a long-term decline in its infrastructure and institutions, and adverse external shocks. Its experience since the mid-1980s, however, illustrates the benefits of effective policy (Figure 7.5).

In Ghana movement on the policy fundamentals meant large rises in many official prices. These increases were needed to deal with the distortions between official and parallel markets and between agriculture and the rest of the economy (Table 7.4). They were supported by strong fiscal adjustment, with an effort to redirect public spending toward the poor. This change in priorities allowed for the rehabilitation and expansion of some social services. Ghana's approach, in other words, was entirely consistent with the development strategy advocated in this Report. Moderating consumption losses by reducing fixed investment was not an option. Investment was already depressed in the mid-1980s, and it has yet to recover to a level that would be sufficient merely to replace worn-out capital. Foreign aid was therefore an essential element in supporting Ghana's recovery in consumption per capita, which grew at 1.6 percent a year in 1985–88. Continued aid will be necessary if investment is to recover and consumption is to continue to grow in the 1990s.

The changes in official prices in Ghana were similar to those made by many countries in the late 1980s. The alternative, which was commonly followed in the early 1980s, was to avoid changes in nominal exchange rates by rationing imports. This led to appreciation of real exchange rates and expansion of parallel markets for foreign exchange. Attempts to control domestic prices usually led to the dominance of parallel product markets, in which prices were more strongly influenced by the black market exchange rate than by the official rate. This happened, for example, in prereform Ghana and in Tanzania. And in countries in which general rationing and price controls were compounded by other sources of acute instability (such as war, as in Angola and Mozambique) rural markets disintegrated. Farmers were forced to withdraw into subsistence production.

In assessing the impact of adjustment on poverty, the main concern is with rural incomes. Rural areas accounted for 80 percent or more of those in poverty in countries such as Ghana in the 1980s. A strategy of rationing imports and reducing official producer prices clearly hurts rural areas. But how have the radical changes adopted in Ghana and other countries influenced the lives of the rural poor? The answer is that many have been helped, but some have been hurt (Box 7.5).

Box 7.5   The effect of macroeconomic adjustment on farmers in Sub-Saharan Africa

Regina Ofo is a farmer in Bendel State in Nigeria. For her, the structural adjustment program of 1986, which included measures to increase farm prices, has meant something concrete: she is better off. Because she earns more from farming, she can afford to buy new clothes for herself and her two daughters, and she was even able to prepare a Christmas feast for the less fortunate in her village. Babatunde Akinola, a former municipal employee, has also benefited. As a result of the scrapping of the government-run Cocoa Marketing Board in 1986 and the subsequent currency devaluations, independent merchants are offering prices for cocoa that are many times higher than prices in the early 1980s. Mr. Akinola spent his pension rehabilitating his father's cocoa farm in Ondo State. His income has risen substantially. Since 1986 he has built a large house, and he is able to send his children to some of the best schools in Nigeria.

Others have been less fortunate. Rising food prices are not always welcome to farmers who have to buy food part of the time. Before the change in policy, Nse Nnachukwu was able to feed his family of six with produce from his plot and his proceeds from petty trading. But higher prices for food and other basic goods have outrun his income. Furthermore, he cannot respond to higher prices by increasing food production because he lives in Imo State, where land is scarce.

Malawi's reforms, which date back to 1981, have included substantial price increases for maize. These increases have both helped and hurt small-scale farmers. Maize farmers—many of whom are poor—tripled their output in the early 1980s and have helped Malawi revive its export trade. But some lost out in the short run. Dester Mlondo is unable to produce enough maize to feed her family year-round. She has to sell her maize at harvest time, when prices are low, to obtain cash for other household needs. The removal of maize subsidies in 1987 has meant that maize becomes expensive in the months before harvest, when Mrs. Mlondo must buy maize to feed her family.

Adjustment measures that favor agriculture will gradually pull up the whole rural economy. In the shorter term they have helped many farmers but hurt others. Even the losers might soon have been worse off without the reforms—but that is little comfort to people such as Mr. Nnachukwu and Mrs. Mlondo. Measures to protect the most vulnerable during adjustment are discussed further in the section on ''Public expenditure restructuring and the poor.''

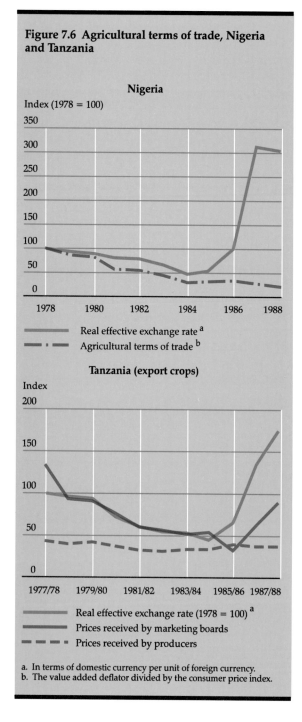

Figure 7.6 Agricultural terms of trade, Nigeria and Tanzania

Nigeria

Index (1978 = 100)

350 — 300 — 250 — 200 — 150 — 100 — 50 — 0

1978   1980   1982   1984   1986   1988

——— Real effective exchange rate [a]
—·—· Agricultural terms of trade [b]

Tanzania (export crops)

Index

200 — 150 — 100 — 50 — 0

1977/78   1979/80   1981/82   1983/84   1985/86   1987/88

——— Real effective exchange rate (1978 = 100) [a]
——— Prices received by marketing boards
— — — Prices received by producers

a. In terms of domestic currency per unit of foreign currency.
b. The value added deflator divided by the consumer price index.

Price reform helps the rural poor by raising their incomes as producers. Sometimes, however, even large changes in the official exchange rate and in prices have failed to have much effect on poverty. Figure 7.6 illustrates the experience of Nigeria and Tanzania. Potential gains from depreciation of the exchange rate have not always been passed on; sometimes, notably in Tanzania, they have been absorbed by inefficient marketing chains. Moreover, many of the poorest farmers produce crops

114

that are little affected by international price and exchange rate changes, and they have suffered from the contraction in economic activity; this was important in Nigeria. Finally, some of the poor in rural areas—in Malawi, for example—are net purchasers of food. These mixed short-run effects do not diminish the case for strong price incentives in agriculture. But they underline one of the central messages of Chapter 4: a coherent overall strategy that includes improved marketing and rural infrastructure is needed to support growth in rural incomes.

Rural areas tend to gain from adjustment, especially in the medium term. Indirect evidence suggests that it is the urban poor who are more at risk. Real urban incomes may fall—but not always because of higher prices, as is often supposed. In many cases poor urban consumers are paying parallel-market prices rather than official prices when adjustment begins, and higher official prices often have neutral, and perhaps favorable, effects on the prices actually paid by the urban poor. The main reason for decreases in urban income is the contraction in the demand for urban labor. In many countries this was unavoidable. Urban spending, especially in the public sector, reached levels in the 1970s that were clearly unsustainable. Even before the adoption of reform measures, both Ghana and Nigeria experienced a radical decline in the position of urban labor. Urban-rural migration has become significant in both countries—three-fifths of all internal migrants in Ghana during 1982–87 came from Accra, the capital.

In this third group of countries the problems of adjustment and poverty are at their most severe. But, as before, the appropriate path is to combine effective action on policy fundamentals with as much support for private consumption as macroeconomic resources allow. Two special factors deserve to be stressed regarding this group. First, price distortions are in many cases still so great that dramatic price reforms may be either neutral or beneficial for the poor, who in many cases have gained little from attempts to control official prices. Second, usually the only short-run option for moderating consumption declines is foreign aid. Given the depth of the structural problems in many countries, a lengthy transition during which aid finances consumption as well as a recovery in investment will probably be necessary.

Macroeconomic policy choices and political feasibility

Protecting the poor through macroeconomic policy has proved easier in some countries than in others. The East Asian countries were in a better position

Box 7.6 The political economy of adjustment

Effective adjustment can ease the burden on the poor in the short run and reduce poverty in the long run. Yet adjustment poses dilemmas for political leaders. The policies often impose costs on constituents—sometimes permanent costs, as when monopoly profits or transfers are cut. They also involve a tradeoff between present and future—a tradeoff that politicians, with elections to win, interest groups to satisfy, and coups to deflect, find awkward. The success of adjustment measures may depend on the feasibility of building coalitions of those who benefit and on careful sequencing with respect to political as well as economic objectives.

Favorable initial conditions, which many East Asian countries enjoy, reduce the political as well as the economic costs of adjustment. The openness of the Malaysian economy, Korea's strong export orientation, and Indonesia's long-standing stress on rural development created important constituencies that quickly benefited from adjustment. This reduced the risks for political leaders and contributed to a virtuous circle of sound policy and satisfactory economic performance.

Severe imbalances and large external shocks increase the temptation to delay adjustment. If people think, as they did in Zambia, that economic difficulties are externally caused and adjustment policies externally imposed, there is a high risk of losing political support. Weak or divided governments and those facing electoral challenges are likely to procrastinate. The governments of Costa Rica and Ghana in the late 1970s and early 1980s, Brazil in 1986, and the Philippines in 1984 all delayed because of political uncertainties. This increased the costs of adjustment.

Some have argued that authoritarian regimes are better at effecting adjustment, since they have no (parliamentary) opposition demanding compromise and they have the luxury of longer time horizons. The governments of Chile after 1973, Korea in the early 1980s, and Ghana from the mid-1980s are examples. But there are many cases of strong reform under democratic accountability—Jamaica in the 1980s, the Philippines in

1986, Turkey in 1983, Costa Rica in the mid-1980s, and so on. In these cases, leaders built on discontent with previous forms of economic management and defended market-oriented policies as "progressive." Under these circumstances the fit between the politics and economics of effective adjustment can be close. Where new economic teams have come to power and the policies of the previous team have been discredited, there is scope for ambitious reform. In such cases demand-reducing and restructuring measures should be introduced as quickly as is technically and economically feasible. Swift action establishes the credibility of the program, limits the opportunity for resistance to coalesce, and increases the likelihood that new leaders will reap the political fruits of reform. These lessons are particularly relevant for the new Eastern European democracies.

A mix of swift action on the fundamentals and efforts to cushion consumption is often justified on welfare grounds. The political case for this approach can also be strong. But there is an important difference between the two rationales. Concern with welfare puts the emphasis on the poor, whereas a preoccupation with politics points the other way, dictating that losses among politically powerful groups (such as formal sector workers) be moderated. In designing programs to compensate losers among the poor, some leakage to such groups may be both economically unavoidable (if the truly disadvantaged are to be reached) and politically advisable.

As painful as they may be, crises can strengthen support for policy change, weaken antireform interest groups, and increase politicians' willingness to rely on technocrats. For those governments that are willing to act, the political risks of undertaking difficult measures can be relieved by outside support. When governments lack the resources to cushion consumption, external capital inflows can play a vital role in the political sustainability of reform. Adjustment in both Ghana and Turkey was facilitated by timely outside support for committed governments.

---

at the beginning of the decade, they reacted swiftly to the shocks by taking macroeconomic and restructuring measures, and they used a pause in investment appropriately to moderate declines in consumption during the transition. Their economies responded powerfully, and the poor were relatively well protected, notably through changes in relative prices. A weaker initial position undoubtedly contributed to the plight of the poor in other areas. But policy was of critical importance, as the progress achieved in Costa Rica and Ghana testifies.

Political factors have a decisive influence on the

choice of policies for dealing with macroeconomic disequilibrium (Box 7.6). Conflicts between political imperatives and the goal of reducing poverty are common. This is especially true when demand-reducing measures are required or when growth-promoting policies help the rural poor but hurt the towns. If experience is a guide, strong executives with a mandate for change seem best placed to pursue reform—and, given the opportunity, it makes sense to act quickly. In any case, external capital flows and measures to compensate losers play a crucial political role as well as a purely economic one.

Public expenditure restructuring and the poor

Macroeconomic and structural adjustment policies can evidently have a significant impact on the poor. In many countries reducing poverty has been facilitated by good macroeconomic policy choices. But many of the poor have suffered and continue to suffer in the wake of the shocks of the 1980s. Even if policy promotes the expansion of labor demand by reducing biases against labor-intensive activities, economies take time to respond, and some groups of laborers or small-scale producers will lose during the transition. Also, dealing with shocks and excessive public debt often involves cuts in public spending, which may hurt the poor directly. Table 7.5 shows how reductions in aggregate spending affected spending on social services in Sub-Saharan Africa and Latin America in the early 1980s. Social spending fell in both regions—but in Sub-Saharan Africa changes in allocation in favor of the social sectors provided a little protection, whereas in Latin America there were actually shifts in composition away from social spending.

With overall public spending under pressure, how far is it possible to protect the poor? There are three main elements in that task.

- *Cushioning consumption.* The poor lack savings and access to credit, and they are ill-equipped to protect their consumption on their own.
- *Maintaining physical and human capital.* Adjustment may mean a long-term setback for the poor if it undermines the resources that enable them to work as small-scale producers and laborers. Health and education, irrigation works, and rural roads are some of the investments that should not be allowed to deteriorate.

Table 7.5 Fiscal contraction and social spending, Sub-Saharan Africa and Latin America

Region and indicator	1980	1985	Change (percent)
Real expenditure per capita (1978 = 100)			
Sub-Saharan Africa			
Total noninterest spending	96	64	−33
Social spending	85	63	−26
Latin America			
Total noninterest spending	110	92	−16
Social spending	107	87	−18
Social spending as a percentage of total noninterest spending			
Sub-Saharan Africa	23	26	13
Latin America	23	20	−16

Note: The figures include all countries in which total real noninterest spending declined during the period.

- *Preparing the way for a recovery in investment.* Although a decrease in public investment is an appropriate initial response to a shock, a subsequent recovery is essential.

There are clearly tradeoffs here, and some of them become sharper in a macroeconomic crisis. Public spending to cushion declines in consumption becomes all the more important, but so does maintaining and expanding the capital stock. Accurate targeting is especially valuable in the face of these difficulties, but by definition, it entails cuts that hurt the rich or middle classes, making it politically as well as administratively awkward. Nevertheless, countries such as Chile and Indonesia have managed to alter their public spending priorities as part of an overall fiscal adjustment.

This section focuses on short-run changes in budgetary expenditures. But changes in government receipts can also be important. In many countries there is a case for reforming the structure of revenues in a manner that both serves long-run efficiency and is broadly progressive; well-designed direct and indirect tax structures and user charges for utilities, energy products, and social services have these characteristics. Where such reforms can be introduced swiftly, increased revenues can reduce the need for spending cuts. A good example is reduced subsidies on petroleum products in Indonesia. Often, however, reform of the tax system takes longer.

Restructuring public expenditure during adjustment

Many countries have cut spending across the board. The Philippines in the mid-1980s is an example. The share of spending on the social sectors, agriculture, and poverty-oriented programs remained roughly constant at about 30 percent of noninterest spending, but because of the overall cutbacks real per capita spending in these areas in 1986 was about two-thirds of the 1981 level. Since overall public spending in the Philippines benefits the nonpoor disproportionately, they also suffered substantial losses from the cuts. But it is the poor who are most vulnerable, and the pattern of spending did not change to protect them.

Indonesia also had to cut its public spending after oil prices declined in the early 1980s. Between 1982–83 and 1987–88 its real public spending fell by 17 percent. But despite an 80 percent increase in interest payments, spending to maintain economic and social infrastructure was protected, and transfers to the provinces increased by 29 percent. The reallocation was feasible because of a substantial reduction in development spending and a real decline in the wage bill. Within development spending, resources shifted from import-intensive industry and mining to human resources. The net effect was to increase the employment content of public spending and preserve adequate resources for maintaining and selectively expanding social and economic infrastructure. The Indonesian government has traditionally avoided explicit transfers, but shifts of public spending into activities with a high employment content helped to maintain the incomes and consumption of the poor.

The pattern of spending within sectors is as important as the pattern among sectors. It is often argued that when social spending is cut, services for the poor are cut most. The evidence is inconclusive. In some African countries primary education and health services suffered disproportionately, and the quality of service declined. Cuts tend to bear hardest on supplies and equipment; personnel costs are harder to adjust. (In Cameroon salaries rose to 99 percent of total recurrent health spending in the fiscal squeeze of 1985–87.)

Chile managed to protect services to the poor during its fiscal adjustment. Despite lower public spending on goods and services overall, basic health and child nutrition programs targeted to the poor expanded. This helped to sustain a continued improvement in social conditions in the 1980s, including further declines in mortality rates for children under 5. In education, too, the government maintained quality by ensuring an adequate supply of materials; expenditure on these items rose in real terms despite cuts in total education spending. The government also tilted its spending in favor of primary education. Survey data confirm that this reallocation was progressive. A longer-term reorientation of public spending on education toward the poor continued in the 1980s despite increasing fiscal austerity (Figure 7.7).

Protecting the poor through transfers
in a macroeconomic crisis

Should transfers rise or fall during adjustment? Reducing transfers may seem an obvious part of growth-oriented fiscal adjustment, but it can add to the burden of the poor. The alternative is better targeting, but this too is difficult at the best of times and rarely gets any easier in a macroeconomic crisis. There is some scope, however, for using three sorts of transfer—subsidies, public employment schemes, and compensation for laid-off workers—to help the poor during adjustment.

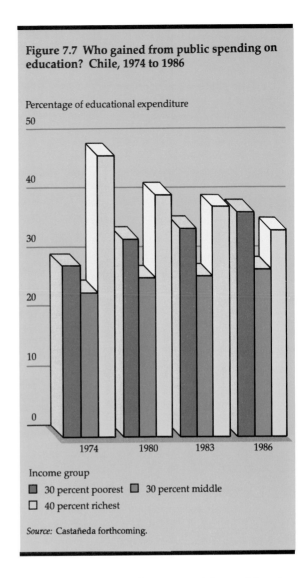

Figure 7.7 Who gained from public spending on education? Chile, 1974 to 1986

Percentage of educational expenditure

Income group
■ 30 percent poorest   ▨ 30 percent middle
□ 40 percent richest

Source: Castañeda forthcoming.

These transfers often form part of the social action programs that many countries have recently introduced (Box 7.7).

SUBSIDIES. General subsidies often benefit the urban poor (and occasionally the rural poor, as in Egypt and in Kerala, India), but leakages to the nonpoor are substantial. As a result, fiscal outlays must be large to have much of an impact on the poor, and the costs of maintaining them during a macroeconomic crisis are high. Better targeting is highly desirable—but difficult.

Jamaica and Sri Lanka, for instance, both shifted from general to targeted food subsidies in the late 1970s and early 1980s. The switch succeeded in reducing aggregate subsidies: in Sri Lanka these declined from 5 percent of GDP in 1975–79 to less than 1 percent in 1984, and in Jamaica they went from a peak of 6 percent of GDP in 1977 to less

The late 1980s saw an increasing number of special multisectoral schemes that sought to mitigate the social costs of adjustment; those in Bolivia, Ghana, and Madagascar are the most advanced and best known. These programs included short-run measures to relieve distress (such as public employment, severance payments, and credit schemes for displaced workers) and other measures (ranging from urban sanitation to provision of textbooks) that form part of a longer-term strategy for reducing poverty. They often involve many donors and local and international NGOs.

Bolivia's Emergency Social Fund (ESF) and Ghana's Programme of Action to Mitigate the Social Costs of Adjustment (PAMSCAD) have entirely different designs. The ESF involved a new institution—essentially a domestic financing agency for projects chosen by local communities and executed by private contractors. Thanks to strong leadership, highly motivated personnel (who received salaries above civil service rates), and minimal government involvement, the scheme was implemented rapidly. By contrast, PAMSCAD works with established government agencies. It includes twenty-three antipoverty interventions that cover public works, credit, training, low-cost water,

health, drugs, nutrition, and shelter, all with a strong orientation toward community involvement and the participation of indigenous NGOs. Problems of foreign and domestic coordination have badly delayed implementation. Both programs have served three important purposes: mobilizing foreign assistance, raising domestic awareness of poverty inside and outside the government, and easing the introduction of difficult adjustment measures.

Neither scheme is an ideal model for other countries, especially in Africa—Bolivia's because of its special, autonomous character and Ghana's because of its complexity. Newer schemes have been less complex than PAMSCAD, but most still have many components and mix short- and long-run measures. This raises problems of coordination and may divert attention and resources from where they are needed most. Sometimes immediate measures to start dealing with long-term problems will be desirable, but they should be compatible with longer-term strategies. The Economic Management and Social Action Project in Madagascar, for example, includes measures to provide drugs and support family planning, but these will feed into longer-term health interventions.

than 1 percent in the mid-1980s. But some of the poor lost out because coverage was incomplete. In Sri Lanka the real value of food stamps declined. Furthermore, there is evidence that income decreased for the poorest fifth of the population, whereas less poor households were protected by the general rise in economic activity and growth in real urban wages. Jamaica did somewhat better, especially in providing food in clinics to pregnant women and children under 5. Self-selection improved targeting for this group.

These and other cases suggest three conclusions. First, when subsidies are already well targeted— say through feeding programs for vulnerable groups that are held in clinics attended by the poor—there is a powerful case for maintaining them. (Chile is again a good example.) In such well-designed systems temporary increases in the ration may be considered. Second, where better targeting is feasible—through food stamps, a shift to goods consumed mainly by the poor, or geographic targeting—it should be pursued. Third, if improved targeting is practically or politically difficult, it may be better to cut subsidies across the board, releasing resources for other programs. The

opportunity cost of subsidies in a period of adjustment is high.

PUBLIC EMPLOYMENT SCHEMES. Most countries that are undergoing adjustment have to cope with a temporary drop in labor demand. Public employment schemes are usually better than subsidies at reaching the poor under these circumstances. Bolivia, Chile, Peru, and, more recently, Ghana and Madagascar have used employment schemes in response to macroeconomic shocks. Similar programs in South Asia provide a safety net for the rural poor. These programs often take the form of traditional public works schemes, but in some countries, including Bolivia, Ghana, and Madagascar, the government acts as a financing agency for labor-intensive projects carried out by private contractors.

The poor may face a temporary decline in real wages owing to reduced demand for labor or shifts in relative prices—higher food prices, for instance. (A study in Bangladesh found that real agricultural wages first fell and then recovered after an increase in rice prices. Full adjustment took three to four years.) Public employment schemes can help the poor in both cases. If targeting is to be through self-selection, however, the wage must be set low.

The public employment programs in Chile and Peru are good examples. At their peak in 1983 Chile's programs provided employment to a remarkable 13 percent of the labor force (Figure 7.8). Afterward, the programs were run down as the labor market recovered. At its peak in 1986 Peru's Programa de Apoyo de Ingreso Temporal (PAIT) employed 3.5 percent of the labor force. Both schemes paid low wages, thus reinforcing targeting through self-selection. In 1986–87 two-thirds of the employees in the Chilean programs were from the poorest 20 percent of the population, and both schemes attracted many women (half of the program's workers in Chile and three-quarters in Peru). Low wages also meant that relatively broad coverage was affordable, especially in Chile, where the total cost of the program was 1.4 percent of GNP at the peak in 1983. Chile's program was financed from domestic sources, partly through lower spending on civil service wages. Peru's program, at its height in 1986, cost only 0.2 percent of GNP and 4 percent of total public investment.

Both schemes were controversial. Chile's aroused much hostility and was viewed by some as a make-work scheme to reemploy sacked public sector workers. Peru's program was popular among workers but became discredited when it was increasingly used for political purposes. Nevertheless, both programs successfully targeted the poor and provided social security for the unemployed during the recession.

Bolivia's Emergency Social Fund (ESF) included employment measures with similar objectives but with a different design: a special agency, substantial donor finance, and the use of private contractors to hire construction workers at market wages. It succeeded in channeling donor finance to local infrastructure projects, and it softened the decline in activity in an economy that was contracting sharply. It recruited male workers almost exclusively and was much less finely targeted than the Chilean and Peruvian schemes—no doubt because it paid market wages. Fewer than half of the ESF workers came from the poorest 40 percent of Bolivian households.

These cases confirm the potential for public employment schemes, especially those targeted to urban labor markets. But can such schemes reach the rural poor, too? Chapter 6 concluded that a mixed strategy of cash-for-work schemes and measures to increase the availability of food through private and public channels can stop a drought from turn-

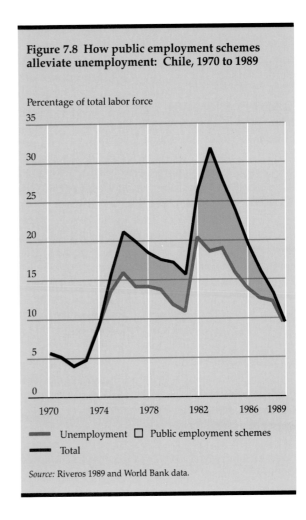

Figure 7.8 How public employment schemes alleviate unemployment: Chile, 1970 to 1989

Percentage of total labor force

Source: Riveros 1989 and World Bank data.

ing into a famine. The temporary shocks to the rural labor market under consideration here are very similar to the reductions in purchasing power that occur in a drought. In one respect adjustment is easier: since the initial source of the shock is not an interrupted food supply, the government can focus on employment without having to worry about the food distribution system. But since there is not a visible crisis, there is less information about destitution and less chance of special foreign assistance. If a government is to use public employment schemes to best effect, it must develop mechanisms for monitoring vulnerable groups, and it must be willing to cut spending that benefits the nonpoor. The demand for work provided through employment schemes can itself supply the government with information on the extent of need.

In Africa donor finance is often available, but the complementary supervisory and material resources are much scarcer than in Latin America and South Asia. It is too early to judge the schemes currently being implemented, although some of them have already proved effective in dealing with drought (for example, in Botswana and Cape Verde in the 1980s). The use of employment schemes to transfer income to the poor should be paralleled by efforts to introduce efficient labor-intensive techniques in infrastructure programs. Ghana provides an example of this parallel approach: a food-for-work scheme run by a local NGO has recently been substantially expanded with the aim of providing employment for the rural poor. Although the organizers expect some benefits in the form of improvements to rural infrastructure, transfers are the main objective. In addition, the Ministry of Transport has adopted efficient labor-intensive methods of building feeder roads. The Ministry works through local contractors, who employ roughly four times as much labor as with other common methods and use 40 percent less foreign exchange than is usual.

COMPENSATING THE LOSERS. The most visible losers in adjustment are often formal sector urban workers who lose their jobs. Governments often target benefits to laid-off workers—for example, through severance or other redeployment payments, special credits, and retraining schemes. Such measures are frequently prominent in social action programs. The newly unemployed often suffer losses, but they are generally not the poorest members of society. Civil servants, for example, are usually well equipped to withstand a spell of unemployment, and in many countries with over-extended civil services, public sector workers have other sources of income. One study of Nigeria found that many laid-off civil servants had maintained their land rights and were able to return to farming (although this was less true of the young).

Reducing public employment is often an essential part of adjustment, especially in Sub-Saharan Africa. But it is politically difficult, and some form of compensation may be necessary. Payment of compensation, however, implies that fewer resources will be available to soften the consumption declines of the poor, protect the capital stock, and support a recovery in investment. By contrast, in Eastern Europe those who lose their jobs are also likely to be among the poor. There, notably in Poland, state employees made up an increasing share of the poor in urban areas in the 1980s. Job losses

in the public sector are likely to be heavy, and they will lead to deepening poverty. Unemployment compensation, which may be politically necessary in the 1990s in any case, will also make sense as a means of reducing poverty.

If compensation is necessary, direct payments are better than special credit and retraining schemes. Special credit programs have been tried in Ghana, Guinea, Mauritania, and Senegal. In general, such programs have had a sorry record and have brought few benefits to the poor (see Chapter 4). Measures to promote investment by small-scale enterprises are an important part of any growth strategy, but they should not be mixed up with compensation schemes. As for training, the emphasis should be on developing a training system that increases the flexibility of skilled labor rather than on special initiatives to equip displaced workers for specific new jobs.

Lessons for adjustment in the 1990s

Even if the 1990s prove less turbulent than the 1980s, many countries will confront the need to adjust. Some will face new adverse shocks, and many will be continuing the process of adjustment that started in the 1980s. The experience of the 1980s suggests that efforts to restructure economies in the wake of a macroeconomic crisis are, by and large, consistent with a medium-term shift toward a pattern of growth and human capital formation that effectively reduces poverty. In the short run, however, some of the poor may lose out. A combination of effective action on the policy fundamentals (notably changes in relative prices to favor agriculture) and efforts to moderate declines in consumption (through a pause in investment, for instance) can help many of the poor in most cases. But shifts in the pattern of public spending toward goods and services consumed by poor people and transfers targeted to them will often be necessary as well. Increased capital inflows can also help to soften the impact of adjustment on the poor, and they could be particularly important in Latin America, Eastern Europe, and Sub-Saharan Africa. But without sound economic policies, increased capital flows can provide only temporary relief. They are no substitute for domestic action to protect the poor.

8 International factors in reducing poverty

Although domestic policies are the essential ingredients of a strategy for reducing poverty, international factors play an important part. This chapter discusses world trade, international debt, and the supply of foreign aid to developing countries. In each case it asks what the implications are for the poor.

Trade and poverty

Trade performance and prospects differ greatly among developing countries. Some middle-income countries have a diversified production base and substantial manufacturing and exports. The newly industrializing economies of East Asia are the most obvious examples, and a number of Latin American countries also fit into this category. Most of these economies, especially those in East Asia, have made substantial headway in reducing poverty. Other middle- and low-income countries have an increasingly diversified economic base but have not yet attained such high levels of development. They include the emerging "second tier" of newly industrializing economies—notably Indonesia, Malaysia, and Thailand—and some low-income countries such as China and India. Many of these, too, have reduced poverty dramatically over the past two decades. Still other countries, including many in Sub-Saharan Africa, produce and export mainly primary commodities and lack a diversified economic base. Very few of them have had much success in reducing poverty.

Given this pattern of trade and poverty, the effects on the poor of changes in international trade relations are likely to differ according to country characteristics. The domestic policies of the developing countries themselves—for example, regarding exchange rates, levels of protection, and other interventions—are largely responsible for the countries' success or failure in world trade. They also have direct and indirect effects on poverty. These and other policies are discussed elsewhere in this Report. This chapter addresses some of the ways in which industrial country trade policies affect the poor in developing countries.

Industrial country protectionism

The developing countries face many obstacles in selling their products abroad. High on the list are the *farm trade policies* of the industrial countries. In OECD countries assistance to farmers through price supports, direct payments, and supply management programs seriously distorts world trade in agricultural commodities. On the whole, these policies raise domestic farm production, leading to more exports, fewer imports, and lower world prices. Price decreases help those developing countries that import the commodities concerned, but they hurt those that are themselves net producers (and are often more efficient producers than their industrial country counterparts).

Nontariff barriers also thwart some agricultural exports from developing countries to OECD markets. Quantitative import restrictions most frequently affect sugar and animal and dairy products, but processed fruits, groundnuts, tobacco, and rice are also common targets. About one-third of the agricultural exports of developing countries appear to be affected by such barriers. The effects can be serious (Box 8.1).

Tariff escalation has a particularly damaging effect

Box 8.1 Industrial country trade policy and the poor in the Dominican Republic

The Dominican Republic demonstrates vividly the impact that industrial countries' trade policies can have on the poor in developing countries. One U.S. trade policy—its sugar import quota—has greatly harmed the country's rural poor, whereas its "807 program," which encourages assembly operations using materials imported from the United States, has apparently helped to generate urban employment.

The U.S. sugar import quota varies with domestic production, but it is largely determined by political interests. The total import quota for all exporting countries was reduced by about 70 percent between 1982 and 1987. The Dominican Republic, which traditionally has had the largest national allocation, saw its quota reduced proportionately. During the same period the European Community (EC), the world's largest sugar exporter, continued to export more than six million tons of sugar a year. The combination of a shrinking preferential U.S. quota and booming, subsidized EC exports wreaked havoc on the world sugar market. Throughout the 1980s the world price was only about one-third of the U.S. protected price. The Dominican Republic is one of the world's more efficient producers of cane sugar, yet it found itself unable to compete at the unprecedentedly depressed world price. At the same time, its access to the U.S. preferential market was shrinking. Its only recourse was to cut sugar production and exports drastically. Four sugar mills were closed by 1990, and production plunged 40 percent following the reduction in the quota.

Since sugar is the main rural economic activity in the Dominican Republic, the repercussions were severe. The average real incomes of cane workers—who were already among the lowest-paid people in the rural economy—collapsed. About two-fifths of the estimated 50,000 expatriate Haitian canecutters lost their jobs, together with perhaps half of their Dominican counterparts. Although most mill employees of the Dominican state sugar company kept their jobs, the field workers had to fall back on subsistence farming, compete for meager wages in the depressed day labor market, or migrate to the towns.

U.S. sugar policy is not, of course, the sole determinant of rural poverty in the Dominican Republic, but it has certainly made development much more difficult. The country's real per capita income has stagnated since the early 1980s, and rural per capita income has fallen by as much as 40 percent. Infant mortality and malnutrition rates, particularly in rural areas, are closer to those prevailing in neighboring Haiti—the poorest country in the Western Hemisphere—than to the average for Latin America. This is in spite of the fact that the per capita GNP of the Dominican Republic is almost equal to the Latin American average.

In sharp contrast, the U.S. 807 program has helped the economy. If an import under the program is assembled from U.S. material (an example would be shirts sewn from U.S. cloth), tariffs are levied only on the value added by the exporter. Since 1980 the number of firms in export processing zones (EPZs), which mainly assemble U.S.-produced parts, has risen from 70 to 330. The firms now account for about half of all manufacturing employment and have since 1980 generated the bulk of the nation's incremental merchandise exports. Employment in EPZ firms—which mainly use semiskilled workers—has increased from 16,000 to 130,000. Since 1980 such firms—stimulated by the U.S. 807 program—have provided one-fifth of the urban jobs created in the Dominican Republic.

U.S. trade policy has substantially altered the shape of the Dominican economy. EPZ exports have replaced sugar as the country's largest foreign exchange generator. Although some new higher-paying jobs have been created for the urban poor, the net effect of the policies has been increased impoverishment in the Dominican Republic.

---

on low-income countries. Industrial countries' tariff duties generally increase—or "escalate"—according to the degree of processing. The purpose of this protection is to retain high value added processing in the developed countries. Products for which escalation is most pronounced include tobacco, rubber, leather, paper, cotton, jute, and iron. Average industrial country tariffs on fruit preparations are double the tariffs on fresh fruit; tariffs on vegetable preparations are more than double those on fresh vegetables. Escalation discourages the processing of commodities in developing countries. More than 70 percent of developing countries' meat, fish, and vegetable exports

are in the primary stage; more than 90 percent of their cocoa and sugar exports are unprocessed. The amount of labor used in processing varies from product to product, but many such activities would be labor-intensive, and low-income countries could have a comparative advantage in them.

Industrial country trade restrictions concerning *textiles and clothing* are another example of how protectionism can hurt low-income countries. Exports of these products by developing countries amount to $30 billion. Much of the world's trade in textiles and clothing is governed by the Multifibre Arrangement, which sets bilaterally negotiated quotas designed to slow the growth of exports from low-cost (mainly developing country) producers (Box 8.2).

The industrial countries have put in place a number of special arrangements with the avowed purpose of stimulating exports from developing countries. The main such arrangement is the generalized system of preferences. With some exceptions, these schemes have done little to offset the damage done by the much broader range of overtly protectionist devices. The benefits from such preferences have been mainly concentrated in a handful of middle-income countries with relatively few poor people (Box 8.3).

Assessing the effects of trade liberalization on developing countries

Developing countries will reap substantial gains from trade liberalization by the industrial countries. It is difficult, however, to make a precise calculation of these benefits. Results would vary from country to country, and many countries would gain only over the long-term. Table 8.1 presents the results for selected developing countries of a simulation exercise showing the short-run changes in exports if trade were completely liberalized.

Table 8.1 The effect of complete trade liberalization on selected countries

Economy	Change in exports (percent)[a]	GNP per capita 1987 (dollars)
High and middle income		
Hong Kong	25.9	8,180
Korea, Rep. of	21.6	2,900
Yugoslavia	14.0	2,480
Dominican Rep.	13.0	740
Tunisia	11.4	1,190
Mauritius	10.5	1,500
Thailand	10.3	850
Morocco	8.9	620
Singapore	7.2	8,010
Brazil	6.8	2,030
Low income		
Sri Lanka	20.9	410
China	13.0	300
Pakistan	10.7	340
Haiti	9.3	360
India	8.6	310
Bangladesh	−1.0	160
Tanzania	−3.3	210
Burundi	−5.5	250
Nepal	−9.6	160
Somalia	−24.3	170

a. Percentage change in value of exports in 1983 attributable to full trade liberalization.
Source: Karsenty and Laird 1987 and World Bank data.

Box 8.2 Bangladesh is not spared from MFA quotas

The emergence of an export-oriented garment industry in Bangladesh—one of the world's poorest countries, with a GNP per capita of only $170 and with 57 percent of its population in poverty—was a great success in the early 1980s. Quota restrictions on Korea's textile exports under the Multifibre Arrangement led Korean exporters to look elsewhere for trade opportunities, and a Korean joint venture was a catalyst in building up an efficient industry in Bangladesh. By the end of 1985 there were about 700 garment factories in the country. From a negligible start around 1980 Bangladesh's garment exports rose to more than $100 million in a couple of years. The garment industry provided employment for many poor people, mostly women. The production and export of garments is a clear example of the kind of efficient labor-intensive activity advocated in this Report.

In 1985 Canada, the United States, and some European countries—notably the United Kingdom and France—imposed export quotas on Bangladeshi garments. About 80 percent of Bangladesh's garment exports were going to the United States at that time, yet their share in total U.S. imports of clothing and textile products was less than 0.5 percent. The initial U.S.

quotas covered only two product groups: cotton coats and men's and boys' shirts. Seven additional groups were brought under quotas in 1986. By 1987 there were thirteen quotas.

Initially, with stocks of garments building up in warehouses, on docks, and aboard ships in U.S. ports, the quotas had a big effect in Bangladesh. Many factories closed. The United States later increased its quotas, and exporters in Bangladesh managed to diversify their markets as well as their products. In 1987 Bangladesh exported over $300 million in thirty-five garment categories, including products made of cotton, wool, and man-made fabrics. These products accounted for nearly 30 percent of the country's exports.

The story does not appear to be over. In 1988 most of Bangladesh's clothing and textile products subject to quotas in the United States were again reaching their quota limits: the overall quota utilization rate was more than 90 percent. The dismantling of the Multifibre Arrangement would reduce the instability in Bangladesh's most important industry, permit the country to fulfill its great potential as a garment exporter, and lead to substantial employment gains for poor workers in the industry.

Box 8.3 The generalized system of preferences: who benefits and how much?

The generalized system of preferences (GSP) is complex. Each industrial country in the scheme—including the United States, Japan, and the members of the European Community—grants its own preferences, and there is considerable variation among them. Most schemes are limited to manufactured exports, but a few cover relatively small quantities of agricultural products. Some donors charge no duties at all on specified products from qualifying countries, and others have duties but at a preferential rate; the least-developed countries are usually given a zero rate.

Most studies agree that the GSP does little to increase trade. It has been estimated that total imports in most preference-granting countries are less than 0.5 percent higher as a result of the system. In the beneficiary countries the effects are generally about 1 or 2 percent of total exports, with important exceptions. The most exhaustive effort to assess the direct trade effects of all the GSP schemes concluded that in 1983 about $6.5 billion of the imports by GSP donors from the preference-receiving countries could be attributed to the various schemes. This represented just 2.3 percent of total imports, which amounted to $280.6 billion.

The gains, with a few exceptions, have been concentrated in a few middle-income economies, particularly Hong Kong, Korea, and Taiwan, China. These econo-mies have received an estimated 44 percent of the total benefit; each gains three times more than the next largest beneficiary, Brazil.

An assessment of the GSP found that of the thirty principal beneficiaries, only four—Bangladesh, China, Haiti, and India—were low-income countries. Except for Haiti, incremental exports attributable to the GSP were tiny.

An effort to work out what the effects would be if GSP schemes were extended without any limitation on product or country coverage found that imports by donors from preference-receivers would increase by about $20.7 billion. But the poorest countries would actually face some loss of trade because they currently enjoy better treatment than other GSP beneficiaries in most markets. The same would also be true of some beneficiaries under the Lomé Convention, a system of trade preferences granted by the EC.

The various GSP schemes may have helped some poor people in the middle-income countries to the extent that the expanded exports were labor-intensive in production, but the poor in low-income countries cannot have gained much at all. The clear tendency to exclude agricultural products from the schemes strengthens this conclusion.

In general, the successful middle-income exporters, which have relatively little poverty, would benefit. The outcome would also be positive for some low-income countries, including those with the largest numbers of poor people, China and India. But for many low-income countries—mainly but not exclusively in Sub-Saharan Africa and mainly exporters of primary products—any benefits from industrial country liberalization would be slow to materialize. Several countries might actually lose in the short run from complete trade liberalization because their existing trade preferences would disappear. Moreover, net food importers would suffer some losses because liberalized trade in agricultural goods would probably raise world food prices.

Much depends on the commodity composition of exports (Figure 8.1). Countries that produce and export mainly primary commodities, such as the low-income African countries, could not be expected to profit much from liberalization in the short run. Tariffs are already low or nonexistent on most such commodities, demand in the importing countries is often insensitive to price, and existing preferences would be lost. Many countries produce few of the goods that might experience a rise in demand as a result of tariff cutting in the Uruguay Round or other forums. And the low-income countries suffer from structural rigidities that make them slow to adopt new patterns of production and exports.

Despite this, industrial country liberalization should continue to be the goal. It would have the following favorable effects.

• Poor people in middle-income countries—who number about 175 million—would probably gain, since many of the exports, especially manufactured exports, that would be stimulated by liberalization are labor-intensive.

• In some sectors, notably textiles and clothing, low-income as well as middle-income countries would be likely to benefit immediately from liberalization. If all bilateral quotas and tariffs under the Multifibre Arrangement were removed, developing countries would realize an estimated benefit of $11.3 billion, or more than one-third of their total exports of clothing and textiles. The expansion of trade brought about by abolition of the Multifibre

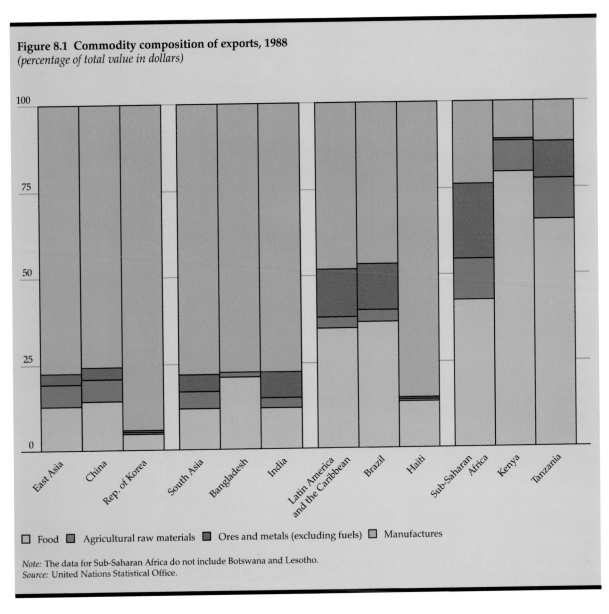

Figure 8.1 Commodity composition of exports, 1988
(percentage of total value in dollars)

☐ Food ▨ Agricultural raw materials ▤ Ores and metals (excluding fuels) ☐ Manufactures

Note: The data for Sub-Saharan Africa do not include Botswana and Lesotho.
Source: United Nations Statistical Office.

Arrangement might raise employment in these countries' textile and clothing industries by 20 to 45 percent. China might gain about $2.3 billion and Bangladesh about $340 million (or 44 percent of its total exports in 1986).

• Trade liberalization would have longer-term effects that would eventually benefit even the low-income countries that are largely dependent on primary commodities. But this would depend on whether these countries adopted policies that would encourage a supply response. If tariff escalation could be substantially reduced, for example, it would be easier to diversify away from primary commodities. One study found that the removal of all industrial country tariffs on processing would increase such activities in developing countries by

almost 80 percent in the case of coffee, 76 percent for wool, and 52 percent for cocoa.

In the end the gains for the poor could be large. But the diversification required in many countries cannot take place overnight. It will take time for the poorest countries to reorient their production and export bases to take advantage of the more liberal trade environment that might emerge from the current round of multilateral trade negotiations. Policy and institutional reforms will be required. These efforts will call for substantial investment, and in the years ahead this is bound to be difficult. External assistance, including debt relief and the provision of concessional finance, will thus have a significant role in these countries for at least the next decade.

Debt and poverty

Limited export earnings are likely to be an important constraint on the development prospects of many countries. Debt burdens are another problem. There are twenty-six severely indebted low-income countries, of which twenty-four are in Sub-Saharan Africa, and nineteen severely indebted middle-income countries. Chapter 1 discussed the debt problems of the second group of countries and the international initiatives for dealing with them. This chapter focuses on the debt burdens of low-income countries.

In absolute terms the debt of the severely indebted low-income countries—$103 billion in 1988—is not high compared with the $516 billion owed by the middle-income group. But some indicators of debt burden are actually much higher for the first group. The ratio of debt to GNP for the low-income countries, for example, was 111 percent in 1988; for the middle-income countries it was 54 percent.

A number of international initiatives for dealing with the debt burdens of low-income countries have been undertaken. Since 1978 many bilateral donors have converted part of the official debt owed by these countries into grants. It is estimated that $3 billion of official debt has been canceled in this way; about $2 billion represented claims on low-income Sub-Saharan African countries. Although this is an important achievement, the canceled debt amounts to only about 3 percent of the total outstanding debt of the low-income African countries at the end of 1988. Moreover, many of these countries will not benefit greatly from further conversions of loans to grants, since most of their concessional loans have already been forgiven.

The agreement reached at the Toronto economic summit in June 1988 provides debt relief on official bilateral nonconcessional debt under the auspices of the Paris Club for severely indebted low-income countries that are undertaking adjustment programs. As of March 1, 1990, the "menu" of options agreed on at Toronto (partial write-offs, longer repayment periods, and more concessional interest rates) had been applied to sixteen Sub-Saharan African countries. The Toronto accords were a breakthrough in dealing with the debt of low-income countries because they officially sanctioned the principle of debt relief. It was acknowledged that these countries could not simply "grow out of debt."

As with the conversions of concessional loans to grants, however, the amount of actual debt relief delivered by the Toronto accords is limited so far. The cash flow savings for twelve Sub-Saharan African countries participating in the Special Program of Assistance in 1989 were about $50 million (in relation to rescheduling under standard terms), or 2 percent of their debt service.

Projections indicate that Toronto-terms reschedulings are likely to have only a small effect on the future stock of debt. If there is no change in the debt-relief options offered by creditors and if Toronto terms are applied repeatedly (that is, if rescheduled debts coming due are again rescheduled on the same terms), the total reduction of debt to all bilateral creditors by the end of 2000 would be about $2.0 billion, or only 11 percent of long-term nonconcessional debt in 1988.

In 1988 interest payments on the external debt of the low-income countries of Sub-Saharan Africa (including Nigeria) totaled about $2.9 billion. This represented about 27 percent of net disbursements of all official development assistance (ODA) to these countries in that year. The ratio of interest payments to pure grants was more substantial—it was 47 percent in Kenya, 52 percent in Ghana, 50 percent in Madagascar, 73 percent in Togo, and 57 percent in Zaire. Such high levels of interest payments severely limit the contributions that aid can make to increasing consumption and investment and reducing poverty.

A number of other low-income countries have had increasing recourse to nonconcessional borrowing as a result of stagnation in aid flows. For example, over the past decade India's ratio of debt service to exports has increased from less than 10 percent to about 30 percent. In 1988 its interest payments on external debt actually exceeded net disbursements of ODA (interest payments were $3.1 billion and net disbursements were $2.1 billion). Pakistan's debt service is about 25 percent of exports. In 1988 interest payments on external debt were about 45 percent of the net disbursements of ODA that it received. If India, Pakistan, and a number of other non-African low-income countries are to avoid the fate of the severely indebted low-income countries, they will clearly need to boost exports substantially. But they will also require continued substantial inflows of external assistance on concessional terms.

Many low-income countries—especially but not exclusively in Sub-Saharan Africa—find themselves with daunting debt and debt service burdens at a time when they need to invest more (in order to improve their long-term prospects) and, simultaneously, to increase the consumption of large numbers of people in poverty. Further efforts by the international community will be needed to reduce their debts and to increase concessional assistance to them. These efforts should be conditional on appropriate policy reform in the countries concerned. Aid and debt relief will be of no avail if appropriate policies are not in place.

Aid and poverty

Official development assistance in 1988 was $51 billion—half the net receipts of external capital by developing countries. For the low-income countries, where most of the world's poor live, aid represents close to 70 percent of net external finance. In many of these countries aid is a much more important source of foreign exchange than are exports (Table 8.2). Given the scale of this effort, it is important to assess the effectiveness of external assistance and to learn from past successes and failures. Aid donors have increasingly recognized this and have been modifying their policies—through improved coordination, for example—to take account of the lessons of experience.

Although many countries have benefited significantly from aid, some of the poorest countries have become trapped in "aid dependency." They

Table 8.2 The relative importance of aid in selected developing countries, 1987

Country	Total aid receipts as a percentage of GNP	Aid receipts from DAC countries as a percentage of exports to OECD markets
Guinea-Bissau	89.3	956.0
Gambia, The	55.6	89.1
Mozambique	51.7	509.2
Chad	28.3	332.2
Malawi	23.6	61.0
Zambia	22.5	53.0
Tanzania	17.0	270.4
Lesotho	15.6	1,041.7
Bangladesh	9.4	105.9
Benin	7.9	108.5
Sierra Leone	7.6	26.4
Kenya	7.5	60.3
Myanmar	3.6	261.6
Pakistan	2.7	18.2
Indonesia	1.9	7.7
India	0.7	11.8
China	0.5	3.9

Source: Organisation for Economic Co-operation and Development 1990.

need aid just to maintain their present low quality of life, when it should go toward improving their long-term prospects. Viewed from the perspective of this Report, another fact about aid is particularly worrying: in many countries aid has done much less than might have been hoped to reduce poverty. In its comprehensive review *Twenty-Five Years of Development Cooperation*, which covers the period 1960–85, the OECD's Development Assistance Committee (DAC) concluded that "the most troubling shortcoming of development aid has been its limited measurable contribution to the reduction—as distinguished from the relief—of extreme poverty, especially in the rural areas of both middle-income and poor countries."

This part of the Report asks why aid has apparently been less effective than it might have been in reducing poverty and examines how future programs can be strengthened and improved. It notes that much aid—especially bilateral aid—has simply not been concerned with economic development or poverty reduction and that although aid specifically devoted to these objectives has had many clear successes, there have also been some problems.

The motives for supplying aid

Aid is provided by three broad groups of donors: bilateral donors, multilateral agencies, and non-governmental organizations. Their respective shares in the total aid receipts of developing countries are shown in Figure 8.2. Box 8.4 discusses some characteristics of the aid they provide.

Bilateral donors, in particular, provide aid for many reasons—political, strategic, commercial, and humanitarian. Reducing poverty is only one motive, and it is usually far from the most important. This has several results.

- Not all aid goes to low-income countries. In 1988 about 41 percent of it was directed to middle- and high-income countries.
- There are great disparities in the per capita allocation of aid, and the most generous per capita allocations do not necessarily go to the poorest countries (see Table 8.3). Despite their poverty, China and India have received almost the least aid per capita.
- Many "aid" programs in donor countries cover an assortment of activities (including commercial and strategic initiatives) which often have, at best, a tenuous connection with development. Only about 8 percent of the U.S. aid program in 1986, for example, could be identified as "develop-

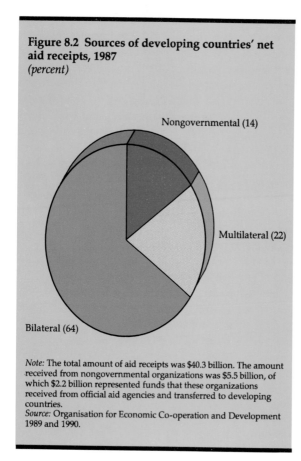

Figure 8.2 Sources of developing countries' net aid receipts, 1987
(percent)

Nongovernmental (14)

Multilateral (22)

Bilateral (64)

Note: The total amount of aid receipts was $40.3 billion. The amount received from nongovernmental organizations was $5.5 billion, of which $2.2 billion represented funds that these organizations received from official aid agencies and transferred to developing countries.
Source: Organisation for Economic Co-operation and Development 1989 and 1990.

ment assistance devoted to low-income countries."

• A substantial amount of bilateral aid is "tied"; recipients are required to buy goods and services from donor countries. Approximately two-thirds of all aid supplied by DAC members is in this category.

• Donors prefer to finance physical capital installations that help their own firms and exporters, and they are reluctant to support the operating ("recurrent") costs of aid-funded undertakings. But many of the initiatives required for reducing poverty in the developing world are in sectors such as health and education that make intensive use of recurrent resources.

In sum, a substantial proportion of aid is provided at least partly for purposes other than to promote development. It stands to reason, therefore, that the impact of aid on poverty has been smaller than it might have been.

Aid for development

When aid has served development, it has done so in two main ways: by providing general budgetary support to countries with balance of payments difficulties and by financing development projects in specific sectors. How far has aid of this sort helped to reduce poverty?

A clear link between aid and the reduction of poverty has been hard to find. The main reason is that aid is only one of many factors influencing poverty and is often far from the most important. Domestic policies, the institutional and managerial capacity of the recipients, and other variables often matter more. Although the overall effects of aid may be unclear, detailed studies of individual countries have highlighted its role in specific instances.

Aid contributed in an important way to growth and declining poverty in Korea, for example. A recent study concluded that aid-financed investments in infrastructure paved the way for the country's successful export-oriented growth in the 1960s, that assistance to education was vital to the development of a literate labor force, and that aid promoted agricultural and rural development.

Korea has moved from an initial heavy dependence on aid toward self-reliance. In the 1950s concessional assistance financed about 70 percent of total imports and accounted for more than 75 percent of all savings. Later, external support from official nonconcessional sources increased; Korea has received a cumulative total of $7 billion in such assistance from the World Bank. The country now receives substantial volumes of private capital from commercial sources.

Table 8.3 Per capita aid receipts, 1988
(dollars)

Country	Aid receipts per capita	GNP per capita
Israel	282.07	8,650
Jordan	108.95	1,500
Gambia, The	102.63	200
Senegal	78.85	650
Zambia	63.73	290
Egypt	29.91	660
Nepal	22.05	180
Ethiopia	21.05	120
Syrian Arab Republic	16.34	1,680
Bangladesh	14.62	170
Pakistan	13.32	350
Myanmar	11.22	. . .[a]
Indonesia	9.34	440
India	2.58	340
China	1.84	330
Nigeria	1.09	290

a. GNP per capita estimated at less than $500.
Source: Organisation for Economic Co-operation and Development 1990 and World Bank data.

Box 8.4 Foreign aid for development

Official aid is disbursed to recipient countries from bilateral and multilateral sources. It comprises grants and loans (with at least a 25 percent grant element) from official sources that have promotion of economic development and welfare as their main objectives. In addition, a great many nongovernmental organizations in industrial countries also provide aid. Measures of aid effort differ considerably depending on the figures used. Among DAC members, the United States is the largest donor in terms of total volume; it provided $10.1 billion in aid in 1988. Japan, with $9.1 billion, was the next largest provider of total aid. But the United States is near the bottom among DAC donors when aid is calculated as a proportion of GNP—the figure is only 0.21 percent. At the other extreme, Norway gives 1.10 percent of GNP. Aid from Arab countries in 1988 totaled $2.3 billion, of which $2.1 billion was from Saudi Arabia and $108 million from Kuwait. Saudi Arabia's ratio of aid to GNP was 2.70, the highest for any donor, and Kuwait's was 0.41, above the average for DAC members (Box figure 8.4).

U.S. aid is mainly directed to countries of key strategic importance such as Egypt and Israel; French and British aid goes disproportionately to former colonies. Some donors—the Nordic countries, for example—have emphasized the reduction of poverty more than others.

Multilateral aid is provided by two main categories of suppliers: the multilateral development banks and the functional agencies of the United Nations system. Net disbursements of concessional assistance from the multilateral development banks totaled about $5 billion in 1988; of this, assistance from IDA accounted for about $3.8 billion. The United Nations assistance agencies, such as the United Nations Children's Fund, the United Nations Development Programme, and the World Food Programme, provided about $3.8 billion.

Nongovernmental organizations in industrial countries supplied about $5.5 billion in financial resources to developing countries in 1987. In addition, they are extremely important in educating the public on development issues.

Bilateral donors are frequently criticized for providing aid for political, strategic, and commercial reasons. But they are able to focus on countries or sectors in which they have particular experience and expertise, and they are often responsible for novel or innovative approaches. Multilateral agencies generally give more weight to developmental criteria, and some play a leading role in the policy dialogue with recipients and in the aid coordination process. But many regard these agencies' approach as excessively technocratic, and the conditionality attached to assistance from the development banks is often a bone of contention. Nongovernmental organizations are particularly adept at local interventions, participatory approaches, and poverty reduction. But they are small, and many have questioned whether they are capable of providing large-scale delivery of services on a sustained basis.

Box figure 8.4 Aid as a percentage of GNP, 1988

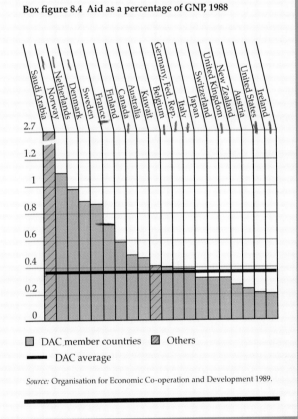

☐ DAC member countries   ▨ Others
━━ DAC average

Source: Organisation for Economic Co-operation and Development 1989.

A number of other countries have moved toward self-reliance, and most of them have also made good progress on poverty. Indonesia, where the headcount index of poverty fell from 58 to 17 percent between 1970 and 1987, is a good example. During that time it received more than $12.9 billion in foreign aid, making it the seventh largest aid recipient. Between 1968 and 1974 all World Bank lending to Indonesia was concessional and was extended through the International Development Association (IDA). Virtually all Bank lending to Indonesia since then has been in the form of nonconcessional loans. The country advanced partly because of its newfound oil wealth, which the authorities managed very well. Nevertheless, there is general agreement that without aid—for agriculture, education, and family planning, for example—the country's efforts to develop and thus to reduce poverty would have made slower progress.

The story is different in other countries—Tanzania, for example. Tanzania's GDP, which had grown by more than 6 percent a year in the immediate postindependence years (1961–67), increased 4.3 percent a year during 1967–73, 2.5 percent during 1973–79, and less than 1.4 percent during 1979–85. All the while, aid poured in. Between 1970 and 1988 the country received about $8.6 billion in concessional assistance.

Tanzania's espousal of African socialism, with its stress on equity and the fight against poverty, appealed greatly to bilateral and multilateral donors. The country's development strategy was based on cooperative "villagization" in agriculture, the provision of health, education, and water to the rural poor, and a headlong drive toward industrialization. But the economywide policies pursued were frequently ineffective; they actually discouraged agriculture and supported large, inefficient state enterprises. The public sector took on a greater role in every aspect of the economy, contributing to severe policy distortions and misallocation of resources. This combination of policies meant that Tanzania's aid-financed initiatives largely failed. Per capita real private consumption has fallen by 43 percent since 1973, and poverty has increased. Whereas Korea and other aid recipients greatly reduced their reliance on aid, Tanzania came to depend on it increasingly. In recent years, however, Tanzania has undertaken significant institutional and policy reforms, and the World Bank and other donors have provided support for these efforts.

Other aid recipients have also traveled the road toward aid dependency. Sudan received about $9.6 billion in foreign aid during 1970–88, making it the ninth largest aid recipient in absolute terms; Zaire received $5.8 billion over the same period. Neither has made much headway on growth or poverty. Mozambique, Niger, Togo, and Zambia are similar cases. Outside Africa, Haiti has also received substantial aid and yet has failed to reduce poverty.

One lesson stands out from this picture: success and failure in aid programs spring from the actions of both donors and recipients. When countries have adopted domestic policies that use aid effectively, and when donors have backed good advice with assistance aimed at overcoming development bottlenecks, the result has been a virtuous circle of growth and diminishing dependence on aid. But

aid recipients have often followed policies that were harmful to both growth and poverty reduction, and donors have not always monitored programs carefully or linked assistance to policy reform.

Projects and poverty

A large part of the aid that flows to poor developing countries finances specific projects. Again, the effect of aid on the poor is difficult to judge. One reason is that sometimes external assistance for specific antipoverty projects indirectly finances other undertakings that may not help the poor and may even hurt them. Nevertheless, observers have generally concluded that projects in at least the following areas have reduced poverty: agricultural research (particularly on crops grown predominantly by the poor) and extension; the introduction of high-yielding varieties of foodgrains in Asia and especially India (the "Green Revolution"); irrigation that benefits many small farmers, especially in Asia; basic infrastructure in rural areas, especially farm-to-market roads in many low-income Sub-Saharan African countries; primary education, basic health care, and nutrition; and relief from natural and man-made disasters.

The World Bank's experience with rural development and urban poverty projects is discussed in Boxes 8.5 and 8.6. Such projects have registered many successes, as have many efforts of other donors. A review of experience reveals, however, that some aid projects intended to reduce poverty have gone wrong, although it is impossible to give a precise number. Among the reasons why some aid projects have been ineffective are the following.

LACK OF COMMITMENT. Some poverty-oriented projects are undertaken mainly to satisfy donors and, often, because the government wants funds for something else. Without a commitment to help the poor, agricultural credit projects intended to benefit small farmers end up making cheap loans available to large farmers, public works projects benefit contracting firms rather than the poor, and the provision of water supply and other basic urban services is diverted to wealthier neighborhoods. Enormous sums have been spent for purposes that have nothing whatever to do with reducing poverty—military expenditures, for example, and lavish "cathedrals in the desert." In 1986 the developing countries spent $159 billion on their armed forces—about five times what they re-

Box 8.5 The World Bank's experience with rural development projects

The World Bank's approach to poverty has varied over the years. During the presidency of Robert S. McNamara (1968–81), the Bank emphasized targeted interventions explicitly designed to benefit the poor in both rural and urban areas. In recent years these projects—mainly begun during the mid- and late 1970s—have been subjected to a number of assessments by the Bank itself. Although it is exceedingly difficult to generalize from a vast body of diverse project experience, several conclusions have emerged.

The basic goal of the Bank's rural development projects was to shift the focus of agricultural development toward smallholder farmers and to increase these farmers' productivity, output, and incomes. Rural development projects usually included agricultural credit to poor farmers, research on crops grown mainly by such farmers, extension services, the construction of infrastructure (primarily rural access roads), and some "directly productive" investments. Many projects had an "area development" focus and were undertaken in areas that suffered extreme poverty even by the rural standards of developing countries. For example, in Funtua State—the site of the Bank's first rural development project in Nigeria—the rural population had the lowest per capita income of any state in the country.

Many projects were "integrated": they involved a specified sequence of actions by a variety of agencies within the recipient countries and by the Bank itself. In fact, the phrase "integrated rural development project" became synonymous in many people's minds with the Bank's whole rural development effort in the 1970s. There were other kinds of rural development projects, too—some nationwide projects, for example, included a substantial component for small farmers or low-income producers but were not targeted on the rural poor in a specific geographic area. Several nationwide agricultural credit projects in Mexico and a nationwide agricultural research and extension project in Brazil are examples.

In 1987 the Bank's Operations Evaluation Department conducted a thorough review of 112 completed rural development projects undertaken during the McNamara years. Total Bank lending for these projects was about $2.7 billion. The review used the simplest and most commonly accepted Bank measure of a project's "success" or "failure"—the economic rate of return. A return of 10 percent normally qualifies as successful. The evaluation found that 63 percent of the projects were successful and that the projects overall had an average rate of return of 17 percent. About 85 percent of the projects appear to have increased food production directly in project areas. Eighty-three projects undertaken between fiscal years 1974 and 1979 are estimated to have benefited about 4.7 million farm families directly. For these projects the cost per beneficiary family at project completion was about $1,100 (as against an estimate of $960 when the projects were first appraised).

By now a number of lessons from these rural development projects have been documented. A few are given here.

• Many integrated projects were too ambitious and complex, and they often placed impossible demands on local leadership and institutions. As a result, they performed worse than projects with simpler designs.

• In many cases the benefits flowing from projects were not sustained beyond project completion. One reason was the Bank's tendency to create independent project management units. Although this may have facilitated implementation over the short term, it was difficult to deal with national bureaucracies once disbursements on projects were completed. Another reason was that project beneficiaries were often not involved in decisions, and they felt that they had little stake in sustaining the projects. Projects that encouraged participation worked better.

• Although there was awareness of the importance of an appropriate policy framework, finance was often granted in unpromising circumstances in the hope that governments would be encouraged to change their policies. As it turned out, the larger policy environment was perhaps the single most important factor in the success or failure of the projects. Government policies on prices, interest rates, and input supplies were frequently at variance with project objectives. Moreover, the projects themselves often proved ineffective levers for influencing overall national policies for agricultural development. Many tended to be successful "enclaves" within national agricultural systems that were still largely inefficient and inattentive to the needs of poor farmers.

The balance sheet of successes and failures for rural development projects during the McNamara years has influenced the Bank's subsequent approaches to rural poverty. Today's projects pay more attention to overall sectoral policies, place greater stress on institutional development, put less emphasis on complex multisectoral approaches, and are increasingly realistic about the feasibility of focusing project benefits precisely on narrow target groups.

Box 8.6 The World Bank's experience with urban poverty projects

In response to the diverse problems of cities in developing countries, the World Bank in the 1970s began to expand its lending for urban development. Lending increased from a modest $10 million in 1972 to more than $2 billion in 1988. Much of this lending has sought to address poverty. In a sample of projects for which poverty data are available, nearly three-quarters had at least 40 percent of their funds allocated to the poor. Almost 60 percent of the Bank's total urban lending since 1972 has gone to shelter operations, although lending for the direct provision of shelter has declined substantially in recent years. Lending for transport and for water supply and sanitation are the other main components of the Bank's urban operations, and there has also been considerable lending for citywide financial and institutional reforms.

As with the rural development programs described in Box 8.5, the Bank's poverty emphasis in urban areas is prominently identified with the McNamara years. The Bank's shelter strategy of the time attracted international attention. It relied primarily on sites and services housing projects and slum-upgrading projects.

In sites and services projects, land parcels equipped with rudimentary urban services were provided to people who then either constructed their own dwellings or contributed to the construction. The projects were designed to reorient typical public sector housing policies in developing countries, which had benefited mainly middle-income households and not the poor. The projects provided beneficiaries with core houses, some infrastructure, social facilities, and employment sites. They also made available financing for plots, houses, and building materials. Typical "upgrading" projects also relied greatly on self-help schemes. They sought to improve infrastructure through a comprehensive package that included water, sanitation, drainage, solid waste removal, roads, and footpaths.

How many of these urban shelter projects were successful? As with rural development projects, it is hard to be precise. About thirteen million households are estimated to have benefited from shelter projects between 1972 and 1989. The Bank's shelter strategy showed that "housing the poor" is possible. The changes in design standards introduced by some of the projects did in fact lower shelter costs—in some cases dramatically. In Zambia, for example, houses in sites and services projects cost less than one-fifth the price

of the least expensive government-subsidized housing. In El Salvador houses in the sites and services project cost less than half as much as the cheapest conventional houses in the public sector.

The shelter projects were, however, not without problems. Assessments of completed projects have provided a number of important lessons.

• The larger policy and institutional environment can hamper urban poverty projects, just as it has rural development projects. The concentration of land in the hands of large property owners often made it difficult to acquire land for housing projects. Zoning regulations also generally discriminated against the poor. The inefficiencies of service-delivery organizations often thwarted efforts to provide municipal services to poor areas.

• It is difficult for urban poverty projects to reach the poorest people. The most comprehensive study conducted by the Bank found that people in the middle rather than the lower part of the urban income distribution tended to gain most.

• Project-level interventions, such as shelter projects, often do not have much influence on the overall urban policies of recipient countries. Some old planning and design criteria gave way to lower-cost solutions, but the laws, codes, and regulations that provide the framework for private housing development were generally left unchanged. The most recent assessment of the Bank's urban projects concluded that in most countries sites and services projects—again like many rural development projects—became "enclaves." Rarely did governments establish programs independent of external donor support. As a result, the direct provision of shelter did not have the broad, long-term impact on the sector that had been expected.

The Bank's new approach to the urban sector stresses broad policy and institutional issues and strives for a sectorwide impact. New priorities include better urban administration, improved mobilization of municipal resources (which may involve the recovery of costs for the supply of services), more efficient urban land markets, and a cleaner urban environment. Project-level interventions, such as the provision of basic urban infrastructure, will continue to be important. But projects will need to pay much greater attention than in the past to these wider issues.

---

ceived in aid. In 1984 they spent almost as much on arms imports as on all their health programs. The continued provision of aid needs to be carefully reexamined if it seems that developing country governments are not serious about reducing poverty.

THE SECTORAL AND MACROECONOMIC CONTEXT. In the 1970s the presumed shortcomings of "trickle-down" approaches to poverty reduction led many donors to emphasize direct, project-specific interventions. Many of these projects were successful. But projects explicitly intended to reduce poverty were often undermined by sectoral and macroeconomic policies such as pricing policies in the agricultural sector and land use policies in urban areas. Moreover, even when projects to reduce poverty were successful on their own terms, many of them were essentially "enclaves" with little influence on national efforts to reduce poverty.

FADDISM. Frequent shifts in donor concerns and policies have often overshadowed the need for stable long-term strategies. A study of six Sub-Saharan African countries concluded that changes of direction were one of the main reasons that aid had not accomplished more. The study found that aid in the 1970s was characterized by "a single-minded emphasis on food security and poverty alleviation that undermined export-crop production and neglected the technological factors affecting improvement in food-crop productivity," whereas in the 1980s there was "a sharp and simplistic swing of donor attention toward efficiency and away from equity concerns." These aid-induced "zigzags" were apparent not only in agriculture but also in education and other sectors. They made projects more complicated, when success in attacking poverty called for sustained attention to a few simpler matters. For instance, the contributions that basic infrastructure can make to reducing poverty in rural areas have often been neglected in the pursuit of a grander vision of "rural development." Faddism also leads to competition among donors for "good" projects. The result has often been that too many donors are doing the same thing in the same country or—even worse—are doing the same thing differently. This wastes effort and means that the total impact of development aid is less than the sum of its parts.

NEGLECT OF INSTITUTIONAL DEVELOPMENT. Reducing poverty through aid calls for more than money; building capacity is crucial. Donors have unduly neglected the institutional and managerial aspects of poverty-oriented projects and programs. The reason is not want of funds; technical assistance accounts for more than a quarter of total aid. Rather, much of this assistance fails to reflect borrowers' priorities. The main form of technical assistance has been the supply of expatriate talent. The United Nations Development Programme (UNDP) estimates that donors support between 75,000 and 100,000 foreign experts a year in developing countries. Donors often prefer to gather these experts in project units outside the normal bureaucratic structure. The result is that aid con-tributes less than it should to institution building in the recipient countries. In recent years attempts have been made to improve this aspect of aid, but much remains to be done.

INADEQUATE PARTICIPATION. Donors and recipients have given too little attention to sociocultural and political factors and have not been sufficiently aware of the important role that the poor themselves can play in initiatives designed to assist them. Evidence supports the view that involving the poor in the design, implementation, and evaluation of projects in a range of sectors would make aid more effective. Involvement of women has contributed to the attainment of objectives in many agricultural development projects in Sub-Saharan Africa; participation of local community organizations has improved performance in many urban poverty projects; organizations of beneficiaries in aid-supported irrigation schemes have made important contributions to the maintenance and operation of project works; and involvement of organized groups of low-income borrowers has facilitated repayment of loans in small-scale credit programs.

Toward a greater role for aid in poverty reduction

This review of successes and failures provides important lessons for future assistance. Although aid will continue to serve many diverse development objectives, an assessment of countries' policies and their likely effects on poverty should play a more important role in allocating aid resources. An aid strategy revised to make external assistance a more effective weapon against poverty should have as its centerpiece appropriately designed support for countries that are pursuing policies intended to reduce poverty. This means looking at the effects on the poor of the whole range of government policies—policies designed to expand the income-earning opportunities of the poor (Chapter 4), extend social services (Chapter 5), effect income transfers and provide safety nets (Chapter 6), and implement structural reforms while incorporating a concern for the effects of these measures on the poor (Chapter 7).

Aid allocation

Such a revised aid strategy has implications for the allocation of aid from both bilateral and multilateral sources. IDA, the World Bank's concessional lending affiliate, already extends about 95 percent of its credits to low-income countries. Poverty—its extent and the efforts that individual countries are making to reduce it—is one of the principal criteria in allocating these resources. In recent years countries that are judged to be doing too little to reduce poverty have received a smaller proportion of resources from IDA. The approach recommended here would reinforce this trend.

Past practice in the World Bank has tended to focus on measuring the effect on poverty of particular projects (by attempting to assess, for example, what proportion of project benefits accrues to the poor). The approach recommended here is economywide. The central question is the impact on the poor of government policies as a whole. The most recent negotiations for the ninth replenishment of IDA stressed the importance of poverty criteria in allocating the organization's resources, and broad assessments of the effects on poverty of general country policies increasingly receive special attention in the economic and sector work undertaken by Bank economists. These efforts should be broadened and intensified so that external assistance from the Bank and other donors can more effectively support the kinds of policies advocated in this Report.

In assessing the overall impact on poverty of country policies and in monitoring their implementation, it is necessary to avoid an excessively mechanistic approach. Decisions will have to be made on the basis of informed judgments concerning the extent to which governments' policies are appropriate for reducing poverty. Other government and donor objectives must also be taken into account. Both the assessment and the monitoring of the influence of government policies on the poor would be greatly facilitated, however, by more systematic compilation of social and income indicators that could measure progress in implementing the two-part approach outlined in this Report. For example, data on per capita expenditures on primary education and nutrition programs could help to measure progress in providing social services to the poor. On the income side, it should be feasible to collect on a systematic and regular basis data on producer prices for small farmers, wages of daily agricultural laborers, urban unskilled wages, and relevant cost of living indices. These would complement direct assessments of the status of the poor, such as those obtained from household expenditure surveys. The World Bank has collected survey data in many countries through its Living Standards Measurement Studies, and additional surveys are in preparation.

Country assistance strategies

A revised aid strategy also has implications for the design of country assistance strategies and the use of a variety of aid instruments. These would vary according to country circumstances; to a large extent they would depend on the domestic policies being pursued by recipient countries.

In countries in which policies are already consistent with the reduction of poverty, assistance to the public sector can be delivered in three ways: balance of payments support linked to the restructuring of public expenditure, "time-slices" of public expenditure programs, and investment projects. The appropriate mix would depend on the most pressing needs of individual countries. Aid for balance of payments support is especially important in debt-distressed low-income countries. It is already a key feature of the Special Program of Assistance for debt-distressed countries in Sub-Saharan Africa that are undertaking adjustment programs. Support for time-slices of public expenditure programs is also under way in a number of cases—for example, in the Bank's support for the education sector in Morocco. If the proposed aid strategy is to be effective, disbursements for both kinds of support would have to be based on agreed changes in the structure of public spending.

A particular use of general budgetary assistance is contingency funding to support safety nets. External shocks and natural disasters often coincide with (or cause) fiscal difficulties. At precisely the time that the need for transfers to the poor is greatest, governments may be least well positioned to supplement or even maintain existing programs. There is a good case for increased external assistance at such times. Emergency food aid already serves this purpose during droughts and famines (Box 8.7). When governments have in place effective safety nets, such as public works schemes, this basic idea could be extended to cover other shocks. Thus, aid programs could include agreements to the effect that external assistance would be increased in the event of adverse macroeconomic shocks to provide temporary relief while efforts to restructure the economy are put in place.

Free-standing investments should also continue to play a central role. Such investments will be vital for building and maintaining basic infrastructure and for undertaking projects in the social sectors. As discussed in Chapter 4, however, the scope for specific investments will vary between, at one end of the range, areas with high productive

Box 8.7 Food aid and poverty

In 1989 food aid to developing countries amounted to approximately $2.5 billion. Food aid constituted 5 to 6 percent of bilateral aid from all DAC members; it represented 12 percent of Canada's aid program and 18 percent of total U.S. assistance. The main multilateral provider is the World Food Programme, which accounts for about 21 percent of all food aid from United Nations sources. Another significant donor is the European Community; in 1989 it contributed 10 percent of all food aid.

A strong argument on behalf of food aid is that much of it represents U.S. and EC production surpluses that would not otherwise benefit developing countries. Since food aid is likely to continue to be a significant component of foreign assistance, it is important that it be an effective instrument for reducing poverty. At the global level allocation of food aid (as of aid in general) could be based more strongly on poverty criteria, as opposed to political considerations. Reform of domestic policies can also greatly improve the effectiveness of this resource in reaching and assisting the poorest within a given country.

Most food aid is provided for general balance of payments support ("program" food aid). Questions about the effectiveness of program food aid mainly concern the appropriateness and efficiency of public sector expenditures. Given good administration and appropriate policies, program food aid can free resources for poverty reduction and other development efforts without interfering with the functioning of local food markets. In India, for example, funds generated by the sale of food aid, together with the associated foreign exchange savings, accounted for 30 to 40 percent of government revenue in the mid-1960s. Some of these resources were used to create the infrastructure for the Green Revolution, which in turn led to considerable increases in food production. Program food aid can

also help to finance measures to protect the standard of living of the poor during adjustment.

Food aid is also provided for emergencies and such specific purposes as food-for-work or supplementary child feeding projects ("project" food aid). An issue with these forms of food aid is whether they are effective in providing transfers and safety nets to the poorest groups. Ensuring food security for the poor is the central objective of such assistance, but this does not necessarily entail physically supplying poor people with food. Simply making more food available in a country can help protect the poor by stabilizing prices, and food aid can be used to finance effective poverty-reducing programs that do not involve food transfers. Direct distribution can, of course, be important in emergency situations where there is a large food deficit and markets are not functioning well. Examples include the famines in Ethiopia, Somalia, and Sudan as well as the severe floods in Bangladesh in 1988, when the World Food Programme coordinated 400,000 tons of food aid through a quick-response capacity developed in dealing with previous floods.

Monetization of food aid through sale in the recipient country is often appropriate and can greatly improve the poverty-reducing potential of this form of assistance. The cash generated can be used to finance such domestic programs as rural employment schemes. Programs of this kind are able to reach the poorest rapidly and effectively. By relying on regular market channels to bring food into deficit areas, they avoid production disincentives and high internal distribution costs. In addition to providing direct assistance, monetized food aid can serve as a resource for investments in human and physical capital and so help to bring about sustained improvements in food security and in the well-being of poor people.

---

potential and, at the other, resource-poor regions that have little productive potential but many poor people.

Since the private sector is central to growth in labor demand, an aid strategy should support this sector. But aid will be effective only if incentives are appropriate. An evaluation of the broad framework of incentives must form an integral part of the overall assessment of country strategies. Balance of payments support can also be important here—provided that it is linked to macroeconomic management that facilitates adequate private investment. Aid can be used to reduce the demand placed on the banking system by the public sector, and this in turn will ease financial pressures on

private investment. It will also continue to have a role in more directly promoting labor-intensive activities in the private sector.

The provision of aid through these instruments cannot, however, be recommended for those countries whose policies are not conducive to meaningful poverty reduction. Yet there are large numbers of poor people in such countries. In these cases difficult decisions will have to be confronted. Directing limited quantities of aid in a highly targeted fashion toward the poorest groups would seem to be the appropriate response. For example, aid could support health clinics that serve poor women and children, immunization programs for children, and well-targeted feeding programs.

Much of the work of agencies such as UNICEF and OXFAM—in Ethiopia, Kampuchea, Sudan, and elsewhere—is precisely of this kind. The World Bank is also undertaking such work, in Zaire, for example. The goal must be to protect the welfare of the poor as far as possible while efforts to reform country policies continue. But large volumes of aid should not go to such countries until policies more consistent with the reduction of poverty are put in place.

Many countries present intermediate cases, and the choices for deploying aid are not so well defined. Again, informed judgments will have to be made on what sorts of initiatives can be effectively supported by development assistance in such countries. If, for example, a country is not providing adequate social services but is doing reasonably well at increasing the incomes of the poor, aid should be directed at improving social services. If policies are not conducive to the productive use of poor people's labor but the provision of social services to the poor is satisfactory, aid can help to maintain the stock of physical capital while efforts to encourage growth-promoting policies continue. So, some assistance to intermediate cases would be justified. But the disbursement of substantial volumes of aid should generally be confined to countries that are pursuing appropriate policies designed to generate income-earning opportunities and are providing social services efficiently to the poor.

Implications for the volume of aid

This strategy implies that an undifferentiated case for more aid cannot be made—whether aid should be increased depends on how many countries are seriously pursuing the reduction of poverty. Nor can it be argued unequivocally that aid should be reallocated from less poor to poorer countries, although the case for disbursing large volumes of aid to middle-income countries is weak. Such a reallocation would again depend on country policies.

There are two important reasons, however, for believing that a more substantial volume of aid will be required in the short- to medium-term. First, the outlook for exports and debt relief is not good for many low-income countries. Second, and more encouragingly, more countries are adopting policies consistent with the priorities urged in this Report. These include the countries eligible for the Special Program of Assistance to Sub-Saharan Africa, and there is guarded optimism that other countries may join their ranks.

At \$51 billion, the total volume of aid in 1988 might seem large in absolute terms. But it is small when viewed in a wider perspective—especially when it is recalled that a substantial part of this amount, mainly that from bilateral sources, is not oriented toward development. Total aid from DAC members amounts to only 0.36 percent of their combined GNP. Moreover, the development assistance provided by industrial country donors in recent years has been only about 5 percent of their military expenditures. These donors spent \$31.6 billion for aid and \$666 billion for military purposes in 1986. In recent years aid has represented only about 1.4 percent of central government expenditures for DAC members (and only about 0.8 percent for the United States). A substantial increase in the resources for fighting poverty in the poorest countries appears entirely affordable. It is a matter of political commitment and the reassessment of donors' priorities.

DAC projects an increase of only 2 percent a year in real terms in its members' aid over the medium term. This would yield aid of \$64 billion in 2000, but it means that the growth of official development assistance would be slower than the growth of members' GNP, which is estimated at about 3 percent in this Report. The ratio of aid to GNP would decline even further.

This chapter has stressed that in the longer term the progress of developing countries—including their progress in reducing poverty—will demand substantially more reliance on the countries' own domestic resources and on their income from foreign trade and considerably less dependence on external official support through aid. But economic self-reliance is still far off for many poor countries. Real growth in aid of only 2 percent a year is an unacceptably weak response to the challenge of global poverty. The international community needs to do better—much better. At a minimum, it should ensure that aid does not fall as a proportion of donors' GNP. A 3 percent annual increase in aid between now and 2000 would produce a total amount of \$73 billion in 2000. Preferably, donors should aim much higher. Aid could reach \$108 billion in 2000 if donors with aid-to-GNP ratios of less than 0.5 increased their aid to that proportion and those with ratios of more than 0.5 maintained their current performance. Attainment by all donors of the widely accepted international target of ODA as 0.7 percent of GNP (with those donors having already attained the target remaining at their current aid ratios) would increase aid to \$144 billion. Moreover, if increases in aid volume were accompanied by significant reallocations toward countries that have policies geared toward the reduction of poverty, the effects on the external resources available to those countries could be even more dramatic.

The goal must be to make aid a more effective weapon in the war against global poverty. This entails challenges for donors and recipients alike.

Donors must be prepared to supply substantial volumes of aid to countries that are serious about reducing poverty. Recipients must increasingly demonstrate that seriousness. Together they can learn from past successes and failures and make aid a more effective instrument for reducing poverty in the future.

9

Prospects for the poor

In the coming decade 850 million people will be born in the developing world. The chance that an individual will be born poor and will grow up in poverty will depend mainly on the region of the world in which he or she is born. But this does not mean that economic policy is unimportant—far from it. Policy choices by domestic governments and the international community can make a critical difference for hundreds of millions of the poor. This chapter examines the prospects for reducing world poverty over the next decade.

Poverty at the end of the century

This Report has emphasized a dual approach to reducing poverty. The elements of this twofold strategy are:

- Efficient labor-intensive growth based on appropriate market incentives, physical infrastructure, institutions, and technological innovation
- Adequate provision of social services, including primary education, basic health care, and family planning services.

In addition, transfers are needed to help those who would not otherwise benefit—the extremely destitute, the sick, and the aged, and safety nets must be provided to protect those most vulnerable to income-reducing shocks.

The projections in this chapter are intended to show what might be achieved if the recommended strategy gained wider acceptance. They do not assume that all countries will fully adopt the strategy. They do assume that where it is in place, countries will persevere and that where it is not, countries will at least move in that direction. More

specific details on domestic policy are discussed below, region by region. The projections are based on the relatively favorable assumptions about global economic conditions described in Chapter 1—growth in industrial countries of about 3 percent a year, falling real interest rates, rising commodity prices over the decade, and a successful conclusion to the trade talks at the Uruguay Round of the GATT and other forums. This is the Report's assessment of the most likely outcome. But fear remains that the problems of the 1980s will persist. The projections should be interpreted, therefore, as indicating what can reasonably be expected. It would be possible to do somewhat better—or much worse.

Table 9.1 shows projected changes in two social indicators: under 5 mortality and primary school enrollment. The projections are based on long-term trends in each region. Under 5 mortality is expected to decline throughout the developing world. In South Asia, for example, the rate is expected to fall dramatically, to 98 per thousand. If the experience of recent years continues, even greater progress can be expected. Moreover, the developing world will have attained or nearly attained universal primary enrollment, although some countries in South Asia and in Sub-Saharan Africa show a significant lag.

In Sub-Saharan Africa a return to long-term trends holds the promise of substantial progress. Under 5 mortality is likely to fall but to remain well above 100. Similarly, the percentage of children attending primary school will increase significantly, although it will still be somewhat lower than in other regions. If these projections are to prove accurate, increased spending on the social sectors

Table 9.1 Social indicators, by developing region, 1985 and 2000

Region	Net primary enrollment ratio		Under 5 mortality	
	1985	2000	1985	2000
Sub-Saharan Africa	56	86	185	136
East Asia	96	100	54	31
China	93	95	44	25
South Asia	74	88	150	98
India	81	96	148	94
Eastern Europe	90	92	25	16
Middle East and North Africa	75	94	119	71
Latin America and the Caribbean	92	100	75	52
Total	84	91	102	67

Note: For under 5 mortality, regional figures are weighted averages, 1985 refers to 1985–90, and 2000 refers to 2000–05.
Source: For 1985, United Nations data and Table 5.1; for projections, World Bank estimates.

will be required. A repetition of the experience of the 1980s would imply much higher mortality among children and lower enrollment rates.

Expanded provision of social services for the poor needs to go hand in hand with a greater emphasis on growth that makes productive use of labor. Table 9.2 shows what the two together might achieve. Between 1985 and 2000 the incidence of poverty in the developing world would fall from 33 percent to 18 percent and the number of poor from 1.1 billion to 825 million. This would be remarkable progress by many standards—but one-seventh of humanity would still be living lives of acute deprivation. Moreover, some regions will progress much faster than others. In Sub-Saharan Africa, the number in poverty will rise by 85 million, to 265 million by the end of the century. The distribution of global poverty will shift dramatically. Asia's share of the world's poor will decline to 53 percent from 72 percent in 1985; Sub-Saharan Africa's will double, from 16 to 32 percent.

If the global economy performs less favorably than forecast, the level of world poverty will be considerably higher. A slowdown in industrial country growth, persistently high real interest rates, rising protectionism, or setbacks in the current debt reduction initiatives could all seriously undermine progress. In that case, by 2000 the number of poor would still be hovering around 1 billion. In most regions the expected improvement in social indicators should prove less vulnerable to external events, but, as in the 1980s, Sub-Saharan Africa may be an exception. If the deterioration in services that occurred in the 1980s were to con-

tinue, the projections of Table 9.1 would not be realized.

Regional differences in poverty

Regional variations reflect differences in the provision of social services, in the rate and pattern of economic growth, and in population growth. They also reflect differences in the structure of poverty and in administrative capacity for dealing with its problems.

East Asia

East Asia has long followed the broad approach to reducing poverty advocated in this Report. By 1985 the number of poor in the region had declined to 280 million, most of whom were in China, and by the end of the decade it is projected to fall to about 70 million. Growth of GDP in the region should remain strong, at almost 7 percent a year. The countries are expected to continue to provide infrastructure and appropriate incentives for efficient, labor-intensive manufacturing, to maintain domestic terms of trade that encourage agricultural growth, and to allocate a substantial share of government spending to investment in human capital. (The Philippines may be an exception; as in the past, macroeconomic imbalances and an unfavorable distribution of land may lead to slow growth and prolonged underemployment.)

Several factors, however, sound a cautionary note. First, since China accounts for three-quarters of the region's population, any setback there will

Table 9.2 Poverty in 2000, by developing region

Region	Incidence of poverty		Number of poor (millions)	
	1985	2000	1985	2000
Sub-Saharan Africa	46.8	43.1	180	265
East Asia	20.4	4.0	280	70
China	20.0	2.9	210	35
South Asia	50.9	26.0	525	365
India	55.0	25.4	420	255
Eastern Europe	7.8	7.9	5	5
Middle East, North Africa, and other Europe	31.0	22.6	60	60
Latin America and the Caribbean	19.1	11.4	75	60
Total	32.7	18.0	1,125	825

Note: The incidence of poverty is the share of the population below the poverty line, which is set at $370 annual income (the higher line used in this Report).
Source: For 1985, Table 2.1; for 2000, World Bank estimates.

have a significant effect on regional poverty. The projected 6.8 percent growth rate of GDP in the 1990s assumes that internal reforms will continue. The projected drop in the number of poor also depends on maintaining the favorable distribution of income that has marked China's development. An erosion of the agricultural terms of trade or a failure of lagging regions to join in growth could compromise China's overall progress, especially in rural areas. At the same time, greater reliance on market forces and decentralization could further undermine the community-level system of health care and social security. The challenge that China faces is to encourage gains in efficiency through market reform while maintaining or replacing social safety nets threatened by reform. If external conditions are unfavorable and internal reforms are not implemented, annual growth is unlikely to exceed 5 percent in the 1990s. This would leave China with 90 million poor by 2000. A fall in the real incomes of the rural poor (caused, for instance, by a shift in relative prices) could easily boost this number to more than 100 million.

A second reason to temper optimism about the region's poor is that the pattern of poverty is changing. Rising incomes and strong employment growth in the middle-income countries of East Asia have meant that the poor are increasingly confined to those groups that are unable to benefit from employment opportunities and rising real wages—notably, the elderly and the infirm. Demographic and social forces are also increasing the need for state provision of health care and safety nets for these groups. Economies such as Korea and Malaysia have the resources and administrative capacity to put social assistance schemes in place, but a higher share of domestic transfers will be needed for this purpose in the future.

Finally, Southeast Asia, in particular, is vulnerable to protectionism in its export markets. In these countries exports are an exceptionally large share of GNP. In several product areas their potential for further growth has run up against industrial country barriers to imports of, for example, garments, shoes, and electronic goods. For East Asia more than any other region, growth prospects and domestic employment opportunities will be improved by further trade liberalization under the GATT.

Sub-Saharan Africa

Sub-Saharan Africa lies at the other extreme. It has the furthest to go in adopting the strategy proposed here, it has faced more severe external problems than most other regions, and its social and physical infrastructures are seriously debilitated. In addition, the region's population is projected to continue growing at more than 3 percent a year for the next decade. Such rapid growth exacerbates the difficulty of eliminating poverty by undermining efforts to increase labor income and increasing the cost of expanding social services.

The sharp rise in poverty projected for Sub-Saharan Africa distinguishes it starkly from other regions. The 3.7 percent annual growth in GDP that underlies the projections is somewhat higher than the average growth achieved over the previous twenty years, but that will be barely adequate to hold living standards steady over the next ten years. In that time span the population will grow by another 165 million, and an additional 70 million people will be living in poverty.

The plight of Sub-Saharan Africa requires a commitment to fundamental changes in domestic policies and development priorities. During the second half of the 1980s many countries introduced major reform programs. These need to be continued and strengthened. In particular, there must be a continued commitment in three critical areas: reducing regional fertility rates, expanding social investment (especially in education and health care), and rehabilitating the physical infrastructure needed to encourage the expansion of agriculture, commerce, and industry. Many of the policies for achieving this objective were described in a recent World Bank report, *Sub-Saharan Africa: From Crisis to Sustainable Growth*. The analysis of future poverty presented here strengthens that report's conclusions.

To see the scale of the task confronting Sub-Saharan Africa, consider what it would take to prevent the number of poor from increasing. Even with a supportive policy environment that includes greater provision of social services and some improvement in income distribution, a growth rate of about 5.5 percent a year—nearly 2 percent higher than the projected rate—would be needed to raise per capita consumption by enough to meet this target. To achieve this, the region would need much more, and better designed, foreign assistance. Such assistance will be effective (and warranted) only if domestic policy is consistent with the reduction of poverty and the development of indigenous capacity.

South Asia

In South Asia there is considerable potential for progress toward reducing poverty, particularly in

India. But there is also a threat of stagnation, especially elsewhere in the subcontinent. Close to half the world's poor live in the region, and what happens to them will go far toward determining the success or failure of efforts to reduce world poverty. Per capita GDP is still low, but it grew at a steady 3 percent during the 1980s and is likely to continue at this rate through the 1990s. If this strong performance can be maintained, the number of poor is projected to fall from 525 million to 365 million.

Poverty in India is projected to fall dramatically. The key to the gains in India will be sustained growth and further internal policy reforms. Fiscal reforms are needed to curb growing government deficits, contain foreign and domestic debt, and ensure adequate savings to support domestic investment. Servicing domestic and foreign debt accounts for a growing share of government spending and may threaten the government's ability to meet its investment targets. If investment remains squeezed by low domestic saving rates and external borrowing, India's growth is unlikely to exceed 2 percent per capita a year over the decade. Such slippage would imply a poverty count of 370 million people by 2000, eroding much of the potential gain.

Additional domestic measures will be needed in the fight against poverty. Further trade liberalization would encourage exports and allow efficient, labor-intensive import substitution. Agriculture needs access to new technology, and rural infrastructure must be expanded and maintained, particularly in lagging subregions. Exports are projected to become a more important source of growth as public spending is trimmed back. Economywide policies must be supplemented with better-targeted interventions. Public works schemes, for example, have proved successful and could be extended and developed.

The prospects for other countries are bleaker, and strong measures are needed to prevent poverty from deepening significantly over the decade. At the projected growth rates, the number of poor in Bangladesh and Pakistan would increase. Although Bangladesh is endowed with fertile land and natural resources, in other respects it resembles Sub-Saharan Africa. Lack of administrative capacity, weak infrastructure, rapid population growth, and highly distorted domestic policies hamper the reduction of poverty. For external assistance to have a significant impact, fundamental efforts are needed to improve aid administration and to direct resources toward improving preventive health care, nutrition, sanitation, and basic ed-

ucation. By contrast, Pakistan has a sizable manufacturing sector, ample administrative skills, and a per capita income twice that of Bangladesh. Despite these advantages, it has made little progress toward improving the social indicators of poverty. Reducing poverty requires a much higher level of investment in social services for the poor.

Aid has generally been used more efficiently in Asia than in Sub-Saharan Africa, but despite the vast numbers of poor, the flow of aid to the region is much smaller in relation to total population or GDP. One important conclusion of this Report is that aid allocations should be based on a demonstrated commitment to the goal of reducing poverty. More aid should be forthcoming where serious efforts are being made to reduce poverty, whether in Africa or in Asia, and the increase should not come at the expense of the other region. Additional aid from industrial countries will be needed.

Latin America and the Caribbean

Nowhere in the developing world are the contrasts between poverty and national wealth more striking than in Latin America and the Caribbean. Despite average per capita incomes that are five to six times those in South Asia and Sub-Saharan Africa, nearly one-fifth of the population still lives in poverty. This is because of the region's exceptionally high degree of income inequality. Raising all the poor in the continent to just above the poverty line would cost only 0.7 percent of regional GDP—the approximate equivalent of a 2 percent income tax on the wealthiest fifth of the population.

Regional prospects for reducing poverty rest heavily on domestic policy reforms in several areas. Credible macroeconomic stabilization measures are of primary importance. Stabilization is a prerequisite for restoring investor confidence, encouraging the return of flight capital, and breaking the cycle of economic crises that has characterized many countries in the region. Policies to promote inequality-reducing growth are equally important. First, reforms to remove biases that favor the use of capital are needed to ensure that future growth will generate productive employment that reaches the poor. This includes reforms in price and financial policy to encourage private investment in efficient labor-intensive and outward-oriented industries. Moreover, since 40 to 50 percent of the poor will still reside in rural areas in the 1990s, the improvements in incentives for agricultural production that occurred in the 1980s need to be complemented by active support for rural development.

Second, there is a need to maintain and in some areas to expand the provision of social services to the poor. Finally, transfers, such as emergency employment schemes of the type undertaken in Bolivia, Chile, and Peru, may be needed to protect the poor, particularly during the stabilization process.

The average GDP growth of 4.2 percent a year projected for Latin America in the 1990s assumes that during the second half of the decade the debt burden will no longer be a serious constraint on regional investment and that programs to restore economic stability will be put in place over the next few years. If, in addition, income distribution improves with growth (as it did in Indonesia and Colombia, for instance, during the 1970s and 1980s), significant progress can be made in reducing regional poverty. The incidence of poverty is forecast to fall from 19 to 11 percent by 2000.

Adverse developments in the global economy, as described in Chapter 1, would darken the outlook for growth and for reducing poverty in the region. If efforts to ease the debt burden failed, terms of trade grew worse, and world demand for the region's exports fell, the result would be to slow growth and probably undermine adjustment efforts. Under these circumstances growth in per capita consumption would not rise above 1 percent, and an additional 25 million people, or 5 percent of the region's population, would be in poverty by 2000. To avert this outcome, political commitment to adjustment programs in the region is needed, along with adequate external assistance and debt relief to prevent the debt crisis from persisting through the 1990s.

Eastern Europe

The condition of the poor in Eastern Europe is unusual because of the state's large role in providing employment, housing, and other services. Poverty is largely an urban problem associated with low real wages and, increasingly, with outright unemployment. In several countries poverty increased during the 1980s. Structural problems accompanied by low productivity growth and chronic material shortages have caused a drop in real wages for a large part of the work force. Although poverty is already serious and threatens to deepen further during the transition to a market-based system, the number of poor in Eastern Europe is much lower than in Sub-Saharan Africa and South Asia.

Per capita GDP growth over the next decade is projected at only 1.5 percent a year, and the incidence of poverty is expected to remain roughly constant at about 8 percent of the population. Two important issues face the region's governments. One is the speed of reform, which will determine the severity of social dislocation and the time required before market reforms boost productivity. The second is the tradeoff between the reduction of fiscal deficits and state interventions—an essential step if markets are to flourish—and the need to maintain state-provided safety nets. A significant part of the work force is likely to be dropped from state employment rolls at the same time as subsidies on food, housing, and services are cut back. Temporary unemployment insurance and worker training programs will therefore be needed.

The potential for raising regional output, productivity, and labor incomes over the medium and long run is enormous. If the institutional and legal transition to a market-based system can be managed quickly and technical and financial assistance (including foreign investment) can be obtained from abroad, consumption growth could be much higher than in the projections. With a broadly unchanged distribution of income, growth in GDP of 4 percent a year over the decade would eliminate absolute poverty.

Middle East and North Africa

Heavy state intervention in domestic markets has also characterized the countries of the Middle East and North Africa, but the challenges facing them differ from those in Eastern Europe. Many North African countries have relied on food subsidies to help the poor, despite ample evidence that subsidies are an extremely inefficient form of transfer. In Algeria, Egypt, Morocco, and Tunisia food subsidies account for a substantial share of the government budget. More cost-effective means of providing transfers to the truly poor are needed. Several countries also have severely distorted domestic markets, persistent current account imbalances (caused by unsustainable fiscal and exchange rate policies), and high debt-to-exports ratios. The prolonged regional conflicts in the Middle East have been extremely costly and have diverted resources from investment and the needs of the poor. Until these conflicts are fully resolved, prospects for the poor will remain bleak.

Assuming that peace comes to the region in the 1990s and that structural adjustment programs are put in place, growth in per capita GDP should average 2.1 percent a year. Despite high population growth (projected to remain at more than 2 percent a year), modest improvements in income distribution and more cost-effective targeting of the poor could hold the number of poor to about 60 million in 2000, the same as in 1985. On less favorable assumptions, the number of poor could rise to about 85 million.

The potential for action

The decade started with momentous changes in the U.S.S.R. and in many Eastern European countries. These may point the way toward a world less gripped by superpower rivalry and more devoted to improving the quality of life. This Report has discussed a quieter but equally momentous change—the steady movement of households out of poverty. Public action has often been immensely effective in supporting this process, but more than a billion people are still poor. In some parts of the world the number in poverty increased in the 1980s.

The projections presented in this chapter are inevitably uncertain, but they do illustrate the benefits that can flow from appropriate public action. Three conclusions are especially clear. First, a less buoyant external environment would place a greater strain on resources in developing countries and would leave many more people in poverty in 2000. Second, a failure to undertake policy reforms, to reduce income inequality, or to safeguard social services and real incomes where progress has already been made would sharply reduce the potential gains. Together, these might stifle all progress toward reducing poverty over the coming decade. Third, the projections show that between 1985 and 2000 the number of poor in Sub-Saharan Africa will rise by perhaps 85 million. Only through exceptionally bold action by the international community and the governments of the region can this be avoided.

Preventing the number of poor from rising in Sub-Saharan Africa while reducing the number elsewhere in the developing world by nearly 400 million (as compared with 1985) is an ambitious, but achievable, target for the end of the century. In many areas the political and economic obstacles are daunting. Effective action to help the poor involves some costs for the nonpoor in both developed and developing countries. But these costs are modest even in the short term, and they are massively outweighed by the advance in human welfare that a sustained attack on poverty would bring.

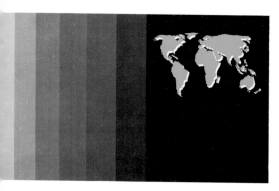

Bibliographical note

This Report has drawn on a wide range of World Bank reports and on numerous outside sources. World Bank sources include ongoing research as well as country economic, sector, and project work. The principal sources for each chapter are noted below. These and other sources are then listed alphabetically by author or organization in two groups: background papers commissioned for this Report and a selected bibliography. The background papers, some of which will be available through the Policy, Research, and External Affairs Working Paper series, synthesize relevant literature and Bank work. The views they express are not necessarily those of the World Bank or of this Report.

In addition to the principal sources listed, many persons, both inside and outside the World Bank, helped with the Report. In particular, the core team wishes to thank Ravi Kanbur, Michael Lipton, Martin Ravallion, and T. N. Srinivasan for their extensive support. Others who provided notes or detailed comments include Surjit Bhalla and Herman van der Tak.

Chapter 1

This chapter draws principally on IMF, OECD, and World Bank sources. Projections and background analysis were prepared by the International Economic Analysis and Prospects Division, International Economics Department, World Bank; Fardoust and Dhareshwar 1990 was an important background source. The preparation of special forecast scenarios was assisted by Robert Lynn, Christian Pedersen, and Karsten Pedersen. The sections on debt draw mainly on World Bank 1989f and on discussions with Constantijn Claessens, Charles Humphreys, Ishrat Husain, and Sweder

van Wijnbergen. Box 1.2 is based on Dornbusch and Edwards 1989, Sachs 1989, and the background paper by Roubini. Box 1.4 draws mainly on van Wijnbergen 1990 and Box 1.5 on Borrell and Yang 1990. Ajay Chhibber, Alan Gelb, and Paul Meo provided valuable comments.

Chapter 2

Numerous World Bank, United Nations, and academic studies on poverty were consulted for the chapter. The three household profiles were inspired by Hartmann and Boyce 1983, Tremblay and Capon 1988, and household survey data from the World Bank's Living Standards Measurement Study project, with help from Paul Glewwe and Dean Joliffe. Gabriela Vega also provided useful suggestions. Box 2.1 is based on the background paper by Anand and Harris and on Haddad and Kanbur 1989 and Ravallion 1988. Box 2.2 draws on the literature on poverty measurement, particularly Sen 1981, with policy applications from Ravallion and van de Walle 1988. The discussion in Box 2.3 is based on Collier and Lal 1986, Collier and others 1986, Drèze forthcoming, and Greer and Thorbecke 1986. Box 2.4 was prepared by Martin Ravallion and Apparao Katikineni from data files provided by ICRISAT, India. Gaurav Datt and Etienne van de Walle made useful comments.

Chapter 3

The discussion on changes in poverty draws on World Bank sources and on work by Elaine K. Chan on poverty decomposition and income distribution. Box 3.1 is based on Keyfitz 1985; and Box 3.2 on Bevan, Collier, and Gunning 1988, Collier forthcoming, Collier and others 1986, Wagao 1986 and material from Douglas Rimmer; Box 3.4 on the background paper by Williamson and Polak. William Ascher made substantial contributions to Box 3.5. Box 3.6 and the discussion of critical tradeoffs are based on the background paper by Bourguignon. Data for figure 3.4 were provided by Juan Luis Londoño.

Chapter 4

This chapter draws extensively on World Bank sources and on the Bank's operational experience. The section on government policy and rural development is based on the background paper by Papanek; on Adelman 1984, Booth 1989, Cavallo and Mundlak 1982, de Janvry and others 1989, Krueger, Schiff, and Valdés 1988, and Schiff and Valdés forthcoming; on Lele 1989 and other materials from the Bank's project on Managing Agricultural Development in Africa; and on material provided by Jean-Jacques Dethier. The discussion of infrastructure and technology draws on Anderson, Herdt, and Scobie 1988, Binswanger 1990, Binswanger, Khandker, and Rosenzweig 1989, Hayami and Ruttan 1985, Hazell and Ramasamy 1988, and Lipton and Longhurst 1989. Sources for the section on encouraging farm-nonfarm linkages include Haggblade and Hazell 1989 and Haggblade, Hazell, and Brown 1989. The section on urban and industrial growth benefited from de Soto 1989, International Labour Organisation 1985, Krueger 1983, Lee 1989, Lee and Anas 1989, and Little, Mazumdar, and Page 1987. The discussion on access to land draws on the background paper on land rights by Bell, on Binswanger and Elgin 1988, and on material provided by Peter Hazell and Peter Hopcraft. The section on access to credit is based on the background paper on credit by Bell and on material prepared by Sharon Holt; other sources include Braverman and Guasch 1989, Hossain 1988, Huppi and Feder 1989, U.S. Agency for International Development 1989, Von Pischke 1989, and Von Pischke, Adams, and Donald 1983. Lynn Bennett, Millard Long, Elizabeth Rhyen, J. D. Von Pischke, and Jacob Yaron provided detailed comments. Material on access to infrastructure and technology came from the background papers by Holt and by the International Fund for Agricultural Development and from Cernea 1985, Korten 1980, Korten and Siy 1988, Lewis and others 1988, and Uphoff 1986. The discussion on resource-poor areas is based on material prepared by Sharon Holt and on Lele and Stone 1989 and Leonard and others 1989; John Doolette contributed material, and Gloria Davis, Jeffrey Leonard,

Augusta Molnar, and Robert Repetto provided comments. Box 4.1 is based on Binswanger 1989 and Box 4.2 on Ahmed and Hossain 1988. Box 4.3 draws on material prepared by Elizabeth King. Box 4.4 is based on background notes by Friedrich Kahnert and Oded Stark. Box 4.6 was prepared by Peter Hazell and Shem Migot-Adholla and draws on Blarel and Place 1990. Box 4.7 draws on material prepared for World Bank 1989c. Box 4.8 is based on Singh and Bara 1988, Box 4.9 on Kahnert 1989, and Box 4.10 on Piazza and Doolette 1990. Douglas Barnes, David Beckmann, Clive Bell, Hans Binswanger, Peter Hazell, Barbara Herz, Peter Hopcraft, Friedrich Kahnert, Robert Liebenthal, Luis Riveros, Ricardo Silveira, Roger Slade, and Norman Uphoff provided valuable comments on the chapter.

Chapter 5

This chapter draws heavily on World Bank experience in education and health. The section on primary education is based mainly on Lockheed, Verspoor, and others 1990 and on World Bank 1986b. The discussion on government intervention in health owes much to World Bank 1987b. Data on under 5 mortality are from United Nations, Department of International Economic and Social Affairs 1988 and Hill and Pebley 1988. The Westinghouse series of Demographic and Health Surveys (DHS) was a valuable source of information on child and maternal mortality, fertility, and family planning indicators. Ralph Henderson made available data generated by the Expanded Programme on Immunization of the World Health Organization. Nutrition information is drawn from United Nations 1987 and has benefited from suggestions by Alan Berg and John Mason. Nancy Birdsall provided material on demographic and family planning issues. Box 5.1 was inspired by work in progress in the Population, Health, and Nutrition Division of the World Bank, under the direction of Anthony Measham. Box 5.2 derives from the background paper by Lau, Jamison, and Louat. Box 5.3 was drafted by Ann Tinker and Box 5.4 by Eleanor Schreiber. The information for Box 5.5 was made available by the UNDP–World Bank Interregional Handpump Project. Barbara Herz, Dennis de Tray, Emmanuel Jimenez, Oded Stark, and Adriaan Verspoor provided detailed comments on the chapter.

Chapter 6

This chapter draws on a range of World Bank and other sources and benefited from discussions with people in and outside the Bank. The discussion of fishing communities is based on a background note by Jean-Philippe Platteau and on Platteau forthcoming. The section on food policies draws on Alderman forthcoming, Alderman and von Braun 1984, Berg 1987, Edirisinghe 1987, Jamaica Statistical Institute and World Bank 1988, Pinstrup-Andersen 1988, Ravallion 1987, Sen 1981, United Nations Children's Fund 1989, and World Bank 1986c. Margaret Grosh provided information on Jamaican policies. The section on public employment schemes draws mainly on Acharya and Panwalkar 1988, Drèze and Sen 1990, and Ravallion 1990. Box 6.1 is based on material from the background papers by Atkinson and by Williamson and Polak and on Howard 1943. Box 6.2 draws on Besley and Kanbur 1988, Ravallion 1990, and background notes by Jean Drèze. Boxes 6.3 and 6.5 are based on material in Drèze forthcoming and Morgan forthcoming. Box 6.4 draws on information in Acharya and Panwalkar 1988. Helpful comments were provided by Alan Berg, Jean Drèze, Judith McGuire, Per Pinstrup-Andersen, Shlomo Reutlinger, Nicholas Stern, Kalanidhi Subbarao, and Joachim von Braun.

Chapter 7

The analysis of the relationship between macroeconomic policy and the poor draws on the background papers by Ahmed and Peters; Berry; Bourguignon, de Melo, and Suwa; and Fox and Morley. Other sources were Beaudry and Sowa 1989, Mazumdar 1989, World Bank country work, and papers prepared for the project on Labor Markets in an Era of Adjustment sponsored by the University of Warwick and the Economic Development Institute of the World Bank. The discussion of public spending is based on the background paper by Gallagher and the analysis of employment schemes in Bolivia, Chile, and Peru on Newman 1988, Universidad de Chile 1987, and Graham 1990. The discussion of compensation for laid-off workers draws on Collier 1988. Box 7.1 is based on Moser 1989, Box 7.2 on the background paper by de Janvry, Fargeix, and Sadoulet, and Box 7.3 on the background paper by Milanovic. Box 7.4 is drawn from Blejer and Guerrero forthcoming and Box 7.5 from *African Farmer* 1990. Box 7.6 was prepared by Stephen Haggard, drawing on Nelson 1990. Box 7.7 benefited from work for the Social Dimensions of Adjustment project undertaken by the African Development Bank, the United Nations Development Programme, and the World

Bank. François Bourguignon, and Frances Stewart provided valuable comments on the chapter. Further assistance came from Perla Aizenman, Benoit Blarel, Fernando Luis Quevedo, and Luis Riveros.

Chapter 8

The discussion of trade and poverty draws on Finger and Messerlin 1989, Finger and Olechowski 1987, Karsenty and Laird 1987, Laird and Yeats 1990, Tyers and Anderson 1986, United Nations Conference on Trade and Development 1989, Whalley 1985, and Yeats 1981 and 1989 and on extensive discussions with Refik Erzan, Sam Laird, Paul Meo, and Alexander Yeats. Essential data were obtained from United Nations Conference on Trade and Development 1988. The discussion of the Multifibre Arrangement profited from the work of Erzan, Goto, and Holmes 1989 and Trela and Whalley 1988. The discussion of debt relies primarily on Greene 1989, Humphreys and Underwood 1989, and World Bank 1989f. Materials of the Development Assistance Committee, especially Organisation for Economic Co-operation and Development 1985, 1989, and 1990, were the principal sources on aid and poverty; Josefina G. Valeriano provided invaluable research assistance. Other published studies on aid that were extremely useful included Cassen and associates 1986, Lele 1989, Mosley 1987, Riddell 1987, and World Bank 1986a. Box 8.1 was prepared by Paula Holmes and Paul Meo and Box 8.2 by Refik Erzan with the assistance of Paula Holmes. Box 8.3 draws mainly on Karsenty and Laird 1987. Box 8.4 owes much to the OECD sources, especially 1989. Box 8.5 is based largely on Ayres 1983 and World Bank 1988c and Box 8.6 on Ayres 1983, World Bank 1983, and recent unpublished World Bank studies. Box 8.7 profited from discussions with Robert Hindle, Shlomo Reutlinger, and Cornelis Tuinenburg. David Beckmann, Michael Carter, and Robert Liebenthal provided valuable comments.

Background papers

Ahmad, Ehtisham, and Christine Allison. ''Poverty, Growth, and Public Policy in Pakistan.''

Ahmad, Ehtisham, and Stephen Ludlow. ''Poverty, Inequality, and Growth in Pakistan.''

Ahmad, Ehtisham, and Yan Wang. ''Inequality and Poverty in China: Institutional Change and Public Policy, 1978–1988.''

Ahmad, Ehtisham, and Gang Zou. ''Deprivation and Prosperity in Chinese History.''

Ahmed, Sadiq, and R. Kyle Peters, Jr. "Adjustment with Poverty Alleviation: Indonesia's Experience."

Anand, Sudhir, and Christopher Harris. "On the Choice of Welfare Indicator in the Analysis of Poverty: An Illustration Using Sri Lankan Data."

Atkinson, Anthony B. "Poverty, Economic Performance, and Income Transfer Policy in OECD Countries."

Bell, Clive. "Credit and Saving."

——. "Land Reform, Tenancy, Productivity, and Employment as Aspects of Property Rights in Land."

Bell, Clive, and Robert Rich. "Rural Poverty and Agricultural Performance in India between 1956–57 and 1983–84."

Berry, Albert. "The Effects of Stabilization and Adjustment on Poverty and Income Distribution: Aspects of the Latin American Experience."

Bhalla, Surjit S. "The Role of Welfare Policies and Income Growth in Improving Living Standards in India and Sri Lanka."

Bourguignon, François. "Optimal Poverty Reduction, Adjustment, and Growth: An Applied Framework."

Bourguignon, François, Jaime de Melo, and A. Suwa. "Distributional Effects of Adjustment Policies: Simulations for Two Archetype Economies."

Chan, Elaine K. "A Compendium of Data on Poverty and Income Distribution."

——. "Decomposing Changes in Poverty."

de Janvry, Alain, André Fargeix, and Elisabeth Sadoulet. "Economic, Welfare, and Political Consequences of Stabilization Policies: A General Equilibrium Approach."

Drèze, Jean P., Peter Lanjouw, and Nicholas Stern. "Identifying and Reaching the Poor: Principles and Some Examples from a North Indian Village."

Fox, M. Louise, and Samuel A. Morley. "Who Paid the Bill? Adjustment and Poverty in Brazil, 1980–1995."

Gallagher, Mark. "Fiscal Duress and the Social Sectors in Developing Countries."

Hill, Kenneth. "Demographic Response to Economic Shock."

Holt, Sharon L. "The Role of Institutions in Poverty Reduction: A Focus on the Productive Sectors."

International Fund for Agricultural Development. "Poverty Alleviation: An IFAD Perspective."

Lau, Lawrence, Dean Jamison, and Frédéric Louat. "Education and Productivity in Developing Countries: An Aggregate Production Function Approach."

Milanovic, Branko. "Poverty in Eastern Europe in the Years of Crisis: Poland, Hungary, and Yugoslavia."

——. "Poverty in Poland in the Years of Crisis, 1978–87."

Papanek, Gustav F. "Growth, Poverty, and Real Wages in Labor-Abundant Countries."

Pissarides, Christopher A. "Macroeconomic Adjustment and Poverty in Selected Developed Countries."

Posarac, Aleksandra. "Poverty in Yugoslavia, 1978–87."

Ravallion, Martin. "The Challenging Arithmetic of Poverty in Bangladesh."

Ravallion, Martin, Gaurav Datt, Dominique van de Walle, and Elaine K. Chan. "Quantifying the Magnitude and Severity of Absolute Poverty in the Developing World in the Mid-1980s."

Roubini, Nouriel. "The Interactions between Macroeconomic Performance and Political Structures and Institutions: The Political Economy of Poverty, Growth, and Development."

Szalai, Julia. "Poverty in Hungary during the Period of Economic Crisis."

Teklu, Tesfaye, and Joachim von Braun. "Coping with Disastrous Drought: The 1984/85 Famine in North Kordofan, Sudan."

Williamson, Jeffrey G., and Ben Polak. "Poverty, Policy, and Industrialization: Lessons from the Distant Past."

Selected bibliography

The word "processed" describes works that are reproduced from typescript by mimeography, xerography, or similar means; such works may not be cataloged or commonly available through libraries, or may be subject to restricted circulation.

Acharya, Meena, and Lynn Bennett. 1983. *Women and the Subsistence Sector: Economic Participation and Household Decisionmaking in Nepal.* World Bank Staff Working Paper 526. Washington, D.C.

Acharya, Sarthi, and V. G. Panwalkar. 1988. "The Maharashtra Employment Guarantee Scheme: Impacts on Male and Female Labour." Prepared for the Population Council Program on Women's Roles and Gender Differences. Tata Institute of Social Sciences, Bombay, India. Processed.

Adelman, Irma. 1984. "Beyond Export-Led Growth." *World Development* 12, 9 (September): 937–49.

African Development Bank, United Nations Development Programme, and World Bank. 1990. *The Social Dimensions of Adjustment in Africa: A Policy Agenda*. Washington, D.C.: World Bank.

African Farmer. 1990. "Farmers Adjust to Economic Reform." Issue 3 (April): 5–16. New York: The Hunger Project.

Ahmed, Raisuddin, and Mahabub Hossain. 1988. "Developmental Impact of Rural Infrastructure: Bangladesh." International Food Policy Research Institute, Washington, D.C., in collaboration with the Bangladesh Institute of Development Studies. Processed.

Alderman, Harold. Forthcoming. "Food Subsidies and the Poor." World Bank, Latin America Technical Department, Washington, D.C. In George Psacharopoulos, ed., *Essays on Poverty, Equity and Growth*.

Alderman, Harold, and Valerie Kozel. 1989. *Formal and Informal Sector Wage Determination in Urban Low-Income Neighborhoods in Pakistan*. Living Standards Measurement Study Working Paper 65. Washington, D.C.: World Bank.

Alderman, Harold, and Joachim von Braun. 1984. *The Effects of the Egyptian Food Ration and Subsidy System on Income Distribution and Consumption*. Research Report 45. Washington, D.C.: International Food Policy Research Institute.

Allison, Christine. 1989. "Poverty, Inequality, and Public Policy in Pakistan." World Bank, Eastern Africa Department, Washington, D.C. Processed.

Anderson, Jock R. 1985. *Research and Agricultural Progress*. Armidale, N.S.W., Australia: University of New England.

Anderson, Jock R., Robert W. Herdt, and Grant M. Scobie. 1988. *Science and Food: The CGIAR and Its Partners*. Washington, D.C.: World Bank.

Ascher, William. 1984. *Scheming for the Poor: The Politics of Redistribution in Latin America*. Cambridge, Mass.: Harvard University Press.

Atkinson, A. B. 1987. "On the Measurement of Poverty." *Econometrica* 55: 749–64.

Ayres, Robert L. 1983. *Banking on the Poor: The World Bank and World Poverty*. Cambridge, Mass.: MIT Press.

Beaton, George H., and Hossein Ghassemi. 1982. "Supplementary Feeding Programs for Young Children in Developing Countries." *American Journal of Clinical Nutrition* 35 (April): 864–916.

Beaudry, P., and N. K. Sowa. 1989. "Labor Markets in an Era of Adjustment: A Case Study of Ghana." Prepared for the Conference on Labor Markets in an Era of Adjustment, Coventry, U.K., August 7–10, sponsored by the Development Economics Research Centre, University of Warwick, and the Economic Development Institute of the World Bank. Processed.

Berg, Alan. 1987. *Malnutrition: What Can Be Done? Lessons from World Bank Experience*. Baltimore, Md.: Johns Hopkins University Press.

Besley, Timothy, and Ravi Kanbur. 1988. "The Principles of Targeting." Discussion Paper 85. Development Economics Research Centre, University of Warwick, Coventry, U.K. Processed.

Bevan, David, Paul Collier, and Jan Gunning. 1988. "The Political Economy of Poverty, Equity and Growth: Indonesia and Nigeria." World Bank, Latin America Technical Department, Washington, D.C. Processed.

Bhende, M. J. 1986. "Credit Markets in Rural South India." *Economic and Political Weekly* 21, 38–39 (September).

Biggs, Tyler S., Donald R. Snodgrass, and Pradeep Srivastava. 1990. "On Minimalist Credit Programs." Development Discussion Paper 331, Economic Policy Series. Harvard Institute for International Development, Cambridge, Mass. Processed.

Binswanger, Hans P. 1989. "Brazilian Policies That Encourage Deforestation in the Amazon." Environment Department Working Paper 16. World Bank, Washington, D.C. Processed.

————. 1990. "The Policy Response of Agriculture." In *Proceedings of the World Bank Annual Conference on Development Economics 1989*. Washington, D.C.: World Bank.

Binswanger, Hans P., and Miranda Elgin. 1988. "What Are the Prospects for Land Reform?" Prepared for the Twentieth International Conference of Agricultural Economists, Buenos Aires, August 24–31. Processed.

Binswanger, Hans P., Shahidur R. Khandker, and Mark R. Rosenzweig. 1989. "How Infrastructure and Financial Institutions Affect Agricultural Output and Investment in India." Policy, Planning, and Research Working Paper 163. World Bank, Latin America and the Caribbean Country Department II, Washington, D.C. Processed.

Binswagner, Hans P., and Jaime B. Quizon. 1986. "What Can Agriculture do for the Poorest Rural Groups?" Agriculture and Rural Development Department Discussion Paper ARU 57. World Bank, Washington, D.C. Processed.

Birdsall, Nancy. 1980. ''Population Growth and Poverty in the Developing World.'' *Population Bulletin* 35, 5 (December): 3–38.

Birdsall, Nancy, and Estelle James. 1989. ''Efficiency and Equity in Social Spending: How and Why Governments Misbehave.'' Policy, Research, and External Affairs Working Paper 274. World Bank, Latin America and the Caribbean Country Department I, Washington, D.C. Processed.

Blarel, Benoit, and Frank Place. 1990. ''Land Tenure and Agricultural Production under Land Scarcity: The Case of Rwanda.'' World Bank, Agriculture and Rural Development Department, Washington, D.C. Processed.

Blejer, Mario I., and Isabel Guerrero. Forthcoming. ''The Impact of Macroeconomic Policies on Income Distribution: An Empirical Study of the Philippines.'' *Review of Economics and Statistics*.

Boateng, E. Oti, and others. 1989. ''A Poverty Profile for Ghana, 1987–88.'' World Bank, Occidental and Central Africa Department, Washington, D.C. Processed.

Booth, Anne. 1989. ''Indonesian Agricultural Development in Comparative Perspective.'' *World Development* 17, 8 (August): 1235–54.

Borrell, Brent, and Maw-Cheng Yang. 1990. ''EC Bananarama 1992.'' International Commodity Markets Paper. World Bank, International Economics Department, Washington D.C. Processed.

Boulier, Bryan L. 1985. *Evaluating Unmet Needs for Contraceptives: Estimates for Thirty-six Developing Countries*. World Bank Staff Working Paper 678. Washington, D.C.

Bourguignon, François, William H. Branson, and Jaime de Melo. 1989. ''Adjustment and Income Distribution: A Counterfactual Analysis.'' Policy, Planning, and Research Working Paper 215. World Bank, Country Economics Department, Washington, D.C. Processed.

Braverman, Avishay, and J. Luis Guasch. 1989. ''Rural Credit in Developing Countries.'' Policy, Planning, and Research Working Paper 219. World Bank, Agriculture and Rural Development Department, Washington, D.C. Processed.

Brown, L. David, and David C. Korten. 1989. ''Understanding Voluntary Organizations: Guidelines for Donors.'' Policy, Planning, and Research Working Paper 258. World Bank, Country Economics Department, Washington, D.C. Processed.

Bulatao, Rodolfo, and others. 1989. ''Africa Region Population Projections: 1989–90 Edition.'' Policy, Planning, and Research Working Paper 330. World Bank, Population and Human Resources Department, Washington, D.C. Processed.

Cassen, Robert, and associates. 1986. *Does Aid Work? Report to an Intergovernmental Task Force*. New York: Clarendon Press.

Castañeda, Tarsicio. Forthcoming. *Innovative Social Policies for Reducing Poverty: Chile in the 1980s*.

Cavallo, Domingo, and Yair Mundlak. 1982. *Agriculture and Economic Growth in an Open Economy: The Case of Argentina*. Research Report 36. Washington, D.C.: International Food Policy Research Institute.

Cernea, Michael M., ed. 1985. *Putting People First: Sociological Variables in Rural Development*. New York: Oxford University Press.

———. 1990. *Population Displacement in Water Resources Development: Current Practice, Issues, and Policy Responses*. Harvard Institute for International Development Discussion Paper. Cambridge, Mass.

Chambers, Robert. 1983. *Rural Development: Putting the Last First*. London: Longman.

Chenery, Hollis, and others. 1974. *Redistribution with Growth*. New York: Oxford University Press.

Chhibber, Ajay. 1986. ''Financing Public Expenditures in Developing Countries: Direct versus Indirect Taxation.'' Resource Mobilization Department Working Paper. World Bank, Washington, D.C. Processed.

Collier, Paul. 1988. ''African Public Sector Retrenchment: An Analytical Survey.'' World Employment Programme Research Working Paper 27. International Labour Office, Geneva. Processed.

———. Forthcoming. ''Aid and Economic Performance in Tanzania.'' In Uma Lele and Ijaz Nabi, eds., *Transitions in Development: The Role of Aid and Commercial Flows*. San Francisco, Calif.: Institute for Contemporary Studies.

Collier, Paul, and Deepak Lal. 1986. *Labour and Poverty in Kenya, 1900–1980*. Oxford: Clarendon Press.

Collier, Paul, Samir Radwan, and Samuel Wangwe, with Albert Wagner. 1986. *Labour and Poverty in Rural Tanzania: Ujamaa and Rural Development in the United Republic of Tanzania*. Oxford: Clarendon Press.

Cornia, Giovanni Andrea, Richard Jolly, and Francis Stewart, eds. 1987. *Adjustment with a Human Face*. 2 vols. Oxford: Clarendon Press.

Cox, Donald, and Emmanuel Jimenez. 1990. "Private Transfers and Public Policy in Developing Countries: A Case Study for Peru." Policy, Planning, and Research Working Paper 345. World Bank, Country Economics Department, Washington, D.C. Processed.

Dandekar, Kumudini. 1983. *Employment Guarantee Scheme: An Employment Opportunity for Women*. Gokhale Institute Study 67. Bombay, India: Orient Longman.

Datt, Gaurav, and Martin Ravallion. 1990. "Regional Disparities, Targeting, and Poverty in India." Policy, Research, and External Affairs Working Paper 375. World Bank, Agriculture and Rural Development Department, Washington, D.C. Processed.

Deaton, Angus, and Anne Case. 1988. *Analysis of Household Expenditures*. Living Standards Measurement Study Working Paper 28. Washington, D.C.: World Bank.

de Janvry, Alain, and Elisabeth Sadoulet. 1988. "Investment Strategies to Combat Rural Poverty: A Proposal for Latin America." Working Paper 459. Giannini Foundation of Agricultural Economics, University of California, Berkeley. Processed.

de Janvry, Alain, and others. 1989. *Rural Development in Latin America: An Evaluation and a Proposal*. IICA Program Paper 12. San Jose, Costa Rica: Instituto Interamericano de Cooperación para la Agricultura.

de Soto, Hernando. 1989. *The Other Path: The Invisible Revolution in the Third World*. New York: Harper and Row.

Donaldson, Graham. 1989. "Government-Sponsored Rural Development: Experience of the World Bank." World Bank, Operations Evaluation Department, Washington, D.C. Processed.

Dornbusch, Rudiger, and Sebastian Edwards. 1989. "Macroeconomic Populism in Latin America." NBER Working Paper 2986. National Bureau of Economic Research, Cambridge, Mass. Processed.

Drabek, Anne Gordon, ed. 1987. "Development Alternatives: The Challenges for NGOs." *World Development* 15 suppl. (Autumn).

Drèze, Jean P. Forthcoming. "Famine Prevention in Africa." In Jean P. Drèze and Amartya K. Sen, eds., *The Political Economy of Hunger*. Oxford: Oxford University Press.

Drèze, Jean, and Amartya Sen. 1990. *Hunger and Public Action*. Oxford: Clarendon Press.

Echeverri-Gent, John. 1988. "Guaranteed Employment in an Indian State." *Asian Survey* 28, 12: 1294–1310.

Edirisinghe, Neville. 1987. *The Food Stamp Scheme in Sri Lanka: Costs, Benefits and Options for Modification*. Research Report 58. Washington, D.C.: International Food Policy Research Institute.

Erzan, Refik, Junichi Goto, and Paula Holmes. 1989. "Effects of the Multi-Fibre Arrangement on Developing Countries' Trade: An Empirical Investigation." Policy, Planning, and Research Working Paper 297. World Bank, International Economics Department, Washington, D.C. Processed.

Erzan, Refik, and Peter Svedberg. 1989. "Protection Facing Exports from Sub-Saharan Africa in the EC, Japan, and the United States." Policy, Planning, and Research Working Paper 320. World Bank, International Economics Department, Washington, D.C. Processed.

Evans, Timothy. 1989. "The Impact of Permanent Disability on Rural Households: River Blindness in Guinea." *IDS Bulletin* 20, 2 (April): 41–48.

Fardoust, Shahrokh, and Ashok Dhareshwar. 1990. "Long-Term Outlook for the World Economy: Issues and Projections for the 1990s." Policy, Research, and External Affairs Working Paper 372. World Bank, International Economics Department, Washington, D.C. Processed.

Finger, J. Michael, and Patrick A. Messerlin. 1989. *The Effects of Industrial Countries' Policies on Developing Countries*. Policy and Research Series 3. Washington, D.C.: World Bank.

Finger, J. Michael, and Andrzej Olechowski, eds. 1987. *The Uruguay Round: A Handbook on the Multilateral Trade Negotiations*. Washington, D.C.: World Bank.

Fitchett, Delbert A. 1988. *Agricultural Trade Protectionism in Japan: A Survey*. World Bank Discussion Paper 28. Washington, D.C.

Food and Agriculture Organization. 1987. *The Fifth World Food Survey*. Rome.

————. 1988. *Rural Poverty in Latin America and the Caribbean*. Prepared for the FAO Regional Conference for Latin America and the Caribbean, Recife, Brazil. Rome. Processed.

Gallagher, Mark, and Osita M. Ogbu. 1989. "Public Expenditures, Resource Use and Social Services in Sub-Saharan Africa." World Bank, Africa Technical Department, Washington, D.C. Processed.

Galway, Katrina, Brent Wolff, and Richard Sturgis. 1987. *Child Survival: Risks and the Road to Health*. Columbia, Md.: Institute for Resource Development/Westinghouse.

Garcia, Marito H., and Per Pinstrup-Andersen. 1987. *The Pilot Food Price Subsidy Scheme in the Philippines: Its Impact on Income, Food Consumption, and Nutritional Status*. Research Report 61. Washington, D.C.: International Food Policy Research Institute.

George, P. S. 1985. *Some Aspects of Procurement and Distribution of Foodgrains in India*. Working Paper on Food Subsidies 1. Washington, D.C.: International Food Policy Research Institute.

Gertler, Paul, and Jacques van der Gaag. Forthcoming. *The Willingness to Pay for Medical Care: Evidence from Developing Countries*. Baltimore, Md.: Johns Hopkins University Press.

Ghai, Dharam, and Samir Radwan, eds. 1983. *Agrarian Policies and Rural Poverty in Africa*. Geneva: International Labour Office.

Glewwe, Paul. 1988. *The Distribution of Welfare in Côte d'Ivoire in 1985*. Living Standards Measurement Study Working Paper 29. Washington, D.C.: World Bank.

———. 1988. *The Distribution of Welfare in Peru in 1985–86*. Living Standards Measurement Study Working Paper 42. Washington, D.C.: World Bank.

Glewwe, Paul, and Dennis de Tray. 1988. *The Poor During Adjustment: A Case Study of Côte d'Ivoire*. Living Standards Measurement Study Working Paper 47. Washington, D.C.: World Bank.

———. 1989. *The Poor in Latin America during Adjustment: A Case Study of Peru*. Living Standards Measurement Study Working Paper 56. Washington, D.C.: World Bank.

Glewwe, Paul, and Kwaku A. Twum-Baah. 1989. "The Distribution of Welfare in Ghana." World Bank, Population and Human Resources Department, Washington, D.C. Processed.

Glewwe, Paul, and Jacques van der Gaag. 1988. *Confronting Poverty in Developing Countries: Definitions, Information, and Policies*. Living Standards Measurement Study Working Paper 48. Washington, D.C.: World Bank.

Golub, Stephen S., and J. M. Finger. 1979. "The Processing of Primary Commodities: Effects of Developed-Country Tariff Escalation and Developing-Country Export Taxes." *Journal of Political Economy* 87, 3 (June): 559–77.

Goto, Junichi. 1989. "The Multifibre Arrangement and Its Effects on Developing Countries." *World Bank Research Observer* 4, 2 (July): 203–27.

Graham, Carol. 1990. "The APRA Government and the Urban Poor: The PAIT Programme in Lima's Pueblos Jovenes." Duke University, Durham, N.C. Processed.

Greene, Joshua. 1989. "The External Debt Problem of Sub-Saharan Africa." *IMF Staff Papers* 36, 4 (December): 836–74.

Greer, Joel, and Erik Thorbecke. 1986. "Food Poverty Profile Applied to Kenyan Smallholders." *Economic Development and Cultural Change* 35 (October): 115–41.

Griffin, Charles C. 1988. *User Charges for Health Care in Principle and Practice*. EDI Seminar Paper 37. Washington, D.C.: World Bank.

Haddad, Lawrence, and Ravi Kanbur. 1989. "How Serious Is the Neglect of Intrahousehold Inequality?" Policy, Planning, and Research Working Paper 296. World Bank, Office of the Vice President, Development Economics, Washington, D.C. Processed.

Haggblade, Steven, and Peter Hazell. 1989. "Agricultural Technology and Farm-Nonfarm Growth Linkages." *Agricultural Economics* 3: 345–64.

Haggblade, Steven, Peter Hazell, and James Brown. 1989. "Farm-Nonfarm Linkages in Rural Sub-Saharan Africa." *World Development* 17, 8 (August): 1173–1201.

Halstead, Scott B., and others, eds. 1985. *Good Health at Low Cost*. New York: Rockefeller Foundation.

Hart, Gillian. 1986. *Power, Labor, and Livelihood: Processes of Change in Rural Java*. Berkeley: University of California Press.

Hartmann, Betsy, and James K. Boyce. 1983. *A Quiet Violence: View from a Bangladesh Village*. London: Zed Press.

Hayami, Yujiro, and Vernon W. Ruttan. 1985. *Agricultural Development: An International Perspective*. Baltimore, Md.: Johns Hopkins University Press.

Hazell, Peter B. R., and C. Ramasamy. 1988. "Green Revolution Reconsidered: The Impact of the High-Yielding Rice Varieties in South India." World Bank, Agriculture and Rural Development Department, Washington, D.C. Processed.

Herz, Barbara, and Anthony R. Measham. 1987. *The Safe Motherhood Initiative: Proposals for Action*. World Bank Discussion Paper 9. Washington, D.C.

Hill, Kenneth, and Ann R. Pebley. 1988. "Levels, Trends and Patterns of Child Mortality in the Developing World." Prepared for the Workshop on Child Survival Programs: Issues for the 1990s, School of Hygiene and Public Health, Johns Hopkins University, Baltimore, Md., November 20–21. Processed.

Hinchliffe, Keith. 1986. "The Monetary and Non-Monetary Returns to Education in Africa." Education and Training Discussion Paper EDT46. World Bank, Washington, D.C. Processed.

Hossain, Mahabub. 1988. *Credit for Alleviation of Rural Poverty: The Grameen Bank in Bangladesh*. Research Report 65. Washington, D.C.: International Food Policy Research Institute in collaboration with the Bangladesh Institute of Development Studies.

Hossain, Mahabub, and Rita Afsar. 1989. *Credit for Women's Involvement in Economic Activities in Rural Bangladesh*. Research Report 105. Dhaka: Bangladesh Institute of Development Studies.

Hossain, Mosharaff. 1987. *The Assault That Failed: A Profile of Absolute Poverty in Six Villages of Bangladesh*. Geneva: United Nations Research Institute for Social Development.

Howard, Donald S. 1943. *The WPA and Federal Relief Policy*. New York: Russell Sage Foundation.

Humphreys, Charles, and John Underwood. 1989. "The External Debt Difficulties of Low-Income Africa." In Ishrat Husain and Ishac Diwan, eds., *Dealing with the Debt Crisis*. Washington, D.C.: World Bank.

Huppi, Monika, and Gershon Feder. 1989. "The Role of Groups and Credit Cooperatives in Rural Lending." World Bank, Agriculture and Rural Development Department, Washington, D.C. Processed.

Iliffe, John. 1987. *The African Poor*. Cambridge: Cambridge University Press.

India, Government of. 1987. *Family Welfare Programme in India: Year Book 1986–87*. New Delhi: Ministry of Health and Family Welfare, Department of Family Welfare.

Institute of Population Studies, Chulalongkorn University. 1989. *Thailand: Health and Population Studies Based on the 1987 Thailand Demographic and Health Survey*. Demographic and Health Surveys Further Analysis Series 1. New York: Population Council.

International Labour Organisation. 1985. *Informal Sector in Africa*. Addis Ababa: Jobs and Skills Programme for Africa.

————. 1988. *Employment Promotion in the Informal Sector in Africa*. Addis Ababa: Jobs and Skills Programme for Africa.

International Monetary Fund. 1989. *World Economic Outlook: A Survey by the Staff of the International Monetary Fund*. Washington, D.C.

————. Various years. *International Financial Statistics Yearbook*. Washington, D.C.

International Rice Research Institute. 1983. *Women in Rice Farming*. Manila.

Islam, Rizwanul, ed. 1987. *Rural Industrialisation and Employment in Asia*. New Delhi: International Labour Organisation, Asian Employment Programme.

Jamaica Statistical Institute and World Bank. 1988. "Living Conditions Survey, Jamaica." Kingston. Processed.

————. 1989. "Survey of Living Conditions, Jamaica." Kingston. Processed.

Jamison, Dean T., and Lawrence J. Lau. 1982. *Farmer Education and Farm Efficiency*. Baltimore, Md.: Johns Hopkins University Press.

Jimenez, Emmanuel. 1987. *Pricing Policy in the Social Sectors: Cost Recovery for Education and Health in Developing Countries*. Baltimore, Md.: Johns Hopkins University Press.

Jodha, N. S. 1985. "Market Forces and Erosion of Common Property Resources." In *Agricultural Markets in the Semi-Arid Tropics: Proceedings of the International Workshop Held at ICRISAT Center, India, 24–28 October 1983*. Patancheru, India: International Crops Research Institute for the Semi-Arid Tropics.

————. 1986. "Common Property Resources and Rural Poor in Dry Regions of India." *Economic and Political Weekly* 21, 27 (July): 1169–81.

Kahnert, Friedrich. 1989. "Assisting Poor Rural Areas through Groundwater Irrigation: Exploratory Proposals for East India, Bangladesh and Nepal." Asia Regional Series IDP44. World Bank, Washington, D.C. Processed.

Kanbur, Ravi S. 1990. *Poverty and the Social Dimensions of Structural Adjustment in Côte d'Ivoire*. Social Dimensions of Adjustment Working Paper 2. Washington, D.C.: World Bank.

Karsenty, Guy, and Sam Laird. 1987. "The GSP, Policy Options and the New Round." *Weltwirtschaftliches Archiv* 123, 2: 262–96.

Keja, Ko, and others. 1986. "Effectiveness of the Expanded Programme on Immunization." *World Health Statistics Quarterly* 39: 161–70.

Keyfitz, Nathan. 1985. "An East Javanese Village in 1953 and 1985: Observations on Development." *Population and Development Review* 11 (December): 695–719.

Khandker, Shahidur R. 1989. "Improving Rural Wages in India." Policy, Planning, and Research Working Paper 276. World Bank, Population and Human Resources Department, Washington, D.C. Processed.

Korten, David. 1980. "Community Organization and Rural Development: A Learning Process Approach." *Public Administration Review* 40, 5 (September–October): 480–511.

Korten, David C., ed. 1986. *Community Management: Asian Experience and Perspectives.* West Hartford, Conn.: Kumarian Press.

Korten, Frances F., and Robert Y. Siy, Jr. 1988. *Transforming a Bureaucracy: The Experience of the Philippine National Irrigation Administration.* West Hartford, Conn.: Kumarian Press.

Krueger, Anne O. 1983. *Trade and Employment in Developing Countries: Synthesis and Conclusions.* Chicago: University of Chicago Press.

Krueger, Anne O., and Vernon W. Ruttan. 1989. "Assistance to Korea." In Anne O. Krueger, Constantine Michalopoulos, and Vernon W. Ruttan, eds. *Aid and Development.* Baltimore, Md.: Johns Hopkins University Press.

Krueger, Anne O., Maurice Schiff, and Alberto Valdés. 1988. "Agricultural Incentives in Developing Countries: Measuring the Effect of Sectoral and Economywide Policies." *World Bank Economic Review* 2, 3 (September): 255–71.

Laird, Sam, and Alexander Yeats. 1990. *Quantitative Methods for Trade Barrier Analysis.* London: Macmillan.

Lal, Deepak, and Hla Myint. 1989. "The Political Economy of Poverty, Equity, and Growth in Some Developing Countries: A Comparative Study." World Bank, Latin America Technical Department, Washington, D.C. Processed.

Ledesma, Antonio J. 1982. *Landless Workers and Rice Farmers: Peasant Subclasses under Agrarian Reform in Two Philippine Villages.* Los Baños, Philippines: International Rice Research Institute.

Lee, Kyu Sik. 1989. *The Location of Jobs in a Developing Metropolis: Patterns of Growth in Bogotá and Cali, Colombia.* New York: Oxford University Press.

Lee, Kyu Sik, and Alex Anas. 1989. "Manufacturers' Responses to Infrastructure Deficiencies in Nigeria: Private Alternatives and Policy Options." Infrastructure and Urban Development Department Discussion Paper INU50. World Bank, Washington, D.C. Processed.

Lele, Uma. 1989. "Aid to African Agriculture: Lessons from Two Decades of Donor Experience." Discussion draft prepared for the Managing Agricultural Development in Africa (MADIA) Symposium. World Bank, Africa Technical Department, Washington, D.C. Processed.

Lele, Uma, and L. Richard Meyers. 1989. *Growth and Structural Change in East Africa: Domestic Policies, Agricultural Performance, and World Bank Assistance, 1963–86.* MADIA Discussion Paper 3. Washington, D.C.: World Bank.

Lele, Uma, and Steven W. Stone. 1989. *Population Pressure, the Environment, and Agricultural Intensification: Variations on the Boserup Hypothesis.* MADIA Discussion Paper 4. Washington, D.C.: World Bank.

Leonard, Jeffrey H., and others. 1989. *Environment and the Poor: Development Strategies for a Common Agenda.* U.S.–Third World Policy Perspectives 11. New Brunswick, N.J.: Transaction Books.

Levy, Victor. 1988. "Aid and Growth in Sub-Saharan Africa: The Recent Experience." *European Economic Review* 32: 1777–95.

Lewis, John P., and others. 1988. *Strengthening the Poor: What Have We Learned?* U.S.–Third World Policy Perspectives 10. Washington, D.C.: Overseas Development Council.

Liedholm, Carl, and Donald Mead. 1987. *Small Scale Industries in Developing Countries: Empirical Evidence and Policy Implications.* MSU International Development Paper 9. East Lansing: Department of Agricultural Economics, Michigan State University.

Lipton, Michael. 1983. *Labor and Poverty.* World Bank Staff Working Paper 616. Washington, D.C.

———. 1985. *Land Assets and Rural Poverty.* World Bank Staff Working Paper 744. Washington, D.C.

———. 1987. *Improving the Impact of Aid for Rural Development.* Discussion Paper 233. Brighton, U.K.: Institute of Development Studies, University of Sussex.

Lipton, Michael, with Richard Longhurst. 1989. *New Seeds and Poor People.* London: Unwin Hyman.

Lipton, Michael, and John Toye. 1990. *Does Aid Work in India? A Country Study of the Impact of Official Development Assistance.* London: Routledge.

Little, Ian M. D., Dipak Mazumdar, and John M. Page, Jr. 1987. *Small Manufacturing Enterprises: A Comparative Analysis of India and Other Economies.* New York: Oxford University Press.

Lockheed, Marlaine, Adriaan Verspoor, and others. 1990. "Improving Primary Education in Developing Countries: A Review of Policy Options." World Bank, Population and Human Resources Department, Washington, D.C. Processed.

Londoño, Juan Luis. 1989. "Income Distribution in Colombia: Turning Points, Catching Up and Other Kuznetsian Tales." Harvard University, Cambridge, Mass. Processed.

Mazumdar, Dipak. 1989. *Microeconomic Issues of Labor Markets in Developing Countries: Analysis and Policy Implications*. EDI Seminar Paper 40. Washington, D.C.: World Bank.

McGregor, J. Allister. 1988. "Credit and the Rural Poor: The Changing Policy Environment in Bangladesh." *Public Administration and Development* 8: 467–81.

Mencher, Joan. 1988. "Women's Work and Poverty: Women's Contribution to Household Maintenance in Two Regions of South India." In Daisy Dwyer and Judith Bruce, eds., *A Home Divided: Women and Income in the Third World*. Palo Alto, Calif.: Stanford University Press.

Migot-Adholla, Shem, and others. n.d. "Land Tenure Reform and Agricultural Development in SubSaharan Africa." World Bank, Agriculture and Rural Development Department, Washington, D.C. Processed.

Morgan, Richard G. Forthcoming. "Social Welfare Programmes and the Reduction of Household Vulnerability in the SADCC States of Southern Africa." In Ehtisham S. Ahmad and others, eds., *Social Security in Developing Countries*. Oxford: Oxford University Press.

Moser, Caroline O. 1989. "The Impact of Recession and Structural Adjustment Policies at the Micro-Level: Low Income Women and Their Households in Guayaquil, Ecuador." Department of Social Administration, London School of Economics and Political Science. Processed.

Mosley, Paul. 1987. *Overseas Aid: Its Defence and Reform*. Brighton, U.K.: Wheatsheaf Books.

Mosley, Paul, and Rudra Prasad Dahal. 1987. "Credit for the Rural Poor: A Comparison of Policy Experiments in Nepal and Bangladesh." *Manchester Papers on Development* 3, 2 (July): 45–59.

Murray, Christopher J. L. 1987. "A Critical Review of International Mortality Data." *Social Science and Medicine* 25, 7: 773–81.

Nelson, Joan M., ed. 1990. *Economic Crises and Policy Choice: The Politics of Adjustment in the Third World*. Princeton, N.J.: Princeton University Press.

Newman, John L. 1988. *Labor Market Activity in Côte d'Ivoire and Peru*. Living Standards Measurement Study Working Paper 36. Washington, D.C.: World Bank.

Oberai, A. S. 1987. *Migration, Urbanisation, and Development*. Training in Population, Human Resources, and Development Planning Background Paper 5. Geneva: International Labour Office.

Organisation for Economic Co-operation and Development. 1985. *Twenty-Five Years of Development Co-operation: A Review*. Paris.

———. 1987. *National Policies and Agricultural Trade*. Paris.

———. 1988. *Voluntary Aid for Development: The Role of Non-Governmental Organisations*. Paris.

———. 1989. *Development Co-operation in the 1990s*. Paris.

———. 1990. *Geographical Distribution of Financial Flows to Developing Countries, 1985–88*. Paris.

Osmani, Siddiqur R., and Omar H. Chowdhury. 1983. "Short Run Impact of Food for Work Programme in Bangladesh." *Bangladesh Development Studies* 11: 135–90.

Paul, Samuel. 1983. *Managing Development Programs: The Lessons of Success*. Boulder, Colo.: Westview Press.

Peek, Peter. 1988. "How Equitable Are Rural Development Projects?" *International Labour Review* 127, 1: 73–89.

Piazza, Alan, and John Doolette. 1990. "The Impact of Combining Agricultural Techniques and Soil Conservation Measures in China's Loess Plateau." In *Proceedings of the 1988 International Conference on Dryland Farming*. College Station: Texas Agricultural Experiment Station, Texas A&M University.

Pinstrup-Andersen, Per. 1988. *Consumer-Oriented Food Subsidies: Cost, Benefits and Policy Options for Developing Countries*. Baltimore, Md.: Johns Hopkins University Press.

Pinstrup-Andersen, Per, and Peter B. R. Hazell. 1985. "The Impact of the Green Revolution and Prospects for the Future." Reprinted from *Food Reviews International* 1, 1. Washington, D.C.: International Food Policy Research Institute.

Pinto, Brian. 1987. "Nigeria during and after the Oil Boom." *World Bank Economic Review* 1, 3 (May): 419–45.

Platteau, Jean-Philippe. Forthcoming. "Traditional Systems of Social Security and Hunger Insurance: Past Achievements and Modern Challenges." In Ehtisham S. Ahmad and others, eds., *Social Security in Developing Countries*. Oxford: Oxford University Press.

Preston, Samuel. 1980. "Causes and Consequences of Mortality Declines in Less Developed Countries During the Twentieth Century." In Richard Easterlin, ed., *Population and Economic Change in Developing Countries*. Chicago: University of Chicago Press.

Psacharopoulos, George. 1985. "Returns to Education: A Further International Update and Implications." *Journal of Human Resources* 20 (Fall): 583–604.

Pulley, Robert V. 1989. *Making the Poor Creditworthy: A Case Study of the Integrated Rural Development Program in India.* World Bank Discussion Paper 58. Washington, D.C.

Ravallion, Martin. 1987. *Markets and Famines.* Oxford: Clarendon Press.

———. 1988. "Expected Poverty under Risk Induced Welfare Variability." *Economic Journal* 98, 393 (December): 1171–82.

———. 1989a. "Income Effects on Undernutrition." *Economic Development and Cultural Change* 38 (April): 489–516.

———. 1989b. "Land-Contingent Poverty Alleviation Schemes." *World Development* 17, 8 (August): 1223–33.

———. 1990. "Reaching the Poor through Rural Public Works: Arguments, Evidence, and Lessons from South Asia." World Bank, Agriculture and Rural Development Department, Washington, D.C. Processed.

———. Forthcoming. "Rural Welfare Effects of Food Price Changes under Induced Wage Responses: Theory and Evidence for Bangladesh." *Oxford Economic Papers.*

Ravallion, Martin, and Lorraine Dearden. 1988. "Social Security in a 'Moral Economy': An Empirical Analysis for Java." *Review of Economics and Statistics* 70, 1 (February): 36–44.

Ravallion, Martin, and Monika Huppi. 1989. "Poverty and Undernutrition in Indonesia during the 1980s." Agriculture and Rural Development Department Working Paper 286. World Bank, Washington, D.C. Processed.

Ravallion, Martin, and Dominique van de Walle. 1988. "Poverty Orderings of Food Pricing Reforms." Discussion Paper 86. Development Economics Research Centre, University of Warwick, Coventry, U.K. Processed.

Riddell, Roger C. 1987. *Foreign Aid Reconsidered.* Baltimore, Md.: Johns Hopkins University Press.

Riveros, Luis A. 1989. "Labor Markets in an Era of Adjustment: The Chilean Case." Prepared for the Conference on Labor Markets in an Era of Adjustment, Coventry, U.K., August 7–10, sponsored by the Development Economics Research Centre, University of Warwick, and the Economic Development Institute of the World Bank. Processed.

Rodgers, Gerry, ed. 1989. *Urban Poverty and the Labor Market: Access to Jobs and Incomes in Asian and Latin American Cities.* Geneva: International Labour Office.

Rodgers, Gerry, and Guy Standing, eds. 1981. *Child Work, Poverty and Underdevelopment.* Geneva: International Labour Office.

Rodrik, Dani. 1989. "Policy Uncertainty and Private Investment in Developing Countries." NBER Working Paper 2999. National Bureau of Economic Research, Cambridge, Mass. Processed.

Sachs, Jeffrey D. 1989. "Social Conflict and Populist Policies in Latin America." NBER Working Paper 2897. National Bureau of Economic Research, Cambridge, Mass. Processed.

Salmen, Lawrence F. 1987. *Listen to the People: Participant-Observer Evaluation of Development Projects.* New York: Oxford University Press.

Sarvekshana, Journal of the National Sample Survey Organization. 1988. *Report of the Third Quinquennial Survey on Employment and Unemployment.* New Delhi: Department of Statistics, Ministry of Planning.

Schiff, Maurice, and Alberto Valdés. Forthcoming. *The Economics of Agricultural Pricing Incentives in Developing Countries.* Vol. 4 of Anne O. Krueger, Maurice Schiff, and Alberto Valdés, eds., *A Comparative Study of the Political Economy of Agricultural Pricing Policies.* Baltimore, Md.: Johns Hopkins University Press.

Sen, Amartya. 1981. *Poverty and Famines: An Essay on Entitlement and Deprivation.* Oxford: Clarendon Press.

Siamwalla, Ammar, and Suthad Setboonsarng. 1989. *Trade, Exchange Rate, and Agricultural Pricing Policies in Thailand.* World Bank Comparative Studies. Washington, D.C.

Singh, K. P., and Niva Bara. 1988. "Integrating Women's Concerns in Farming Systems Research/Extension: A Project in the Tribal Areas of Bihar (India)." Presented at the Farming Systems Symposium, University of Arkansas, October 10–12. Processed.

Sinn, Hans-Werner. 1988. "The Sahel Problem." *Kyklos* 41, 2; 187–213.

Spinanger, Dean. 1987. "Will the Multi-Fibre Arrangement Keep Bangladesh Humble?" *World Economy* 10, 1 (March): 75–84.

Srinivasan, T. N., and Pranab K. Bardhan, eds. 1988. *Rural Poverty in South Asia.* New York: Columbia University Press.

Steinberg, David I. 1985. "Foreign Aid and the Development of the Republic of Korea: The Effectiveness of Concessional Assistance." AID Special Study 42. U.S. Agency for International Development, Washington, D.C. Processed.

Streeten, Paul. 1987. *What Price Food? Agricultural Price Policies in Developing Countries.* New York: St. Martin's Press.

Subbarao, Kalanidhi. Forthcoming. "Interventions to Combat Household-Level Food Insecurity: A Review of India's Experience." In S. Guhan, Barbara Harriss, and Robert Cassen, eds., *Poverty in India.* Delhi: Oxford University Press.

Summers, Robert, and Alan Heston. 1988. "A New Set of International Comparisons of Real Product and Price Levels Estimates for 130 Countries, 1950–1985." *Review of Income and Wealth* (March): 1–24.

Tendler, Judith. 1989. "What Ever Happened to Poverty Alleviation?" *World Development* 17, 7 (July): 1033–44.

Trela, Irene, and John Whalley. 1988. "Do Developing Countries Lose from the MFA?" NBER Working Paper 2618. National Bureau of Economic Research, Cambridge, Mass. Processed.

Tremblay, Hélène, and Pat Capon. 1988. *Families of the World: Family Life at the Close of the Twentieth Century.* Vol. 1: *The Americas and the Caribbean.* New York: Farrar, Straus and Giroux.

Tyers, Rodney, and Kym Anderson. 1986. "Distortions in World Food Markets: A Quantitative Assessment." Background paper for *World Development Report 1986.* World Bank, World Development Report Office, Washington, D.C. Processed.

United Nations. 1987. "First Report on the World Nutrition Situation." Administrative Committee on Coordination, Subcommittee on Nutrition, Geneva. Processed.

———. 1989. "Update on the Nutrition Situation: Recent Trends in Nutrition in 33 Countries." Administrative Committee on Coordination, Subcommittee on Nutrition, Geneva. Processed.

United Nations Children's Fund. 1988. *Children on the Front Line: The Impact of Apartheid, Destabilization and Warfare on Children in Southern and South Africa.* New York.

———. 1989. *Improving Child Survival and Nutrition: The Joint WHO/UNICEF Nutrition Support Programme in Iringa, Tanzania.* Dar es Salaam.

———. 1990. *The State of the World's Children.* New York: Oxford University Press.

United Nations Conference on Trade and Development. 1988. *Handbook of International Trade and Development Statistics: Supplement 1987.* New York.

———. 1989. *Uruguay Round: Papers on Selected Issues.* New York.

United Nations, Department of International Economic and Social Affairs. 1988. *Mortality of Children under Age 5: World Estimates and Projections, 1950–2025.* Population Studies 105. New York.

United Nations Educational, Scientific, and Cultural Organization. Various years. *Statistical Yearbook.* Paris.

Universidad de Chile. Facultad de Ciencias Económicas y Administrativas, Departamento Economía. 1987. *Estudio sobre los Programas Especiales de Empleo.* Vols. 1–3. Santiago.

Uphoff, Norman. 1986. *Local Institutional Development: An Analytical Sourcebook with Cases.* West Hartford, Conn.: Kumarian Press.

U.S. Agency for International Development. 1989. *A.I.D. Microenterprise Stock-taking: Synthesis Report.* AID Evaluation Occasional Paper. Washington, D.C.

U.S. Arms Control and Disarmament Agency. 1988. *World Military Expenditures and Arms Transfers 1988.* Washington, D.C.: Government Printing Office.

van Wijnbergen, Sweder. 1989. "Growth, External Debt, and the Real Exchange Rate in Mexico." Policy, Planning, and Research Working Paper 257. World Bank, Latin America and the Caribbean Country Department II, Washington, D.C. Processed.

———. 1990. "Mexico's External Debt Restructuring in 1989/90: An Economic Analysis." World Bank, Latin America and the Caribbean Regional Office, Washington, D.C. Processed.

von Braun, Joachim, Eileen Kennedy, and Howarth Bouis. 1989. "Comparative Analyses of the Effects of Increased Commercialization of Subsistence Agriculture on Production, Consumption, and Nutrition." International Food Policy Research Institute, Washington, D.C. Processed.

Von Pischke, J. D. 1989. "Finance at the Frontier: Debt Capacity and the Role of Credit in Developing the Private Economy." World Bank, Economic Development Institute, Washington, D.C. Processed.

Von Pischke, J. D., Dale Adams, and Gordon Donald. 1983. *Rural Financial Markets in Developing Countries: Their Use and Abuse.* Baltimore, Md.: Johns Hopkins University Press.

Wagao, Imanne Hamisi. 1986. "The Impact of Global Recession on Living Standards—Tanzania." Economics Department, University of Dar es Salaam. Processed.

Walker, Thomas S., and John G. Ryan, with others. Forthcoming. *Against the Odds: Village and Household Economies in India's Semi-Arid Tropics.* Baltimore, Md.: Johns Hopkins University Press.

Watanabe, Barbara, and Eva Mueller. 1984. "A Poverty Profile for Rural Botswana." *World Development* 12, 2 (February): 115–27.

Webster, Leila. 1989. "World Bank Lending for Small and Medium Enterprises: Fifteen Years of Experience." World Bank, Industry and Energy Department, Washington, D.C. Processed.

Whalley, John. 1985. *Trade Liberalization among Major World Trading Areas.* Cambridge, Mass.: MIT Press.

Williamson, Jeffrey G. 1986. "Migration and Urbanization in the Third World." Harvard Institute for Economic Research Discussion Paper 1245. Cambridge, Mass. Processed.

Wilson, Francis, and Mamphela Ramphele. 1989. *Uprooting Poverty: The South African Challenge.* New York: W. W. Norton.

World Bank. 1983. *Learning by Doing: World Bank Lending for Urban Development, 1972–82.* Washington, D.C.

———. 1986a. *Aid for Development: The Key Issues. Supporting Materials for the Report of the Task Force on Concessional Flows.* Development Committee pamphlet 8. Washington, D.C.

———. 1986b. *Financing Education in Developing Countries: An Exploration of Policy Options.* Washington, D.C.

———. 1986c. *Poverty and Hunger: Issues and Options for Food Security in Developing Countries.* A World Bank Policy Study. Washington, D.C.

———. *World Development Report 1986.* New York: Oxford University Press.

———. 1987a. *The Aga Khan Rural Support Program in Pakistan: An Interim Evaluation.* A World Bank Operations Evaluation Study. Washington, D.C.

———. 1987b. *Financing Health Services in Developing Countries: An Agenda for Reform.* A World Bank Policy Study. Washington, D.C.

———. 1988a. *Education in Sub-Saharan Africa: Policies for Adjustment, Revitalization, and Expansion.* A World Bank Policy Study. Washington, D.C.

———. 1988b. "The Philippines: The Challenge of Poverty." Report 7144–PH. Asia Country Department II, Washington, D.C. Processed.

———. 1988c. *Rural Development: World Bank Experience, 1965–86.* A World Bank Operations Evaluation Study. Washington, D.C.

———. 1988d. *World Development Report 1988.* New York: Oxford University Press.

———. 1989a. "Feeding Latin America's Children." Latin America and the Caribbean Technical Department, Washington, D.C. Processed.

———. 1989b. *India: Poverty, Employment, and Social Services.* A World Bank Country Study. Washington, D.C.

———. 1989c. *Sub-Saharan Africa: From Crisis to Sustainable Growth.* A Long-Term Perspective Study. Washington, D.C.

———. 1989d. *Trends in Developing Economies.* Washington, D.C.

———. 1989e. *Women in Pakistan: An Economic and Social Strategy.* Washington, D.C.

———. 1989f. *World Debt Tables 1989–90: External Debt of Developing Countries.* Washington, D.C.

———. 1989g. *World Development Report 1989.* New York: Oxford University Press.

World Health Organization. Various years. *World Health Statistics Annual.* Geneva.

Yeats, Alexander J. 1981. "Agricultural Protectionism: An Analysis of Its International Economic Effects and Options for Institutional Reform." *Trade and Development* 3 (Winter): 1–29.

———. 1989. "Shifting Patterns of Comparative Advantage: Manufactured Exports of Developing Countries." Policy, Planning, and Research Working Paper 165. World Bank, International Economics Department, Washington, D.C. Processed.

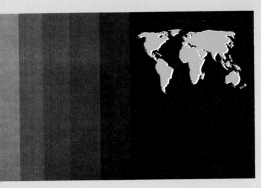

Statistical appendix

The tables in this statistical appendix present summary data on the population, national accounts, trade, and external debt of the low- and middle-income economies, the high-income economies, and all reporting economies as a group. Readers should refer to the "Definitions and data notes" for an explanation of the country groupings and to the technical notes to the World Development Indicators for definitions of the concepts used.

Table A.1 Population growth, 1965 to 1990, and projected to 2000

Country group	1989 population (millions)	Average annual growth (percent)			
		1965–73	1973–80	1980–90	1990–2000
Low- and middle-income economies	4,037	2.5	2.1	2.1	1.9
Low-income economies	2,947	2.6	2.1	2.0	1.9
Middle-income economies	1,090	2.4	2.3	2.1	1.9
Sub-Saharan Africa	479	2.6	2.8	3.2	3.1
East Asia	1,566	2.7	1.7	1.5	1.4
South Asia	1,132	2.4	2.4	2.3	1.9
Europe, Middle East, and North Africa	404	1.9	2.1	2.1	2.1
Latin America and the Caribbean	422	2.7	2.4	2.1	1.8
Severely indebted middle-income economies	506	2.5	2.3	2.1	1.8
High-income economies	789	1.0	0.8	0.7	0.5
OECD members	755	1.0	0.7	0.6	0.5
Total reporting economies	4,826	2.2	1.9	1.8	1.7
Oil exporters	609	2.7	2.7	2.7	2.4

Table A.2 Population and GNP per capita, 1980, and growth rates, 1965 to 1989

Country group	1980 GNP (billions of dollars)	1980 population (millions)	1980 GNP per capita (dollars)	Average annual growth of GNP per capita (percent)					
				1965–73	1973–80	1980–86	1987	1988	1989[a]
Low- and middle-income economies	2,406	3,359	700	4.0	2.6	1.5	2.7	3.4	1.2
Low-income economies	784	2,459	320	3.6	2.4	4.0	3.9	6.8	1.8
Middle-income economies	1,622	900	1,760	4.6	2.4	0.1	1.8	1.1	0.8
Sub-Saharan Africa	213	362	570	3.0	0.1	−2.8	−4.4	−0.8	0.5
East Asia	586	1,363	420	5.4	4.4	6.6	8.0	8.7	3.1
South Asia	220	922	240	1.0	2.0	3.2	0.9	6.1	2.3
Europe, Middle East, and North Africa	590	335	1,740	5.6	2.1	0.8	−0.6	0.1	0.6
Latin America and the Caribbean	716	348	2,000	4.1	2.4	−1.6	1.5	−0.8	−0.8
Severely indebted middle-income economies	791	419	1,840	4.2	2.6	−1.5	1.2	−0.4	−0.7
High-income economies	7,923	742	10,740	3.5	2.2	1.7	2.5	3.5	3.1
OECD members	7,663	716	10,750	3.5	2.2	1.9	2.8	3.7	3.1
Total reporting economies	10,329	4,101	2,520	2.7	1.5	0.9	1.8	2.7	1.7
Oil exporters	964	479	1,980	4.6	2.8	−1.6	−2.5	0.5	..

a. Preliminary.

Table A.3 Population and composition of GDP, selected years, 1965 to 1989
(billions of dollars, unless otherwise specified)

Country group and indicator	1965	1973	1980	1985	1986	1987	1988	1989[a]
Low- and middle-income economies								
GDP	377	849	2,406	2,521	2,598	2,818	3,159	..
Domestic absorption	375	842	2,446	2,522	2,618	2,801	3,178	..
Net exports	1	7	−39	0	−20	17	−19	..
Population (millions)	2,377	2,897	3,359	3,718	3,794	3,874	3,952	4,037
Low-income economies								
GDP	168	312	784	824	785	812	923	984
Domestic absorption	170	310	788	853	816	823	941	..
Net exports	−2	2	−4	−29	−31	−11	−18	..
Population (millions)	1,741	2,129	2,459	2,714	2,770	2,828	2,884	2,947
Middle-income economies								
GDP	209	537	1,622	1,698	1,813	2,006	2,236	..
Domestic absorption	206	532	1,658	1,669	1,803	1,978	2,237	..
Net exports	3	5	−36	29	10	28	−1	..
Population (millions)	635	768	900	1,003	1,025	1,046	1,068	1,090
Sub-Saharan Africa								
GDP	29	65	213	195	164	150	161	156
Domestic absorption	29	64	211	194	170	152	162	..
Net exports	0	2	2	0	−6	−1	−1	..
Population (millions)	243	299	362	422	435	449	464	479
East Asia								
GDP	93	215	586	645	650	732	889	1,026
Domestic absorption	93	213	585	645	635	699	860	..
Net exports	0	2	1	0	14	34	29	..
Population (millions)	980	1,208	1,363	1,470	1,492	1,516	1,538	1,566
South Asia								
GDP	69	97	220	277	294	325	348	345
Domestic absorption	72	99	236	291	308	332	358	351
Net exports	−3	−2	−15	−14	−13	−7	−10	−6
Population (millions)	645	781	922	1,033	1,058	1,082	1,107	1,132
Europe, Middle East, and North Africa								
GDP	73	186	590	668	741	796	..	..
Domestic absorption	73	183	611	693	..	..	..	..
Net exports	0	3	−21	−25	..	..	..	..
Population (millions)	250	290	335	372	380	388	396	404

Table A.3 *(continued)*

Country group and indicator	1965	1973	1980	1985	1986	1987	1988	1989[a]
Latin America and the Caribbean								
GDP	99	254	716	682	698	739	852	..
Domestic absorption	96	253	726	650	681	720	830	..
Net exports	3	1	−10	31	16	19	22	..
Population (millions)	239	295	348	388	397	405	414	422
Severely indebted middle-income economies								
GDP	109	280	791	755	784	822	943	955
Domestic absorption	106	278	807	721	769	802	918	..
Net exports	3	2	−15	34	16	20	25	..
Population (millions)	294	357	419	466	476	486	496	506
High-income economies								
GDP	1,406	3,330	7,914	8,938	10,860	12,599	14,108	15,237
Domestic absorption	1,396	3,297	7,867	8,914	10,807	12,560	14,049	15,173
Net exports	10	33	47	24	53	39	59	64
Population (millions)	647	701	742	768	773	779	784	789
OECD members								
GDP	1,391	3,283	7,652	8,700	10,633	12,347	13,836	14,943
Domestic absorption	1,382	3,255	7,666	8,679	10,568	12,298	13,767	14,868
Net exports	9	28	−14	21	65	50	68	75
Population (millions)	632	681	716	738	742	746	751	755
Total reporting economies								
GDP	1,783	4,180	10,320	11,459	13,458	15,417	17,267	..
Domestic absorption	1,772	4,139	10,313	11,435	13,425	15,361	17,227	..
Net exports	11	41	8	24	32	56	40	..
Population (millions)	3,024	3,598	4,101	4,485	4,567	4,653	4,736	4,826
Oil exporters								
GDP	78	226	965	1,005	844	850	926	..
Domestic absorption	75	209	861	985	872	848	938	..
Net exports	3	17	104	19	−28	2	−12	..
Population (millions)	321	398	479	547	562	578	593	609

Note: Components may not sum to totals because of rounding. Domestic absorption includes private consumption, general government consumption, and gross domestic investment. Net exports includes goods and nonfactor services.
a. Preliminary.

Table A.4 GDP, 1980, and growth rates, 1965 to 1989

Country group	1980 GDP (billions of dollars)	Average annual growth of GDP (percent)					
		1965–73	1973–80	1980–86	1987	1988	1989[a]
Low- and middle-income economies	2,406	6.6	4.8	3.8	4.5	5.4	3.3
Low-income economies	784	6.0	4.6	6.1	6.1	8.9	4.2
Middle-income economies	1,622	6.9	4.9	2.5	3.5	3.0	2.8
Sub-Saharan Africa	213	5.9	2.7	0.3	−1.1	2.5	3.5
East Asia	586	7.9	6.5	7.9	9.6	10.0	5.1
South Asia	220	3.6	4.1	5.6	3.2	8.9	4.8
Europe, Middle East, and North Africa	590	7.5	4.2	3.2	1.4	2.4	..
Latin America and the Caribbean	716	6.5	5.1	0.9	3.0	1.2	1.5
Severely indebted middle-income economies	791	6.4	5.2	1.0	2.6	1.6	1.4
High-income economies	7,914	4.6	3.0	2.5	3.4	4.3	3.6
OECD members	7,652	4.5	2.9	2.6	3.4	4.3	3.6
Total reporting economies	10,319	4.9	3.4	2.8	3.7	4.6	3.4
Oil exporters	965	7.3	4.9	0.8	0.3	3.0	..

a. Preliminary.

161

Table A.5 GDP structure of production, selected years, 1965 to 1988
(percentage of GDP)

Country group	1965 Agriculture	1965 Industry	1973 Agriculture	1973 Industry	1980 Agriculture	1980 Industry	1985 Agriculture	1985 Industry	1986 Agriculture	1986 Industry	1987 Agriculture	1987 Industry	1988a Agriculture	1988a Industry
Low- and middle-income economies	30	30	24	34	19	38	19	36	19	35	18	37	17	37
Low-income economies	43	27	39	32	32	37	33	33	32	32	31	33	31	34
Middle-income economies	19	32	15	35	12	38	12	37	13	37	13	38	10	39
Sub-Saharan Africa	40	17	33	24	28	32	34	26	34	23	31	25	31	25
East Asia	41	35	34	40	26	44	25	42	24	42	23	43	22	43
South Asia	41	19	43	19	35	22	31	24	29	25	29	25	30	24
Europe, Middle East, and North Africa	22	33	17	38	14	41	..	..	..	..	..	..	..	..
Latin America and the Caribbean	15	32	12	33	9	36	10	36	11	35	9	37	6	37
Severely indebted middle-income economies	16	32	13	33	10	36	11	35	11	34	10	37	7	38
High-income economies	5	40	5	38	3	37	3	34	3	32	3	31	..	..
OECD members	5	40	5	38	3	36	3	34	3	32	3	31	..	..
Total reporting economies	10	38	9	37	7	37	6	35	6	33	5	32	..	..
Oil exporters	19	32	14	38	11	48	13	38	13	34	12	36	..	..

a. Preliminary.

Table A.6 Sector growth rates, 1965 to 1989
(average annual percentage change)

Country group	Agriculture 1965–73	Agriculture 1973–80	Agriculture 1980–89	Industry 1965–73	Industry 1973–80	Industry 1980–89	Services 1965–73	Services 1973–80	Services 1980–89
Low- and middle-income economies	3.0	2.3	3.7	8.8	4.9	5.3	7.3	6.1	3.8
Low-income economies	2.9	1.8	4.3	10.7	7.0	8.7	6.3	5.3	6.1
Middle-income economies	3.2	3.0	2.7	8.0	4.0	3.2	7.6	6.3	3.1
Sub-Saharan Africa	2.2	−0.3	1.8	13.9	4.2	−0.2	4.1	3.1	1.5
East Asia	3.2	2.5	5.3	12.7	9.2	10.3	10.5	7.3	7.9
South Asia	3.1	2.2	2.7	3.9	5.6	7.2	4.0	5.3	6.1
Europe, Middle East, and North Africa	3.4	3.2	..	8.6	1.4	..	8.1	8.4	..
Latin America and the Caribbean	3.0	3.7	2.5	6.8	5.1	1.1	7.3	5.4	1.7
Severely indebted middle-income economies	3.1	3.6	2.7	6.8	5.4	1.0	7.2	5.4	1.7
High-income economies	1.4	0.5	2.3	3.9	2.2	1.9	4.5	3.4	3.0
OECD members	1.4	0.5	2.2	3.7	2.0	2.2	4.5	3.3	3.0
Total reporting economies	2.2	1.8	3.2	4.8	2.8	2.5	4.9	3.9	3.2
Oil exporters	3.3	2.1	2.7	9.4	3.3	−0.1	6.4	8.0	2.4

Note: Figures in italics are for years other than those specified.

Table A.7 Consumption, investment, and saving, selected years, 1965 to 1988
(percentage of GDP)

Country group and indicator	1965	1973	1980	1985	1986	1987	1988[a]
Low- and middle-income economies							
Consumption	79.4	76.1	74.7	75.9	76.6	75.2	74.8
Investment	20.4	23.2	26.9	24.1	24.2	24.1	25.6
Saving	18.9	21.7	23.6	21.2	20.8	22.3	22.6
Low-income economies							
Consumption	81.8	76.7	74.6	76.5	76.4	74.4	74.2
Investment	19.1	22.7	25.8	27.0	27.5	27.0	27.8
Saving	17.8	21.0	24.4	22.4	22.4	24.2	24.4
Middle-income economies							
Consumption	77.3	75.7	74.7	75.7	76.8	75.6	75.2
Investment	21.3	23.3	27.5	22.7	22.7	23.0	24.9
Saving	19.9	22.2	23.2	20.7	20.1	21.5	21.9
Sub-Saharan Africa							
Consumption	84.0	79.1	78.6	87.8	89.0	85.5	85.0
Investment	14.3	18.3	20.5	12.2	14.6	15.4	15.4
Saving	13.8	16.9	18.2	8.8	6.7	8.1	8.3
East Asia							
Consumption	77.6	71.6	69.1	69.1	67.7	65.6	65.9
Investment	22.3	27.3	30.7	30.9	30.1	29.8	30.9
Saving	22.3	25.8	29.7	29.5	31.1	33.3	33.3
South Asia							
Consumption	87.5	84.7	84.8	81.1	81.8	81.0	80.8
Investment	16.8	17.0	22.1	23.9	22.8	21.3	22.1
Saving	11.9	14.9	15.3	18.0	17.2	17.9	18.0
Europe, Middle East, and North Africa							
Consumption	78.1	73.1	73.1	75.4	76.9	78.8	..
Investment	21.9	25.3	30.5	28.3	..	..	..
Saving	17.8	24.2	25.8	22.3	21.1	18.8	..
Latin America and the Caribbean							
Consumption	76.4	78.4	77.2	77.8	80.2	77.7	75.9
Investment	20.3	21.2	24.2	17.6	17.4	19.7	21.5
Saving	21.1	19.4	20.3	16.8	14.9	17.9	19.6
Severely indebted middle-income economies							
Consumption	76.0	77.8	76.8	76.8	79.3	77.0	75.0
Investment	20.9	21.5	25.1	18.7	18.7	20.5	22.4
Saving	21.0	19.5	20.5	18.0	16.1	18.8	20.9
High-income economies							
Consumption	82.6	76.3	77.4	80.0	79.6	79.3	78.0
Investment	16.7	22.7	22.0	19.7	19.9	20.4	21.6
Saving	17.7	24.1	23.2	20.4	20.7	20.9	22.2
OECD members							
Consumption	79.6	76.4	78.2	80.1	79.6	79.2	78.0
Investment	19.8	22.7	22.0	19.6	19.8	20.4	21.5
Saving	20.8	24.1	22.3	20.1	20.6	20.9	22.1
Total reporting economies							
Consumption	82.0	76.2	76.7	79.2	79.1	78.6	77.5
Investment	17.5	22.9	23.2	20.7	20.7	21.1	22.4
Saving	18.0	23.7	23.3	20.5	20.7	21.1	22.2
Oil exporters							
Consumption	76.2	69.9	63.5	74.8	79.2	75.8	76.1
Investment	19.9	22.5	25.7	23.3	24.2	23.9	25.2
Saving	18.6	25.2	35.0	23.8	20.2	22.8	22.1

a. Preliminary.

Table A.8 Growth of export volume, 1965 to 1988

Country group and commodity	Average annual change in export volume (percent)					
	1965–73	1973–80	1980–86	1986	1987	1988
By commodity						
Low- and middle-income economies	5.3	3.8	4.8	5.9	7.4	7.3
Manufactures	11.6	12.8	9.5	8.4	17.6	10.2
Food	2.4	4.2	3.1	−0.7	7.2	−0.1
Nonfood	2.1	0.4	2.2	5.3	1.4	9.8
Metals and minerals	4.8	6.5	1.2	6.4	13.4	−4.1
Fuels	5.6	−0.4	2.0	7.1	−7.0	6.6
Total reporting economies	8.7	4.6	2.9	4.9	6.0	6.3
Manufactures	10.7	6.1	4.5	2.2	7.0	8.4
Food	4.6	6.8	2.9	11.4	11.7	−2.1
Nonfood	3.1	0.9	2.5	1.4	17.2	11.1
Metals and minerals	6.8	8.6	1.5	5.9	2.1	−8.0
Fuels	8.7	0.5	−1.9	12.1	−4.3	..
By country group						
Low- and middle-income economies	5.3	3.8	4.8	5.9	7.4	7.3
Manufactures	11.6	12.8	9.5	8.4	17.6	10.2
Primary goods	4.4	1.2	2.1	4.1	0.3	4.9
Low-income economies	9.6	2.2	2.9	9.2	3.9	7.6
Manufactures	1.8	8.5	10.0	15.5	23.5	15.8
Primary goods	11.2	1.1	0.6	6.7	−4.7	3.1
Middle-income economies	4.0	4.4	5.3	4.9	8.5	7.2
Manufactures	16.7	13.8	9.5	7.0	16.4	8.9
Primary goods	2.5	1.2	2.6	3.3	2.1	5.6
Sub-Saharan Africa	15.1	0.2	−2.0	−0.1	−1.8	1.2
Manufactures	7.6	5.6	4.8	2.9	4.3	5.3
Primary goods	15.4	0.0	−2.5	−0.4	−2.3	0.8
East Asia	9.7	8.7	9.7	15.9	14.3	9.4
Manufactures	17.5	15.5	13.3	19.2	24.9	12.8
Primary goods	7.3	4.7	5.7	11.7	−0.2	3.6
South Asia	−0.7	5.8	4.1	9.1	11.2	6.7
Manufactures	0.6	8.2	3.5	10.4	20.9	7.5
Primary goods	−1.8	3.1	5.0	7.7	0.0	5.5
Europe, Middle East, and North Africa	..	..	..	..	..	..
Manufactures	..	..	..	..	..	..
Primary goods	..	..	..	..	..	..
Latin America and the Caribbean	−0.9	0.9	3.4	−4.2	3.9	8.1
Manufactures	16.6	10.1	8.1	−10.6	5.5	19.3
Primary goods	−1.7	−0.5	2.3	−2.2	3.5	4.8
Severely indebted middle-income economies	−0.3	1.9	3.9	−3.5	2.9	11.4
Manufactures	16.9	12.1	9.0	−8.3	6.1	20.0
Primary goods	−1.1	0.3	2.5	−1.9	1.9	8.6
High-income economies	9.9	4.8	2.4	4.6	5.5	6.0
Manufactures	10.6	5.5	3.9	1.3	5.3	8.1
Primary goods	8.9	3.5	−0.6	12.9	6.0	1.3
OECD members	9.4	5.4	3.6	3.4	6.0	5.3
Manufactures	10.6	5.2	3.7	1.4	4.5	7.4
Primary goods	6.7	5.9	3.1	9.5	10.0	−0.4
Oil exporters	8.7	0.0	−4.6	12.5	−4.4	10.9
Manufactures	11.7	3.9	9.5	7.3	13.6	11.4
Primary goods	8.6	−0.1	−5.6	13.1	−6.4	10.9

Table A.9 Change in export prices and terms of trade, 1965 to 1988
(average annual percentage change)

Country group	1965–73	1973–80	1980–86	1986	1987	1988
Export prices						
Low- and middle-income economies	6.2	14.7	−4.9	−10.6	11.0	6.1
Manufactures	6.4	8.2	−2.2	9.4	8.6	8.9
Food	5.9	8.6	−2.7	7.6	−7.0	14.4
Nonfood	4.6	10.2	−4.8	−1.1	21.7	2.8
Metals and minerals	2.5	4.7	−4.4	−4.8	11.4	28.2
Fuels	8.3	26.0	−10.1	−46.7	22.0	−15.0
High-income OECD members						
Total	4.8	10.3	−1.4	12.2	11.4	8.3
Manufactures	4.5	10.9	−0.3	19.0	13.7	7.0
Terms of trade						
Low- and middle-income economies	0.1	2.5	−2.7	−10.9	2.3	−0.2
Low-income economies	−4.9	4.1	−3.0	−16.0	4.3	−1.1
Middle-income economies	1.8	1.9	−2.7	−9.1	1.8	0.1
Sub-Saharan Africa	−8.5	4.8	−4.0	−21.5	2.9	−4.4
East Asia	−0.6	1.2	−1.3	−6.1	0.5	1.1
South Asia	3.7	−3.4	1.5	3.1	1.2	2.0
Europe, Middle East, and North Africa	..	..	..	..	..	..
Latin America and the Caribbean	3.8	2.3	−3.3	−14.0	−2.3	1.7
Severely indebted middle-income economies	4.3	1.7	−2.2	−11.4	1.6	0.2
High-income economies	−1.2	−2.1	0.5	7.0	0.2	0.5
OECD members	−1.0	−3.3	1.1	10.6	−0.5	0.7
Oil exporters	0.3	11.5	−7.3	−40.8	11.7	−16.5

Table A.10 Growth of long-term debt of low- and middle-income economies, 1970 to 1989
(average annual percentage change, nominal)

Country group	1970–73	1973–80	1980–86	1987	1988	1989
Low- and middle-income economies						
Debt outstanding and disbursed	18.0	22.2	13.2	13.2	−1.9	1.1
Official	15.3	17.8	15.3	21.9	0.8	5.7
Private	20.7	25.6	12.0	7.2	−4.0	−2.6
Low-income economies						
Debt outstanding and disbursed	16.9	16.6	14.0	25.9	5.0	6.4
Official	14.9	14.2	13.8	23.1	4.0	8.0
Private	26.1	23.8	14.6	31.7	7.0	3.4
Middle-income economies						
Debt outstanding and disbursed	18.4	24.2	13.0	9.6	−4.1	−0.7
Official	15.6	20.7	16.3	21.3	−1.1	4.3
Private	20.1	25.9	11.7	3.8	−5.9	−3.8
Sub-Saharan Africa						
Debt outstanding and disbursed	20.2	23.8	13.7	26.4	0.9	4.9
Official	17.2	22.3	17.5	27.0	1.6	11.3
Private	25.6	26.2	8.4	25.2	−0.5	−8.0
East Asia						
Debt outstanding and disbursed	23.7	22.7	15.8	13.7	−0.2	1.1
Official	27.0	17.9	16.4	24.8	1.5	3.3
Private	20.7	26.6	15.5	6.8	−1.4	−0.6
South Asia						
Debt outstanding and disbursed	11.6	11.2	12.5	18.3	5.9	9.7
Official	12.4	10.4	9.3	16.7	4.4	5.5
Private	1.6	24.5	30.3	23.1	10.3	21.3
Europe, Middle East, and North Africa						
Debt outstanding and disbursed	22.2	28.9	12.4	15.4	−2.3	4.1
Official	16.4	25.6	15.9	18.6	−2.0	5.9
Private	29.9	32.1	9.4	11.9	−2.6	2.0
Latin America and the Caribbean						
Debt outstanding and disbursed	16.8	21.6	13.1	7.4	−4.8	−3.9
Official	11.6	15.2	17.4	24.0	1.0	2.9
Private	18.9	23.5	12.2	2.6	−6.8	−6.5
Severely indebted middle-income economies						
Debt outstanding and disbursed	16.9	23.9	14.4	9.4	−4.7	−3.1
Official	12.7	17.5	22.9	23.9	0.7	3.1
Private	18.5	25.7	12.5	4.4	−6.9	−5.9

Table A.11 Investment, saving, and current account balance before official transfers, 1965 to 1988
(percentage of GNP)

Country	Gross domestic investment			Gross national saving			Balance of payments: current account balance before official transfers		
	1965–73	1973–80	1980–88	1965–73[a]	1973–80	1980–88	1965–73	1973–80	1980–88
Latin America and the Caribbean									
*Argentina	19.7	23.4	14.4	20.1	22.6	10.0	0.4	−0.7	−4.5
*Bolivia	25.4	24.9	12.1	16.8	18.5	1.6	−8.6	−6.4	−10.5
*Brazil	21.3	23.9	20.7	23.1	19.3	18.5	1.9	−4.6	−2.2
*Chile	14.3	17.3	17.5	11.9	12.1	8.9	−2.4	−5.2	−8.7
Colombia	18.9	18.8	20.2	15.8	19.0	16.7	−3.2	0.2	−3.5
*Costa Rica	21.8	25.5	27.9	13.0	13.8	17.7	−8.8	−11.7	−10.2
*Ecuador	19.0	26.7	23.3	12.7	21.2	17.4	−6.2	−5.6	−5.9
Guatemala	13.3	18.7	13.4	11.6	16.4	9.3	−1.7	−2.3	−4.2
*Honduras	18.6	24.9	17.5	14.0	14.6	7.8	−4.6	−10.2	−9.7
Jamaica	32.0	20.2	23.8	23.7	13.6	13.7	−8.4	−6.6	−10.2
*Mexico	20.6	24.2	23.5	16.5	20.2	21.9	−4.0	−4.0	−1.6
*Nicaragua	20.1	18.7	21.8	13.5	9.0	−5.6	−6.5	−9.7	−27.4
*Peru	24.1	23.9	27.4	19.5	19.7	22.7	−4.6	−4.1	−4.6
*Uruguay	12.0	15.7	12.6	12.0	11.3	9.8	0.0	−4.4	−2.8
*Venezuela	31.1	34.2	22.5	31.9	35.8	24.2	0.8	1.6	1.7
Sub-Saharan Africa									
Cameroon	16.6	21.8	21.6	..	17.0	16.9	..	−4.8	−4.7
*Congo, People's Rep.	29.3	34.0	38.2	4.2	10.3	24.5	−25.2	−23.6	−13.8
*Côte d'Ivoire	22.8	29.1	19.4	..	16.8	8.0	..	−12.3	−11.5
Ethiopia	12.8	9.5	12.7	11.0	6.9	5.6	−1.8	−2.5	−7.1
Ghana	12.3	8.7	7.8	8.7	..	2.7	−3.5	−1.8	−5.1
Kenya	22.6	26.2	25.7	17.2	16.4	18.7	−5.5	−9.8	−7.0
Liberia	19.1	28.7	15.0	..	27.5	6.9	..	−1.2	−8.1
Malawi	20.0	29.7	18.3	..	10.7	7.2	..	−19.0	−11.1
Niger	9.7	23.8	16.3	..	9.7	1.9	..	−14.1	−14.3
Nigeria	16.3	22.8	13.9	11.8	24.4	12.3	−4.5	1.6	−1.6
*Senegal	14.7	17.5	16.0	..	4.2	0.2	..	−13.3	−15.8
Sierra Leone	13.8	14.1	14.2	9.8	−1.0	7.8	−4.0	−15.1	−6.3
Sudan	11.9	16.2	13.4	11.0	9.6	..	−0.9	−6.6	..
Tanzania	19.9	23.9	19.0	17.3	13.8	10.2	−2.6	−10.0	−8.8
Zaire	13.7	15.0	15.2	29.3	8.6	5.4	15.6	−6.4	−9.8
Zambia	31.9	28.5	18.2	34.3	19.9	4.3	2.4	−8.6	−14.0
East Asia									
Indonesia	15.8	24.5	27.6	13.7	24.6	24.4	−2.1	0.1	−3.2
Korea, Republic of	23.9	31.2	30.3	17.6	25.9	31.7	−6.3	−5.3	1.4
Malaysia	22.3	28.7	32.4	22.6	29.4	29.1	0.2	0.6	−3.4
Papua New Guinea	27.8	22.0	27.1	..	11.7	5.2	..	−10.4	−21.9
*Philippines	20.6	29.1	22.1	18.7	24.3	17.9	−1.9	−4.8	−4.1
Thailand	24.3	26.9	25.6	20.5	21.9	21.4	−3.8	−5.0	−4.2
South Asia									
India	17.2	21.3	24.0	14.0	21.0	21.7	−3.3	−0.3	−2.2
Pakistan	16.1	17.5	19.0	..	11.7	15.1	..	−5.9	−3.9
Sri Lanka	15.8	20.6	26.4	11.2	13.4	15.9	−4.6	−7.2	−10.5
Europe, Middle East, and North Africa									
Algeria	32.6	44.6	36.0	30.5	39.0	35.3	−2.2	−5.6	−0.7
Egypt, Arab Republic of	14.0	29.3	27.7	9.3	18.2	15.6	−4.6	−11.1	−12.1
*Hungary	..	32.0	27.9	..	..	..	..	..	..
*Morocco	15.1	25.9	26.1	13.6	16.8	19.8	−1.5	−9.0	−6.3
*Poland	..	..	28.3	..	..	25.4	..	−5.6	−2.9
Portugal	26.6	29.7	30.3	..	..	29.4	..	..	−0.9
Tunisia	23.3	29.9	27.9	17.8	23.2	22.1	−5.5	−6.7	−5.8
Turkey	18.5	21.8	22.9	17.5	18.1	20.2	−1.0	−3.7	−2.7
Yugoslavia	29.9	35.6	37.0	27.2	32.9	38.0	−2.6	−2.7	1.0

Note: An asterisk indicates a severely indebted middle-income economy. Figures in italics are for years other than those specified.
a. Excludes transfers, 1965–69.

Table A.12 Composition of debt outstanding, 1970 to 1988
(percentage of total long-term debt)

Country	Debt from official sources			Debt from private sources			Debt at floating rate		
	1970–72	1980–82	1988	1970–72	1980–82	1988	1973–75	1980–82	1988
Latin America and the Caribbean									
*Argentina	12.6	9.0	17.7	87.4	91.0	82.3	6.6	29.2	80.2
*Bolivia	58.2	49.3	81.1	41.8	50.7	18.9	7.3	28.4	21.7
*Brazil	30.7	11.9	24.3	69.3	88.1	75.7	26.1	45.9	62.0
*Chile	46.0	11.1	26.9	54.0	88.9	73.1	8.3	23.4	65.5
Colombia	68.1	46.1	52.8	31.9	53.9	47.2	5.4	33.7	40.5
*Costa Rica	39.8	36.8	51.5	60.2	63.2	48.5	15.5	42.4	43.6
*Ecuador	51.4	30.6	38.7	48.6	69.4	61.3	8.2	36.5	66.7
Guatemala	47.5	71.0	74.5	52.5	29.0	25.5	3.5	5.6	10.5
*Honduras	73.8	62.2	79.7	26.3	37.8	20.4	1.8	19.1	18.2
Jamaica	7.4	68.3	82.9	92.6	31.7	17.1	4.7	17.3	25.7
*Mexico	19.5	10.9	18.1	80.5	89.1	81.9	32.0	61.7	72.0
*Nicaragua	65.3	58.0	80.2	34.7	42.0	19.8	44.2	42.1	20.6
*Peru	15.6	39.4	45.0	84.4	60.6	55.0	16.1	22.9	29.4
*Uruguay	44.2	21.1	21.7	55.8	78.9	78.3	10.1	28.5	69.6
*Venezuela	30.8	3.6	1.5	69.2	96.4	98.5	17.2	57.9	72.8
Sub-Saharan Africa									
Cameroon	82.2	56.6	69.3	17.8	43.4	30.6	1.8	11.3	8.2
*Congo, People's Rep.	84.0	43.9	49.1	16.0	56.1	50.9	0.0	10.9	40.2
*Côte d'Ivoire	51.4	22.9	40.8	48.6	77.1	59.2	19.3	37.5	35.8
Ethiopia	87.3	90.9	83.5	12.7	9.1	16.5	1.5	2.1	6.7
Ghana	56.5	87.9	88.5	43.5	12.1	11.5	0.0	0.0	3.7
Kenya	58.3	55.0	73.4	41.7	45.0	26.6	2.1	10.2	3.6
Liberia	81.1	73.5	81.7	19.0	26.5	18.3	0.0	16.9	9.3
Malawi	85.8	72.2	95.6	14.2	27.8	4.4	2.3	21.9	3.8
Niger	97.0	41.0	76.9	2.9	59.0	23.1	0.0	13.4	6.4
Nigeria	68.8	14.7	37.9	31.2	85.3	62.1	0.7	48.8	40.1
*Senegal	59.2	67.8	93.0	40.8	32.2	7.0	24.6	12.0	2.5
Sierra Leone	60.6	66.4	81.4	39.4	33.6	18.6	3.8	0.1	0.6
Sudan	86.9	75.4	78.6	13.1	24.6	21.4	2.2	9.4	0.8
Tanzania	63.7	75.8	93.3	36.3	24.2	6.7	0.4	0.3	2.5
Zaire	42.5	65.9	90.0	57.5	34.1	10.0	32.8	11.9	5.4
Zambia	22.0	69.7	87.5	78.0	30.3	12.5	20.7	10.2	13.4
East Asia									
Indonesia	72.1	51.9	58.3	27.9	48.1	41.7	4.9	15.0	25.8
Korea, Republic of	35.2	34.3	38.2	64.8	65.7	61.8	11.8	29.0	23.8
Malaysia	51.0	21.9	23.1	49.0	78.1	76.9	17.4	36.7	42.3
Papua New Guinea	6.1	23.9	33.7	93.8	76.1	66.3	0.0	23.2	17.1
*Philippines	22.6	31.3	44.8	77.4	68.7	55.2	7.3	24.0	41.4
Thailand	40.1	39.1	46.0	59.9	60.9	54.0	0.4	22.4	27.2
South Asia									
India	95.1	83.9	60.7	4.9	16.1	39.3	0.0	3.0	15.1
Pakistan	90.6	92.6	93.6	9.4	7.4	6.4	0.0	3.2	8.8
Sri Lanka	81.6	79.5	82.8	18.4	20.5	17.2	0.0	12.9	4.4
Europe, Middle East, and North Africa									
Algeria	47.2	20.5	23.7	52.8	79.5	76.3	34.0	23.5	35.8
Egypt, Arab Republic of	70.3	82.1	85.8	29.7	17.9	14.2	3.1	2.3	1.4
*Hungary	0.0	12.0	10.6	0.0	88.0	89.5	0.0	81.3	60.2
*Morocco	79.1	55.9	74.7	20.9	44.1	25.3	2.7	27.2	38.4
*Poland	0.0	0.0	65.5	0.0	0.0	34.5	0.0	0.0	63.3
Portugal	29.3	24.7	18.1	70.7	75.3	81.9	0.0	33.9	36.3
Tunisia	71.4	59.9	71.6	28.6	40.1	28.4	0.0	13.6	16.5
Turkey	92.5	63.3	54.8	7.5	36.7	45.2	0.8	23.0	33.5
Yugoslavia	37.5	23.6	34.5	62.5	76.4	65.5	3.2	10.1	46.8

Note: An asterisk indicates a severely indebted middle-income economy.

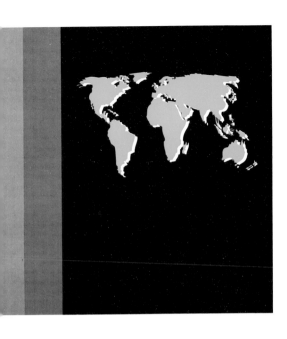

World Development Indicators

Contents

Key

In each table, economies are listed in their group in ascending order of GNP per capita except those for which no GNP per capita can be calculated. These are italicized, in alphabetical order, at the end of their group. The reference numbers below reflect the order in the tables.

Figures in the colored bands are summary measures for groups of economies. The letter *w* after a summary measure indicates that it is a weighted average; *m*, a median value; *t*, a total.

All growth rates are in real terms.

Data cutoff date is April 30, 1990.

. . = not available.
0 and 0.0 = zero or less than half the unit shown.
Blank means not applicable.

Figures in italics are for years or periods other than those specified.

Afghanistan	37	Hong Kong	102	Papua New Guinea	51
Algeria	81	Hungary	82	Paraguay	63
Angola	77	India	22	Peru	66
Argentina	84	Indonesia	34	Philippines	44
Australia	104	*Iran, Islamic Republic of*	94	Poland	73
Austria	110	*Iraq*	95	Portugal	90
Bangladesh	5	Ireland	99	*Romania*	96
Belgium	108	Israel	100	Rwanda	20
Benin	28	Italy	106	Saudi Arabia	97
Bhutan	9	Jamaica	60	Senegal	46
Bolivia	43	Japan	120	*Sierra Leone*	41
Botswana	58	Jordan	67	Singapore	101
Brazil	76	*Kampuchea, Democratic*	39	Somalia	7
Burkina Faso	13	Kenya	24	South Africa	80
Burundi	15	Korea, Republic of	89	Spain	98
Cameroon	59	Kuwait	107	Sri Lanka	31
Canada	113	Lao People's Democratic Rep.	10	Sudan	36
Central African Republic	26	*Lebanon*	78	Sweden	117
Chad	3	Lesotho	30	Switzerland	121
Chile	68	*Liberia*	40	Syrian Arab Republic	69
China	21	Libya	93	Tanzania	4
Colombia	62	Madagascar	12	Thailand	57
Congo, People's Republic of the	55	Malawi	6	Togo	25
Costa Rica	70	Malaysia	74	Trinidad and Tobago	88
Côte d'Ivoire	50	Mali	14	Tunisia	64
Denmark	114	Mauritania	35	Turkey	65
Dominican Republic	49	Mauritius	72	Uganda	16
Ecuador	61	Mexico	71	United Arab Emirates	111
Egypt, Arab Republic of	48	Morocco	52	United Kingdom	105
El Salvador	56	Mozambique	1	United States	118
Ethiopia	2	*Myanmar*	38	Uruguay	83
Finland	116	Nepal	11	Venezuela	87
France	112	Netherlands	109	*Viet Nam*	42
Gabon	86	New Zealand	103	Yemen Arab Republic	45
Germany, Federal Republic of	115	*Nicaragua*	79	Yemen, People's Dem. Rep. of	33
Ghana	29	Niger	19	Yugoslavia	85
Greece	91	Nigeria	17	Zaire	8
Guatemala	54	Norway	119	Zambia	18
Guinea	32	Oman	92	Zimbabwe	47
Haiti	27	Pakistan	23		
Honduras	53	Panama	75		

Note: For economies with populations of less than 1 million, see Box A.1; for nonreporting nonmember economies, see Box A.2.

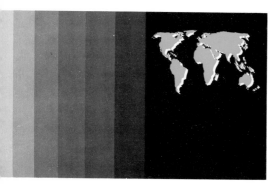

Introduction

The World Development Indicators provide information on the main features of social and economic development. Most of the data collected by the World Bank are on the low- and middle-income economies. Because comparable data for high-income economies are readily available, these are also included here. Additional information on some of these and other countries may be found in other World Bank publications, notably the *World Bank Atlas*, *World Tables*, *World Debt Tables*, and *Social Indicators of Development*. Data available for nonreporting nonmembers are summarized in the main tables and shown by country in Box A.2.

In these notes the term ''country'' does not imply political independence but may refer to any territory whose authorities present for it separate social or economic statistics. As in the past, the Bank classifies economies for certain operational and analytical purposes according to gross national product (GNP) per capita. The definitions and data notes at the beginning of the main Report provide a detailed description of the country groups.

Although every effort has been made to standardize the data, full comparability cannot be ensured, and care must be taken in interpreting the indicators. The statistics are drawn from sources thought to be most authoritative, but the data are subject to considerable margins of error. Variations in national statistical practices also reduce the comparability of data, which should thus be construed only as indicating trends and characterizing major differences among economies, rather than taken as precise quantitative indications of those differences.

The indicators in Table 1 give a summary profile of economies. Data in the other tables fall into the following broad areas: production, domestic absorption, fiscal and monetary accounts, core international transactions, external finance, and human resources.

In this edition, changes have been made to a number of tables. While these are described more fully in the technical notes, the objectives of the changes may be of interest.

As an outgrowth of the World Development Report's focus this year on poverty, the reporting of income distribution (Table 30) has been modified. Illiteracy, female as well as overall, is reported as a basic indicator (Table 1).

Social indicators have been rearranged. The age structure of the population is again reported, at the expense of estimates of population momentum (Table 26). Education (Table 29) adds indicators on primary net enrollment and pupil-teacher ratios and drops male enrollment measures (which can still be gauged from total and female measures). Gender-relative indicators are added (Table 32) for risk of dying by age 5 as well as persistence in primary school. To accommodate these additions, Table 27 takes over the indicator showing when net reproduction rate will equal 1; estimates for births attended by health staff and infant mortality rates are moved to Table 28.

Data on external debt are compiled directly by the Bank on the basis of reports from developing member countries through the Debtor Reporting System. Other data are drawn mainly from the United Nations and its specialized agencies, the International Monetary Fund, and country reports to the World Bank. Bank staff estimates are also used to improve currency or consistency. For most countries, national accounts estimates are obtained from member governments through World Bank economic missions. In some instances these are adjusted by Bank staff to conform to international definitions and concepts to provide better consistency and to incorporate latest estimates.

For ease of reference, only ratios and rates of growth are usually shown; absolute values are generally available from other World Bank publications, notably the 1989–90 edition of the *World Tables*. Most growth rates are calculated for two periods, 1965–80 and 1980–88, and are computed, unless otherwise noted, by using the least-squares regression method. Because this method takes into account all observations in a period, the resulting growth rates reflect general trends that are not unduly influenced by exceptional values, particularly at the end points. To exclude the effects of inflation, constant price economic indicators are used in calculating growth rates. Details of this methodology are given at the beginning of the technical notes. Data in italics indicate that they are for years or periods other than those specified—up to two years earlier for economic indicators and up to three years on either side for social indicators, since the latter tend to be collected less regularly and change less dramatically over short periods of time. All dollar figures are U.S. dollars, unless otherwise stated. The various methods used for converting from national currency figures are described in the technical notes.

Differences between figures in this year's and last year's edition reflect not only updating revisions in the countries themselves but revisions to historical series and changes in methodology. In addition, the Bank reviews methodologies in an effort to improve the international comparability and analytical significance of the indicators.

As in the Report itself, the main criterion used to classify economies in the World Development Indicators is GNP per capita. These income groups broadly distinguish countries at different stages of economic development. Many of the economies are further classified by geographical location. Other classifications include severely indebted middle-income economies and all oil exporters. Severely indebted middle-income economies is a group of nineteen countries that replaces previous editions' 17 highly indebted economies, which contained a mix of low- and middle-income economies. For a list of countries in each group, see the definitions and data notes. The major classifications used in the tables this year are 42 low-income economies with per capita incomes of $545 or less in 1988, 54 middle-income economies with per capita incomes of $546 to $5,999, including Angola, a new Bank member, and 25 high-income economies. For a final group of 9 nonreporting nonmember economies, paucity of data, differences in methods of computing national income, and difficulties of conversion are such that only aggregates are shown in the main tables. Some selected indicators for these countries, however, are included in Box A.2.

Economies with populations of less than 1 million are not shown separately in the main tables, but basic indicators for these countries and territories, and for Puerto Rico, are in a separate table in Box A.1.

The summary measures are overall estimates. Countries for which individual estimates are not shown, because of size, nonreporting, or insufficient history, have been implicitly included by assuming they follow the trend of reporting countries during such periods. This gives a more consistent aggregate measure by standardizing country coverage for each period shown. Group aggregates also include countries with less than 1 million population, even though country-specific data for these countries do not appear in the tables. Where missing information accounts for a third or more of the overall estimate, however, the group measure is reported as not available.

Throughout the World Development Indicators, the data for China do not include Taiwan, China. However, footnotes to Tables 14, 15, 16, and 18 provide estimates of the international transactions for Taiwan, China.

The table format of this edition follows that used in previous years. In each group, economies are listed in ascending order of GNP per capita, except those for which no such figure can be calculated. These are italicized and in alphabetical order at the end of the group deemed to be appropriate. This order is used in all tables except Table 19, which covers only high-income OPEC and OECD countries. The alphabetical list in the key shows the reference number for each economy; here, too, italics indicate economies with no estimates of GNP per capita. Economies in the high-income group marked by the symbol † are those classified by the United Nations or otherwise regarded by their authorities as developing.

The colored bands show summary measures—

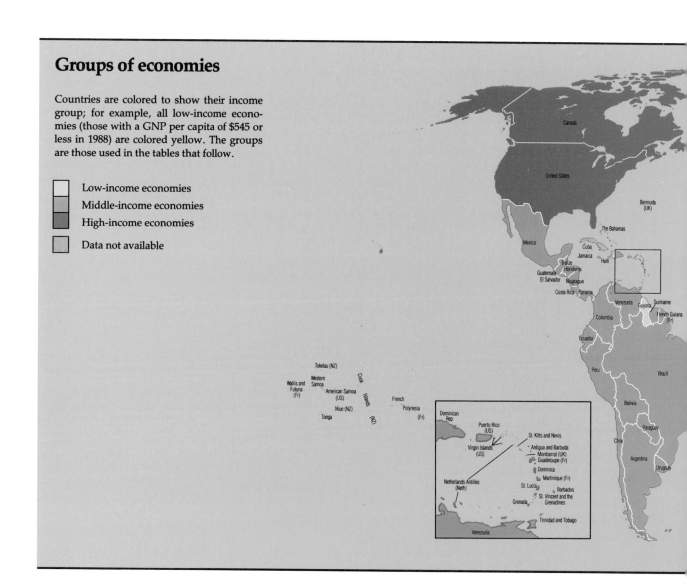

Groups of economies

Countries are colored to show their income group; for example, all low-income economies (those with a GNP per capita of $545 or less in 1988) are colored yellow. The groups are those used in the tables that follow.

Low-income economies
Middle-income economies
High-income economies

Data not available

totals, weighted averages, or median values—calculated for groups of economies. The methodology used for computing the summary measures is described in the technical notes. For these numbers, *w* indicates that the summary measures are weighted averages; *m*, median values; and *t*, totals. The coverage of economies is not uniform for all indicators, and the variation from measures of central tendency can be large; therefore readers should exercise caution in comparing the summary measures for different indicators, groups, and years or periods.

The technical notes and footnotes to tables should be referred to in any use of the data. These notes outline the methods, concepts, definitions, and data sources used in compiling the tables. A separate section gives details of these sources, which contain comprehensive definitions and descriptions of concepts used. It should also be noted that country notes to the *World Tables* provide additional explanations of sources used, breaks in comparability, and other exceptions to standard statistical practices that have been identified by Bank staff on national accounts and international transactions.

Comments and questions relating to the World Development Indicators should be addressed to:
Socio-Economic Data Division
International Economics Department
The World Bank
1818 H Street, N.W.
Washington, D.C. 20433.

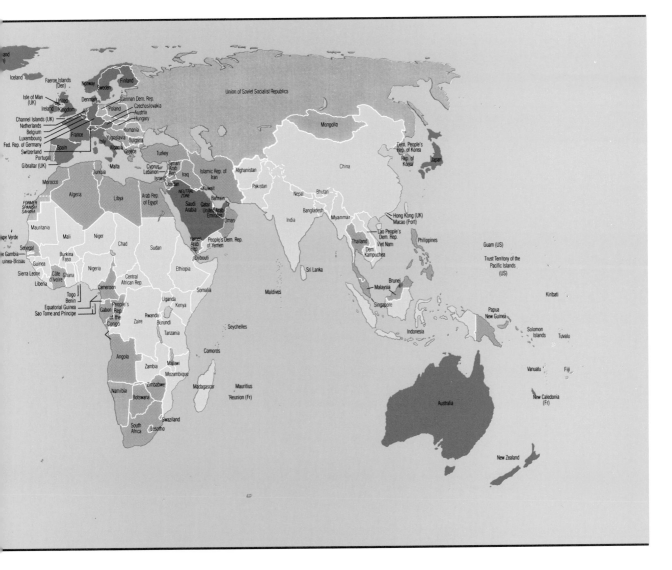

Population

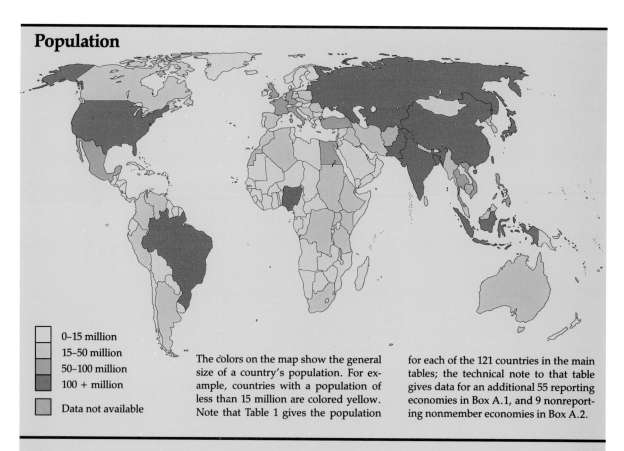

☐	0–15 million
☐	15–50 million
☐	50–100 million
■	100 + million
☐	Data not available

The colors on the map show the general size of a country's population. For example, countries with a population of less than 15 million are colored yellow. Note that Table 1 gives the population for each of the 121 countries in the main tables; the technical note to that table gives data for an additional 55 reporting economies in Box A.1, and 9 nonreporting nonmember economies in Box A.2.

Fertility and mortality

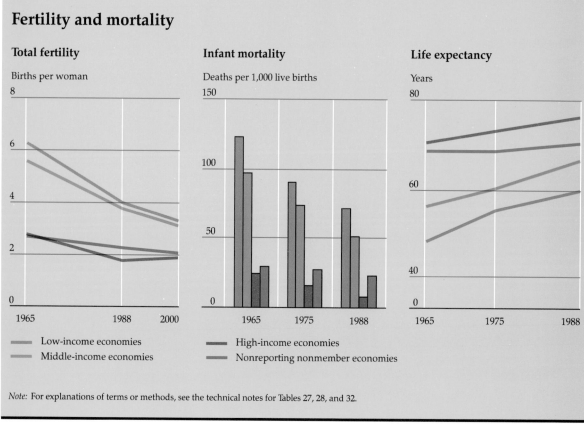

Total fertility
Births per woman

Infant mortality
Deaths per 1,000 live births

Life expectancy
Years

—— Low-income economies
—— Middle-income economies
—— High-income economies
—— Nonreporting nonmember economies

Note: For explanations of terms or methods, see the technical notes for Tables 27, 28, and 32.

Share of agriculture in GDP

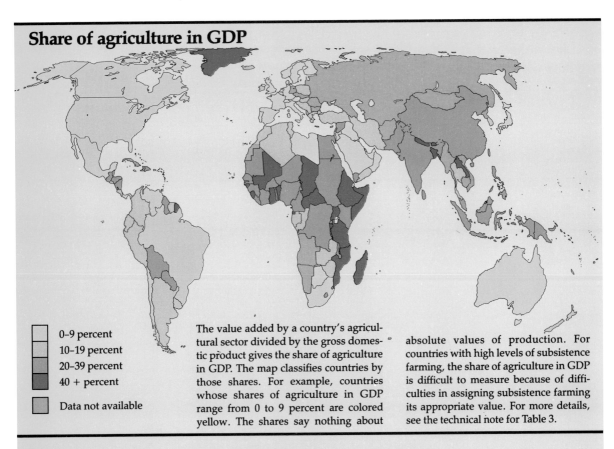

0–9 percent
10–19 percent
20–39 percent
40 + percent

Data not available

The value added by a country's agricultural sector divided by the gross domestic product gives the share of agriculture in GDP. The map classifies countries by those shares. For example, countries whose shares of agriculture in GDP range from 0 to 9 percent are colored yellow. The shares say nothing about absolute values of production. For countries with high levels of subsistence farming, the share of agriculture in GDP is difficult to measure because of difficulties in assigning subsistence farming its appropriate value. For more details, see the technical note for Table 3.

External balances of low- and middle-income countries

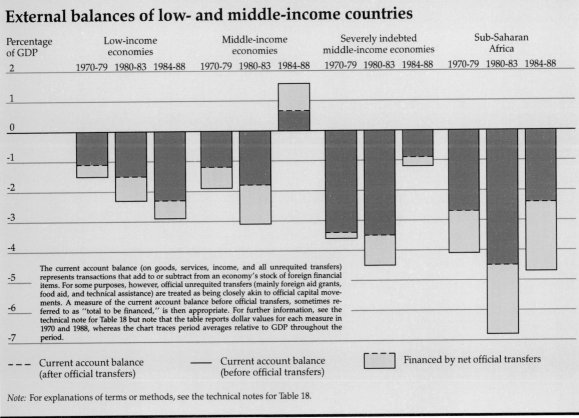

Percentage of GDP	Low-income economies			Middle-income economies			Severely indebted middle-income economies			Sub-Saharan Africa		
	1970-79	1980-83	1984-88	1970-79	1980-83	1984-88	1970-79	1980-83	1984-88	1970-79	1980-83	1984-88

The current account balance (on goods, services, income, and all unrequited transfers) represents transactions that add to or subtract from an economy's stock of foreign financial items. For some purposes, however, official unrequited transfers (mainly foreign aid grants, food aid, and technical assistance) are treated as being closely akin to official capital movements. A measure of the current account balance before official transfers, sometimes referred to as "total to be financed," is then appropriate. For further information, see the technical note for Table 18 but note that the table reports dollar values for each measure in 1970 and 1988, whereas the chart traces period averages relative to GDP throughout the period.

– – – Current account balance (after official transfers)

——— Current account balance (before official transfers)

Financed by net official transfers

Note: For explanations of terms or methods, see the technical notes for Table 18.

Table 1. Basic indicators

		Population (millions) mid-1988	Area (thousands of square kilometers)	GNP per capita[a] Dollars 1988	GNP per capita[a] Average annual growth rate (percent) 1965-88	Average annual rate of inflation[a] (percent) 1965-80	Average annual rate of inflation[a] (percent) 1980-88	Life expectancy at birth (years) 1988	Adult illiteracy (percent) Female 1985	Adult illiteracy (percent) Total 1985
	Low-income economies	**2,884.0 t**	**36,997 t**	**320 w**	**3.1 w**	**8.8 w**	**8.9 w**	**60 w**	**58 w**	**44 w**
	China and India	**1,904.0 t**	**12,849 t**	**340 w**	**4.0 w**	**2.8 w**	**5.8 w**	**63 w**	**56 w**	**42 w**
	Other low-income	**980.0 t**	**24,149 t**	**280 w**	**1.5 w**	**18.2 w**	**13.8 w**	**54 w**	**62 w**	**51 w**
1	Mozambique	14.9	802	100	..	..	33.6	48	78	62
2	Ethiopia	47.4	1,222	120	-0.1	3.4	2.1	47	..	38
3	Chad	5.4	1,284	160	-2.0	6.2	3.2	46	89	75
4	Tanzania	24.7	945	160	-0.5	9.9	25.7	53	..	..
5	Bangladesh	108.9	144	170	0.4	14.9	11.1	51	78	67
6	Malawi	8.0	118	170	1.1	7.2	12.6	47	69	59
7	Somalia	5.9	638	170	0.5	10.3	38.4	47	94	88
8	Zaire	33.4	2,345	170	-2.1	24.5	56.1	52	55	39
9	Bhutan	1.4	47	180	..	..	8.9	48	..	..
10	Lao PDR	3.9	237	180	..	..	..	49	24	16
11	Nepal	18.0	141	180	..	7.8	8.7	51	88	74
12	Madagascar	10.9	587	190	-1.8	7.7	17.3	50	38	33
13	Burkina Faso	8.5	274	210	1.2	6.5	3.2	47	94	87
14	Mali	8.0	1,240	230	1.6	9.3	3.7	47	89	83
15	Burundi	5.1	28	240	3.0	6.4	4.0	49	74	66
16	Uganda	16.2	236	280	-3.1	21.2	100.7	48	55	43
17	Nigeria	110.1	924	290	0.9	13.7	11.6	51	69	58
18	Zambia	7.6	753	290	-2.1	6.4	33.5	53	33	24
19	Niger	7.3	1,267	300	-2.3	7.5	3.6	45	91	86
20	Rwanda	6.7	26	320	1.5	12.5	4.1	49	67	53
21	China	1,088.4	9,561	330	5.4	0.1	4.9	70	45	31
22	India	815.6	3,288	340	1.8	7.5	7.4	58	71	57
23	Pakistan	106.3	796	350	2.5	10.3	6.5	55	81	70
24	Kenya	22.4	580	370	1.9	7.3	9.6	59	51	41
25	Togo	3.4	57	370	0.0	6.9	6.1	53	72	59
26	Central African Rep.	2.9	623	380	-0.5	8.5	6.7	50	71	60
27	Haiti	6.3	28	380	0.4	7.3	7.9	55	65	62
28	Benin	4.4	113	390	0.1	7.5	8.0	51	84	74
29	Ghana	14.0	239	400	-1.6	22.8	46.1	54	57	47
30	Lesotho	1.7	30	420	5.2	8.0	12.2	56	16	26
31	Sri Lanka	16.6	66	420	3.0	9.4	11.0	71	17	13
32	Guinea	5.4	246	430	..	..	..	43	83	72
33	Yemen, PDR	2.4	333	430	..	..	4.5	51	75	59
34	Indonesia	174.8	1,905	440	4.3	34.2	8.5	61	35	26
35	Mauritania	1.9	1,026	480	-0.4	7.7	9.4	46	..	..
36	Sudan	23.8	2,506	480	0.0	11.5	33.5	50	..	..
37	*Afghanistan*	..	652	..	..	4.9	..	..	..	..
38	*Myanmar*	40.0	677	..	..	..	..	60	..	..
39	*Kampuchea, Dem.*	..	181	..	..	..	..	..	..	..
40	*Liberia*	2.4	111	..	..	6.3	..	50	77	65
41	*Sierra Leone*	3.9	72	..	..	7.8	..	42	79	71
42	*Viet Nam*	64.2	330	..	..	..	..	66	..	..
	Middle-income economies	**1,068.0 t**	**37,352 t**	**1,930 w**	**2.3 w**	**20.4 w**	**66.7 w**	**66 w**	**31 w**	**26 w**
	Lower-middle-income	**741.7 t**	**24,451 t**	**1,380 w**	**2.6 w**	**21.7 w**	**80.8 w**	**65 w**	**32 w**	**27 w**
43	Bolivia	6.9	1,099	570	-0.6	15.7	482.8	53	35	26
44	Philippines	59.9	300	630	1.6	11.7	15.6	64	15	14
45	Yemen Arab Rep.	8.5	195	640	..	..	11.6	47	97	86
46	Senegal	7.0	197	650	-0.8	6.5	8.1	48	81	72
47	Zimbabwe	9.3	391	650	1.0	5.8	12.1	63	33	26
48	Egypt, Arab Rep.	50.2	1,001	660	3.6	7.3	10.6	63	70	56
49	Dominican Rep.	6.9	49	720	2.7	6.6	16.8	66	23	23
50	Côte d'Ivoire	11.2	322	770	0.9	9.5	3.8	53	69	57
51	Papua New Guinea	3.7	463	810	0.5	8.1	4.7	54	65	55
52	Morocco	24.0	447	830	2.3	6.0	7.7	61	78	67
53	Honduras	4.8	112	860	0.6	5.6	4.7	64	42	41
54	Guatemala	8.7	109	900	1.0	7.1	13.3	62	53	45
55	Congo, People's Rep.	2.1	342	910	3.5	6.7	0.8	53	45	37
56	El Salvador	5.0	21	940	-0.5	7.0	16.8	63	31	28
57	Thailand	54.5	513	1,000	4.0	6.3	3.1	65	12	9
58	Botswana	1.2	582	1,010	8.6	8.1	10.0	67	31	29
59	Cameroon	11.2	475	1,010	3.7	8.9	7.0	56	55	44
60	Jamaica	2.4	11	1,070	-1.5	12.8	18.7	73	..	..
61	Ecuador	10.1	284	1,120	3.1	10.9	31.2	66	20	18
62	Colombia	31.7	1,139	1,180	2.4	17.4	24.1	68	13	12
63	Paraguay	4.0	407	1,180	3.1	9.4	22.1	67	15	12
64	Tunisia	7.8	164	1,230	3.4	6.7	7.7	66	59	46
65	Turkey	53.8	779	1,280	2.6	20.7	39.3	64	38	26
66	Peru	20.7	1,285	1,300	0.1	20.5	119.1	62	22	15
67	Jordan	3.9	89	1,500	..	..	2.2	66	37	25

Note: For data comparability and coverage, see the technical notes. Figures in italics are for years other than those specified.

	Population (millions) mid-1988	Area (thousands of square kilometers)	GNP per capita[a] Dollars 1988	GNP per capita[a] Average annual growth rate (percent) 1965-88	Average annual rate of inflation[a] (percent) 1965-80	Average annual rate of inflation[a] (percent) 1980-88	Life expectancy at birth (years) 1988	Adult illiteracy (percent) Female 1985	Adult illiteracy (percent) Male 1985
68 Chile	12.8	757	1,510	0.1	129.9	20.8	72	..	6
69 Syrian Arab Rep.	11.6	185	1,680	2.9	8.3	12.9	65	57	40
70 Costa Rica	2.7	51	1,690	1.4	11.3	26.9	75	7	6
71 Mexico	83.7	1,958	1,760	2.3	13.0	73.8	69	12	10
72 Mauritius	1.1	2	1,800	2.9	11.8	7.8	67	23	17
73 Poland	37.9	313	1,860	..	..	30.5	72	..	..
74 Malaysia	16.9	330	1,940	4.0	4.9	1.3	70	34	27
75 Panama	2.3	77	2,120	2.2	5.4	3.3	72	12	12
76 Brazil	144.4	8,512	2,160	3.6	31.5	188.7	65	24	22
77 *Angola*	9.4	1,247	..	..	..	..	45	..	59
78 *Lebanon*	..	10	..	..	9.3	..	..	..	..
79 *Nicaragua*	3.6	130	..	−2.5	8.9	86.6	64	..	..
Upper-middle-income	**326.3 t**	**12,901 t**	**3,240 w**	**2.3 w**	**18.9 w**	**45.0 w**	**68 w**	**31 w**	**24 w**
80 South Africa	34.0	1,221	2,290	0.8	10.1	13.9	61	..	..
81 Algeria	23.8	2,382	2,360	2.7	10.5	4.4	64	63	50
82 Hungary	10.6	93	2,460	5.1	2.6	6.4	70	c	c
83 Uruguay	3.1	177	2,470	1.3	57.8	57.0	72	4	5
84 Argentina	31.5	2,767	2,520	0.0	78.2	290.5	71	5	5
85 Yugoslavia	23.6	256	2,520	3.4	15.3	66.9	72	14	9
86 Gabon	1.1	268	2,970	0.9	12.7	0.9	53	47	38
87 Venezuela	18.8	912	3,250	−0.9	10.4	13.0	70	15	13
88 Trinidad and Tobago	1.2	5	3,350	0.9	14.0	5.3	71	5	4
89 Korea, Rep. of	42.0	99	3,600	6.8	18.7	5.0	70	..	..
90 Portugal	10.3	92	3,650	3.1	11.7	20.1	74	20	16
91 Greece	10.0	132	4,800	2.9	10.5	18.9	77	12	8
92 Oman	1.4	212	5,000	6.4	19.9	−6.5	64	..	..
93 Libya	4.2	1,760	5,420	−2.7	15.4	0.1	61	50	33
94 *Iran, Islamic Rep.*	48.6	1,648	..	..	15.6	..	63	61	49
95 *Iraq*	17.6	438	..	..	..	..	64	13	11
96 *Romania*	23.0	238	..	..	..	..	70	c	c
Low- and middle-income	**3,952.0 t**	**74,349 t**	**750 w**	**2.7 w**	**16.5 w**	**46.8 w**	**62 w**	**51 w**	**40 w**
Sub-Saharan Africa	**463.9 t**	**22,240 t**	**330 w**	**0.2 w**	**12.5 w**	**15.5 w**	**51 w**	**65 w**	**52 w**
East Asia	**1,538.0 t**	**14,017 t**	**540 w**	**5.2 w**	**8.7 w**	**5.6 w**	**66 w**	**41 w**	**29 w**
South Asia	**1,106.8 t**	**5,158 t**	**320 w**	**1.8 w**	**8.3 w**	**7.5 w**	**57 w**	**72 w**	**59 w**
Europe, M.East, & N.Africa	**395.6 t**	**11,420 t**	**2,000 w**	**2.4 w**	**13.2 w**	**25.8 w**	**64 w**	**53 w**	**41 w**
Latin America & Caribbean	**413.6 t**	**20,293 t**	**1,840 w**	**1.9 w**	**29.4 w**	**117.4 w**	**67 w**	**19 w**	**17 w**
Severely indebted	**495.5 t**	**20,057 t**	**1,730 w**	**2.0 w**	**28.3 w**	**107.9 w**	**66 w**	**23 w**	**20 w**
High-income economies	**784.2 t**	**33,739 t**	**17,080 w**	**2.3 w**	**7.9 w**	**4.9 w**	**76 w**	**..**	**..**
OECD members	**751.1 t**	**31,057 t**	**17,470 w**	**2.3 w**	**7.7 w**	**4.7 w**	**76 w**	**..**	**..**
†Other	**33.1 t**	**2,682 t**	**8,380 w**	**3.1 w**	**15.9 w**	**10.8 w**	**71 w**	**..**	**..**
97 †Saudi Arabia	14.0	2,150	6,200	3.8	17.2	−4.2	64	..	..
98 Spain	39.0	505	7,740	2.3	12.3	10.1	77	8	6
99 Ireland	3.5	70	7,750	2.0	12.0	8.0	74	..	..
100 †Israel	4.4	21	8,650	2.7	25.2	136.6	76	7	5
101 †Singapore	2.6	1	9,070	7.2	4.9	1.2	74	21	14
102 †Hong Kong	5.7	1	9,220[b]	6.3	8.1	6.7	77	19	12
103 New Zealand	3.3	269	10,000	0.8	10.2	11.4	75	c	c
104 Australia	16.5	7,687	12,340	1.7	9.3	7.8	76	c	c
105 United Kingdom	57.1	245	12,810	1.8	11.1	5.7	75	c	c
106 Italy	57.4	301	13,330	3.0	11.4	11.0	77	4	c
107 †Kuwait	2.0	18	13,400	−4.3	16.4	−3.9	73	37	30
108 Belgium	9.9	31	14,490	2.5	6.7	4.8	75	c	c
109 Netherlands	14.8	37	14,520	1.9	7.5	2.0	77	c	c
110 Austria	7.6	84	15,470	2.9	6.0	4.0	75	c	c
111 †United Arab Emirates	1.5	84	15,770	..	..	0.1	71	..	..
112 France	55.9	552	16,090	2.5	8.4	7.1	76	c	c
113 Canada	26.0	9,976	16,960	2.7	7.1	4.6	77	c	c
114 Denmark	5.1	43	18,450	1.8	9.3	6.3	75	c	c
115 Germany, Fed. Rep.	61.3	249	18,480	2.5	5.2	2.8	75	c	c
116 Finland	5.0	338	18,590	3.2	10.5	7.1	75	c	c
117 Sweden	8.4	450	19,300	1.8	8.0	7.5	77	c	c
118 United States	246.3	9,373	19,840	1.6	6.5	4.0	76	c	c
119 Norway	4.2	324	19,990	3.5	7.7	5.6	77	c	c
120 Japan	122.6	378	21,020	4.3	7.7	1.3	78	c	c
121 Switzerland	6.6	41	27,500	1.5	5.3	3.8	77	c	c
Total reporting economies	**4,736.2 t**	**108,088 t**	**3,470 w**	**1.5 w**	**9.8 w**	**14.1 w**	**64 w**	**50 w**	**39 w**
Oil exporters	**593.3 t**	**17,292 t**	**1,500 w**	**2.0 w**	**15.1 w**	**21.4 w**	**61 w**	**43 w**	**35 w**
Nonreporting nonmembers	**364.5 t**	**25,399 t**	**..**	**..**	**..**	**..**	**70 w**	**..**	**..**

Note: For economies with populations of less than 1 million, see Box A.1. For nonreporting nonmember economies, see Box A.2.   † Economies classified by United Nations or otherwise regarded by their authorities as developing.   a. See the technical notes.   b. GNP data refer to GDP.   c. According to Unesco, illiteracy is less than 5 percent.

Table 2. Growth of production

		GDP		Agriculture		Industry		(Manufacturing)[a]		Services, etc.	
		\multicolumn{12}{c}{Average annual growth rate (percent)}									
		1965–80	1980–88	1965–80	1980–88	1965–80	1980–88	1965–80	1980–88	1965–80	1980–88
	Low-income economies	5.4 w	6.4 w	2.6 w	4.4 w	8.8 w	8.7 w	8.2 w	9.7 w	6.0 w	6.0 w
	China and India	5.3 w	8.7 w	2.7 w	5.4 w	8.2 w	11.4 w	8.0 w	10.5 w	6.3 w	8.6 w
	Other low-income	5.5 w	2.0 w	2.3 w	2.3 w	10.0 w	1.7 w	9.1 w	5.9 w	5.7 w	3.4 w
1	Mozambique	..	−2.8	..	−0.8	..	−7.1	..	..	..	−3.1
2	Ethiopia	2.7	1.4	1.2	−1.1	3.5	3.5	5.1	3.7	5.2	3.6
3	Chad [b]	0.1	3.9	−0.3	2.6	−0.6	7.7	..	..	0.2	4.2
4	Tanzania	3.7	2.0	1.6	4.0	4.2	−2.0	5.6	−2.5	6.7	1.0
5	Bangladesh [b]	2.4	3.7	1.5	2.1	3.8	4.9	6.8	2.4	3.4	5.2
6	Malawi	5.6	2.6	4.1	2.7	6.3	3.0	..	..	6.7	2.4
7	Somalia	3.4	3.2	..	3.9	..	2.3	..	−0.1	..	1.2
8	Zaire[b]	1.4	1.9	..	3.2	..	2.5	..	1.7	..	0.3
9	Bhutan	..	..	..	..	..	..	..	..	..	..
10	Lao PDR	..	..	..	..	..	..	..	..	..	..
11	Nepal	1.9	4.7	1.1	4.4	..	..	..	..	..	..
12	Madagascar [b]	1.8	0.6	..	2.2	..	−1.0	..	..	..	−0.1
13	Burkina Faso	..	5.5	..	6.4	..	3.7	..	..	..	5.5
14	Mali [b]	3.9	3.2	2.8	0.3	1.8	8.1	..	..	7.6	5.8
15	Burundi	5.6	4.3	6.7	3.1	17.4	5.8	6.0	6.1	1.4	6.3
16	Uganda	0.8	1.4	1.2	0.3	−4.1	6.4	−3.7	2.3	1.1	3.4
17	Nigeria	6.9	−1.1	1.7	1.0	13.1	−3.2	14.6	−2.9	7.6	−0.4
18	Zambia[b]	1.9	0.7	2.2	4.1	2.1	0.3	5.3	2.5	1.5	0.0
19	Niger [b]	0.3	−1.2	−3.4	2.8	11.4	−4.3	..	..	3.4	−8.0
20	Rwanda[b]	4.9	2.1	..	0.3	..	3.6	..	3.4	..	3.4
21	China[b]	6.4	10.3	2.8	6.8	10.0	12.4	9.5[c]	11.0 [c]	10.3	11.3
22	India	3.6	5.2	2.5	2.3	4.2	7.6	4.5	8.3	4.4	6.1
23	Pakistan	5.1	6.5	3.3	4.3	6.4	7.2	5.7	8.1	5.9	7.4
24	Kenya	6.4	4.2	4.9	3.3	9.8	2.8	10.5	4.6	6.4	5.5
25	Togo[b]	4.5	0.5	1.9	4.2	6.8	0.0	..	−0.5	5.4	−1.7
26	Central African Rep.	2.6	2.1	2.1	2.6	5.3	2.0	..	0.2	2.0	1.7
27	Haiti[b]	2.9	−0.2	..	..	..	..	..	..	..	..
28	Benin	2.1	2.4	..	4.2	..	5.8	..	7.4	..	−1.0
29	Ghana[b]	1.4	2.1	1.6	0.5	1.4	1.9	2.5	3.1	1.1	4.9
30	Lesotho	5.7	2.9	..	1.8	..	1.6	..	12.4	..	4.1
31	Sri Lanka	4.0	4.3	2.7	2.7	4.7	4.4	3.2	6.2	4.6	5.3
32	Guinea[b]	..	..	..	..	..	..	..	..	..	..
33	Yemen, PDR	..	..	..	..	..	..	..	..	..	..
34	Indonesia[b]	8.0	5.1	4.3	3.1	11.9	5.1	12.0	13.1	7.3	6.4
35	Mauritania	2.0	1.6	−2.0	1.5	2.2	4.9	..	..	6.5	−0.5
36	Sudan	3.8	2.5	2.9	2.7	3.1	3.6	..	5.0	4.9	2.0
37	*Afghanistan*	2.9	..	..	..	..	..	..	..	..	..
38	*Myanmar*	..	..	..	..	..	..	..	..	..	..
39	*Kampuchea, Dem.*	..	..	..	..	..	..	..	..	..	..
40	Liberia	3.3	−1.3	5.5	1.2	2.2	−6.0	10.0	−5.0	2.4	−0.8
41	*Sierra Leone*	2.8	0.2	3.9	2.2	−0.8	−4.9	0.7	−2.0	4.3	0.7
42	*Viet Nam*	..	..	..	..	..	..	..	..	..	..
	Middle-income economies	6.1 w	2.9 w	3.2 w	2.7 w	5.9 w	3.2 w	8.2 w	3.8 w	7.2 w	3.1 w
	Lower-middle-income	6.5 w	2.6 w	3.3 w	2.8 w	7.8 w	2.5 w	7.9 w	2.4 w	7.0 w	2.6 w
43	Bolivia[b]	4.5	−1.6	3.8	2.1	3.9	−5.7	5.9	−5.6	5.4	−0.2
44	Philippines[b]	5.9	0.1	4.6	1.8	8.0	−1.8	7.5	−0.3	5.2	0.7
45	Yemen Arab Rep.[b]	..	6.5	..	2.9	..	11.5	..	12.8	..	6.2
46	Senegal[b]	2.0	3.3	1.3	3.2	4.8	3.8	3.5	3.4	1.3	3.2
47	Zimbabwe	5.0	2.7	..	2.5	..	1.7	..	2.1	..	3.4
48	Egypt, Arab Rep.	6.8	5.7	2.7	2.6	6.9	5.1	..	5.6	9.4	7.3
49	Dominican Rep.[b]	7.9	2.2	6.3	0.8	10.9	2.5	8.9	1.0	7.3	2.5
50	Côte d'Ivoire	6.8	2.2	3.3	1.6	10.4	−2.4	9.1	8.2	8.6	4.2
51	Papua New Guinea[b]	4.1	3.2	3.2	2.7	..	5.6	..	1.0	..	2.0
52	Morocco[b]	5.6	4.2	2.4	6.6	6.1	2.8	..	4.2	6.8	4.2
53	Honduras	5.0	1.7	2.0	1.1	6.8	0.8	7.5	1.9	6.2	2.4
54	Guatemala[b]	5.9	−0.2	..	..	..	..	..	..	..	..
55	Congo, People's Rep.[b]	6.3	4.0	3.1	2.0	9.9	5.1	..	7.1	4.7	3.5
56	El Salvador [b]	4.3	0.0	3.6	−1.4	5.3	0.4	4.6	0.3	4.3	0.7
57	Thailand[b]	7.2	6.0	4.6	3.7	9.5	6.6	11.2	6.8	7.6	6.8
58	Botswana[b]	14.2	11.4	9.7	−5.9	24.0	15.1	13.5	5.0	11.5	10.3
59	Cameroon[b]	5.1	5.4	4.2	2.4	7.8	7.8	7.0	6.2	4.8	5.5
60	Jamaica[b]	1.3	0.6	0.5	0.9	−0.1	0.0	0.4	1.6	2.7	0.9
61	Ecuador[b]	8.7	2.0	3.4	4.3	13.7	2.2	11.5	0.6	7.6	1.1
62	Colombia	5.8	3.4	4.5	2.4	5.7	5.1	6.4	2.9	6.4	2.7
63	Paraguay[b]	6.9	1.7	4.9	2.7	9.1	0.1	7.0	1.3	7.5	2.0
64	Tunisia	6.6	3.4	5.5	2.4	7.4	2.4	9.9	6.0	6.5	4.4
65	Turkey	6.3	5.3	3.2	3.6	7.2	6.7	7.5	7.9	7.6	5.1
66	Peru[b]	3.9	1.1	1.0	3.6	4.4	0.4	3.8	1.6	4.3	1.2
67	Jordan	..	4.2	..	6.0	..	3.6	..	3.4	..	4.4

		Average annual growth rate (percent)									
		GDP		Agriculture		Industry		(Manufacturing)[a]		Services, etc.	
		1965-80	1980-88	1965-80	1980-88	1965-80	1980-88	1965-80	1980-88	1965-80	1980-88
68	Chile[b]	1.9	1.9	1.6	3.8	0.8	2.2	0.6	2.0	2.7	1.3
69	Syrian Arab Rep.[b]	8.7	0.5	4.8	0.5	11.8	1.4	..	..	9.0	0.2
70	Costa Rica[b]	6.2	2.4	4.2	2.5	8.7	2.3	..	..	6.0	2.5
71	Mexico[b]	6.5	0.5	3.2	1.2	7.6	-0.1	7.4	0.2	6.6	0.7
72	Mauritius	5.2	5.7	..	4.0	..	9.0	..	11.4	..	4.6
73	Poland[b]	..	..	..	..	..	..	..	..	..	..
74	Malaysia[b]	7.3	4.6	..	3.7	..	6.1	..	7.3	..	3.6
75	Panama[b]	5.5	2.6	2.4	2.5	5.9	-0.8	4.7	0.7	6.0	3.5
76	Brazil	8.8	2.9	3.8	3.5	10.1	2.6	9.8	2.2	9.5	3.1
77	Angola	..	..	..	..	..	..	..	..	..	..
78	Lebanon[b]	-1.2	..	..	..	..	..	..	..	..	..
79	Nicaragua[b]	2.6	-0.3	3.3	-0.2	4.2	0.4	5.2	0.6	1.4	-0.9
	Upper-middle-income	5.6 w	3.3 w	3.2 w	2.5 w	4.7 w	3.7 w	..	..	7.5 w	3.7 w
80	South Africa	3.8	1.3	..	1.7	..	0.2	..	0.2	..	2.6
81	Algeria[b]	6.8	3.5	5.7	5.6	7.1	3.8	9.5	6.1	6.7	2.7
82	Hungary[b]	5.6	1.6	2.7	2.4	6.4	1.0	..	..	6.2	1.9
83	Uruguay	2.4	-0.4	1.0	0.3	3.1	-1.8	..	-0.5	2.3	0.2
84	Argentina[b]	3.5	-0.2	1.4	1.4	3.3	-0.8	2.7	-0.2	4.0	-0.2
85	Yugoslavia	6.0	1.4	3.1	1.2	7.8	1.3	..	..	5.5	1.4
86	Gabon[b]	9.5	-0.2	..	..	..	..	..	..	..	..
87	Venezuela[b]	3.7	0.9	3.9	3.8	1.5	-0.1	5.8	3.3	6.3	1.4
88	Trinidad and Tobago	5.1	-6.1	0.0	4.5	5.0	-8.6	2.6	-9.5	5.8	-3.4
89	Korea, Rep. of[b]	9.6	9.9	3.0	3.7	16.4	12.6	18.7	13.5	9.6	8.9
90	Portugal[b]	5.3	0.8	..	-0.9	..	1.0	..	0.0	..	1.3
91	Greece	5.6	1.4	2.3	-0.1	7.1	0.4	8.4	0.0	6.2	2.5
92	Oman[b]	13.0	12.7	..	9.4	..	15.1	..	37.9	..	12.2
93	Libya	4.2	..	10.7	..	1.2	..	13.7	..	15.5	..
94	Iran, Islamic Rep.	6.2	..	4.5	..	2.4	..	10.0	..	13.6	..
95	Iraq	..	..	..	..	..	..	..	..	..	..
96	Romania	..	..	..	..	..	..	..	..	..	..
	Low- and middle-income	5.8 w	4.3 w	2.8 w	3.7 w	6.8 w	5.3 w	8.2 w	5.9 w	6.9 w	3.9 w
	Sub-Saharan Africa	4.8 w	0.8 w	1.3 w	1.8 w	9.4 w	-0.8 w	8.7 w	0.2 w	5.0 w	1.4 w
	East Asia	7.2 w	8.5 w	3.2 w	5.7 w	10.8 w	10.3 w	10.6 w	10.2 w	8.6 w	8.0 w
	South Asia	3.7 w	5.1 w	2.5 w	2.5 w	4.4 w	7.3 w	4.6 w	7.9 w	4.5 w	6.1 w
	Europe, M.East, & N.Africa	6.1 w	..	3.5 w	..	4.9 w	..	..	..	8.6 w	..
	Latin America & Caribbean	6.0 w	1.5 w	3.3 w	2.5 w	6.0 w	1.1 w	7.0 w	1.3 w	6.6 w	1.6 w
	Severely indebted	6.0 w	1.5 w	3.2 w	2.7 w	6.2 w	1.0 w	7.1 w	1.3 w	6.6 w	1.6 w
	High-income economies	3.7 w	2.8 w	0.8 w	2.3 w	3.2 w	1.9 w	3.6 w	3.2 w	3.7 w	3.0 w
	OECD members	3.6 w	2.9 w	0.8 w	2.3 w	3.1 w	2.2 w	3.6 w	3.2 w	3.7 w	3.0 w
	†Other	8.0 w	-1.3 w	..	12.7 w	..	-7.0 w	..	6.0 w	..	4.6 w
97	†Saudi Arabia[b]	11.3	-3.3	4.1	15.2	11.6	-6.0	8.1	7.9	10.5	2.6
98	Spain[b]	4.6	2.5	2.6	0.9	5.1	0.4	5.9	0.4	4.1	2.1
99	Ireland	5.0	1.7	..	2.2	..	1.7	..	..	..	0.6
100	†Israel[b]	6.8	3.2	..	..	..	..	..	..	..	..
101	†Singapore[b]	10.1	5.7	2.8	-5.1	11.9	4.5	13.2	4.8	9.4	6.6
102	†Hong Kong	8.6	7.3	..	..	..	..	..	..	..	..
103	New Zealand[b]	2.4	2.2	..	3.3	..	4.2	..	3.5	..	2.0
104	Australia[b]	4.0	3.3	2.7	4.4	3.0	2.2	1.3	1.1	5.7	3.7
105	United Kingdom	2.4	2.8	-1.6[d]	3.4	-0.5[d]	1.9	-1.2[d]	1.5	2.2[d]	2.5
106	Italy[b]	4.3	2.2	0.8	1.0	4.0	1.1	5.1	1.9	4.1	2.7
107	†Kuwait[b]	1.2	-1.1	..	23.6	..	-2.3	..	1.4	..	-0.9
108	Belgium[b]	3.8	1.4	0.4	2.5	4.4	1.1	4.6	2.3	3.7	1.2
109	Netherlands[b]	3.8	1.6	4.7	4.1	4.0	0.8	4.8	..	4.4	1.6
110	Austria[b]	4.1	1.7	2.1	0.7	4.3	1.1	4.5	1.6	4.2	1.9
111	†United Arab Emirates	..	-4.5	..	9.3	..	-8.7	..	2.7	..	3.7
112	France[b]	4.0	1.8	1.0	2.3	4.3	0.1	5.2	-0.4	4.6	2.4
113	Canada	5.1	3.3	0.8	2.7	3.5	3.0	3.9	3.6	6.9	3.2
114	Denmark	2.7	2.2	0.9	3.3	1.9	3.4	3.2	2.4	3.2	2.0
115	Germany, Fed. Rep.[b]	3.3	1.8	1.4	1.9	2.8	0.4	3.3	1.0	3.7	2.1
116	Finland	4.0	2.8	0.0	-1.1	4.2	2.7	4.9	3.0	4.8	3.3
117	Sweden	2.9	1.7	-0.2	1.8	2.3	2.9	2.4	2.9	3.4	0.8
118	United States[b]	2.7	3.3	1.0	3.2	1.7	2.9	2.5	3.9	3.4	3.3
119	Norway	4.4	3.8	-0.4	1.3	5.7	4.7	2.6	1.8	4.1	3.4
120	Japan[b]	6.5	3.9	0.8	0.8	8.5	4.9	9.4	6.7	5.2	3.1
121	Switzerland[b]	2.0	1.9	..	..	..	..	..	..	..	..
	Total reporting economies	4.1 w	3.1 w	2.0 w	3.2 w	3.9 w	2.5 w	4.3 w	3.8 w	4.2 w	3.2 w
	Oil exporters	6.4 w	1.0 w	3.1 w	2.7 w	6.3 w	-0.1 w	7.7 w	3.7 w	7.6 w	2.4 w
	Nonreporting nonmembers	..	..	..	..	..	..	..	..	..	..

a. Because manufacturing is generally the most dynamic part of the industrial sector, its growth rate is shown separately. b. GDP and its components are at purchaser values. c. World Bank estimate. d. Data refer to the period 1973-80.

Table 3. Structure of production

		GDP[a] (millions of dollars)		Distribution of gross domestic product (percent)							
				Agriculture		Industry		(Manufacturing)[b]		Services, etc.	
		1965	1988	1965	1988	1965	1988	1965	1988	1965	1988
	Low-income economies	161,340 t	886,620 t	44 w	33 w	28 w	36 w	21 w	..	28 w	32 w
	China and India	117,730 t	610,250 t	44 w	32 w	32 w	40 w	24 w	..	24 w	28 w
	Other low-income	42,660 t	273,080 t	45 w	33 w	17 w	27 w	9 w	..	38 w	40 w
1	Mozambique	..	1,100	..	62	..	20	..	..	..	18
2	Ethiopia	1,180	4,950	58	42	14	17	7	12	28	40
3	Chad[c]	290	920	42	47	15	18	12	15	43	35
4	Tanzania	790	2,740	46	66	14	7	8	4	40	27
5	Bangladesh[c]	4,380	19,320	53	46	11	14	5	7	36	40
6	Malawi	220	1,080	50	37	13	18	..	..	37	44
7	Somalia	220	970	71	65	6	9	3	5	24	25
8	Zaire[c]	3,140	6,470	21	31	26	34	16	7	53	35
9	Bhutan[c]	..	300	..	44	..	28	..	6	..	28
10	Lao PDR	..	500	..	59	..	20	..	7	..	21
11	Nepal	730	2,860	65	56	11	17	3	6	23	27
12	Madagascar [c]	670	1,880	*31*	41	*16*	16	*11*	..	*53*	43
13	Burkina Faso	260	1,750	53	39	20	23	..	13	27	38
14	Mali[c]	*260*	1,940	*65*	49	9	12	5	5	25	39
15	Burundi	150	960	..	56	..	15	..	10	..	29
16	Uganda	1,100	3,950	52	72	13	7	8	6	35	20
17	Nigeria	5,850	29,370	54	34	13	36	6	*18*	33	29
18	Zambia[c]	1,060	4,000	14	14	54	43	6	25	32	43
19	Niger [c]	670	2,400	68	36	3	23	2	9	29	41
20	Rwanda[c]	150	2,310	75	38	7	22	2	15	18	40
21	China[c]	67,200	372,320	44	32	39	46	31[d]	33[d]	17	21
22	India	50,530	237,930	44	32	22	30	16	19	34	38
23	Pakistan	5,450	34,050	40	26	20	24	14	17	40	49
24	Kenya	920	7,380	35	31	18	20	11	12	47	49
25	Togo[c]	190	1,360	45	34	21	21	10	8	34	45
26	Central African Rep.	140	1,080	46	44	16	12	4	8	38	44
27	Haiti[c]	350	2,500	..	31	..	38	..	15	..	31
28	Benin	220	1,710	59	40	8	13	..	6	33	47
29	Ghana[c]	2,050	5,230	44	49	19	16	10	10	38	34
30	Lesotho	50	330	65	21	5	28	1	13	30	52
31	Sri Lanka	1,770	6,400	28	26	21	27	17	15	51	47
32	*Guinea*[c]	..	2,540	..	30	..	32	..	5	..	38
33	Yemen, PDR	..	*840*	..	*16*	..	*23*	..	..	..	*61*
34	Indonesia[c]	3,840	83,220	56	24	13	36	8	19	31	40
35	Mauritania	160	900	32	38	36	21	4	..	32	41
36	Sudan	1,330	11,240	54	33	9	15	4	8	37	52
37	*Afghanistan*	600	..	..	..	..	..	..	..	..	..
38	*Myanmar*	..	..	..	..	..	..	..	..	..	..
39	*Kampuchea, Dem.*	..	..	..	..	..	..	..	..	..	..
40	*Liberia*	270	*990*	27	*37*	40	*28*	3	*5*	34	*35*
41	*Sierra Leone*	320	1,270	34	46	28	12	6	3	38	42
42	*Viet Nam*	..	..	..	..	..	..	..	..	..	..
	Middle-income economies	199,900 t	2,200,750 t	20 w	12 w	33 w	40 w	19 w	24 w	46 w	50 w
	Lower-middle-income	111,840 t	1,061,910 t	22 w	14 w	28 w	38 w	19 w	25 w	50 w	50 w
43	Bolivia[c]	710	4,310	23	24	31	27	15	17	46	49
44	Philippines[c]	6,010	39,210	26	23	28	34	20	25	46	44
45	Yemen Arab Rep.[c]	..	5,910	..	23	..	26	..	12	..	50
46	Senegal[c]	810	4,980	25	22	18	29	14	19	56	49
47	Zimbabwe	960	5,650	18	11	35	43	20	31	47	46
48	Egypt, Arab Rep.	4,550	34,330	29	21	27	25	..	14	45	54
49	Dominican Rep.[c]	890	4,630	23	23	22	34	16	16	55	43
50	Côte d'Ivoire	760	*7,650*	47	*36*	19	25	11	*16*	33	*39*
51	Papua New Guinea[c]	340	3,520	42	34	18	31	..	9	41	36
52	Morocco[c]	2,950	21,990	23	17	28	34	16	18	49	49
53	Honduras	460	3,860	40	25	19	21	12	*13*	41	54
54	Guatemala[c]	1,330	8,100	..	..	..	..	..	..	..	..
55	Congo, People's Rep.[c]	200	2,150	19	15	19	30	..	8	62	54
56	El Salvador [c]	800	5,470	29	14	22	22	18	18	49	65
57	Thailand[c]	4,390	57,950	32	17	23	35	14	24	45	48
58	Botswana[c]	50	1,940	34	3	19	55	12	5	47	42
59	Cameroon[c]	810	12,900	33	26	20	30	10	13	47	44
60	Jamaica[c]	970	3,220	10	6	37	42	17	21	53	52
61	Ecuador [c]	1,150	10,320	27	15	22	36	18	21	50	49
62	Colombia	5,910	39,070	27	19	27	34	19	20	47	47
63	Paraguay[c]	440	6,040	37	30	19	25	16	17	45	46
64	Tunisia	880	8,750	22	14	24	32	9	16	54	54
65	Turkey	7,660	64,360	34	17	25	36	16	26	41	46
66	Peru[c]	5,020	25,670	18	12	30	*36*	17	*24*	53	*51*
67	Jordan	..	3,900	..	10	..	25	..	12	..	65

Note: For data comparability and coverage, see the technical notes. Figures in italics are for years other than those specified.

		GDP[a] (millions of dollars)		Agriculture		Industry		(Manufacturing)[b]		Services, etc.	
		1965	1988	1965	1988	1965	1988	1965	1988	1965	1988
68	Chile[c]	5,940	22,080	9	..	40	..	24	..	52	..
69	Syrian Arab Rep.[c]	1,470	14,950	29	38	22	16	..	..	49	46
70	Costa Rica[c]	590	4,650	24	18	23	28	..	..	53	54
71	Mexico[c]	21,640	176,700	14	9	27	35	20	26	59	56
72	Mauritius	190	1,600	16	13	23	33	14	25	61	54
73	Poland[c]	..	..	..	..	..	..	..	..	..	..
74	Malaysia[c]	3,130	34,680	28	..	25	..	9	..	47	..
75	Panama[c]	660	5,490	18	9	19	18	12	8	63	73
76	Brazil	19,450	323,610	19	9	33	43	26	29	48	49
77	Angola	..	..	..	..	..	..	..	..	..	..
78	Lebanon[c]	1,150	..	12	..	21	..	..	..	67	..
79	Nicaragua[c]	570	3,200	25	21	24	34	18	24	51	46
	Upper-middle-income	88,200 t	1,138,840 t	18 w	..	39 w	..	..	..	42 w	..
80	South Africa	10,540	78,970	10	6	42	45	23	25	48	49
81	Algeria[c]	3,170	51,900	15	13	34	43	11	12	51	44
82	Hungary[c,e]	..	28,000	..	14	..	37	..	..	..	49
83	Uruguay	930	6,680	15	11	32	29	..	24	53	60
84	Argentina[c]	16,500	79,440	17	13	42	44	33	31	42	44
85	Yugoslavia	11,190	61,710	23	14	42	49	..	..	35	37
86	Gabon[c]	230	3,320	26	11	34	51	..	..	40	38
87	Venezuela[c]	9,820	63,750	6	6	40	36	..	22	55	58
88	Trinidad and Tobago	690	4,400	8	5	48	31	..	9	44	64
89	Korea, Rep. of [c]	3,000	171,310	38	11	25	43	18	32	37	46
90	Portugal[c]	3,740	41,700	..	9	..	37	..	..	..	54
91	Greece	5,270	40,900	24	16	26	29	16	18	49	56
92	Oman[c]	60	8,150	61	3	23	43	0	6	16	54
93	Libya	1,500	..	5	..	63	..	3	..	33	..
94	Iran, Islamic Rep.	6,170	..	26	..	36	..	12	..	38	..
95	Iraq	2,430	..	18	..	46	..	8	..	36	..
96	Romania	..	..	..	..	..	..	..	..	..	..
	Low- and middle-income	363,680 t	3,060,950 t	31 w	18 w	31 w	39 w	20 w	..	38 w	44 w
	Sub-Saharan Africa	27,490 t	149,550 t	43 w	34 w	18 w	27 w	9 w	..	39 w	39 w
	East Asia	92,420 t	893,410 t	41 w	22 w	35 w	43 w	27 w	..	24 w	36 w
	South Asia	64,510 t	312,070 t	44 w	33 w	21 w	27 w	15 w	17 w	35 w	39 w
	Europe, M.East, & N.Africa	69,200 t	..	24 w	..	34 w	..	..	..	40 w	..
	Latin America & Caribbean	95,330 t	808,340 t	16 w	10 w	33 w	39 w	23 w	27 w	51 w	52 w
	Severely indebted	105,150 t	897,390 t	17 w	10 w	34 w	39 w	23 w	27 w	50 w	52 w
	High-income economies	1,391,700 t	13,867,530 t	5 w	..	41 w	..	30 w	..	55 w	..
	OECD members	1,373,380 t	13,603,060 t	5 w	..	41 w	..	30 w	..	55 w	..
	†Other	11,020 t	234,370 t	6 w	..	54 w	..	11 w	..	41 w	..
97	†Saudi Arabia[c]	2,300	72,620	8	8	60	43	9	8	31	50
98	Spain[c]	23,750	340,320	15	6	36	37	..	27	49	57
99	Ireland	2,340	27,820	..	10	..	38	..	..	..	52
100	†Israel[c]	3,590	44,960	..	..	..	..	..	..	..	..
101	†Singapore[c]	970	23,880	3	0	24	38	15	30	74	61
102	†Hong Kong	2,150	44,830	2	0	40	29	24	22	58	70
103	New Zealand[c]	5,410	39,800	..	10	..	33	..	23	..	57
104	Australia[c]	22,920	245,950	9	4	39	34	26	18	51	61
105	United Kingdom	89,100	702,370	3	2	46	42	34	27	51	56
106	Italy[c]	72,150	828,850	10	4	37	40	25	27	53	56
107	†Kuwait[c]	2,100	19,970	0	1	70	51	3	10	29	48
108	Belgium[c]	16,840	153,810	5	2	42	34	31	24	53	64
109	Netherlands[c]	19,640	228,280	..	5	..	37	..	24	..	58
110	Austria[c]	9,480	127,200	9	4	46	45	33	32	45	51
111	†United Arab Emirates	..	23,850	..	2	..	55	..	9	..	44
112	France[c]	99,660	949,440	8	4	38	37	27	27	54	59
113	Canada	46,730	435,860	6	4	41	40	26	23	53	56
114	Denmark	8,940	90,530	9	5	36	37	23	25	55	58
115	Germany, Fed. Rep.[c]	114,790	1,201,820	4	2	53	51	40	44	43	47
116	Finland	7,540	91,690	16	7	37	43	23	29	47	50
117	Sweden	19,880	159,880	6	4	40	43	28	30	53	54
118	United States[c]	700,970	4,847,310	3	2	38	33	28	22	59	65
119	Norway[c]	7,080	91,050	8	4	33	45	21	21	59	51
120	Japan[c]	91,110	2,843,710	9	3	43	41	32	29	48	57
121	Switzerland[c]	13,920	184,830	..	..	..	..	..	..	..	..
	Total reporting economies	1,755,990 t	17,018,400 t	10 w	..	39 w	..	28 w	..	52 w	..
	Oil exporters	77,910 t	921,070 t	19 w	12 w	32 w	35 w	14 w	16 w	48 w	51 w
	Nonreporting nonmembers	..	..	..	..	..	..	..	..	..	..

a. See the technical notes.   b. Because manufacturing is generally the most dynamic part of the industrial sector, its share of GDP is shown separately.   c. GDP and its components are shown at purchaser values.   d. World Bank estimate.   e. Services, etc. include the unallocated share of GDP.

Table 4. Agriculture and food

		Value added in agriculture (millions of current dollars)		Cereal imports (thousands of metric tons)		Food aid in cereals (thousands of metric tons)		Fertilizer consumption (hundreds of grams of plant nutrient per hectare of arable land)		Average index of food production per capita (1979–81=100)
		1970	1988	1974	1988	1974/75	1987/88	1970/71	1987/88	1986–88
	Low-income economies	**89,156 t**	**289,209 t**	**22,757 t**	**32,469 t**	**6,002 t**	**6,977 t**	**171 w**	**706 w**	**112 w**
	China and India	**60,621 t**	**197,397 t**	**11,294 t**	**18,502 t**	**1,582 t**	**570 t**	**241 w**	**997 w**	**117 w**
	Other low-income	**28,109 t**	**90,501 t**	**11,462 t**	**13,967 t**	**4,420 t**	**6,407 t**	**72 w**	**318 w**	**102 w**
1	Mozambique	..	679	62	527	34	466	22	21	83
2	Ethiopia	931	2,090	118	1,157	54	825	4	39	89
3	Chad[a]	142	430	37	61	20	15	7	17	103
4	Tanzania	473	1,795	431	120	148	72	31	92	89
5	Bangladesh[a]	3,636	8,882	1,866	3,010	2,076	1,397	157	770	92
6	Malawi	119	402	17	44	0	109	52	203	85
7	Somalia	167	636	42	236	111	152	29	40	100
8	Zaire[a]	585	2,008	343	415	1	177	8	9	98
9	Bhutan	..	130	3	30	0	2	..	10	118
10	Lao PDR	..	297	53	115	8	21	2	6	123
11	Nepal	579	1,601	18	52	0	21	27	232	100
12	Madagascar [a]	266	775	114	217	7	76	61	21	97
13	Burkina Faso	126	685	99	128	28	38	3	57	116
14	Mali[a]	207	952	281	109	107	26	31	59	97
15	Burundi	159	535	7	15	6	4	5	20	100
16	Uganda	929	2,859	36	28	..	29	14	2	121
17	Nigeria	5,080	10,105	389	333	7	0	2	94	103
18	Zambia[a]	191	568	93	128	5	140	73	183	96
19	Niger [a]	420	866	155	151	73	19	1	8	83
20	Rwanda[a]	135	880	3	11	19	8	3	20	82
21	China[a]	36,705	120,779	6,033	15,517	0	347	410	2,361	132
22	India	23,916	76,618	5,261	2,985	1,582	223	137	517	105
23	Pakistan	3,352	8,935	1,274	602	584	657	146	829	107
24	Kenya	484	2,265	15	86	2	119	238	421	89
25	Togo[a]	85	464	6	110	11	16	3	76	88
26	Central African Rep.	60	469	7	40	1	6	12	4	87
27	Haiti[a]	..	782	83	205	25	154	4	25	95
28	Benin	121	680	7	121	9	11	36	49	110
29	Ghana[a]	1,030	2,577	177	228	33	110	13	38	108
30	Lesotho	23	67	48	107	14	55	10	125	80
31	Sri Lanka	545	1,685	951	940	271	361	555	1,094	79
32	Guinea[a]	..	761	63	222	49	26	19	6	93
33	Yemen, PDR	..	132	148	459	0	31	..	118	85
34	Indonesia[a]	4,340	20,055	1,919	1,702	301	319	133	1,068	117
35	Mauritania	58	339	115	219	48	51	11	55	89
36	Sudan	757	3,716	125	702	46	604	28	40	89
37	Afghanistan	..	..	5	236	10	104	24	97	..
38	Myanmar	..	..	26	..	9	0	21	125	..
39	Kampuchea, Dem.	..	..	223	150	226	6	11	2	..
40	Liberia	91	..	42	103	3	56	63	94	92
41	Sierra Leone	108	581	72	119	10	58	17	3	101
42	Viet Nam	..	..	1,854	417	64	65	513	651	117
	Middle-income economies	**49,929 t**	**274,894 t**	**42,929 t**	**77,525 t**	**1,925 t**	**5,915 t**	**330 w**	**648 w**	**99 w**
	Lower-middle-income	**31,837 t**	**149,950 t**	**24,538 t**	**38,685 t**	**1,631 t**	**5,911 t**	**304 w**	**611 w**	**100 w**
43	Bolivia[a]	202	1,023	209	328	22	290	7	19	95
44	Philippines[a]	1,996	9,005	817	1,322	89	471	287	612	90
45	Yemen Arab Rep.[a]	118	1,387	158	754	33	160	1	58	118
46	Senegal[a]	208	1,100	341	461	27	109	17	40	106
47	Zimbabwe	214	615	56	93	0	14	446	505	81
48	Egypt, Arab Rep.	1,942	7,257	3,877	8,479	610	1,738	1,312	3,505	111
49	Dominican Rep.[a]	345	1,082	252	601	16	278	334	556	95
50	Côte d'Ivoire	462	2,728	172	494	4	1	74	90	104
51	Papua New Guinea[a]	240	1,196	71	180	..	0	58	381	92
52	Morocco[a]	789	3,770	891	1,643	75	340	117	376	106
53	Honduras	212	956	52	144	31	146	156	190	76
54	Guatemala[a]	..	..	138	166	9	320	298	656	92
55	Congo, People's Rep.[a]	49	331	34	113	2	1	114	25	92
56	El Salvador [a]	292	740	75	217	4	177	1,043	1,262	87
57	Thailand[a]	1,837	9,795	97	303	0	97	59	328	101
58	Botswana[a]	28	57	21	150	5	53	15	7	69
59	Cameroon[a]	364	3,405	81	282	4	2	34	71	97
60	Jamaica[a]	93	180	340	418	1	208	873	914	101
61	Ecuador [a]	401	1,547	152	563	13	33	133	232	97
62	Colombia	1,806	7,364	502	864	28	90	287	945	100
63	Paraguay[a]	191	1,788	71	2	10	2	98	69	106
64	Tunisia	245	1,187	307	2,116	59	393	76	222	111
65	Turkey	3,383	11,125	1,276	380	16	1	157	637	98
66	Peru[a]	1,351	..	637	1,857	37	355	300	622	96
67	Jordan	44	377	171	874	79	29	74	362	111

Note: For data comparability and coverage, see the technical notes. Figures in italics are for years other than those specified.

		Value added in agriculture (millions of current dollars)		Cereal imports (thousands of metric tons)		Food aid in cereals (thousands of metric tons)		Fertilizer consumption (hundreds of grams of plant nutrient per hectare of arable land)		Average index of food production per capita (1979–81 = 100)
		1970	1988	1974	1988	1974/75	1987/88	1970/71	1987/88	1986–88
68	Chile [a]	558	..	1,737	339	323	14	313	544	105
69	Syrian Arab Rep.[a]	435	5,728	339	1,044	47	26	68	404	93
70	Costa Rica[a]	222	853	110	318	1	235	1,001	1,806	89
71	Mexico[a]	4,462	15,958	2,881	5,650	..	32	232	753	93
72	Mauritius	30	211	160	177	22	32	2,095	3,075	106
73	Poland[a]	..	..	4,185	3,114	..	1	1,678	2,223	108
74	Malaysia[a]	1,198	..	1,023	2,387	1	..	489	1,596	106
75	Panama[a]	149	..	63	93	3	..	387	657	95
76	Brazil	4,392	27,849	2,485	1,387	31	21	186	485	108
77	*Angola*	..	..	149	313	0	103	33	29	87
78	*Lebanon*[a]	136	..	354	537	26	54	1,354	671	..
79	*Nicaragua*[a]	193	..	44	206	3	87	215	433	71
	Upper-middle-income	**18,586** t	..	**18,392** t	**38,840** t	**294** t	**4** t	**377** w	**728** w	**98** w
80	South Africa	1,362	4,624	127	212	..	..	422	541	84
81	Algeria[a]	492	6,546	1,816	6,130	54	4	163	320	106
82	Hungary[a]	1,010	4,019	408	203	..	..	1,497	2,595	111
83	Uruguay	268	744	70	44	6	0	485	420	103
84	Argentina[a]	2,250	10,089	0	3	..	..	26	45	97
85	Yugoslavia	2,212	*8,518*	992	297	..	..	770	1,328	100
86	Gabon[a]	60	375	24	59	..	..	..	46	97
87	Venezuela[a]	826	3,753	1,270	3,054	..	..	170	1,580	94
88	Trinidad and Tobago	40	210	208	212	..	..	880	450	71
89	Korea, Rep. of [a]	2,311	18,561	2,679	9,369	234	..	2,450	3,920	98
90	Portugal[a]	..	*3,180*	1,861	1,383	..	..	428	1,026	103
91	Greece	1,569	*6,461*	1,341	859	..	..	861	1,542	97
92	Oman[a]	40	..	52	293	..	..	..	417	..
93	Libya	93	..	612	1,435	..	..	62	416	119
94	Iran, Islamic Rep.	2,120	..	2,076	4,644	..	..	60	658	99
95	*Iraq*	579	..	870	4,442	..	..	34	397	105
96	*Romania*	..	..	1,381	30	..	..	565	1,301	117
	Low- and middle-income	**140,632** t	**558,529** t	**65,686** t	**109,994** t	**7,928** t	**12,891** t	**238** w	**680** w	**109** w
	Sub-Saharan Africa	15,421 t	50,851 t	4,108 t	8,214 t	910 t	3,583 t	33 w	85 w	94 w
	East Asia	50,416 t	194,504 t	17,259 t	37,462 t	923 t	1,327 t	380 w	1,326 w	123 w
	South Asia	32,884 t	103,969 t	9,404 t	7,645 t	4,522 t	2,660 t	135 w	586 w	100 w
	Europe, M.East, & N.Africa	19,480 t	..	23,247 t	39,511 t	1,010 t	2,880 t	474 w	960 w	103 w
	Latin America & Caribbean	18,622 t	81,703 t	11,537 t	16,946 t	563 t	2,441 t	176 w	451 w	100 w
	Severely indebted	**21,461** t	**91,994** t	**16,496** t	**21,242** t	**664** t	**2,134** t	**336** w	**613** w	**100** w
	High-income economies	**87,956** t	..	**73,681** t	**78,693** t			**999** w	**1,172** w	**101** w
	OECD members	87,148 t	..	70,120 t	68,319 t			1,001 w	1,163 w	102 w
	†Other	765 t	..	3,562 t	10,374 t			645 w	3,131 w	85 w
97	†Saudi Arabia[a]	219	5,526	482	5,179			54	3,678	..
98	Spain[a]	..	*15,721*	4,675	3,416			593	989	115
99	Ireland	559	*2,712*	640	408			3,067	6,815	98
100	†Israel[b]	295	..	1,176	1,799	53	2	1,401	2,237	101
101	†Singapore [a]	44	101	682	1,054			2,500	13,750	87
102	†Hong Kong	62	*174*	657	690			..	..	24
103	New Zealand[a]	897	*2,826*	92	158			7,745	7,086	108
104	Australia[a]	2,173	*8,227*	2	27			232	286	97
105	United Kingdom	2,971	..	7,540	3,620			2,631	3,555	109
106	Italy[a]	8,465	*31,062*	8,101	7,502			896	1,901	101
107	†Kuwait [a]	8	..	101	417			..	750	..
108	Belgium[a]	934	*3,042*	4,585c	4,620c			5,648c	5,098c	113c
109	Netherlands[a]	1,827	*8,456*	7,199	6,354			7,493	6,877	113
110	Austria[a]	992	*3,844*	164	135			2,426	2,214	107
111	†United Arab Emirates	..	453	132	458			..	1,632	..
112	France [a]	9,366	*30,780*	654	951			2,435	2,990	106
113	Canada	3,280	..	1,513	595			191	484	111
114	Denmark	882	*4,130*	462	211			2,234	2,330	118
115	Germany, Fed. Rep.[a]	5,951	*16,541*	7,164	4,181			4,263	4,208	112
116	Finland	1,205	*5,153*	222	230			1,930	2,164	99
117	Sweden	1,394	*4,582*	300	189			1,646	1,357	99
118	United States[a]	27,828	*89,811*	460	1,811			816	937	94
119	Norway	624	*2,876*	713	460			2,443	2,704	110
120	Japan[a]	12,467	*65,384*	19,557	28,018			3,547	4,327	104
121	Switzerland[a]	..	..	1,458	788			3,831	4,306	108
	Total reporting economies	**226,275** t	..	**139,368** t	**188,687** t	**7,981** t	**12,894** t	**480** w	**831** w	**107** w
	Oil exporters	22,367 t	114,085 t	18,105 t	45,171 t	1,038 t	2,155 t	143 w	607 w	104 w
	Nonreporting nonmembers	..	..	**15,326** t	**43,584** t	..	..	**572** w	**1,268** w	**110** w

a. Value added in agriculture data are at purchaser values.   b. Value added in agriculture data refer to net domestic product at factor cost.   c. Includes Luxembourg.

185

Table 5. Commercial energy

		Average annual energy growth rate (percent)				Energy consumption per capita (kilograms of oil equivalent)		Energy imports as a percentage of merchandise exports	
		Energy production		Energy consumption					
		1965-80	1980-88	1965-80	1980-88	1965	1988	1965	1988
	Low-income economies	10.0 w	4.4 w	8.2 w	5.3 w	126 w	322 w	6 w	11 w
	China and India	9.1 w	5.8 w	8.8 w	5.5 w	146 w	424 w	4 w	6 w
	Other low-income	12.4 w	0.3 w	5.0 w	4.2 w	73 w	122 w	8 w	17 w
1	Mozambique	19.8	−39.0	2.2	2.0	81	86	13	43
2	Ethiopia	7.5	6.4	4.1	2.2	10	20	8	59
3	Chad	. .	. .	. .	. .	. .	18	22	. .
4	Tanzania	7.3	3.4	3.7	2.4	37	36	10	44
5	Bangladesh	. .	14.0	. .	7.6	. .	50	. .	24
6	Malawi	18.2	4.3	8.0	0.2	25	42	7	9
7	Somalia	. .	. .	16.7	1.8	14	66	8	20
8	Zaire	9.4	4.3	3.6	1.5	74	74	6	2
9	Bhutan	. .	. .	. .	. .	. .	. .	. .	. .
10	Lao PDR	. .	−0.2	4.2	2.0	24	37	. .	. .
11	Nepal	18.4	11.6	6.2	9.4	6	23	10	29
12	Madagascar	3.9	9.3	3.5	1.5	34	39	8	45
13	Burkina Faso	. .	. .	10.5	. .	7	. .	11	7
14	Mali	38.6	9.3	7.0	2.9	14	21	16	31
15	Burundi	. .	11.6	6.0	8.2	5	20	11	8
16	Uganda	−0.5	4.1	−0.5	4.0	36	25	1	14
17	Nigeria	17.3	−1.4	12.9	6.6	34	150	7	2
18	Zambia	25.7	1.4	4.0	0.6	464	376	6	6
19	Niger	. .	15.7	12.5	3.2	8	43	9	15
20	Rwanda	8.8	5.5	15.2	4.4	8	41	10	63
21	China	10.0	5.5	9.8	5.5	178	580	0	2
22	India	5.6	6.9	5.8	5.4	100	211	8	20
23	Pakistan	6.5	6.6	3.5	6.2	135	210	7	27
24	Kenya	13.1	8.3	4.5	0.2	110	94	13	41
25	Togo	2.9	11.4	10.7	−1.5	27	54	4	6
26	Central African Rep.	6.7	0.7	2.2	3.7	22	30	9	14
27	Haiti	. .	4.3	8.4	1.6	24	57	6	13
28	Benin	. .	7.8	9.9	4.7	21	46	10	72
29	Ghana	17.7	−6.1	7.8	−3.5	76	125	6	15
30	Lesotho	. .	. .	. .	. .	. .	. .	. . [a]	. . [a]
31	Sri Lanka	10.4	8.6	2.2	3.7	106	162	6	25
32	Guinea	16.5	. .	2.3	1.1	56	78	. .	. .
33	Yemen, PDR	. .	. .	−6.4	2.5	. .	653	. .	. .
34	Indonesia	9.9	1.0	8.4	4.5	91	229	3	14
35	Mauritania	. .	. .	9.5	0.3	48	111	3	6
36	Sudan	17.8	1.6	2.0	0.9	67	58	5	37
37	*Afghanistan*	15.7	0.9	5.6	11.3	30	. .	8	. .
38	*Myanmar*	8.4	4.8	4.9	5.1	39	74	4	5
39	*Kampuchea, Dem.*	. .	6.5	7.6	2.1	19	. .	7	. .
40	*Liberia*	14.6	−0.9	7.9	−8.4	182	164	6	12
41	*Sierra Leone*	. .	. .	0.8	−0.8	109	76	11	11
42	*Viet Nam*	5.3	1.2	−2.6	1.9	. .	93	. .	. .
	Middle-income economies	3.7 w	3.3 w	6.6 w	2.7 w	585 w	1,086 w	8 w	9 w
	Lower-middle-income	7.0 w	4.7 w	6.8 w	2.4 w	429 w	797 w	9 w	10 w
43	Bolivia	9.5	−0.2	7.7	−1.5	156	249	1	3
44	Philippines	9.0	9.0	5.8	−1.0	160	244	12	16
45	Yemen Arab Rep.	. .	. .	21.0	10.7	7	102	. .	. .
46	Senegal	. .	. .	7.4	−1.2	79	155	8	18
47	Zimbabwe	−0.7	−0.0	5.2	0.6	441	527	7	5
48	Egypt, Arab Rep.	10.7	6.3	6.2	6.7	313	607	11	4
49	Dominican Rep.	10.9	5.4	11.5	2.3	127	332	8	36
50	Côte d'Ivoire	11.1	. .	8.6	. .	101	. .	5	12
51	Papua New Guinea	13.7	6.4	13.0	2.4	56	243	11	9
52	Morocco	2.5	−0.1	7.9	2.4	124	239	5	17
53	Honduras	14.0	6.7	7.6	3.2	111	203	5	14
54	Guatemala	12.5	7.4	6.8	−0.5	150	168	9	14
55	Congo, People's Rep.	41.1	7.5	7.8	4.4	90	245	10	5
56	El Salvador	9.0	3.4	7.0	1.6	140	215	5	14
57	Thailand	9.0	35.2	10.1	6.6	82	331	11	14
58	Botswana	8.8	2.6	9.5	2.3	191	415	. . [a]	. . [a]
59	Cameroon	13.0	14.9	6.3	6.1	67	152	6	1
60	Jamaica	−0.9	5.1	6.1	−2.8	703	855	12	22
61	Ecuador	35.0	−3.6	11.9	0.5	162	573	11	3
62	Colombia	1.0	11.1	6.0	2.2	413	755	1	4
63	Paraguay	. .	11.8	9.7	4.6	84	224	16	12
64	Tunisia	20.4	−1.7	8.5	5.6	170	499	12	10
65	Turkey	4.3	8.9	8.5	7.3	258	822	12	24
66	Peru	6.6	−1.1	5.0	0.7	395	478	3	1
67	Jordan	. .	7.5	9.3	6.9	226	723	33	42

Note: For data comparability and coverage, see the technical notes. Figures in italics are for years other than those specified.

		Average annual energy growth rate (percent)				Energy consumption per capita (kilograms of oil equivalent)		Energy imports as a percentage of merchandise exports	
		Energy production		Energy consumption					
		1965–80	*1980–88*	*1965–80*	*1980–88*	*1965*	*1988*	*1965*	*1988*
68	Chile	1.8	2.8	3.0	1.6	652	832	5	4
69	Syrian Arab Rep.	56.3	4.6	12.4	4.1	212	913	13	18
70	Costa Rica	8.2	7.7	8.8	2.9	267	557	8	12
71	Mexico	9.7	2.4	7.9	0.7	605	1,305	4	1
72	Mauritius	2.1	6.7	7.2	2.8	160	402	6	9
73	Poland	4.0	2.1	4.8	1.1	2,027	3,453	. .	*15*
74	Malaysia	36.9	15.6	6.7	5.9	313	784	11	5
75	Panama	6.9	9.8	5.8	4.2	576	1,627	61	57
76	Brazil	8.6	9.0	9.9	3.6	286	813	14	13
77	*Angola*	. .	. .	. .	. .	. .	. .	. .	. .
78	*Lebanon*	2.0	−4.0	2.0	3.4	713	. .	51	. .
79	*Nicaragua*	2.6	−0.2	6.5	1.8	172	252	6	42
	Upper-middle-income	**2.3** *w*	**2.4** *w*	**6.4** *w*	**2.9** *w*	**912** *w*	**1,766** *w*	**7** *w*	**8** *w*
80	South Africa	5.1	4.9	4.3	3.3	1,744	2,439	5[a]	0[a]
81	Algeria	5.3	5.2	11.9	6.2	226	1,094	0	2
82	Hungary	0.8	1.4	3.8	1.0	1,825	3,068	12	15
83	Uruguay	4.7	10.6	1.3	−1.3	765	769	13	10
84	Argentina	4.5	2.6	4.3	2.1	975	1,523	8	4
85	Yugoslavia	3.5	2.3	6.0	3.1	898	2,159	7	18
86	Gabon	13.7	0.3	14.7	3.0	153	1,134	3	1
87	Venezuela	−3.1	−0.9	4.6	2.1	2,319	2,354	0	0
88	Trinidad and Tobago	3.8	−3.4	6.6	0.2	2,776	5,255	60	10
89	Korea, Rep. of	4.1	9.7	12.1	5.5	238	1,515	18	10
90	Portugal	3.6	4.7	6.5	2.7	506	1,324	13	21
91	Greece	10.5	8.2	8.5	2.5	615	1,986	29	11
92	Oman	23.0	10.3	30.5	7.7	14	2,012	77	2
93	Libya	0.6	−5.0	18.2	4.8	222	2,719	2	*1*
94	*Iran, Islamic Rep.*	3.6	5.1	8.9	2.7	537	875	0	. .
95	*Iraq*	6.2	5.3	7.4	5.3	399	781	0	. .
96	*Romania*	4.3	0.7	6.6	0.8	1,536	3,459	. .	. .
	Low- and middle-income	**5.5** *w*	**3.8** *w*	**7.2** *w*	**3.8** *w*	**253** *w*	**525** *w*	**7** *w*	**9** *w*
	Sub-Saharan Africa	**15.3** *w*	**0.1** *w*	**5.6** *w*	**2.7** *w*	**71** *w*	**95** *w*	**7** *w*	**11** *w*
	East Asia	**9.8** *w*	**5.2** *w*	**9.4** *w*	**5.3** *w*	**168** *w*	**474** *w*	**6** *w*	**8** *w*
	South Asia	**5.8** *w*	**5.6** *w*	**5.7** *w*	**5.5** *w*	**99** *w*	**182** *w*	**7** *w*	**22** *w*
	Europe, M.East, & N.Africa	**4.4** *w*	**3.2** *w*	**6.2** *w*	**2.8** *w*	**746** *w*	**1,343** *w*	**9** *w*	**16** *w*
	Latin America & Caribbean	**1.9** *w*	**2.6** *w*	**6.9** *w*	**1.9** *w*	**515** *w*	**952** *w*	**8** *w*	**7** *w*
	Severely indebted	**2.4** *w*	**2.2** *w*	**6.1** *w*	**1.6** *w*	**675** *w*	**1,084** *w*	**7** *w*	**9** *w*
	High-income economies	**3.1** *w*	**0.1** *w*	**3.1** *w*	**1.1** *w*	**3,707** *w*	**5,098** *w*	**11** *w*	**9** *w*
	OECD members	**2.1** *w*	**1.7** *w*	**3.0** *w*	**1.0** *w*	**3,748** *w*	**5,181** *w*	**11** *w*	**9** *w*
	†Other	**7.7** *w*	**−6.6** *w*	**5.7** *w*	**3.2** *w*	**1,943** *w*	**3,028** *w*	**7** *w*	**8** *w*
97	†Saudi Arabia	11.5	−10.3	7.2	5.0	1,759	3,098	0	*1*
98	Spain	3.6	7.0	6.5	1.5	901	1,902	31	17
99	Ireland	0.1	5.9	3.9	1.5	1,504	2,610	14	5
100	†Israel	−15.2	−14.2	4.4	1.4	1,574	1,972	14	13
101	†Singapore	. .	. .	10.8	−0.6	670	4,464	17	16
102	†Hong Kong	. .	. .	8.4	3.9	413	1,544	4	2
103	New Zealand	4.7	6.9	3.6	3.5	2,622	4,339	7	5
104	Australia	10.5	5.7	5.0	1.6	3,287	5,157	11	6
105	United Kingdom	3.6	1.7	0.9	0.8	3,481	3,756	13	6
106	Italy	1.3	0.9	3.7	−0.3	1,568	2,608	16	9
107	†Kuwait	−1.6	−0.0	2.1	3.7	. .	4,637	0	0
108	Belgium[b]	−3.9	9.1	2.9	−0.0	3,402	4,781	. .	. .
109	Netherlands	15.4	−1.8	5.0	1.3	3,134	5,235	12	9
110	Austria	0.8	−0.7	4.0	0.6	2,060	3,396	10	7
111	†United Arab Emirates	14.7	−0.1	36.6	8.4	105	6,481	4	2
112	France	−0.9	7.8	3.7	0.4	2,468	3,704	16	9
113	Canada	5.7	4.2	4.5	1.6	6,007	9,683	8	4
114	Denmark	2.6	57.6	2.4	0.9	2,911	3,902	13	6
115	Germany, Fed. Rep.	−0.1	0.4	3.0	−0.2	3,197	4,421	8	6
116	Finland	3.8	8.1	5.1	2.6	2,233	5,550	11	9
117	Sweden	4.9	6.6	2.5	2.4	4,162	6,617	12	6
118	United States	1.1	0.4	2.3	0.9	6,535	7,655	8	14
119	Norway	12.4	6.6	4.1	3.2	4,650	9,516	11	4
120	Japan	−0.4	3.7	6.1	1.9	1,474	3,306	19	14
121	Switzerland	3.7	1.7	3.1	2.0	2,501	4,193	8	4
	Total reporting economies	**4.0** *w*	**1.4** *w*	**4.0** *w*	**1.9** *w*	**1,010** *w*	**1,289** *w*	**10** *w*	**9** *w*
	Oil exporters	**5.8** *w*	**−1.0** *w*	**7.4** *w*	**3.0** *w*	**389** *w*	**790** *w*	**5** *w*	**5** *w*
	Nonreporting nonmembers	**4.6** *w*	**2.8** *w*	**4.4** *w*	**2.8** *w*	**2,509** *w*	**4,777** *w*	. .	. .

a. Figures for the South African Customs Union, comprising South Africa, Namibia, Lesotho, Botswana, and Swaziland, are included in South African data. Trade among the component territories is excluded.   b. Includes Luxembourg.

Table 6. Structure of manufacturing

	Value added in manufacturing (millions of current dollars)		Distribution of manufacturing value added (percent; current prices)									
			Food, beverages, and tobacco		Textiles and clothing		Machinery and transport equipment		Chemicals		Other[a]	
	1970	1987	1970	1987	1970	1987	1970	1987	1970	1987	1970	1987
Low-income economies	45,816 t	..										
China and India	38,394 t	..										
Other low-income	6,285 t	..										
1 Mozambique	..	..	51	..	13	..	5	..	3	..	28	..
2 Ethiopia	149	564	46	49	31	19	0	2	2	4	21	27
3 Chad [b]	51	106	..	..	..	..	..	..	..	..	..	..
4 Tanzania	116	146	36	32	28	23	5	9	4	6	26	30
5 Bangladesh[b]	387	1,313	30	26	47	32	3	5	11	16	10	21
6 Malawi	..	..	51	33	17	21	3	3	10	17	20	26
7 Somalia	26	51	88	59	6	13	0	2	1	13	6	13
8 Zaire[b]	286	374	38	..	16	..	7	..	10	..	29	..
9 Bhutan	..	16	..	..	..	..	..	..	..	..	..	..
10 Lao PDR	..	47	..	..	..	..	..	..	..	..	..	..
11 Nepal	32	165	..	..	..	..	..	..	..	..	..	..
12 Madagascar [b]	118	..	36	49	28	25	6	5	7	9	23	12
13 Burkina Faso	..	220	69	..	9	..	2	..	1	..	19	..
14 Mali[b]	25	100	36	..	40	..	4	..	5	..	14	..
15 Burundi	16	96	53	..	25	..	0	..	6	..	16	..
16 Uganda	158	162	40	..	20	..	2	..	4	..	34	..
17 Nigeria	543	5,196	36	..	26	..	1	..	6	..	31	..
18 Zambia[b]	181	568	49	46	9	11	5	14	10	6	27	23
19 Niger [b]	30	189	..	..	..	..	..	..	..	..	..	..
20 Rwanda[b]	8	314	86	65	0	3	3	0	2	5	8	28
21 China[b]	30,466[c]	92,800[c]	..	12	..	14	..	25	..	11	..	38
22 India	7,928	43,331	13	12	21	15	20	26	14	15	32	32
23 Pakistan	1,462	5,001	24	34	38	19	6	9	9	14	23	24
24 Kenya	174	839	31	38	9	11	18	13	7	11	35	27
25 Togo[b]	25	94	..	..	..	..	..	..	..	..	..	..
26 Central African Rep.	12	79	..	..	..	..	..	..	..	..	..	..
27 Haiti[b]	..	..	..	..	..	..	..	..	..	..	..	..
28 Benin	19	83	..	..	..	..	..	..	..	..	..	..
29 Ghana[b]	252	501	34	..	16	..	4	..	4	..	41	..
30 Lesotho	3	37	..	..	..	..	..	..	..	..	..	..
31 Sri Lanka	321	967	26	..	19	..	10	..	11	..	33	..
32 Guinea[b]	..	117	..	..	..	..	..	..	..	..	..	..
33 Yemen, PDR	..	..	..	..	..	..	..	..	..	..	..	..
34 Indonesia[b]	994	12,876	..	22	..	13	..	8	..	9	..	48
35 Mauritania	10	..	..	..	..	..	..	..	..	..	..	..
36 Sudan	140	1,111	39	..	34	..	3	..	5	..	19	..
37 *Afghanistan*	..	..	..	..	..	..	..	..	..	..	..	..
38 *Myanmar*	..	..	..	..	..	..	..	..	..	..	..	..
39 *Kampuchea, Dem.*	..	..	..	..	..	..	..	..	..	..	..	..
40 *Liberia*	15	47	..	..	..	..	..	..	..	..	..	..
41 *Sierra Leone*	22	24	..	65	..	1	..	0	..	4	..	30
42 *Viet Nam*	..	..	..	..	..	..	..	..	..	..	..	..
Middle-income economies	63,448 t	451,574 t										
Lower-middle-income	36,839 t	225,539 t										
43 Bolivia[b]	135	675	33	30	34	7	1	1	6	4	26	58
44 Philippines[b]	1,622	8,424	39	43	8	8	8	8	13	10	32	30
45 Yemen Arab Rep.[b]	10	578	20	..	50	..	..	..	1	..	28	..
46 Senegal[b]	141	868	51	48	19	15	2	6	6	7	22	24
47 Zimbabwe	293	1,637	24	34	16	16	9	9	11	9	40	32
48 Egypt, Arab Rep.	..	4,244	17	..	35	..	9	..	12	..	27	..
49 Dominican Rep.[b]	275	843	74	..	5	..	1	..	6	..	14	..
50 Côte d'Ivoire	149	1,191	27	..	16	..	10	..	5	..	42	..
51 Papua New Guinea[b]	35	227	25	..	1	..	37	..	5	..	33	..
52 Morocco[b]	641	3,398	..	..	..	..	..	..	..	..	..	..
53 Honduras	91	515	58	..	10	..	1	..	4	..	28	..
54 Guatemala[b]	..	..	42	45	14	9	4	3	12	13	27	30
55 Congo, People's Rep.[b]	..	147	65	42	4	10	1	4	8	8	22	35
56 El Salvador [b]	194	809	40	37	30	14	3	5	8	16	18	28
57 Thailand[b]	1,130	11,543	43	29	13	18	9	13	6	7	29	33
58 Botswana[b]	5	82	..	52	..	7	..	0	..	6	..	36
59 Cameroon[b]	119	1,632	47	..	16	..	..	5	4	..	28	..
60 Jamaica[b]	221	639	46	..	7	..	..	..	10	..	36	..
61 Ecuador[b]	305	2,073	43	32	14	13	3	6	8	8	32	41
62 Colombia	1,487	7,244	31	36	20	14	8	8	11	13	29	30
63 Paraguay[b]	99	735	56	..	16	..	1	..	5	..	21	..
64 Tunisia	121	1,265	29	20	18	19	4	4	13	9	36	47
65 Turkey	1,930	15,863	26	17	15	15	8	15	7	11	45	43
66 Peru[b]	1,430	6,232	25	25	14	12	7	8	7	11	47	43
67 Jordan	32	552	21	22	14	3	7	1	6	7	52	67

Note: For data comparability and coverage, see the technical notes. Figures in italics are for years other than those specified.

	Value added in manufacturing (millions of current dollars)		Distribution of manufacturing value added (percent; current prices)									
			Food, beverages, and tobacco		Textiles and clothing		Machinery and transport equipment		Chemicals		Other[a]	
	1970	1987	1970	1987	1970	1987	1970	1987	1970	1987	1970	1987
68 Chile[b]	2,092	..	17	26	12	7	11	4	5	8	55	56
69 Syrian Arab Rep.[b]	..	..	37	24	40	10	3	3	2	15	20	48
70 Costa Rica[b]	..	..	48	..	12	..	6	..	7	..	28	..
71 Mexico[b]	8,449	36,381	28	24	15	12	13	14	11	12	34	39
72 Mauritius	26	358	75	27	6	52	5	2	3	4	12	15
73 Poland[b]	..	..	20	14	19	16	24	31	8	6	28	34
74 Malaysia[b]	500	..	26	21	3	6	8	22	9	15	54	37
75 Panama[b]	127	422	41	47	9	7	1	3	5	8	44	34
76 Brazil	10,429	78,995	16	15	13	10	22	21	10	12	39	42
77 Angola	..	..	..	..	..	..	..	..	..	..	..	..
78 Lebanon[b]	..	..	27	..	19	..	1	..	3	..	49	..
79 Nicaragua[b]	159	759	53	54	14	12	2	2	8	10	23	22
Upper-middle-income	26,419 t	..										
80 South Africa	3,914	17,790	15	14	13	9	17	19	10	12	45	47
81 Algeria[b]	682	7,196	32	20	20	17	9	13	4	3	35	47
82 Hungary[b]	..	..	12	7	13	10	28	35	8	12	39	37
83 Uruguay	..	1,690	34	29	21	19	7	11	6	9	32	32
84 Argentina[b]	5,750	22,024	20	21	18	12	17	15	7	11	38	41
85 Yugoslavia	..	..	10	14	15	17	23	25	7	7	45	37
86 Gabon[b]	..	..	37	..	7	..	6	..	6	..	44	..
87 Venezuela[b]	2,140	10,779	30	18	13	7	9	8	8	8	39	59
88 Trinidad and Tobago	198	416	18	43	3	6	7	6	2	4	70	42
89 Korea, Rep. of [b]	1,880	42,286	26	12	17	17	11	28	11	8	36	35
90 Portugal[b]	..	..	18	17	19	25	13	13	10	10	39	34
91 Greece	1,642	7,170	20	20	20	25	13	10	7	8	40	36
92 Oman[b]	..	464	..	..	..	..	..	..	..	..	..	..
93 Libya	81	..	64	..	5	..	0	..	12	..	20	..
94 Iran, Islamic Rep.	1,501	..	30	..	20	..	18	..	6	..	26	..
95 Iraq	325	..	26	14	14	9	7	10	3	16	50	50
96 Romania	..	..	..	..	..	..	..	..	..	..	..	..
Low- and middle-income	110,929 t	..										
Sub-Saharan Africa	3,376 t	..										
East Asia	38,947 t	..										
South Asia	10,359 t	51,621 t										
Europe, M.East, & N.Africa	..	..										
Latin America & Caribbean	34,698 t	180,987 t										
Severely indebted	38,028 t	202,164 t										
High-income economies	608,635 t	2,895,002 t										
OECD members	604,270 t	2,855,538 t										
†Other	2,387 t	32,313 t										
97 †Saudi Arabia[b]	372	6,085	..	..	..	..	..	..	..	..	..	..
98 Spain[b]	..	66,408	13	18	15	9	16	21	11	11	45	40
99 Ireland	785	..	31	27	19	6	13	26	7	17	30	25
100 †Israel[b]	..	..	15	12	14	8	23	32	7	8	41	39
101 †Singapore[b]	379	5,741	12	5	5	4	28	52	4	12	51	27
102 †Hong Kong	1,013	9,825	4	6	41	40	16	19	2	2	36	33
103 New Zealand[b]	1,777	7,101	24	26	13	10	15	16	4	6	43	43
104 Australia[b]	9,051	31,547	16	18	9	7	24	21	7	8	43	45
105 United Kingdom	36,044	116,553	13	14	9	6	31	32	10	11	37	36
106 Italy[b]	30,942	175,443	10	8	13	14	24	32	13	10	40	36
107 †Kuwait[b]	120	1,902	5	10	4	7	1	4	4	6	86	73
108 Belgium[b]	8,226	32,303	17	19	12	8	22	23	9	13	40	36
109 Netherlands[b]	8,545	39,759	17	19	8	4	27	27	13	13	36	37
110 Austria[b]	4,873	30,879	17	17	12	8	19	25	6	6	45	43
111 †United Arab Emirates	..	2,155	..	14	..	1	..	..	..	..	..	84
112 France[b]	38,861	191,692	12	13	10	8	26	30	8	9	44	41
113 Canada	17,001	..	16	15	8	6	23	26	7	9	46	45
114 Denmark	2,929	17,230	20	22	8	5	24	23	8	10	40	40
115 Germany, Fed. Rep.[b]	70,888	359,754	13	10	8	4	32	40	9	13	38	33
116 Finland	2,588	19,132	13	12	10	6	20	25	6	7	51	50
117 Sweden	8,477	33,282	10	10	6	2	30	34	5	9	49	45
118 United States[b]	253,863	868,233	12	12	8	5	31	35	10	10	39	38
119 Norway	2,416	12,337	15	21	7	2	23	25	7	8	49	44
120 Japan[b]	73,339	689,295	8	10	8	5	34	37	11	10	40	38
121 Switzerland[b]	..	..	10	..	7	..	31	..	9	..	42	..
Total reporting economies	722,228 t	3,551,267 t										
Oil exporters	19,643 t	128,122 t										
Nonreporting nonmembers	..	..										

a. Includes unallocable data; see the technical notes.   b. Value added in manufacturing data are at purchaser values.   c. World Bank estimate.

Table 7. Manufacturing earnings and output

	Earnings per employee					Total earnings as a percentage of value added				Gross output per employee (1980=100)			
	Growth rate		Index (1980=100)										
	1970-80	1980-87	1985	1986	1987	1970	1985	1986	1987	1970	1985	1986	1987
Low-income economies													
China and India													
Other low-income													
1 Mozambique	..	..	..	..	..	..	..	..	..	..	..	..	..
2 Ethiopia	−4.7	−0.1	85	96	105	24	20	19	20	61	114	112	119
3 Chad	..	..	..	..	..	..	..	..	..	..	..	..	..
4 Tanzania	..	−12.7	51	42	..	42	35	34	..	122	99	76	..
5 Bangladesh	−3.0	−2.9	90	81	78	26	30	29	29	116	113	106	111
6 Malawi	..	1.6	115	..	..	37	39	..	..	120	139	..	..
7 Somalia	−5.1	..	..	..	..	28	..	27	..	..	..	..	..
8 Zaire	..	..	..	..	..	..	..	..	..	..	..	..	..
9 Bhutan	..	..	..	..	..	..	..	..	..	..	..	..	..
10 Lao PDR	..	..	..	..	..	..	..	..	..	..	..	..	..
11 Nepal	..	..	..	..	..	..	..	..	..	..	..	..	..
12 Madagascar	−0.9	−10.3	66	..	..	36	40	..	..	91	55	..	..
13 Burkina Faso	..	..	..	..	..	..	..	..	..	..	..	..	..
14 Mali	..	..	..	..	..	46	..	..	..	139	..	..	..
15 Burundi	−7.8	..	..	..	..	..	..	..	..	..	..	..	..
16 Uganda	..	..	..	..	..	..	..	..	..	..	..	..	..
17 Nigeria	..	−9.6	..	..	..	18	..	..	..	105	..	..	..
18 Zambia	−3.2	..	..	..	..	34	..	..	..	109	..	..	..
19 Niger	..	..	..	..	..	..	..	..	..	..	..	..	..
20 Rwanda	..	..	..	..	..	22	10	10	..	..	..	..	..
21 China	..	4.2	114	124	..	..	13	15	..	..	131	131	..
22 India	0.5	4.9	120	127	138	47	46	48	48	83	149	157	174
23 Pakistan	3.3	6.2	132	138	..	21	20	20	..	51	145	149	..
24 Kenya	−3.4	−2.3	79	83	87	53	48	48	48	38	107	113	108
25 Togo	..	..	..	..	..	..	..	..	..	..	..	..	..
26 Central African Rep.	..	..	..	..	..	..	49	..	..	..	74	85	..
27 Haiti	−3.3	3.4	104	116	153	..	..	..	..	..	..	..	..
28 Benin	..	..	..	..	..	..	..	..	..	..	..	..	..
29 Ghana	..	..	..	..	..	23	..	..	..	193	..	..	..
30 Lesotho	..	..	..	..	..	..	28	..	..	..	..	..	..
31 Sri Lanka	..	0.8	102	102	..	..	..	..	..	70	135	132	..
32 Guinea	..	..	..	..	..	..	..	..	..	..	..	..	..
33 Yemen, PDR	..	..	..	..	..	..	..	..	..	..	..	..	..
34 Indonesia	5.0	6.0	139	144	..	26	19	19	..	42	141	156	..
35 Mauritania	..	..	..	..	..	..	..	..	..	..	..	..	..
36 Sudan	..	..	..	..	..	31	..	..	..	..	..	..	..
37 *Afghanistan*	..	..	..	..	..	..	..	..	..	..	..	..	..
38 *Myanmar*	..	..	..	..	..	..	..	..	..	..	..	..	..
39 *Kampuchea, Dem.*	..	..	..	..	..	..	..	..	..	..	..	..	..
40 *Liberia*	..	1.6	107	99	..	..	..	..	..	..	..	..	..
41 *Sierra Leone*	..	..	..	..	..	..	..	..	..	..	..	..	..
42 *Viet Nam*	..	..	..	..	..	..	..	..	..	..	..	..	..
Middle-income economies													
Lower-middle-income													
43 Bolivia	0.0	−10.3	63	41	50	43	26	24	28	65	37	35	34
44 Philippines	−3.7	2.6	109	120	..	21	22	21	20	102	105	112	..
45 Yemen Arab Rep.	..	..	..	..	..	..	..	..	..	..	..	166	169
46 Senegal	−4.9	−0.1	..	..	..	..	44	44	..	..	..	..	..
47 Zimbabwe	1.6	−0.4	105	104	103	43	42	40	40	98	92	89	90
48 Egypt, Arab Rep.	4.1	..	..	..	..	54	..	..	..	76	..	..	..
49 Dominican Rep.	−1.0	−4.4	79	..	..	35	..	..	..	63	..	..	..
50 Côte d'Ivoire	−0.9	..	..	..	..	27	..	..	..	52	..	..	..
51 Papua New Guinea	3.0	−2.9	..	..	..	42	..	..	..	..	..	..	..
52 Morocco	..	..	81	73	..	..	..	..	..	..	98	92	..
53 Honduras	..	..	..	..	..	..	..	..	..	..	..	..	..
54 Guatemala	−3.2	−1.4	99	93	..	..	23	27	..	..	..	..	..
55 Congo, People's Rep.	..	−0.1	..	..	..	34	49	..	..	..	..	..	..
56 El Salvador	2.4	−9.3	63	..	..	28	20	..	..	71	87	..	..
57 Thailand	1.0	7.0	143	146	..	25	24	23	24	68	138	138	..
58 Botswana	2.6	−4.5	85	..	..	..	46	..	..	..	60	..	..
59 Cameroon	..	..	..	..	..	29	..	..	..	..	..	..	..
60 Jamaica	−0.2	..	..	..	..	43	..	..	..	..	..	..	..
61 Ecuador	3.3	−1.5	94	99	95	27	40	36	35	83	104	109	114
62 Colombia	−0.2	3.8	116	116	134	25	18	16	18	86	128	123	146
63 Paraguay	..	..	..	..	..	..	..	..	..	..	..	..	..
64 Tunisia	4.2	..	..	..	..	44	..	..	..	95	..	..	..
65 Turkey	6.1	−3.5	84	81	86	26	21	16	17	108	139	154	170
66 Peru	..	−5.0	75	87	..	..	13	18	..	82	64	63	..
67 Jordan	..	−1.1	101	100	101	37	31	31	22	..	155	144	161

Note: For data comparability and coverage, see the technical notes. Figures in italics are for years other than those specified.

	Earnings per employee					Total earnings as a percentage of value added				Gross output per employee (1980=100)			
	Growth rate		Index (1980=100)										
	1970–80	1980–87	1985	1986	1987	1970	1985	1986	1987	1970	1985	1986	1987
68 Chile	8.2	−3.5	97	98	84	19	14	17	15	60	..	..	..
69 Syrian Arab Rep.	2.8	−1.4	..	..	..	33	33	23	..	72	..	..	..
70 Costa Rica	..	..	..	..	..	41	..	..	..	..	..	..	..
71 Mexico	1.2	−3.5	91	87	..	44	26	26	..	77	112	107	..
72 Mauritius	1.8	−1.8	84	86	94	34	46	44	43	139	80	72	74
73 Poland	..	..	..	..	..	..	..	..	..	..	..	..	..
74 Malaysia	2.0	5.2	135	134	138	29	30	30	29	96	..	..	..
75 Panama	0.2	3.3	125	128	126	32	34	34	34	67	87	96	..
76 Brazil	4.0	..	..	..	..	22	..	..	..	68	108	108	104
77 *Angola*	..	..	..	..	..	..	..	..	..	..	..	..	..
78 *Lebanon*	..	..	..	..	..	..	..	..	..	..	..	..	..
79 *Nicaragua*	..	−14.5	69	31	..	16	22	22	..	206	113	109	..
Upper-middle-income													
80 South Africa	2.7	0.0	106	102	101	46	47	46	46	..	..	..	..
81 Algeria	−1.0	..	..	..	..	45	..	..	..	120	..	..	..
82 Hungary	3.7	1.5	108	111	111	28	34	34	33	41	111	111	113
83 Uruguay	..	0.3	96	109	116	..	22	25	26	..	108	113	120
84 Argentina	−1.5	2.5	105	111	103	30	21	21	19	71	87	103	103
85 Yugoslavia	1.3	−1.4	91	97	93	39	29	33	30	59	100	98	89
86 Gabon	..	..	..	..	..	..	..	..	..	..	..	..	..
87 Venezuela	3.8	−0.6	110	106	107	31	26	27	31	118	109	106	110
88 Trinidad and Tobago	..	2.3	..	..	..	..	79	67	..	..	..	..	..
89 Korea, Rep. of	10.0	5.6	125	128	145	25	27	26	27	40	140	146	165
90 Portugal	2.5	−1.9	89	95	..	34	39	39	..	..	123	..	..
91 Greece	4.9	..	..	..	..	32	..	..	..	56	..	..	..
92 Oman	..	..	..	..	..	..	..	..	..	..	..	..	..
93 Libya	..	..	..	..	..	37	..	..	..	45	..	..	..
94 *Iran, Islamic Rep.*	..	..	..	..	..	25	..	..	..	85	..	..	..
95 *Iraq*	..	..	..	..	..	36	25	25	..	..	..	..	..
96 *Romania*	..	..	..	..	..	..	..	..	..	..	..	..	..

Low- and middle-income
  Sub-Saharan Africa
  East Asia
  South Asia
  Europe, M.East, & N.Africa
  Latin America & Caribbean

Severely indebted

High-income economies
  OECD members
  †Other

	Earnings per employee					Total earnings as a percentage of value added				Gross output per employee (1980=100)			
	Growth rate		Index (1980=100)										
	1970–80	1980–87	1985	1986	1987	1970	1985	1986	1987	1970	1985	1986	1987
97 †Saudi Arabia	..	0.9	..	..	..	52	40	38	40	..	127	112	139
98 Spain	4.4	..	100	101	112	49	33	33	33	44	205	187	..
99 Ireland	4.1	1.6	102	105	110	36	59	..	..	..	..	..	..
100 †Israel	8.8	−6.4	102	65	70	36	38	32	29	..	..	..	..
101 †Singapore	3.6	6.2	153	148	146	..	..	..	..	73	114	111	121
102 †Hong Kong	6.4	4.9	113	124	143	..	63	60	61	..	..	..	..
103 New Zealand	1.2	−1.6	95	..	..	62	59	..	..	..	121	..	..
104 Australia	2.9	1.9	106	113	115	53	48	52	52	..	111	113	117
105 United Kingdom	1.7	2.9	112	115	123	52	43	43	43	61	137	129	..
106 Italy	4.1	0.7	101	100	108	41	42	42	43	51	128	126	135
107 †Kuwait	..	3.7	119	..	..	12	43	..	..	..	153	..	..
108 Belgium	4.6	0.3	95	104	104	46	46	47	47	51	122	127	131
109 Netherlands	2.5	0.9	100	108	..	52	50	52	..	68	116	127	..
110 Austria	3.4	1.5	106	110	113	47	56	56	56	64	116	111	118
111 †United Arab Emirates	..	..	..	..	..	..	61	..	..	..	..	..	..
112 France	..	1.2	107	..	..	..	66	..	..	..	112	105	107
113 Canada	1.8	−0.1	102	101	96	53	46	45	46	68	120	..	..
114 Denmark	2.5	0.3	97	100	103	56	52	53	53	64	108	101	95
115 Germany, Fed. Rep.	3.5	1.4	102	107	110	46	42	43	43	60	117	107	104
116 Finland	2.6	2.4	110	115	118	47	43	50	46	73	122	123	128
117 Sweden	0.4	0.4	98	100	102	52	37	37	35	75	123	120	125
118 United States	0.1	1.4	106	108	109	47	40	39	39	63	116	116	124
119 Norway	2.6	1.6	105	107	109	50	57	59	58	75	121	118	120
120 Japan	3.1	1.8	110	112	113	32	35	37	35	45	124	116	122
121 Switzerland	..	..	..	..	..	..	..	..	..	..	..	..	..

Total reporting economies
  Oil exporters

Nonreporting nonmembers

Table 8. Growth of consumption and investment

		Average annual growth rate (percent)					
		General government consumption		Private consumption, etc.		Gross domestic investment	
		1965–80	1980–88	1965–80	1980–88	1965–80	1980–88
	Low-income economies	**6.3 w**	**7.0 w**	**4.1 w**	**5.2 w**	**8.8 w**	**8.0 w**
	China and India	**5.3 w**	**9.2 w**	**4.0 w**	**6.8 w**	**8.3 w**	**11.7 w**
	Other low-income	**8.4 w**	**2.4 w**	**4.4 w**	**2.8 w**	**9.7 w**	**−2.3 w**
1	Mozambique	. .	−4.6	. .	−1.0	. .	−6.6
2	Ethiopia	6.4	5.6	3.0	1.3	−0.1	2.0
3	Chad	. .	. .	. .	. .	. .	. .
4	Tanzania	a	8.4	3.4	1.8	6.2	0.3
5	Bangladesh	a	a	2.7	3.8	0.0	2.5
6	Malawi	5.6	3.8	4.0	3.1	9.0	−8.3
7	Somalia	11.7	−0.3	4.8	0.5	12.4	0.6
8	Zaire	0.7	16.3	1.2	−1.8	6.7	−1.6
9	Bhutan	. .	. .	. .	. .	. .	. .
10	Lao PDR	. .	. .	. .	. .	. .	. .
11	Nepal	. .	. .	. .	. .	. .	. .
12	Madagascar	2.0	−0.8	1.1	−0.4	1.5	−0.7
13	Burkina Faso	8.7	10.0	2.1	2.9	8.8	4.3
14	Mali	1.9	3.1	4.9	3.4	1.8	2.8
15	Burundi	7.3	5.4	6.1	2.3	9.0	8.8
16	Uganda	a	. .	1.4	. .	−5.7	. .
17	Nigeria	13.9	−1.5	5.0	−0.1	14.7	−14.5
18	Zambia	5.1	−5.4	−0.9	4.5	−3.6	−4.5
19	Niger	2.9	1.5	−2.4	1.7	6.3	−10.2
20	Rwanda	6.2	3.0	4.2	1.6	9.0	7.4
21	China	5.6	9.4	5.2	7.4	10.7	14.4
22	India	4.7	8.8	2.7	5.8	4.5	4.3
23	Pakistan	4.7	11.0	4.8	4.3	2.4	6.5
24	Kenya	10.6	1.1	5.7	5.1	7.2	−1.1
25	Togo	9.5	3.9	5.0	−1.8	9.0	−1.6
26	Central African Rep.	−1.1	−2.4	4.2	2.0	−5.4	8.8
27	Haiti	1.9	−1.4	2.3	0.4	14.8	−5.1
28	Benin	0.7	1.4	2.3	1.9	10.4	−11.5
29	Ghana	3.8	−0.3	1.4	2.3	−1.3	4.9
30	Lesotho	12.3	. .	8.8	. .	17.3	. .
31	Sri Lanka	1.1	10.0	4.0	4.6	11.5	−0.9
32	Guinea	. .	. .	. .	. .	. .	. .
33	Yemen, PDR	. .	. .	. .	. .	. .	. .
34	Indonesia	11.4	2.9	5.9	7.2	16.1	1.9
35	Mauritania	10.0	−4.3	1.9	4.3	19.2	−5.3
36	Sudan	0.2	−5.3	4.3	3.7	6.4	−5.1
37	*Afghanistan*	. .	. .	. .	. .	. .	. .
38	*Myanmar*	. .	. .	. .	. .	. .	. .
39	*Kampuchea, Dem.*	. .	. .	. .	. .	. .	. .
40	*Liberia*	3.4	*1.3*	3.2	*0.8*	6.4	*−16.7*
41	*Sierra Leone*	a	*−3.3*	4.2	*−3.0*	−1.0	*−5.1*
42	*Viet Nam*	. .	. .	. .	. .	. .	. .
	Middle-income economies	**7.7 w**	**2.5 w**	**6.6 w**	**2.5 w**	**8.6 w**	**−0.6 w**
	Lower-middle-income	**7.4 w**	**2.7 w**	**6.2 w**	**2.2 w**	**8.5 w**	**−1.6 w**
43	Bolivia	8.0	−5.2	4.0	−1.1	4.4	−19.5
44	Philippines	7.7	0.8	5.0	2.2	8.5	−10.9
45	Yemen Arab Rep.	. .	4.3	. .	3.6	. .	−9.1
46	Senegal	3.1	−0.9	1.7	2.7	3.9	2.0
47	Zimbabwe	10.6	6.2	5.1	−2.4	0.9	−1.4
48	Egypt, Arab Rep.	a	4.4	5.5	4.1	11.3	1.5
49	Dominican Rep.	0.2	2.8	7.9	0.5	13.5	4.6
50	Côte d'Ivoire	13.2	−2.6	7.5	1.9	10.7	−11.4
51	Papua New Guinea	0.1	−0.6	3.9	1.9	1.4	−1.5
52	Morocco	10.9	4.7	4.7	2.7	11.4	3.7
53	Honduras	6.9	4.9	4.9	1.9	6.8	−0.6
54	Guatemala	6.2	2.0	5.1	0.1	7.4	−3.4
55	Congo, People's Rep.	5.5	*11.3*	1.3	*7.1*	4.5	*0.6*
56	El Salvador	7.0	3.3	4.1	−0.1	6.6	0.1
57	Thailand	9.5	5.2	6.2	5.1	8.0	5.0
58	Botswana	12.0	*13.8*	9.2	*2.4*	21.0	*−1.5*
59	Cameroon	5.0	7.8	4.2	4.2	9.9	0.4
60	Jamaica	9.8	−1.5	2.0	*2.4*	−3.3	*−1.2*
61	Ecuador	12.2	−2.2	6.8	1.8	9.5	−3.7
62	Colombia	6.7	3.2	5.9	2.5	5.8	0.3
63	Paraguay	5.1	3.7	6.5	1.1	13.5	−2.1
64	Tunisia	7.2	3.9	8.3	3.3	4.6	−6.1
65	Turkey	6.1	2.8	5.7	5.7	8.8	4.4
66	Peru	6.3	0.3	4.9	2.0	0.3	−3.9
67	Jordan	. .	4.7	. .	6.6	. .	−5.5

Note: For data comparability and coverage, see the technical notes. Figures in italics are for years other than those specified

		General government consumption		Private consumption, etc.		Gross domestic investment	
		1965-80	*1980-88*	*1965-80*	*1980-88*	*1965-80*	*1980-88*
68	Chile	4.0	−0.5	0.9	0.6	0.5	−0.5
69	Syrian Arab Rep.	15.1	−1.3	11.9	−0.7	13.9	−1.5
70	Costa Rica	6.8	0.4	5.2	2.7	9.4	5.8
71	Mexico	8.5	2.7	5.8	0.3	8.5	−6.9
72	Mauritius	7.1	2.4	5.9	3.6	8.3	14.0
73	Poland	. .	2.8	. .	1.7	. .	1.6
74	Malaysia	8.5	2.2	6.0	0.9	10.4	0.0
75	Panama	7.4	*3.5*	4.6	*4.3*	5.9	*−3.2*
76	Brazil	6.7	2.9	8.9	2.5	11.3	0.0
77	*Angola*	. .	. .	. .	. .	. .	. .
78	*Lebanon*	. .	. .	. .	. .	. .	. .
79	*Nicaragua*	6.6	*16.0*	2.0	*−8.1*	. .	*4.0*
	Upper-middle-income	**8.0** w	. .	**7.1** w	**2.9** w	**8.7** w	**−0.5** w
80	South Africa	5.3	3.8	3.3	2.2	4.1	−5.8
81	Algeria	8.6	5.1	8.8	1.4	15.9	−0.8
82	Hungary	a	1.3	5.7	1.3	7.0	−1.0
83	Uruguay	3.2	1.1	2.4	−0.7	8.0	−9.2
84	Argentina	3.2	0.0	3.0	0.4	4.6	−7.7
85	Yugoslavia	3.6	0.7	7.9	0.1	6.5	−0.4
86	Gabon	10.7	3.3	. .	6.2	14.1	−4.9
87	Venezuela	. .	0.4	. .	0.3	. .	−4.7
88	Trinidad and Tobago	8.9	−3.1	6.3	−11.3	12.1	−19.1
89	Korea, Rep. of	7.7	5.3	7.8	7.5	15.9	10.5
90	Portugal	8.1	2.4	6.7	2.1	4.6	−1.3
91	Greece	6.6	2.6	4.9	3.2	5.3	−3.9
92	Oman	. .	a	. .	13.6	. .	18.4
93	Libya	19.7	. .	19.1	. .	7.3	. .
94	*Iran, Islamic Rep.*	14.6	. .	10.1	. .	11.5	. .
95	*Iraq*	. .	. .	. .	. .	. .	. .
96	*Romania*	. .	. .	. .	. .	. .	. .
	Low- and middle-income	**7.3** w	**4.0** w	**5.6** w	**3.5** w	**8.6** w	**2.7** w
	Sub-Saharan Africa	**8.2** w	**1.4** w	**3.5** w	**0.9** w	**9.1** w	**−7.3** w
	East Asia	**6.7** w	**7.1** w	**5.8** w	**6.6** w	**11.4** w	**9.7** w
	South Asia	**4.6** w	**8.9** w	**3.0** w	**5.6** w	**4.2** w	**4.2** w
	Europe, M.East, & N.Africa	**9.4** w	. .	. .	. .	**8.9** w	. .
	Latin America & Caribbean	**6.5** w	**2.0** w	**6.4** w	**1.2** w	**8.3** w	**−3.2** w
	Severely indebted	**6.7** w	**2.0** w	**6.3** w	**1.4** w	**8.4** w	**−3.1** w
	High-income economies	**2.7** w	**2.6** w	**3.9** w	**3.0** w	**3.4** w	**3.7** w
	OECD members	**2.7** w	**2.6** w	**3.8** w	**3.0** w	**3.3** w	**3.7** w
	†Other	. .	. .	. .	. .	**14.4** w	. .
97	†Saudi Arabia	a	. .	20.0	. .	27.5	. .
98	Spain	5.1	4.7	4.8	1.8	3.7	3.7
99	Ireland	6.1	0.1	4.3	−1.4	6.3	−3.3
100	†Israel	8.8	1.0	6.0	4.8	5.9	1.4
101	†Singapore	10.2	7.9	8.0	4.7	13.3	2.6
102	†Hong Kong	7.7	5.4	9.0	7.1	8.6	3.0
103	New Zealand	3.4	1.1	2.3	1.6	2.2	3.9
104	Australia	5.0	3.7	4.1	3.0	2.8	2.7
105	United Kingdom	2.3	1.1	2.2	3.8	0.6	6.4
106	Italy	3.4	3.0	4.1	2.5	3.4	1.5
107	†Kuwait	a	*3.9*	9.3	*0.8*	11.9	*−2.3*
108	Belgium	4.6	0.6	4.3	1.3	2.9	0.5
109	Netherlands	2.9	1.0	4.8	1.2	1.8	2.3
110	Austria	3.7	1.4	4.4	2.1	4.5	1.7
111	†United Arab Emirates	. .	. .	. .	. .	. .	. .
112	France	3.6	2.3	4.7	2.3	3.9	0.9
113	Canada	4.8	1.9	4.9	3.0	5.1	4.6
114	Denmark	4.8	1.3	2.3	2.2	1.2	4.5
115	Germany, Fed. Rep.	3.5	1.5	4.0	1.6	1.7	1.2
116	Finland	5.3	3.7	3.8	4.3	2.9	2.0
117	Sweden	4.0	1.6	2.5	1.8	0.9	2.2
118	United States	1.2	3.5	3.1	3.6	2.6	5.0
119	Norway	5.5	3.4	3.9	3.1	4.2	3.2
120	Japan	5.1	2.7	6.0	3.2	6.7	4.9
121	Switzerland	2.7	2.7	2.5	1.6	0.8	4.8
	Total reporting economies	**3.3** w	**2.9** w	**4.2** w	**3.1** w	**4.4** w	**3.4** w
	Oil exporters	**11.2** w	. .	**7.1** w	**2.1** w	**11.5** w	**−2.5** w
	Nonreporting nonmembers	. .	. .	. .	. .	. .	. .

Average annual growth rate (percent)

a. General government consumption figures are not available separately; they are included in private consumption, etc.

Table 9. Structure of demand

| | | \multicolumn{12}{c}{Distribution of gross domestic product (percent)} |
| | | General government consumption | | Private consumption, etc. | | Gross domestic investment | | Gross domestic savings | | Exports of goods and nonfactor services | | Resource balance | |
		1965	1988	1965	1988	1965	1988	1965	1988	1965	1988	1965	1988
	Low-income economies	**11 w**	**10 w**	**70 w**	**65 w**	**19 w**	**28 w**	**18 w**	**26 w**	**7 w**	**13 w**	**−1 w**	**−3 w**
	China and India	**12 w**	**9 w**	**68 w**	**61 w**	**21 w**	**32 w**	**20 w**	**30 w**	**4 w**	**11 w**	**0 w**	**−2 w**
	Other low-income	**9 w**	**12 w**	**78 w**	**74 w**	**14 w**	**18 w**	**12 w**	**14 w**	**17 w**	**19 w**	**−3 w**	**−4 w**
1	Mozambique	..	22	..	93	..	33	..	−15	..	15	..	−47
2	Ethiopia	11	24	77	72	13	16	12	4	12	11	−1	−11
3	Chad	20	22	74	89	12	12	6	−12	19	23	−6	−24
4	Tanzania	10	12	74	93	15	21	16	−5	26	16	1	−26
5	Bangladesh	9	9	83	88	11	12	8	3	10	8	−4	−9
6	Malawi	16	14	84	78	14	16	0	8	19	23	−14	−8
7	Somalia	8	10	84	86	11	34	8	3	17	8	−3	−30
8	Zaire	9	24	61	68	14	11	30	8	36	37	15	−2
9	Bhutan	..	..	..	..	..	..	..	..	..	..	..	..
10	Lao PDR	..	12	..	66	..	31	..	21	..	18	..	−9
11	Nepal	a	10	100	80	6	20	0	10	8	13	−6	−10
12	Madagascar	23	12	74	80	10	16	4	8	16	21	−6	−9
13	Burkina Faso	9	26	87	78	12	25	4	−4	9	15	−8	−29
14	Mali	*10*	10	*84*	93	*18*	15	*5*	−4	*12*	15	*−13*	−18
15	Burundi	7	17	89	78	6	18	4	5	10	12	−2	−13
16	Uganda	10	*8*	78	*87*	11	*13*	12	*5*	26	*11*	1	−8
17	Nigeria	5	12	83	73	14	13	12	15	13	25	−2	2
18	Zambia	15	17	45	69	25	11	40	14	49	28	15	3
19	Niger	6	11	90	85	8	10	3	4	9	17	−5	−6
20	Rwanda	14	12	81	82	10	16	5	6	12	8	−5	−10
21	China	14	7	61	56	24	38	25	37	4	14	1	−1
22	India	9	12	76	67	17	24	15	21	4	7	−2	−3
23	Pakistan	11	14	76	73	21	18	13	13	8	14	−8	−5
24	Kenya	15	19	70	59	14	26	15	22	31	19	1	−3
25	Togo	8	17	76	69	22	21	17	14	20	34	−6	−7
26	Central African Rep.	22	10	67	90	21	12	11	−1	27	17	−11	−12
27	Haiti	8	11	90	86	7	10	2	4	13	13	−5	−6
28	Benin	11	12	87	89	11	12	3	0	13	18	−8	−12
29	Ghana	14	9	77	84	18	12	8	6	17	19	−10	−6
30	Lesotho	18	28	109	145	11	47	−26	−73	16	23	−38	−120
31	Sri Lanka	13	10	74	78	12	23	13	13	38	26	1	−10
32	Guinea	..	10	..	71	..	22	..	19	..	26	..	−3
33	Yemen, PDR	..	..	..	..	..	..	..	..	..	..	..	..
34	Indonesia	5	9	87	65	8	22	8	25	5	25	0	4
35	Mauritania	19	14	54	76	14	18	27	10	42	51	13	−8
36	Sudan	12	9	79	85	10	10	9	7	15	4	−1	−3
37	*Afghanistan*	a	..	99	..	11	..	1	..	11	..	−10	..
38	*Myanmar*	..	..	..	..	..	..	..	..	..	..	..	..
39	*Kampuchea, Dem.*	16	..	71	..	13	..	12	..	12	..	−1	..
40	*Liberia*	12	..	61	..	17	..	27	..	50	..	10	..
41	*Sierra Leone*	8	6	83	77	12	*11*	8	*17*	30	*31*	−3	6
42	*Viet Nam*	..	..	..	..	..	..	..	..	..	..	..	..
	Middle-income economies	**11 w**	**15 w**	**67 w**	**59 w**	**21 w**	**25 w**	**21 w**	**27 w**	**17 w**	**27 w**	**0 w**	**3 w**
	Lower-middle-income	**10 w**	**12 w**	**71 w**	**64 w**	**19 w**	**23 w**	**18 w**	**24 w**	**14 w**	**21 w**	**−1 w**	**2 w**
43	Bolivia	9	20	74	73	22	11	17	6	21	16	−5	−4
44	Philippines	9	9	70	73	21	17	21	18	17	25	0	1
45	Yemen Arab Rep.	..	20	..	80	..	13	..	0	..	16	..	−13
46	Senegal	17	16	75	74	12	15	8	9	24	26	−4	−5
47	Zimbabwe	12	19	65	57	15	21	23	24	..	27	8	3
48	Egypt, Arab Rep.	19	14	67	78	18	20	14	8	18	22	−4	−12
49	Dominican Rep.	19	6	75	78	10	24	6	16	16	34	−4	−7
50	Côte d'Ivoire	11	19	61	59	22	14	29	22	37	33	7	8
51	Papua New Guinea	34	21	64	58	22	26	2	21	18	45	−20	−5
52	Morocco	12	15	76	62	10	24	12	23	18	25	1	0
53	Honduras	10	17	75	72	15	16	15	11	27	23	0	−5
54	Guatemala	7	8	82	84	13	14	10	8	17	16	−3	−6
55	Congo, People's Rep.	14	22	80	58	22	22	5	20	36	42	−17	−2
56	El Salvador	9	13	79	81	15	13	12	6	27	16	−2	−6
57	Thailand	10	11	72	63	20	28	19	26	16	34	−1	−2
58	Botswana	24	..	89	..	6	..	−13	..	32	..	−19	..
59	Cameroon	13	10	75	76	13	17	12	14	24	16	−1	−3
60	Jamaica	8	15	69	66	27	27	23	19	33	49	−4	−8
61	Ecuador	9	11	80	68	14	23	11	21	16	27	−3	−2
62	Colombia	8	11	75	67	16	21	17	22	11	16	1	2
63	Paraguay	7	6	79	72	15	24	14	23	15	26	−1	−2
64	Tunisia	15	16	71	65	28	19	14	19	19	43	−13	0
65	Turkey	12	9	74	65	15	24	13	26	6	24	−1	2
66	Peru	10	8	59	68	34	29	31	24	16	10	−3	−4
67	Jordan	..	27	..	76	..	26	..	−3	..	54	..	−29

Note: For data comparability and coverage, see the technical notes. Figures in italics are for years other than those specified.

194

		Distribution of gross domestic product (percent)											
		General government consumption		Private consumption, etc.		Gross domestic investment		Gross domestic savings		Exports of goods and nonfactor services		Resource balance	
		1965	1988	1965	1988	1965	1988	1965	1988	1965	1988	1965	1988
68	Chile	11	11	73	65	15	17	16	24	14	37	1	7
69	Syrian Arab Rep.	14	16	76	72	10	17	10	13	17	11	0	−4
70	Costa Rica	13	15	78	59	20	26	9	26	23	36	−10	0
71	Mexico	6	10	75	67	20	20	19	23	8	16	−2	2
72	Mauritius	13	11	74	64	17	25	13	25	36	72	−4	0
73	Poland	..	8	..	56	..	33	..	35	..	23	..	3
74	Malaysia	15	14	61	49	20	26	24	36	42	67	4	10
75	Panama	11	..	73	..	18	..	16	..	36	..	−2	..
76	Brazil	11	12	67	60	20	23	22	28	8	10	2	5
77	*Angola*	..	..	..	..	..	..	..	..	..	..	..	..
78	*Lebanon*	10	..	81	..	22	..	9	..	36	..	−13	..
79	*Nicaragua*	8	..	74	..	21	..	18	..	29	..	−3	..
	Upper-middle-income	12 *w*	..	62 *w*	..	24 *w*	..	25 *w*	..	20 *w*	..	1 *w*	..
80	South Africa	11	18	62	56	28	20	27	25	26	29	0	5
81	Algeria	15	16	66	53	22	31	19	31	22	16	−3	−1
82	Hungary	a	11	75	61	26	25	25	28	..	38	−1	3
83	Uruguay	15	13	68	73	11	10	18	14	19	22	7	4
84	Argentina	8	11	69	71	19	14	22	18	8	10	3	4
85	Yugoslavia	18	*14*	52	*47*	30	*39*	30	*40*	22	*24*	0	*1*
86	Gabon	11	22	52	45	31	27	37	33	43	44	6	6
87	Venezuela	10	10	56	66	25	30	34	25	26	22	9	−6
88	Trinidad and Tobago	12	22	67	57	26	18	21	21	65	39	−5	3
89	Korea, Rep. of	9	10	83	51	15	30	8	38	9	41	−7	9
90	Portugal	12	14	68	66	25	30	20	21	27	35	−5	−10
91	Greece	12	21	73	68	26	18	15	11	9	23	−11	−7
92	Oman	..	..	..	..	..	..	..	..	..	..	..	..
93	Libya	14	..	36	..	29	..	50	..	53	..	21	..
94	*Iran, Islamic Rep.*	13	..	63	..	17	..	24	..	20	..	6	..
95	*Iraq*	20	..	50	..	16	..	31	..	38	..	15	..
96	*Romania*	..	..	..	..	..	..	..	..	..	..	..	..
	Low- and middle-income	11 *w*	13 *w*	68 *w*	61 *w*	20 *w*	26 *w*	20 *w*	27 *w*	13 *w*	23 *w*	−1 *w*	2 *w*
	Sub-Saharan Africa	10 *w*	15 *w*	73 *w*	72 *w*	14 *w*	15 *w*	14 *w*	12 *w*	23 *w*	23 *w*	1 *w*	−4 *w*
	East Asia	13 *w*	10 *w*	64 *w*	56 *w*	22 *w*	31 *w*	23 *w*	34 *w*	8 *w*	30 *w*	0 *w*	3 *w*
	South Asia	8 *w*	12 *w*	77 *w*	70 *w*	17 *w*	22 *w*	14 *w*	18 *w*	6 *w*	8 *w*	−3 *w*	−4 *w*
	Europe, M.East, & N.Africa	13 *w*	..	65 *w*	..	22 *w*	..	20 *w*	..	19 *w*	..	−2 *w*	..
	Latin America & Caribbean	9 *w*	11 *w*	69 *w*	65 *w*	20 *w*	22 *w*	21 *w*	24 *w*	13 *w*	15 *w*	1 *w*	2 *w*
	Severely indebted	9 *w*	11 *w*	69 *w*	64 *w*	21 *w*	22 *w*	22 *w*	25 *w*	14 *w*	16 *w*	1 *w*	3 *w*
	High-income economies	17 *w*	17 *w*	63 *w*	61 *w*	20 *w*	22 *w*	21 *w*	22 *w*	12 *w*	21 *w*	1 *w*	0 *w*
	OECD members	17 *w*	17 *w*	63 *w*	61 *w*	20 *w*	22 *w*	20 *w*	22 *w*	12 *w*	20 *w*	1 *w*	0 *w*
	†Other	14 *w*	22 *w*	50 *w*	53 *w*	24 *w*	25 *w*	34 *w*	25 *w*	54 *w*	63 *w*	10 *w*	−2 *w*
97	†Saudi Arabia	18	33	34	47	14	27	48	20	60	38	34	−6
98	Spain	8	15	68	63	28	23	24	22	10	19	−3	−1
99	Ireland	15	16	68	55	26	18	17	27	35	64	−9	10
100	†Israel	20	31	65	59	29	17	15	10	19	32	−13	−6
101	†Singapore	10	11	80	48	22	37	10	41	123	..	−12	4
102	†Hong Kong	7	7	64	60	36	28	29	33	71	136	−7	5
103	New Zealand	13	15	62	60	26	22	26	26	22	28	−1	3
104	Australia	13	19	69	58	20	24	18	23	15	17	−2	−1
105	United Kingdom	16	19	63	64	21	21	20	17	18	23	−1	−4
106	Italy	14	15	63	62	23	23	24	23	13	18	1	0
107	†Kuwait	13	25	26	60	16	20	60	15	68	41	45	−5
108	Belgium	13	16	64	63	23	18	23	21	36	68	0	3
109	Netherlands	15	18	70	59	16	19	15	23	43	55	−1	4
110	Austria	13	17	57	56	30	27	30	27	25	37	−1	0
111	†United Arab Emirates	..	21	..	44	..	26	..	36	..	55	..	10
112	France	16	19	57	60	26	21	27	21	13	22	1	0
113	Canada	14	19	60	59	26	22	26	23	19	26	0	1
114	Denmark	16	25	72	54	13	18	12	21	29	32	−2	3
115	Germany, Fed. Rep.	15	19	67	55	18	21	18	26	19	33	0	6
116	Finland	14	19	58	54	30	27	29	27	20	25	−2	0
117	Sweden	18	26	72	53	11	19	10	21	22	32	−1	1
118	United States	19	20	63	67	17	15	18	13	6	11	1	−2
119	Norway	15	20	56	52	30	28	29	28	41	36	−1	0
120	Japan	8	9	64	57	27	31	28	33	11	13	1	3
121	Switzerland	11	12	60	58	30	31	30	31	29	36	−1	0
	Total reporting economies	15 *w*	16 *w*	64 *w*	61 *w*	20 *w*	22 *w*	20 *w*	23 *w*	12 *w*	21 *w*	0 *w*	1 *w*
	Oil exporters	11 *w*	16 *w*	66 *w*	59 *w*	20 *w*	25 *w*	24 *w*	24 *w*	23 *w*	25 *w*	5 *w*	0 *w*
	Nonreporting nonmembers	..	..	..	..	..	..	..	..	..	..	..	..

a. General government consumption figures are not available separately; they are included in private consumption, etc.

Table 10. Structure of consumption

Percentage share of total household consumption[a]

	Food		Clothing and footwear	Gross rents, fuel and power		Medical care	Education	Transport and communication		Other consumption	
	Total	Cereals and tubers		Total	Fuel and power			Total	Motor cars	Total	Other consumer durables
Low-income economies											
China and India											
Other low-income											
1 Mozambique	..	..	..	..	..	..	..	..	..	..	..
2 Ethiopia	50	24	6	14	7	3	2	8	1	17	2
3 Chad	..	..	..	..	..	..	..	..	..	..	..
4 Tanzania	64	32	10	8	3	3	3	2	0	10	3
5 Bangladesh	59	36	8	17	7	2	1	3	0	10	3
6 Malawi	55	28	5	12	2	3	4	7	2	15	3
7 Somalia	..	..	..	..	..	..	..	..	..	..	..
8 Zaire	55	15	10	11	3	3	1	6	0	14	3
9 Bhutan	..	..	..	..	..	..	..	..	..	..	..
10 Lao PDR	..	..	..	..	..	..	..	..	..	..	..
11 Nepal	57	38	12	14	6	3	1	1	0	13	2
12 Madagascar	59	26	6	12	6	2	4	4	1	14	1
13 Burkina Faso	..	..	..	..	..	..	..	..	..	..	..
14 Mali	57	22	6	8	6	2	4	10	1	13	1
15 Burundi	..	..	..	..	..	..	..	..	..	..	..
16 Uganda	..	..	..	..	..	..	..	..	..	..	..
17 Nigeria	52	18	7	10	2	3	4	4	1	20	6
18 Zambia	37	8	10	11	5	7	13	5	1	16	1
19 Niger	..	..	..	..	..	..	..	..	..	..	..
20 Rwanda	30	11	11	16	6	3	4	9	..	28	9
21 China	61[b]	..	13	8	3	1	1	1	..	15	..
22 India	52	18	11	10	3	3	4	7	0	13	3
23 Pakistan	54	17	9	15	6	3	3	1	0	15	5
24 Kenya	39	16	7	12	2	3	9	8	1	22	6
25 Togo	..	..	..	..	..	..	..	..	..	..	..
26 Central African Rep.	..	..	..	..	..	..	..	..	..	..	..
27 Haiti	..	..	..	..	..	..	..	..	..	..	..
28 Benin	37	12	14	12	2	5	4	14	2	15	5
29 Ghana	50	..	13	11	..	3	5[c]	3	..	15	..
30 Lesotho	..	..	..	..	..	..	..	..	..	..	..
31 Sri Lanka	43	18	7	6	3	2	3	15	1	25	5
32 Guinea	..	..	..	..	..	..	..	..	..	..	..
33 Yemen, PDR	..	..	..	..	..	..	..	..	..	..	..
34 Indonesia	48	21	7	13	7	2	4	4	0	22	5
35 Mauritania	..	..	..	..	..	..	..	..	..	..	..
36 Sudan	60	..	5	15	4	5	3	2	..	11	..
37 *Afghanistan*	..	..	..	..	..	..	..	..	..	..	..
38 *Myanmar*	..	..	..	..	..	..	..	..	..	..	..
39 *Kampuchea, Dem.*	..	..	..	..	..	..	..	..	..	..	..
40 *Liberia*	..	..	..	..	..	..	..	..	..	..	..
41 *Sierra Leone*	56	22	4	15	6	2	3	12	..	9	1
42 *Viet Nam*	..	..	..	..	..	..	..	..	..	..	..
Middle-income economies											
Lower-middle-income											
43 Bolivia	33	..	9	12	1	5	7	12	..	22	..
44 Philippines	51	20	4	19	5	2	4	4	2	16	2
45 Yemen Arab Rep.	..	..	..	..	..	..	..	..	..	..	..
46 Senegal	50	15	11	12	4	2	5	6	0	14	2
47 Zimbabwe	40	9	11	13	5	4	7	6	1	20	3
48 Egypt, Arab Rep.	50	10	11	9	3	3	6	4	1	18	3
49 Dominican Rep.	46	13	3	15	5	8	3	4	0	21	8
50 Côte d'Ivoire	40	14	10	5	1	9	4	10	..	23	3
51 Papua New Guinea	..	..	..	..	..	..	..	..	..	..	..
52 Morocco	40	12	11	9	2	4	6	8	1	22	5
53 Honduras	39	..	9	21	..	8	5[c]	3	..	15	..
54 Guatemala	36	10	10	14	5	13	4	3	0	20	5
55 Congo, People's Rep.	42	19	6	11	4	3	1	17	1	20	4
56 El Salvador	33	12	9	7	2	8	5	10	1	28	7
57 Thailand	30	7	16	7	3	5	5	13	0	24	5
58 Botswana	35	13	8	15	5	4	9	8	2	22	7
59 Cameroon	24	8	7	17	3	11	9	12	1	21	3
60 Jamaica	39	..	4	15	7	3[d]	..	17	..	22	..
61 Ecuador	30	..	10	7[e]	1[e]	5	6[c]	12[f]	..	30	..
62 Colombia	29	..	6	12	2	7	6	13	..	27	..
63 Paraguay	30	6	12	21	4	2	3	10	1	22	3
64 Tunisia	37	7	10	13	4	6	9	7	1	18	5
65 Turkey	40	8	15	13	7	4	1	5	..	22	..
66 Peru	35	8	7	15	3	4	6	10	0	24	7
67 Jordan	35	..	5	6	..	5	8	6	..	35	..

Note: For data comparability and coverage, see the technical notes. Figures in italics are for years other than those specified.

		Percentage share of total household consumption[a]										
		Food		Clothing and footwear	Gross rents, fuel and power		Medical care	Education	Transport and communication		Other consumption	
		Total	Cereals and tubers		Total	Fuel and power			Total	Motor cars	Total	Other consumer durables
68	Chile	29	7	8	13	2	5	6	11	0	29	5
69	Syrian Arab Rep.	..	..	..	..	..	..	..	..	..	..	..
70	Costa Rica	33	8	8	9	1	7	8	8	0	28	9
71	Mexico	35[b]	..	10	8	..	5	5	12	..	25	..
72	Mauritius	24	7	5	19	3	5	7	11	1	29	4
73	Poland	29	..	9	7	2	6	7	8	2	34	9
74	Malaysia	30	..	5	9	..	5	8	16	..	27	..
75	Panama	38	7	3	11	3	8	9	7	0	24	6
76	Brazil	35	9	10	11	2	6	5	8	1	27	8
77	Angola	..	..	..	..	..	..	..	..	..	..	..
78	Lebanon	..	..	..	..	..	..	..	..	..	..	..
79	Nicaragua	..	..	..	..	..	..	..	..	..	..	..
	Upper-middle-income											
80	South Africa	26	..	7	12	..	4[d]	..	17	..	34	..
81	Algeria	..	..	..	..	..	..	..	..	..	..	..
82	Hungary	25	..	9	10	5	5	7	9	2	35	8
83	Uruguay	31	7	7	12	2	6	4	13	0	27	5
84	Argentina	35	4	6	9	2	4	6	13	0	26	6
85	Yugoslavia	27	..	10	9	4	6	5	11	2	32	9
86	Gabon	..	..	..	..	..	..	..	..	..	..	..
87	Venezuela	38	..	4	8	..	8	7[c]	10	..	25	..
88	Trinidad and Tobago	..	..	..	..	..	..	..	..	..	..	..
89	Korea, Rep. of	35	14	6	11	5	5	9	9	..	25	5
90	Portugal	34	..	10	8	3	6	5	13	3	24	7
91	Greece	30	..	8	12	3	6	5	13	2	26	5
92	Oman	..	..	..	..	..	..	..	..	..	..	..
93	Libya	..	..	..	..	..	..	..	..	..	..	..
94	Iran, Islamic Rep.	37	10	9	23	2	6	5	6	1	14	5
95	Iraq	..	..	..	..	..	..	..	..	..	..	..
96	Romania	..	..	..	..	..	..	..	..	..	..	..

Low- and middle-income
  Sub-Saharan Africa
  East Asia
  South Asia
  Europe, M.East, & N.Africa
  Latin America & Caribbean

Severely indebted

High-income economies
  OECD members
  †Other

97	†Saudi Arabia	..	..	..	..	..	..	..	..	..	..	..
98	Spain	24	3	7	16	3	7	5	13	3	28	6
99	Ireland	22	4	5	11	5	10	7	11	3	33	5
100	† Israel	22	..	4	20	2	10	14	10	..	20	..
101	† Singapore	19	..	8	11	..	7	12	13	..	30	..
102	† Hong Kong	12	1	9	15	2	6	5	9	1	44	15
103	New Zealand	12	2	6	14	2	9	6	19	6	34	9
104	Australia	13	2	5	21	2	10	8	13	4	31	7
105	United Kingdom	12	2	6	17	4	8	6	14	4	36	7
106	Italy	19	2	8	14	4	10	7	11	3	31	7
107	† Kuwait	..	..	..	..	..	..	..	..	..	..	..
108	Belgium	15	2	6	17	7	10	9	11	3	31	7
109	Netherlands	13	2	6	18	6	11	8	10	3	33	8
110	Austria	16	2	9	17	5	10	8	15	3	26	7
111	† United Arab Emirates	..	..	..	..	..	..	..	..	..	..	..
112	France	16	2	6	17	5	13	7	13	3	29	7
113	Canada	11	2	6	21	4	5	12	14	5	32	8
114	Denmark	13	2	5	19	5	8	9	13	5	33	7
115	Germany, Fed. Rep.	12	2	7	18	5	13	6	13	4	31	9
116	Finland	16	3	4	15	4	9	8	14	4	34	6
117	Sweden	13	2	5	19	4	11	8	11	2	32	7
118	United States	13	2	6	18	4	14	8	14	5	27	7
119	Norway	15	2	6	14	5	10	8	14	6	32	7
120	Japan	16	4	6	17	3	10	8	9	1	34	6
121	Switzerland	17	..	4	17	6	15	..	9	..	38	..

Total reporting economies
  Oil exporters

Nonreporting nonmembers

a. Data refer to either 1980 or 1985. b. Includes beverages and tobacco. c. Refers to government expenditure. d. Excludes government expenditure. e. Excludes fuel. f. Includes fuel.

Table 11. Central government expenditure

	Percentage of total expenditure												Total expenditure as a percentage of GNP		Overall surplus/deficit as a percentage of GNP	
	Defense		Education		Health		Housing, amenities; social security and welfare[a]		Economic services		Other[a]					
	1972	1988	1972	1988	1972	1988	1972	1988	1972	1988	1972	1988	1972	1988	1972	1988
Low-income economies	..	..	..	..	..	..	..	..	..	..	..	..	..	..	..	..
China and India	..	..	..	..	..	..	..	..	..	..	..	..	..	..	..	..
Other low-income	..	10.6 w	20.5 w	9.0 w	5.5 w	2.8 w	..	6.2 w	..	..	..	51.1 w	15.6 w	24.1 w	..	−3.0 w
1 Mozambique	..	..	..	..	..	..	..	..	..	..	..	..	..	..	..	..
2 Ethiopia	14.3	..	14.4	10.6	5.7	3.6	4.4	9.3	22.9	30.1	52.6	46.5	13.7	35.2	−1.4	−6.8
3 Chad	24.6	..	14.8	..	4.4	..	1.7	..	21.8	..	32.7	..	14.9	..	−2.7	..
4 Tanzania	11.9	..	17.3	..	7.2	..	2.1	..	39.0	..	22.6	..	19.7	..	−5.0	..
5 Bangladesh[b]	5.1	..	14.8	..	5.0	..	9.8	..	39.3	..	25.9	..	9.4	..	−1.9	..
6 Malawi[b]	3.1	5.6	15.8	10.0	5.5	5.9	5.8	2.0	33.1	27.0	36.7	49.4	22.1	32.0	−6.2	−8.6
7 Somalia[b]	23.3	..	5.5	..	7.2	..	1.9	..	21.6	..	40.5	..	13.5	..	0.6	..
8 Zaire	11.1	..	15.2	..	2.3	..	2.0	..	13.3	..	56.1	..	19.8	..	−3.8	..
9 Bhutan	..	..	..	..	..	..	..	..	..	..	..	..	..	..	..	..
10 Lao PDR	..	..	..	..	..	..	..	..	..	..	..	..	..	..	..	..
11 Nepal	7.2	5.6	7.2	10.9	4.7	4.3	0.7	3.3	57.2	51.2	23.0	24.7	8.5	19.7	−1.2	−6.2
12 Madagascar	3.6	..	9.1	..	4.2	..	9.9	..	40.5	..	32.7	..	20.8	..	−2.5	..
13 Burkina Faso	11.5	17.9	20.6	14.0	8.2	5.2	6.6	..	15.5	7.0	37.6	55.9	11.1	16.8	0.3	0.4
14 Mali	..	8.4	..	9.8	..	2.6	..	3.3	..	18.4	..	57.5	..	28.2	..	−5.5
15 Burundi	10.3	..	23.4	..	6.0	..	2.7	..	33.9	..	23.8	..	19.9	..	0.0	..
16 Uganda	23.1	26.3	15.3	15.0	5.3	2.4	7.3	2.9	12.4	14.8	36.6	38.6	21.8	10.3	−8.1	−3.0
17 Nigeria[b]	40.2	2.8	4.5	2.8	3.6	0.8	0.8	1.5	19.6	35.9	31.4	56.2	8.3	27.8	..	−10.3
18 Zambia[b]	0.0	0.0	19.0	8.3	7.4	4.7	1.3	2.3	26.7	21.0	45.7	63.7	34.0	26.0	−13.8	−9.8
19 Niger	..	..	..	..	..	..	..	..	..	..	..	..	..	..	..	..
20 Rwanda	25.6	..	22.2	..	5.7	..	2.6	..	22.0	..	21.9	..	12.5	..	−2.7	..
21 China	..	..	..	..	..	..	..	..	..	..	..	..	..	..	..	..
22 India	26.2	19.3	2.3	2.9	1.5	1.8	3.2	5.4	19.9	21.7	46.9	49.0	10.5	17.8	−3.2	−7.9
23 Pakistan	39.9	29.5	1.2	2.6	1.1	0.9	3.2	8.7	21.4	34.5	33.2	23.8	16.9	21.7	−6.9	−7.0
24 Kenya[b]	6.0	9.2	21.9	21.5	7.9	6.1	3.9	3.5	30.1	19.8	30.2	39.9	21.0	28.6	−3.9	−6.6
25 Togo	..	11.1	..	19.9	..	5.2	..	8.5	..	31.2	..	24.1	..	32.5	..	−2.6
26 Central African Rep.	..	..	..	..	..	..	..	..	..	..	..	..	..	25.7	..	..
27 Haiti	..	..	..	..	..	..	..	..	..	..	..	..	14.5	..	..	..
28 Benin	..	..	..	..	..	..	..	..	..	..	..	..	..	..	..	..
29 Ghana[b]	7.9	3.2	20.1	25.7	6.3	9.0	4.1	11.9	15.1	19.2	46.6	31.1	19.5	14.0	−5.8	0.4
30 Lesotho	0.0	..	22.4	..	7.4	..	6.0	..	21.6	..	42.7	..	14.5	..	3.5	..
31 Sri Lanka	3.1	9.6	13.0	7.8	6.4	5.4	19.5	11.7	20.2	29.2	37.7	36.3	25.4	31.4	−5.3	−12.8
32 Guinea	..	..	..	..	..	..	..	..	..	..	..	..	..	..	..	..
33 Yemen, PDR	..	..	..	..	..	..	..	..	..	..	..	..	..	..	..	..
34 Indonesia	18.6	8.3	7.4	10.0	1.4	1.8	0.9	1.7	30.5	..	41.3	78.2	15.1	22.7	−2.5	−3.3
35 Mauritania	..	..	..	..	..	..	..	..	..	..	..	..	..	..	..	..
36 Sudan[b]	24.1	..	9.3	..	5.4	..	1.4	..	15.8	..	44.1	..	19.2	..	−0.8	..
37 Afghanistan	..	..	..	..	..	..	..	..	..	..	..	..	..	..	..	..
38 Myanmar	31.6	12.9	15.0	13.4	6.1	4.9	7.5	13.2	20.1	38.6	19.7	16.9	..	..	..	..
39 Kampuchea, Dem.	..	..	..	..	..	..	..	..	..	..	..	..	..	..	..	..
40 Liberia	5.3	..	15.2	..	9.8	..	3.5	..	25.8	..	40.5	..	16.7	27.1	1.1	..
41 Sierra Leone[b]	3.6	..	15.5	..	5.3	..	2.7	..	24.6	..	48.3	..	23.9	..	−4.4	..
42 Viet Nam	..	..	..	..	..	..	..	..	..	..	..	..	..	..	..	..
Middle-income economies	12.2 w	12.9 w	12.6 w	..	6.1 w	..	16.7 w	16.6 w	25.7 w	..	26.7 w	..	18.5 w	19.9 w	−2.8 w	−3.9 w
Lower-middle-income	11.3 w	12.9 w	17.5 w	13.3 w	5.7 w	4.0 w	16.2 w	10.6 w	23.1 w	16.1 w	26.2 w	43.1 w	14.9 w	15.4 w	−3.4 w	−3.7 w
43 Bolivia	18.8	14.5	31.3	18.4	6.3	1.9	0.0	25.6	12.5	17.1	31.3	22.5	9.6	15.8	−1.8	−0.1
44 Philippines[b]	10.9	11.6	16.3	15.7	3.2	4.6	4.3	2.2	17.6	31.9	47.7	34.1	13.4	15.6	−2.0	−2.8
45 Yemen Arab Rep.	33.8	31.2	4.0	17.6	2.9	3.6	0.0	0.0	0.9	6.3	58.4	41.3	13.4	31.8	−2.2	−13.1
46 Senegal	..	..	..	..	..	..	..	..	..	..	..	..	18.8	..	−2.8	..
47 Zimbabwe	..	16.3	..	22.0	..	7.5	..	3.8	..	23.1	..	27.3	..	38.7	..	−9.1
48 Egypt, Arab Rep.	..	..	..	..	..	..	..	..	..	..	..	..	..	..	..	..
49 Dominican Rep.	8.5	..	14.2	..	11.7	..	11.8	..	35.4	..	18.3	..	17.7	..	−0.2	..
50 Côte d'Ivoire	..	..	..	..	..	..	..	..	..	..	..	..	..	..	..	..
51 Papua New Guinea[b]	..	4.5	..	15.9	..	9.6	..	1.7	..	21.2	..	47.1	..	31.7	..	−1.9
52 Morocco	12.3	15.1	19.2	17.0	4.8	3.0	8.4	7.3	25.6	21.4	29.7	36.0	22.8	29.2	−3.9	−4.6
53 Honduras	12.4	..	22.3	..	10.2	..	8.7	..	28.3	..	18.1	..	16.1	..	−2.9	..
54 Guatemala	..	..	..	..	..	..	..	..	..	..	..	..	9.9	12.1	−2.2	−1.1
55 Congo, People's Rep.	..	..	..	..	..	..	..	..	..	..	..	..	..	..	..	..
56 El Salvador[b]	6.6	25.7	21.4	17.1	10.9	7.1	7.6	4.4	14.4	17.6	39.0	28.1	12.8	11.3	−1.0	−0.3
57 Thailand	20.2	18.7	19.9	19.3	3.7	6.2	7.0	5.4	25.6	19.5	23.5	30.9	16.7	16.4	−4.2	1.0
58 Botswana[b]	0.0	12.1	10.0	18.1	6.0	7.4	21.7	11.0	28.0	21.2	34.5	30.2	33.7	50.9	−23.8	21.9
59 Cameroon	..	..	..	..	..	..	..	..	..	..	..	..	..	..	..	..
60 Jamaica	..	..	..	..	..	..	..	..	..	..	..	..	..	..	..	..
61 Ecuador[b]	15.7	..	27.5	..	4.5	..	0.8	..	28.9	..	22.6	..	13.4	17.1	0.2	−2.4
62 Colombia	..	..	..	..	..	..	..	..	..	..	..	..	13.1	14.7	−2.5	−0.7
63 Paraguay	13.8	..	12.1	..	3.5	..	18.3	..	19.6	..	32.7	..	13.1	..	−1.7	..
64 Tunisia	4.9	5.7	30.5	14.6	7.4	5.9	8.8	22.0	23.3	24.4	25.1	27.3	23.1	37.1	−0.9	−4.8
65 Turkey	15.5	10.4	18.1	12.7	3.2	2.4	3.1	3.1	42.0	22.1	18.1	49.3	22.7	22.0	−2.2	−4.0
66 Peru[b]	14.5	20.0	23.6	15.3	5.5	5.8	1.8	..	30.9	18.9	23.6	40.1	16.1	14.6	−0.9	−5.7
67 Jordan	33.5	26.5	9.4	13.0	3.8	5.4	10.5	9.5	26.6	15.7	16.2	30.0	52.3	49.9	−7.6	−15.7

Note: For data comparability and coverage, see the technical notes. Figures in italics are for years other than those specified.

Percentage of total expenditure

	Defense		Education		Health		Housing, amenities; social security and welfare[a]		Economic services		Other[a]		Total expenditure as a percentage of GNP		Overall surplus/deficit as a percentage of GNP	
	1972	1988	1972	1988	1972	1988	1972	1988	1972	1988	1972	1988	1972	1988	1972	1988
68 Chile	6.1	10.4	14.3	12.0	8.2	6.3	39.8	39.2	15.3	11.2	16.3	20.9	43.2	33.4	−13.0	−0.2
69 Syrian Arab Rep.	37.2	40.4	11.3	10.4	1.4	1.5	3.6	4.5	39.9	25.0	6.7	18.2	28.8	28.3	−3.5	−2.7
70 Costa Rica	2.8	2.2	28.3	16.2	3.8	19.3	26.7	26.7	21.8	12.3	16.7	23.3	18.9	28.0	−4.5	−4.7
71 Mexico	4.5	1.4	16.4	7.4	4.5	1.1	25.4	9.3	35.8	11.4	13.4	69.3	11.4	27.9	−2.9	−10.0
72 Mauritius	0.8	0.8	13.5	12.7	10.3	7.6	18.0	16.6	13.9	23.8	43.4	38.6	16.3	24.8	−1.2	0.3
73 Poland	..	..	..	..	..	..	..	..	..	..	..	..	..	40.4	..	−2.4
74 Malaysia	18.5	..	23.4	..	6.8	..	4.4	..	14.2	..	32.7	..	26.5	31.3	−9.4	−8.0
75 Panama	0.0	5.9	20.7	15.6	15.1	16.7	10.8	16.0	24.2	6.1	29.1	39.7	27.6	34.4	−6.5	−4.4
76 Brazil	8.3	4.0	8.3	4.8	6.7	9.5	35.0	24.2	23.3	12.1	18.3	45.4	17.4	25.1	−0.3	−12.2
77 Angola	..	..	..	..	..	..	..	..	..	..	..	..	..	..	..	..
78 Lebanon	..	..	..	..	..	..	..	..	..	..	..	..	..	..	..	..
79 Nicaragua	12.3	..	16.6	..	4.0	..	16.4	..	27.2	..	23.4	..	15.5	58.0	−3.9	−16.3
Upper-middle-income	13.6 w	..	7.5 w	..	..	..	17.1 w	..	..	..	..	..	24.3 w	..	−1.9 w	..
80 South Africa	..	..	..	..	..	..	..	..	..	..	..	..	21.8	33.1	−4.2	−5.7
81 Algeria	..	..	..	..	..	..	..	..	..	..	..	..	..	..	..	..
82 Hungary	..	4.8	..	2.1	..	1.7	..	28.7	..	34.8	..	27.8	..	58.3	..	−0.2
83 Uruguay	5.6	10.2	9.5	7.1	1.6	4.8	52.3	49.5	9.8	8.3	21.2	20.1	25.0	23.7	−2.5	−0.7
84 Argentina	10.0	6.9	20.0	6.9	..	2.1	20.0	32.0	30.0	17.7	20.0	34.4	19.6	21.6	−4.9	−4.1
85 Yugoslavia	20.5	55.1	0.0	0.0	24.8	0.0	35.6	11.2	12.0	16.3	7.0	17.3	21.1	7.5	−0.4	0.0
86 Gabon[b]	..	..	..	..	..	..	..	..	..	..	..	..	40.1	..	−12.9	..
87 Venezuela	10.3	5.8	18.6	19.6	11.7	10.0	9.2	11.7	25.4	17.3	24.8	35.6	18.1	21.8	−0.2	−2.1
88 Trinidad and Tobago	..	..	..	..	..	..	..	..	..	..	..	..	..	..	..	..
89 Korea, Rep. of	25.8	27.1	15.8	19.0	1.2	2.2	5.9	8.5	25.6	17.1	25.7	26.0	18.0	15.7	−3.9	1.6
90 Portugal	..	5.4	..	9.5	..	7.8	..	25.7	..	9.4	..	42.3	27.5	45.3	..	−11.0
91 Greece	14.9	..	9.1	..	7.4	..	30.6	..	26.4	..	11.7	..	..	..	−1.7	..
92 Oman	39.3	38.2	3.7	10.7	5.9	4.8	3.0	8.3	24.4	12.9	23.6	25.1	62.1	49.3	−15.3	−12.6
93 Libya	..	..	..	..	..	..	..	..	..	..	..	..	..	..	..	..
94 Iran, Islamic Rep.	24.1	14.2	10.4	19.6	3.6	6.0	6.1	17.4	30.6	15.7	25.2	27.1	30.8	..	−4.6	..
95 Iraq	..	..	..	..	..	..	..	..	..	..	..	..	..	..	..	..
96 Romania	5.4	..	2.9	..	0.5	..	16.2	..	61.8	..	13.1	..	..	..	..	..
Low- and middle-income	14.1 w	13.6 w	12.9 w	..	5.7 w	..	14.4 w	..	..	..	..	39.7 w	15.9 w	20.9 w	..	−4.7 w
Sub-Saharan Africa	..	..	..	..	..	..	..	..	..	..	..	..	..	..	..	..
East Asia	..	..	..	..	..	..	..	..	..	..	..	..	..	..	..	..
South Asia	..	20.3 w	..	3.7 w	..	2.1 w	..	7.2 w	..	24.3 w	..	42.4 w	..	18.8 w	..	−8.0 w
Europe, M.East, & N.Africa	..	..	..	..	..	..	..	..	..	..	..	..	..	..	−4.2 w	..
Latin America & Caribbean	6.7 w	5.8 w	15.4 w	11.0 w	6.5 w	..	20.3 w	16.6 w	17.0 w	13.5 w	34.1 w	53.1 w	11.9 w	13.0 w	−1.9 w	−3.2 w
Severely indebted	7.3 w	6.4 w	15.6 w	10.8 w	5.9 w	4.4 w	18.9 w	17.2 w	16.9 w	19.2 w	35.4 w	42.0 w	12.2 w	14.4 w	−2.2 w	−3.8 w
High-income economies	21.8 w	13.4 w	..	4.8 w	11.1 w	12.4 w	41.9 w	36.5 w	13.0 w	9.0 w	12.2 w	23.9 w	22.7 w	28.9 w	−1.9 w	−3.3 w
OECD members	21.7 w	13.3 w	..	4.7 w	11.2 w	12.6 w	42.3 w	36.9 w	13.0 w	8.9 w	11.8 w	23.6 w	22.3 w	28.6 w	−1.8 w	−3.4 w
†Other	..	..	..	..	..	..	..	..	..	..	..	..	..	..	..	..
97 †Saudi Arabia	..	..	..	..	..	..	..	..	..	..	..	..	..	..	..	..
98 Spain	6.5	..	8.3	..	0.9	..	49.8	..	17.5	..	17.0	..	19.6	34.1	−0.5	−4.5
99 Ireland	..	2.8	..	11.8	..	12.4	..	30.3	..	15.4	..	27.3	32.7	58.1	−5.5	−10.7
100 †Israel	42.9	27.2	7.1	9.6	3.6	3.7	7.1	21.2	7.1	11.7	32.2	26.6	43.9	50.6	−15.7	−9.9
101 †Singapore	35.3	14.6	15.7	14.4	7.8	3.6	3.9	11.0	9.9	15.6	27.3	40.8	16.7	35.0	1.3	−2.7
102 †Hong Kong	..	..	..	..	..	..	..	..	..	..	..	..	..	..	..	..
103 New Zealand[b]	5.8	4.7	16.9	11.1	14.8	12.4	25.6	29.7	16.5	9.2	20.4	32.9	31.1	49.1	−4.2	0.7
104 Australia	14.2	9.2	4.2	7.0	7.0	9.6	20.3	28.6	14.4	7.0	39.9	38.6	20.2	28.7	0.3	−1.3
105 United Kingdom	16.7	12.6	2.6	2.2	12.2	13.6	26.5	30.9	11.1	6.9	30.8	33.8	31.8	37.6	−2.7	−0.8
106 Italy	6.3	3.3	16.1	7.6	13.5	10.4	44.8	35.4	18.4	10.5	0.9	32.7	29.5	51.3	−8.7	−14.2
107 †Kuwait	8.4	13.9	15.0	14.2	5.5	7.7	14.2	20.1	16.6	18.1	40.1	26.1	34.4	35.7	17.4	23.5
108 Belgium	6.7	4.9	15.5	12.2	1.5	1.8	41.0	43.3	18.9	9.1	16.4	28.7	39.3	52.4	−4.3	−8.3
109 Netherlands	6.8	5.1	15.2	11.9	12.1	10.9	38.1	39.6	9.1	9.4	18.7	23.2	41.0	55.7	0.0	−4.3
110 Austria	3.3	2.6	10.2	9.3	10.1	12.8	53.8	47.5	11.2	11.3	11.4	16.4	29.6	40.1	−0.2	−5.1
111 †United Arab Emirates[b]	24.4	..	16.5	..	4.3	..	6.1	..	18.3	..	30.5	..	4.0	..	0.3	..
112 France	..	..	..	..	..	..	..	..	..	..	..	..	32.3	43.1	0.7	−2.3
113 Canada	7.6	7.7	3.5	3.1	7.6	5.9	35.3	37.3	19.5	11.7	26.5	34.3	20.1	23.4	−1.3	−3.0
114 Denmark	7.3	5.1	16.0	9.0	10.0	1.3	41.6	41.1	11.3	7.2	13.7	36.2	32.6	41.2	2.7	4.7
115 Germany, Fed. Rep.	12.4	8.9	1.5	0.6	17.5	18.2	46.9	49.4	11.3	7.1	10.4	15.8	24.2	29.9	0.7	−1.5
116 Finland	6.1	5.3	15.3	13.9	10.6	10.6	28.4	36.1	27.9	20.1	11.6	14.1	24.3	30.2	1.2	0.3
117 Sweden	12.5	6.8	14.8	9.2	3.6	1.1	44.3	54.2	10.6	8.0	14.3	20.7	27.9	40.8	−1.2	2.2
118 United States	32.2	24.8	3.2	1.7	8.6	12.5	35.3	31.5	10.6	6.5	10.1	23.0	19.1	22.9	−1.5	−3.2
119 Norway	9.7	8.3	9.9	8.2	12.3	10.7	39.9	36.1	20.2	19.5	8.0	17.2	35.0	41.5	−1.5	0.2
120 Japan[b]	..	..	..	..	..	..	..	..	..	..	..	..	12.7	17.0	−1.9	−3.5
121 Switzerland	15.1	..	4.2	..	10.0	..	39.5	..	18.4	..	12.8	..	13.3	..	0.9	..
Total reporting economies	20.8 w	13.3 w	..	5.4 w	10.4 w	..	38.3 w	33.7 w	14.4 w	10.1 w	16.1 w	26.1 w	21.9 w	28.2 w	−2.1 w	−3.6 w
Oil exporters	15.0 w	..	14.5 w	..	..	..	..	..	31.2 w	..	24.0 w	..	22.0 w	..	0.2 w	−4.5 w
Nonreporting nonmembers	..	..	..	..	..	..	..	..	..	..	..	..	..	..	..	..

a. See the technical notes.   b. Refers to budgetary data.

Table 12. Central government current revenue

	Percentage of total current revenue													Total current revenue as a percentage of GNP	
	Tax revenue														
	Taxes on income, profit, and capital gain		Social security contributions		Domestic taxes on goods and services		Taxes on international trade and transactions		Other taxes[a]		Nontax revenue				
	1972	1988	1972	1988	1972	1988	1972	1988	1972	1988	1972	1988		1972	1988
Low-income economies	..	..	..	..	..	..	..	..	..	..	..	..		..	..
China and India	..	..	..	..	..	..	..	..	..	..	..	..		..	..
Other low-income	..	28.0 w	..	..	..	27.4 w	..	19.3 w	..	..	..	21.2 w		..	19.5 w
1 Mozambique	..	..	..	..	..	..	..	..	..	..	..	..		..	..
2 Ethiopia	23.0	30.4	0.0	0.0	29.8	22.4	30.4	19.1	5.6	2.2	11.1	25.9		10.5	25.5
3 Chad	16.7	..	0.0	..	12.3	..	45.2	..	20.5	..	5.3	..		10.8	..
4 Tanzania	29.9	25.8	0.0	0.0	29.1	57.4	21.7	8.6	0.5	3.1	18.8	5.1		15.8	15.2
5 Bangladesh[b]	3.7	11.7	0.0	0.0	22.4	33.2	18.0	31.5	3.8	7.1	52.2	16.5		8.6	8.6
6 Malawi[b]	31.4	33.7	0.0	..	24.2	33.0	20.0	16.0	0.5	0.4	23.8	16.8		16.0	20.6
7 Somalia[b]	10.7	..	0.0	..	24.7	..	45.3	..	5.2	..	14.0	..		13.7	..
8 Zaire	22.2	26.8	2.2	0.7	12.7	14.6	57.9	42.5	1.4	2.3	3.7	13.8		14.3	15.3
9 Bhutan	..	..	..	..	..	..	..	..	..	..	..	..		..	..
10 Lao PDR	..	..	..	..	..	..	..	..	..	..	..	..		..	..
11 Nepal	4.1	8.4	0.0	0.0	26.5	36.1	36.7	31.1	19.0	5.4	13.7	19.1		5.2	10.3
12 Madagascar	13.1	..	7.2	..	29.9	..	33.6	..	5.5	..	10.8	..		18.3	..
13 Burkina Faso	16.8	16.2	0.0	7.4	18.0	23.3	51.8	22.6	3.2	9.8	10.2	20.7		11.4	17.7
14 Mali	..	8.1	..	4.5	..	21.7	..	27.5	..	29.2	..	9.1		..	16.0
15 Burundi	18.1	..	1.2	..	18.3	..	40.3	..	15.6	..	6.5	..		11.5	..
16 Uganda	22.1	6.0	0.0	0.0	32.8	24.3	36.3	69.6	0.3	0.0	8.5	0.0		13.7	8.2
17 Nigeria[b]	43.0	39.9	0.0	0.0	26.3	5.1	17.5	6.6	0.2	−14.5	13.0	62.9		9.4	18.5
18 Zambia[b]	49.7	37.9	0.0	0.0	20.2	40.3	14.3	17.3	0.1	0.5	15.6	4.0		23.2	15.8
19 Niger	..	..	..	..	..	..	..	..	..	..	..	..		..	..
20 Rwanda	17.9	..	4.4	..	14.1	..	41.7	..	13.8	..	8.1	..		9.8	..
21 China	..	..	..	..	..	..	..	..	..	..	..	..		..	..
22 India	21.3	14.5	0.0	0.0	44.5	35.3	20.1	30.3	0.9	0.3	13.2	19.5		10.2	14.0
23 Pakistan	13.6	11.9	0.0	0.0	35.9	33.0	34.2	31.0	0.5	0.3	15.8	23.8		12.5	16.5
24 Kenya[b]	35.6	28.5	0.0	0.0	19.9	41.2	24.3	18.9	1.4	1.4	18.8	10.1		18.0	21.5
25 Togo	..	35.7	..	7.8	..	9.6	..	35.4	..	1.1	..	10.4		..	25.3
26 Central African Rep.	..	23.9	..	0.0	..	13.1	..	45.2	..	11.4	..	6.4		..	13.1
27 Haiti	..	11.8	..	0.0	..	42.2	..	21.4	..	10.3	..	14.3		..	10.8
28 Benin	..	..	..	..	..	..	..	..	..	..	..	..		..	..
29 Ghana[b]	18.4	28.7	0.0	0.0	29.4	28.3	40.6	35.2	0.2	0.1	11.5	7.8		15.1	13.8
30 Lesotho	14.3	11.1	0.0	0.0	2.0	10.3	62.9	67.8	9.5	0.1	11.3	10.5		11.7	21.7
31 Sri Lanka	19.1	11.1	0.0	0.0	34.7	40.8	35.4	29.9	2.1	4.3	8.7	13.9		20.1	19.0
32 Guinea	..	..	..	..	..	..	..	..	..	..	..	..		..	..
33 Yemen, PDR	..	..	..	..	..	..	..	..	..	..	..	..		..	..
34 Indonesia	45.5	55.9	0.0	0.0	22.8	24.5	17.6	5.6	3.5	3.0	10.6	11.0		13.4	19.2
35 Mauritania	..	..	..	..	..	..	..	..	..	..	..	..		..	..
36 Sudan[b]	11.8	..	0.0	..	30.4	..	40.5	..	1.5	..	15.7	..		18.0	..
37 Afghanistan	..	..	..	..	..	..	..	..	..	..	..	..		..	..
38 Myanmar	28.7	6.7	0.0	0.0	34.2	39.8	13.4	14.3	0.0	0.0	23.8	39.2		..	..
39 Kampuchea, Dem.	..	..	..	..	..	..	..	..	..	..	..	..		..	..
40 Liberia	40.4	33.9	0.0	0.0	20.3	25.1	31.6	34.6	3.1	2.3	4.6	4.2		17.0	17.0
41 Sierra Leone [b]	32.7	20.1	0.0	0.0	14.6	22.4	42.4	53.6	0.3	0.9	9.9	3.0		19.5	7.3
42 Viet Nam	..	..	..	..	..	..	..	..	..	..	..	..		..	..
Middle-income economies	21.1 w	25.0 w	..	..	20.8 w	28.4 w	13.1 w	12.2 w	..	..	23.5 w	..		16.1 w	15.7 w
Lower-middle-income	22.0 w	26.5 w	..	..	27.6 w	35.9 w	19.4 w	14.7 w	..	..	14.8 w	19.6 w		11.9 w	11.7 w
43 Bolivia	15.4	2.7	0.0	9.6	24.5	59.7	30.9	20.6	23.9	1.2	3.2	6.3		16.9	11.8
44 Philippines[b]	13.8	21.5	0.0	0.0	24.3	37.5	23.0	24.5	29.7	2.2	9.3	14.3		12.4	14.3
45 Yemen Arab Rep.	6.1	19.7	0.0	0.0	10.3	10.3	56.5	20.7	9.6	9.3	17.5	40.0		8.0	23.4
46 Senegal	17.5	..	0.0	..	24.5	..	30.9	..	23.9	..	3.2	..		16.9	..
47 Zimbabwe	..	47.3	..	0.0	..	24.9	..	15.0	..	1.1	..	11.7		..	32.0
48 Egypt, Arab Rep.	..	14.9	..	14.2	..	11.3	..	13.2	..	8.1	..	38.3		..	34.3
49 Dominican Rep.	17.9	16.3	3.9	4.0	19.0	25.8	40.4	39.9	1.7	1.9	17.0	12.1		17.2	16.4
50 Côte d'Ivoire	..	..	..	..	..	..	..	..	..	..	..	..		..	..
51 Papua New Guinea[b]	..	43.6	..	0.0	..	11.8	..	25.9	..	1.7	..	17.1		..	23.5
52 Morocco	16.4	19.0	5.9	5.0	45.7	46.1	13.2	12.7	6.1	7.0	12.6	10.2		18.5	24.4
53 Honduras	19.2	..	3.0	..	33.8	..	28.2	..	2.3	..	13.5	..		13.2	..
54 Guatemala	12.7	20.3	0.0	0.0	36.1	27.5	26.2	37.2	15.6	6.8	9.4	8.2		8.9	10.3
55 Congo, People's Rep.	19.4	..	0.0	..	40.3	..	26.5	..	6.3	..	7.5	..		18.4	..
56 El Salvador [b]	15.2	21.1	0.0	0.0	25.6	43.8	36.1	21.1	17.2	7.7	6.0	6.3		11.6	10.5
57 Thailand	12.1	19.9	0.0	0.0	46.3	46.3	28.7	22.9	1.8	2.9	11.2	8.0		12.5	17.4
58 Botswana[b]	19.9	43.3	0.0	0.0	2.4	1.4	47.2	13.8	0.4	0.1	30.0	41.5		30.7	74.1
59 Cameroon	..	31.3	..	5.4	..	14.9	..	18.7	..	4.0	..	25.8		..	18.9
60 Jamaica	..	..	..	..	..	..	..	..	..	..	..	..		..	..
61 Ecuador [b]	19.6	48.6	0.0	0.0	19.1	25.6	52.4	19.6	5.1	3.7	3.8	2.6		13.6	14.2
62 Colombia	37.1	27.0	13.7	8.6	15.2	27.7	19.8	19.1	7.1	6.2	7.1	11.5		10.6	13.8
63 Paraguay	8.8	13.8	10.4	13.3	26.1	25.3	24.8	10.9	17.0	23.0	12.9	13.6		11.5	10.6
64 Tunisia	15.9	13.3	7.1	8.8	31.6	22.1	21.8	24.7	7.8	5.7	15.7	25.4		23.6	33.2
65 Turkey	30.8	39.5	0.0	0.0	31.0	32.0	14.6	6.6	6.1	3.3	17.5	18.5		20.6	17.9
66 Peru[b]	17.3	19.6	0.0	0.0	32.7	52.2	15.4	21.5	21.2	−0.1	13.5	6.7		15.2	9.0
67 Jordan	9.0	9.8	0.0	0.0	14.9	14.9	34.7	31.1	7.1	7.4	34.2	36.8		26.6	29.2

Note: For data comparability and coverage, see the technical notes. Figures in italics are for years other than those specified.

		Percentage of total current revenue												
		Tax revenue												
		Taxes on income, profit, and capital gain		Social security contributions		Domestic taxes on goods and services		Taxes on international trade and transactions		Other taxes[a]		Nontax revenue		Total current revenue as a percentage of GNP	
		1972	1988	1972	1988	1972	1988	1972	1988	1972	1988	1972	1988	1972	1988
68	Chile	14.3	22.6	28.6	5.8	28.6	36.0	14.3	9.5	0.0	−0.2	14.3	26.2	30.2	31.7
69	Syrian Arab Rep.	6.8	32.3	0.0	0.0	10.4	6.1	17.3	5.8	12.1	23.1	53.4	32.7	25.1	22.6
70	Costa Rica	17.7	12.7	13.4	26.5	38.1	30.2	18.1	21.1	1.6	0.1	11.0	9.5	15.7	22.3
71	Mexico	37.3	26.8	18.6	11.8	32.2	68.5	13.6	3.4	−8.5	−18.1	6.8	7.5	10.1	18.0
72	Mauritius	22.7	10.9	0.0	4.0	23.3	18.6	40.2	50.8	5.5	5.2	8.2	10.5	15.6	25.1
73	Poland	..	30.4	..	21.4	..	30.4	..	6.2	..	6.5	..	5.1	..	38.7
74	Malaysia	25.2	32.2	0.1	0.7	24.2	18.0	27.9	17.3	1.4	2.0	21.2	29.8	20.3	25.1
75	Panama	23.3	21.9	22.4	24.7	13.2	14.4	16.0	10.0	7.7	3.2	17.3	25.8	21.8	31.9
76	Brazil	20.0	11.5	27.7	16.6	35.4	13.6	7.7	1.7	3.1	2.8	6.2	53.8	18.9	34.4
77	Angola	..	..	..	..	..	..	..	..	..	..	..	..	..	..
78	Lebanon	..	..	..	..	..	..	..	..	..	..	..	..	..	..
79	Nicaragua	9.5	12.5	14.0	12.2	37.3	50.1	24.4	6.9	9.0	10.2	5.8	8.1	12.6	40.7
	Upper-middle-income	20.5 w	..	..	..	15.2 w	..	8.1 w	..	..	..	30.1 w	..	22.6 w	..
80	South Africa	54.8	52.7	1.2	1.2	21.5	31.8	4.6	2.9	5.0	2.8	12.8	8.6	21.2	27.7
81	Algeria	..	..	..	..	..	..	..	..	..	..	..	..	..	..
82	Hungary	..	15.6	..	24.5	..	40.2	..	5.4	..	2.5	..	11.7	..	58.2
83	Uruguay	4.7	7.9	30.0	25.6	24.5	44.7	6.1	12.2	22.0	5.2	12.6	4.4	22.7	22.1
84	Argentina	0.0	8.5	33.3	26.4	0.0	35.0	33.3	10.3	0.0	11.0	33.3	8.8	14.7	19.7
85	Yugoslavia	0.0	0.0	52.3	0.0	24.5	60.1	19.5	38.4	0.0	0.0	3.7	1.5	20.7	7.5
86	Gabon[b]	18.2	44.2	6.0	0.0	9.5	6.5	44.9	16.2	4.2	1.9	17.2	31.2	28.3	47.1
87	Venezuela	54.2	61.7	6.0	3.2	6.7	4.8	6.1	13.7	1.1	1.9	25.9	14.7	18.5	28.2
88	Trinidad and Tobago	..	..	..	..	..	..	..	..	..	..	..	..	..	..
89	Korea, Rep. of	29.0	30.3	0.7	3.8	41.7	37.3	10.7	14.0	5.3	4.9	12.6	9.6	13.1	18.3
90	Portugal	..	25.2	..	22.7	..	32.0	..	3.0	..	91.2	..	8.8	..	33.5
91	Greece	12.2	17.9	24.5	34.9	35.5	36.3	6.7	0.5	12.0	0.2	9.2	10.2	25.4	35.8
92	Oman	71.1	19.0	0.0	0.0	0.0	0.8	3.0	3.0	2.3	0.8	23.6	76.4	47.4	35.9
93	Libya	..	..	..	..	..	..	..	..	..	..	..	..	..	..
94	Iran, Islamic Rep.	7.9	13.4	2.7	9.5	6.4	8.0	14.6	9.0	4.9	5.6	63.6	54.4	26.2	19.4
95	Iraq	..	..	..	..	..	..	..	..	..	..	..	..	..	..
96	Romania	6.0	0.0	8.2	16.5	0.0	0.0	0.0	0.0	0.0	12.3	85.8	71.2	..	..
	Low- and middle-income	20.6 w	23.4 w	..	..	25.2 w	29.3 w	15.4 w	14.9 w	..	..	22.1 w	..	13.5 w	16.5 w
	Sub-Saharan Africa	..	..	..	..	..	..	..	..	..	..	..	..	..	..
	East Asia	..	..	..	..	..	..	..	..	..	..	..	..	..	..
	South Asia	..	13.7 w	..	..	..	35.5 w	..	29.6 w	..	..	..	20.6 w	..	14.9 w
	Europe, M.East, & N.Africa	..	..	..	..	..	..	..	..	..	..	..	..	..	..
	Latin America & Caribbean	25.5 w	24.4 w	..	..	20.1 w	37.7 w	12.1 w	13.4 w	..	..	11.1 w	12.1 w	10.4 w	10.4 w
	Severely indebted	23.4 w	25.0 w	..	..	21.9 w	39.5 w	12.0 w	13.4 w	..	..	10.9 w	11.9 w	10.5 w	11.2 w
	High-income economies	44.0 w	37.8 w	..	..	23.3 w	20.0 w	2.3 w	1.1 w	..	..	6.5 w	8.5 w	22.0 w	25.5 w
	OECD members	44.3 w	38.1 w	..	..	23.5 w	20.1 w	2.2 w	1.1 w	..	..	6.2 w	7.8 w	21.7 w	25.2 w
	†Other	..	..	..	..	..	..	..	..	..	..	..	..	..	..
97	†Saudi Arabia	..	..	..	..	..	..	..	..	..	..	..	..	..	..
98	Spain	15.9	24.6	38.9	41.0	23.4	19.4	10.0	4.8	0.7	1.7	11.1	8.5	19.7	27.8
99	Ireland	28.3	35.8	9.0	13.1	32.1	30.2	16.7	7.1	3.2	3.1	10.6	10.7	30.1	46.7
100	†Israel	40.0	42.9	0.0	7.0	20.0	32.3	20.0	3.8	10.0	1.8	10.0	12.1	31.3	41.6
101	†Singapore	24.4	19.1	0.0	0.0	17.6	14.5	11.1	2.7	15.5	9.7	31.4	54.0	21.5	29.6
102	†Hong Kong	..	..	..	..	..	..	..	..	..	..	..	..	..	..
103	New Zealand[b]	61.4	51.4	0.0	0.0	19.9	26.3	4.1	2.8	4.5	2.0	10.0	17.5	29.8	46.6
104	Australia	58.3	61.6	0.0	0.0	21.9	22.1	5.2	4.6	2.1	0.5	12.5	11.3	22.2	27.5
105	United Kingdom	39.4	38.0	15.6	18.5	27.1	30.6	1.7	0.1	5.4	2.5	10.8	10.2	32.6	36.4
106	Italy	16.6	37.1	39.2	37.3	31.7	24.2	0.4	0.0	4.3	−1.0	7.7	2.3	24.9	36.9
107	†Kuwait	68.8	0.9	0.0	0.0	19.7	0.7	1.5	1.6	0.2	0.1	9.9	96.7	55.2	51.9
108	Belgium	31.3	36.8	32.4	34.8	28.9	22.9	1.0	0.0	3.3	2.2	3.1	3.3	35.1	45.0
109	Netherlands	32.5	26.5	36.7	40.4	22.3	22.1	0.5	0.0	3.4	2.5	4.7	8.6	43.4	51.0
110	Austria	20.7	19.6	30.0	36.5	28.3	25.7	5.4	1.6	10.2	8.2	5.5	8.3	29.7	35.5
111	†United Arab Emirates[b]	0.0	..	0.0	..	0.0	..	0.0	..	0.0	..	100.0	..	0.2	..
112	France	16.8	17.4	37.0	42.4	37.9	29.4	0.3	0.0	3.0	3.1	4.9	7.6	33.4	41.4
113	Canada	54.0	51.8	8.8	14.9	15.9	18.9	11.0	3.8	−0.6	0.0	10.9	10.7	21.1	20.5
114	Denmark	40.0	38.6	5.1	2.8	42.1	42.2	3.1	0.1	2.8	3.1	6.8	13.3	35.5	42.9
115	Germany, Fed. Rep.	19.7	17.7	46.6	54.9	28.1	22.6	0.8	0.0	0.8	0.1	4.0	4.6	25.3	28.5
116	Finland	30.0	28.9	7.8	10.3	47.7	46.3	3.1	0.9	5.8	3.9	5.5	9.8	26.5	29.8
117	Sweden	27.0	17.8	21.6	29.7	34.0	29.0	1.5	0.6	4.7	9.6	11.3	13.3	32.4	42.9
118	United States	59.4	51.5	21.6	34.2	7.1	3.6	1.6	1.7	2.5	0.8	5.7	8.1	17.6	19.7
119	Norway	22.6	16.1	20.6	23.2	48.0	41.2	1.6	0.6	1.0	1.3	6.2	17.7	36.8	46.1
120	Japan[b]	..	..	..	..	..	..	..	..	..	..	..	..	11.2	13.6
121	Switzerland	13.9	..	37.3	..	21.5	..	16.7	..	2.6	..	8.0	..	14.5	..
	Total reporting economies	40.6 w	35.7 w	..	..	23.2 w	20.7 w	3.8 w	2.6 w	..	..	8.0 w	9.7 w	20.9 w	24.5 w
	Oil exporters	26.4 w	..	..	..	24.2 w	..	10.9 w	..	..	..	..	..	20.2 w	..
	Nonreporting nonmembers	..	..	..	..	..	..	..	..	..	..	..	..	..	..

a. See the technical notes.   b. Refers to budgetary data.

Table 13. Money and interest rates

		Monetary holdings, broadly defined					Average annual inflation (GDP deflator)	Nominal interest rates of banks (average annual percentage)			
		Average annual nominal growth rate (percent)		Average outstanding as a percentage of GDP				Deposit rate		Lending rate	
		1965–80	1980–88	1965	1980	1988	1980–88	1980	1988	1980	1988
	Low-income economies										
	China and India										
	Other low-income										
1	Mozambique	..	..	..	..	..	33.6	..	..	..	..
2	Ethiopia	12.7	11.9	12.5	25.3	43.5	2.1	..	7.50	..	6.00
3	Chad	12.5	14.4	9.3	20.0	26.4	3.2	5.50	4.31	11.00	10.79
4	Tanzania	*19.7*	21.5	..	37.2	24.8	25.7	4.00	17.46	11.50	29.63
5	Bangladesh	..	23.8	..	16.9	..	11.1	8.25	12.00	11.33	16.00
6	Malawi	15.4	*17.7*	17.6	20.3	*25.0*	12.6	7.92	13.50	16.67	22.25
7	Somalia	20.4	42.4	12.7	17.8	17.2	38.4	4.50	*16.25*	7.50	33.67
8	Zaire	28.2	59.4	11.1	8.9	10.4	56.1	..	..	..	..
9	Bhutan	..	26.5	..	..	..	8.9	..	..	..	..
10	Lao PDR	..	..	..	..	*8.1*	..	7.20	14.00	4.80	15.00
11	Nepal	17.9	19.3	8.4	21.9	31.1	..	4.00	8.50	14.00	15.00
12	Madagascar	12.2	16.3	19.6	27.6	26.1	17.3	5.63	11.50	9.50	..
13	Burkina Faso	17.1	12.9	9.3	18.5	24.9	3.2	13.55	5.25	9.38	7.29
14	Mali	14.4	12.3	..	17.9	23.4	3.7	13.71	5.25	9.38	6.63
15	Burundi	15.7	9.9	10.1	13.3	17.0	4.0	2.50	4.00	12.00	12.00
16	Uganda	*23.1*	*77.8*	..	12.7	*7.8*	100.7	6.80	26.00	10.80	35.00
17	Nigeria	28.5	11.9	9.9	21.5	24.6	11.6	5.27	*13.09*	8.43	*13.96*
18	Zambia	12.7	*28.9*	..	32.6	*30.6*	33.5	7.00	11.44	9.50	18.39
19	Niger	18.3	*6.1*	3.8	13.3	*18.1*	3.6	6.19	5.25	9.38	8.00
20	Rwanda	19.0	10.5	15.8	13.6	17.3	4.1	6.25	6.25	13.50	12.00
21	China	..	25.9	..	33.5	63.4	4.9	5.40	..	..	..
22	India	15.3	*17.0*	23.7	36.2	*45.4*	7.4	..	..	16.50	16.50
23	Pakistan	14.7	14.4	40.7	38.7	40.2	6.5	..	..	..	..
24	Kenya	*18.6*	14.9	..	37.7	37.9	9.6	5.75	10.33	10.58	15.00
25	Togo	20.3	8.9	10.9	29.0	38.1	6.1	12.71	6.71	9.38	7.13
26	Central African Rep.	12.7	6.3	13.5	18.9	18.1	6.7	5.50	7.44	10.50	12.25
27	Haiti	20.3	*8.1*	9.9	26.1	*16.4*	7.9	10.00	..	..	..
28	Benin	17.3	5.1	10.6	21.1	18.2	8.0	13.71	5.25	9.38	7.13
29	Ghana	25.9	45.0	20.3	16.2	12.3	46.1	11.50	16.50	19.00	25.58
30	Lesotho	..	18.8	..	..	47.3	12.2	*9.60*	9.58	11.00	13.67
31	Sri Lanka	15.4	16.0	32.3	35.3	37.1	11.0	14.50	13.23	19.00	12.42
32	Guinea	..	..	..	..	..	..	..	..	..	..
33	Yemen, PDR	15.2	11.1	..	114.8	174.8	4.5	..	..	..	..
34	Indonesia	54.4	23.8	..	13.2	28.5	8.5	6.00	17.72	..	22.10
35	Mauritania	20.7	12.1	5.7	20.5	23.8	9.4	..	6.00	..	12.00
36	Sudan	21.6	28.1	14.1	32.5	23.3	33.5	6.00	..	..	..
37	*Afghanistan*	14.0	*16.2*	14.4	26.8	..	..	9.00	*9.00*	13.00	*13.00*
38	*Myanmar*	11.5	10.3	..	..	..	..	1.50	*1.50*	8.00	*8.00*
39	*Kampuchea, Dem.*	..	..	..	..	..	..	..	..	..	..
40	*Liberia*	..	..	..	..	..	..	10.30	5.43	18.40	13.36
41	*Sierra Leone*	15.9	50.6	11.7	20.6	14.5	..	9.17	16.33	11.00	28.00
42	*Viet Nam*	..	..	..	..	..	..	..	..	..	..
	Middle-income economies										
	Lower-middle-income										
43	Bolivia	24.3	*589.2*	10.9	16.2	*21.7*	482.8	18.00	..	28.00	..
44	Philippines	17.7	16.1	19.9	19.0	21.1	15.6	12.25	11.32	14.00	15.92
45	Yemen Arab Rep.	..	20.4	..	61.8	60.3	11.6	9.33	9.50	..	..
46	Senegal	15.6	7.6	15.3	26.6	22.5	8.1	6.19	5.25	9.38	6.96
47	Zimbabwe	..	*18.1*	..	*54.6*	44.0	12.1	3.52	9.68	17.54	13.00
48	Egypt, Arab Rep.	17.7	22.2	35.3	52.2	86.8	10.6	8.33	11.00	13.33	17.00
49	Dominican Rep.	18.5	*22.4*	18.0	21.8	*29.5*	16.8	..	..	..	..
50	Côte d'Ivoire	20.4	7.1	21.8	25.8	32.3	3.8	13.55	5.25	9.38	7.13
51	Papua New Guinea	..	8.9	..	32.9	31.3	4.7	6.90	9.27	11.15	12.68
52	Morocco	15.7	14.5	29.4	42.4	50.5	7.7	4.88	8.50	7.00	9.00
53	Honduras	14.8	11.7	15.4	22.8	33.0	4.7	7.00	8.63	18.50	15.38
54	Guatemala	16.3	14.7	15.2	20.5	22.2	13.3	9.00	12.17	11.00	15.17
55	Congo, People's Rep.	14.2	8.6	16.5	14.7	21.5	0.8	6.50	7.81	11.00	11.79
56	El Salvador	14.3	17.1	21.6	28.1	28.5	16.8	..	..	..	..
57	Thailand	17.9	18.0	23.6	37.6	65.0	3.1	12.00	9.50	18.00	15.00
58	Botswana	..	25.1	..	30.7	34.3	10.0	5.00	5.00	8.48	7.83
59	Cameroon	19.1	10.8	11.7	18.3	18.3	7.0	7.50	7.21	13.00	13.46
60	Jamaica	17.2	25.9	24.3	35.6	59.6	18.7	10.29	17.92	13.00	23.00
61	Ecuador	22.6	31.8	15.6	20.2	16.1	31.2	..	34.00	12.00	26.00
62	Colombia	26.5	..	19.8	23.7	..	24.1	..	28.28	19.00	28.22
63	Paraguay	21.3	20.0	12.1	19.8	15.6	22.1	..	..	..	..
64	Tunisia	17.4	*15.5*	30.2	42.1	..	7.7	2.50	7.37	7.25	9.87
65	Turkey	27.5	50.3	23.0	17.2	22.8	39.3	10.95	*35.40*	25.67	*50.00*
66	Peru	25.9	*100.8*	18.7	16.3	..	119.1	..	..	..	..
67	Jordan	19.1	12.8	..	88.8	152.2	2.2	..	..	..	..

Note: For data comparability and coverage, see the technical notes. Figures in italics are for years other than those specified.

		Monetary holdings, broadly defined					Average annual inflation (GDP deflator)	Nominal interest rates of banks (average annual percentage)			
		Average annual nominal growth rate (percent)		Average outstanding as a percentage of GDP				Deposit rate		Lending rate	
		1965–80	1980–88	1965	1980	1988	1980–88	1980	1988	1980	1988
68	Chile	139.9	..	16.3	21.3	..	20.8	37.46	26.60	47.14	38.28
69	Syrian Arab Rep.	21.9	19.8	24.6	40.9	..	12.9	5.00	..	..	..
70	Costa Rica	24.6	26.7	19.3	38.8	36.1	26.9	..	15.18	..	28.69
71	Mexico	21.9	62.6	25.1	27.5	14.0	73.8	20.63	52.93	25.20	52.70
72	Mauritius	21.8	20.2	27.3	41.1	58.9	7.8	9.25	10.00	12.19	14.96
73	Poland	..	26.7	..	58.4	32.9	30.5	3.00	21.00	8.00	16.67
74	Malaysia	21.5	13.0	26.3	69.8	117.4	1.3	6.23	3.00	7.75	7.25
75	Panama	..	..	..	..	..	3.3	..	..	..	..
76	Brazil	43.4	..	20.6	18.0	..	188.7	115.00	859.43	..	..
77	Angola	..	..	..	..	..	..	..	..	..	..
78	Lebanon	16.2	42.3	83.4	..	..	..	..	..	..	..
79	Nicaragua	15.0	..	15.4	21.0	..	86.6	7.50	..	..	..
	Upper-middle-income										
80	South Africa	14.0	15.8	56.6	49.5	52.1	13.9	5.54	13.54	9.50	15.33
81	Algeria	22.3	17.5	32.1	58.5	..	5.6	..	..	..	..
82	Hungary	..	7.6	..	46.5	43.0	6.4	3.00	9.00	9.00	13.00
83	Uruguay	65.8	57.1	28.0	31.2	36.3	57.0	50.30	67.82	66.62	101.98
84	Argentina	86.0	284.0	..	22.2	19.6	290.5	79.40	432.75	..	430.38
85	Yugoslavia	25.7	67.0	43.6	59.1	50.3	66.9	5.88	279.21	11.50	455.17
86	Gabon	25.2	6.5	16.2	15.2	24.6	0.9	7.50	8.17	12.50	11.79
87	Venezuela	22.3	16.4	17.3	36.3	43.6	13.0	..	8.95	..	8.50
88	Trinidad and Tobago	23.1	12.4	21.3	32.0	..	5.3	6.57	6.03	10.00	12.58
89	Korea, Rep. of	35.5	19.5	11.1	31.7	44.6	5.0	19.50	10.00	18.00	10.13
90	Portugal	19.5	21.4	77.7	96.3	98.7	20.1	18.20	..	18.50	..
91	Greece	21.4	25.1	35.0	61.6	80.0	18.9	14.50	17.32	21.25	22.89
92	Oman	..	17.7	..	12.3	28.6	−6.5	..	7.57	..	9.40
93	Libya	29.2	2.1	14.2	34.7	..	0.1	5.13	5.50	7.00	7.00
94	Iran, Islamic Rep.	28.6	..	21.6	..	..	..	..	..	..	..
95	Iraq	..	..	19.7	..	..	..	..	..	..	..
96	Romania	..	7.5	..	33.2	..	..	..	..	..	..

Low- and middle-income
Sub-Saharan Africa
East Asia
South Asia
Europe, M.East, & N.Africa
Latin America & Caribbean

Severely indebted

High-income economies
OECD members
†Other

97	†Saudi Arabia	32.1	9.4	16.4	18.6	63.7	−4.2	..	..	16.85	12.43
98	Spain	19.7	9.7	59.2	75.2	65.3	10.1	13.05	9.06	15.96	8.29
99	Ireland	16.1	6.0	..	58.1	45.0	8.0	12.00	3.63	..	..
100	†Israel	52.7	137.9	15.3	56.9	65.0	136.6	..	19.39	176.93	61.43
101	†Singapore	17.6	12.1	58.4	74.4	116.1	1.2	9.37	2.74	11.72	5.96
102	†Hong Kong	..	16.4	..	69.3	..	6.7	11.0	16.32	12.63	20.84
103	New Zealand	12.8	12.7	56.5	53.4	11.5	11.4	8.58	11.92	10.58	18.52
104	Australia	13.1	13.2	50.0	46.6	47.7	7.8	..	..	..	..
105	United Kingdom	13.8	13.2	47.8	46.1	5.7	5.7	14.13	5.35	16.17	10.29
106	Italy	18.0	12.2	69.0	82.7	74.8	11.0	12.70	6.69	19.03	13.57
107	†Kuwait	17.8	5.3	28.1	33.1	88.2	−3.9	4.50	4.50	6.80	6.80
108	Belgium	10.4	6.8	59.2	57.0	58.0	4.8	7.69	4.54	..	8.92
109	Netherlands	14.7	5.8	54.4	79.0	87.7	2.0	5.96	3.48	13.50	7.77
110	Austria	13.3	7.3	48.9	72.6	84.9	4.0	5.00	2.73	..	..
111	†United Arab Emirates	..	11.8	..	19.0	66.2	0.1	9.47	..	12.13	..
112	France	15.0	9.9	53.7	69.7	74.6	7.1	6.25	5.01	18.73	15.65
113	Canada	15.3	7.8	40.2	64.4	64.0	4.6	12.86	9.54	14.27	10.83
114	Denmark	11.5	15.6	46.0	42.6	..	6.3	10.80	7.75	17.20	12.59
115	Germany, Fed. Rep.	10.1	5.7	46.1	60.4	64.9	2.8	7.95	3.29	12.04	8.33
116	Finland	14.7	14.3	39.1	39.5	50.8	7.1	9.00	7.75	9.77	9.72
117	Sweden	10.7	10.7	46.8	46.5	49.8	7.5	11.25	8.88	15.12	13.32
118	United States	9.2	9.3	64.0	58.8	66.3	4.0	13.07	7.73	15.27	9.31
119	Norway	12.6	12.2	51.9	51.6	62.1	5.6	5.07	8.03	12.63	14.28
120	Japan	17.2	8.8	106.7	134.0	177.4	1.3	5.50	1.76	8.35	5.03
121	Switzerland	7.1	8.0	101.1	107.4	123.0	3.8	7.75	2.69	5.56	5.07

Total reporting economies
Oil exporters

Nonreporting nonmembers

Table 14. Growth of merchandise trade

		Merchandise trade (millions of dollars)		Average annual growth rate[a] (percent)				Terms of trade (1980 = 100)	
		Exports 1988	Imports 1988	Exports 1965–80	Exports 1980–88	Imports 1965–80	Imports 1980–88	1985	1988
	Low-income economies	**107,355** t	**131,444** t	**5.6** w	**4.1** w	**4.5** w	**2.6** w	**92** m	**93** m
	China and India	**62,140** t	**77,751** t	**4.8** w	**10.0** w	**4.5** w	**10.2** w	**104** m	**101** m
	Other low-income	**45,215** t	**53,693** t	**5.9** w	**0.5** w	**4.5** w	**-3.2** w	**91** m	**93** m
1	Mozambique	104	706	..	..	..	..	..	..
2	Ethiopia	374	1,099	−0.5	−0.7	−0.9	7.2	99	104
3	Chad	148	366	..	..	..	..	..	..
4	Tanzania	373	1,185	−4.0	−5.4	1.6	0.5	90	94
5	Bangladesh	1,231	2,987	..	6.1	..	3.3	124	111
6	Malawi	301	412	4.1	3.3	3.3	−3.4	69	72
7	Somalia	58	354	3.8	−9.7	5.8	−4.1	91	91
8	Zaire	2,207	1,954	4.7	−2.9	−2.9	0.2	82	96
9	Bhutan	..	..	..	..	..	..	..	..
10	Lao PDR	58	188	..	..	..	..	..	..
11	Nepal	186	628	−2.3	5.5	3.0	7.0	91	93
12	Madagascar	282	382	0.7	−3.5	−0.4	−1.8	104	95
13	Burkina Faso	249	697	6.8	6.5	5.8	2.2	80	69
14	Mali	255	513	11.0	7.0	6.2	3.7	82	88
15	Burundi	123	165	3.0	8.4	2.0	1.1	100	81
16	Uganda	298	518	−3.9	2.6	−5.3	4.6	96	78
17	Nigeria	7,390	6,324	11.4	−3.6	15.2	−13.7	90	40
18	Zambia	1,073	889	1.7	−3.7	−5.5	−4.8	71	107
19	Niger	369	430	12.8	−4.9	6.6	−4.2	109	83
20	Rwanda	113	370	7.7	1.3	8.7	5.8	102	108
21	China*	47,540	55,251	5.5	11.9	7.9	13.1	95	84
22	India	14,600	22,500	3.7	4.7	1.6	5.4	114	119
23	Pakistan	4,362	7,521	4.3	8.4	0.4	3.8	88	106
24	Kenya	1,034	1,989	0.3	0.1	1.7	−0.6	92	91
25	Togo	334	411	4.6	−0.3	8.6	−3.8	91	80
26	Central African Rep.	132	236	−0.4	0.1	−1.1	3.5	87	94
27	Haiti	207	300	7.0	−2.6	8.4	−2.4	97	101
28	Benin	225	413	5.2	2.4	6.7	2.7	90	94
29	Ghana	882	1,091	−1.8	1.1	−1.4	−1.4	91	78
30	Lesotho	55	534	.. [b]	.. [b]	.. [b]	.. [b]	.. [b]	.. [b]
31	Sri Lanka	1,472	2,241	0.5	5.8	−1.2	3.4	99	102
32	Guinea	584	468	..	..	..	..	..	..
33	Yemen, PDR	80	598	−13.7	1.9	−7.5	4.4	99	76
34	Indonesia	19,677	15,732	9.6	2.9	14.2	−2.1	94	70
35	Mauritania	433	353	2.7	9.7	5.4	2.4	112	104
36	Sudan	486	1,223	−0.3	2.7	2.3	−7.9	90	86
37	Afghanistan	..	..	..	..	..	..	..	..
38	Myanmar	299	611	−2.1	−7.0	−1.7	−8.0	70	72
39	Kampuchea, Dem.	..	..	..	..	..	..	..	..
40	Liberia	382	308	4.5	−3.2	1.5	−9.8	91	103
41	Sierra Leone	106	156	−3.8	−3.2	−2.7	−13.1	100	94
42	Viet Nam	..	..	..	..	..	..	..	..
	Middle-income economies	**341,143** t	**338,711** t	**2.4** w	**5.8** w	**5.9** w	**0.6** w	**92** m	**86** m
	Lower-middle-income	**172,809** t	**163,123** t	**5.8** w	**6.0** w	**5.2** w	**−0.2** w	**92** m	**87** m
43	Bolivia	541	700	2.8	−0.5	5.0	−2.6	84	57
44	Philippines	7,074	8,159	4.7	0.4	2.9	−1.7	92	110
45	Yemen Arab Rep.	853	1,310	2.8	35.6	23.3	−10.0	93	40
46	Senegal	761	1,147	2.4	7.0	4.1	2.8	100	96
47	Zimbabwe	1,589	1,325	3.4	1.5	−1.8	−6.0	84	83
48	Egypt, Arab Rep.	4,499	10,771	2.7	6.2	6.0	1.5	84	62
49	Dominican Rep.	893	1,608	1.7	0.0	5.5	2.3	66	76
50	Côte d'Ivoire	2,359	1,542	5.6	1.5	8.0	−2.2	96	92
51	Papua New Guinea	1,464	1,589	12.8	6.4	1.3	1.1	95	89
52	Morocco	3,624	4,818	3.7	5.0	6.5	1.8	89	103
53	Honduras	919	940	3.1	2.8	2.5	−0.3	93	102
54	Guatemala	1,074	1,548	4.8	−2.0	4.6	−3.0	87	87
55	Congo, People's Rep.	912	611	12.5	4.6	1.0	−2.1	94	49
56	El Salvador	573	975	2.4	−4.4	2.7	−0.6	96	86
57	Thailand	15,806	17,876	8.5	11.3	4.1	6.2	74	82
58	Botswana	1,418	1,031	.. [b]	.. [b]	.. [b]	.. [b]	.. [b]	.. [b]
59	Cameroon	1,639	1,484	5.2	6.8	5.6	2.5	92	64
60	Jamaica	832	1,428	−0.3	−4.5	−1.9	−0.5	95	97
61	Ecuador	2,203	1,714	15.1	5.7	6.8	−2.8	94	50
62	Colombia	5,339	4,515	1.4	8.2	5.3	−3.5	98	68
63	Paraguay	919	878	7.9	15.7	4.6	4.9	82	102
64	Tunisia	2,397	3,692	10.8	3.0	10.4	−1.6	83	77
65	Turkey	11,662	14,340	5.5	15.3	7.7	10.3	91	115
66	Peru	2,694	2,750	2.3	−2.5	−0.2	−3.2	81	80
67	Jordan	875	2,751	13.7	6.5	9.7	0.3	93	102
*	Data for Taiwan, China, are:	60,382	44,584	19.0	13.9	15.1	8.5	104	105

Note: For data comparability and coverage, see the technical notes. Figures in italics are for years other than those specified.

		Merchandise trade (millions of dollars)		Average annual growth rate [a] (percent)				Terms of trade (1980 = 100)	
		Exports 1988	Imports 1988	Exports 1965-80	Exports 1980-88	Imports 1965-80	Imports 1980-88	1985	1988
68	Chile	7,052	4,833	7.9	4.5	2.6	−6.0	79	94
69	Syrian Arab Rep.	1,345	2,223	11.4	−0.5	8.5	−8.2	97	56
70	Costa Rica	1,270	1,409	7.0	2.9	5.7	−0.3	95	98
71	Mexico	20,658	18,903	7.6	5.5	5.7	−4.9	98	67
72	Mauritius	1,110	1,115	3.1	12.1	6.4	8.7	90	117
73	Poland	13,211	12,064	. .	4.7	. .	2.3	106	116
74	Malaysia	20,848	16,584	4.4	9.4	2.9	0.4	87	74
75	Panama	2,352	2,815	. .	1.2	. .	−5.6	94	104
76	Brazil	33,689	14,691	9.3	6.0	8.2	−2.9	89	117
77	*Angola*	. .	. .	. .	. .	. .	. .	. .	. .
78	*Lebanon*	. .	. .	. .	. .	. .	. .	. .	. .
79	*Nicaragua*	236	791	2.3	−6.3	1.3	0.4	85	84
	Upper-middle-income	**168,333** *t*	**175,588** *t*	**0.9** *w*	**4.4** *w*	**6.8** *w*	**1.4** *w*	**91** *m*	**75** *m*
80	South Africa	19,714	16,664	6.1[b]	0.2[b]	0.1[b]	−6.6[b]	75[b]	73[b]
81	Algeria	7,674	7,432	1.5	3.4	13.0	−5.9	97	41
82	Hungary	9,922	9,326	. .	5.4	. .	1.7	92	75
83	Uruguay	1,402	1,177	4.6	2.1	1.2	−4.2	87	99
84	Argentina	9,134	5,324	4.7	0.1	1.8	−8.0	90	86
85	Yugoslavia	12,779	13,329	5.6	0.9	6.6	−1.3	111	120
86	Gabon	1,204	998	8.1	−2.2	10.5	0.8	90	54
87	Venezuela	10,234	11,581	−9.5	0.4	8.7	−3.9	93	41
88	Trinidad and Tobago	1,160	1,247	−5.5	−6.0	−5.8	−15.0	96	55
89	Korea, Rep. of	60,696	51,811	27.2	14.7	15.2	9.9	106	108
90	Portugal	10,218	16,038	3.4	11.6	3.7	6.3	85	107
91	Greece	5,400	11,978	11.9	4.6	5.2	3.4	88	89
92	Oman	*3,941*	*1,822*	. .	. .	. .	. .	. .	. .
93	Libya	5,640	6,386	3.3	−5.4	15.8	−14.8	91	*47*
94	*Iran, Islamic Rep.*	. .	9,454	. .	. .	. .	. .	. .	. .
95	*Iraq*	*9,014*	10,268	. .	. .	. .	. .	. .	. .
96	*Romania*	. .	. .	. .	. .	. .	. .	. .	. .
	Low- and middle-income	**448,498** *t*	**470,155** *t*	**3.2** *w*	**5.4** *w*	**5.6** *w*	**1.1** *w*	**92** *m*	**89** *m*
	Sub-Saharan Africa	**28,871** *t*	**32,738** *t*	**6.6** *w*	**−0.7** *w*	**4.9** *w*	**−5.0** *w*	**91** *m*	**92** *m*
	East Asia	**173,653** *t*	**167,930** *t*	**9.7** *w*	**10.4** *w*	**8.6** *w*	**6.9** *w*	**94** *m*	**84** *m*
	South Asia	**21,712** *t*	**35,950** *t*	**1.7** *w*	**5.4** *w*	**0.6** *w*	**4.4** *w*	**95** *m*	**104** *m*
	Europe, M.East, & N.Africa	**102,798** *t*	**138,333** *t*	. .	**0.3** *w*	. .	**0.3** *w*	**92** *m*	**83** *m*
	Latin America & Caribbean	**101,750** *t*	**78,540** *t*	**−2.0** *w*	**3.2** *w*	**4.4** *w*	**−4.1** *w*	**90** *m*	**86** *m*
	Severely indebted	**127,659** *t*	**101,688** *t*	**−1.0** *w*	**3.6** *w*	**5.6** *w*	**−2.3** *w*	**92** *m*	**92** *m*
	High-income economies	**2,178,528** *t*	**2,265,978** *t*	**7.0** *w*	**3.4** *w*	**4.4** *w*	**4.9** *w*	**95** *m*	**98** *m*
	OECD members	**2,024,259** *t*	**2,110,250** *t*	**7.2** *w*	**4.1** *w*	**4.2** *w*	**5.1** *w*	**94** *m*	**103** *m*
	†Other	**154,269** *t*	**155,728** *t*	**6.0** *w*	**−4.2** *w*	**10.4** *w*	**0.6** *w*	**96** *m*	**64** *m*
97	†Saudi Arabia	*23,138*	*20,465*	8.8	*−16.3*	25.9	*−9.3*	95	*54*
98	Spain	40,458	60,434	12.4	7.7	4.4	7.2	90	103
99	Ireland	18,736	15,558	9.8	7.8	4.8	3.2	107	112
100	†Israel	9,605	15,030	8.9	7.6	6.3	4.4	94	92
101	†Singapore	39,205	43,765	4.7	7.3	7.0	4.9	101	101
102	†Hong Kong	63,161	63,894	9.5	12.3	8.3	10.4	103	105
103	New Zealand	8,785	7,304	4.2	3.9	1.1	3.5	97	110
104	Australia	*25,283*	*29,318*	5.5	5.8	0.9	*3.0*	89	*74*
105	United Kingdom	145,076	189,466	4.8	3.1	1.4	4.9	96	93
106	Italy	128,534	135,514	7.7	3.8	3.5	4.3	95	108
107	†Kuwait	7,160	5,348	−1.9	−2.9	11.8	*−5.5*	95	*54*
108	Belgium[c]	88,953	91,098	7.8	4.7	5.2	2.8	87	89
109	Netherlands	103,206	99,743	8.0	4.7	4.4	3.4	91	91
110	Austria	28,111	36,579	8.2	4.3	6.1	4.0	90	98
111	†United Arab Emirates	*12,000*	*7,226*	10.9	*0.1*	20.5	*−7.1*	91	*54*
112	France	161,702	176,745	8.5	3.4	4.3	2.6	94	101
113	Canada	111,364	112,180	5.4	6.4	2.6	8.4	122	119
114	Denmark	27,816	26,458	5.4	5.8	1.7	5.2	96	107
115	Germany, Fed. Rep.	322,555	248,999	7.2	4.6	5.3	3.3	88	106
116	Finland	21,639	20,911	5.9	3.5	3.1	4.2	96	114
117	Sweden	49,867	45,793	4.9	5.5	1.8	3.3	89	95
118	United States	315,313	458,682	6.4	1.2	5.5	8.9	114	118
119	Norway	22,503	23,212	8.2	6.3	3.0	3.5	97	67
120	Japan	264,772	183,252	11.4	5.3	4.9	5.0	112	157
121	Switzerland	50,633	56,325	6.2	4.3	4.5	4.5	88	103
	Total reporting economies	**2,627,026** *t*	**2,736,133** *t*	**6.1** *w*	**3.8** *w*	**4.6** *w*	**4.1** *w*	**93** *m*	**92** *m*
	Oil exporters	**161,995** *t*	**163,458** *t*	**3.0** *w*	**−3.6** *w*	**9.3** *w*	**−5.5** *w*	**94** *m*	**54** *m*
	Nonreporting nonmembers	. .	. .	. .	. .	. .	. .	. .	. .

a. See the technical notes.   b. Figures for the South African Customs Union, comprising South Africa, Namibia, Lesotho, Botswana, and Swaziland, are included in South African data. Trade among the component territories is excluded.   c. Includes Luxembourg.

Table 15. Structure of merchandise imports

	Food		Fuels		Other primary commodities		Machinery and transport equipment		Other manufactures	
Percentage share of merchandise imports										
	1965	1988	1965	1988	1965	1988	1965	1988	1965	1988
Low-income economies	22 w	7 w	5 w	9 w	10 w	6 w	28 w	34 w	34 w	44 w
China and India	28 w	3 w	3 w	5 w	19 w	7 w	26 w	35 w	24 w	50 w
Other low-income	17 w	11 w	7 w	14 w	4 w	6 w	29 w	31 w	42 w	37 w
1 Mozambique	17	21	8	6	7	9	24	..	45	..
2 Ethiopia	6	5	6	23	6	3	37	34	44	36
3 Chad	13	..	19	..	3	..	23	..	42	..
4 Tanzania	10	6	9	14	2	2	34	46	45	32
5 Bangladesh	..	23	..	10	..	9	..	20	..	38
6 Malawi	15	6	5	6	3	2	21	44	57	41
7 Somalia	31	22	5	4	8	8	24	39	33	27
8 Zaire	18	23	7	3	5	6	33	31	37	36
9 Bhutan	..	..	..	..	..	..	..	..	..	..
10 Lao PDR	27	..	15	..	6	..	18	..	33	..
11 Nepal	22	6	5	8	14	6	37	22	22	57
12 Madagascar	19	5	5	33	2	3	25	37	48	22
13 Burkina Faso	23	19	4	3	14	4	19	33	40	41
14 Mali	20	13	6	16	5	1	23	43	47	26
15 Burundi	16	11	6	5	9	4	15	19	55	62
16 Uganda	7	6	1	9	3	2	38	45	51	38
17 Nigeria	9	18	6	2	3	6	34	31	48	43
18 Zambia	9	7	10	9	3	1	33	38	45	46
19 Niger	12	21	6	8	6	10	21	30	55	32
20 Rwanda	12	11	7	21	5	7	28	28	50	33
21 China*	36	2	0	2	25	6	12	41	27	49
22 India	22	5	5	13	14	9	37	20	22	53
23 Pakistan	20	14	3	19	5	13	38	28	34	25
24 Kenya	10	11	11	22	3	4	34	31	42	31
25 Togo	15	34	3	5	5	10	31	21	45	31
26 Central African Rep.	13	11	7	8	2	3	29	36	49	43
27 Haiti	25	14	6	8	6	2	14	25	48	51
28 Benin	18	14	6	31	7	3	17	16	53	37
29 Ghana	12	8	4	17	3	3	33	36	48	37
30 Lesotho[a]	..	..	..	..	..	..	..	..	..	..
31 Sri Lanka	41	17	8	17	4	3	12	27	34	37
32 Guinea	..	..	..	..	..	..	..	..	..	..
33 Yemen, PDR	19	16	40	40	5	2	10	21	26	19
34 Indonesia	6	3	3	18	2	5	39	39	50	36
35 Mauritania	9	21	4	5	1	2	56	36	30	36
36 Sudan	23	7	5	19	4	2	21	36	47	36
37 *Afghanistan*	17	..	4	..	1	..	8	..	69	..
38 *Myanmar*	15	5	4	2	5	2	18	43	58	48
39 *Kampuchea, Dem.*	6	..	7	..	2	..	26	..	58	..
40 *Liberia*	16	20	8	22	3	2	34	28	39	28
41 *Sierra Leone*	17	23	9	8	3	4	30	19	41	46
42 *Viet Nam*	..	..	..	..	..	..	..	..	..	..
Middle-income economies	15 w	11 w	8 w	10 w	11 w	10 w	31 w	34 w	36 w	35 w
Lower-middle-income	16 w	12 w	8 w	11 w	8 w	8 w	33 w	33 w	35 w	37 w
43 Bolivia	19	15	1	3	3	3	35	52	42	27
44 Philippines	20	10	10	13	7	7	33	20	30	50
45 Yemen Arab Rep.	41	28	6	8	6	6	26	22	21	35
46 Senegal	36	40	6	12	4	3	15	16	38	30
47 Zimbabwe	13	8	8	6	3	3	31	35	46	48
48 Egypt, Arab Rep.	26	19	7	2	12	8	23	29	31	41
49 Dominican Rep.	23	16	10	17	4	4	24	26	40	38
50 Côte d'Ivoire	18	18	6	15	3	3	28	27	46	37
51 Papua New Guinea	23	24	5	10	3	2	25	34	45	30
52 Morocco	36	12	5	13	10	17	18	24	31	34
53 Honduras	11	8	6	15	1	2	26	30	56	45
54 Guatemala	11	6	7	10	2	3	29	27	50	54
55 Congo, People's Rep.	15	24	6	7	1	3	34	25	44	42
56 El Salvador	15	15	5	8	4	4	28	19	48	53
57 Thailand	6	4	9	11	6	12	31	37	49	36
58 Botswana[a]	..	..	..	..	..	..	..	..	..	..
59 Cameroon	11	23	5	1	4	2	28	35	51	39
60 Jamaica	20	14	9	11	5	5	23	22	43	48
61 Ecuador	10	5	9	3	4	4	33	62	44	26
62 Colombia	8	9	1	4	10	7	45	37	35	43
63 Paraguay	24	15	14	18	4	8	31	35	28	25
64 Tunisia	16	18	6	7	7	14	31	22	41	39
65 Turkey	6	2	10	20	10	8	37	34	37	36
66 Peru	17	19	3	1	5	4	41	44	34	33
67 Jordan	28	19	6	16	6	5	18	23	42	38
* Data for Taiwan, China, are:	13	6	5	9	25	14	29	36	29	35

Note: For data comparability and coverage, see the technical notes. Figures in italics are for years other than those specified.

		Food		Fuels		Other primary commodities		Machinery and transport equipment		Other manufactures	
		1965	1988	1965	1988	1965	1988	1965	1988	1965	1988
68	Chile	20	2	6	6	10	2	35	46	30	44
69	Syrian Arab Rep.	22	17	10	11	9	5	16	28	43	39
70	Costa Rica	9	5	5	12	2	2	29	28	54	52
71	Mexico	5	16	2	1	10	8	50	36	33	38
72	Mauritius	34	17	5	9	3	4	16	16	43	53
73	Poland	..	*11*	..	*17*	..	*11*	..	*32*	..	*29*
74	Malaysia	25	15	12	6	10	5	22	47	32	28
75	Panama	11	9	21	21	2	1	21	24	45	44
76	Brazil	20	14	21	28	9	7	22	25	28	26
77	*Angola*	..	..	..	..	..	..	..	..	..	..
78	*Lebanon*	28	..	9	..	9	..	17	..	36	..
79	*Nicaragua*	12	25	5	11	2	3	30	17	51	44
	Upper-middle-income	**13 w**	**10 w**	**8 w**	**10 w**	**14 w**	**12 w**	**29 w**	**35 w**	**35 w**	**34 w**
80	South Africa [a]	5	2	5	0	11	3	42	47	37	47
81	Algeria	26	30	0	2	6	5	15	27	52	35
82	Hungary	12	7	12	16	22	10	27	30	28	36
83	Uruguay	7	9	17	13	16	8	24	34	36	36
84	Argentina	6	4	10	8	21	7	25	43	38	38
85	Yugoslavia	16	7	6	18	19	12	28	27	32	36
86	Gabon	16	22	5	2	2	3	38	36	40	37
87	Venezuela	12	11	1	0	5	3	44	40	39	45
88	Trinidad and Tobago	11	19	50	12	2	5	16	26	22	38
89	Korea, Rep. of	15	6	7	12	26	17	13	35	38	30
90	Portugal	16	13	8	14	19	9	27	30	30	34
91	Greece	15	17	8	5	11	8	35	30	30	40
92	Oman	27	15	19	3	4	2	15	41	34	39
93	Libya	13	*15*	4	*1*	3	2	36	*33*	43	*49*
94	*Iran, Islamic Rep.*	16	..	0	..	6	..	36	..	42	..
95	*Iraq*	24	..	0	..	7	..	25	..	44	..
96	*Romania*	..	..	..	..	..	..	..	..	..	..
	Low- and middle-income	**17 w**	**10 w**	**7 w**	**10 w**	**11 w**	**9 w**	**30 w**	**35 w**	**35 w**	**37 w**
	Sub-Saharan Africa	**14 w**	**16 w**	**6 w**	**9 w**	**4 w**	**5 w**	**30 w**	**30 w**	**44 w**	**38 w**
	East Asia	**21 w**	**6 w**	**6 w**	**8 w**	**15 w**	**11 w**	**23 w**	**38 w**	**34 w**	**38 w**
	South Asia	**29 w**	**9 w**	**4 w**	**14 w**	**11 w**	**9 w**	**32 w**	**22 w**	**26 w**	**45 w**
	Europe, M.East, & N.Africa	**..**	**14 w**	**..**	**13 w**	**..**	**9 w**	**..**	**32 w**	**..**	**32 w**
	Latin America & Caribbean	**12 w**	**12 w**	**9 w**	**9 w**	**8 w**	**6 w**	**34 w**	**35 w**	**36 w**	**38 w**
	Severely indebted	**14 w**	**12 w**	**7 w**	**11 w**	**14 w**	**7 w**	**32 w**	**33 w**	**33 w**	**37 w**
	High-income economies	**19 w**	**10 w**	**11 w**	**9 w**	**19 w**	**8 w**	**20 w**	**34 w**	**31 w**	**40 w**
	OECD members	**19 w**	**10 w**	**11 w**	**9 w**	**20 w**	**9 w**	**20 w**	**34 w**	**31 w**	**39 w**
	†Other	**21 w**	**9 w**	**10 w**	**7 w**	**12 w**	**5 w**	**19 w**	**33 w**	**37 w**	**46 w**
97	†Saudi Arabia	29	*17*	1	*1*	5	2	27	*34*	38	*46*
98	Spain	19	11	10	11	16	9	27	38	28	30
99	Ireland	18	12	8	6	10	5	25	34	39	44
100	†Israel	16	8	6	8	12	5	28	30	38	49
101	†Singapore	23	7	13	14	19	6	14	42	30	30
102	†Hong Kong	25	7	3	2	13	6	13	27	46	58
103	New Zealand	7	7	7	5	10	5	33	37	43	45
104	Australia	5	*5*	8	*5*	10	*4*	37	*39*	41	*47*
105	United Kingdom	30	10	11	5	25	8	11	37	23	41
106	Italy	24	13	16	9	24	12	15	29	21	37
107	†Kuwait	21	17	1	1	7	2	33	39	39	41
108	Belgium [b]	14	11	9	7	21	9	24	24	32	48
109	Netherlands	15	15	10	9	13	6	25	28	37	41
110	Austria	14	6	7	6	13	8	31	36	35	44
111	†United Arab Emirates	15	4	3	3	7	1	34	43	41	49
112	France	19	10	15	8	18	8	20	33	27	41
113	Canada	10	6	7	4	9	5	40	55	34	31
114	Denmark	14	12	11	6	11	7	25	28	39	47
115	Germany, Fed. Rep.	22	11	8	8	21	9	13	29	35	43
116	Finland	10	6	10	10	12	8	35	39	34	38
117	Sweden	12	6	11	7	12	7	30	39	36	40
118	United States	19	6	10	10	20	5	14	43	36	36
119	Norway	10	6	7	4	12	8	38	39	32	43
120	Japan	22	17	20	21	38	20	9	13	11	30
121	Switzerland	16	7	6	4	11	5	24	32	43	52
	Total reporting economies	**18 w**	**10 w**	**10 w**	**9 w**	**18 w**	**8 w**	**22 w**	**34 w**	**32 w**	**40 w**
	Oil exporters	**14 w**	**13 w**	**7 w**	**4 w**	**8 w**	**5 w**	**34 w**	**37 w**	**39 w**	**42 w**
	Nonreporting nonmembers	**..**	**..**	**..**	**..**	**..**	**..**	**..**	**..**	**..**	**..**

a. Figures for the South African Customs Union, comprising South Africa, Namibia, Lesotho, Botswana, and Swaziland, are included in South African data. Trade among the component territories is excluded.   b. Includes Luxembourg.

Table 16. Structure of merchandise exports

Percentage share of merchandise exports

	Fuels minerals, and metals		Other primary commodities		Machinery and transport equipment		Other manufactures		(Textiles and clothing)[a]	
	1965	1988	1965	1988	1965	1988	1965	1988	1965	1988
Low-income economies	**21** w	**25** w	**53** w	**23** w	**1** w	**4** w	**23** w	**49** w	**11** w	..
China and India	**8** w	**10** w	**45** w	**18** w	**2** w	**6** w	**45** w	**67** w	..	..
Other low-income	**30** w	**44** w	**60** w	**29** w	**1** w	**1** w	**8** w	**24** w	**4** w	..
1 Mozambique	14	3	83	89	0	..	2	..	1	..
2 Ethiopia	1	3	98	96	1	0	0	1	0	..
3 Chad	4	..	93	..	0	..	4	..	..	..
4 Tanzania	4	6	83	75	0	3	13	15	1	..
5 Bangladesh	..	2	..	29	..	0	..	69	..	67
6 Malawi	0	0	99	83	0	5	1	12	0	..
7 Somalia	6	0	80	95	4	0	10	5	..	..
8 Zaire	72	64	20	29	0	1	8	6	0	..
9 Bhutan	..	..	..	..	..	..	..	..	..	..
10 Lao PDR	..	25	..	65	..	0	..	10	..	..
11 Nepal	0	4	78	29	0	2	22	65	..	27
12 Madagascar	4	14	90	70	1	3	4	13	1	3
13 Burkina Faso	1	0	94	98	1	1	4	1	0	..
14 Mali	1	0	96	70	1	1	2	29	0	..
15 Burundi	1	0	94	83	0	0	6	16	0	..
16 Uganda	14	4	86	96	0	0	1	0	0	..
17 Nigeria	32	88	65	10	0	0	2	2	0	0
18 Zambia	97	95	3	3	0	1	0	1	0	..
19 Niger	0	76	95	20	1	1	4	3	0	..
20 Rwanda	40	9	60	90	0	0	1	1	..	..
21 China*	6	10	48	17	3	4	43	69	..	24
22 India	10	9	41	18	1	11	48	62	36	25
23 Pakistan	2	1	62	30	1	2	35	67	29	54
24 Kenya	13	20	81	63	0	2	6	15	0	..
25 Togo	49	69	48	23	1	1	3	8	0	..
26 Central African Rep.	1	0	45	60	0	0	54	40	0	..
27 Haiti	14	4	61	23	2	13	23	61	..	60
28 Benin	1	36	94	38	2	7	3	19	0	..
29 Ghana	13	32	85	65	1	0	2	3	0	..
30 Lesotho[b]	..	..	..	..	..	..	..	..	..	..
31 Sri Lanka	2	7	97	50	0	3	1	40	0	32
32 Guinea	..	..	..	..	..	..	..	..	..	..
33 Yemen, PDR	80	90	14	9	2	1	4	0	2	..
34 Indonesia	43	49	53	22	3	1	1	28	0	8
35 Mauritania	94	32	5	65	1	0	0	2	0	..
36 Sudan	1	13	98	80	1	3	0	4	0	..
37 *Afghanistan*	0	..	86	..	0	..	13	..	1	..
38 *Myanmar*	5	3	94	86	0	7	0	3	0	..
39 *Kampuchea, Dem.*	0	..	99	..	0	..	1	..	..	..
40 *Liberia*	72	54	25	44	1	0	3	1	0	..
41 *Sierra Leone*	25	21	14	21	0	1	60	58	0	..
42 *Viet Nam*	..	..	..	..	..	..	..	..	..	..
Middle-income economies	**35** w	**21** w	**50** w	**21** w	**2** w	**19** w	**13** w	**40** w	**3** w	..
Lower-middle-income	**27** w	**24** w	**58** w	**30** w	**1** w	**16** w	**12** w	**30** w	**2** w	..
43 Bolivia	92	89	3	8	0	1	4	2	0	1
44 Philippines	11	12	84	26	0	10	6	52	1	7
45 Yemen Arab Rep.	9	88	91	1	0	9	0	2	..	..
46 Senegal	9	25	88	50	1	6	2	18	1	3
47 Zimbabwe	45	13	40	47	1	3	15	37	6	3
48 Egypt, Arab Rep.	8	64	72	10	0	0	20	25	15	..
49 Dominican Rep.	10	21	88	53	0	6	2	20	0	..
50 Côte d'Ivoire	2	3	93	85	1	3	4	9	0	..
51 Papua New Guinea	1	63	89	32	0	1	10	4	..	..
52 Morocco	40	21	55	29	0	2	5	48	1	18
53 Honduras	7	10	89	79	0	0	4	11	1	..
54 Guatemala	0	3	86	59	1	3	13	35	4	..
55 Congo, People's Rep.	5	72	32	17	2	1	61	10	0	..
56 El Salvador	2	3	81	68	1	3	16	26	6	..
57 Thailand	11	3	84	45	0	11	4	41	0	17
58 Botswana[b]	..	..	..	..	..	..	..	..	..	..
59 Cameroon	17	53	77	35	3	2	2	10	0	1
60 Jamaica	28	15	41	26	0	3	31	56	4	14
61 Ecuador	2	45	96	48	0	2	2	4	1	0
62 Colombia	18	26	75	49	0	1	6	24	2	6
63 Paraguay	0	0	92	88	0	0	8	12	0	0
64 Tunisia	31	19	51	17	0	6	19	58	3	30
65 Turkey	9	6	89	30	0	7	2	57	1	32
66 Peru	45	58	54	20	0	3	1	18	0	7
67 Jordan	27	43	54	10	11	6	7	41	0	5
* Data for Taiwan, China, are:	2	1	56	7	4	34	37	58	5	15

Note: For data comparability and coverage, see the technical notes. Figures in italics are for years other than those specified.

		Percentage share of merchandise exports									
		Fuels minerals, and metals		Other primary commodities		Machinery and transport equipment		Other manufactures		(Textiles and clothing)[a]	
		1965	1988	1965	1988	1965	1988	1965	1988	1965	1988
68	Chile	89	67	7	18	1	3	4	12	0	0
69	Syrian Arab Rep.	7	50	83	25	1	3	9	22	7	6
70	Costa Rica	0	1	84	59	1	7	15	33	3	..
71	Mexico	22	38	62	7	1	33	15	22	3	2
72	Mauritius	0	0	100	39	0	4	0	58	0	47
73	Poland	..	19	..	14	..	33	..	34	..	5
74	Malaysia	35	18	59	37	2	26	4	19	0	4
75	Panama	35	13	63	66	0	1	2	20	0	5
76	Brazil	9	21	83	31	2	18	7	30	1	3
77	Angola	..	..	..	..	..	..	..	..	..	..
78	Lebanon	13	..	53	..	14	..	20	..	2	..
79	Nicaragua	4	2	90	89	0	0	6	9	1	..
	Upper-middle-income	41 w	18 w	37 w	13 w	3 w	25 w	20 w	45 w	4 w	..
80	South Africa[b]	24	11	44	9	3	3	29	77	1	..
81	Algeria	58	96	38	1	2	1	2	3	0	0
82	Hungary	5	8	25	22	32	31	37	38	9	7
83	Uruguay	0	1	95	52	0	3	5	44	2	13
84	Argentina	1	5	93	70	1	5	5	20	0	3
85	Yugoslavia	11	9	33	13	24	31	33	48	8	8
86	Gabon	50	59	39	27	1	3	10	11	0	..
87	Venezuela	97	90	1	1	0	3	2	6	0	0
88	Trinidad and Tobago	84	61	9	6	0	1	7	32	1	0
89	Korea, Rep. of	15	2	25	5	3	39	56	54	27	22
90	Portugal	4	4	34	16	3	17	58	64	24	30
91	Greece	8	15	78	30	2	3	11	52	3	31
92	Oman	90	91	10	2	0	5	0	2	..	0
93	Libya	99	99	1	0	1	1	0	1	0	..
94	Iran, Islamic Rep.	87	..	8	..	0	..	4	..	4	..
95	Iraq	95	..	4	..	0	..	1	..	0	..
96	Romania	..	..	..	..	..	..	..	..	..	..
	Low- and middle-income	30 w	22 w	53 w	21 w	1 w	16 w	17 w	42 w	5 w	..
	Sub-Saharan Africa	34 w	45 w	58 w	38 w	1 w	2 w	6 w	14 w	0 w	..
	East Asia	17 w	10 w	58 w	16 w	2 w	23 w	21 w	51 w	2 w	..
	South Asia	6 w	7 w	57 w	24 w	1 w	8 w	36 w	61 w	27 w	..
	Europe, M.East, & N.Africa	..	..	..	..	..	..	..	..	..	..
	Latin America & Caribbean	43 w	35 w	50 w	29 w	1 w	14 w	6 w	23 w	1 w	..
	Severely indebted	35 w	30 w	45 w	26 w	5 w	17 w	15 w	27 w	..	..
	High-income economies	12 w	9 w	20 w	12 w	29 w	40 w	38 w	40 w	7 w	4 w
	OECD members	9 w	7 w	21 w	12 w	31 w	41 w	39 w	40 w	7 w	5 w
	†Other	57 w	31 w	13 w	6 w	4 w	23 w	26 w	40 w	11 w	14 w
97	†Saudi Arabia	98	90	1	1	1	4	1	5	0	..
98	Spain	9	7	51	20	10	34	29	39	6	4
99	Ireland	3	2	63	28	5	32	29	39	7	5
100	†Israel	6	2	28	13	2	18	63	67	9	6
101	†Singapore	21	15	44	11	11	47	24	28	6	5
102	†Hong Kong	2	2	11	6	6	25	81	66	43	29
103	New Zealand	1	8	94	68	0	6	5	19	0	2
104	Australia	13	37	73	38	5	8	10	17	1	1
105	United Kingdom	7	10	10	8	41	39	41	43	7	4
106	Italy	8	3	14	8	30	36	47	53	15	13
107	†Kuwait	84	90	9	1	4	4	3	5	0	..
108	Belgium[c]	13	8	11	12	20	26	55	53	12	7
109	Netherlands	12	12	32	25	21	21	35	42	9	4
110	Austria	8	5	16	8	20	34	55	53	12	9
111	†United Arab Emirates	99	79	1	4	0	0	0	16	..	..
112	France	8	5	21	19	26	35	45	41	10	5
113	Canada	28	18	35	20	15	38	22	24	1	1
114	Denmark	2	4	55	32	22	25	21	39	4	5
115	Germany, Fed. Rep.	7	4	5	6	46	48	42	42	5	5
116	Finland	3	5	40	14	12	28	45	53	2	4
117	Sweden	9	6	23	10	35	43	33	41	2	2
118	United States	8	6	27	17	37	47	28	31	3	2
119	Norway	21	51	28	11	17	15	34	23	2	1
120	Japan	2	1	7	1	31	65	60	33	17	2
121	Switzerland	3	4	7	4	30	33	60	60	10	5
	Total reporting economies	15 w	11 w	27 w	14 w	25 w	35 w	34 w	41 w	7 w	..
	Oil exporters	67 w	71 w	25 w	7 w	3 w	8 w	7 w	15 w	1 w	..
	Nonreporting nonmembers	..	..	..	..	..	..	..	..	..	..

a. Textiles and clothing is a subgroup of other manufactures. b. Figures for the South African Customs Union, comprising South Africa, Namibia, Lesotho, Botswana, and Swaziland, are included in South African data. Trade among the component territories is excluded. c. Includes Luxembourg.

209

Table 17. OECD imports of manufactured goods: origin and composition

		Value of imports of manufactures, by origin (millions of dollars)		Composition of 1988 imports of manufactures by high-income OECD countries (percent)[a]				
		1968	1988[a]	Textiles and clothing	Chemicals	Electrical machinery and electronics	Transport equipment	Others
	Low-income economies	1,281 t	37,243 t	43 w	7 w	5 w	2 w	44 w
	China and India	759 t	26,942 t	42 w	7 w	6 w	0 w	45 w
	Other low-income	523 t	10,300 t	45 w	6 w	1 w	6 w	42 w
1	Mozambique	6	5	12	3	10	2	72
2	Ethiopia	6	53	10	10	1	1	78
3	Chad	0	1	7	1	4	0	88
4	Tanzania	0	14	6	5	15	2	72
5	Bangladesh	0	774	84	0	0	0	16
6	Malawi	0	17	90	0	1	0	9
7	Somalia	1	5	1	2	18	10	70
8	Zaire	38	382	0	3	0	0	96
9	Bhutan	0	1	17	16	0	8	60
10	Lao PDR	0	2	77	5	4	1	13
11	Nepal	2	173	90	0	0	0	9
12	Madagascar	0	5	10	4	6	3	77
13	Burkina Faso	30	36	62	2	1	1	34
14	Mali	7	33	66	13	0	0	20
15	Burundi	4	2	6	2	7	14	71
16	Uganda	0	6	2	1	2	2	94
17	Nigeria	12	160	2	26	2	1	68
18	Zambia	9	32	22	0	1	4	73
19	Niger	0	367	0	98	0	0	2
20	Rwanda	0	1	3	17	11	0	69
21	China	206	19,874	42	8	8	0	42
22	India	553	7,069	41	4	1	0	54
23	Pakistan	161	2,159	79	0	0	0	21
24	Kenya	14	95	7	3	4	2	84
25	Togo	1	13	2	1	3	1	93
26	Central African Rep.	12	51	0	0	0	0	100
27	Haiti	12	398	50	3	17	0	30
28	Benin	0	15	1	1	3	47	48
29	Ghana	16	49	1	3	2	10	85
30	Lesotho[b]	. .	. .	. .	. .	. .	. .	. .
31	Sri Lanka	6	824	74	1	0	0	24
32	Guinea	30	133	0	38	0	0	62
33	Yemen, PDR	2	3	1	0	53	12	34
34	Indonesia	10	3,339	33	3	1	0	62
35	Mauritania	0	3	25	5	3	6	61
36	Sudan	2	18	14	8	2	24	52
37	*Afghanistan*	10	50	91	1	0	1	8
38	*Myanmar*	3	22	37	8	0	2	52
39	*Kampuchea, Dem.*	0	1	19	0	4	0	77
40	*Liberia*	25	904	0	0	0	65	34
41	*Sierra Leone*	80	69	0	0	1	0	99
42	*Viet Nam*	1	0	. .	. .	. .	. .	. .
	Middle-income economies	3,371 t	183,671 t	22 w	5 w	17 w	7 w	49 w
	Lower-middle-income	1,080 t	63,138 t	22 w	6 w	21 w	8 w	43 w
43	Bolivia	1	24	23	7	0	6	65
44	Philippines	107	3,732	34	4	29	0	32
45	Yemen Arab Rep.	0	31	1	0	2	3	94
46	Senegal	9	37	7	33	6	4	50
47	Zimbabwe	12	553	7	0	0	0	93
48	Egypt, Arab Rep.	28	448	62	5	2	1	31
49	Dominican Rep.	5	1,202	46	1	6	0	47
50	Côte d'Ivoire	5	199	24	3	1	2	70
51	Papua New Guinea	3	20	5	0	1	11	82
52	Morocco	18	1,468	62	19	5	2	12
53	Honduras	3	109	62	2	0	1	35
54	Guatemala	4	143	70	8	0	3	18
55	Congo, People's Rep.	8	97	0	0	0	0	100
56	El Salvador	1	110	56	0	25	0	18
57	Thailand	25	5,892	28	2	14	1	55
58	Botswana[b]	. .	. .	. .	. .	. .	. .	. .
59	Cameroon	1	58	36	2	1	1	59
60	Jamaica	58	563	40	54	1	0	5
61	Ecuador	3	50	14	5	2	1	79
62	Colombia	34	779	24	4	0	0	72
63	Paraguay	4	53	18	13	0	0	69
64	Tunisia	11	1,295	62	15	8	1	14
65	Turkey	23	4,356	71	5	2	1	21
66	Peru	8	346	52	8	4	0	36
67	Jordan	0	123	4	50	5	2	40

Note: For data comparability and coverage, see the technical notes. Figures in italics are for years other than those specified.

		Value of imports of manufactures, by origin (millions of dollars)		Composition of 1988 imports of manufactures by high-income OECD countries (percent)[a]				
		1968	1988[a]	Textiles and clothing	Chemicals	Electrical machinery and electronics	Transport equipment	Others
68	Chile	9	335	13	31	1	4	51
69	Syrian Arab Rep.	1	23	32	8	2	3	55
70	Costa Rica	2	421	65	1	11	1	22
71	Mexico	295	18,557	4	5	35	13	43
72	Mauritius	0	635	83	1	0	0	16
73	Poland	222	2,637	22	16	6	11	45
74	Malaysia	28	6,047	16	3	58	0	23
75	Panama[c]	20	794	5	3	1	63	29
76	Brazil	107	11,472	8	9	6	14	63
77	Angola	2	202	0	0	0	0	100
78	Lebanon	18	185	17	2	3	1	78
79	Nicaragua	2	5	5	6	32	2	55
	Upper-middle-income	**2,291 t**	**120,533 t**	**23 w**	**5 w**	**15 w**	**6 w**	**52 w**
80	South Africa[b]	491	3,101	4	15	1	2	78
81	Algeria	13	239	1	21	1	18	60
82	Hungary	119	2,310	24	21	9	3	42
83	Uruguay	14	277	58	2	1	1	39
84	Argentina	86	1,539	11	17	1	2	68
85	Yugoslavia	270	6,699	27	8	9	11	45
86	Gabon	9	115	0	69	1	1	29
87	Venezuela	20	528	2	24	3	7	64
88	Trinidad and Tobago	37	304	1	74	0	0	25
89	Korea, Rep. of	247	42,367	25	2	19	8	46
90	Portugal	336	8,394	40	7	8	6	39
91	Greece	82	3,728	56	4	3	6	31
92	Oman	1	278	0	0	3	34	62
93	Libya	5	280	0	88	1	0	11
94	Iran, Islamic Rep.	107	478	90	1	1	0	8
95	Iraq	4	133	1	9	4	13	73
96	Romania	87	2,150	30	8	3	3	56
	Low- and middle-income	**4,653 t**	**220,913 t**	**26 w**	**5 w**	**15 w**	**6 w**	**48 w**
	Sub-Saharan Africa	**343 t**	**4,412 t**	**16 w**	**14 w**	**1 w**	**14 w**	**55 w**
	East Asia	**925 t**	**127,935 t**	**24 w**	**3 w**	**18 w**	**4 w**	**51 w**
	South Asia	**724 t**	**11,037 t**	**54 w**	**3 w**	**1 w**	**0 w**	**42 w**
	Europe, M.East, & N.Africa	**1,374 t**	**35,947 t**	**41 w**	**10 w**	**7 w**	**6 w**	**36 w**
	Latin America & Caribbean	**795 t**	**38,472 t**	**11 w**	**9 w**	**20 w**	**12 w**	**49 w**
	Severely indebted	**1,038 t**	**44,143 t**	**14 w**	**8 w**	**20 w**	**11 w**	**47 w**
	High-income economies	**85,975 t**	**1,226,247 t**	**6 w**	**13 w**	**11 w**	**19 w**	**51 w**
	OECD members	**84,267 t**	**1,176,481 t**	**5 w**	**13 w**	**11 w**	**20 w**	**51 w**
	†Other	**1,708 t**	**49,766 t**	**22 w**	**6 w**	**18 w**	**2 w**	**51 w**
97	†Saudi Arabia	8	2,095	0	47	1	1	51
98	Spain	470	21,512	5	10	6	27	51
99	Ireland	363	11,618	8	24	12	2	55
100	†Israel	261	6,589	8	14	11	2	64
101	†Singapore	36	13,858	6	5	33	2	54
102	†Hong Kong	1,264	24,141	39	1	16	1	44
103	New Zealand	79	1,447	11	25	6	3	54
104	Australia	368	4,989	3	36	4	6	51
105	United Kingdom	7,988	81,223	6	18	10	11	55
106	Italy	5,646	87,765	17	8	7	10	58
107	†Kuwait	6	164	1	17	7	17	59
108	Belgium[d]	5,255	62,739	9	20	6	20	45
109	Netherlands	3,929	56,100	7	31	8	8	45
110	Austria	1,086	21,553	10	9	13	5	62
111	†United Arab Emirates	0	366	27	22	5	2	44
112	France	6,125	99,708	6	18	9	23	45
113	Canada	6,262	64,535	1	8	6	41	44
114	Denmark	1,024	14,319	8	15	11	5	62
115	Germany, Fed. Rep.	16,278	227,674	5	14	10	21	49
116	Finland	748	13,767	4	8	8	5	75
117	Sweden	2,901	35,210	2	9	9	19	61
118	United States	16,484	161,794	2	12	13	20	53
119	Norway	774	7,394	2	22	7	9	60
120	Japan	5,760	164,334	1	3	19	30	46
121	Switzerland	2,724	38,624	6	21	10	2	61
	Total reporting economies	**90,627 t**	**1,447,161 t**	**9 w**	**12 w**	**12 w**	**17 w**	**50 w**
	Oil exporters	**1,347 t**	**35,670 t**	**8 w**	**13 w**	**20 w**	**10 w**	**49 w**
	Nonreporting nonmembers	**1,025 t**	**8,871 t**	**9 w**	**27 w**	**5 w**	**8 w**	**51 w**

Note: Includes only high-income OECD economies. a. All Australian data refer to 1987. b. Figures are for South Africa, Botswana, and Lesotho. c. Excludes the Canal Zone. d. Includes Luxembourg.

Table 18. Balance of payments and reserves

| | | Current account balance (millions of dollars) | | | | Net workers' remittances (millions of dollars) | | Net direct private investment (millions of dollars) | | Gross international reserves | | In months of import coverage |
| | | After official transfers | | Before official transfers | | | | | | Millions of dollars | | |
		1970	1988	1970	1988	1970	1988	1970	1988	1970	1988	1988
	Low-income economies									**3,673 t**	**47,187 t**	**3.5 w**
	China and India									**1,023 t**	**32,937 t**	**4.6 w**
	Other low-income									**2,650 t**	**14,250 t**	**2.3 w**
1	Mozambique	..	−359[a]	..	−733[a]	..	..	..	0[a]	..	..	..
2	Ethiopia	−32	−389[a]	−43	−510[a]	..	..	4	..	72	171	1.5
3	Chad	2	−17[a]	−33	−252[a]	−6	0[a]	1	0[a]	2	66	1.7
4	Tanzania	−36	−235	−37	−743	..	..	..	..	65	78	0.6
5	Bangladesh	−114[a]	−289	−234[a]	−1,112	0	737	..	0	..	829	2.9
6	Malawi	−35	−53	−46	−134	−4	..	9	0	29	151	3.7
7	Somalia	−6	−107[a]	−18	−349[a]	..	..	5	−11	21	23	0.6
8	Zaire	−64	−693	−141	−888	−98	0	42	11	189	372	1.4
9	Bhutan	..	−68	..	−68	..	..	..	..	..	47	..
10	Lao PDR	..	−92	..	−118	..	..	..	..	6	16	0.9
11	Nepal	−1[a]	−245	−25[a]	−251	..	0	..	0	94	283	4.5
12	Madagascar	10	−127[a]	−42	−261[a]	−26	..	10	0[a]	37	224	3.7
13	Burkina Faso	9	−66[a]	−21	−310[a]	16	215[a]	0	0[a]	36	325	4.6
14	Mali	−2	−104	−22	−350	−1	49	−1	1	1	44	0.7
15	Burundi	2[a]	−62	−2[a]	−163	..	..	0[a]	1	15	76	2.9
16	Uganda	20	−163[a]	19	−289[a]	−5	..	4	1	57	49	0.8
17	Nigeria	−368	−1,024	−412	−1,045	..	−34	205	836	223	933	1.3
18	Zambia	108	−174	107	−234	−48	−21	−297	0	515	139	1.2
19	Niger	0	−94	−32	−248	−3	−45	0	..	19	237	4.7
20	Rwanda	7	−119	−12	−258	−4	−17	0	21	8	118	3.2
21	China*	−81[a]	−3,760	−81[a]	−3,802	0[a]	129	..	2,344	..	23,751	5.0
22	India	−380[a]	−6,870[a]	−590[a]	−7,220[a]	80[a]	2,850[a]	0[a]	280[a]	1,023	9,186	3.8
23	Pakistan	−667	−1,164	−705	−1,685	86	2,018	23	145	195	1,193	1.5
24	Kenya	−49	−454	−86	−711	..	−3	14	7	220	296	1.3
25	Togo	3	−50	−14	−122	−3	13	0	12	35	237	4.5
26	Central African Rep.	−12	−21[a]	−24	−181[a]	−4	29[a]	1	0[a]	1	113	3.9
27	Haiti	11	−53	4	−183	13	64	3	10	4	20	0.5
28	Benin	−3	−105[a]	−23	−177[a]	0	87[a]	7	1[a]	16	9	0.2
29	Ghana	−68	−59[a]	−76	−232[a]	−9	−2	68	5[a]	43	310	2.7
30	Lesotho	18[a]	−73	−1[a]	−130	..	..	..	21	..	56	1.2
31	Sri Lanka	−59	−404	−71	−611	3	357	0	43	43	248	1.1
32	Guinea	..	−209[a]	..	−279[a]	..	..	..	7[a]	..	..	..
33	Yemen, PDR	−4	−383	−4	−436	52	253	−1	..	59	97	1.3
34	Indonesia	−310	−1,189	−376	−1,500	..	99	83	542	160	6,322	3.3
35	Mauritania	−5	−8	−13	−179	−6	−26	1	2	3	77	1.4
36	Sudan	−42	−775[a]	−43	−1,144[a]	..	300[a]	−1	0[a]	22	107	0.6
37	*Afghanistan*	..	26	..	−243	..	..	..	..	49	657	9.1
38	*Myanmar*	−63	−208[a]	−81	−307[a]	..	..	..	..	98	180	2.7
39	*Kampuchea, Dem.*	..	..	..	..	..	..	..	..	..	..	..
40	*Liberia*	−16[a]	−118	−27[a]	−163	−18[a]	−51	28[a]	39	..	0	0.0
41	*Sierra Leone*	−16	−74[a]	−20	−86[a]	..	0	8	39	39	7	0.4
42	*Viet Nam*	..	−1,086	..	−1,099	..	..	..	..	243	..	..
	Middle-income economies									**16,396 t**	**120,433 t**	**2.9 w**
	Lower-middle-income									**7,173 t**	**56,716 t**	**2.4 w**
43	Bolivia	4	−306	2	−429	..	1	−76	30	46	473	5.0
44	Philippines	−48	−406	−138	−694	..	388	−29	986	255	2,169	2.2
45	Yemen Arab Rep.	−34[a]	−695[a]	−52[a]	−785[a]	39[a]	190[a]	..	0[a]	..	285	1.6
46	Senegal	−16	−262	−66	−467	−16	78	5	−73	22	22	0.2
47	Zimbabwe	−14[a]	9[a]	−26[a]	−56[a]	..	..	..	4	59	341	2.2
48	Egypt, Arab Rep.	−148	−1,868[a]	−452	−2,848[a]	29	3,386[a]	..	973[a]	165	2,261	1.8
49	Dominican Rep.	−102	−128	−103	−218	25	328	72	106	32	261	1.4
50	Côte d'Ivoire	−38	−1,278	−73	−1,335	−56	−480	31	..	119	29	0.1
51	Papua New Guinea	−89[a]	−163	−239[a]	−380	..	42	..	89	..	419	2.6
52	Morocco	−124	467	−161	164	27	1,289	20	85	142	836	1.5
53	Honduras	−64	−314	−68	−431	..	..	8	47	20	57	0.5
54	Guatemala	−8	−402	−8	−506	..	0	29	96	79	416	2.6
55	Congo, People's Rep.	−45[a]	67	−53[a]	7	−3[a]	−46	30[a]	43	9	8	0.1
56	El Salvador	9	14[a]	7	−242[a]	..	..	4	−55[a]	64	354	3.0
57	Thailand	−250	−1,671	−296	−1,859	..	..	43	1,093	911	7,112	3.6
58	Botswana	−30[a]	491	−35[a]	309	..	..	6[a]	40	..	2,258	17.7
59	Cameroon	−30	−881[a]	−47	−881[a]	−11	3[a]	16	34[a]	81	163	0.7
60	Jamaica	−153	74	−149	4	29	65	161	−16	139	147	0.8
61	Ecuador	−113	−597	−122	−657	..	..	89	80	76	568	2.1
62	Colombia	−293	−355[a]	−333	−355[a]	6	384[a]	39	186[a]	207	3,700	5.4
63	Paraguay	−16	−150	−19	−173	..	..	4	11	18	338	3.0
64	Tunisia	−53	212	−88	93	20	539	16	59	60	976	2.5
65	Turkey	−44	1,500	−57	1,139	273	1,755	58	352	440	3,912	2.5
66	Peru	202	−1,128	146	−1,285	..	..	−70	44	339	1,213	2.9
67	Jordan	−20	285[a]	−130	−281[a]	..	813[a]	..	0[a]	258	414	1.2
*	Data for Taiwan, China, are:	1[a]	10,177[a]	2[a]	10,174[a]	..	..	61[a]	−3,161[a]	627	79,430	16.0

Note: For data comparability and coverage, see the technical notes. Figures in italics are for years other than those specified.

		Current account balance (millions of dollars)				Net workers' remittances (millions of dollars)		Net direct private investment (millions of dollars)		Gross international reserves		
		After official transfers		Before official transfers						Millions of dollars		In months of import coverage
		1970	1988	1970	1988	1970	1988	1970	1988	1970	1988	1988
68	Chile	−91	−168	−95	−282	..	..	−79	109	392	3,788	5.2
69	Syrian Arab Rep.	−69	−76	−72	−604	7	210	..	0	57	342	1.6
70	Costa Rica	−74	−143	−77	−356	..	0	26	76	16	677	3.9
71	Mexico	−1,068	−2,905	−1,098	−3,068	..	264	323	2,594	756	6,327	2.1
72	Mauritius	8	−45	5	−65	..	0	2	31	46	463	3.6
73	Poland	..	−107	..	−107	..	0	..	−7	..	2,249	1.5
74	Malaysia	8	1,802	2	1,618	..	0	94	649	667	7,491	4.0
75	Panama	−64	737	−79	625	..	..	33	−36	16	72	0.2
76	Brazil	−837	4,448a	−861	4,448a	..	0a	407	2,681a	1,190	1,118	0.4
77	Angola	..	367	..	367	..	..	..	360	..	..	..
78	Lebanon	..	..	..	..	..	..	..	..	405	4,761	..
79	Nicaragua	−40	..	−43	..	..	..	15	..	49	..	..
	Upper-middle-income									9,223 t	63,717 t	3.7 w
80	South Africa	−1,215	1,292	−1,253	1,207	..	..	318	4	1,057	2,204	1.1
81	Algeria	−125	−2,040	−163	−2,040	178	279	45	−48	352	3,191	4.0
82	Hungary	−61	−389a	−61	−389a	..	..	..	..	697	2,521	2.3
83	Uruguay	−45	34	−55	13	..	..	..	−2	186	1,602	10.3
84	Argentina	−163	−1,615	−160	−1,615	..	..	11	1,147	682	5,157	4.7
85	Yugoslavia	−372	2,487	−378	2,487	441	4,893	..	0	143	3,074	2.2
86	Gabon	−3	−616	−15	−627	−8	−151	−1	121	15	71	0.4
87	Venezuela	−104	−4,692	−98	−4,661	−87	−203	−23	89	1,047	7,793	5.4
88	Trinidad and Tobago	−109	−184	−104	−184	3	0	83	26	43	148	1.0
89	Korea, Rep. of	−623	14,161	−706	14,117	..	..	66	720	610	12,478	2.6
90	Portugal	−158a	−601	−158a	−1,320	504a	3,381	15a	820	1,565	11,719	7.1
91	Greece	−422	−958	−424	−2,894	333	1,675	50	907	318	5,012	3.8
92	Oman	..	851	..	844	..	−681	..	33	13	1,173	6.6
93	Libya	645	−2,259	758	−2,222	−134	−496	139	43	1,596	5,798	9.0
94	Iran, Islamic Rep.	−507	..	−511	..	..	..	25	..	217	..	..
95	Iraq	105	..	104	..	..	..	24	..	472	..	..
96	Romania	−23	..	−23	..	..	..	..	..	..	..	..
Low- and middle-income										20,069 t	167,620 t	3.1 w
Sub-Saharan Africa										2,028 t	7,861 t	1.9 w
East Asia										2,885 t	60,151 t	3.6 w
South Asia										1,453 t	11,987 t	3.1 w
Europe, M.East, & N.Africa										7,165 t	50,836 t	3.4 w
Latin America & Caribbean										5,481 t	34,553 t	2.8 w
Severely indebted										6,042 t	36,607 t	2.5 w
High-income economies										75,667 t	842,605 t	3.3 w
OECD members										72,938 t	787,004 t	3.3 w
†Other										2,729 t	55,601 t	3.7 w
97	†Saudi Arabia	71	−9,583	152	−6,283	−183	−4,935	20	−1,175	670	22,438	7.9
98	Spain	79	−3,730	79	−5,220	469	1,413	179	5,788	1,851	42,835	6.9
99	Ireland	−198	625	−228	−1,034	..	..	32	91	698	5,234	2.8
100	†Israel	−562	−678	−766	−4,097	..	..	40	183	452	4,433	2.6
101	†Singapore	−572	1,660	−585	1,683	..	..	93	1,066	1,012	17,073	4.2
102	†Hong Kong	225	1,199	225	1,199	..	..	..	282	..	..	..
103	New Zealand	−232	−780	−222	−704	16	312	137	119	258	2,845	2.7
104	Australia	−777	−11,256	−682	−11,100	..	..	778	−460	1,709	16,853	3.6
105	United Kingdom	1,985	−26,590	2,393	−20,763	..	..	−190	−13,078	2,918	51,899	2.0
106	Italy	800	−5,363	1,096	−2,614	446	1,229	498	1,337	5,547	62,067	4.3
107	†Kuwait	853a	4,713	853a	4,853	..	−1,179	−8a	−262	209	2,965	3.6
108	Belgiumb	717	3,334	904	5,085	38	−30	140	1,365	2,963	23,321	2.1
109	Netherlands	−588	5,282	−617	5,785	−49	−204	−15	2	3,362	34,102	3.2
110	Austria	−75	−642	−73	−569	−7	284	104	294	1,806	16,043	3.7
111	†United Arab Emirates	90a	2,700	100a	2,800	..	..	..	..	..	4,769	5.8
112	France	−204	−3,522	18	875	−641	−1,950	248	−5,986	5,199	58,944	2.9
113	Canada	1,008	−8,258	960	−7,905	..	..	508	−3,306	4,733	22,422	1.8
114	Denmark	−544	−1,819	−510	−1,686	..	..	75	−23	488	11,433	3.3
115	Germany, Fed. Rep.	852	48,499	1,899	60,320	−1,366	−4,188	−303	−8,722	13,879	97,576	3.6
116	Finland	−239	−3,006	−232	−2,578	..	..	−41	−1,752	455	7,171	2.8
117	Sweden	−265	−2,567	−160	−1,424	..	−10	−104	−4,406	775	10,982	2.1
118	United States	2,330	−126,620	4,680	−113,740	−650	−820	−6,130	40,920	15,237	144,177	2.7
119	Norway	−242	−3,671	−200	−2,858	..	−50	32	−23	813	13,753	4.3
120	Japan	1,980	79,590	2,160	82,610	..	..	−260	−34,710	4,876	106,668	4.4
121	Switzerland	72	8,326	114	8,311	−313	−1,549	..	−6,913	5,317	58,367	7.9
Total reporting economies										95,736 t	1,010,225 t	3.3 w
Oil exporters										7,082 t	81,171 t	3.4 w
Nonreporting nonmembers										..	..	..

a. World Bank estimate.   b. Includes Luxembourg.

Table 19. Official development assistance from OECD & OPEC members

		1965	1970	1975	1980	1984	1985	1986	1987	1988	1989[a]
OECD						Millions of U.S. dollars					
99	Ireland	0	0	8	30	35	39	62	51	57	47
103	New Zealand	..	14	66	72	55	54	75	87	104	87
104	Australia	119	212	552	667	777	749	752	627	1,101	1,017
105	United Kingdom	472	500	904	1,854	1,429	1,530	1,737	1,871	2,645	2,588
106	Italy	60	147	182	683	1,133	1,098	2,404	2,615	3,193	..
108	Belgium	102	120	378	595	446	440	547	687	597	
109	Netherlands	70	196	608	1,630	1,268	1,136	1,740	2,094	2,231	2,089
110	Austria	10	11	79	178	181	248	198	201	301	279
112	France	752	971	2,093	4,162	3,788	3,995	5,105	6,525	6,865	..
113	Canada	96	337	880	1,075	1,625	1,631	1,695	1,885	2,347	..
114	Denmark	13	59	205	481	449	440	695	859	922	926
115	Germany, Fed. Rep.	456	599	1,689	3,567	2,782	2,942	3,832	4,391	4,731	4,953
116	Finland	2	7	48	110	178	211	313	433	608	705
117	Sweden	38	117	566	962	741	840	1,090	1,375	1,590	1,813
118	United States	4,023	3,153	4,161	7,138	8,711	9,403	9,564	9,115	10,141	..
119	Norway	11	37	184	486	540	574	798	890	985	919
120	Japan	244	458	1,148	3,353	4,319	3,797	5,634	7,342	9,134	..
121	Switzerland	12	30	104	253	285	302	422	547	617	559
	Total	6,480	6,968	13,855	27,296	28,742	29,429	36,663	41,595	48,167	..
OECD						As a percentage of donor GNP					
99	Ireland	0.00	0.00	0.09	0.16	0.22	0.24	0.28	0.19	0.20	0.17
103	New Zealand	..	0.23	0.52	0.33	0.25	0.25	0.30	0.26	0.27	0.22
104	Australia	0.53	0.59	0.65	0.48	0.45	0.48	0.47	0.34	0.46	0.37
105	United Kingdom	0.47	0.41	0.39	0.35	0.33	0.33	0.31	0.28	0.32	0.31
106	Italy	0.10	0.16	0.11	0.15	0.28	0.26	0.40	0.35	0.39	..
108	Belgium	0.60	0.46	0.59	0.50	0.58	0.55	0.48	0.48	0.40	..
109	Netherlands	0.36	0.61	0.75	0.97	1.02	0.91	1.01	0.98	0.98	0.93
110	Austria	0.11	0.07	0.21	0.23	0.28	0.38	0.21	0.17	0.24	0.22
112	France	0.76	0.66	0.62	0.63	0.77	0.78	0.70	0.74	0.72	..
113	Canada	0.19	0.41	0.54	0.43	0.50	0.49	0.48	0.47	0.50	..
114	Denmark	0.13	0.38	0.58	0.74	0.85	0.80	0.89	0.88	0.89	0.93
115	Germany, Fed. Rep.	0.40	0.32	0.40	0.44	0.45	0.47	0.43	0.39	0.39	0.41
116	Finland	0.02	0.06	0.18	0.22	0.35	0.40	0.45	0.49	0.59	0.63
117	Sweden	0.19	0.38	0.82	0.78	0.80	0.86	0.85	0.88	0.89	0.98
118	United States	0.58	0.32	0.27	0.27	0.24	0.24	0.23	0.20	0.21	..
119	Norway	0.16	0.32	0.66	0.87	1.03	1.01	1.17	1.09	1.10	1.02
120	Japan	0.27	0.23	0.23	0.32	0.34	0.29	0.29	0.31	0.32	..
121	Switzerland	0.09	0.15	0.19	0.24	0.30	0.31	0.30	0.31	0.32	0.30
OECD						National currencies					
99	Ireland (millions of pounds)	0	0	4	15	32	37	46	34	37	35
103	New Zealand (millions of dollars)	..	13	55	74	95	109	143	146	158	145
104	Australia (millions of dollars)	106	189	402	591	873	966	1,121	895	1,404	1,283
105	United Kingdom (millions of pounds)	169	208	409	798	1,070	1,180	1,194	1,142	1,485	1,578
106	Italy (billions of lire)	38	92	119	585	1,991	2,097	3,578	3,389	4,156	..
108	Belgium (millions of francs)	5,100	6,000	13,902	17,399	25,527	26,145	24,525	25,648	21,949	..
109	Netherlands (millions of guilders)	253	710	1,538	3,241	4,069	3,773	4,263	4,242	4,400	4,430
110	Austria (millions of schillings)	260	286	1,376	2,303	3,622	5,132	3,023	2,541	3,717	3,691
112	France (millions of francs)	3,713	5,393	8,971	17,589	33,107	35,894	35,357	39,218	40,814	..
113	Canada (millions of dollars)	104	353	895	1,257	2,104	2,227	2,354	2,500	2,888	..
114	Denmark (millions of kroner)	90	443	1,178	2,711	4,650	4,657	5,623	5,848	6,196	6,769
115	Germany, Fed. Rep. (millions of deutsche marks)	1,824	2,192	4,155	6,484	7,917	8,661	8,323	8,004	8,292	9,318
116	Finland (millions of markkaa)	6	29	177	414	1,070	1,308	1,587	1,902	2,550	3,025
117	Sweden (millions of kronor)	197	605	2,350	4,069	6,129	7,226	7,765	8,718	9,742	11,688
118	United States (millions of dollars)	4,023	3,153	4,161	7,138	8,711	9,403	9,564	9,115	10,141	..
119	Norway (millions of kroner)	79	264	962	2,400	4,407	4,946	5,901	5,998	6,412	6,345
120	Japan (billions of yen)	88	165	341	760	1,026	749	950	1,062	1,169	..
121	Switzerland (millions of francs)	52	131	268	424	672	743	759	815	900	914
OECD						Summary					
	ODA (billions of U.S. dollars, nominal prices)	6.48	6.97	13.86	27.30	28.74	29.43	36.66	41.59	48.17	..
	ODA as a percentage of GNP	0.48	0.34	0.35	0.37	0.36	0.35	0.35	0.35	0.36	..
	ODA (billions of U.S. dollars, constant 1980 prices)	20.68	18.83	21.85	27.30	28.74	29.14	30.55	30.81	33.22	..
	GNP (trillions of U.S. dollars, nominal prices)	1.35	2.04	3.96	7.39	8.03	8.49	10.39	12.05	13.48	..
	GDP deflator[b]	0.31	0.37	0.63	1.00	1.00	1.01	1.20	1.35	1.45	1.44

						Amount					
		1976	1979	1980	1982	1983	1984	1985	1986	1987	1988
OPEC						Millions of U.S. dollars					
17	Nigeria	80	29	35	58	35	51	45	52	30	14
81	Algeria	11	281	81	129	37	52	54	114	39	13
87	Venezuela	109	110	135	125	142	90	32	85	24	49
93	Libya	98	145	376	44	144	24	57	68	63	129
94	Iran, Islamic Rep.	751	−20	−72	−193	10	52	−72	69	−10	39
95	Iraq	123	658	864	52	−10	−22	−32	−21	−37	−28
97	Saudi Arabia	2,791	3,941	5,682	3,854	3,259	3,194	2,630	3,517	2,888	2,098
107	Kuwait	706	971	1,140	1,161	997	1,020	771	715	316	108
111	United Arab Emirates	1,028	968	1,118	406	351	88	122	87	15	−17
	Qatar	180	282	277	139	20	10	8	18	0	4
	Total OAPEC	4,937	7,246	9,538	5,785	4,798	4,366	3,610	4,498	3,284	2,307
	Total OPEC	5,877	7,365	9,636	5,775	4,985	4,559	3,615	4,704	3,328	2,409
OPEC						As a percentage of donor GNP					
17	Nigeria	0.19	0.04	0.04	0.08	0.04	0.06	0.06	0.11	0.13	0.03
81	Algeria	0.07	0.90	0.20	0.31	0.08	0.10	0.10	0.19	0.06	0.02
87	Venezuela	0.35	0.23	0.23	0.19	0.22	0.16	0.00	0.08	0.02	0.04
93	Libya	0.66	0.60	1.16	0.15	0.51	0.10	0.24	0.34	0.25	0.52
94	Iran, Islamic Rep.	1.16	−0.02	−0.08	−0.15	0.01	0.03	−0.04	0.04	−0.01	0.02
95	Iraq	0.76	1.97	2.36	0.13	−0.02	−0.05	−0.07	−0.05	−0.08	−0.05
97	Saudi Arabia	5.95	5.16	4.87	2.50	2.69	3.20	2.98	4.67	3.88	2.70
107	Kuwait	4.82	3.52	3.52	4.34	3.83	3.95	3.17	2.91	1.23	0.41
111	United Arab Emirates	8.95	5.08	4.21	1.39	1.26	0.32	0.45	0.41	0.07	−0.07
	Qatar	7.35	6.07	4.16	2.22	0.40	0.18	0.15	0.47	0.00	0.08
	Total OAPEC	4.23	3.31	3.22	1.81	1.70	1.60	1.39	1.80	1.10	0.86
	Total OPEC	2.32	1.75	1.85	0.96	0.82	0.76	0.61	0.95	0.63	0.45

						Net bilateral flows to low-income economies					
		1965	1970	1975	1980	1983	1984	1985	1986	1987	1988
OECD						As a percentage of donor GNP					
99	Ireland	. .	. .	. .	. .	0.03	0.03	0.05	0.06	0.07	−0.07
103	New Zealand	. .	. .	0.14	0.01	0.00	0.00	0.00	0.00	0.06	0.03
104	Australia	0.08	0.09	0.10	0.04	0.05	0.06	0.05	0.04	0.05	0.11
105	United Kingdom	0.23	0.15	0.11	0.11	0.10	0.09	0.09	0.09	0.09	0.10
106	Italy	0.04	0.06	0.01	0.01	0.05	0.09	0.12	0.16	0.16	0.16
108	Belgium	0.56	0.30	0.31	0.24	0.21	0.20	0.23	0.20	0.14	0.10
109	Netherlands	0.08	0.24	0.24	0.30	0.26	0.29	0.27	0.32	0.31	0.31
110	Austria	0.06	0.05	0.02	0.03	0.02	0.01	0.02	0.01	0.04	−0.04
112	France	0.12	0.09	0.10	0.08	0.09	0.14	0.14	0.13	0.14	0.14
113	Canada	0.10	0.22	0.24	0.11	0.13	0.15	0.15	0.12	0.14	0.14
114	Denmark	0.02	0.10	0.20	0.28	0.31	0.28	0.32	0.32	0.32	0.36
115	Germany, Fed. Rep.	0.14	0.10	0.12	0.08	0.13	0.11	0.14	0.12	0.11	0.11
116	Finland	. .	. .	0.06	0.08	0.12	0.13	0.17	0.18	0.18	0.23
117	Sweden	0.07	0.12	0.41	0.36	0.33	0.30	0.31	0.38	0.29	0.31
118	United States	0.26	0.14	0.08	0.03	0.03	0.03	0.04	0.03	0.03	0.04
119	Norway	0.04	0.12	0.25	0.31	0.39	0.34	0.40	0.47	0.38	0.42
120	Japan	0.13	0.11	0.08	0.08	0.09	0.07	0.09	0.10	0.07	0.07
121	Switzerland	0.02	0.05	0.10	0.08	0.10	0.12	0.12	0.12	0.10	0.10
	Total	0.20	0.13	0.11	0.07	0.08	0.07	0.09	0.09	0.09	0.09

a. Preliminary estimates.   b. See the technical notes.

Table 20. Official development assistance: receipts

		Net disbursement of ODA from all sources							Per capita (dollars)	As a percentage of GNP
		Millions of dollars								
		1982	1983	1984	1985	1986	1987	1988	1988	1988
	Low-income economies	12,969 t	12,443 t	12,500 t	13,946 t	16,853 t	18,591 t	21,912 t	7.6 w	2.4 w
	China and India	2,168 t	2,509 t	2,471 t	2,532 t	3,254 t	3,300 t	4,087 t	2.1 w	0.6 w
	Other low-income	10,801 t	9,934 t	10,029 t	11,414 t	13,599 t	15,291 t	17,825 t	18.2 w	6.6 w
1	Mozambique	208	211	259	300	422	651	886	59.3	70.6
2	Ethiopia	200	339	364	715	636	634	970	20.5	17.4
3	Chad	65	95	115	182	165	198	264	48.9	28.8
4	Tanzania	684	594	558	487	681	882	978	39.6	31.2
5	Bangladesh	1,341	1,049	1,200	1,152	1,455	1,635	1,592	14.6	8.2
6	Malawi	121	117	158	113	198	280	366	46.0	30.6
7	Somalia	462	343	350	353	511	580	433	73.4	42.9
8	Zaire	348	315	312	325	448	627	580	17.4	9.0
9	Bhutan	11	13	18	24	40	42	42	30.3	14.0
10	Lao PDR	38	30	34	37	48	58	77	19.6	14.4
11	Nepal	200	201	198	236	301	347	399	22.2	13.0
12	Madagascar	242	183	153	188	316	321	305	28.0	16.2
13	Burkina Faso	213	184	189	198	284	281	298	34.9	16.0
14	Mali	210	215	321	380	372	366	427	53.5	22.0
15	Burundi	127	140	141	142	187	202	187	36.5	17.1
16	Uganda	133	137	163	182	198	279	359	22.1	8.4
17	Nigeria	37	48	33	32	59	69	120	1.1	0.4
18	Zambia	317	217	239	328	464	430	478	63.3	12.0
19	Niger	257	175	161	304	307	353	371	51.1	15.5
20	Rwanda	151	150	165	181	211	245	253	38.0	11.0
21	China	524	669	798	940	1,134	1,462	1,990	1.8	0.5
22	India	1,644	1,840	1,673	1,592	2,120	1,839	2,098	2.6	0.8
23	Pakistan	916	735	749	801	970	879	1,408	13.3	3.7
24	Kenya	485	400	411	438	455	572	808	36.0	9.4
25	Togo	77	112	110	114	174	126	199	58.9	14.7
26	Central African Rep.	90	93	114	104	139	176	196	68.4	17.5
27	Haiti	128	134	135	153	175	218	147	23.5	5.9
28	Benin	81	86	77	95	138	138	162	36.3	9.0
29	Ghana	141	110	216	203	371	373	474	33.9	9.1
30	Lesotho	93	108	101	94	88	107	108	64.4	26.3
31	Sri Lanka	416	473	466	484	570	502	599	36.1	8.5
32	Guinea	90	68	123	119	175	213	262	48.5	10.3
33	Yemen, PDR	143	106	103	113	71	74	76	32.3	7.2
34	Indonesia	906	744	673	603	711	1,246	1,632	9.3	2.1
35	Mauritania	187	176	175	209	225	182	184	96.6	18.4
36	Sudan	740	962	622	1,128	945	898	918	38.6	7.8
37	*Afghanistan*	9	14	7	17	2	45	72	..	..
38	*Myanmar*	319	302	275	356	416	367	451	11.3	..
39	*Kampuchea, Dem.*	44	37	17	13	13	14	18	..	..
40	*Liberia*	109	118	133	90	97	78	65	26.8	..
41	*Sierra Leone*	82	66	61	66	87	68	102	26.0	..
42	*Viet Nam*	136	106	109	114	147	111	148	2.3	..
	Middle-income economies	10,621 t	9,998 t	10,352 t	10,538 t	11,741 t	12,851 t	11,931 t	12.4 w	0.7 w
	Lower-middle-income	9,969 t	9,473 t	9,869 t	9,947 t	10,981 t	12,000 t	11,089 t	15.8 w	1.0 w
43	Bolivia	148	174	172	202	322	318	392	56.7	9.1
44	Philippines	333	429	397	486	956	770	854	14.3	2.2
45	Yemen Arab Rep.	412	328	326	283	257	348	223	26.3	3.8
46	Senegal	285	323	368	295	567	641	568	81.2	11.4
47	Zimbabwe	216	208	298	237	225	294	273	29.3	4.3
48	Egypt, Arab Rep.	1,441	1,463	1,794	1,791	1,716	1,773	1,537	30.6	4.3
49	Dominican Rep.	136	100	188	207	93	130	118	17.1	2.5
50	Côte d'Ivoire	137	156	128	125	186	254	439	39.1	4.5
51	Papua New Guinea	311	333	322	259	263	322	379	101.9	10.8
52	Morocco	774	398	352	785	403	447	482	20.1	2.2
53	Honduras	158	190	286	272	283	258	321	66.4	7.3
54	Guatemala	64	76	65	83	135	241	235	27.0	2.9
55	Congo, People's Rep.	93	108	98	71	110	152	89	41.5	4.1
56	El Salvador	218	290	261	345	341	426	420	83.4	7.7
57	Thailand	389	431	475	481	496	504	563	10.3	1.0
58	Botswana	101	104	102	96	102	156	151	127.7	7.8
59	Cameroon	212	129	186	159	224	213	284	25.4	2.2
60	Jamaica	180	181	170	169	178	168	193	80.3	6.0
61	Ecuador	53	64	136	136	147	203	137	13.6	1.3
62	Colombia	97	86	88	62	63	78	61	1.9	0.2
63	Paraguay	85	51	50	50	66	81	76	18.7	1.3
64	Tunisia	210	205	178	163	222	274	316	40.5	3.2
65	Turkey	647	356	242	179	339	376	307	5.7	0.4
66	Peru	188	297	310	316	272	292	272	13.2	1.1
67	Jordan	798	787	687	538	564	579	425	108.8	9.3

Note: For data comparability and coverage, see the technical notes. Figures in italics are for years other than those specified.

		Net disbursement of ODA from all sources							Per capita (dollars)	As a percentage of GNP
		Millions of dollars							1988	1988
		1982	1983	1984	1985	1986	1987	1988		
68	Chile	−8	0	2	40	−5	21	44	3.4	0.2
69	Syrian Arab Rep.	962	813	641	610	728	684	191	16.4	1.3
70	Costa Rica	80	252	218	280	196	228	187	69.9	4.0
71	Mexico	140	132	83	144	252	155	173	2.1	0.1
72	Mauritius	48	41	36	28	56	65	59	56.4	3.0
73	Poland	..	..	..	..	..	..	..	..	..
74	Malaysia	135	177	327	229	192	363	104	6.1	0.3
75	Panama	41	47	72	69	52	40	22	9.3	..
76	Brazil	208	101	161	123	178	289	210	1.5	0.1
77	*Angola*	60	75	95	92	131	135	159	16.8	..
78	*Lebanon*	187	127	77	83	62	101	141	..	..
79	*Nicaragua*	121	120	114	102	150	141	213	58.8	..
	Upper-middle-income	**652** *t*	**525** *t*	**483** *t*	**591** *t*	**760** *t*	**852** *t*	**841** *t*	**3.3** *w*	**0.1** *w*
80	South Africa	..	..	..	..	..	..	..	..	..
81	Algeria	136	95	122	173	165	214	171	7.2	0.3
82	Hungary	..	..	..	..	..	..	..	..	..
83	Uruguay	4	3	4	5	27	18	41	13.4	0.5
84	Argentina	30	48	49	39	88	99	152	4.8	0.2
85	Yugoslavia	−8	3	3	11	19	35	44	1.9	0.1
86	Gabon	62	64	76	61	79	82	106	98.3	3.2
87	Venezuela	13	10	14	11	16	19	18	0.9	0.0
88	Trinidad and Tobago	6	5	5	7	19	34	8	6.8	0.2
89	Korea, Rep. of	34	8	−37	−9	−18	11	10	0.2	0.0
90	Portugal	49	43	97	101	139	64	102	9.9	0.2
91	Greece	12	13	13	11	19	35	35	3.5	0.1
92	Oman	133	71	67	78	84	16	1	0.4	..
93	Libya	12	6	5	5	11	6	6	1.3	..
94	*Iran, Islamic Rep.*	3	48	13	16	27	71	82	1.7	..
95	*Iraq*	6	13	4	26	33	91	10	0.6	..
96	*Romania*	..	..	..	..	..	..	..	..	..
	Low- and middle-income	**23,589** *t*	**22,442** *t*	**22,852** *t*	**24,484** *t*	**28,594** *t*	**31,442** *t*	**33,842** *t*	**8.8** *w*	**1.3** *w*
	Sub-Saharan Africa	7,496 *t*	7,305 *t*	7,595 *t*	8,616 *t*	10,572 *t*	11,902 *t*	13,416 *t*	28.9 *w*	8.8 *w*
	East Asia	2,989 *t*	3,121 *t*	3,243 *t*	3,262 *t*	4,080 *t*	5,071 *t*	5,985 *t*	3.9 *w*	0.7 *w*
	South Asia	4,852 *t*	4,623 *t*	4,585 *t*	4,655 *t*	5,888 *t*	5,630 *t*	6,616 *t*	6.0 *w*	1.9 *w*
	Europe, M.East, & N.Africa	5,953 *t*	4,930 *t*	4,738 *t*	4,999 *t*	4,867 *t*	5,233 *t*	4,217 *t*	13.3 *w*	1.1 *w*
	Latin America & Caribbean	2,295 *t*	2,460 *t*	2,689 *t*	2,949 *t*	3,181 *t*	3,601 *t*	3,600 *t*	8.7 *w*	0.4 *w*
	Severely indebted	**2,757** *t*	**2,803** *t*	**2,891** *t*	**3,430** *t*	**4,145** *t*	**4,305** *t*	**4,590** *t*	**10.3** *w*	**0.5** *w*
	High-income economies	..	..	..	..	..	..	..	..	..
	OECD members	..	..	..	..	..	..	..	..	..
	†Other	1,477 *t*	2,084 *t*	1,948 *t*	2,553 *t*	2,711 *t*	2,124 *t*	1,993 *t*	62.5 *w*	0.5 *w*
97	†Saudi Arabia	57	44	36	29	31	22	19	1.5	0.0
98	Spain									
99	Ireland									
100	†Israel	857	1,345	1,256	1,978	1,937	1,251	1,241	279.3	2.8
101	†Singapore	20	15	41	24	29	23	22	8.2	0.1
102	†Hong Kong	8	9	14	20	18	19	22	3.9	0.0
103	New Zealand									
104	Australia									
105	United Kingdom									
106	Italy									
107	†Kuwait	6	5	4	4	5	3	6	3.0	0.0
108	Belgium									
109	Netherlands									
110	Austria									
111	†United Arab Emirates	5	4	3	4	34	115	−12	−8.0	−0.1
112	France									
113	Canada									
114	Denmark									
115	Germany, Fed. Rep.									
116	Finland									
117	Sweden									
118	United States									
119	Norway									
120	Japan									
121	Switzerland									
	Total reporting economies	**25,067** *t*	**24,525** *t*	**24,800** *t*	**27,037** *t*	**31,304** *t*	**33,566** *t*	**35,836** *t*	**9.2** *w*	**1.2** *w*
	Oil exporters	4,376 *t*	4,084 *t*	4,192 *t*	4,036 *t*	4,556 *t*	5,176 *t*	4,580 *t*	7.8 *w*	0.7 *w*
	Nonreporting nonmembers	**16** *t*	**13** *t*	**12** *t*	**24** *t*	**33** *t*	**46** *t*	**42** *t*	**1.3** *w*	..

Table 21. Total external debt

		Long-term debt (millions of dollars)				Use of IMF credit (millions of dollars)		Short-term debt (millions of dollars)		Total external debt (millions of dollars)	
		Public and publicly guaranteed		Private nonguaranteed							
		1970	1988	1970	1988	1970	1988	1970	1988	1970	1988
	Low-income economies										
	China and India										
	Other low-income										
1	Mozambique	..	3,801	0	238	0	41	..	326	..	4,406
2	Ethiopia	169	2,790	0	0	0	55	..	133	..	2,978
3	Chad	33	300	0	0	3	17	..	29	..	346
4	Tanzania	250	4,091	15	9	0	69	..	560	..	4,729
5	Bangladesh	0	9,330	0	0	0	840	..	50	..	10,219
6	Malawi	122	1,190	0	3	0	106	..	51	..	1,349
7	Somalia	77	1,754	0	0	0	165	..	116	..	2,035
8	Zaire	311	7,013	0	0	0	786	..	675	..	8,475
9	Bhutan	..	68	0	0	0	0	..	0	..	68
10	Lao PDR	8	816	0	0	0	3	..	6	..	824
11	Nepal	3	1,088	0	0	0	53	..	23	..	1,164
12	Madagascar	89	3,317	0	0	0	190	..	95	..	3,602
13	Burkina Faso	21	805	0	0	0	3	..	59	..	866
14	Mali	238	1,928	0	0	9	74	..	65	..	2,067
15	Burundi	7	749	0	0	8	33	..	12	..	794
16	Uganda	138	1,438	0	0	0	252	..	235	..	1,925
17	Nigeria	452	28,630	115	337	0	0	..	1,752	..	30,718
18	Zambia	624	4,194	30	0	0	940	..	1,364	..	6,498
19	Niger	32	1,286	0	256	0	95	..	105	..	1,742
20	Rwanda	2	585	0	0	3	4	..	44	..	632
21	China	..	32,196	0	0	0	1,013	..	8,806	..	42,015
22	India	7,838	49,695	100	1,473	0	2,573	..	3,772	..	57,513
23	Pakistan	3,064	13,944	5	84	45	557	..	2,425	..	17,010
24	Kenya	319	4,241	88	627	0	455	..	564	..	5,888
25	Togo	40	1,067	0	0	0	78	..	66	..	1,210
26	Central African Rep.	24	584	0	0	0	50	..	39	..	673
27	Haiti	40	683	0	0	3	47	..	92	..	823
28	Benin	41	904	0	0	0	4	..	147	..	1,055
29	Ghana	488	2,238	10	32	46	762	..	67	..	3,099
30	Lesotho	8	270	0	0	0	5	..	6	..	281
31	Sri Lanka	317	4,139	0	113	79	359	..	577	..	5,189
32	Guinea	312	2,312	0	0	3	61	..	190	..	2,563
33	Yemen, PDR	1	1,970	0	0	0	6	..	118	..	2,093
34	Indonesia	2,453	41,258	461	4,397	139	623	..	6,322	..	52,600
35	Mauritania	27	1,823	0	0	0	71	..	183	..	2,076
36	Sudan	298	8,044	0	374	31	905	..	2,530	..	11,853
37	*Afghanistan*	..	..	..	..	..	..	..	..	..	..
38	*Myanmar*	106	4,217	0	0	17	8	..	96	..	4,321
39	*Kampuchea, Dem.*	..	..	..	..	..	..	..	..	..	..
40	*Liberia*	158	1,101	0	0	4	309	..	222	..	1,632
41	*Sierra Leone*	59	510	0	0	0	109	..	108	..	727
42	*Viet Nam*	..	..	..	..	..	..	..	..	..	..
	Middle-income economies										
	Lower-middle-income										
43	Bolivia	480	4,451	11	200	6	197	..	607	..	5,456
44	Philippines	625	23,475	919	992	69	1,093	..	3,888	..	29,448
45	Yemen Arab Rep.	..	2,378	0	0	0	0	..	570	..	2,948
46	Senegal	100	2,985	31	34	0	318	..	280	..	3,617
47	Zimbabwe	229	2,231	0	50	0	70	..	308	..	2,659
48	Egypt, Arab Rep.	1,714	42,128	0	1,131	49	190	..	6,522	..	49,970
49	Dominican Rep.	212	3,216	141	118	7	218	..	372	..	3,923
50	Côte d'Ivoire	256	8,088	11	3,700	0	509	..	1,828	..	14,125
51	Papua New Guinea	36	1,269	173	860	0	6	..	135	..	2,270
52	Morocco	712	18,567	15	200	28	956	..	200	..	19,923
53	Honduras	90	2,739	19	98	0	37	..	444	..	3,318
54	Guatemala	106	2,131	14	113	0	88	..	301	..	2,633
55	Congo, People's Rep.	124	4,098	0	0	0	15	..	650	..	4,763
56	El Salvador	88	1,630	88	55	7	11	..	110	..	1,806
57	Thailand	324	13,375	402	3,530	0	662	..	2,964	..	20,530
58	Botswana	17	494	0	0	0	0	..	5	..	499
59	Cameroon	131	2,939	9	427	0	100	..	763	..	4,229
60	Jamaica	160	3,512	822	43	0	483	..	267	..	4,304
61	Ecuador	193	9,353	49	25	14	405	..	1,082	..	10,864
62	Colombia	1,297	13,853	283	1,538	55	0	..	1,609	..	17,001
63	Paraguay	112	2,091	0	28	0	0	..	375	..	2,493
64	Tunisia	541	5,886	..	235	13	277	..	275	..	6,672
65	Turkey	1,844	31,054	42	535	74	299	..	7,704	..	39,592
66	Peru	856	12,475	1,799	1,423	10	801	..	3,880	..	18,579
67	Jordan	119	3,955	0	0	0	48	..	1,529	..	5,532

Note: For data comparability and coverage, see the technical notes. Figures in italics are for years other than those specified.

| | | Long-term debt (millions of dollars) | | | | Use of IMF credit (millions of dollars) | | Short-term debt (millions of dollars) | | Total external debt (millions of dollars) | |
| | | Public and publicly guaranteed | | Private nonguaranteed | | | | | | | |
		1970	1988	1970	1988	1970	1988	1970	1988	1970	1988
68	Chile	2,067	13,760	501	2,361	2	1,322	..	2,202	..	19,645
69	Syrian Arab Rep.	233	3,685	0	0	10	0	..	1,205	..	4,890
70	Costa Rica	134	3,531	112	317	0	71	..	611	..	4,530
71	Mexico	3,196	81,207	2,770	7,458	0	4,805	..	8,097	..	101,567
72	Mauritius	32	652	0	57	0	103	..	49	..	861
73	Poland	..	33,661	0	0	0	0	..	8,476	..	42,137
74	Malaysia	390	16,101	50	2,340	0	0	..	2,100	..	20,541
75	Panama	194	3,625	0	0	0	328	..	1,667	..	5,620
76	Brazil	3,421	89,841	1,706	11,514	0	3,333	..	9,903	..	114,592
77	*Angola*	..	..	..	..	..	..	..	..	..	..
78	*Lebanon*	64	229	0	0	0	0	..	270	..	499
79	*Nicaragua*	147	6,744	0	0	8	0	..	1,308	..	8,052
Upper-middle-income											
80	South Africa	..	..	..	..	..	..	..	1,621	..	24,850
81	Algeria	945	23,229	0	0	0	0	..	1,621	..	24,850
82	Hungary	..	14,791	0	0	0	634	..	2,136	..	17,561
83	Uruguay	269	2,953	29	86	18	309	..	477	..	3,825
84	Argentina	1,880	48,166	3,291	1,378	0	3,678	..	5,714	..	58,936
85	Yugoslavia	1,199	13,949	854	5,392	0	1,310	..	1,033	..	21,684
86	Gabon	91	2,128	0	0	0	133	..	402	..	2,663
87	Venezuela	718	25,413	236	4,883	0	0	..	4,361	..	34,657
88	Trinidad and Tobago	101	1,718	0	0	0	115	..	163	..	1,995
89	Korea, Rep. of	1,816	21,349	175	6,027	0	0	..	9,780	..	37,156
90	Portugal	485	13,950	268	615	0	0	..	2,603	..	17,168
91	Greece	905	17,482	388	1,315	0	0	..	4,717	..	23,514
92	Oman	..	2,488	0	0	0	0	..	452	..	2,940
93	Libya	..	..	..	..	..	..	..	..	..	..
94	*Iran, Islamic Rep.*	..	..	..	..	..	..	..	..	..	..
95	*Iraq*	..	..	..	..	..	..	..	..	..	..
96	*Romania*	..	1,946	0	0	0	144	..	700	..	2,790

Low- and middle-income
  Sub-Saharan Africa
  East Asia
  South Asia
  Europe, M.East, & N.Africa
  Latin America & Caribbean

Severely indebted

High-income economies
  OECD members
  †Other

97 †Saudi Arabia
98 Spain
99 Ireland
100 †Israel
101 †Singapore

102 †Hong Kong
103 New Zealand
104 Australia
105 United Kingdom
106 Italy

107 †Kuwait
108 Belgium
109 Netherlands
110 Austria
111 †United Arab Emirates

112 France
113 Canada
114 Denmark
115 Germany, Fed. Rep.
116 Finland

117 Sweden
118 United States
119 Norway
120 Japan
121 Switzerland

Total reporting economies
  Oil exporters

Nonreporting nonmembers

Table 22. Flow of public and private external capital

	Disbursements (millions of dollars)				Repayment of principal (millions of dollars)				Net flow[a] (millions of dollars)			
	Public and publicly guaranteed		Private nonguaranteed		Public and publicly guaranteed		Private nonguaranteed		Public and publicly guaranteed		Private nonguaranteed	
	1970	1988	1970	1988	1970	1988	1970	1988	1970	1988	1970	1988
Low-income economies												
China and India												
Other low-income												
1 Mozambique	..	146	0	14	..	8	0	4	..	138	0	10
2 Ethiopia	28	465	0	0	15	160	0	0	13	305	0	0
3 Chad	6	59	0	0	3	2	0	0	3	57	0	0
4 Tanzania	51	191	8	0	10	45	3	1	40	146	5	−1
5 Bangladesh	0	890	0	0	0	177	0	0	0	714	0	0
6 Malawi	40	116	0	9	3	29	0	6	37	86	0	3
7 Somalia	4	47	0	0	1	1	0	0	4	46	0	0
8 Zaire	32	328	0	0	28	67	0	0	3	261	0	0
9 Bhutan	..	30	0	0	..	1	0	0	..	30	0	0
10 Lao PDR	6	119	0	0	1	7	0	0	4	112	0	0
11 Nepal	1	202	0	0	2	18	0	0	−2	184	0	0
12 Madagascar	11	230	0	0	5	80	0	0	5	150	0	0
13 Burkina Faso	2	92	0	0	2	22	0	0	0	69	0	0
14 Mali	23	154	0	0	0	32	0	0	23	122	0	0
15 Burundi	1	99	0	0	0	19	0	0	1	80	0	0
16 Uganda	27	212	0	0	4	23	0	0	23	189	0	0
17 Nigeria	56	693	25	83	38	483	30	90	18	209	−5	−7
18 Zambia	351	130	23	0	35	115	13	0	316	16	10	0
19 Niger	12	150	0	28	2	31	0	26	11	119	0	2
20 Rwanda	0	82	0	0	0	9	0	0	0	73	0	0
21 China	..	8,868	0	0	..	2,097	0	0	..	6,771	0	0
22 India	883	5,945	25	272	289	1,677	25	440	594	4,269	0	−168
23 Pakistan	489	1,622	3	55	114	828	1	26	375	794	2	29
24 Kenya	35	291	41	196	17	216	12	65	17	75	30	131
25 Togo	5	73	0	0	2	23	0	0	3	50	0	0
26 Central African Rep.	2	84	0	0	2	4	0	0	−1	79	0	0
27 Haiti	4	46	0	0	3	15	0	0	1	31	0	0
28 Benin	2	51	0	0	1	10	0	0	1	41	0	0
29 Ghana	42	344	0	9	14	134	0	7	28	210	0	2
30 Lesotho	0	51	0	0	0	16	0	0	0	36	0	0
31 Sri Lanka	66	402	..	0	30	200	..	6	36	202	..	−6
32 Guinea	90	308	0	0	11	112	0	0	80	197	0	0
33 Yemen, PDR	1	247	0	0	0	75	0	0	1	171	0	0
34 Indonesia	441	6,304	195	1,080	59	4,774	61	788	383	1,530	134	292
35 Mauritania	5	129	0	0	3	78	0	0	1	51	0	0
36 Sudan	53	373	0	0	22	44	0	0	30	329	0	0
37 *Afghanistan*	..	..	..	..	..	..	..	..	..	..	..	..
38 *Myanmar*	22	287	0	0	20	67	0	0	2	220	0	0
39 *Kampuchea, Dem.*	..	..	..	..	..	..	..	..	..	..	..	..
40 *Liberia*	7	34	0	0	11	8	0	0	−4	26	0	0
41 *Sierra Leone*	8	20	0	0	11	5	0	0	−3	14	0	0
42 *Viet Nam*	..	..	..	..	..	..	..	..	..	..	..	..
Middle-income economies												
Lower-middle-income												
43 Bolivia	55	328	3	0	17	132	2	0	38	196	1	0
44 Philippines	141	1,372	276	0	74	1,220	186	100	67	152	90	−100
45 Yemen Arab Rep.	..	261	0	0	..	137	0	0	..	124	0	0
46 Senegal	19	272	1	8	5	124	3	8	14	148	−2	0
47 Zimbabwe	0	233	0	43	5	308	0	44	−5	−75	0	−2
48 Egypt, Arab Rep.	397	1,467	0	180	310	635	0	147	87	832	0	33
49 Dominican Rep.	38	108	22	0	7	91	20	10	31	17	2	−10
50 Côte d'Ivoire	78	440	4	850	29	224	2	414	49	216	2	436
51 Papua New Guinea	43	164	111	164	0	198	20	168	43	−34	91	−4
52 Morocco	168	1,008	8	8	37	533	3	8	131	476	5	0
53 Honduras	29	290	10	14	3	144	3	26	26	146	7	−12
54 Guatemala	37	262	6	0	20	252	2	3	17	10	4	−3
55 Congo, People's Rep.	20	410	0	0	6	187	0	0	15	223	0	0
56 El Salvador	8	190	24	0	6	93	16	15	2	96	8	−15
57 Thailand	51	1,467	169	979	23	1,519	107	701	28	−52	62	279
58 Botswana	6	51	0	0	0	39	0	0	6	11	0	0
59 Cameroon	29	553	11	115	5	149	2	228	24	405	9	−112
60 Jamaica	15	204	165	0	6	200	164	7	9	3	1	−7
61 Ecuador	41	623	7	0	16	266	11	5	26	357	−4	−5
62 Colombia	253	2,234	0	112	78	1,623	59	98	174	611	−59	14
63 Paraguay	15	98	0	0	7	175	0	1	8	−77	0	−1
64 Tunisia	89	885	..	54	47	673	..	45	42	212	..	9
65 Turkey	329	5,565	1	161	128	3,706	3	138	201	1,859	−2	23
66 Peru	148	412	240	0	100	140	233	10	48	272	7	−10
67 Jordan	14	753	0	0	3	586	0	0	12	167	0	0

Note: For data comparability and coverage, see the technical notes.   Figures in italics are for years other than those specified.

	Disbursements (millions of dollars)				Repayment of principal (millions of dollars)				Net flow[a] (millions of dollars)			
	Public and publicly guaranteed		Private nonguaranteed		Public and publicly guaranteed		Private nonguaranteed		Public and publicly guaranteed		Private nonguaranteed	
	1970	1988	1970	1988	1970	1988	1970	1988	1970	1988	1970	1988
68 Chile	408	891	247	669	166	389	41	209	242	502	206	461
69 Syrian Arab Rep.	60	435	0	0	31	260	0	0	29	176	0	0
70 Costa Rica	30	94	30	30	21	132	20	16	9	−38	10	15
71 Mexico	772	4,706	603	1,140	475	3,087	542	3,155	297	1,619	61	−2,015
72 Mauritius	2	212	0	17	1	101	0	4	1	111	0	13
73 Poland	..	569	0	0	..	830	0	0	..	−262	0	0
74 Malaysia	45	1,687	12	615	47	3,023	9	885	−2	−1,336	3	−270
75 Panama	67	5	0	0	24	4	0	0	44	1	0	0
76 Brazil	892	5,534	900	170	256	2,980	200	657	636	2,553	700	−487
77 *Angola*	..	..	..	..	..	..	..	..	..	..	..	..
78 *Lebanon*	12	26	0	0	2	22	0	0	10	5	0	0
79 *Nicaragua*	44	579	0	0	16	82	0	0	28	497	0	0
Upper-middle-income												
80 South Africa	..	..	..	..	..	..	..	..	..	..	..	..
81 Algeria	313	5,922	0	0	35	4,534	0	0	279	1,388	0	0
82 Hungary	..	2,097	0	0	..	1,779	0	0	..	318	0	0
83 Uruguay	37	283	13	0	47	255	4	58	−10	28	9	−58
84 Argentina	482	1,676	424	160	344	1,190	428	150	139	486	−4	10
85 Yugoslavia	179	696	465	1,129	170	808	204	965	9	−112	261	164
86 Gabon	26	161	0	0	9	31	0	0	17	130	0	0
87 Venezuela	216	1,777	67	0	42	1,231	25	1,190	174	546	41	−1,190
88 Trinidad and Tobago	8	183	0	0	10	60	0	0	−3	123	0	0
89 Korea, Rep. of	444	2,721	32	1,127	198	4,890	7	1,202	246	−2,168	25	−75
90 Portugal	18	2,879	20	75	63	3,220	22	99	−45	−341	−1	−24
91 Greece	163	2,271	144	187	62	2,032	37	147	101	239	107	40
92 Oman	..	414	0	0	..	348	0	0	..	66	0	0
93 Libya	..	..	..	..	..	..	..	..	..	..	..	..
94 *Iran, Islamic Rep.*	..	..	..	..	..	..	..	..	..	..	..	..
95 *Iraq*	..	..	..	..	..	..	..	..	..	..	..	..
96 *Romania*	..	94	0	0	..	3,359	0	0	..	−3,266	0	0

Low- and middle-income
Sub-Saharan Africa
East Asia
South Asia
Europe, M.East, & N.Africa
Latin America & Caribbean

Severely indebted

High-income economies
OECD members
†Other

97 †Saudi Arabia
98 Spain
99 Ireland
100 †Israel
101 †Singapore

102 †Hong Kong
103 New Zealand
104 Australia
105 United Kingdom
106 Italy

107 †Kuwait
108 Belgium
109 Netherlands
110 Austria
111 †United Arab Emirates

112 France
113 Canada
114 Denmark
115 Germany, Fed. Rep.
116 Finland

117 Sweden
118 United States
119 Norway
120 Japan
121 Switzerland

Total reporting economies
Oil exporters

Nonreporting nonmembers

a. Disbursements less repayments of principal may not equal net flow because of rounding.

Table 23. Total external public and private debt and debt service ratios

		Total long-term debt outstanding and disbursed				Total interest payments on long-term debt (millions of dollars)		Total long-term debt service as a percentage of			
		Millions of dollars		As a percentage of GNP				GNP		Exports of goods and services	
		1970	1988	1970	1988	1970	1988	1970	1988	1970	1988

Low-income economies
China and India
Other low-income

		1970	1988	1970	1988	1970	1988	1970	1988	1970	1988
1	Mozambique	..	4,039	..	399.7	..	15	..	2.7	..	10.4
2	Ethiopia	169	2,790	9.5	50.6	6	78	1.2	4.3	11.4	37.4
3	Chad	33	300	9.9	33.2	0	4	0.9	0.7	4.2	2.7
4	Tanzania	265	4,100	20.7	140.1	8	41	1.6	3.0	6.3	17.8
5	Bangladesh	0	9,330	0.0	48.5	0	139	0.0	1.6	0.0	20.5
6	Malawi	122	1,193	43.2	85.9	4	29	2.3	4.6	7.8	19.0
7	Somalia	77	1,754	24.4	185.2	0	3	0.3	0.4	2.1	4.9
8	Zaire	311	7,013	9.1	118.0	9	98	1.1	2.8	4.4	6.9
9	Bhutan	..	68	..	27.9	..	1	..	0.5	..	..
10	Lao PDR	8	816	..	153.5	0	2	..	1.8	..	143.5
11	Nepal	3	1,088	0.3	34.6	0	19	0.3	1.2	3.2	8.5
12	Madagascar	89	3,317	10.4	192.7	2	81	0.8	9.3	3.7	39.0
13	Burkina Faso	21	805	6.6	43.4	0	14	0.7	2.0	7.1	11.9
14	Mali	238	1,928	71.4	100.8	0	15	0.2	2.5	1.4	14.2
15	Burundi	7	749	3.1	69.8	0	16	0.3	3.3	2.3	25.1
16	Uganda	138	1,438	7.3	34.3	5	20	0.5	1.0	2.9	14.0
17	Nigeria	567	28,967	4.3	102.5	28	1,411	0.7	7.0	7.1	25.7
18	Zambia	654	4,194	37.5	116.7	32	62	4.6	4.9	8.0	14.2
19	Niger	32	1,542	5.0	66.0	1	74	0.4	5.6	4.0	32.6
20	Rwanda	2	585	0.9	25.5	0	8	0.2	0.7	1.5	9.6
21	China	..	32,196	..	8.7	..	1,593	..	1.0	..	6.9
22	India	7,938	51,168	13.9	19.3	193	2,554	0.9	1.8	23.7	24.9
23	Pakistan	3,069	14,027	30.6	37.6	78	436	1.9	3.5	23.9	24.1
24	Kenya	406	4,869	26.3	58.5	17	194	3.0	5.7	9.1	25.3
25	Togo	40	1,067	16.0	81.6	1	68	1.0	7.0	3.1	18.3
26	Central African Rep.	24	584	13.5	53.3	1	7	1.7	1.1	5.1	5.9
27	Haiti	40	683	10.2	27.7	0	8	1.0	0.9	7.2	8.8
28	Benin	41	904	15.1	49.3	0	8	0.7	1.0	2.5	5.4
29	Ghana	498	2,270	22.9	44.6	12	64	1.2	4.0	5.5	20.6
30	Lesotho	8	270	7.7	36.5	0	7	0.5	3.0	4.5	5.2
31	Sri Lanka	317	4,253	16.1	61.6	12	125	2.1	4.8	11.0	17.6
32	Guinea	312	2,312	..	94.7	4	31	..	5.9	..	21.9
33	Yemen, PDR	1	1,970	..	199.4	0	31	..	10.8	0.0	46.5
34	Indonesia	2,914	45,655	30.0	61.7	46	2,918	1.7	11.5	13.9	39.6
35	Mauritania	27	1,823	13.9	196.2	0	33	1.8	11.9	3.4	21.6
36	Sudan	298	8,418	14.8	74.6	12	19	1.7	0.6	10.6	9.5
37	*Afghanistan*	..	..	..	..	..	..	..	..	..	..
38	*Myanmar*	106	4,217	..	..	3	39	..	..	..	..
39	*Kampuchea, Dem.*	..	..	..	..	..	..	..	..	..	..
40	*Liberia*	158	1,101	39.2	..	6	6	4.3	..	8.0	..
41	*Sierra Leone*	59	510	14.2	..	3	3	3.1	..	10.8	5.9
42	*Viet Nam*	..	..	..	..	..	..	..	..	..	..

Middle-income economies
Lower-middle-income

		1970	1988	1970	1988	1970	1988	1970	1988	1970	1988
43	Bolivia	491	4,651	49.3	114.9	7	95	2.6	5.6	12.6	32.9
44	Philippines	1,544	24,467	21.8	62.6	44	1,638	4.3	7.6	23.0	27.7
45	Yemen Arab Rep.	..	2,378	..	41.7	..	56	..	3.4	..	16.0
46	Senegal	131	3,019	15.5	63.6	2	117	1.1	5.2	4.0	19.3
47	Zimbabwe	229	2,281	15.5	37.3	5	150	0.6	8.2	2.3	27.9
48	Egypt, Arab Rep.	1,714	43,259	22.5	126.7	56	729	4.8	4.4	38.0	16.6
49	Dominican Rep.	353	3,334	23.9	77.3	13	151	2.7	5.8	15.3	14.4
50	Côte d'Ivoire	267	11,788	19.5	135.1	12	447	3.1	12.4	7.5	31.9
51	Papua New Guinea	209	2,129	33.4	64.2	10	153	4.8	15.6	24.5	30.9
52	Morocco	727	18,767	18.6	89.8	25	814	1.7	6.5	9.2	25.1
53	Honduras	109	2,837	15.6	68.3	4	128	1.4	7.2	4.9	28.6
54	Guatemala	120	2,244	6.5	28.3	7	104	1.6	4.5	8.2	27.2
55	Congo, People's Rep.	124	4,098	46.5	205.0	3	75	3.4	13.1	11.5	28.7
56	El Salvador	176	1,685	17.3	31.5	9	66	3.1	3.3	12.0	18.8
57	Thailand	726	16,905	10.2	29.7	33	1,184	2.3	6.0	14.0	15.7
58	Botswana	17	494	21.3	37.9	0	34	0.7	5.7	1.0	4.0
59	Cameroon	140	3,366	12.6	27.0	5	192	1.0	4.6	4.0	27.0
60	Jamaica	982	3,554	73.1	127.2	64	217	17.4	15.2	43.5	24.8
61	Ecuador	242	9,378	14.8	94.2	10	297	2.2	5.7	14.0	21.4
62	Colombia	1,580	15,392	22.5	42.1	59	1,213	2.8	8.0	19.3	42.3
63	Paraguay	112	2,119	19.2	36.4	4	114	1.8	5.0	11.8	24.6
64	Tunisia	541	6,121	38.6	64.2	18	380	4.7	11.5	19.7	25.5
65	Turkey	1,886	31,589	15.0	46.1	44	2,424	1.4	9.1	22.6	35.2
66	Peru	2,655	13,898	37.3	56.1	162	174	7.0	1.3	40.0	8.7
67	Jordan	119	3,955	22.9	94.0	2	239	0.9	19.6	3.6	31.9

Note: For data comparability and coverage, see the technical notes. Figures in italics are for years other than those specified

		Total long-term debt outstanding and disbursed				Total interest payments on long-term debt (millions of dollars)		Total long-term debt service as a percentage of			
		Millions of dollars		As a percentage of GNP				GNP		Exports of goods and services	
		1970	1988	1970	1988	1970	1988	1970	1988	1970	1988
68	Chile	2,568	16,121	32.1	79.3	104	1,019	3.9	7.9	24.5	19.1
69	Syrian Arab Rep.	233	3,685	10.8	25.0	6	119	1.7	2.6	11.3	21.1
70	Costa Rica	246	3,847	25.3	89.2	14	185	5.7	7.7	19.9	19.9
71	Mexico	5,966	88,665	16.2	52.4	283	7,590	3.5	8.2	44.3	43.5
72	Mauritius	32	709	14.3	37.1	2	43	1.4	7.7	3.2	10.4
73	Poland	. .	33,661	. .	51.1	. .	829	. .	2.5	. .	10.0
74	Malaysia	440	18,441	10.8	56.3	25	1,498	2.0	16.5	4.5	22.3
75	Panama	194	3,625	19.5	81.2	7	4	3.1	0.2	7.7	0.2
76	Brazil	5,128	101,356	12.2	29.6	224	11,686	1.6	4.5	21.8	42.0
77	Angola	. .	. .	. .	. .	. .	. .	. .	. .	. .	. .
78	Lebanon	64	229	4.2	. .	1	16	0.2	. .	. .	. .
79	Nicaragua	147	6,744	19.5	. .	7	73	3.1	. .	10.6	. .
	Upper-middle-income										
80	South Africa	. .	. .	. .	. .			. .	. .	. .	. .
81	Algeria	945	23,229	19.8	46.6	10	1,809	0.9	12.7	4.0	77.0
82	Hungary	. .	14,791	. .	54.9	. .	1,100	. .	10.7	0.0	23.3
83	Uruguay	298	3,039	12.5	39.8	17	257	2.9	7.5	23.6	30.3
84	Argentina	5,171	49,544	23.8	58.6	338	2,803	5.1	4.9	51.7	36.0
85	Yugoslavia	2,053	19,341	15.0	38.9	104	1,401	3.5	6.4	19.7	17.6
86	Gabon	91	2,128	28.8	65.6	3	57	3.8	2.7	5.7	6.2
87	Venezuela	954	30,296	7.5	49.0	53	2,675	0.9	8.2	4.2	39.7
88	Trinidad and Tobago	101	1,718	13.3	43.2	6	88	2.1	3.7	4.6	9.2
89	Korea, Rep. of	1,991	27,376	22.3	16.2	76	2,081	3.1	4.8	20.4	11.5
90	Portugal	753	14,565	12.1	35.6	34	1,163	1.9	11.0	8.7	30.3
91	Greece	1,293	18,797	12.7	35.9	63	1,468	1.6	7.0	14.7	32.1
92	Oman	. .	2,488	. .	34.7	. .	182	. .	7.4	. .	. .
93	Libya	. .	. .	. .	. .	. .	. .	. .	. .	. .	. .
94	Iran, Islamic Rep.	. .	. .	. .	. .	. .	. .	. .	. .	. .	. .
95	Iraq	. .	. .	. .	. .	. .	. .	. .	. .	. .	. .
96	Romania	. .	1,946	. .	. .	. .	420	. .	. .	. .	. .

Low- and middle-income
Sub-Saharan Africa
East Asia
South Asia
Europe, M.East, & N.Africa
Latin America & Caribbean

Severely indebted

High-income economies
  OECD members
  †Other

97 †Saudi Arabia
98 Spain
99 Ireland
100 †Israel
101 †Singapore

102 †Hong Kong
103 New Zealand
104 Australia
105 United Kingdom
106 Italy

107 †Kuwait
108 Belgium
109 Netherlands
110 Austria
111 †United Arab Emirates

112 France
113 Canada
114 Denmark
115 Germany, Fed. Rep.
116 Finland

117 Sweden
118 United States
119 Norway
120 Japan
121 Switzerland

Total reporting economies
  Oil exporters

Nonreporting nonmembers

Note: Public and private debt includes public, publicly guaranteed, and private nonguaranteed debt; data are shown only when they are available for all categories.

Table 24. External public debt and debt service ratios

	External public debt outstanding and disbursed				Interest payments on external public debt (millions of dollars)		Debt service as a percentage of			
	Millions of dollars		As a percentage of GNP				GNP		Exports of goods and services	
	1970	1988	1970	1988	1970	1988	1970	1988	1970	1988
Low-income economies	..	248,548 *t*	..	27.6 *w*	..	9,662 *t*	..	2.4 *w*	..	17.0 *w*
China and India	..	81,891 *t*	..	12.8 *w*	..	4,005 *t*	..	1.2 *w*	..	10.8 *w*
Other low-income	10,424 *t*	166,656 *t*	15.2 *w*	64.4 *w*	257 *t*	5,658 *t*	1.1 *w*	5.3 *w*	7.1 *w*	25.3 *w*
1 Mozambique	..	3,801	..	376.1	..	12	..	2.0	..	7.8
2 Ethiopia	169	2,790	9.5	50.6	6	78	1.2	4.3	11.4	37.4
3 Chad	33	300	9.9	33.2	0	4	0.9	0.7	4.2	2.7
4 Tanzania	250	4,091	19.5	139.8	7	40	1.3	2.9	5.3	17.1
5 Bangladesh	0	9,330	0.0	48.5	0	139	0.0	1.6	0.0	20.5
6 Malawi	122	1,190	43.2	85.7	4	28	2.3	4.1	7.8	17.2
7 Somalia	77	1,754	24.4	185.2	0	3	0.3	0.4	2.1	4.9
8 Zaire	311	7,013	9.1	118.0	9	98	1.1	2.8	4.4	6.9
9 Bhutan	..	68	..	27.9	..	1	..	0.5	..	..
10 Lao PDR	8	816	..	153.5	0	2	..	1.8	..	143.5
11 Nepal	3	1,088	0.3	34.6	0	19	0.3	1.2	3.2	8.5
12 Madagascar	89	3,317	10.4	192.7	2	81	0.8	9.3	3.7	39.0
13 Burkina Faso	21	805	6.6	43.4	0	14	0.7	2.0	7.1	11.9
14 Mali	238	1,928	71.4	100.8	0	15	0.2	2.5	1.4	14.2
15 Burundi	7	749	3.1	69.8	0	16	0.3	3.3	2.3	25.1
16 Uganda	138	1,438	7.3	34.3	5	20	0.5	1.0	2.9	14.0
17 Nigeria	452	28,630	3.4	101.3	20	1,385	0.4	6.6	4.3	24.2
18 Zambia	624	4,194	35.8	116.7	29	62	3.7	4.9	6.4	14.2
19 Niger	32	1,286	5.0	55.1	1	54	0.4	3.6	4.0	21.1
20 Rwanda	2	585	0.9	25.5	0	8	0.2	0.7	1.5	9.6
21 China	..	32,196	..	8.7	..	1,593	..	1.0	..	6.9
22 India	7,838	49,695	13.7	18.7	187	2,412	0.8	1.5	22.2	21.8
23 Pakistan	3,064	13,944	30.6	37.4	77	430	1.9	3.4	23.8	23.5
24 Kenya	319	4,241	20.6	51.0	13	149	2.0	4.4	6.0	19.4
25 Togo	40	1,067	16.0	81.6	1	68	1.0	7.0	3.1	18.3
26 Central African Rep.	24	584	13.5	53.3	1	7	1.7	1.1	5.1	5.9
27 Haiti	40	683	10.2	27.7	0	8	1.0	0.9	7.2	8.8
28 Benin	41	904	15.1	49.3	0	8	0.7	1.0	2.5	5.4
29 Ghana	488	2,238	22.5	43.9	12	61	1.2	3.8	5.5	19.7
30 Lesotho	8	270	7.7	36.5	0	7	0.5	3.0	4.5	5.2
31 Sri Lanka	317	4,139	16.1	59.9	12	123	2.1	4.7	11.0	17.2
32 Guinea	312	2,312	..	94.7	4	31	..	5.9	..	21.9
33 Yemen, PDR	1	1,970	..	199.4	0	31	..	10.8	0.0	46.5
34 Indonesia	2,453	41,258	25.3	55.7	25	2,528	0.9	9.9	7.0	34.1
35 Mauritania	27	1,823	13.9	196.2	0	33	1.8	11.9	3.4	21.6
36 Sudan	298	8,044	14.8	71.3	12	19	1.7	0.6	10.6	9.5
37 *Afghanistan*	..	..	..	..	..	..	..	..	..	..
38 *Myanmar*	106	4,217	..	..	3	39	..	..	..	..
39 *Kampuchea, Dem.*	..	..	..	..	..	..	..	..	..	..
40 *Liberia*	158	1,101	39.2	..	6	6	4.3	..	8.0	..
41 *Sierra Leone*	59	510	14.2	..	3	3	3.1	..	10.8	5.9
42 *Viet Nam*	..	..	..	..	..	..	..	..	..	..
Middle-income economies	28,754 *t*	662,972 *t*	11.5 *w*	40.8 *w*	1,236 *t*	43,700 *t*	1.7 *w*	5.5 *w*	11.1 *w*	21.6 *w*
Lower-middle-income	20,310 *t*	472,636 *t*	12.1 *w*	44.7 *w*	825 *t*	30,161 *t*	1.7 *w*	5.2 *w*	12.6 *w*	23.0 *w*
43 Bolivia	480	4,451	48.2	109.9	7	95	2.3	5.6	11.3	32.9
44 Philippines	625	23,475	8.8	60.1	26	1,515	1.4	7.0	7.5	25.6
45 Yemen Arab Rep.	..	2,378	..	41.7	..	56	..	3.4	..	16.0
46 Senegal	100	2,985	11.9	62.9	2	114	0.8	5.0	2.9	18.4
47 Zimbabwe	229	2,231	15.5	36.5	5	139	0.6	7.3	2.3	24.8
48 Egypt, Arab Rep.	1,714	42,128	22.5	123.4	56	624	4.8	3.7	38.0	13.9
49 Dominican Rep.	212	3,216	14.4	74.5	4	144	0.8	5.5	4.5	13.4
50 Côte d'Ivoire	256	8,088	18.7	92.7	12	219	2.9	5.1	7.1	13.0
51 Papua New Guinea	36	1,269	5.8	38.3	1	80	0.2	8.4	1.1	16.5
52 Morocco	712	18,567	18.2	88.8	24	809	1.6	6.4	8.7	24.8
53 Honduras	90	2,739	12.9	65.9	3	121	0.8	6.4	2.8	25.5
54 Guatemala	106	2,131	5.7	26.9	6	98	1.4	4.4	7.4	26.5
55 Congo, People's Rep.	124	4,098	46.5	205.0	3	75	3.4	13.1	11.5	28.7
56 El Salvador	88	1,630	8.6	30.4	4	61	0.9	2.9	3.6	16.6
57 Thailand	324	13,375	4.6	23.5	16	926	0.6	4.3	3.3	11.3
58 Botswana	17	494	21.3	37.9	0	34	0.7	5.7	1.0	4.0
59 Cameroon	131	2,939	11.8	23.6	4	101	0.8	2.0	3.2	11.9
60 Jamaica	160	3,512	11.9	125.7	9	213	1.1	14.8	2.8	24.2
61 Ecuador	193	9,353	11.8	93.9	7	294	1.4	5.6	8.6	21.1
62 Colombia	1,297	13,853	18.5	37.9	44	1,135	1.7	7.5	12.0	39.8
63 Paraguay	112	2,091	19.2	35.9	4	114	1.8	4.9	11.8	24.5
64 Tunisia	541	5,886	38.6	61.7	18	369	4.7	10.9	19.7	24.2
65 Turkey	1,844	31,054	14.7	45.3	42	2,364	1.4	8.9	21.9	34.1
66 Peru	856	12,475	12.0	50.3	43	164	2.0	1.2	11.6	8.1
67 Jordan	119	3,955	22.9	94.0	2	239	0.9	19.6	3.6	31.9

Note: For data comparability and coverage, see the technical notes.   Figures in italics are for years other than those specified

		External public debt outstanding and disbursed				Interest payments on external public debt (millions of dollars)		Debt service as a percentage of			
		Millions of dollars		As a percentage of GNP				GNP		Exports of goods and services	
		1970	1988	1970	1988	1970	1988	1970	1988	1970	1988
68	Chile	2,067	13,760	25.8	67.7	78	868	3.1	6.2	19.2	14.9
69	Syrian Arab Rep.	233	3,685	10.8	25.0	6	119	1.7	2.6	11.3	21.1
70	Costa Rica	134	3,531	13.8	81.8	7	160	2.9	6.8	10.0	17.4
71	Mexico	3,196	81,207	8.7	48.0	216	6,554	1.9	5.7	23.6	30.3
72	Mauritius	32	652	14.3	34.1	2	41	1.4	7.4	3.2	10.1
73	Poland	..	33,661	..	51.1	..	829	..	2.5	..	10.0
74	Malaysia	390	16,101	9.5	49.1	22	1,220	1.7	13.0	3.8	17.5
75	Panama	194	3,625	19.5	81.2	7	4	3.1	0.2	7.7	0.2
76	Brazil	3,421	89,841	8.2	26.3	135	10,117	0.9	3.8	12.5	35.9
77	Angola	..	..	..	..	..	..	..	..	..	..
78	Lebanon	64	229	4.2	..	1	16	0.2	..	..	..
79	Nicaragua	147	6,744	19.5	..	7	73	3.1	..	10.6	..
	Upper-middle-income	8,444 t	190,336 t	10.3 w	33.6 w	411 t	13,539 t	1.7 w	6.0 w	8.9 w	19.7 w
80	South Africa	..	..	..	..	..	..	..	..	..	..
81	Algeria	945	23,229	19.8	46.6	10	1,809	0.9	12.7	4.0	77.0
82	Hungary	..	14,791	..	54.9	..	1,100	..	10.7	..	23.3
83	Uruguay	269	2,953	11.3	38.7	16	257	2.7	6.7	21.7	27.3
84	Argentina	1,880	48,166	8.6	57.0	121	2,560	2.1	4.4	21.6	32.6
85	Yugoslavia	1,199	13,949	8.8	28.0	73	951	1.8	3.5	10.0	9.7
86	Gabon	91	2,128	28.8	65.6	3	57	3.8	2.7	5.7	6.2
87	Venezuela	718	25,413	5.6	41.1	40	2,043	0.6	5.3	2.9	25.5
88	Trinidad and Tobago	101	1,718	13.3	43.2	6	88	2.1	3.7	4.6	9.2
89	Korea, Rep. of	1,816	21,349	20.3	12.6	71	1,563	3.0	3.8	19.5	9.1
90	Portugal	485	13,950	7.8	34.1	29	1,110	1.5	10.6	6.8	29.3
91	Greece	905	17,482	8.9	33.4	41	1,355	1.0	6.5	9.4	29.8
92	Oman	..	2,488	..	34.7	..	182	0.0	7.4	..	..
93	Libya	..	..	..	..	..	..	..	..	..	..
94	Iran, Islamic Rep.	..	..	..	..	..	..	..	..	..	..
95	Iraq	..	..	..	..	..	..	..	..	..	..
96	Romania	..	1,946	..	..	..	420	..	..	..	..
	Low- and middle-income	47,015 t	911,520 t	12.5 w	36.1 w	1,680 t	53,362 t	1.2 w	4.4 w	10.3 w	20.5 w
	Sub-Saharan Africa	5,369 t	112,353 t	12.5 w	78.2 w	169 t	3,128 t	1.1 w	4.3 w	5.3 w	16.5 w
	East Asia	5,667 t	150,401 t	15.0 w	20.1 w	162 t	9,456 t	0.4 w	3.6 w	5.9 w	13.3 w
	South Asia	11,327 t	82,541 t	14.3 w	24.0 w	279 t	3,164 t	0.9 w	1.8 w	18.1 w	21.5 w
	Europe, M.East, & N.Africa	8,784 t	231,433 t	13.6 w	50.5 w	304 t	12,384 t	1.8 w	7.1 w	10.2 w	25.2 w
	Latin America & Caribbean	15,868 t	334,792 t	10.5 w	40.6 w	767 t	25,229 t	1.6 w	4.7 w	13.1 w	28.1 w
	Severely indebted	15,268 t	406,298 t	10.2 w	44.4 w	745 t	27,968 t	1.6 w	4.7 w	12.0 w	26.2 w

High-income economies
OECD members
†Other

97	†Saudi Arabia										
98	Spain										
99	Ireland										
100	†Israel										
101	†Singapore										
102	†Hong Kong										
103	New Zealand										
104	Australia										
105	United Kingdom										
106	Italy										
107	†Kuwait										
108	Belgium										
109	Netherlands										
110	Austria										
111	†United Arab Emirates										
112	France										
113	Canada										
114	Denmark										
115	Germany, Fed. Rep.										
116	Finland										
117	Sweden										
118	United States										
119	Norway										
120	Japan										
121	Switzerland										
	Total reporting economies	..	..	..	..	..	..	..	..	..	..
	Oil exporters	..	..	..	..	..	..	..	..	..	..
	Nonreporting nonmembers	..	..	..	..	..	..	..	..	..	..

Table 25. Terms of external public borrowing

	Commitments (millions of dollars)		Average interest rate (percent)		Average maturity (years)		Average grace period (years)		Public loans with variable interest rates, as a percentage of public debt	
	1970	1988	1970	1988	1970	1988	1970	1988	1970	1988
Low-income economies	..	35,770 t	..	5.3 w	..	21 w	..	6 w	..	19.4 w
China and India	..	18,070 t	..	6.7 w	..	16 w	..	5 w	..	24.8 w
Other low-income	3,390 t	17,701 t	3.2 w	3.9 w	29 w	26 w	9 w	8 w	0.2 w	16.7 w
1 Mozambique	..	294	..	2.2	..	23	..	6	..	4.9
2 Ethiopia	21	487	4.4	3.0	32	24	7	7	0.1	6.7
3 Chad	10	176	5.7	0.9	8	41	1	10	0.0	0.1
4 Tanzania	284	220	1.2	0.8	39	41	11	10	1.6	2.5
5 Bangladesh	0	994	0.0	1.5	0	33	0	10	0.0	0.0
6 Malawi	14	123	3.9	0.9	29	41	6	10	0.0	3.8
7 Somalia	22	24	0.0	2.5	20	28	16	7	0.0	1.1
8 Zaire	258	350	6.5	4.1	13	28	4	8	0.0	5.4
9 Bhutan	..	28	..	5.9	..	17	..	4	..	0.0
10 Lao PDR	12	86	3.0	0.3	28	46	4	30	0.0	0.0
11 Nepal	17	217	2.8	0.9	27	39	6	10	0.0	0.7
12 Madagascar	23	352	2.3	2.4	39	31	9	9	0.0	10.5
13 Burkina Faso	9	108	2.3	2.6	37	31	8	8	0.0	0.5
14 Mali	34	131	1.1	1.2	25	35	10	9	0.0	0.1
15 Burundi	1	205	2.8	1.0	4	38	2	11	0.0	0.3
16 Uganda	12	252	3.8	2.4	28	36	7	9	0.0	0.6
17 Nigeria	65	1,461	6.0	7.6	14	16	4	5	2.7	40.6
18 Zambia	557	64	4.2	3.8	27	20	9	7	0.0	13.4
19 Niger	19	159	1.2	1.4	40	31	8	9	0.0	7.7
20 Rwanda	9	64	0.8	1.7	50	35	11	8	0.0	0.0
21 China	..	10,086	..	7.1	..	13	..	4	..	39.1
22 India	954	7,984	2.5	6.3	34	20	8	6	0.0	15.6
23 Pakistan	951	2,020	2.8	5.2	32	23	12	6	0.0	8.8
24 Kenya	50	679	2.6	1.9	37	22	8	9	0.1	4.1
25 Togo	3	114	4.7	1.6	17	38	4	11	0.0	3.7
26 Central African Rep.	7	76	2.0	0.9	36	36	8	10	0.0	0.0
27 Haiti	5	0	4.8	0.0	10	0	1	0	0.0	1.1
28 Benin	7	162	1.8	2.3	32	32	7	8	0.0	3.9
29 Ghana	51	431	2.0	1.0	37	35	10	8	0.0	3.7
30 Lesotho	0	191	4.4	4.6	22	24	2	5	0.0	1.0
31 Sri Lanka	81	827	3.0	1.9	27	35	5	10	0.0	4.5
32 Guinea	68	271	2.9	1.4	13	30	5	8	0.0	10.5
33 Yemen, PDR	63	664	0.0	2.9	21	24	11	6	0.0	0.0
34 Indonesia	530	5,740	2.6	5.2	34	21	9	7	0.0	28.6
35 Mauritania	7	111	6.1	1.1	11	38	3	10	0.0	6.4
36 Sudan	95	472	1.8	2.0	17	35	9	8	0.0	0.8
37 *Afghanistan*	..	..	..	..	..	..	..	..	..	..
38 *Myanmar*	48	0	4.1	0.0	16	0	5	0	0.0	0.8
39 *Kampuchea, Dem.*	..	..	..	..	..	..	..	..	..	..
40 *Liberia*	12	0	6.7	0.0	19	0	5	0	0.0	9.3
41 *Sierra Leone*	25	0	2.9	1.0	27	12	6	3	10.6	0.6
42 *Viet Nam*	..	..	..	..	..	..	..	..	..	..
Middle-income economies	8,195 t	58,340 t	6.2 w	7.2 w	16 w	13 w	4 w	5 w	2.8 w	52.6 w
Lower-middle-income	5,823 t	36,009 t	6.1 w	6.9 w	17 w	16 w	5 w	5 w	3.2 w	49.7 w
43 Bolivia	24	309	1.9	5.4	48	27	4	7	0.0	22.7
44 Philippines	171	2,341	7.3	5.4	12	22	2	7	0.8	43.2
45 Yemen Arab Rep.	..	463	..	4.8	..	16	..	4	..	0.8
46 Senegal	7	320	3.8	1.8	24	31	7	9	0.0	2.5
47 Zimbabwe	..	448	..	7.1	..	19	..	4	..	22.9
48 Egypt, Arab Rep.	704	1,762	5.3	6.4	21	23	8	7	0.0	1.4
49 Dominican Rep.	20	169	2.4	7.5	28	15	5	4	0.0	31.5
50 Côte d'Ivoire	71	659	5.8	5.7	19	16	5	5	9.0	52.2
51 Papua New Guinea	91	219	6.4	3.5	22	20	8	6	0.0	28.6
52 Morocco	187	1,156	4.6	6.9	20	18	3	4	0.0	38.8
53 Honduras	23	251	4.1	7.3	30	17	7	5	0.0	18.9
54 Guatemala	50	444	3.7	5.9	26	17	6	5	10.3	11.1
55 Congo, People's Rep.	31	486	2.8	8.3	17	10	6	2	0.0	40.2
56 El Salvador	12	369	4.7	4.0	24	33	6	8	0.0	3.9
57 Thailand	106	1,999	6.8	5.3	19	18	4	6	0.0	34.4
58 Botswana	38	103	0.6	2.4	39	29	10	8	0.0	13.6
59 Cameroon	42	922	4.7	4.5	29	14	8	4	0.0	9.4
60 Jamaica	24	174	6.0	6.7	16	18	3	4	0.0	26.1
61 Ecuador	78	515	6.2	6.2	20	18	4	5	0.0	66.9
62 Colombia	363	2,488	6.0	8.2	21	13	5	4	0.0	45.0
63 Paraguay	14	312	5.6	6.4	25	21	6	7	0.0	13.8
64 Tunisia	144	1,114	3.5	4.6	28	21	6	6	0.0	17.2
65 Turkey	484	4,568	3.6	7.0	19	12	5	5	0.9	34.1
66 Peru	125	350	7.4	7.6	14	21	4	18	0.0	32.7
67 Jordan	35	999	3.8	7.5	15	11	5	3	0.0	29.0

Note: For data comparability and coverage, see the technical notes.   Figures in italics are for years other than those specified

		Commitments (millions of dollars)		Average interest rate (percent)		Average maturity (years)		Average grace period (years)		Public loans with variable interest rates, as a percentage of public debt	
		1970	1988	1970	1988	1970	1988	1970	1988	1970	1988
68	Chile	361	649	6.8	6.8	12	13	4	3	0.0	76.7
69	Syrian Arab Rep.	14	275	4.4	7.3	9	17	2	4	0.0	1.1
70	Costa Rica	58	338	5.6	8.9	28	21	6	6	7.5	47.5
71	Mexico	858	2,579	8.0	8.2	12	15	3	3	5.7	78.6
72	Mauritius	14	176	0.0	7.7	24	15	2	3	6.0	19.2
73	Poland	..	1,042	..	6.4	..	6	..	3	..	63.3
74	Malaysia	84	2,259	6.1	6.1	19	15	5	6	0.0	48.5
75	Panama	111	0	6.1	0.0	15	0	4	0	0.0	60.2
76	Brazil	1,439	5,003	6.8	9.5	14	11	3	4	11.8	70.0
77	Angola	..	..	..	..	..	..	..	..	..	..
78	Lebanon	7	40	2.9	7.5	22	27	1	4	0.0	15.3
79	Nicaragua	23	563	7.1	5.1	18	19	4	3	0.0	20.6
	Upper-middle-income	2,372 t	22,331 t	6.5 w	7.6 w	14 w	9 w	4 w	4 w	1.6 w	59.6 w
80	South Africa	..	..	..	..	..	..	..	..	..	..
81	Algeria	378	8,457	5.6	7.6	12	6	3	2	2.8	35.8
82	Hungary[a]	..	1,782	..	7.0	..	9	..	7	..	60.2
83	Uruguay	71	293	8.0	9.5	12	10	3	1	0.7	71.6
84	Argentina	494	2,432	7.3	7.8	12	16	3	5	0.0	82.5
85	Yugoslavia	199	369	7.1	9.2	17	7	6	5	3.3	64.9
86	Gabon	33	152	5.1	7.7	11	16	2	6	0.0	7.6
87	Venezuela	188	2,129	7.6	8.1	8	10	2	3	2.6	86.8
88	Trinidad and Tobago	3	190	7.6	7.5	10	5	1	5	0.0	37.4
89	Korea, Rep. of	691	1,071	5.8	7.6	19	20	6	4	1.2	30.5
90	Portugal	59	3,195	4.3	7.7	17	9	4	5	0.0	37.8
91	Greece	246	1,914	7.2	6.3	9	9	4	6	3.5	52.2
92	Oman	..	285	..	7.5	..	10	..	6	..	39.8
93	Libya	..	..	..	..	..	..	..	..	..	..
94	Iran, Islamic Rep.	..	..	..	..	..	..	..	..	..	..
95	Iraq	..	..	..	..	..	..	..	..	..	..
96	Romania	..	0	..	0.0	..	0	..	0	..	21.9
	Low- and middle-income	12,539 t	94,110 t	5.1 w	6.5 w	21 w	16 w	6 w	5 w	1.7 w	43.5 w
	Sub-Saharan Africa	1,900 t	10,329 t	3.6 w	4.0 w	26 w	24 w	8 w	7 w	0.9 w	19.2 w
	East Asia	1,688 t	23,885 t	5.0 w	6.2 w	23 w	17 w	6 w	5 w	0.5 w	35.8 w
	South Asia	2,052 t	12,073 t	2.7 w	5.3 w	32 w	23 w	10 w	7 w	0.0 w	11.2 w
	Europe, M.East, & N.Africa	2,526 t	28,102 t	5.0 w	7.0 w	18 w	11 w	5 w	4 w	1.3 w	36.3 w
	Latin America & Caribbean	4,373 t	19,722 t	6.9 w	8.1 w	14 w	14 w	4 w	4 w	4.0 w	68.1 w
	Severely indebted	4,208 t	23,198 t	7.0 w	7.6 w	14 w	14 w	3 w	5 w	4.2 w	66.3 w
	High-income economies OECD members †Other										
97	†Saudi Arabia										
98	Spain										
99	Ireland										
100	†Israel										
101	†Singapore										
102	†Hong Kong										
103	New Zealand										
104	Australia										
105	United Kingdom										
106	Italy										
107	†Kuwait										
108	Belgium										
109	Netherlands										
110	Austria										
111	†United Arab Emirates										
112	France										
113	Canada										
114	Denmark										
115	Germany, Fed. Rep.										
116	Finland										
117	Sweden										
118	United States										
119	Norway										
120	Japan										
121	Switzerland										
	Total reporting economies Oil exporters	..	..	..	..	..	..	..	..	..	..
	Nonreporting nonmembers	..	..	..	..	..	..	..	..	..	..

a. Includes debt in convertible currencies only.

Table 26. Population growth and projections

		Average annual growth of population[a] (percent)			Population (millions)			Hypothetical size of stationary population (millions)	Age structure of population (percent) 0–14 years		15–64 years	
		1965–80	1980–88	1988–2000	1988	2000[a]	2025[a]		1988	2025	1988	2025
	Low-income economies	**2.3 w**	**2.0 w**	**1.9 w**	**2,884 t**	**3,620 t**	**5,200 t**		**35.7 w**	**27.1 w**	**59.8**	**65.1 w**
	China and India	**2.2 w**	**1.6 w**	**1.5 w**	**1,904 t**	**2,283 t**	**2,917 t**		**31.8 w**	**22.1 w**	**63.2**	**67.4 w**
	Other low-income	**2.6 w**	**2.8 w**	**2.6 w**	**980 t**	**1,337 t**	**2,284 t**		**43.4 w**	**33.4 w**	**53.4**	**62.2 w**
1	Mozambique	2.5	2.7	3.1	15	21	41	93	43.9	38.6	53.0	58.2
2	Ethiopia	2.7	2.9	3.3	47	70	156	471	47.2	43.7	49.5	53.8
3	Chad	2.0	2.4	2.7	5	7	14	30	41.6	37.7	54.9	58.3
4	Tanzania	3.3	3.5	3.4	25	37	74	158	48.8	37.9	49.0	59.2
5	Bangladesh	2.7	2.8	2.4	109	145	219	346	44.7	28.2	52.1	67.4
6	Malawi	2.9	3.4	3.5	8	12	26	79	46.4	43.4	51.0	54.0
7	Somalia	2.7	3.0	3.1	6	9	17	41	45.8	40.2	51.4	56.7
8	Zaire	2.8	3.1	3.0	33	47	87	173	46.2	35.4	51.4	61.0
9	Bhutan	1.6	2.1	2.4	1	2	3	5	40.0	33.0	56.7	62.7
10	Lao PDR	1.9	2.6	2.9	4	6	10	19	43.7	35.0	53.5	60.9
11	Nepal	2.4	2.6	2.5	18	24	37	61	42.7	29.8	54.9	65.2
12	Madagascar	2.5	2.8	2.6	11	15	24	42	46.2	31.5	50.7	64.7
13	Burkina Faso	2.1	2.6	2.9	9	12	23	52	45.1	39.0	51.9	58.3
14	Mali	2.1	2.4	3.0	8	11	24	63	46.6	41.8	50.5	55.7
15	Burundi	1.9	2.8	3.1	5	7	15	33	45.3	39.6	51.5	57.8
16	Uganda	2.9	3.2	3.5	16	24	51	128	48.4	41.5	49.2	56.2
17	Nigeria	2.5	3.3	3.1	110	159	302	617	48.0	36.4	49.4	60.4
18	Zambia	3.0	3.7	3.5	8	11	24	56	49.0	39.7	48.6	57.6
19	Niger	2.6	3.5	3.3	7	11	24	82	46.7	44.8	50.5	52.8
20	Rwanda	3.3	3.3	3.8	7	10	23	70	47.7	44.0	49.7	53.6
21	China	2.2	1.3	1.3	1,088	1,275	1,566	1,835	27.7	20.5	66.7	66.6
22	India	2.3	2.2	1.8	816	1,007	1,350	1,862	37.2	24.0	58.4	68.4
23	Pakistan	3.1	3.2	3.1	106	154	285	556	45.0	34.9	52.4	61.5
24	Kenya	3.6	3.8	3.4	22	34	62	113	50.9	31.9	46.1	64.7
25	Togo	3.0	3.5	3.3	3	5	9	19	47.7	36.5	49.3	60.4
26	Central African Rep.	1.9	2.7	2.6	3	4	7	13	42.6	34.7	54.9	61.7
27	Haiti	2.0	1.8	1.9	6	8	11	17	39.3	27.1	56.8	67.3
28	Benin	2.7	3.2	2.9	4	6	11	21	47.2	34.4	50.0	62.2
29	Ghana	2.2	3.4	3.0	14	20	36	66	46.6	34.0	50.2	62.4
30	Lesotho	2.3	2.7	2.6	2	2	4	6	43.1	30.5	53.3	64.7
31	Sri Lanka	1.8	1.5	1.1	17	19	24	28	32.8	21.0	61.8	65.9
32	Guinea	1.5	2.4	2.6	5	7	14	34	42.1	40.5	54.3	56.2
33	Yemen, PDR	2.1	3.0	3.0	2	3	6	11	45.2	35.1	52.0	61.8
34	Indonesia	2.4	2.1	1.7	175	213	282	370	37.3	23.3	58.9	68.2
35	Mauritania	2.3	2.6	2.7	2	3	5	13	43.9	41.2	52.6	56.1
36	Sudan	2.8	3.1	2.7	24	33	57	107	44.8	34.7	52.1	61.6
37	*Afghanistan*	2.4	..	..	..	..	..	..	..	..	..	..
38	*Myanmar*	2.3	2.1	2.0	40	50	69	94	37.9	23.9	58.0	68.6
39	*Kampuchea, Dem.*	0.3	..	..	..	..	..	..	..	..	..	..
40	*Liberia*	3.0	3.2	2.8	2	3	6	11	45.1	33.9	51.5	62.3
41	*Sierra Leone*	2.0	2.4	2.6	4	5	10	25	43.0	40.2	54.0	56.4
42	*Viet Nam*	..	2.4	2.0	64	83	117	160	40.0	24.0	55.7	68.8
	Middle-income economies	**2.4 w**	**2.2 w**	**1.9 w**	**1,068 t**	**1,342 t**	**1,923 t**		**36.6 w**	**26.0 w**	**58.6 w**	**65.3 w**
	Lower-middle-income	**2.5 w**	**2.3 w**	**2.0 w**	**742 t**	**940 t**	**1,354 t**		**38.0 w**	**26.0 w**	**57.7 w**	**65.9 w**
43	Bolivia	2.5	2.7	2.7	7	10	16	27	43.9	31.5	52.9	64.2
44	Philippines	2.9	2.5	1.9	60	75	103	139	40.3	23.9	56.2	68.4
45	Yemen Arab Rep.	2.3	3.4	3.6	8	13	29	86	48.4	43.7	48.5	54.3
46	Senegal	2.9	3.0	3.2	7	10	21	48	46.8	40.2	50.5	57.4
47	Zimbabwe	3.1	3.7	2.7	9	13	20	29	45.8	25.4	50.8	68.7
48	Egypt, Arab Rep.	2.1	2.6	2.3	50	66	97	140	40.4	24.9	55.4	67.1
49	Dominican Rep.	2.7	2.4	1.8	7	9	11	15	38.5	23.2	57.9	68.0
50	Côte d'Ivoire	4.1	4.0	3.8	11	18	38	94	49.0	40.7	49.0	56.5
51	Papua New Guinea	2.4	2.4	2.2	4	5	7	11	41.3	27.4	56.0	67.9
52	Morocco	2.5	2.7	2.4	24	32	47	69	41.2	26.1	54.5	68.0
53	Honduras	3.2	3.6	2.9	5	7	11	18	45.1	28.1	51.1	66.9
54	Guatemala	2.8	2.9	2.8	9	12	21	35	45.8	30.7	51.3	64.8
55	Congo, People's Rep.	2.8	3.5	3.3	2	3	7	17	44.9	40.3	51.0	56.7
56	El Salvador	2.7	1.3	2.1	5	6	10	16	45.1	27.7	51.8	67.4
57	Thailand	2.9	1.9	1.3	54	64	83	103	34.2	21.6	61.4	68.2
58	Botswana	3.5	3.4	2.6	1	2	2	4	47.4	25.3	48.8	68.9
59	Cameroon	2.7	3.2	3.2	11	16	33	75	46.6	38.3	49.7	58.3
60	Jamaica	1.3	1.5	0.5	2	3	3	4	34.8	21.1	58.0	68.2
61	Ecuador	3.1	2.7	2.2	10	13	19	26	40.5	24.0	55.3	68.0
62	Colombia	2.5	2.1	1.6	32	38	50	63	35.9	22.3	59.8	68.2
63	Paraguay	2.8	3.2	2.7	4	6	9	13	40.6	26.9	55.7	66.3
64	Tunisia	2.1	2.5	2.2	8	10	14	19	38.7	23.7	57.3	68.3
65	Turkey	2.5	2.3	2.0	54	68	91	120	35.4	23.2	60.3	67.7
66	Peru	2.8	2.2	2.1	21	26	37	49	39.1	23.7	57.2	68.3
67	Jordan	2.5	3.7	3.6	4	6	12	22	47.2	34.4	50.0	61.9

Note: For data comparability and coverage, see the technical notes. Figures in italics are for years other than those specified.

		Average annual growth of population [a] (percent)			Population (millions)			Hypothetical size of stationary population (millions)	Age structure of population (percent)			
									0–14 years		15–64 years	
		1965–80	1980–88	1988–2000	1988	2000[a]	2025[a]		1988	2025	1988	2025
68	Chile	1.7	1.7	1.3	13	15	19	23	30.8	21.3	63.1	65.7
69	Syrian Arab Rep.	3.4	3.6	3.6	12	18	36	74	48.3	36.0	49.1	60.3
70	Costa Rica	2.7	2.3	2.0	3	3	5	6	36.4	22.1	59.7	66.2
71	Mexico	3.1	2.2	1.9	84	105	142	184	38.6	22.8	57.7	68.2
72	Mauritius	1.6	1.0	0.8	1	1	1	2	29.5	19.3	66.5	67.5
73	Poland	0.8	0.8	0.5	38	40	45	50	25.2	19.7	64.9	62.0
74	Malaysia	2.5	2.6	2.2	17	22	30	40	37.2	23.4	58.9	67.2
75	Panama	2.6	2.2	1.6	2	3	4	5	35.9	21.9	59.4	67.2
76	Brazil	2.4	2.2	1.8	144	178	236	303	35.7	22.8	59.8	66.9
77	*Angola*	2.8	2.5	3.0	9	14	27	69	45.0	40.6	52.6	56.3
78	*Lebanon*	1.7	..	..	..	..	..	..	..	..	..	..
79	*Nicaragua*	3.1	3.4	3.0	4	5	9	14	46.1	28.4	51.0	66.4
	Upper-middle-income	**2.0 w**	**1.8 w**	**1.7 w**	**326 t**	**402 t**	**569 t**		**33.4 w**	**26.0 w**	**60.5 w**	**64.0 w**
80	South Africa	2.4	2.3	2.3	34	45	65	96	38.2	25.3	58.1	67.1
81	Algeria	3.1	3.1	2.9	24	33	52	78	44.4	25.7	52.2	68.4
82	Hungary	0.4	−0.1	−0.2	11	10	10	10	19.9	17.4	66.7	61.7
83	Uruguay	0.4	0.6	0.6	3	3	4	4	26.2	20.1	62.7	64.1
84	Argentina	1.6	1.4	1.1	32	36	44	53	30.1	21.5	61.0	65.0
85	Yugoslavia	0.9	0.7	0.6	24	25	28	30	23.5	18.7	67.6	62.4
86	Gabon	3.6	3.9	2.7	1	1	3	7	38.2	39.4	56.9	56.4
87	Venezuela	3.5	2.8	2.2	19	24	34	45	38.7	23.3	57.7	67.5
88	Trinidad and Tobago	1.1	1.7	1.4	1	1	2	2	33.1	22.1	61.6	65.6
89	Korea, Rep. of	2.0	1.2	0.9	42	47	54	56	27.3	18.0	67.9	66.0
90	Portugal	0.4	0.7	0.4	10	11	11	11	21.8	16.4	65.6	63.5
91	Greece	0.7	0.5	0.2	10	10	10	10	19.9	16.0	66.3	60.9
92	Oman	3.7	4.7	3.9	1	2	5	11	45.5	38.1	52.0	57.3
93	Libya	4.3	4.3	3.6	4	6	14	35	46.0	39.5	51.2	56.7
94	*Iran, Islamic Rep.*	3.1	3.0	3.1	49	70	129	247	43.7	34.0	53.5	61.3
95	*Iraq*	3.4	3.6	3.4	18	26	49	90	46.7	33.1	50.6	62.5
96	*Romania*	1.1	0.4	0.5	23	25	27	31	23.8	20.0	66.2	63.6
	Low- and middle-income	**2.3 w**	**2.0 w**	**1.9 w**	**3,952 t**	**4,961 t**	**7,123 t**		**36.0 w**	**26.8 w**	**59.5 w**	**65.2 w**
	Sub-Saharan Africa	**2.7 w**	**3.2 w**	**3.1 w**	**464 t**	**672 t**	**1,310 t**		**46.9 w**	**38.0 w**	**50.2 w**	**58.8 w**
	East Asia	**2.3 w**	**1.5 w**	**1.4 w**	**1,538 t**	**1,824 t**	**2,293 t**		**30.3 w**	**21.3 w**	**64.6 w**	**67.0 w**
	South Asia	**2.4 w**	**2.3 w**	**2.0 w**	**1,107 t**	**1,401 t**	**1,987 t**		**38.7 w**	**26.1 w**	**57.2 w**	**67.2 w**
	Europe, M.East, & N.Africa	**2.0 w**	**2.1 w**	**2.1 w**	**396 t**	**505 t**	**769 t**		**36.5 w**	**28.7 w**	**57.9 w**	**63.4 w**
	Latin America & Caribbean	**2.5 w**	**2.2 w**	**1.8 w**	**414 t**	**514 t**	**699 t**		**36.9 w**	**23.5 w**	**58.6 w**	**67.1 w**
	Severely indebted	**2.4 w**	**2.1 w**	**1.8 w**	**496 t**	**614 t**	**844 t**		**36.5 w**	**24.5 w**	**58.5 w**	**66.2 w**
	High-income economies	**0.9 w**	**0.7 w**	**0.6 w**	**783 t**	**840 t**	**918 t**		**20.5 w**	**17.9 w**	**66.8 w**	**60.6 w**
	OECD members	**0.8 w**	**0.6 w**	**0.5 w**	**751 t**	**796 t**	**847 t**		**19.9 w**	**16.8 w**	**67.1 w**	**60.6 w**
	†Other	**3.5 w**	**2.9 w**	**2.5 w**	**32 t**	**43 t**	**71 t**		**35.1 w**	**30.3 w**	**59.9 w**	**60.2 w**
97	†Saudi Arabia	4.7	4.2	..	14	..	..	..	45.2	..	52.4	..
98	Spain	1.0	0.5	0.4	39	41	43	41	21.3	16.2	65.9	63.0
99	Ireland	1.2	0.5	0.3	4	4	4	5	27.7	19.8	61.2	64.9
100	†Israel	2.8	1.7	1.7	4	5	7	9	32.0	21.3	59.9	65.2
101	†Singapore	1.6	1.1	1.0	3	3	3	4	24.0	18.0	70.8	61.5
102	†Hong Kong	2.0	1.5	0.9	6	6	7	6	21.9	16.0	69.2	61.3
103	New Zealand	1.3	0.8	0.7	3	4	4	4	23.6	18.3	67.1	62.8
104	Australia	1.8	1.4	1.4	17	20	23	24	22.6	18.1	66.6	63.0
105	United Kingdom	0.2	0.2	0.3	57	59	61	61	19.0	17.4	65.5	61.2
106	Italy	0.5	0.2	0.1	57	58	56	46	17.5	14.1	68.4	60.5
107	†Kuwait	7.1	4.4	2.8	2	3	4	5	37.6	21.3	59.2	65.8
108	Belgium	0.3	0.0	0.0	10	10	10	9	18.4	16.0	67.2	60.1
109	Netherlands	0.9	0.5	0.5	15	16	16	14	18.0	15.6	68.9	59.7
110	Austria	0.3	0.0	0.1	8	8	8	7	18.0	15.4	67.1	60.4
111	†United Arab Emirates	16.5	4.8	2.3	1	2	3	3	31.0	22.1	67.0	61.2
112	France	0.7	0.4	0.4	56	59	63	63	20.5	17.3	66.0	60.6
113	Canada	1.3	0.9	0.9	26	29	32	32	21.3	16.9	68.4	60.7
114	Denmark	0.5	0.0	0.0	5	5	5	5	17.6	15.7	67.1	60.2
115	Germany, Fed. Rep.	0.3	−0.1	0.0	61	61	58	50	15.2	15.0	69.6	59.0
116	Finland	0.3	0.5	0.2	5	5	5	5	19.4	16.4	67.8	58.9
117	Sweden	0.5	0.2	0.4	8	9	9	9	17.6	17.6	64.7	59.3
118	United States	1.0	1.0	0.8	246	270	307	316	21.6	18.0	66.0	61.2
119	Norway	0.6	0.3	0.4	4	4	5	5	19.6	17.1	64.5	61.0
120	Japan	1.2	0.6	0.4	123	129	131	121	19.6	15.7	68.9	58.8
121	Switzerland	0.5	0.3	0.4	7	7	7	6	17.0	16.1	68.2	58.4
	Total reporting economies	**2.1 w**	**1.8 w**	**1.7 w**	**4,735 t**	**5,801 t**	**8,041 t**		**33.4 w**	**25.7 w**	**60.7 w**	**64.6 w**
	Oil exporters	**2.7 w**	**2.7 w**	**2.4 w**	**592 t**	**790 t**	**1,261 t**		**41.4 w**	**29.6 w**	**55.1 w**	**64.2 w**
	Nonreporting nonmembers	**1.0 w**	**0.9 w**	**0.6 w**	**365 t**	**392 t**	**450 t**		**25.5 w**	**20.1 w**	**64.1 w**	**63.4 w**

a. For the assumptions used in the projections, see the technical notes.

Table 27. Demography and fertility

		Crude birth rate per thousand population		Crude death rate per thousand population		Women of childbearing age as a percentage of population		Total fertility rate			Assumed year of reaching net reproduction rate of 1	Married women of childbearing age using contraception[b] (percent)
		1965	1988	1965	1988	1965	1988	1965	1988	2000[a]		1986
	Low-income economies	42 w	31 w	16 w	10 w	46 w	50 w	6.3 w	4.0 w	3.3 w		
	China and India	41 w	26 w	14 w	9 w	46 w	53 w	6.3 w	3.1 w	2.5 w		
	Other low-income	46 w	41 w	21 w	13 w	46 w	46 w	6.4 w	5.6 w	4.7 w		
1	Mozambique	49	45	27	17	47	45	6.8	6.3	6.1	2045	..
2	Ethiopia	43	51	20	20	46	43	5.8	7.5	7.2	2055	..
3	Chad	45	44	28	19	47	46	6.0	5.9	6.0	2045	..
4	Tanzania	49	48	22	13	45	43	6.6	6.7	5.8	2040	..
5	Bangladesh	47	40	21	15	44	46	6.8	5.5	4.3	2025	25
6	Malawi	56	54	26	20	46	45	7.8	7.6	7.3	2055	..
7	Somalia	50	49	26	19	45	44	6.7	6.8	6.5	2050	..
8	Zaire	47	45	21	14	46	45	6.0	6.0	5.4	2040	..
9	Bhutan	42	39	23	17	48	48	6.0	5.5	5.3	2035	..
10	Lao PDR	45	47	23	17	47	46	6.1	6.6	5.4	2035	..
11	Nepal	46	42	24	15	50	47	6.0	5.8	4.6	2030	15
12	Madagascar	47	43	22	16	47	44	6.6	6.0	4.8	2030	..
13	Burkina Faso	48	47	26	18	47	45	6.4	6.5	6.2	2045	..
14	Mali	50	50	27	19	46	45	6.5	7.0	6.9	2050	5
15	Burundi	47	47	24	16	48	45	6.4	6.8	6.0	2045	9
16	Uganda	49	51	19	17	44	43	7.0	7.3	6.5	2050	5
17	Nigeria	51	47	23	15	45	43	6.9	6.6	5.6	2040	..
18	Zambia	49	50	20	13	46	44	6.6	6.7	6.0	2045	..
19	Niger	48	51	29	20	43	44	6.8	7.1	7.3	2060	..
20	Rwanda	52	53	17	18	45	43	7.5	8.0	7.2	2055	..
21	China	38	21	10	7	44	55	6.4	2.4	2.1	2000	74
22	India	45	32	20	11	47	49	6.2	4.2	3.0	2015	35
23	Pakistan	48	46	21	13	43	46	7.0	6.6	5.4	2040	11
24	Kenya	52	47	20	11	40	41	8.0	6.9	5.3	2035	17
25	Togo	50	50	22	14	46	44	6.5	6.7	5.5	2040	..
26	Central African Rep.	34	42	24	15	47	46	4.5	5.7	5.2	2035	..
27	Haiti	43	35	20	13	47	49	6.2	4.7	3.8	2025	5
28	Benin	49	47	24	15	44	44	6.8	6.4	5.2	2035	..
29	Ghana	47	45	18	13	45	44	6.8	6.3	5.1	2035	13
30	Lesotho	42	41	18	13	47	46	5.8	5.7	4.5	2030	..
31	Sri Lanka	33	22	8	6	47	53	4.9	2.5	2.1	1995	62
32	Guinea	46	48	29	22	47	46	5.9	6.5	6.5	2050	..
33	Yemen, PDR	50	48	26	15	45	46	7.0	6.6	5.4	2035	..
34	Indonesia	43	28	20	9	47	51	5.5	3.4	2.5	2005	45
35	Mauritania	47	48	26	19	46	45	6.5	6.5	6.5	2050	..
36	Sudan	47	44	24	16	46	45	6.7	6.4	5.4	2035	..
37	*Afghanistan*	53	..	29	..	49	..	7.1	..	..	..	..
38	*Myanmar*	40	30	18	10	46	49	5.8	3.9	2.8	2010	..
39	*Kampuchea, Dem.*	44	..	20	..	47	..	6.2	..	..	..	..
40	*Liberia*	46	45	20	16	46	44	6.4	6.4	5.2	2035	6
41	*Sierra Leone*	48	48	31	23	47	46	6.4	6.5	6.5	2050	..
42	*Viet Nam*	..	31	..	7	..	48	..	4.0	2.8	2010	58
	Middle-income economies	38 w	29 w	13 w	8 w	45 w	49 w	5.6 w	3.8 w	3.1 w		
	Lower-middle-income	41 w	30 w	13 w	8 w	44 w	49 w	6.1 w	3.9 w	3.1 w		
43	Bolivia	46	42	21	14	46	46	6.6	6.0	4.8	2030	..
44	Philippines	42	31	12	7	44	49	6.8	3.8	2.7	2010	44
45	Yemen Arab Rep.	49	54	27	20	47	43	7.0	8.0	7.2	2055	..
46	Senegal	47	45	23	16	46	44	6.4	6.5	6.2	2045	12
47	Zimbabwe	55	38	17	8	42	46	8.0	5.3	3.4	2015	43
48	Egypt, Arab Rep.	43	34	19	9	43	47	6.8	4.5	3.5	2020	38
49	Dominican Rep.	47	31	13	7	43	51	7.0	3.7	2.7	2010	50
50	Côte d'Ivoire	52	50	22	14	44	42	7.4	7.3	6.4	2050	..
51	Papua New Guinea	43	36	20	12	47	47	6.2	5.2	4.0	2020	..
52	Morocco	49	35	18	9	45	48	7.1	4.7	3.5	2020	36
53	Honduras	51	39	17	8	44	45	7.4	5.5	4.2	2025	41
54	Guatemala	46	40	17	8	44	44	6.7	5.7	4.5	2030	23
55	Congo, People's Rep.	42	47	18	15	47	43	5.7	6.5	6.3	2050	..
56	El Salvador	46	36	13	8	44	45	6.7	4.8	3.8	2025	47
57	Thailand	41	22	10	7	44	53	6.3	2.5	2.1	1995	66
58	Botswana	53	38	19	7	45	44	6.9	5.1	3.1	2015	33
59	Cameroon	40	45	20	13	46	42	5.2	6.5	5.8	2045	..
60	Jamaica	38	23	9	6	42	50	5.7	2.6	2.1	1995	..
61	Ecuador	45	32	13	7	43	48	6.8	4.2	3.1	2015	44
62	Colombia	43	26	11	6	43	52	6.5	3.1	2.2	2000	65
63	Paraguay	41	35	8	6	41	49	6.6	4.5	3.7	2025	38
64	Tunisia	44	31	16	7	43	49	7.0	4.1	2.9	2010	50
65	Turkey	41	30	15	8	44	50	5.8	3.7	2.8	2010	77
66	Peru	45	31	16	9	44	49	6.7	4.0	2.9	2010	46
67	Jordan	53	42	21	6	45	43	8.0	6.4	5.2	2035	..

Note: For data comparability and coverage, see the technical notes. Figures in italics are for years other than those specified.

		Crude birth rate per thousand population		Crude death rate per thousand population		Women of childbearing age as a percentage of population		Total fertility rate			Assumed year of reaching net reproduction rate of 1	Married women of childbearing age using contraception[b] (percent)
		1965	1988	1965	1988	1965	1988	1965	1988	2000[a]		1986
68	Chile	34	23	11	6	45	53	4.8	2.7	2.1	2000	..
69	Syrian Arab Rep.	48	45	16	7	41	43	7.7	6.7	5.5	2040	..
70	Costa Rica	45	27	8	4	42	52	6.3	3.2	2.4	2005	69
71	Mexico	45	28	11	6	43	50	6.7	3.5	2.4	2005	53
72	Mauritius	36	19	8	7	45	56	5.0	2.0	1.8	2030	78
73	Poland	17	16	7	10	47	48	2.5	2.2	2.1	1990	..
74	Malaysia	40	30	12	5	43	51	6.3	3.7	2.8	2010	51
75	Panama	40	26	9	5	44	51	5.7	3.1	2.2	2000	58
76	Brazil	39	28	11	8	45	51	5.6	3.4	2.4	2005	66
77	*Angola*	49	47	29	20	47	45	6.4	6.4	6.5	2050	..
78	*Lebanon*	40	..	12	..	42	..	6.2	..	..	..	..
79	*Nicaragua*	49	41	16	7	43	45	7.2	5.4	4.2	2025	..
	Upper-middle-income	**31** w	**26** w	**12** w	**8** w	**47** w	**49** w	**4.5** w	**3.5** w	**3.1** w		
80	South Africa	40	35	16	10	46	49	6.1	4.4	3.5	2020	..
81	Algeria	50	37	18	8	44	45	7.4	5.4	3.8	2020	..
82	Hungary	13	12	11	13	48	47	1.8	1.8	1.8	2030	73
83	Uruguay	21	17	10	10	49	46	2.8	2.4	2.1	1995	..
84	Argentina	23	21	9	9	50	47	3.1	2.9	2.3	2005	..
85	Yugoslavia	21	15	9	9	50	49	2.7	2.0	2.0	2030	..
86	Gabon	31	42	22	16	48	47	4.1	5.5	6.0	2045	..
87	Venezuela	42	30	8	5	44	50	6.1	3.7	2.7	2010	..
88	Trinidad and Tobago	33	26	8	6	46	53	4.3	2.9	2.3	2005	53
89	Korea, Rep. of	35	16	11	6	46	56	4.9	1.8	1.8	2030	70
90	Portugal	23	12	10	9	48	48	3.1	1.6	1.6	2030	..
91	Greece	18	11	8	10	51	47	2.3	1.6	1.6	2030	..
92	Oman	50	45	24	7	46	43	7.2	7.1	5.9	2045	..
93	Libya	49	44	17	9	45	44	7.4	6.8	5.9	2050	..
94	*Iran, Islamic Rep.*	46	41	18	8	42	47	7.1	5.6	4.7	2040	..
95	*Iraq*	49	42	18	8	45	44	7.2	6.3	5.1	2035	..
96	*Romania*	15	16	9	11	50	48	1.9	2.1	2.1	1985	..
	Low- and middle-income	**41** w	**30** w	**15** w	**10** w	**46** w	**50** w	**6.1** w	**3.9** w	**3.3** w		
	Sub-Saharan Africa	**48** w	**47** w	**22** w	**16** w	**45** w	**44** w	**6.6** w	**6.7** w	**5.9** w		
	East Asia	**39** w	**23** w	**11** w	**7** w	**45** w	**54** w	**6.2** w	**2.7** w	**2.2** w		
	South Asia	**45** w	**34** w	**20** w	**12** w	**47** w	**48** w	**6.3** w	**4.5** w	**3.4** w		
	Europe, M.East, & N.Africa	**35** w	**31** w	**15** w	**10** w	**46** w	**47** w	**5.1** w	**4.3** w	**3.7** w		
	Latin America & Caribbean	**40** w	**28** w	**12** w	**7** w	**45** w	**50** w	**5.8** w	**3.6** w	**2.6** w		
	Severely indebted	**37** w	**28** w	**12** w	**8** w	**45** w	**49** w	**5.4** w	**3.6** w	**2.8** w		
	High-income economies	**19** w	**14** w	**10** w	**9** w	**47** w	**50** w	**2.8** w	**1.8** w	**1.9** w		
	OECD members	**19** w	**13** w	**10** w	**9** w	**47** w	**50** w	**2.7** w	**1.7** w	**1.8** w		
	†Other	**35** w	**29** w	**11** w	**6** w	**45** w	**48** w	**5.4** w	**4.5** w	**4.0** w		
97	†Saudi Arabia	48	42	20	8	44	42	7.3	7.1	..	..	..
98	Spain	21	12	8	9	49	48	2.9	1.6	1.6	2030	59
99	Ireland	22	15	12	9	42	48	4.0	2.3	2.1	1990	..
100	†Israel	26	22	6	7	46	48	3.8	3.0	2.3	2005	..
101	†Singapore	31	18	6	5	45	59	4.7	1.9	1.9	2030	..
102	†Hong Kong	27	14	6	5	45	55	4.7	1.6	1.6	2030	72
103	New Zealand	23	16	9	8	45	52	3.6	1.9	1.9	2030	..
104	Australia	20	15	9	7	47	52	3.0	1.9	1.9	2030	..
105	United Kingdom	18	14	12	11	45	48	2.9	1.8	1.8	2030	..
106	Italy	19	10	10	9	48	49	2.7	1.3	1.4	2030	..
107	†Kuwait	48	26	7	3	45	50	7.4	3.7	2.6	2010	..
108	Belgium	17	12	12	11	44	48	2.6	1.6	1.6	2030	..
109	Netherlands	20	13	8	8	47	52	3.0	1.6	1.6	2030	72
110	Austria	18	12	13	11	43	48	2.7	1.5	1.6	2030	..
111	†United Arab Emirates	41	23	14	4	47	47	6.8	4.7	3.7	2020	..
112	France	18	14	11	9	43	48	2.8	1.8	1.8	2030	..
113	Canada	21	14	8	7	47	53	3.1	1.7	1.7	2030	73
114	Denmark	18	12	10	12	47	50	2.6	1.5	1.6	2030	..
115	Germany, Fed. Rep.	18	11	12	11	45	48	2.5	1.5	1.5	2030	78
116	Finland	17	13	10	10	48	49	2.4	1.7	1.7	2030	..
117	Sweden	16	13	10	12	47	47	2.4	2.0	2.0	2030	..
118	United States	19	16	9	9	45	51	2.9	1.9	1.9	2030	..
119	Norway	18	14	10	11	45	48	2.9	1.8	1.8	2030	..
120	Japan	19	11	7	7	56	50	2.0	1.7	1.7	2030	64
121	Switzerland	19	12	10	9	48	50	2.6	1.6	1.7	2030	..
	Total reporting economies	**36** w	**28** w	**14** w	**10** w	**46** w	**50** w	**5.4** w	**3.6** w	**3.1** w		
	Oil exporters	**45** w	**35** w	**18** w	**9** w	**45** w	**48** w	**6.4** w	**4.7** w	**3.8** w		
	Nonreporting nonmembers	**20** w	**18** w	**8** w	**10** w	**47** w	**47** w	**2.7** w	**2.3** w	**2.1** w		

a. For assumptions used in the projections, see the technical note to Table 26.   b. Figures include women whose husbands practice contraception; see the technical notes.

Table 28. Health and nutrition

	Population per Physician		Population per Nursing person		Births attended by health staff (percent)	Babies with low birth weight (percent)	Infant mortality rate (per thousand live births)		Daily calorie supply (per capita)	
	1965	1984	1965	1984	1985	1985	1965	1988	1965	1986
Low-income economies	**9,760 w**	**5,580 w**	**6,010 w**	**2,200 w**			**124 w**	**72 w**	**1,993 w**	**2,384 w**
China and India	**2,930 w**	**1,640 w**	**4,420 w**	**1,710 w**			**114 w**	**59 w**	**2,001 w**	**2,463 w**
Other low-income	**28,080 w**	**13,910 w**	**10,170 w**	**3,250 w**			**149 w**	**98 w**	**1,976 w**	**2,226 w**
1 Mozambique	18,000	*37,960*	5,370	*5,760*	28	15	179	139	1,979	1,595
2 Ethiopia	70,190	78,970	5,970	5,400	58	..	165	135	1,824	1,749
3 Chad	72,480	*38,360*	13,610	3,390	..	11	183	130	2,399	1,717
4 Tanzania	21,700	26,200	2,100	8,130	74	14	138	104	1,832	2,192
5 Bangladesh	8,100	*6,730*	..	8,980	..	31	144	118	1,971	1,927
6 Malawi	47,320	11,330	40,980	*3,110*	59	10	200	149	2,244	2,310
7 Somalia	36,840	16,080	3,950	1,530	2	..	165	130	2,167	2,138
8 Zaire	34,740	..	..	..	..	..	141	96	2,187	2,163
9 Bhutan	..	*23,310*	..	*2,990*	3	..	171	127	..	..
10 Lao PDR	24,320	*1,360*	4,880	*530*	..	39	148	108	1,956	2,391
11 Nepal	46,180	32,710	*87,650*	4,680	10	..	171	126	1,901	2,052
12 Madagascar	10,620	9,780	3,650	..	62	9	201	119	2,462	2,440
13 Burkina Faso	73,960	57,220	4,150	*1,680*	..	18	193	137	2,009	2,139
14 Mali	51,510	25,390	3,360	*1,350*	27	17	207	168	1,858	2,073
15 Burundi	55,910	21,120	7,320	3,040	12	14	142	73	2,391	2,343
16 Uganda	11,110	*21,900*	3,130	*2,060*	..	10	121	101	2,360	2,344
17 Nigeria	29,530	7,990	6,160	*1,020*	..	25	177	103	2,185	2,146
18 Zambia	11,380	*7,150*	5,820	740	..	14	121	78	..	..
19 Niger	65,540	39,730	6,210	460	47	20	180	133	1,994	2,432
20 Rwanda	72,480	*34,680*	7,450	3,650	..	17	141	120	1,665	1,830
21 China	1,600	1,000	3,000	1,710	..	6	90	31	1,926	2,630
22 India	4,880	2,520	6,500	1,700	33	30	150	97	2,111	2,238
23 Pakistan	..	2,910	9,910	4,900	24	25	149	107	1,761	2,315
24 Kenya	13,280	9,970	1,930	950	..	13	112	70	2,289	2,060
25 Togo	23,240	8,700	4,990	1,240	..	20	156	92	2,378	2,207
26 Central African Rep.	34,020	23,530	3,000	2,210	..	15	157	102	2,135	1,949
27 Haiti	14,000	7,180	12,890	2,290	20	17	178	116	2,000	1,902
28 Benin	32,390	15,940	2,540	*1,750*	34	10	166	115	2,009	2,184
29 Ghana	13,740	14,890	3,730	*640*	73	17	120	88	1,950	1,759
30 Lesotho	20,060	18,610	4,700	..	28	10	142	98	2,065	2,303
31 Sri Lanka	5,820	*5,520*	3,220	*1,290*	87	28	63	21	2,153	2,400
32 Guinea	47,050	46,420	4,110	*5,160*	..	18	191	143	1,923	1,776
33 Yemen, PDR	12,870	*4,370*	1,850	*1,060*	10	13	197	118	1,982	2,298
34 Indonesia	31,700	*9,460*	9,490	*1,260*	43	14	128	68	1,800	2,579
35 Mauritania	36,530	12,120	..	1,200	23	10	178	125	2,064	2,322
36 Sudan	23,500	10,100	3,360	1,250	20	15	160	106	1,938	2,208
37 *Afghanistan*	15,770	..	24,430	..	..	..	206	..	2,294	..
38 *Myanmar*	11,860	*3,740*	11,370	*900*	97	16	125	68	1,917	2,609
39 *Kampuchea, Dem.*	22,410	..	3,670	..	..	..	134	..	2,276	..
40 *Liberia*	12,560	*9,340*	2,330	*1,370*	89	..	176	130	2,154	2,381
41 *Sierra Leone*	16,840	13,630	4,470	1,090	25	14	209	152	1,837	1,854
42 *Viet Nam*	..	*1,000*	..	620	..	18	..	44	..	2,297
Middle-income economies	**4,060 w**	**2,520 w**	**2,190 w**	**980 w**			**98 w**	**52 w**	**2,458 w**	**2,846 w**
Lower-middle-income	**4,910 w**	**3,030 w**	**2,190 w**	**1,090 w**			**107 w**	**57 w**	**2,378 w**	**2,733 w**
43 Bolivia	3,300	1,540	3,990	2,480	36	15	160	108	1,869	2,143
44 Philippines	..	6,700	1,140	2,740	..	18	72	44	1,924	2,372
45 Yemen Arab Rep.	56,150	6,010	..	2,580	12	9	197	128	2,008	2,318
46 Senegal	19,490	*13,060*	2,440	2,030	..	10	126	78	2,479	2,350
47 Zimbabwe	8,010	6,700	990	*1,000*	69	15	103	49	2,105	2,132
48 Egypt, Arab Rep.	2,300	*770*	2,030	*780*	24	7	172	83	2,400	3,342
49 Dominican Rep.	1,700	1,760	1,640	1,210	57	16	110	63	1,872	2,477
50 Côte d'Ivoire	20,640	..	2,000	..	20	14	149	95	2,359	2,562
51 Papua New Guinea	12,640	*6,070*	620	*880*	34	25	143	61	1,905	2,205
52 Morocco	12,120	*15,580*	2,290	920	..	9	145	71	2,167	2,915
53 Honduras	5,370	1,510	1,530	670	50	20	128	68	1,963	2,068
54 Guatemala	3,690	2,180	8,250	850	19	10	112	57	2,027	2,307
55 Congo, People's Rep.	14,210	*8,320*	950	590	..	12	129	117	2,259	2,619
56 El Salvador	..	2,830	1,300	930	35	15	120	57	1,859	2,160
57 Thailand	7,160	6,290	4,970	710	33	12	88	30	2,101	2,331
58 Botswana	27,450	*6,900*	17,710	*700*	52	8	112	41	2,019	2,201
59 Cameroon	26,720	5,830	..	..	..	13	143	92	2,079	2,028
60 Jamaica	1,990	2,040	340	490	89	8	49	11	2,231	2,590
61 Ecuador	3,000	820	2,320	610	27	10	112	62	1,940	2,058
62 Colombia	2,500	1,240	890	660	51	15	86	39	2,174	2,542
63 Paraguay	1,850	1,460	1,550	1,000	22	6	73	41	2,627	2,853
64 Tunisia	8,000	*2,150*	..	*370*	60	7	145	48	2,201	2,994
65 Turkey	2,900	1,380	..	*1,030*	78	7	165	75	2,659	3,229
66 Peru	1,650	1,040	900	..	55	9	130	86	2,325	2,246
67 Jordan	4,690	1,140	1,800	1,300	75	7	114	43	2,314	2,991

Note: For data comparability and coverage, see the technical notes. Figures in italics are for years other than those specified.

		Population per				Births attended by health staff (percent)	Babies with low birth weight (percent)	Infant mortality rate (per thousand live births)		Daily calorie supply (per capita)	
		Physician		Nursing person							
		1965	1984	1965	1984	1985	1985	1965	1988	1965	1986
68	Chile	2,120	1,230	600	370	97	7	101	20	2,592	2,579
69	Syrian Arab Rep.	5,400	1,260	..	1,440	37	9	114	46	2,195	3,260
70	Costa Rica	2,010	960	630	450	93	9	72	18	2,366	2,803
71	Mexico	2,080	1,240	980	880	..	15	82	46	2,644	3,132
72	Mauritius	3,930	1,900	2,030	580	90	9	65	22	2,271	2,748
73	Poland	800	490	410	190	..	8	42	16	3,229	3,336
74	Malaysia	6,200	1,930	1,320	1,010	82	9	55	23	2,247	2,730
75	Panama	2,130	980	1,600	390	83	8	56	22	2,255	2,446
76	Brazil	2,500	1,080	3,100	1,210	73	8	104	61	2,402	2,656
77	Angola	13,150	17,790	3,820	1,020	15	17	192	135	1,897	1,880
78	Lebanon	1,010	..	2,030	..	..	..	56	..	2,489	..
79	Nicaragua	2,560	1,500	1,390	530	..	15	121	60	2,398	2,495
	Upper-middle-income	**2,380 w**	**1,220 w**	**2,190 w**	**680 w**			**82 w**	**42 w**	**2,629 w**	**3,117 w**
80	South Africa	2,050	..	490	..	..	12	124	70	2,623	2,924
81	Algeria	8,590	2,340	11,770	330	..	9	154	72	1,681	2,715
82	Hungary	630	310	240	170	99	10	39	16	3,171	3,569
83	Uruguay	880	520	590	..	..	8	47	23	2,811	2,648
84	Argentina	600	370	610	980	..	6	58	31	3,210	3,210
85	Yugoslavia	1,200	550	850	260	..	7	72	25	3,289	3,563
86	Gabon	..	2,790	760	270	92	16	153	101	1,881	2,521
87	Venezuela	1,210	700	560	..	82	9	65	35	2,321	2,494
88	Trinidad and Tobago	3,810	950	560	260	90	..	42	16	2,497	3,082
89	Korea, Rep. of	2,680	1,160	2,970	580	65	9	62	24	2,256	2,907
90	Portugal	1,240	410	1,160	..	..	8	65	14	2,517	3,151
91	Greece	710	350	600	450	..	6	34	12	3,049	3,688
92	Oman	23,790	1,700	6,420	760	60	14	194	38	..	..
93	Libya	3,860	690	850	350	76	5	138	80	1,925	3,601
94	Iran, Islamic Rep.	3,890	2,690	4,270	1,050	..	9	152	64	2,204	3,313
95	Iraq	5,000	1,740	2,910	1,660	50	9	119	68	2,150	2,932
96	Romania	760	570	400	280	99	6	44	24	2,978	3,373
	Low- and middle-income	**8,270 w**	**4,790 w**	**5,020 w**	**1,900 w**			**117 w**	**67 w**	**2,116 w**	**2,507 w**
	Sub-Saharan Africa	**33,200 w**	**23,850 w**	**5,420 w**	**2,460 w**			**160 w**	**108 w**	**2,092 w**	**2,096 w**
	East Asia	**5,600 w**	**2,390 w**	**4,050 w**	**1,570 w**			**92 w**	**37 w**	**1,937 w**	**2,594 w**
	South Asia	**6,220 w**	**3,570 w**	**8,380 w**	**2,710 w**			**147 w**	**99 w**	**2,060 w**	**2,228 w**
	Europe, M.East, & N.Africa	**4,760 w**	**2,430 w**	**3,440 w**	**1,160 w**			**115 w**	**62 w**	**2,610 w**	**3,177 w**
	Latin America & Caribbean	**2,370 w**	**1,230 w**	**2,090 w**	**1,020 w**			**95 w**	**53 w**	**2,457 w**	**2,700 w**
	Severely indebted	**3,010 w**	**2,560 w**	**1,620 w**	**1,180 w**			**88 w**	**51 w**	**2,537 w**	**2,768 w**
	High-income economies	**940 w**	**470 w**	**470 w**	**140 w**			**25 w**	**9 w**	**3,083 w**	**3,376 w**
	OECD members	**870 w**	**450 w**	**420 w**	**130 w**			**24 w**	**8 w**	**3,100 w**	**3,390 w**
	†Other	**4,430 w**	**800 w**	**2,510 w**	**260 w**			**69 w**	**36 w**	**2,323 w**	**3,001 w**
97	†Saudi Arabia	9,400	690	6,060	320	78	6	148	69	1,853	3,004
98	Spain	800	320	1,220	260	96	..	38	9	2,822	3,359
99	Ireland	950	680	170	140	..	4	25	7	3,546	3,632
100	†Israel	400	350	300	110	99	7	27	11	2,784	3,061
101	†Singapore	1,900	1,310	600	..	100	7	26	7	2,297	2,840
102	†Hong Kong	2,520	1,070	1,250	240	..	4	27	7	2,504	2,859
103	New Zealand	820	580	570	80	99	5	20	11	3,237	3,463
104	Australia	720	440	150	110	99	6	19	9	3,118	3,326
105	United Kingdom	870	..	200	120	98	7	20	9	3,353	3,256
106	Italy	1,850	230	790	..	..	7	36	10	3,091	3,523
107	†Kuwait	790	640	270	200	99	7	64	15	2,945	3,021
108	Belgium	700	330	590	110	100	5	24	9	..	..
109	Netherlands	860	450	270	170	..	4	14	8	3,108	3,326
110	Austria	720	390	350	180	..	6	28	8	3,231	3,428
111	†United Arab Emirates	..	1,020	..	390	96	..	108	25	2,705	3,733
112	France	830	320	380	110	..	5	22	8	3,217	3,336
113	Canada	770	510	190	120	99	6	24	7	3,212	3,462
114	Denmark	740	400	190	60	..	6	19	8	3,395	3,633
115	Germany, Fed. Rep.	640	380	500	230	..	5	24	8	3,102	3,528
116	Finland	1,300	440	180	60	..	4	17	6	3,111	3,122
117	Sweden	910	390	310	100	100	4	13	6	2,888	3,064
118	United States	670	470	310	70	100	7	25	10	3,224	3,645
119	Norway	790	450	340	60	100	4	17	8	3,032	2,864
120	Japan	970	660	410	180	100	5	18	5	2,687	2,864
121	Switzerland	710	700	270	130	..	5	18	7	3,412	3,437
	Total reporting economies	**6,630 w**	**4,070 w**	**4,000 w**	**1,600 w**			**97 w**	**57 w**	**2,321 w**	**2,653 w**
	Oil exporters	**17,920 w**	**5,130 w**	**5,740 w**	**1,010 w**			**134 w**	**71 w**	**2,128 w**	**2,737 w**
	Nonreporting nonmembers	**540 w**	**380 w**	**300 w**	**170 w**			**30 w**	**24 w**	**3,151 w**	**3,395 w**

Table 29. Education

	Percentage of age group enrolled in education										Primary net enrollment (percent)		Primary pupil-teacher ratio	
	Primary				Secondary				Tertiary (total)					
	Total		Female		Total		Female							
	1965	1987	1965	1987	1965	1987	1965	1987	1965	1987	1975	1987	1965	1987
Low-income economies	73 w	104 w	..	95 w	20 w	37 w	..	29 w	2 w	..	..	..	..	..
China and India	83 w	117 w	..	106 w	25 w	41 w	..	33 w	2 w	..	..	..	..	..
Other low-income	49 w	76 w	37 w	68 w	9 w	26 w	5 w	16 w	1 w	3 w	..	..	..	..
1 Mozambique	37	68	26	59	3	5	2	4	0	0	..	45	..	..
2 Ethiopia	11	37	6	28	2	15	1	12	0	1	..	27	41	..
3 Chad	34	51	13	29	1	6	0	2	..	0	..	38	83	..
4 Tanzania	32	66	25	66	2	4	1	3	0	0	..	50	52	33
5 Bangladesh	49	59	31	49	13	18	3	11	1	5	..	53	45	48
6 Malawi	44	66	32	59	2	4	1	3	0	1	..	49	..	..
7 Somalia	10	15	4	10	2	9	1	6	0	3	16	..	26	..
8 Zaire	70	76	45	64	5	22	2	13	0	2	..	..	37	..
9 Bhutan	7	24	1	17	0	4	..	1	..	..	..	..	..	..
10 Lao PDR	40	111	30	100	2	23	1	19	0	2	..	..	37	..
11 Nepal	20	82	4	..	5	26	2	..	1	5	..	..	..	..
12 Madagascar	65	..	59	..	8	21	5	19	1	4	..	..	71	..
13 Burkina Faso	12	32	8	24	1	6	1	4	0	1	..	27	47	65
14 Mali	24	23	16	17	4	6	2	4	0	1	..	18	46	38
15 Burundi	26	67	15	50	1	4	1	3	0	1	..	..	40	..
16 Uganda	67	70	50	63	4	13	2	9	0	1	..	..	..	..
17 Nigeria	32	77	24	..	5	..	3	..	0	..	..	..	33	..
18 Zambia	53	97	46	92	7	17	3	13	..	1	..	..	51	..
19 Niger	11	29	7	20	1	6	0	3	..	1	..	..	42	..
20 Rwanda	53	67	43	66	2	6	1	5	0	0	..	64	67	..
21 China	89	132	..	124	24	43	..	37	1	2	..	98	..	..
22 India	74	98	57	81	27	39	13	27	5	..	..	..	42	..
23 Pakistan	40	52	20	35	12	19	5	11	2	5	..	..	42	41
24 Kenya	54	96	40	93	4	23	2	19	0	1	88	..	34	..
25 Togo	55	101	32	78	5	24	2	12	0	3	..	73	50	..
26 Central African Rep.	56	66	28	51	2	12	1	6	..	1	..	49	54	63
27 Haiti	50	95	44	89	5	17	3	16	0	..	..	..	..	..
28 Benin	34	63	21	43	3	16	2	9	0	3	..	50	41	33
29 Ghana	69	71	57	63	13	40	7	32	1	2	..	..	32	24
30 Lesotho	94	113	114	125	4	..	4	..	0	..	..	..	57	..
31 Sri Lanka	93	104	86	102	35	66	35	69	2	4	..	..	..	..
32 Guinea	31	30	19	18	5	9	2	4	0	1	..	23	..	..
33 Yemen, PDR	23	..	10	..	11	..	5	..	..	..	..	..	..	..
34 Indonesia	72	118	65	115	12	46	7	..	1	..	72	..	..	..
35 Mauritania	13	52	6	42	1	16	0	9	..	3	..	..	20	..
36 Sudan	29	49	21	41	4	20	2	17	1	2	..	..	48	..
37 Afghanistan	16	..	5	..	2	..	1	..	0	..	..	..	53	..
38 Myanmar	71	..	65	..	15	..	11	..	1	..	..	..	..	..
39 Kampuchea, Dem.	77	..	56	..	9	..	4	..	1	..	..	..	48	..
40 Liberia	41	35	23	..	5	..	3	..	1	3	..	..	..	..
41 Sierra Leone	29	..	21	..	5	..	3	..	0	..	..	..	32	..
42 Viet Nam	..	102	..	99	..	42	..	40	..	..	..	..	..	..
Middle-income economies	92 w	104 w	86 w	101 w	26 w	54 w	22 w	54 w	6 w	17 w	..	..	36 w	29 w
Lower-middle-income	92 w	104 w	86 w	101 w	23 w	49 w	20 w	50 w	6 w	16 w	..	..	37 w	29 w
43 Bolivia	73	91	60	85	18	37	15	35	5	17	73	83	28	27
44 Philippines	113	106	111	106	41	68	40	69	19	38	95	..	31	..
45 Yemen Arab Rep.	9	91	1	40	0	26	..	6	..	2	22	..	56	..
46 Senegal	40	60	29	49	7	15	3	10	1	3	..	50	43	54
47 Zimbabwe	110	136	92	132	6	45	5	36	0	4	..	..	..	..
48 Egypt, Arab Rep.	75	90	60	79	26	69	15	58	7	20	..	..	39	..
49 Dominican Rep.	87	133	87	135	12	47	12	56	2	19	..	..	53	..
50 Côte d'Ivoire	60	70	41	58	6	19	2	12	0	..	..	..	47	..
51 Papua New Guinea	44	70	35	64	4	12	2	9	..	2	..	..	19	31
52 Morocco	57	71	35	56	11	37	5	30	1	10	47	57	39	26
53 Honduras	80	106	79	108	10	32	9	..	1	9	..	..	..	..
54 Guatemala	50	77	45	70	8	21	7	..	2	9	53	..	33	35
55 Congo, People's Rep.	114	..	94	..	10	..	5	..	1	7	..	..	60	..
56 El Salvador	82	79	79	81	17	29	17	30	2	18	..	71	34	45
57 Thailand	78	95	74	..	14	28	11	..	2	20	..	..	35	..
58 Botswana	65	114	71	117	3	32	3	33	..	3	58	..	40	..
59 Cameroon	94	109	75	100	5	26	2	20	0	3	69	..	47	..
60 Jamaica	109	105	106	106	51	65	50	67	3	4	90	..	..	..
61 Ecuador	91	117	88	116	17	56	16	57	3	30	78	..	37	..
62 Colombia	84	114	86	115	17	56	16	56	3	14	..	..	36	..
63 Paraguay	102	102	96	99	13	30	13	30	4	..	83	..	30	..
64 Tunisia	91	116	65	107	16	40	9	34	2	6	..	95	56	31
65 Turkey	101	117	83	113	16	46	9	34	4	10	..	84	46	31
66 Peru	99	122	90	120	25	65	21	61	8	25	..	..	36	..
67 Jordan	95	..	83	..	38	..	23	..	2	..	..	..	38	..

Note: For data comparability and coverage, see the technical notes. Figures in italics are for years other than those specified.

		Percentage of age group enrolled in education										Primary net enrollment (percent)		Primary pupil-teacher ratio	
		Primary				Secondary				Tertiary (total)					
		Total		Female		Total		Female							
		1965	1987	1965	1987	1965	1987	1965	1987	1965	1987	1975	1987	1965	1987
68	Chile	124	103	122	104	34	70	36	71	6	18	94	..	52	..
69	Syrian Arab Rep.	78	110	52	104	28	59	13	48	8	18	87	99	36	26
70	Costa Rica	106	98	105	97	24	41	25	43	6	25	92	85	27	31
71	Mexico	92	118	90	116	17	53	13	53	4	16	..	100	47	32
72	Mauritius	101	106	97	107	26	51	18	50	3	1	82	94	34	23
73	Poland	104	101	102	101	69	80	69	82	18	18	96	99	28	16
74	Malaysia	90	102	84	102	28	59	22	59	2	7	..	..	..	22
75	Panama	102	106	99	104	34	59	36	63	7	28	87	..	30	..
76	Brazil	108	103	108	..	16	39	16	45	2	11	71	84	28	..
77	Angola	39	..	26	..	5	..	4	..	0	..	..	..	..	..
78	Lebanon	106	..	93	..	26	..	20	..	14	..	..	..	..	..
79	Nicaragua	69	99	69	104	14	43	13	58	2	8	65	76	34	32
	Upper-middle-income	92 w	104 w	86 w	101 w	32 w	67 w	27 w	65 w	7 w	20 w	..	..	34 w	30 w
80	South Africa	90	..	88	..	15	..	14	..	4	..	..	88	43	29
81	Algeria	68	96	53	81	7	55	5	46	1	9	77	95	23	14
82	Hungary	101	97	100	97	..	70	..	70	13	15	..	..	..	..
83	Uruguay	106	110	106	109	44	73	46	..	8	42	..	..	..	..
84	Argentina	101	110	102	110	28	74	31	78	14	39	96	..	20	..
85	Yugoslavia	106	95	103	94	65	80	59	79	13	19	..	..	31	..
86	Gabon	134	..	122	..	11	..	5	..	..	5	81	..	39	..
87	Venezuela	94	107	94	107	27	54	28	59	7	27	..	..	34	..
88	Trinidad and Tobago	93	100	90	100	36	82	34	85	2	4	87	88	34	24
89	Korea, Rep. of	101	101	99	101	35	88	25	86	6	36	99	99	62	37
90	Portugal	84	124	83	121	42	56	34	..	5	12	91	..	32	..
91	Greece	110	104	109	104	49	90	41	89	10	26	97	..	36	..
92	Oman	..	97	..	92	..	38	..	29	..	2	32	80	..	..
93	Libya	78	..	44	..	14	..	4	..	1	10	..	94	31	..
94	Iran, Islamic Rep.	63	114	40	105	18	48	11	39	2	5	..	..	32	29
95	Iraq	74	98	45	91	28	49	14	38	4	13	79	86	22	25
96	Romania	101	97	100	98	39	79	32	80	10	10	..	..	23	..
	Low- and middle-income	78 w	104 w	62 w	96 w	22 w	41 w	14 w	35 w	3 w	8 w	..	..	..	..
	Sub-Saharan Africa	41 w	68 w	30 w	57 w	4 w	17 w	2 w	12 w	0 w	1 w	..	..	42 w	..
	East Asia	88 w	125 w	..	120 w	23 w	45 w	..	40 w	1 w	5 w	..	..	..	..
	South Asia	68 w	89 w	52 w	73 w	24 w	35 w	12 w	24 w	4 w	..	..	..	42 w	..
	Europe, M.East, & N.Africa	83 w	97 w	71 w	90 w	32 w	57 w	26 w	50 w	7 w	12 w	..	..	36 w	..
	Latin America & Caribbean	98 w	108 w	96 w	110 w	19 w	49 w	19 w	53 w	4 w	17 w	..	..	34 w	..
	Severely indebted	99 w	104 w	97 w	103 w	27 w	53 w	26 w	55 w	8 w	19 w	..	..	33 w	27 w
	High-income economies	104 w	102 w	105 w	103 w	62 w	93 w	59 w	96 w	21 w	39 w	..	..	25 w	..
	OECD members	104 w	103 w	106 w	103 w	63 w	94 w	61 w	97 w	21 w	39 w	..	..	25 w	..
	†Other	75 w	87 w	68 w	85 w	27 w	62 w	25 w	59 w	7 w	17 w	..	..	26 w	..
97	†Saudi Arabia	24	71	11	65	4	44	1	35	1	13	42	..	22	..
98	Spain	115	113	114	113	38	102	29	107	6	30	100	..	34	..
99	Ireland	108	100	108	100	51	98	50	103	12	24	91		..	..
100	†Israel	95	95	95	97	48	83	51	87	20	34	..	..	..	19
101	†Singapore	105	..	100	..	45	..	41	..	10	..	100	..	29	..
102	†Hong Kong	103	106	99	105	29	74	25	76	5	..	92	..	29	..
103	New Zealand	106	107	104	106	75	85	74	86	15	36	100	..	22	..
104	Australia	99	106	99	105	62	98	61	99	16	29	98	98	28	17
105	United Kingdom	92	106	92	106	66	83	66	85	12	22	97	..	..	..
106	Italy	112	95	110	97	47	75	41	74	11	24	97	..	22	..
107	†Kuwait	116	94	103	92	52	82	43	79	..	17	68	79	23	12
108	Belgium	109	100	108	100	75	99	72	100	15	33	..	83	21	10
109	Netherlands	104	115	104	116	61	104	57	103	17	31	92	..	31	..
110	Austria	106	101	105	101	52	80	52	81	9	29	89	..	20	11
111	†United Arab Emirates	..	99	..	100	..	60	..	66	0	9	..	88	..	25
112	France	134	113	133	113	56	92	59	96	18	31	98	100	30	..
113	Canada	105	105	104	104	56	104	55	104	26	58	..	97	26	..
114	Denmark	98	99	99	99	83	107	67	107	14	30	..	..	11	..
115	Germany, Fed. Rep.	..	103	..	101	..	94	..	92	9	30	..	..	17	..
116	Finland	92	101	89	101	76	106	80	114	11	38	..	..	23	..
117	Sweden	95	100	96	..	62	91	60	92	13	31	100	100	20	..
118	United States	100	100	..	100	..	98	..	99	40	60	72	..	25	..
119	Norway	97	95	98	95	64	95	62	97	11	35	100	..	21	..
120	Japan	100	102	100	102	82	96	81	97	13	28	99	..	29	..
121	Switzerland	87	..	87	..	37	..	35	..	8	24	..	..	..	..
	Total reporting economies	83 w	104 w	70 w	97 w	28 w	50 w	23 w	46 w	7 w	15 w	..	..	35 w	..
	Oil exporters	68 w	104 w	59 w	105 w	15 w	52 w	10 w	49 w	2 w	15 w	..	..	37 w	..
	Nonreporting nonmembers	104 w	105 w	103 w	101 w	67 w	93 w	73 w	72 w	27 w	23 w	..	..	..	..

Table 30. Income distribution and ICP estimates of GDP

	ICP estimates of GDP per capita[a] (United States = 100) 1985	Percentage share of household income, by percentile group of households[b]						
		Year	Lowest 20 percent	Second quintile	Third quintile	Fourth quintile	Highest 20 percent	Highest 10 percent
Low-income economies								
China and India								
Other low-income								
1 Mozambique	..		..	..	..	..	..	..
2 Ethiopia	1.6		..	..	..	..	..	..
3 Chad	..		..	..	..	..	..	..
4 Tanzania	2.6		..	..	..	..	..	..
5 Bangladesh[c]	5.0	1981–82	9.3	13.1	16.8	21.8	39.0	24.9
6 Malawi	3.6		..	..	..	..	..	..
7 Somalia	..		..	..	..	..	..	..
8 Zaire	..		..	..	..	..	..	..
9 Bhutan	..		..	..	..	..	..	..
10 Lao PDR	..		..	..	..	..	..	..
11 Nepal	..		..	..	..	..	..	..
12 Madagascar	3.9		..	..	..	..	..	..
13 Burkina Faso	..		..	..	..	..	..	..
14 Mali	2.4		..	..	..	..	..	..
15 Burundi	..		..	..	..	..	..	..
16 Uganda	..		..	..	..	..	..	..
17 Nigeria	7.2		..	..	..	..	..	..
18 Zambia	4.7		..	..	..	..	..	..
19 Niger	..		..	..	..	..	..	..
20 Rwanda	3.8		..	..	..	..	..	..
21 China	..		..	..	..	..	..	..
22 India[c]	4.5	1983	8.1	12.3	16.3	22.0	41.4	26.7
23 Pakistan[d]	8.1	1984–85	7.8	11.2	15.0	20.6	45.6	31.3
24 Kenya	5.3		..	..	..	..	..	..
25 Togo	..		..	..	..	..	..	..
26 Central African Rep.	..		..	..	..	..	..	..
27 Haiti	..		..	..	..	..	..	..
28 Benin	6.5		..	..	..	..	..	..
29 Ghana[c]	..	1987	6.5	10.9	15.7	22.3	44.6	29.1
30 Lesotho	..		..	..	..	..	..	..
31 Sri Lanka[e]	11.2	1985–86	4.8	8.5	12.1	18.4	56.1	43.0
32 Guinea	..		..	..	..	..	..	..
33 Yemen, PDR	..		..	..	..	..	..	..
34 Indonesia[c]	..	1987	8.8	12.4	16.0	21.5	41.3	26.5
35 Mauritania	..		..	..	..	..	..	..
36 Sudan	..		..	..	..	..	..	..
37 *Afghanistan*	..		..	..	..	..	..	..
38 *Myanmar*	..		..	..	..	..	..	..
39 *Kampuchea, Dem.*	..		..	..	..	..	..	..
40 *Liberia*	..		..	..	..	..	..	..
41 *Sierra Leone*	3.0		..	..	..	..	..	..
42 *Viet Nam*	..		..	..	..	..	..	..
Middle-income economies								
Lower-middle-income								
43 Bolivia	..		..	..	..	..	..	..
44 Philippines[d]	10.8	1985	5.5	9.7	14.8	22.0	48.0	32.1
45 Yemen Arab Rep.	..		..	..	..	..	..	..
46 Senegal	7.0		..	..	..	..	..	..
47 Zimbabwe	9.9		..	..	..	..	..	..
48 Egypt, Arab Rep.	15.8		..	..	..	..	..	..
49 Dominican Rep.	..		..	..	..	..	..	..
50 Côte d'Ivoire[c]	10.2	1986	5.0	8.0	13.1	21.3	52.7	36.3
51 Papua New Guinea	..		..	..	..	..	..	..
52 Morocco[d]	13.1	1984–85	9.8	13.0	16.4	21.4	39.4	25.4
53 Honduras	..		..	..	..	..	..	..
54 Guatemala	..	1979–81	5.5	8.6	12.2	18.7	55.0	40.8
55 Congo, People's Rep.	16.4		..	..	..	..	..	..
56 El Salvador	..		..	..	..	..	..	..
57 Thailand	16.0		..	..	..	..	..	..
58 Botswana	16.1	1985–86	2.5	6.5	11.8	20.2	59.0	42.8
59 Cameroon	14.0		..	..	..	..	..	..
60 Jamaica[c]	..	1988	5.4	9.9	14.4	21.2	49.2	33.4
61 Ecuador	..		..	..	..	..	..	..
62 Colombia[e]	..	1988	4.0	8.7	13.5	20.8	53.0	37.1
63 Paraguay	..		..	..	..	..	..	..
64 Tunisia	19.8		..	..	..	..	..	..
65 Turkey	21.8		..	..	..	..	..	..
66 Peru[c]	..	1985	4.4	8.5	13.7	21.5	51.9	35.8
67 Jordan	..		..	..	..	..	..	..

Note: For data comparability and coverage, see the technical notes. Figures in italics are for years other than those specified.

		ICP estimates of GDP per capita[a] (United States = 100) 1985	Percentage share of household income, by percentile group of households[b]					
			Year	Lowest 20 percent	Second quintile	Third quintile	Fourth quintile	Highest 20 percent	Highest 10 percent
68	Chile	..		..	..	..	..	..	..
69	Syrian Arab Rep.	..		..	..	..	..	..	..
70	Costa Rica[e]	..	1986	3.3	8.3	13.2	20.7	54.5	38.8
71	Mexico	..		..	..	..	..	..	..
72	Mauritius	24.8		..	..	..	..	..	..
73	Poland[e]	24.5	1987	9.7	14.2	18.0	22.9	35.2	21.0
74	Malaysia[e]	..	1987	4.6	9.3	13.9	21.2	51.2	34.8
75	Panama	..		..	..	..	..	..	..
76	Brazil	..	1983	2.4	5.7	10.7	18.6	62.6	46.2
77	*Angola*	..		..	..	..	..	..	..
78	*Lebanon*	..		..	..	..	..	..	..
79	*Nicaragua*	..		..	..	..	..	..	..

Upper-middle-income

80	South Africa	..		..	..	..	..	..	..
81	Algeria	..		..	..	..	..	..	..
82	Hungary[e]	31.2	1983	10.9	15.3	18.7	22.8	32.4	18.7
83	Uruguay	..		..	..	..	..	..	..
84	Argentina	..		..	..	..	..	..	..
85	Yugoslavia[e]	29.2	1987	6.1	11.0	16.5	23.7	42.8	26.6
86	Gabon	..		..	..	..	..	..	..
87	Venezuela[e]	..	1987	4.7	9.2	14.0	21.5	50.6	34.2
88	Trinidad and Tobago	..		..	..	..	..	..	..
89	Korea, Rep. of	24.1		..	..	..	..	..	..
90	Portugal	33.8		..	..	..	..	..	..
91	Greece	35.5		..	..	..	..	..	..
92	Oman	..		..	..	..	..	..	..
93	Libya	..		..	..	..	..	..	..
94	*Iran, Islamic Rep.*	27.9		..	..	..	..	..	..
95	*Iraq*	..		..	..	..	..	..	..
96	*Romania*	..		..	..	..	..	..	..

Low- and middle-income
 Sub-Saharan Africa
 East Asia
 South Asia
 Europe, M.East, & N.Africa
 Latin America & Caribbean

Severely indebted

High-income economies
 OECD members
 †Other

97	†Saudi Arabia	..		..	..	..	..	..	..
98	Spain	46.0	1980–81	6.9	12.5	17.3	23.2	40.0	24.5
99	Ireland	40.9		..	..	..	..	..	..
100	†Israel	..	1979	6.0	12.1	17.8	24.5	39.6	23.5
101	†Singapore	..	1982–83	5.1	9.9	14.6	21.4	48.9	33.5
102	†Hong Kong	61.7	1980	5.4	10.8	15.2	21.6	47.0	31.3
103	New Zealand	60.9	1981–82	5.1	10.8	16.2	23.2	44.7	28.7
104	Australia	71.1	1985	4.4	11.1	17.5	24.8	42.2	25.8
105	United Kingdom	66.1	1979	5.8	11.5	18.2	25.0	39.5	23.3
106	Italy	65.6	1986	6.8	12.0	16.7	23.5	41.0	25.3
107	†Kuwait	..		..	..	..	..	..	..
108	Belgium	64.7	1978–79	7.9	13.7	18.6	23.8	36.0	21.5
109	Netherlands	68.2	1983	6.9	13.2	17.9	23.7	38.3	23.0
110	Austria	66.1		..	..	..	..	..	..
111	†United Arab Emirates	..		..	..	..	..	..	..
112	France	69.3	1979	6.3	12.1	17.2	23.5	40.8	25.5
113	Canada	92.5	1987	5.7	11.8	17.7	24.6	40.2	24.1
114	Denmark	74.2	1981	5.4	12.0	18.4	25.6	38.6	22.3
115	Germany, Fed. Rep.	73.8	1984	6.8	12.7	17.8	24.1	38.7	23.4
116	Finland	69.5	1981	6.3	12.1	18.4	25.5	37.6	21.7
117	Sweden	76.9	1981	8.0	13.2	17.4	24.5	36.9	20.8
118	United States	100.0	1985	4.7	11.0	17.4	25.0	41.9	25.0
119	Norway	84.4	1979	6.2	12.8	18.9	25.3	36.7	21.2
120	Japan	71.5	1979	8.7	13.2	17.5	23.1	37.5	22.4
121	Switzerland	..	1982	5.2	11.7	16.4	22.1	44.6	29.8

Total reporting economies
 Oil exporters

Nonreporting nonmembers

a. ICP refers to the United Nations' International Comparison Program; data are preliminary Phase V results.   b. These estimates should be treated with caution; see the technical notes for details of different distribution measures, as in the following footnotes.   c. Per capita expenditure.   d. Household expenditure.   e. Per capita income.

Table 31. Urbanization

	Urban population				Percentage of urban population				Number of cities of over 500,000 persons	
	As a percentage of total population		Average annual growth rate (percent)		In largest city		In cities of over 500,000 persons			
	1965	1988	1965–80	1980–88	1960	1980	1960	1980	1960	1980
Low-income economies	17 w	35 w	3.5 w	..	11 w	13 w	30 w	43 w	59 t	165 t
China and India	18 w	40 w	3.0 w	..	6 w	6 w	36 w	43 w	49 t	114 t
Other low-income	14 w	25 w	4.9 w	5.2 w	24 w	28 w	17 w	43 w	10 t	51 t
1 Mozambique	5	24	10.2	11.0	75	83	0	83	0	1
2 Ethiopia	8	13	4.9	5.2	30	37	0	37	0	1
3 Chad	9	31	7.8	7.4	..	39	0	0	0	0
4 Tanzania	5	30	11.7	11.6	34	50	0	50	0	1
5 Bangladesh	6	13	6.4	5.6	20	30	20	51	1	3
6 Malawi	5	14	7.5	7.9	..	19	0	0	0	0
7 Somalia	20	37	5.5	5.6	..	34	0	0	0	0
8 Zaire	26	39	4.6	4.6	14	28	14	38	1	2
9 Bhutan	3	5	3.9	4.9	..	..	0	0	0	0
10 Lao PDR	8	18	5.3	6.1	69	48	0	0	0	0
11 Nepal	4	9	6.4	7.4	41	27	0	0	0	0
12 Madagascar	12	24	5.5	5.9	44	36	0	36	0	1
13 Burkina Faso	5	9	4.1	5.4	..	41	0	0	0	0
14 Mali	13	19	4.4	3.5	32	24	0	0	0	0
15 Burundi	2	7	6.7	9.5	..	..	0	0	0	0
16 Uganda	7	10	4.7	5.1	38	52	0	52	0	1
17 Nigeria	17	34	5.7	6.3	13	17	22	58	2	9
18 Zambia	23	54	7.2	6.7	..	35	0	35	0	1
19 Niger	7	18	7.2	8.0	..	31	0	0	0	0
20 Rwanda	3	7	7.5	8.2	..	..	0	0	0	0
21 China	18	50	2.3	..	6	6	42	45	38	78
22 India	19	27	3.9	4.0	7	6	26	39	11	36
23 Pakistan	24	31	4.3	4.5	20	21	33	51	2	7
24 Kenya	9	22	8.1	8.2	40	57	0	57	0	1
25 Togo	11	25	6.6	7.0	..	60	0	0	0	0
26 Central African Rep.	27	45	4.3	4.9	40	36	0	0	0	0
27 Haiti	18	29	4.2	4.0	42	56	0	56	0	1
28 Benin	11	40	9.0	7.8	..	63	0	63	0	1
29 Ghana	26	33	3.2	4.2	25	35	0	48	0	2
30 Lesotho	6	19	7.5	7.2	..	..	0	0	0	0
31 Sri Lanka	20	21	2.3	1.3	28	16	0	16	0	1
32 Guinea	12	24	4.9	5.7	37	80	0	80	0	1
33 Yemen, PDR	30	42	3.5	4.7	61	49	0	0	0	0
34 Indonesia	16	27	4.8	4.8	20	23	34	50	3	9
35 Mauritania	10	40	9.5	7.8	..	39	0	0	0	0
36 Sudan	13	21	5.6	4.1	30	31	0	31	0	1
37 *Afghanistan*	9	..	6.0	..	33	..	0	..	0	..
38 *Myanmar*	21	24	3.2	2.3	23	23	23	23	1	2
39 *Kampuchea, Dem.*	11	..	−0.5	..	..	..	..	..	..	..
40 *Liberia*	22	43	6.2	5.8	..	..	0	0	0	0
41 *Sierra Leone*	15	26	4.4	5.0	37	47	0	0	0	0
42 *Viet Nam*	..	..	..	3.9	..	21	..	50	..	4
Middle-income economies	42 w	58 w	3.9 w	3.3 w	29 w	31 w	34 w	47 w	51 t	113 t
Lower-middle-income	40 w	56 w	4.0 w	3.5 w	29 w	32 w	32 w	47 w	31 t	70 t
43 Bolivia	40	50	3.1	4.3	47	44	0	44	0	1
44 Philippines	32	41	4.1	3.7	27	30	27	34	1	2
45 Yemen Arab Rep.	5	23	10.2	8.8	..	25	0	0	0	0
46 Senegal	33	38	3.3	4.0	53	65	0	65	0	1
47 Zimbabwe	14	27	6.0	6.2	40	50	0	50	0	1
48 Egypt, Arab Rep.	41	48	2.8	3.5	38	39	53	53	2	3
49 Dominican Rep.	35	59	5.2	4.3	50	54	0	54	0	1
50 Côte d'Ivoire	23	45	7.5	6.6	27	34	0	34	0	1
51 Papua New Guinea	5	15	8.2	4.5	..	25	0	0	0	0
52 Morocco	32	47	4.3	4.4	16	26	16	50	1	4
53 Honduras	26	42	5.5	5.6	31	33	0	0	0	0
54 Guatemala	34	33	2.7	2.9	41	36	41	36	1	1
55 Congo, People's Rep.	34	41	4.5	4.8	77	56	0	0	0	0
56 El Salvador	39	44	3.2	1.9	26	22	0	0	0	0
57 Thailand	13	21	5.1	4.7	65	69	65	69	1	1
58 Botswana	4	22	12.6	8.4	..	..	..	..	..	..
59 Cameroon	16	47	8.1	7.2	26	21	0	21	0	1
60 Jamaica	38	51	2.8	2.6	77	66	0	66	0	1
61 Ecuador	37	55	4.7	4.7	31	29	0	51	0	2
62 Colombia	54	69	3.7	3.0	17	26	28	51	3	4
63 Paraguay	36	46	3.8	4.5	44	44	0	44	0	1
64 Tunisia	40	54	4.0	2.9	40	30	40	30	1	1
65 Turkey	34	47	4.2	3.4	18	24	32	42	3	4
66 Peru	52	69	4.3	3.1	38	39	38	44	1	2
67 Jordan	46	67	4.3	5.1	31	37	0	37	0	1

Note: For data comparability and coverage, see the technical notes. Figures in italics are for years other than those specified.

		Urban population				Percentage of urban population				Number of cities of over 500,000 persons	
		As a percentage of total population		Average annual growth rate (percent)		In largest city		In cities of over 500,000 persons			
		1965	1988	1965–80	1980–88	1960	1980	1960	1980	1960	1980
68	Chile	72	85	2.6	2.3	38	44	38	44	1	1
69	Syrian Arab Rep.	40	51	4.6	4.5	35	33	35	55	1	2
70	Costa Rica	38	45	4.0	1.9	67	64	0	64	0	1
71	Mexico	55	71	4.4	3.1	28	32	36	48	3	7
72	Mauritius	37	42	2.5	0.8	..	..	..	..	..	..
73	Poland	50	61	1.9	1.4	17	15	41	47	5	8
74	Malaysia	26	41	4.5	4.9	19	27	0	27	0	1
75	Panama	44	54	3.5	3.0	61	66	0	66	0	1
76	Brazil	50	75	4.5	3.6	14	15	35	52	6	14
77	*Angola*	13	27	6.4	5.8	44	64	0	64	0	1
78	*Lebanon*	50	..	4.5	..	64	..	64	..	1	..
79	*Nicaragua*	43	59	4.7	4.6	41	47	0	47	0	1
	Upper-middle-income	**45** *w*	**62** *w*	**3.6** *w*	**2.8** *w*	**31** *w*	**30** *w*	**38** *w*	**48** *w*	**20** *t*	**43** *t*
80	South Africa	47	58	3.3	3.4	16	13	44	53	4	7
81	Algeria	38	44	3.7	3.9	27	12	27	12	1	1
82	Hungary	43	60	2.0	1.2	45	37	45	37	1	1
83	Uruguay	81	85	0.7	0.8	56	52	56	52	1	1
84	Argentina	76	86	2.2	1.8	46	45	54	60	3	5
85	Yugoslavia	31	49	3.0	2.5	11	10	11	23	1	3
86	Gabon	21	44	7.3	6.7	..	..	..	..	..	..
87	Venezuela	70	83	4.8	2.6	26	26	26	44	1	4
88	Trinidad and Tobago	30	67	5.6	3.9	..	..	0	0	0	0
89	Korea, Rep. of	32	69	5.8	3.7	35	41	61	77	3	7
90	Portugal	24	32	1.7	1.9	47	44	47	44	1	1
91	Greece	48	62	2.0	1.3	51	57	51	70	1	2
92	Oman	4	10	7.6	8.7	..	..	..	..	..	..
93	Libya	26	68	9.8	6.7	57	64	0	64	0	1
94	*Iran, Islamic Rep.*	37	54	5.1	4.1	26	28	26	47	1	6
95	*Iraq*	51	73	5.3	4.8	35	55	35	70	1	3
96	*Romania*	38	49	3.0	0.3	22	17	22	17	1	1
	Low- and middle-income	**24** *w*	**41** *w*	**3.7** *w*	**6.9** *w*	**16** *w*	**18** *w*	**31** *w*	**44** *w*	**110** *t*	**278** *t*
	Sub-Saharan Africa	**14** *w*	**28** *w*	**5.8** *w*	**6.2** *w*	**28** *w*	**36** *w*	**6** *w*	**41** *w*	**3** *t*	**28** *t*
	East Asia	**19** *w*	**46** *w*	**3.0** *w*	**..**	**11** *w*	**13** *w*	**41** *w*	**47** *w*	**46** *t*	**102** *t*
	South Asia	**18** *w*	**26** *w*	**4.0** *w*	**4.0** *w*	**11** *w*	**11** *w*	**25** *w*	**40** *w*	**15** *t*	**49** *t*
	Europe, M.East, & N.Africa	**37** *w*	**50** *w*	**3.5** *w*	**3.1** *w*	**28** *w*	**28** *w*	**31** *w*	**40** *w*	**22** *t*	**43** *t*
	Latin America & Caribbean	**53** *w*	**71** *w*	**4.0** *w*	**3.2** *w*	**27** *w*	**29** *w*	**32** *w*	**49** *w*	**20** *t*	**49** *t*
	Severely indebted	**50** *w*	**66** *w*	**3.8** *w*	**3.1** *w*	**26** *w*	**28** *w*	**33** *w*	**47** *w*	**24** *t*	**56** *t*
	High-income economies	**71** *w*	**78** *w*	**1.4** *w*	**0.8** *w*	**19** *w*	**19** *w*	**47** *w*	**55** *w*	**107** *t*	**157** *t*
	OECD members	**72** *w*	**77** *w*	**1.3** *w*	**0.7** *w*	**18** *w*	**18** *w*	**47** *w*	**55** *w*	**104** *t*	**152** *t*
	†Other	**68** *w*	**83** *w*	**4.6** *w*	**3.5** *w*	**58** *w*	**49** *w*	**51** *w*	**54** *w*	**3** *t*	**5** *t*
97	†Saudi Arabia	39	76	8.5	5.8	15	18	0	33	0	2
98	Spain	61	77	2.2	1.3	13	17	37	44	5	6
99	Ireland	49	58	2.1	1.1	51	48	51	48	1	1
100	†Israel	81	91	3.5	2.1	46	35	46	35	1	1
101	†Singapore	100	100	1.6	1.1	100	100	100	100	1	1
102	†Hong Kong	89	93	2.1	1.7	100	100	100	100	1	1
103	New Zealand	79	84	1.6	0.9	25	30	0	30	0	1
104	Australia	83	86	2.0	1.4	26	24	62	68	4	5
105	United Kingdom	87	92	0.5	0.4	24	20	61	55	15	17
106	Italy	62	68	1.0	0.5	13	17	46	52	7	9
107	†Kuwait	78	95	8.2	5.1	75	30	0	0	0	0
108	Belgium	93	97	0.4	0.2	17	14	28	24	2	2
109	Netherlands	86	88	1.2	0.5	9	9	27	24	3	3
110	Austria	51	57	0.8	0.6	51	39	51	39	1	1
111	†United Arab Emirates	41	78	23.7	4.2	..	..	..	..	..	..
112	France	67	74	1.3	0.5	25	23	34	34	4	6
113	Canada	73	76	1.5	1.0	14	18	31	62	2	9
114	Denmark	77	86	1.1	0.3	40	32	40	32	1	1
115	Germany, Fed. Rep.	79	86	0.7	0.1	20	18	48	45	11	11
116	Finland	44	60	2.5	0.4	28	27	0	27	0	1
117	Sweden	77	84	0.9	0.3	15	15	15	35	1	3
118	United States	72	74	1.2	1.0	13	12	61	77	40	65
119	Norway	48	74	3.0	0.9	50	32	50	32	1	1
120	Japan	67	77	2.1	0.7	18	22	35	42	5	9
121	Switzerland	53	61	1.0	1.3	19	22	19	22	1	1
	Total reporting economies	**34** *w*	**47** *w*	**2.7** *w*	**4.9** *w*	**17** *w*	**18** *w*	**35** *w*	**46** *w*	**217** *t*	**435** *t*
	Oil exporters	**30** *w*	**46** *w*	**4.8** *w*	**4.3** *w*	**24** *w*	**26** *w*	**31** *w*	**49** *w*	**16** *t*	**50** *t*
	Nonreporting nonmembers	**53** *w*	**67** *w*	**2.1** *w*	**1.6** *w*	**9** *w*	**7** *w*	**20** *w*	**30** *w*	**31** *t*	**58** *t*

Table 32. Women in development

	Health and welfare							Education							
	Risk of dying by age 5		Life expectancy at birth (years)				Maternal mortality (per 100,000 live births)	Persistence to grade 4 as a percentage of cohort				Females per 100 males			
			Female		Male			Female		Male		Primary		Secondary[a]	
	Female 1988	Male 1988	1965	1988	1965	1988	1980	1970	1984	1970	1984	1970	1987	1970	1987
Low-income economies	**89** w	**97** w	**50** w	**60** w	**48** w	**60** w	..	..	..	..	..	..	..	..	..
China and India	**67** w	**74** w	**52** w	**63** w	**50** w	**64** w		..	..	..	..	..	..	..	..
Other low-income	**132** w	**142** w	**45** w	**56** w	**43** w	**53** w		**64** w	**75** w	**72** w	**73** w	**61** w	**67** w	**44** w	**60** w
1 Mozambique	190	210	39	50	36	47	479[b]	..	..	..	..	..	78	..	54
2 Ethiopia	183	203	43	49	42	46	2,000[b]	57	45	56	50	46	61	32	63
3 Chad	198	221	38	47	35	45	700	..	..	..	..	34	40	9	18
4 Tanzania	135	153	45	55	41	52	370[b]	82	88	88	89	65	99	38	66
5 Bangladesh	175	160	44	51	45	51	600	..	..	..	30	47	66	..	45
6 Malawi	234	248	40	48	38	47	250	55	64	60	65	59	80	36	60
7 Somalia	200	223	40	49	37	46	1,100	46	59	51	65	33	..	27	..
8 Zaire	139	157	45	54	42	51	800[b]	56	..	65	..	58	..	26	..
9 Bhutan	186	178	40	47	41	49	..	..	26	..	29	5	..	3	..
10 Lao PDR	158	178	42	51	39	48	..	..	..	..	..	59	78	36	73
11 Nepal	187	173	40	51	41	52	..	..	..	..	..	18	..	16	..
12 Madagascar	160	178	45	51	42	50	300	65	..	63	..	86	94	70	85
13 Burkina Faso	188	208	40	49	37	46	600	71	84	68	82	57	59	33	46
14 Mali	209	237	39	49	37	46	..	52	68	89	75	55	59	29	42
15 Burundi	98	113	45	51	42	47	..	47	84	45	84	49	..	17	..
16 Uganda	147	167	47	50	44	47	300	..	..	..	..	65	..	31	..
17 Nigeria	151	170	43	53	40	49	1,500	64	..	66	..	59	..	49	..
18 Zambia	108	124	46	55	43	52	110	93	97	99	..	80	..	49	..
19 Niger	204	226	38	47	35	43	420[b]	75	76	74	88	53	..	35	42
20 Rwanda	184	205	51	50	47	47	210	63	82	65	81	79	97	44	35
21 China	30	40	57	66	53	69	44	..	76	..	77	..	83	..	69
22 India	118	120	44	58	46	58	500	42	..	45	..	60	..	39	..
23 Pakistan	139	128	45	55	47	55	600	56	..	60	..	36	49	25	39
24 Kenya	95	110	50	61	46	57	510[b]	84	75	84	73	71	93	42	70
25 Togo	132	150	44	55	40	52	476[b]	85	77	88	70	45	63	26	32
26 Central African Rep.	150	169	41	52	40	49	600	67	67	67	74	49	62	20	37
27 Haiti	137	158	47	57	44	53	340	..	..	..	..	..	..	..	..
28 Benin	152	170	43	52	41	49	1,680[b]	59	64	67	63	45	51	44	..
29 Ghana	126	144	49	56	46	52	1,070[b]	77	..	82	..	75	80	35	66
30 Lesotho	125	142	50	58	47	54	..	87	86	70	75	150	125	111	153
31 Sri Lanka	19	27	64	73	63	68	90	94	97	73	99	89	93	101	106
32 Guinea	210	233	36	43	34	42	..	..	62	..	67	46	45	26	31
33 Yemen, PDR	157	175	41	53	39	50	..	68	..	56	..	25	..	25	..
34 Indonesia	75	90	45	62	43	59	800	67	78	89	99	84	..	59	79
35 Mauritania	192	214	39	48	36	45	119	..	91	..	96	39	70	13	44
36 Sudan	158	177	41	51	39	49	607[b]	..	81	..	80	61	..	40	..
37 *Afghanistan*	..	..	35	..	35	..	..	64	..	71	..	16	..	16	..
38 *Myanmar*	79	94	49	62	46	59	140	39	..	58	..	89	..	65	..
39 *Kampuchea, Dem.*	..	..	46	..	43	..	..	..	..	..	..	70	..	43	..
40 *Liberia*	173	192	44	52	41	48	173	..	..	..	..	49	..	30	..
41 *Sierra Leone*	235	260	34	43	31	41	450	..	..	..	..	67	..	40	..
42 *Viet Nam*	46	59	..	68	..	64	110	..	..	..	..	..	..	..	..
Middle-income economies	**59** w	**69** w	**59** w	**68** w	**55** w	**63** w		**77** w	**84** w	**76** w	**89** w	**85** w	**88** w	**89** w	**101** w
Lower-middle-income	**64** w	**75** w	**57** w	**67** w	**54** w	**62** w		**70** w	**82** w	**71** w	**86** w	**85** w	**88** w	**85** w	**94** w
43 Bolivia	140	158	47	56	42	51	480	..	..	..	..	69	87	64	..
44 Philippines	45	58	57	66	54	62	80	..	82	..	76	..	97	..	..
45 Yemen Arab Rep.	193	215	41	48	39	47	..	44	71	31	76	10	29	3	12
46 Senegal	109	125	42	50	40	46	530[b]	..	88	..	92	63	69	39	51
47 Zimbabwe	55	67	50	65	46	61	150[b]	74	87	80	87	79	..	63	..
48 Egypt, Arab Rep.	98	107	50	64	48	61	500	85	..	93	..	61	75	48	68
49 Dominican Rep.	73	80	57	68	54	64	56	..	52	..	70	99	100	..	..
50 Côte d'Ivoire	137	156	44	54	40	51	..	77	82	83	83	57	..	27	44
51 Papua New Guinea	69	84	44	55	44	53	1,000	76	..	84	..	57	79	37	57
52 Morocco	84	100	51	63	48	59	327[b]	..	77	..	79	51	63	40	66
53 Honduras	71	85	51	66	48	62	82	38	63	35	59	99	..	79	..
54 Guatemala	63	77	50	65	48	60	110	33	62	73	73	79	..	65	..
55 Congo, People's Rep.	166	180	47	56	41	50	..	86	82	89	89	78	95	43	76
56 El Salvador	63	77	56	67	53	58	74	56	..	56	..	92	102	77	92
57 Thailand	28	38	58	68	54	63	270	71	..	69	..	88	..	69	..
58 Botswana	41	52	49	69	46	65	300	97	95	90	95	113	107	88	107
59 Cameroon	116	133	47	58	44	55	303	59	85	58	86	74	85	36	64
60 Jamaica	10	14	67	75	64	71	100	..	..	..	..	100	97	103	..
61 Ecuador	74	81	57	68	55	64	220	69	..	70	..	93	96	76	91
62 Colombia	39	49	61	71	57	66	130	57	75	51	67	101	..	73	..
63 Paraguay	44	56	67	69	63	65	469	70	75	71	76	89	92	91	98
64 Tunisia	50	63	52	67	51	65	1,000[c]	..	90	..	94	64	81	38	75
65 Turkey	89	97	55	66	52	63	207	76	97	81	98	73	89	37	60
66 Peru	105	114	52	64	49	60	310	..	..	..	..	85	..	74	..
67 Jordan	49	60	52	68	49	65	..	90	99	92	..	78	96	53	95

Note: For data comparability and coverage, see the technical notes. Figures in italics are for years other than those specified.

		Health and welfare						Maternal mortality (per 100,000 live births) 1980	Education							
		Risk of dying by age 5		Life expectancy at birth (years)					Persistence to grade 4 as a percentage of cohort				Females per 100 males			
				Female		Male			Female		Male		Primary		Secondary[a]	
		Female 1988	Male 1988	1965	1988	1965	1988		1970	1984	1970	1984	1970	1987	1970	1987
68	Chile	20	25	63	75	57	68	55	86	96	83	97	98	95	130	108
69	Syrian Arab Rep.	55	67	54	67	51	64	280	92	96	95	97	57	87	36	70
70	Costa Rica	18	22	66	77	63	73	26	93	92	91	90	96	94	111	105
71	Mexico	51	57	61	73	58	66	92	..	72	..	95	92	94	..	88
72	Mauritius	21	29	63	70	59	63	99	97	99	97	99	94	98	66	92
73	Poland	17	22	72	76	66	68	12	99	..	97	..	93	95	251	263
74	Malaysia	22	30	60	72	56	68	59	..	100	..	99	88	95	69	98
75	Panama	21	29	65	74	62	70	90	97	90	97	89	92	92	99	105
76	Brazil	62	75	59	68	55	63	150	56	..	54	..	99	..	99	..
77	Angola	207	229	37	47	34	43	..	..	..	..	..	55	..	77	..
78	Lebanon	..	..	64	..	60	..	..	..	..	..	..	83	..	67	..
79	Nicaragua	66	80	52	65	49	62	65	48	64	45	58	101	107	89	168
	Upper-middle-income	46 w	55 w	62 w	70 w	59 w	65 w		89 w	89 w	86 w	97 w	85 w	89 w	95 w	112 w
80	South Africa	81	97	54	64	49	58	550c	..	..	..	..	98	..	95	..
81	Algeria	83	91	51	65	49	63	129	90	..	95	..	60	79	40	73
82	Hungary	15	22	72	74	67	67	28	90	97	99	97	93	95	202	190
83	Uruguay	22	28	72	76	65	69	56	..	99	..	99	91	95	129	..
84	Argentina	30	40	69	74	63	68	85	92	..	69	..	98	97	156	172
85	Yugoslavia	25	30	68	75	64	69	27	91	..	99	..	91	94	86	94
86	Gabon	147	166	44	54	41	51	124b	73	80	78	78	91	98	43	81
87	Venezuela	36	45	65	73	61	67	65	84	82	61	89	99	..	102	..
88	Trinidad and Tobago	15	20	67	74	63	69	81	78	99	74	96	97	98	113	100
89	Korea, Rep. of	22	31	58	73	55	66	34	96	100	96	99	92	94	65	87
90	Portugal	13	17	68	78	62	71	15	92	..	92	..	95	97	98	114
91	Greece	13	15	72	79	69	74	12	97	98	96	99	92	94	98	101
92	Oman	35	46	45	66	43	63	..	82	96	82	99	16	85	..	65
93	Libya	84	100	51	63	48	59	..	92	..	95	..	59	..	21	..
94	Iran, Islamic Rep.	74	89	52	64	52	62	..	75	79	74	99	55	80	49	68
95	Iraq	81	89	53	65	51	63	..	84	90	90	92	41	82	41	62
96	Romania	24	31	70	73	66	68	180	90	..	89	..	97	95	151	233
	Low- and middle-income	81 w	90 w	52 w	62 w	50 w	61 w		61 w	78 w	64 w	79 w	69 w	81 w	59 w	75 w
	Sub-Saharan Africa	154 w	172 w	43 w	52 w	41 w	49 w		66 w	73 w	69 w	74 w	60 w	77 w	40 w	59 w
	East Asia	37 w	47 w	56 w	66 w	52 w	67 w		..	78 w	..	81 w	..	84 w	..	71 w
	South Asia	124 w	123 w	45 w	57 w	46 w	57 w		45 w	..	48 w	..	57 w	..	40 w	..
	Europe, M.East, & N.Africa	74 w	84 w	58 w	66 w	55 w	62 w		84 w	88 w	87 w	94 w	70 w	82 w	86 w	104 w
	Latin America & Caribbean	57 w	67 w	60 w	70 w	56 w	64 w		64 w	75 w	59 w	86 w	96 w	96 w	100 w	110 w
	Severely indebted	56 w	67 w	61 w	69 w	57 w	63 w		73 w	79 w	69 w	87 w	92 w	92 w	122 w	131 w
	High-income economies	10 w	12 w	74 w	79 w	67 w	73 w		95 w	97 w	94 w	96 w	95 w	95 w	94 w	100 w
	OECD members	9 w	11 w	74 w	79 w	68 w	73 w		96 w	97 w	94 w	96 w	96 w	95 w	95 w	100 w
	†Other	37 w	46 w	64 w	73 w	59 w	68 w		95 w	94 w	94 w	94 w	74 w	94 w	69 w	105 w
97	†Saudi Arabia	72	86	50	65	47	62	52	93	93	91	93	46	80	16	66
98	Spain	9	11	74	80	69	74	10	76	97	76	96	99	93	84	101
99	Ireland	8	10	73	77	69	72	7	..	..	..	..	96	95	124	101
100	†Israel	11	15	74	77	71	74	5	96	98	96	98	92	98	131	121
101	†Singapore	7	10	68	77	64	71	11	99	..	99	..	88	..	103	..
102	†Hong Kong	7	10	71	80	64	75	4	94	..	92	..	90	92	74	104
103	New Zealand	11	15	74	78	68	72	..	..	98	..	98	94	95	94	98
104	Australia	10	13	74	80	68	73	11	..	97	..	94	94	95	91	98
105	United Kingdom	9	12	74	78	68	73	7	..	..	..	..	95	95	94	96
106	Italy	9	12	73	80	68	74	13	..	..	..	..	94	..	86	..
107	†Kuwait	14	20	65	76	61	71	18	96	92	98	93	73	95	74	67
108	Belgium	9	13	74	78	68	72	10	87	85	85	..	94	96	87	103
109	Netherlands	8	10	76	80	71	74	5	99	..	96	..	96	98	91	111
110	Austria	9	13	73	79	66	72	11	95	99	92	100	95	94	95	93
111	†United Arab Emirates	23	32	59	73	56	69	..	97	95	93	92	61	94	..	99
112	France	8	10	75	81	68	72	13	97	96	90	99	95	94	107	108
113	Canada	8	10	75	81	69	73	2	95	97	92	93	95	93	95	95
114	Denmark	9	11	75	78	70	72	4	98	100	96	100	97	96	102	105
115	Germany, Fed. Rep.	8	11	73	78	67	72	11	97	97	96	96	96	96	93	97
116	Finland	7	9	73	78	66	72	5	..	99	..	98	90	95	112	112
117	Sweden	6	8	76	80	72	74	4	98	..	96	..	96	95	92	104
118	United States	10	13	74	79	67	72	9	..	96	..	94	95	94	98	..
119	Norway	9	11	76	80	71	74	..	99	99	98	99	105	95	97	103
120	Japan	5	7	73	81	68	76	15	100	100	100	100	96	95	101	99
121	Switzerland	7	9	75	81	69	74	5	94	99	93	99	98	97	93	..
	Total reporting economies	69 w	77 w	57 w	65 w	54 w	63 w		67 w	83 w	69 w	83 w	76 w	84 w	67 w	79 w
	Oil exporters	87 w	99 w	50 w	63 w	48 w	59 w		73 w	80 w	82 w	97 w	73 w	85 w	54 w	77 w
	Nonreporting nonmembers	25 w	31 w	72 w	75 w	65 w	66 w		94 w	98 w	99 w	98 w	..	..	..	..

a. See the technical notes. b. Data refer to maternal mortality in hospitals and other medical institutions only. c. Community data from rural areas only.

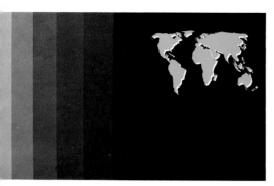

Technical notes

This thirteenth edition of the World Development Indicators provides economic and social indicators for selected periods or years in a form suitable for comparing economies and groups of economies.

The main criterion of country classification is gross national product (GNP) per capita. With the inclusion of a new World Bank member, Angola, the main tables now include country data on 121 economies. As in last year's edition, since only sparse data are available for nine nonreporting nonmember economies, these countries are not included in the main tables. Summary measures for them are shown in the main tables where available, and selected country data are presented in Box A.2. Box A.1, Basic indicators for economies with populations of less than 1 million, covers another fifty-five economies. As in last year's edition, the table on labor force is not included because of the continuing lack of new data. This table will be reinserted when the 1990 round of census results has been tabulated and collected by the International Labour Office (ILO). Other changes are outlined in the introduction.

Considerable effort has been made to standardize the data; nevertheless, statistical methods, coverage, practices, and definitions differ widely. In addition, the statistical systems in many developing economies are still weak, and this affects the availability and reliability of the data. Moreover, intercountry and intertemporal comparisons always involve complex technical problems, which cannot be fully and unequivocally resolved. The data are drawn from sources thought to be most authoritative, but many of them are subject to considerable margins of error. Readers are urged to take these limitations into account in interpreting the indicators, particularly when making comparisons across economies.

To facilitate international comparisons, national accounts constant price data series with base years other than 1980 have been partially rebased to 1980. This is accomplished by rescaling, which moves the year in which current and constant price versions of the same time series have the same value, without altering the trend of either. Components of gross domestic product (GDP) are individually rescaled and summed to provide GDP and its subaggregates. In this process, a rescaling deviation may occur between constant price GDP by industrial origin and GDP by expenditure. Such rescaling deviations are absorbed under the heading *private consumption, etc.*, because GDP by industrial origin is usually the more reliable estimate.

This approach takes into account the effects of changes in intersectoral relative prices between the original and the new base period. Because private consumption is calculated as a residual, the national accounting identities are maintained. It does, however, involve incorporating in private consumption whatever statistical discrepancies arise for expenditure in the rebasing process. The value added in the services sector also includes a statistical discrepancy as reported by the original source.

The summary measures are calculated by simple addition when a variable is expressed in reasonably comparable units of account. Economic indicators that do not seem naturally additive are usually combined by a price-weighting scheme. The summary measures for social indicators are weighted by population. It should be emphasized, however, that use of a single base year raises problems over a period encompassing profound structural changes and significant changes in relative prices, such as occurred from 1965 to 1988.

The Bank's statistical publications will soon shift to a 1987 base year. With some exceptions, use of 1987 rather than 1980 values as country weights will not greatly alter the group indexes and growth rates reported here. Most exceptions relate to oil exporters and reflect declining shares of group

Box A.1 Basic indicators for economies with populations of less than 1 million

		Area (thousands of square kilometers)	GNP per capita[a]		Average annual rate of inflation[a] (percent)		Life expectancy at birth (years) 1988	Adult illiteracy	
	Population (thousands) mid-1988		Dollars 1988	Average annual growth rate (percent) 1965–88	1965–80	1980–88		Female 1985	Total 1985
1 Guinea-Bissau	940	36	190	−1.9	..	49.0	40	83	69
2 Gambia, The	822	11	200	1.1	8.1	13.9	44	85	75
3 Equatorial Guinea	336	28	410	..	..	..	46	..	63
4 Maldives	202	b	410	2.3	..	7.1	60	..	..
5 Guyana	799	215	420	−4.4	8.1	15.9	63	5	4
6 Comoros	442	2	440	0.6	..	5.8	56	..	..
7 São Tomé and Principe	119	1	490	−0.1	..	18.1	65	..	..
8 Solomon Islands	303	29	630	..	7.7	13.1	64	..	..
9 Western Samoa	159	3	640	..	..	10.5	66	..	..
10 Kiribati	67	1	650	..	..	5.7	55	..	..
11 Cape Verde	360	4	680	..	..	8.9	65	61	53
12 Swaziland	735	17	810	2.2	9.1	11.4	56	34	32
13 Tonga	97	1	830	..	..	..	66	..	..
14 Vanuatu	147	12	840	..	..	4.3	64	..	..
15 St. Vincent and the Grenadines	112	b	1,200	2.0	10.9	4.3	70	..	..
16 Belize	180	23	1,500	2.4	7.1	2.2	67	..	..
17 Fiji	732	18	1,520	1.9	10.4	5.7	71	19	15
18 St. Lucia	145	1	1,540	2.7	9.3	3.9	71	..	..
19 Dominica	82	1	1,680	0.6	12.8	5.8	74	..	..
20 Grenada	94	b	1,720	..	11.2	7.4	69	..	..
21 Suriname	427	163	2,460	1.1	..	5.8	67	10	10
22 St. Kitts and Nevis	42	b	2,630	3.6	9.7	6.2	69	..	..
23 Antigua and Barbuda	78	b	3,690	0.6	..	..	73	..	..
24 Seychelles	68	b	3,800	3.2	12.2	3.9	70	..	..
25 Malta	348	b	5,190	7.4	3.5	1.9	73	18	16
26 Barbados	254	b	6,010	2.3	11.3	6.1	75	..	..
27 Cyprus	687	9	6,260	..	..	6.4	76	..	..
28 Bahrain	473	1	6,340	..	..	−1.3	68	36	27
29 Qatar	411	11	9,930	..	..	..	70	..	..
30 Bahamas, The	244	14	10,700	1.0	6.4	6.2	68	..	..
31 Iceland	249	103	20,190	3.3	26.8	38.0	78	..	..
32 Luxembourg	375	3	22,400	4.1	6.7	4.2	75	..	..
33 *American Samoa*	37	b	c	..	..	..	..	..	..
34 *Aruba*	60	b	c	..	..	..	..	..	..
35 *Bermuda*	57	b	c	..	8.1	10.7	..	..	..
36 *Brunei*	241	6	c	..	..	−4.4	75	..	..
37 *Channel Islands*	137	..	c	..	..	..	76	..	..
38 *Djibouti*	..	23	d	..	..	..	47	..	..
39 *Faeroe Islands*	47	1	c	..	..	..	..	..	..
40 *Fed. States of Micronesia*	99	..	c	..	..	..	..	..	..
41 *French Guiana*	88	90	e	..	7.4	..	73	..	..
42 *French Polynesia*	186	4	c	..	..	..	72	..	..
43 *Gibraltar*	30	b	e	..	..	..	..	..	..
44 *Greenland*	55	342	c	..	..	..	..	..	..
45 *Guadeloupe*	338	2	e	..	8.7	..	74	..	..
46 *Guam*	130	1	c	..	..	..	73	..	..
47 *Isle of Man*	66	..	c	..	..	..	..	..	..
48 *Marshall Islands*	41	..	c	..	..	..	..	..	..
49 *Macao*	442	b	e	..	..	..	71	..	..
50 *Martinique*	335	1	e	..	9.2	..	75	..	..
51 *Netherlands Antilles*	183	1	c	..	..	..	66	..	..
52 *New Caledonia*	158	19	c	..	..	..	68	..	..
53 *Puerto Rico[f]*	3,321	9	e	..	..	4.5	75	..	..
54 *Reunion*	576	3	e	..	..	..	71	..	..
55 *Virgin Islands (U.S.)*	106	b	c	1.9	6.0	4.5	70	..	..

Note: Economies in italics are those for which 1988 GNP per capita cannot be calculated; figures in italics are for years other than those specified. a. See the technical note to Table 1. b. Less than 500 square kilometers. c. GNP per capita estimated to be in the high-income range. d. GNP per capita estimated to be in the lower-middle-income range. e. GNP per capita estimated to be in the upper-middle-income range. f. Population is more than 1 million.

Box A.2 Selected indicators for nonreporting nonmember economies

Indicator	USSR 1965	USSR 1988	Democratic People's Republic of Korea 1965	Democratic People's Republic of Korea 1988	German Democratic Republic 1965	German Democratic Republic 1988	Czechoslovakia 1965	Czechoslovakia 1988	Cuba 1965	Cuba 1988
Population (millions)	232	286	12	21	17	17	14	16	8	10
Urban population (percentage of total)	52	67	45	66	73	77	51	67	58	74
Life expectancy at birth (years)	69	70	57	70	70	73	69	71	67	76
Crude birth rate (per thousand)	18	18	44	20	17	13	16	14	34	18
Crude death rate (per thousand)	7	11	12	5	14	13	10	12	8	7
Population per physician	480	270	..	420	870	440	540	280	1,150	530
Total fertility rate	2.5	2.4	6.5	2.5	2.5	1.8	2.4	2	4.4	1.9
Infant mortality (per 1,000 live births)	28	25	63	27	25	8	26	13	38	12
Low birth weight (percent)	..	..	..	..	..	6	..	6	..	8
Risk of dying by age 5 (female)	..	24	..	26	..	8	..	13	..	13
Risk of dying by age 5 (male)	..	33	..	35	..	11	..	17	..	16
Daily calorie supply (per capita)	3,205	3,399	2,329	3,232	3,204	3,814	3,383	3,448	2,374	3,124
Food production per capita index (1979–81 = 100)	85	111	72	111	73	118	73	119	81	103
Education, primary (female)	103	..	..	..	111	*105*	97	96	119	100
Education, primary (total)	103	*106*	..	..	109	106	99	96	121	104
Area (thousands of square kilometers)	..	22,402	..	121	..	108	..	128	..	111
Population projected to year 2000 (millions)	..	307	..	25	..	16	..	16	..	12

Note: For data comparability and coverage, see the technical notes. Figures in italics are for years other than those specified.

GNP, trade, and so on from 1980 to 1987. This is most notable for Sub-Saharan Africa, with the dramatic decline in Nigeria's weight. In contrast, changing the base year for country series themselves, as described above, is likely to alter trends significantly. Differences of half a percentage point a year in growth rates could be quite common; larger changes may occur for economies that have undergone significant structural change, such as oil exporters.

The World Development Indicators, unlike the *World Tables*, provide data for (usually) two reference points, rather than annual time series. For summary measures that cover many years, the calculation is based on the same country composition over time and across topics. The World Development Indicators do so by permitting group measures to be compiled only if the country data available for a given year account for at least two-thirds of the full group, as defined by the 1980 benchmarks. So long as that criterion is met, uncurrent reporters (and those not providing ample history) are, for years with missing data, assumed to behave like the sample of the group that does provide estimates. Readers should keep in mind that the purpose is to maintain an appropriate relationship across topics, despite myriad problems with country data, and that nothing meaningful can be deduced about behavior at the country level by working back from group indicators. In addition, the weighting process may result in discrepancies between summed subgroup figures and overall totals. This is explained more fully in the introduction to the *World Tables*.

All growth rates shown are calculated from constant price series and, unless otherwise noted, have been computed using the least-squares method. The least-squares growth rate, r, is estimated by fitting a least-squares linear regression trend line to the logarithmic annual values of the variable in the relevant period. More specifically, the regression equation takes the form $\log X_t = a + bt + e_t$, where this is equivalent to the logarithmic transformation of the compound growth rate equation, $X_t = X_o (1 + r)^t$. In these equations, X is the variable, t is time, and $a = \log X_o$ and $b = \log (1 + r)$ are the parameters to be estimated; e is the error term. If b^* is the least-squares estimate of b, then the average annual percentage growth rate, r, is obtained as [antilog (b^*)] $- 1$ and multiplied by 100 to express it as a percentage.

Table 1. Basic indicators

For basic indicators for economies with populations of less than 1 million, see Box A.1. For selected indicators for nonreporting nonmember economies, see Box A.2.

Population numbers for mid-1988 are World Bank estimates. These are normally projections from the most recent population censuses or surveys, which, in some cases, are very dated. Note that refugees not permanently settled in the country of asylum are generally considered to be part of the population of their country of origin.

Bulgaria		Albania		Mongolia		Namibia		Indicator
1965	1988	1965	1988	1965	1988	1965	1988	
8	9	2	3	1	2	1	1	Population (millions)
46	69	32	35	42	51	28	55	Urban population (percentage of total)
69	72	66	72	50	62	45	57	Life expectancy at birth (years)
15	13	35	25	42	36	46	44	Crude birth rate (per thousand)
8	12	9	6	16	9	22	12	Crude death rate (per thousand)
600	280	2,100	..	710	100	..	..	Population per physician
2.1	1.9	5.4	3.1	5.9	4.9	6.1	6.0	Total fertility rate
31	14	87	27	113	66	145	104	Infant mortality (per 1,000 live births)
..	..	..	..	..	..	..	..	Low birth weight (percent)
..	14	..	29	..	76	..	118	Risk of dying by age 5 (female)
..	18	..	34	..	91	..	137	Risk of dying by age 5 (male)
3,452	3,642	2,389	2,713	2,597	2,847	1,904	1,824	Daily calorie supply (per capita)
78	102	85	95	138	99	114	86	Food production per capita index (1979–81 = 100)
102	103	87	99	97	103	..	..	Education, primary (female)
103	104	92	100	98	102	..	..	Education, primary (total)
..	111	..	29	..	1,565	..	824	Area (thousands of square kilometers)
..	8	..	4	..	3	..	2	Population projected to year 2000 (millions)

The data on *area* are from the Food and Agriculture Organization.

GNP per capita figures in U.S. dollars are calculated according to the *World Bank Atlas* method, which is described below.

GNP per capita does not, by itself, constitute or measure welfare or success in development. It does not distinguish between the aims and ultimate uses of a given product, nor does it say whether it merely offsets some natural or other obstacle, or harms or contributes to welfare. For example, GNP is higher in colder countries, where people spend money on heating and warm clothes, than in balmy climates, where people are comfortable wearing light clothes in the open air.

More generally, GNP abstracts from environmental issues, particularly natural resource use. The Bank has joined with others to see how national accounts might provide insights into these issues. The possibility of developing "satellite" accounts is being considered; such accounts could delve into practical and conceptual difficulties, such as assigning a meaningful economic value to resources that markets do not yet perceive as "scarce" and allocating costs that are essentially global within a framework that is inherently national.

GNP measures the total domestic and foreign value added claimed by residents. It comprises GDP (defined in the note for Table 2) plus net factor income from abroad, which is the income residents receive from abroad for factor services (labor and capital) less similar payments made to nonresidents who contributed to the domestic economy.

In estimating GNP per capita, the Bank recognizes that perfect cross-country comparability of GNP per capita estimates cannot be achieved. Beyond the classic, strictly intractable index number problem, two obstacles stand in the way of adequate comparability. One concerns the GNP and population estimates themselves. There are differences in national accounting and demographic reporting systems and in the coverage and reliability of underlying statistical information among various countries. The other relates to the use of official exchange rates for converting GNP data, expressed in different national currencies, to a common denomination—conventionally the U.S. dollar—to compare them across countries.

Recognizing that these shortcomings affect the comparability of the GNP per capita estimates, the World Bank has introduced several improvements in the estimation procedures. Through its regular review of member countries' national accounts, the Bank systematically evaluates the GNP estimates, focusing on the coverage and concepts employed and, where appropriate, making adjustments to improve comparability. As part of the review, Bank staff estimates of GNP (and sometimes of population) may be developed for the most recent period.

The Bank also systematically assesses the appropriateness of official exchange rates as conversion factors. An alternative conversion factor is used (and reported in the *World Tables*) when the official exchange rate is judged to diverge by an exceptionally large margin from the rate effectively applied to foreign transactions. This applies to only a small number of countries. For all other countries the Bank calculates GNP per capita using the *Atlas* method.

The *Atlas* conversion factor for any year is the average of the exchange rate for that year and the exchange rates for the two preceding years, after adjusting them for differences in relative inflation between the country and the United States. This three-year average smooths fluctuations in prices and exchange rates for each country. The resulting GNP in U.S. dollars is divided by the midyear population for the latest of the three years to derive GNP per capita.

Some sixty low- and middle-income economies have suffered declining real GNP per capita in constant prices during the 1980s. In addition, significant currency and terms of trade fluctuations have affected relative income levels. For this reason the levels and ranking of GNP per capita estimates, calculated by the *Atlas* method, have sometimes changed in ways not necessarily related to the relative domestic growth performance of the economies.

The following formulas describe the procedures for computing the conversion factor for year t:

$$(e^{*}_{t-2,t}) = \frac{1}{3} \left[e_{t-2} \left(\frac{P_t}{P_{t-2}} \middle/ \frac{P^{\$}_t}{P^{\$}_{t-2}} \right) + e_{t-1} \left(\frac{P_t}{P_{t-1}} \middle/ \frac{P^{\$}_t}{P^{\$}_{t-1}} \right) + e_t \right]$$

and for calculating GNP per capita in U.S. dollars for year t:

$$(Y^{\$}_t) = (Y_t / N_t \div e^{*}_{t-2,t})$$

where

Y_t = current GNP (local currency) for year t
P_t = GNP deflator for year t
e_t = annual average exchange rate (local currency/U.S. dollar) for year t
N_t = midyear population for year t
$P^{\$}_t$ = U.S. GNP deflator for year t.

Because of problems associated with the availability of comparable data and the determination of conversion factors, information on GNP per capita is not shown for nonreporting nonmarket economies.

The use of official exchange rates to convert national currency figures to U.S. dollars does not reflect the relative domestic purchasing powers of currencies. The United Nations International Comparison Program (ICP) has developed measures of real GDP on an internationally comparable scale, using purchasing power parities (PPPs) instead of exchange rates as conversion factors. Table 30 shows the most recent ICP estimates. Information on the ICP has been published in four studies and in a number of other reports. The most recent study is Phase V, parts of which have already been published by the European Communities (EC)—covering Europe and Africa—and the Organisation for Economic Co-operation and Development (OECD).

The ICP has covered more than seventy countries in five phases, at five-year intervals. The Bank is currently reviewing the data and methodology underlying the latest estimates and will include an updated comparison of ICP and *Atlas* numbers in a future edition of the *Atlas* or another statistical publication.

The ICP figures reported in Table 30 are preliminary and may be revised. The United Nations and its regional economic commissions, as well as other international agencies, such as the EC, the OECD, and the World Bank, are working to improve the methodology and to extend annual purchasing power comparisons to all countries. However, exchange rates remain the only generally available means of converting GNP from national currencies to U.S. dollars.

The *average annual rate of inflation* is measured by the growth rate of the GDP implicit deflator for each of the periods shown. The GDP deflator is first calculated by dividing, for each year of the period, the value of GDP at current values by the value of GDP at constant values, both in national currency. The least-squares method is then used to calculate the growth rate of the GDP deflator for the period. This measure of inflation, like any other, has limitations. For some purposes, however, it is used as an indicator of inflation because it is the most broadly based measure, showing annual price movements for all goods and services produced in an economy.

Life expectancy at birth indicates the number of years a newborn infant would live if prevailing patterns of mortality at the time of its birth were to stay the same throughout its life. Data are from the U.N. Population Division, supplemented by World Bank estimates.

Adult illiteracy is defined here as the proportion of the over-15 population who cannot, with understanding, read and write a short, simple statement on their everyday life. This is only one of three widely accepted definitions, and its application is subject to qualifiers in a number of countries.

The summary measures for GNP per capita, life expectancy, and adult illiteracy in this table are weighted by population. Those for average annual rates of inflation are weighted by the 1980 share of country GDP valued in current U.S. dollars.

Tables 2 and 3. Growth and structure of production

Most of the definitions used are those of the *U.N. System of National Accounts* (SNA), Series F, No. 2, Revision 3. Estimates are obtained from national sources, sometimes reaching the World Bank through other international agencies but more often collected during World Bank staff missions.

World Bank staff review the quality of national accounts data and in some instances, through mission work or technical assistance, help adjust national series. Because of the sometimes limited capabilities of statistical offices and basic data problems, strict international comparability cannot be achieved, especially in economic activities that are difficult to measure such as parallel market transactions, the informal sector, or subsistence agriculture.

GDP measures the total output of goods and services for final use produced by residents and non-residents, regardless of the allocation to domestic and foreign claims. It is calculated without making deductions for depreciation of "manmade" assets or depletion and degradation of natural resources. Although SNA envisages estimates of GDP by industrial origin to be at producer prices, many countries still report such details at factor cost. International comparability of the estimates is affected by the use of differing country practices in valuation systems for reporting value added by production sectors. As a partial solution, GDP estimates are shown at purchaser values if the components are on this basis, and such instances are footnoted. However, for a few countries in Tables 2 and 3, GDP at purchaser values has been replaced by GDP at factor cost. Note that in editions before 1986, *GDP at producer prices* and *GDP at purchaser values* were referred to for convenience as *GDP at factor cost* and *GDP at market prices*, respectively.

The figures for GDP are dollar values converted from domestic currencies using single-year official exchange rates. For a few countries where the official exchange rate does not reflect the rate effectively applied to actual foreign exchange transactions, an alternative conversion factor is used (and reported in the *World Tables*). Note that this table does not use the three-year averaging technique applied to GNP per capita in Table 1.

Agriculture covers forestry, hunting, and fishing as well as agriculture. In developing countries with high levels of subsistence farming, much of agricultural production is either not exchanged or not exchanged for money. This increases the difficulty of measuring the contribution of agriculture to GDP and reduces the reliability and comparability of such numbers. *Industry* comprises value added in mining; *manufacturing* (also reported as a subgroup); construction; and electricity, water, and gas. Value added in all other branches of economic activity, including imputed bank service charges, import duties, and any statistical discrepancies noted by national compilers, are categorized as *services, etc.*

Partially rebased 1980 series in domestic currencies, as explained at the beginning of the technical notes, are used to compute the growth rates in Table 2. The sectoral shares of GDP in Table 3 are based on current price series.

In calculating the summary measures for each indicator in Table 2, partially rebased constant 1980

U.S. dollar values for each economy are calculated for each of the years of the periods covered; the values are aggregated across countries for each year; and the least-squares procedure is used to compute the growth rates. The average sectoral percentage shares in Table 3 are computed from group aggregates of sectoral GDP in current U.S. dollars.

Table 4. Agriculture and food

The basic data for *value added in agriculture* are from the World Bank's national accounts series at current prices in national currencies. Value added in current prices in national currencies is converted to U.S. dollars by applying the single-year conversion procedure, as described in the technical note for Tables 2 and 3.

The figures for the remainder of this table are from the Food and Agriculture Organization (FAO). *Cereal imports* are measured in grain equivalents and defined as comprising all cereals in the *Standard International Trade Classification* (SITC), Revision 2, Groups 041–046. *Food aid in cereals* covers wheat and flour, bulgur, rice, coarse grains, and the cereal component of blended foods. The figures are not directly comparable because of reporting and timing differences. Cereal imports are based on calendar-year data reported by recipient countries, and food aid in cereals is based on data for crop years reported by donors and international organizations, including the International Wheat Council and the World Food Programme. Furthermore, food aid information from donors may not correspond to actual receipts by beneficiaries during a given period because of delays in transportation and recording, or because aid is sometimes not reported to the FAO or other relevant international organizations. Food aid imports may also not show up in customs records. The earliest available food aid data are for 1974. The time reference for food aid is the crop year, July to June.

Fertilizer consumption measures the plant nutrients used in relation to arable land. Fertilizer products cover nitrogenous, potash, and phosphate fertilizers (which include ground rock phosphate). Arable land is defined as land under temporary crops (double-cropped areas are counted once), temporary meadows for mowing or pastures, land under market or kitchen gardens, and land temporarily fallow or lying idle, as well as land under permanent crops. The time reference for fertilizer consumption is the crop year, July to June.

The *average index of food production per capita* shows the average annual quantity of food produced per capita in 1986–88 in relation to the average produced annually in 1979–81. The estimates are derived by dividing the quantity of food production by the total population. For this index food is defined as comprising nuts, pulses, fruits, cereals, vegetables, sugar cane, sugar beet, starchy roots, edible oils, livestock, and livestock products. Quantities of food production are measured net of animal feed, seeds for use in agriculture, and food lost in processing and distribution.

The summary measures for fertilizer consumption are weighted by total arable land area; the summary measures for food production are weighted by population.

Table 5. Commercial energy

The data on energy are primarily from U.N. sources. They refer to commercial forms of primary energy—petroleum and natural gas liquids, natural gas, solid fuels (coal, lignite, and so on), and primary electricity (nuclear, geothermal, and hydroelectric power)—all converted into oil equivalents. Figures on liquid fuel consumption include petroleum derivatives that have been consumed in nonenergy uses. For converting primary electricity into oil equivalents, a notional thermal efficiency of 34 percent has been assumed. The use of firewood, dried animal excrement, and other traditional fuels, although substantial in some developing countries, is not taken into account because reliable and comprehensive data are not available.

Energy imports refer to the dollar value of energy imports—Section 3 in the SITC, Revision 1—and are expressed as a percentage of earnings from merchandise exports.

Because data on energy imports do not permit a distinction between petroleum imports for fuel and those for use in the petrochemicals industry, these percentages may overestimate the dependence on imported energy.

The summary measures of energy production and consumption are computed by aggregating the respective volumes for each of the years covered by the periods and then applying the least-squares growth rate procedure. For energy consumption per capita, population weights are used to compute summary measures for the specified years.

The summary measures of energy imports as a percentage of merchandise exports are computed from group aggregates for energy imports and merchandise exports in current dollars.

Table 6. Structure of manufacturing

The basic data for *value added in manufacturing* are from the World Bank's national accounts series at current prices in national currencies. Value added in current prices in national currencies is converted to U.S. dollars by applying the single-year conversion procedure, as described in the technical note for Tables 2 and 3.

The data for *distribution of manufacturing value added* among industries are provided by the United Nations Industrial Development Organization, and distribution calculations are from national currencies in current prices.

The classification of manufacturing industries is in accordance with the U.N. *International Standard*

Industrial Classification of All Economic Activities (ISIC), Revision 2. *Food, beverages, and tobacco* comprise ISIC Division 31; *textiles and clothing*, Division 32; *machinery and transport equipment*, Major Groups 382–84; and *chemicals*, Major Groups 351 and 352. *Other* comprises wood and related products (Division 33), paper and related products (Division 34), petroleum and related products (Major Groups 353–56), basic metals and mineral products (Divisions 36 and 37), fabricated metal products and professional goods (Major Groups 381 and 385), and other industries (Major Group 390). When data for textiles, machinery, or chemicals are shown as not available, they are also included in *other*.

Summary measures given for value added in manufacturing are totals calculated by the aggregation method noted at the beginning of the technical notes.

Table 7. Manufacturing earnings and output

Four indicators are shown—two relate to real earnings per employee, one to labor's share in total value added generated, and one to labor productivity in the manufacturing sector. The indicators are based on data from the United Nations Industrial Development Organization (UNIDO), although the deflators are from other sources, as explained below.

Earnings per employee are in constant prices and are derived by deflating nominal earnings per employee by the country's consumer price index (CPI). The CPI is from the International Monetary Fund's *International Financial Statistics*. *Total earnings as a percentage of value added* are derived by dividing total earnings of employees by value added in current prices, to show labor's share in income generated in the manufacturing sector. *Gross output per employee* is in constant prices and is presented as an index of overall labor productivity in manufacturing with 1980 as the base year. To derive this indicator, UNIDO data on gross output per employee in current prices are adjusted using the implicit deflators for value added in manufacturing or in industry, taken from the World Bank's national accounts data files.

To improve cross-country comparability, UNIDO has, where possible, standardized the coverage of establishments to those with five or more employees.

The concepts and definitions are in accordance with the *International Recommendations for Industrial Statistics*, published by the United Nations. Earnings (wages and salaries) cover all remuneration to employees paid by the employer during the year. The payments include (a) all regular and overtime cash payments and bonuses and cost of living allowances; (b) wages and salaries paid during vacation and sick leave; (c) taxes and social insurance contributions and the like, payable by the employees and deducted by the employer; and (d) payments in kind.

The value of gross output is estimated on the basis of either production or shipments. On the production basis it consists of (a) the value of all products of the establishment, (b) the value of industrial services rendered to others, (c) the value of goods shipped in the same condition as received, (d) the value of electricity sold, and (e) the net change in the value of work-in-progress between the beginning and the end of the reference period. In the case of estimates compiled on a shipment basis, the net change between the beginning and the end of the reference period in the value of stocks of finished goods is also included. "Value added" is defined as the current value of gross output less the current cost of (a) materials, fuels, and other supplies consumed, (b) contract and commission work done by others, (c) repair and maintenance work done by others, and (d) goods shipped in the same condition as received.

The term "employees" in this table combines two categories defined by the U.N., regular employees and persons engaged. Together these groups comprise regular employees, working proprietors, active business partners, and unpaid family workers; they exclude homeworkers. The data refer to the average number of employees working during the year.

Tables 8 and 9. Growth of consumption and investment; structure of demand

GDP is defined in the note for Tables 2 and 3, but for these two tables it is in purchaser values.

General government consumption includes all current expenditure for purchases of goods and services by all levels of government. Capital expenditure on national defense and security is regarded as consumption expenditure.

Private consumption, etc., is the market value of all goods and services, including durable products (such as cars, washing machines, and home computers) purchased or received as income in kind by households and nonprofit institutions. It excludes purchases of dwellings but includes imputed rent for owner-occupied dwellings (see the note to Table 10 for details). In practice, it includes any statistical discrepancy in the use of resources. At constant prices, it also includes the rescaling deviation from partial rebasing, which is explained in the beginning of the technical notes.

Gross domestic investment consists of outlays on additions to the fixed assets of the economy plus net changes in the level of inventories.

Gross domestic savings are calculated by deducting total consumption from GDP.

Exports of goods and nonfactor services represent the value of all goods and nonfactor services provided to the rest of the world; they include merchandise, freight, insurance, travel, and other nonfactor services. The value of factor services, such as investment income, interest, and labor income, is excluded. Current transfers are also excluded.

The *resource balance* is the difference between exports of goods and nonfactor services and imports of goods and nonfactor services.

Partially rebased 1980 series in constant domestic currency units are used to compute the indicators in Table 8. Table 9 uses national accounts series in current domestic currency units.

The summary measures are calculated by the method explained in the note to Tables 2 and 3.

Table 10. Structure of consumption

Percentage shares of selected items in total household consumption expenditure are computed from details of GDP (expenditure at national market prices) defined in the U.N. System of National Accounts (SNA), mostly as collected for International Comparison Program (ICP) Phases IV (1980) and V (1985). For countries not covered by the ICP, less detailed national accounts estimates are included, where available, in order to present a general idea of the broad structure of consumption. The data cover eighty-four countries (including Bank staff estimates for China) and refer to the most recent estimates, generally for 1980 and 1985. Where they refer to other years the figures are shown in italics. *Consumption* here refers to private (nongovernment) consumption as defined in the SNA and in the notes to Tables 2 and 3, 4, and 9, except that education and medical care comprise government as well as private outlays. This ICP concept of "enhanced consumption" reflects who uses rather than who pays for consumption goods, and it improves international comparability because it is less sensitive to differing national practices regarding the financing of health and education services.

Cereals and tubers, a major subitem of *food,* comprise the main staple products: rice, flour, bread, all other cereals and cereal preparations, potatoes, yams, and other tubers. For high-income OECD members, however, this subitem does not include tubers. *Gross rents, fuel and power* consist of actual and imputed rents and repair and maintenance charges, as well as the subitem *fuel and power* (for heating, lighting, cooking, air conditioning, and so forth). Note that this item excludes energy used for transport (rarely reported to be more than 1 percent of total consumption in low- and middle-income economies). As mentioned, *medical care* and *education* include government as well as private consumption expenditure. *Transport and communication* also includes the purchase of *motor cars,* which are reported as a subitem. *Other consumption,* the residual group, includes beverages and tobacco, nondurable household goods and household services, recreational services, and services (including meals) supplied by hotels and restaurants; carry-out food is recorded here. It also includes the separately reported subitem *other consumer durables,* comprising household appliances, furniture, floor coverings, recreational equipment, and watches and jewelry.

Estimating the structure of consumption is one of the weakest aspects of national accounting in low- and middle-income economies. The structure is estimated through household expenditure surveys and similar survey techniques. It therefore shares any bias inherent in the sample frame. Since, conceptually, expenditure is not identical to consumption, other apparent discrepancies occur and data for some countries should be treated with caution. For example, some countries limit surveys to urban areas or, even more narrowly, to capital cities. This tends to produce lower than average shares for food and high shares for transport and communication, gross rents, fuel and power, and other consumption. Controlled food prices and incomplete national accounting for subsistence activities also contribute to low food shares.

Table 11. Central government expenditure

The data on central government finance in Tables 11 and 12 are from the IMF *Government Finance Statistics Yearbook* (1989) and IMF data files. The accounts of each country are reported using the system of common definitions and classifications found in the IMF *Manual on Government Finance Statistics* (1986).

For complete and authoritative explanations of concepts, definitions, and data sources, see these IMF sources. The commentary that follows is intended mainly to place these data in the context of the broad range of indicators reported in this edition.

The shares of *total expenditure* and *current revenue* by category are calculated from series in national currencies. Because of differences in coverage of available data, the individual components of central government expenditure and current revenue shown in these tables may not be strictly comparable across all economies.

Moreover, inadequate statistical coverage of state, provincial, and local governments dictates the use of central government data; this may seriously understate or distort the statistical portrayal of the allocation of resources for various purposes, especially in countries where lower levels of government have considerable autonomy and are responsible for many economic and social services. In addition, "central government" can mean either of two accounting concepts: consolidated or budgetary. For most countries, central government finance data have been consolidated into one overall account, but for others only the budgetary central government accounts are available. Since all central government units are not included in the budgetary accounts, the overall picture of central government activities is incomplete. Countries reporting budgetary data are footnoted.

It must be emphasized that for these and other reasons the data presented, especially those for education and health, are not comparable across countries. In many economies private health and education services are substantial; in others public services represent the major component of total expenditure but may be financed by lower levels of government. Caution should therefore be exercised in using the data for cross-country comparisons. Central government expenditure comprises the expenditure by all government offices, departments, establishments, and other bodies that are agencies or instruments of the central authority of a country. It includes both current and capital (development) expenditure.

Defense comprises all expenditure, whether by defense or other departments, on the maintenance of military forces, including the purchase of military supplies and equipment, construction, recruiting, and training. Also in this category are closely related items such as military aid programs.

Education comprises expenditure on the provision, management, inspection, and support of pre-primary, primary, and secondary schools; of universities and colleges; and of vocational, technical, and other training institutions. Also included is expenditure on the general administration and regulation of the education system; on research into its objectives, organization, administration, and methods; and on such subsidiary services as transport, school meals, and school medical and dental services. Note that Table 10 provides an alternative measure of expenditure on education, private as well as public, relative to household consumption.

Health covers public expenditure on hospitals, maternity and dental centers, and clinics with a major medical component; on national health and medical insurance schemes; and on family planning and preventive care. Note that Table 10 provides a more comprehensive measure of expenditure on medical care, private as well as public, relative to household consumption.

Housing, amenities; social security and welfare cover expenditure on housing, such as income-related schemes; on provision and support of housing and slum clearance activities; on community development; and on sanitary services. These categories also cover compensation for loss of income to the sick and temporarily disabled; payments to the elderly, the permanently disabled, and the unemployed; family, maternity, and child allowances; and the cost of welfare services, such as care of the aged, the disabled, and children. Many expenditures relevant to environmental defense, such as pollution abatement, water supply, sanitary affairs, and refuse collection, are included indistinguishably in this category.

Economic services comprise expenditure associated with the regulation, support, and more efficient operation of business; economic development; redress of regional imbalances; and creation of employment opportunities. Research, trade promotion, geological surveys, and inspection and regulation of particular industry groups are among the activities included.

Other covers items not included elsewhere; for a few economies it also includes amounts that could not be allocated to other components (or adjustments from accrual to cash accounts).

Total expenditure is more narrowly defined than the measure of general government consumption given in Table 9, because it excludes consumption expenditure by state and local governments. At the same time, central government expenditure is more broadly defined because it includes government's gross domestic investment and transfer payments.

Overall surplus/deficit is defined as current and capital revenue and grants received, less total expenditure and lending minus repayments.

Summary measures for the components of central government expenditure are computed from group totals for expenditure components and central government expenditure in current dollars. Those for total expenditure as a percentage of GNP and for overall surplus/deficit as a percentage of GNP are computed from group totals for the above total expenditures and overall surplus/deficit in current dollars, and GNP in current dollars, respectively. Since 1988 data are not available for more than half the countries, 1987 data are used as weights for the summary measures in this table.

Table 12. Central government current revenue

Information on data sources and comparability is given in the note to Table 11. Current revenue by source is expressed as a percentage of *total current revenue,* which is the sum of tax revenue and nontax revenue and is calculated from national currencies.

Tax revenue comprises compulsory, unrequited, nonrepayable receipts for public purposes. It includes interest collected on tax arrears and penalties collected on nonpayment or late payment of taxes and is shown net of refunds and other corrective transactions. *Taxes on income, profit, and capital gain* are taxes levied on the actual or presumptive net income of individuals, on the profits of enterprises, and on capital gains, whether realized on land sales, securities, or other assets. *Social security contributions* include employers' and employees' social security contributions as well as those of self-employed and unemployed persons. *Domestic taxes on goods and services* include general sales and turnover or value added taxes, selective excises on goods, selective taxes on services, taxes on the use of goods or property, and profits of fiscal monopolies. *Taxes on international trade and transactions* include import duties, export duties, profits of export or import monopolies, exchange profits, and exchange taxes. *Other taxes* include employers' payroll or labor taxes, taxes on property, and taxes not allocable to other categories. They may include negative values that are adjustments, for instance, for taxes collected on behalf of state and local governments and not allocable to individual tax categories.

Nontax revenue comprises receipts that are not a compulsory nonrepayable payment for public purposes, such as fines, administrative fees, or entrepreneurial income from government ownership of property. Proceeds of grants and borrowing, funds arising from the repayment of previous lending by governments, incurrence of liabilities, and proceeds from the sale of capital assets are not included.

Summary measures for the components of current revenue are computed from group totals for revenue components and total current revenue in current dollars; those for current revenue as a percentage of GNP are computed from group totals for total current revenue and GNP in current dollars. Since 1988 data are not available for more than half the countries, 1987 data are used as weights for the summary measures for this table.

Table 13. Money and interest rates

The data on monetary holdings are based on the IMF's *International Financial Statistics* (IFS). *Monetary holdings, broadly defined,* comprise the monetary and quasi-monetary liabilities of a country's financial institutions to residents other than the central government. For most countries, monetary holdings are the sum of money (IFS line 34) and quasi-money (IFS line 35). Money comprises the economy's means of payment: currency outside banks and demand deposits. Quasi-money comprises time and savings deposits and similar bank accounts that the issuer will readily exchange for money. Where nonmonetary financial institutions are important issuers of quasi-monetary liabilities, these are also included in the measure of monetary holdings.

The growth rates for monetary holdings are calculated from year-end figures, while the average of the year-end figures for the specified year and the previous year is used for the ratio of monetary holdings to GDP.

The *nominal interest rates of banks,* also from IFS, represent the rates paid by commercial or similar banks to holders of their quasi-monetary liabilities (deposit rate) and charged by the banks on loans to prime customers (lending rate). The data are, however, of limited international comparability partly because coverage and definitions vary, and partly because countries differ in the scope available to banks for adjusting interest rates to reflect market conditions.

Since interest rates (and growth rates for monetary holdings) are expressed in nominal terms, much of the variation among countries stems from differences in inflation. For easy reference, the Table 1 indicator of recent inflation is repeated in this table.

Table 14. Growth of merchandise trade

This year, a significant change has been made to the data source of Table 14. For low- and middle-income countries, the main data source for current trade values has changed from the U.N. Commodity Trade data file to the World Bank data file. The latter includes data collected from World Bank member countries before more detailed data are reported to the U.N.

The statistics on merchandise trade for high-income countries continue to be primarily from the U.N. trade data system, which accords with the U.N. *Yearbook of International Trade Statistics*—that is, the data are based on countries' customs returns. In some cases, data from secondary sources permit coverage adjustments for significant components of a country's foreign trade not subject to regular customs reports. Such cases are identified in the country notes to the *World Tables*. Values in these tables are in current U.S. dollars.

Merchandise *exports* and *imports*, with some exceptions, cover international movements of goods across customs borders. Exports are valued f.o.b. (free on board) and imports c.i.f. (cost, insurance, and freight), unless otherwise specified in the foregoing sources. These values are in current dollars; note that they do not include trade in services.

The growth rates of merchandise exports and imports are in constant terms and are calculated from quantum indexes of exports and imports. Quantum indexes are obtained from the export or import value index as deflated by the corresponding price index. To calculate these quantum indexes, the World Bank uses its own price indexes, which are based on international prices for primary commodities and unit value indexes for manufactures. These price indexes are country-specific and disaggregated by broad commodity groups. This ensures consistency between data for a group of countries and those for individual countries. Such consistency will increase as the World Bank continues to improve its trade price indexes for an increasing number of countries. These growth rates can differ from those derived from national practices because national price indexes may use different base years and weighting procedures from those used by the World Bank.

The *terms of trade*, or the net barter terms of trade, measure the relative movement of export prices against that of import prices. Calculated as the ratio of a country's index of average export prices to its average import price index, this indicator shows changes over a base year in the level of export prices as a percentage of import prices. The terms of trade index numbers are shown for 1985 and 1988, where 1980 = 100. The price indexes are from the source cited above for the growth rates of exports and imports.

The summary measures for the growth rates are calculated by aggregating the 1980 constant U.S. dollar price series for each year and then applying the least-squares growth rate procedure for the periods shown. Note again that these values do not include trade in services.

Tables 15 and 16. Structure of merchandise imports and exports

The shares in these tables are derived from trade values in current dollars reported in the U.N. trade

data system and the U.N. *Yearbook of International Trade Statistics*, supplemented by other secondary sources and World Bank estimates, as explained in the note to Table 14.

Merchandise *exports* and *imports* are also defined in the note to Table 14.

The categorization of exports and imports follows the *Standard International Trade Classification* (SITC), Series M, No. 34, Revision 1. Estimates from secondary sources also usually follow this definition. For some countries, data for certain commodity categories are unavailable and the full breakdown cannot be shown.

In Table 15, *food* commodities are those in SITC Sections 0, 1, and 4 and Division 22 (food and live animals, beverages, oils and fats, and oilseeds and nuts), less Division 12 (tobacco). *Fuels* are the commodities in SITC Section 3 (mineral fuels, lubricants and related materials). *Other primary commodities* comprise SITC Section 2 (crude materials, excluding fuels), less Division 22 (oilseeds and nuts), plus Divisions 12 (tobacco) and 68 (nonferrous metals). *Machinery and transport equipment* are the commodities in SITC Section 7. *Other manufactures*, calculated residually from the total value of manufactured imports, represent SITC Sections 5 through 9, less Section 7 and Division 68.

In Table 16, *fuels, minerals, and metals* are the commodities in SITC Section 3 (mineral fuels and lubricants and related materials), Divisions 27 and 28 (minerals and crude fertilizers, and metalliferous ores), and Division 68 (nonferrous metals). *Other primary commodities* comprise SITC Sections 0, 1, 2, and 4 (food and live animals, beverages and tobacco, inedible crude materials, oils, fats, and waxes), less Divisions 27 and 28. *Machinery and transport equipment* are the commodities in SITC Section 7. *Other manufactures* represent SITC Sections 5 through 9, less Section 7 and Division 68. *Textiles and clothing*, representing SITC Divisions 65 and 84 (textiles, yarns, fabrics, and clothing), are shown as a subgroup of *other manufactures*.

The summary measures in Table 15 are weighted by total merchandise imports of individual countries in current dollars, those in Table 16 by total merchandise exports of individual countries in current dollars. (See the note to Table 14.)

Table 17. OECD imports of manufactured goods: origin and composition

The data are from the U.N., reported by high-income OECD economies, which are the OECD members excluding Greece, Portugal, and Turkey.

The table reports the value of *imports of manufactures* of high-income OECD countries by the economy of origin, and the composition of such imports by major manufactured product groups.

The table replaces one in past editions on the origin and destination of manufactured exports, which was based on exports reported by individual economies. Since there was a lag of several years in reporting by many developing economies, estimates based on various sources were used to fill the gaps. Until these estimates can be improved, this table, based on up-to-date and consistent but less comprehensive data, is included instead. Manufactured imports of the predominant markets from individual economies are the best available proxy of the magnitude and composition of the manufactured exports of these economies to all destinations taken together.

Manufactured goods are the commodities in *Standard International Trade Classification* (SITC), Revision 1, Sections 5 through 9 (chemical and related products, basic manufactures, manufactured articles, machinery and transport equipment, and other manufactured articles and goods not elsewhere classified), excluding Division 68 (nonferrous metals). This definition is somewhat broader than the one used to define exporters of manufactures.

The major manufactured product groups reported are defined as follows: *textiles and clothing* (SITC Sections 65 and 84), *chemicals* (SITC Section 5), *electrical machinery and electronics* (SITC Section 72), *transport equipment* (SITC Section 73), and *others*, defined as the residual. SITC Revision 1 data are used for the year 1968, whereas the equivalent data in Revision 2 are used for the year 1988.

Table 18. Balance of payments and reserves

The statistics for this table are mostly as reported by the IMF but do include recent estimates by World Bank staff and, in rare instances, the Bank's own coverage or classification adjustments to enhance international comparability. Values in this table are in U.S. dollars converted at current exchange rates.

The *current account balance after official transfers* is the difference between (a) exports of goods and services (factor and nonfactor) as well as inflows of unrequited transfers (private and official) and (b) imports of goods and services as well as all unrequited transfers to the rest of the world.

Current account balance before official transfers is the current account balance that treats net official unrequited transfers as akin to official capital movements. The difference between the two balance of payments measures is essentially foreign aid in the form of grants, technical assistance, and food aid, which, for most developing countries, tends to make current account deficits smaller than the financing requirement.

Net workers' remittances cover payments and receipts of income by migrants who are employed or expect to be employed for more than a year in their new economy, where they are considered residents. These remittances are classified as private unrequited transfers and are included in the balance of payments current account balance, whereas those derived from shorter-term stays are included in services as labor income. The distinction accords with internationally agreed guidelines, but many developing countries classify

workers' remittances as a factor income receipt (and hence a component of GNP). The World Bank adheres to international guidelines in defining GNP and, therefore, may differ from national practices.

Net direct private investment is the net amount invested or reinvested by nonresidents in enterprises in which they or other nonresidents exercise significant managerial control, including equity capital, reinvested earnings, and other capital. The net figures are obtained by subtracting the value of direct investment abroad by residents of the reporting country.

Gross international reserves comprise holdings of monetary gold, special drawing rights (SDRs), the reserve position of members in the IMF, and holdings of foreign exchange under the control of monetary authorities. The data on holdings of international reserves are from IMF data files. The gold component of these reserves is valued throughout at year-end (December 31) London prices: that is, $37.37 an ounce in 1970 and $410.25 an ounce in 1988. The reserve levels for 1970 and 1988 refer to the end of the year indicated and are in current dollars at prevailing exchange rates. Because of differences in the definition of international reserves, in the valuation of gold, and in reserve management practices, the levels of reserve holdings published in national sources do not have strictly comparable significance. Reserve holdings at the end of 1988 are also expressed in terms of the number of months of imports of goods and services they could pay for.

The summary measures are computed from group aggregates for gross international reserves and total imports of goods and services in current dollars.

Table 19. Official development assistance from OECD & OPEC members

Official development assistance (ODA) consists of net disbursements of loans and grants made on concessional financial terms by official agencies of the members of the Development Assistance Committee (DAC) of the Organisation for Economic Cooperation and Development (OECD) and members of the Organization of Petroleum Exporting Countries (OPEC), to promote economic development and welfare. Although this definition is meant to exclude purely military assistance, the borderline is sometimes blurred; the definition used by the country of origin usually prevails. ODA also includes the value of technical cooperation and assistance. All data shown are supplied by the OECD, and all U.S. dollar values are converted at official exchange rates.

Amounts shown are net disbursements to developing countries and multilateral institutions. The disbursements to multilateral institutions are now reported for all DAC members on the basis of the date of issue of notes; some DAC members previously reported on the basis of the date of encashment. *Net bilateral flows to low-income countries* exclude unallocated bilateral flows and all disbursements to multilateral institutions.

The nominal values shown in the summary for ODA from high-income OECD countries were converted at 1980 prices using the dollar GDP deflator. This deflator is based on price increases in OECD countries (excluding Greece, Portugal, and Turkey) measured in dollars. It takes into account the parity changes between the dollar and national currencies. For example, when the dollar depreciates, price changes measured in national currencies have to be adjusted upward by the amount of the depreciation to obtain price changes in dollars.

The table, in addition to showing totals for OPEC, shows totals for the Organization of Arab Petroleum Exporting Countries (OAPEC). The donor members of OAPEC are Algeria, Iraq, Kuwait, Libya, Qatar, Saudi Arabia, and United Arab Emirates. ODA data for OPEC and OAPEC are also obtained from the OECD.

Table 20. Official development assistance: receipts

Net disbursements of ODA from all sources consist of loans and grants made on concessional financial terms by all bilateral official agencies and multilateral sources to promote economic development and welfare. They include the value of technical cooperation and assistance. The disbursements shown in this table are not strictly comparable with those shown in Table 19 since the receipts are from all sources; disbursements in Table 19 refer only to those made by high-income members of the OECD and members of OPEC. Net disbursements equal gross disbursements less payments to the originators of aid for amortization of past aid receipts. Net disbursements of ODA are shown per capita and as a percentage of GNP.

The summary measures of per capita ODA are computed from group aggregates for population and for ODA. Summary measures for ODA as a percentage of GNP are computed from group totals for ODA and for GNP in current U.S. dollars.

Table 21. Total external debt

The data on debt in this and successive tables are from the World Bank Debtor Reporting System, supplemented by World Bank estimates. That system is concerned solely with developing economies and does not collect data on external debt for other groups of borrowers or from economies that are not members of the World Bank. The dollar figures on debt shown in Tables 21 through 25 are in U.S. dollars converted at official exchange rates.

The data on debt include private nonguaranteed debt reported by twenty-five developing countries and complete or partial estimates for an additional twenty-three countries.

Public loans are external obligations of public debtors, including the national government, its agencies, and autonomous public bodies. *Publicly guaranteed loans* are external obligations of private debtors that are guaranteed for repayment by a public entity. These two categories are aggregated in the tables. *Private nonguaranteed loans* are external obligations of private debtors that are not guaranteed for repayment by a public entity.

Use of IMF credit denotes repurchase obligations to the IMF for all uses of IMF resources, excluding those resulting from drawings in the reserve tranche. It is shown for the end of the year specified. It comprises purchases outstanding under the credit tranches, including enlarged access resources, and all of the special facilities (the buffer stock, compensatory financing, Extended Fund, and oil facilities), Trust Fund loans and operations under the Enhanced Structural Adjustment facilities. Use of IMF credit outstanding at year-end (a stock) is converted to U.S. dollars at the dollar-SDR exchange rate in effect at year-end.

Short-term debt is debt with an original maturity of one year or less. Available data permit no distinctions between public and private nonguaranteed short-term debt.

Total external debt is defined for the purpose of this Report as the sum of public, publicly guaranteed, and private nonguaranteed long-term debt, use of IMF credit, and short-term debt.

Table 22. Flow of public and private external capital

Data on *disbursements* and *repayment of principal* (amortization) are for public, publicly guaranteed, and private nonguaranteed long-term loans. The *net flow* estimates are disbursements less the repayment of principal.

Table 23. Total external public and private debt and debt service ratios

Data on *total long-term debt outstanding and disbursed* in this table cover public and publicly guaranteed debt and private nonguaranteed debt. *Debt service as a percentage of exports of goods and services* is one of several conventional measures used to assess the ability to service debt. The average ratios of debt service to GNP for the economy groups are weighted by GNP in current dollars. The average ratios of debt service to exports of goods and services are weighted by exports of goods and services in current dollars.

Table 24. External public debt and debt service ratios

External public debt outstanding and disbursed represents public and publicly guaranteed loans drawn at year-end, net of repayments of principal and write-offs. For estimating external public debt as a percentage of GNP, the debt figures are converted into U.S. dollars from currencies of repayment at end-of-year official exchange rates. GNP is converted from national currencies to U.S. dollars by applying the conversion procedure described in the technical note to Tables 2 and 3.

Interest payments are actual payments made on the outstanding and disbursed public and publicly guaranteed debt in foreign currencies, goods, or services; they include commitment charges on undisbursed debt if information on those charges is available.

Debt service is the sum of actual repayments of principal (amortization) and actual payments of interest made in foreign currencies, goods, or services on external public and publicly guaranteed debt. Procedures for estimating total long-term debt as a percentage of GNP, average ratios of debt service to GNP, and average ratios of debt service to exports of goods and services are the same as those described in the note to Table 23.

The summary measures are computed from group aggregates of debt service and GNP in current dollars.

Table 25. Terms of external public borrowing

Commitments refer to the public and publicly guaranteed loans for which contracts were signed in the year specified. They are reported in currencies of repayment and converted into U.S. dollars at average annual official exchange rates.

Figures for *interest rates*, *maturities*, and *grace periods* are averages weighted by the amounts of the loans. Interest is the major charge levied on a loan and is usually computed on the amount of principal drawn and outstanding. The maturity of a loan is the interval between the agreement date, when a loan agreement is signed or bonds are issued, and the date of final repayment of principal. The grace period is the interval between the agreement date and the date of the first repayment of principal.

Public loans with variable interest rates, as a percentage of public debt, refer to interest rates that float with movements in a key market rate; for example, the London interbank offered rate (LIBOR) or the U.S. prime rate. This column shows the borrower's exposure to changes in international interest rates.

The summary measures in this table are weighted by the amounts of the loans.

Table 26. Population growth and projections

The introduction outlines the changes to the next seven tables.

Population growth rates are period averages calculated from midyear populations.

Population estimates for mid-1988 and estimates of fertility and mortality are made by the World Bank from data provided by the U.N. Population Division, the U.N. Statistical Office, and country statistical offices. Estimates take into account the results of the latest population censuses, which, in some cases, are neither recent nor accurate. Note that refugees not permanently settled in the country of asylum are generally considered to be part of the population of their country of origin.

The projections of population for 2000, 2025, and the year in which the population will eventually become stationary (see definition below) are made for each economy separately. Information on total population by age and sex, fertility, mortality, and international migration is projected on the basis of generalized assumptions until the population becomes stationary.

A stationary population is one in which age- and sex-specific mortality rates have not changed over a long period, during which fertility rates have remained at replacement level; that is, when the net reproduction rate (NRR) equals 1 (the note to Table 27 defines NRR). In such a population, the birth rate is constant and equal to the death rate, the age structure is constant, and the growth rate is zero.

Population projections are made age cohort by age cohort. Mortality, fertility, and migration are projected separately and the results are applied iteratively to the 1985 base-year age structure. For the projection period 1985 to 2005, the changes in mortality are country specific: increments in life expectancy and decrements in infant mortality are based on previous trends for each country. When female secondary school enrollment is high, mortality is assumed to decline more quickly. Infant mortality is projected separately from adult mortality.

Projected fertility rates are also based on previous trends. For countries in which fertility has started to decline (termed "fertility transition"), this trend is assumed to continue. It has been observed that no country with a life expectancy of less than 50 years has experienced a fertility decline; for these countries fertility transition is delayed, and then the average decline of the group of countries in fertility transition is applied. Countries with below-replacement fertility are assumed to have constant total fertility rates until 1995–2000 and then to regain replacement level by 2030.

International migration rates are based on past and present trends in migration flows and migration policy. Among the sources consulted are estimates and projections made by national statistical offices, international agencies, and research institutions. Because of the uncertainty of future migration trends, it is assumed in the projections that net migration rates will reach zero by 2025.

The estimates of the size of the stationary population are speculative. *They should not be regarded as predictions.* They are included to show the implications of recent fertility and mortality trends on the basis of generalized assumptions. A fuller description of the methods and assumptions used to calculate the estimates is contained in the World Bank's *World Population Projections, 1989–90 Edition.*

Table 27. Demography and fertility

The *crude birth rate* and *crude death rate* indicate respectively the number of live births and deaths occurring per thousand population in a year. They come from the sources mentioned in the note to Table 26.

Women of childbearing age as a percentage of population refers to women age 15 to 49.

The *total fertility rate* represents the number of children that would be born to a woman if she were to live to the end of her childbearing years and bear children at each age in accordance with prevailing age-specific fertility rates. The rates given are from the sources mentioned in Table 26.

The *net reproduction rate* (NRR), which measures the number of daughters a newborn girl will bear during her lifetime, assuming fixed age-specific fertility and mortality rates, reflects the extent to which a cohort of newborn girls will reproduce themselves. An NRR of 1 indicates that fertility is at replacement level: at this rate women will bear, on average, only enough daughters to replace themselves in the population. As with the size of the stationary population, the assumed year of reaching replacement-level fertility is speculative and should not be regarded as a prediction.

Married women of childbearing age using contraception refers to women who are practicing, or whose husbands are practicing, any form of contraception. Contraceptive usage is generally measured for women age 15 to 49. A few countries use measures relating to other age groups, especially 15 to 44.

Data are mainly derived from demographic and health surveys, contraceptive prevalence surveys, World Bank country data, and Mauldin and Segal's article ''Prevalence of Contraceptive Use: Trends and Issues'' in volume 19 of *Studies in Family Planning* (1988). For a few countries for which no survey data are available, program statistics are used; these include India and several African countries. Program statistics may understate contraceptive prevalence because they do not measure use of methods such as rhythm, withdrawal, or abstinence, or of contraceptives not obtained through the official family planning program. The data refer to rates prevailing in a variety of years, generally not more than two years before the year specified in the table.

All summary measures are country data weighted by each country's share in the aggregate population.

Table 28. Health and nutrition

The estimates of *population per physician* and *per nursing person* are derived from World Health Organization (WHO) data and are supplemented by data obtained directly by the World Bank from national sources. The data refer to a variety of years, generally no more than two years before the year specified. The figure for physicians, in addition to the total number of registered practitioners in the country, includes medical assistants whose medical training is less than that of qualified physicians but who nevertheless dispense similar medical services, including simple operations. Nursing persons include graduate, practical, assistant, and auxiliary nurses, as well as paraprofessional personnel such as health workers, first aid workers, traditional birth attendants, and so on. The inclusion of auxiliary and paraprofessional personnel provides more realistic estimates of available nursing care. Because definitions of doctors and nursing personnel vary–and because the data shown are for a variety of years—the data for these two indicators are not strictly comparable across countries.

Data on *births attended by health staff* show the percentage of births recorded where a recognized health service worker was in attendance. The data are from WHO and supplemented by UNICEF data; they are based on national sources. The data are derived mostly from official community reports and hospital records, and some reflect only births in hospitals and other medical institutions. Sometimes smaller private and rural hospitals are excluded, and sometimes even relatively primitive local facilities are included. The coverage is therefore not always comprehensive, and the figures should be treated with extreme caution.

The percentage of *babies with low birth weight* relates to children born weighing less than 2,500 grams. Low birth weight is frequently associated with maternal malnutrition and tends to raise the risk of infant mortality and to lead to poor growth in infancy and childhood, thus increasing the incidence of other forms of retarded development. The figures are derived from both WHO and UNICEF sources and are based on national data. The data are not strictly comparable across countries since they are compiled from a combination of surveys and administrative records that may not have representative national coverage.

The *infant mortality rate* is the number of infants who die before reaching one year of age, per thousand live births in a given year. The data are from the U.N. publication *Mortality of Children under Age 5: Projections, 1950–2025* as well as from the World Bank.

The *daily calorie supply per capita* is calculated by dividing the calorie equivalent of the food supplies in an economy by the population. Food supplies comprise domestic production, imports less exports, and changes in stocks; they exclude animal feed, seeds for use in agriculture, and food lost in processing and distribution. These estimates are from the Food and Agriculture Organization.

The summary measures in this table are country figures weighted by each country's share in the aggregate population.

Table 29. Education

The data in this table refer to a variety of years, generally not more than two years distant from those specified; however, figures for females sometimes refer to a year earlier than that for overall totals. The data are mostly from Unesco.

Primary school enrollment data are estimates of children of all ages enrolled in primary school. Figures are expressed as the ratio of pupils to the population of school-age children. Although many countries consider primary school age to be 6 to 11 years, others do not. The differences in country practices in the ages and duration of schooling are reflected in the ratios given. For some countries with universal primary education, the gross enrollment ratios may exceed 100 percent because some pupils are younger or older than the country's standard primary school age.

The data on *secondary* school enrollment are calculated in the same manner, but again the definition of secondary school age differs among countries. It is most commonly considered to be 12 to 17 years. Late entry of more mature students as well as repetition and the phenomenon of "bunching" in final grades can influence these ratios.

The *tertiary* enrollment ratio is calculated by dividing the number of pupils enrolled in all postsecondary schools and universities by the population in the 20–24 age group. Pupils attending vocational schools, adult education programs, two-year community colleges, and distance education centers (primarily correspondence courses) are included. The distribution of pupils across these different types of institutions varies among countries. The youth population—that is, 20 to 24 years—has been adopted by Unesco as the denominator since it represents an average tertiary level cohort even though people above and below this age group may be registered in tertiary institutions.

Primary net enrollment is the percentage of school-age children who are enrolled in school. Unlike gross enrollment, the net ratios correspond to the country's primary school age group. This indicator gives a much clearer idea of how many children in the age group are actually enrolled in school, without the number being inflated by over- (or under-) age children.

The *primary pupil-teacher ratio* is the number of pupils enrolled in school in a country, divided by the number of teachers in the education system.

The summary measures in this table are country enrollment rates weighted by each country's share in the aggregate population.

Table 30. Income distribution and ICP estimates of GDP

The data in this table refer to the ICP estimates of GDP and the distribution of income or expenditure accruing to percentile groups of households ranked by total household income, per capita income, or expenditure.

The first column presents preliminary results of the U.N. International Comparison Program (ICP), Phase V, for 1985. ICP recasts traditional national accounts through special price collections and disaggregation of GDP by expenditure components. More comprehensive ICP results are expected to be available by the mid-1990s. The figures given here are subject to change and should be regarded as indicative only. ICP Phase V details are pre-

pared by national statistical offices. The results are coordinated by the U.N. Statistical Office (UNSO) with support from other international agencies, particularly the Statistical Office of the European Communities (Eurostat) and the Organisation for Economic Co-operation and Development (OECD). The World Bank, the Economic Commission for Europe, and the Economic and Social Commission for Asia and the Pacific also contribute to this exercise.

A total of sixty-four countries participated in ICP Phase V, and preliminary results are now available for fifty-seven. For one country (Nepal), total GDP data were not available, and comparisons were made for consumption only; two countries with populations of less than 1 million—Luxembourg, with 81.3 as its estimated index of GDP per capita; and Swaziland, with 13.6—have been omitted from this table. Data for the remaining seven countries, all Caribbean, are expected soon.

Although the GDP per capita figures are presented as indexes to the U.S. value, the underlying data are expressed in U.S. dollars. However, these dollar values, which are different from those shown in Tables 1 and 3 (see the technical notes for these tables), are obtained by special conversion factors designed to equalize purchasing powers of currencies in the respective countries. This conversion factor, commonly known as the purchasing power parity (PPP), is defined as the number of units of a country's currency required to buy the same amounts of goods and services in the domestic market as one dollar would buy in the United States. The computation of PPPs involves obtaining implicit quantities from national accounts expenditure data and specially collected price data and revaluing the implicit quantities in each country at a single set of average prices. The PPP rate thus equalizes dollar prices in every country, and intercountry comparisons of GDP based on them reflect differences in quantities of goods and services free of any price-level differentials. This procedure is designed to bring intercountry comparisons in line with intertemporal real value comparisons that are based on constant price series.

The figures presented here are the results of a two-step exercise. Countries within a region or group such as the OECD are first compared using their own group average prices. Next, since group average prices may differ from each other, making the countries belonging to different groups not comparable, the group prices are adjusted to make them comparable at the world level. The adjustments, done by UNSO, are based on price differentials observed in a network of "link" countries representing each group. However, the linking is done in a manner that retains in the world comparison the relative levels of GDP observed in the group comparisons.

The two-step process was adopted because the relative GDP levels and ranking of two countries may change when more countries are brought into the comparison. It was felt that this should not be allowed to happen within geographic regions; that is, that the relationship of, say, Ghana and Senegal should not be affected by the prices prevailing in the United States. Thus overall GDP per capita levels are calculated at "regional" prices and then linked together. The linking is done by revaluing GDPs of all the countries at average "world" prices and reallocating the new regional totals on the basis of each country's share in the original comparison.

Such a method does not permit the comparison of more detailed quantities (such as food consumption). Hence these subaggregates and more detailed expenditure categories are calculated using world prices. These quantities are indeed comparable internationally, but they do not add up to the indicated GDPs because they are calculated at a different set of prices.

Some countries belong to several regional groups. Some groups have priority; others are equal. Thus fixity is always maintained between members of the European Communities, even within the OECD and world comparison. For Finland and Austria, however, the bilateral relationship that prevails within the OECD comparison is also the one used within the global comparison. However, a significantly different relationship (based on Central European prices) prevails in the comparison within that group, and this is the relationship presented in the separate publication of the European comparison.

For further details on the ICP procedures, readers may consult the ICP Phase IV report, *World Comparisons of Purchasing Power and Real Product for 1980* (New York: United Nations, 1986).

The income distribution data cover rural and urban areas for all countries. The data refer to different years between 1979 and 1988 and are drawn from a variety of sources. These include the Economic Commission for Latin America and the Caribbean, the Luxembourg Income Study, the OECD, the U.N.'s *National Accounts Statistics: Compendium of Income Distribution Statistics, 1985*, the World Bank, and national sources. Data for many countries have been updated, and some of the income distribution data previously published have been deleted because they refer to years long past.

In many countries the collection of income distribution data is not systematically organized or integrated with the official statistical system. The data are derived from surveys designed for other purposes, most often consumer expenditure surveys, that also collect information on income. These surveys use a variety of income concepts and sample designs, and in many cases their geographic coverage is too limited to provide reliable nationwide estimates of income distribution. Although the data presented here represent the best available estimates, they do not avoid all these problems and should be interpreted with caution.

Similarly, the scope of the indicator is limited for certain countries, and data for other countries are not fully comparable. Because households vary in size, a distribution in which households are ranked according to per capita household income, rather than according to total household income, is superior for many purposes. The distinction is important because households with low per capita incomes frequently are large households, whose total income may be high, whereas many households with low household incomes may be small households with high per capita income. Information on the distribution of per capita household income exists for only a few countries and is infrequently updated. Where possible, distributions are ranked according to per capita income; where this is not possible, distributions are ranked by per capita expenditure, household income, or household expenditure. Since the size of household is likely to be small for low-income households (for instance, single-person households and couples without children), the distribution of household income may overstate the income inequality. Also, since household savings tend to increase faster as income levels increase, the distribution of expenditure is inclined to understate the income inequality. The World Bank's Living Standards Measurement Study and the Social Dimensions of Adjustment project, covering Sub-Saharan African countries, are assisting a few countries in improving their collection and analysis of data on income distribution.

Table 31. Urbanization

The data on *urban population as a percentage of total population* are from the U.N. publication *Prospects of World Urbanization, 1988*, supplemented by data from the World Bank.

The growth rates of urban population are calculated from the World Bank's population estimates; the estimates of urban population shares are calculated from the sources just cited. Data on urban agglomeration in large cities are from the U.N.'s *Patterns of Urban and Rural Population Growth, 1980*.

Because the estimates in this table are based on different national definitions of what is urban, cross-country comparisons should be interpreted with caution. Data on urban agglomeration in large cities are from population censuses.

The summary measures for urban population as a percentage of total population are calculated from country percentages weighted by each country's share in the aggregate population; the other summary measures in this table are weighted in the same fashion, using urban population.

Table 32. Women in development

This table provides some basic indicators disaggregated to show differences between the sexes that illustrate the condition of women in society. The measures reflect the demographic status of women and their access to health and education services.

Statistical anomalies become even more apparent when social indicators are analyzed by gender, because reporting systems are often weak in areas related specifically to women. Indicators drawn from censuses and surveys, such as those on population, tend to be about as reliable for women as for men; but indicators based largely on administrative records, such as maternal and infant mortality, are less reliable. More resources are now being devoted to develop better information on these topics, but the reliability of data, even in the series shown, still varies significantly.

The *risk of dying by age 5* (also referred to as the under-5 mortality rate) shows the probability of a newborn baby dying before reaching age 5. The rates are derived from life tables based on estimated current life expectancy at birth and on infant mortality rates. In general throughout the world more males are born than females. Under good nutritional and health conditions and in times of peace, male children under 5 have a higher death rate than females. These columns show that female-male differences in the risk of dying by age 5 vary substantially. In industrial market economies, female babies have a 23 percent lower risk of dying by age 5 than male babies; the risk of dying by age 5 is actually higher for females than for males in some lower-income economies. This suggests differential treatment of males and females with respect to food and medical care.

Such discrimination particularly affects very young girls, who may get a smaller share of scarce food or receive less prompt costly medical attention. This pattern of discrimination is not uniformly associated with development. There are low- and middle-income countries (and regions within countries) where the relative risk of dying by age 5 for females relative to males approximates the pattern found in industrial countries. In many other countries, however, the numbers starkly demonstrate the need to associate women more closely with development. The health and welfare indicators in both Table 28 and in this table's maternal mortality column draw attention, in particular, to the conditions associated with childbearing. This activity still carries the highest risk of death for women of reproductive age in developing countries. The indicators reflect, but do not measure, both the availability of health services for women and the general welfare and nutritional status of mothers.

Life expectancy at birth is defined in the note to Table 1.

Maternal mortality refers to the number of female deaths that occur during childbirth, per 100,000 live births. Because deaths during childbirth are defined more widely in some countries to include complications of pregnancy or the period after childbirth, or of abortion, and because many pregnant women die because of lack of suitable health care, maternal mortality is difficult to measure consistently and reliably across countries. The data in these two series are drawn from diverse national sources and collected by the World Health Organization (WHO), although many national administrative systems are weak and do not record vital events in a systematic way. The data are derived mostly from official community reports and hospital records, and some reflect only deaths in hospitals and other medical institutions. Sometimes smaller private and rural hospitals are excluded, and sometimes even relatively primitive local facilities are included. The coverage is therefore not always comprehensive, and the figures should be treated with extreme caution.

Clearly, many maternal deaths go unrecorded, particularly in countries with remote rural populations; this accounts for some of the very low numbers shown in the table, especially for several African countries. Moreover, it is not clear whether an increase in the number of mothers in hospital reflects more extensive medical care for women or more complications in pregnancy and childbirth because of poor nutrition, for instance. (Table 28 shows data on low birth weight.)

These time series attempt to bring together readily available information not always presented in international publications. WHO warns that there are inevitably gaps in the series, and it has invited countries to provide more comprehensive figures. They are reproduced here, from the 1986 WHO publication *Maternal Mortality Rates,* supplemented by the UNICEF publication *The State of the World's Children 1989,* as part of the international effort to highlight data in this field. The data refer to any year from 1977 to 1984.

The *education* indicators, based on Unesco sources, show the extent to which females have equal access to schooling.

Persistence to grade 4 is the percentage of children starting primary school in 1970 and 1984, respectively, who continued to the fourth grade by 1973 and 1987. Figures in italics represent earlier or later cohorts. The data are based on enrollment records. The slightly higher persistence ratios for females in some African countries may indicate male participation in activities such as animal herding.

All things being equal, and opportunities being the same, the ratios for *females per 100 males* should be close to 100. However, inequalities may cause the ratios to move in different directions. For example, the number of females per 100 males will rise at secondary school level if male attendance declines more rapidly in the final grades because of males' greater job opportunities, conscription into the army, or migration in search of work. In addition, since the numbers in these columns refer mainly to general secondary education, they do not capture those (mostly males) enrolled in technical and vocational schools or in full-time apprenticeships, as in Eastern Europe.

All summary measures are country data weighted by each country's share in the aggregate population.

Data sources

Production and domestic absorption	U.N. Department of International Economic and Social Affairs. Various years. *Statistical Yearbook.* New York. ———. Various years. *World Energy Supplies.* Statistical Papers, series J. New York. International Comparison Program Phases IV (1980) and V (1985) reports, and data from ECE, ESCAP, Eurostat, OECD, and U.N. FAO, IMF, UNIDO, and World Bank data; national sources.
Fiscal and monetary accounts	International Monetary Fund. 1989. *Government Finance Statistics Yearbook.* Vol. 11. Washington, D.C. ———. Various years. *International Financial Statistics.* Washington, D.C. U.N. Department of International Economic and Social Affairs. Various years. *World Energy Supplies.* Statistical Papers, series J. New York. IMF data.
Core international transactions	International Monetary Fund. Various years. *International Financial Statistics.* Washington, D.C. U.N. Conference on Trade and Development. Various years. *Handbook of International Trade and Development Statistics.* Geneva. U.N. Department of International Economic and Social Affairs. Various years. *Monthly Bulletin of Statistics.* New York. ———. Various years. *Yearbook of International Trade Statistics.* New York. FAO, IMF, U.N., and World Bank data.
External finance	Organisation for Economic Co-operation and Development. Various years. *Development Co-operation.* Paris. ———. 1988. *Geographical Distribution of Financial Flows to Developing Countries.* Paris. IMF, OECD, and World Bank data; World Bank Debtor Reporting System.
Human resources	Institute for Resource Development/Westinghouse. 1987. *Child Survival: Risks and the Road to Health.* Columbia, Md. Mauldin, W. Parker, and Sheldon J. Segal. 1988. ''Prevalence of Contraceptive Use: Trends and Issues.'' *Studies in Family Planning* 19, no. 6: 335-53. Sivard, Ruth. 1985. *Women—A World Survey.* Washington, D.C.: World Priorities. U.N. Department of International Economic and Social Affairs. Various years. *Demographic Yearbook.* New York. ———. Various years. *Population and Vital Statistics Report.* New York. ———. Various years. *Statistical Yearbook.* New York. ———. 1980. *Patterns of Urban and Rural Population Growth.* New York. ———. 1984. *Recent Levels and Trends of Contraceptive Use as Assessed in 1983.* New York. ———. 1988. *Mortality of Children under Age 5: Projections 1950–2025.* New York. ———. 1989. *Prospects of World Urbanization.* New York. ———. 1989. *World Population Prospects: 1988.* New York. U.N. Educational Scientific and Cultural Organization. Various years. *Statistical Yearbook.* Paris. UNICEF. 1989. *The State of the World's Children 1989.* Oxford: Oxford University Press. World Health Organization. Various years. *World Health Statistics Annual.* Geneva. ———. 1986. *Maternal Mortality Rates: A Tabulation of Available Information,* 2nd edition. Geneva. ———. Various years. *World Health Statistics Report.* Geneva. FAO and World Bank data.

 The World Bank

More than a billion people in the developing world live in poverty, and millions in Sub-Saharan Africa and Latin America are experiencing increasing deprivation. Ten years after *World Development Report 1980* looked at the causes and extent of poverty, this thirteenth annual Report returns to the subject to examine what has gone right and wrong and to look toward the future. It recommends that countries and the development community pursue a twofold strategy for reducing poverty— a strategy that has already shown promise.

The first necessity is to promote broadly based growth that will generate income-earning opportunities for the poor. The second is to ensure, by improving access to education, health care, and other social services, that the poor can take advantage of these opportunities. Transfers and other special arrangements are needed for those who are not able to benefit fully from the increased opportunities—for example, the needy aged, the ill, and the disabled—and those buffeted by economic shocks and setbacks. But the main elements of the strategy are designed to enable the poor to make effective use of their principal asset—their ability to work. The Report urges the development community to allocate larger shares of aid budgets to those countries which have shown in their policies a genuine commitment to reducing poverty.

The world economy emerged from the shocks and transformations of the 1980s in better shape than might have been expected. The current trends, if they continue, would create a good economic foundation for meeting the challenge of poverty and creating brighter prospects for large populations in the developing world in the last years of the twentieth century. Great progress has already been made in the past three decades. Even during the so-called lost decade of the 1980s, living standards continued to improve for most of the world's poor. What is needed now is political commitment—on the part of the developing countries, the industrial countries, and the international community.

Like previous issues, this Report contains a World Development Indicators annex with comprehensive, up-to-date data on social and economic development in more than 180 countries and territories. These data will also be available on diskette for use with personal computers.

Cover design by Joyce C. Petruzzelli

ISBN 0-19-520851-X (PB)
ISBN 0-19-520850-1 (HC)